Margaret Stokes

Christian Iconography or, the History of Christian Art In the Middle Ages

Vol. II: Trinity, Agels, Devils, Death, The Soul, The Christian Scheme, Appendices

Margaret Stokes

Christian Iconography or, the History of Christian Art in the Middle Ages
Vol. II: Trinity, Agels, Devils, Death, The Soul, The Christian Scheme, Appendices

ISBN/EAN: 9783337259105

Printed in Europe, USA, Canada, Australia, Japan

Cover: Foto ©Thomas Meinert / pixelio.de

More available books at **www.hansebooks.com**

CHRISTIAN ICONOGRAPHY;

OR,

THE HISTORY OF CHRISTIAN ART IN THE MIDDLE AGES.

BY THE LATE

ADOLPHE NAPOLÉON DIDRON.

TRANSLATED FROM THE FRENCH BY E. J. MILLINGTON, AND COMPLETED
WITH ADDITIONS AND APPENDICES

BY

MARGARET STOKES.

IN TWO VOLUMES.

Vol. II.

TRINITY: ANGELS: DEVILS: DEATH: THE SOUL: THE CHRISTIAN SCHEME:
APPENDICES.

WITH NUMEROUS ILLUSTRATIONS.

LONDON: GEORGE BELL AND SONS, YORK STREET,
COVENT GARDEN.
1891.

CONTENTS OF VOL. II.

	PAGE
THE TRINITY	1
HISTORY OF THE DOCTRINE OF THE TRINITY	1
DEFINITION OF THE DIVINE PERSONS	6
MANIFESTATIONS OF THE TRINITY	13
WORSHIP OF THE TRINITY	28
CHRONOLOGICAL ICONOGRAPHY OF THE TRINITY	34
ATTRIBUTES OF THE TRINITY	63
ICONOGRAPHY OF ANGELS	85
ICONOGRAPHY OF DEVILS	109
ICONOGRAPHY OF DEATH	153
ICONOGRAPHY OF THE SOUL	173
ICONOGRAPHY OF THE CHRISTIAN SCHEME	188
MYTHOLOGICAL LEGENDS IN THE SPECULUM HUMANÆ SALVATIONIS	211
INFLUENCE OF THE DRAMA ON ICONOGRAPHY	233
MEDIÆVAL ART AND THE ANTIQUE	244
APPENDIX I.: ADDITIONAL NOTES	255
APPENDIX II.: 'BYZANTINE GUIDE TO PAINTING'	265
APPENDIX III.: TEXT OF THE BIBLIA PAUPERUM	403
DESCRIPTIVE LIST OF ILLUSTRATIONS IN VOLS. I. AND II.	431
INDEX	440

LIST OF ILLUSTRATIONS TO VOL. II.

	PAGE
AN ANGEL ASSISTING THE CREATOR	14
THE TRINITY IN COMBAT WITH BEHEMOTH AND LEVIATHAN	17
THE TRINITY AT THE BAPTISM OF CHRIST	19
THE TRINITY OF EVIL	22
THE TRINITY OF ABSOLUTE EVIL	23
FIGURE OF TIME WITH THREE FACES	25
THE TRINITY IN THREE HUMAN PERSONS OF IDENTICAL FIGURE	42
THE THREE DIVINE PERSONS FUSED ONE INTO THE OTHER	44
THE TRINITY UNDER THE FORM OF THREE CIRCLES.	46
THE DIVINE TRIPLICITY, CONTAINED WITHIN THE UNITY	51
THE THREE FACES OF THE TRINITY ON ONE SINGLE HEAD AND ONE SINGLE BODY	53
THE THREE DIVINE FACES WITH TWO EYES AND ONE SINGLE BODY	57
THE DIVINE PERSONS DISTINCT	64
THE HOLY GHOST DESCENDING FROM THE FATHER UPON THE SON	69
THE HOLY GHOST PROCEEDING FROM THE FATHER AND THE SON, AND RE-ASCENDING FROM THE SON TO THE FATHER	70
THE HOLY GHOST, NOT PROCEEDING EITHER FROM THE FATHER OR THE SON	72
THE THREE DIVINE HEADS WITHIN A SINGLE TRIANGLE	73
THE TRINITY IN ONE GOD SUPPORTING THE WORLD.	76
THE TRINITY IN ONE SINGLE GOD HOLDING THE BALANCES AND THE COMPASSES	78
THE TRINITY IN HUMAN FORM WITH CRUCIFORM NIMBUS AND AUREOLE OF FLAME	81
SERAPH OF ST. FRANCIS	90
THRONES: FIERY TWO-WINGED WHEELS	91
SCULPTURED ANGEL, CHARTRES, THIRTEENTH CENTURY	92
ANGELS (PIERO DELLA FRANCESCA)	93
ANGEL WITHOUT FEET OR LEGS	94
ANGEL OF THE ASCENSION	95

SIX-WINGED ANGEL HOLDING LANCE, WINGS CROSSED ON BREAST,
 ARRAYED IN ROBE AND MANTLE 97
ANGELS FROM CATHEDRAL OF CHARTRES . . . 100, 101, 102
ST. JOHN THE BAPTIST 108
LUCIFER BEFORE THE FALL 109
FALL OF LUCIFER 111, 112
FOUR-HEADED DEMON 113
PERSONIFICATION OF RIVER 115
FIRE DEMON 117
SATAN IN MISSAL OF POITIERS 119
DEVIL IN CAMPO SANTO, PISA 120
PERSIAN DEVIL 122
EGYPTIAN DEVIL 123
TURKISH DEVIL 124
SATAN WITH SERPENT HORNS 125
THE ABYSS 127
CHRIST TEMPTED 128
TEMPTATION OF ST. PAPHNUTIUS 129
ST. JULIANA AND THE DEVIL 130
DEMONS ON THE TOMB OF DAGOBERT 131
CHARTRES: THE DEMON IN MAN 133
THE DEMON AS SATYR 134
BEAST WITH SEVEN HEADS 137
THE DEVIL AS SERPENT 139
THE TEMPTATION OF ADAM AND EVE 140
VAMPIRE, CAMPO SANTO, PISA 141
DEMON ON THE CASQUE OF GOLIATH 142
DIABOLISM, HUMOROUS FIGURES OF 143, 144
EXORCISM 145
SEAL OF LUCIFER 147
WRITING OF ASMODEUS 148
IMPIETY: AMIENS CATHEDRAL 149
COVETOUSNESS: AMIENS CATHEDRAL 150
THANATOS 154
TRIUMPH OF DEATH 156, 160, 161
DEATH AS A WOMAN 158, 159
DEATH AS A DEMON 162
WICKED SOUL CAST INTO HELL 164
SATAN OF JOB, CAMPO SANTO, PISA 165
THE LADDER OF THE SOUL 167
DEATH AS A CROWNED SKELETON ON TOMB . . . 169
DEATH AS ECCE HOMO 169
DEATH AND THE FOOL 170

LIST OF ILLUSTRATIONS.

	PAGE
THE DANCE OF DEATH	171
DEATH AS A SKELETON	172
PSYCHE IN DESPAIR, SEATED ON A ROCK AND BEWAILING THE FLIGHT OF CUPID	174
THE BUTTERFLY AND THE SOUL	175, 176
MARTYRDOM OF ST. STEPHEN: SCULPTURE ON PORCH OF ST. TROPHIMUS AT ARLES	177
SOUL BORNE TO HEAVEN BY ANGELS	178
WEIGHING OF SOULS IN THE BALANCE	179, 180
HERMES LIFTING THE SOUL FROM THE SHADES	181
HERMES LEADING A SOUL TO CHARON	181
ST. MICHAEL AND THE DRAGON	182, 184, 185
ADORATION OF THE CROSS	196
DESCENT OF CHRIST INTO HELL	198
SAMSON AND THE LION	198
DAVID SLAYING GOLIATH	198
CHRIST AND THE HUMAN-HEADED SERPENT	201
HERCULES AND THE HUMAN-HEADED HYDRA	202
DANIEL AMONG LIONS; HABBAKKUK AND THE ANGEL	210
THE LEGEND OF THE OSTRICH	215
THE SOULS OF THE MARTYRS DIONYSIUS, RUSTICUS, AND ELEUTHERIUS APPEAR AS DOVES	239
BAS-RELIEF AT NOTRE DAME, PARIS	241

CHRISTIAN ICONOGRAPHY.

THE TRINITY.

THE three Divine Persons are merged in one single God, just as the three images representing them combine to form one single group. The doctrines of our holy faith, and the works of art—Theology and Iconography—walk hand in hand, the one in describing, the other in pourtraying the Trinity. The three Persons have hitherto been each considered separately. It now remains only to exhibit them grouped together, united between themselves, and represented as Trinities.

HISTORY OF THE DOCTRINE OF THE TRINITY.

The doctrine of the Trinity, which had been almost entirely unknown to the Pagans, and but imperfectly revealed to the Jewish race, was made clearly and completely manifest from the very earliest origin of Christianity. It unfolded tself in all its extent, and with all the various and important results connected with it, during the successive centuries of the Christian era, and conformably with them. Considerable research and enquiry has been made as to the ideas entertained by Pagans on the subject of the Trinity, and the amount of knowledge possessed by them of the unity of the divine essence, and the triplicity of persons, or hypotases. Plato appears to have foreseen the Christian doctrine, but only as objects perceived at a distance, which the eye can scarcely reach, or seizes but imperfectly. The doctrine attributed to that Greek philosopher, and which seems rather to be deducible from his general theory, than openly avowed by himself, is that the divine triplicity ought to be called Goodness, Intelligence, and the Soul or cause of all things.*

The Platonists, and the philosophers of the school of Alexandria in particular, delighted in scrutinising, elucidating, filling up, and amplifying beyond measure, the idea of the master. Plotinus and Longinus, who are followed by Jamblichus and Porphyry, admit one single God in three persons; but Numerius insists upon three Gods. Numerius acknowledges the Father, the Creator, and the World.† He seems to make of each of these three Gods a trinity of Idealism, Intelligence, and Power. Amelius and Theodore also discover three Trinities in that of Plato, and pretend that there are three Goodnesses, three Intelligences, three Souls.‡ Seneca seems to approximate to the doctrine of Christianity in a curious passage of his writings, in which he names, as primal cause of every event, first—God, who can do all things; next—incorporeal Reason, by which the greatest works are performed; lastly—the Divine Spirit circulating throughout everything. To these three moving causes he adds Fatality or Destiny, that is to say, the reciprocal union of these causes and their mutual combination.§

Comparing this text with what Greek mythology teaches in reference to the three great divinities, who, the offspring of one common Father, are the supreme heads of the world

---

* "Τὸ εὖ, ὁ νοῦς, or, ὁ λόγος, ἡ ψυχή." See the *Études sur la Théodicée de Platon et d'Aristote,* par M. Jules Simon, pp. 148, 151, 175. In the Greek paintings of Mount Athos, the philosopher Plato is constantly represented amongst the number of those Pagans who had a knowledge, although imperfect, of the truth. He is an old man, with a long beard, and appears to be uttering the following words, which are painted on a rouleau that he holds in his left hand: "The old is new and the new old, the Father is in the Son, and the Son is in the Father. The Unity is divided into three, and the Trinity re-united in one." The language is not literally that of the Greek philosopher, but it is attributed to him by Byzantine artists as presenting the result of his doctrine.

† "Πατὴρ, ποιητής, ποίημα."

‡ See a thesis in M. Jules Simon, entitled *Commentaire du Timée de Platon, par Proclus,* p. 105.

§ "Id actum est, mihi crede, ab illo, quisquis formator universi fuit, sive ille DEUS est, potens omnium; sive incorporalis RATIO, ingentium operum artifex; sive divinus SPIRITUS, per omnia maxima, minima et æquali intentione diffusus; sive FATUM et immutabilis causarum inter se cohærentium series."—Ap. Senecam, *De Consolatione ad Helviam,* cap. viii.

which they share between them, it must be confessed that the doctrine of the Trinity was at least vaguely known to the Pagans. In fact, amongst the Hindoos, a divine "Trimourti" directs all the phenomena of the Universe.* Amongst the Greeks, Jupiter, Neptune, and Pluto reign upon the three different stages composing the edifice of the world.

At the summit, in the highest region of the air, hovers Jupiter, the king of heaven; in the centre Neptune, commanding the sea; at the foot, Pluto governs earth and hell, which form his covering. They are all three sons of one single parent, of the old Saturn, himself the son of Cœlus and Terra. When any Greek deity associates in himself universal functions, he generally has three different names. Thus the feminine power, corresponding with the three male divinities who have just been named, is called in heaven Luna, Diana on the earth, Hecate or Proserpine in hell.

The ancients, those more especially who were scholars of Pythagoras, and scrutators of celestial arithmetic, delighted to repeat that God regarded with favour an uneven number, and more particularly the number three. The number three, which can be divided only by itself, or by the unit, was the image of God, who can be compared only with himself, that is to say with the absolute Unity. The Pagans seem to have imagined that nothing could be complete unless it were capable of being divided by three, and thus presenting itself to the mind under a threefold aspect; beauty was symbolised by the three Graces; life, by the three Fates; justice by the three Judges; and vengeance by the three Eumenides. Any combination whatever, in use among the Greeks, will be found to be divisible into three members; thus every column has a basement on which the shaft is fixed, and the shaft again is surmounted by a capital.

The above ideas concerning numbers, and the mysterious properties of the number three, prevailed during the entire

* The Hindoo "Trimourti" is composed of Brâhma, Siva, and Vishnoo. Brâhma presides over the earth, and is the creative god; Siva is the destructive god, and reigns over fire; to Vishnoo, the conservative god, belongs the empire of the water, upon which he moves.—M. Guignaut, *Religions de l'Antiquité*, vol. i., c. 2 and 3.

course of the middle ages, and even in the present day they still engage our attention. Geometricians have observed that no material object can exist, without possessing the three dimensions, length, breadth, and height. Physiologists assert life itself to be composed of three particular lives; intellectual life, the seat of which is in the brain; digestive life, of which the centre is the stomach; and locomotive life, which resides in the muscular power. Certain psychologists, taking possession of the intellectual and cerebral life, which is the most elevated of the three material existences, divide it into intelligence properly so called, love, and volition, whence severally flow, faculties, feelings, and actions. Many modern philosophers, admitting that division and terminology, declare man to be in himself a little world; a sort of finite deity, and that the chief attributes of divinity are wisdom, goodness, and power.* Christianity is the most complete development, the highest, and at the same time the most universal of all truths; by it past truths are revealed, purified, and filtered, if the expression may be allowed; by it truths that are yet future are prepared. It was fitting, therefore, that Christianity should proclaim God to be a Divine Unity in three persons. "Fides Catholica hæc est; ut unum Deum in Trinitate, et Trinitatem in unitate veneremur." "And the Catholic faith is this, that we worship

* To live, to think, to act, are, according to Hindoo metaphysics, the three modes of the Divine existence. Cambry (*Monuments Celtiques*, in 8vo. p. 157,) considers they should be rather—to be, to think, and to speak. "Man," says M. P. Leroux, in his works, "is in his nature and by essence, sensation, feeling, and intelligence, indivisibly united." This psychological definition of man reminds us of the Trinity of the St. Simonians, Industry, Science, and Religion, which have for their aim or object, the union of the useful, the true, and the good or beautiful. According to M. de la Mennais (*Esquisse d'une philosophie*), "Man, regarded in an elevated point of view, exhibits the laws of intelligence, volition and love, closely connected in his being, with the laws of organism. Man exerts himself in three spheres of activity, united, because man is one single being; but distinct, because referring to different aims or objects: Industry, of which the object is the useful; Art, whose aim is beauty; and Science, which has for its object truth. French eclecticism and the whole range of German philosophy, that of Hegel in particular, hold nearly the same language. It would be out of place here to pursue further this inventory of modern philosophy; what has been already said will suffice to prove the high estimation in which the number three is held even in our own day. We lean, far more than we are willing to allow, to the doctrines of Pythagoras and the learned schoolmen of the middle ages.

one God in Trinity, and Trinity in Unity.* These words Dante translates as follows:

"Quell' uno e due e tre che sempre vive,
E regna sempre in tre e due ed uno,
Non circonscritto e tuto circonscrive,
. Tre volte era cantato da ciascuno
Di quelli spirti.*   *   *   *
  Divina Commedia, Paradiso, c. xiv. l. 28.†

In Jacobus de Voragine, in the legend of the Apostle St. Thomas, we find a psychological and material justification of the triplicity resolving itself into unity. This passage, dating from the earliest period of Christianity,‡ leads from the exposition of the dogma of the Trinity to the definition of the Divine persons, and is therefore here given.

St. Thomas, on his arrival in India, began to heal the sick, and to preach the truths of Christianity. "The Apostle began by instructing them in the twelve degrees of the virtues; the first of these degrees was the belief in one God, single in essence, and triple in person. He gave them three self-evident or palpable examples of the Trinity of persons in one single substance. The first, that there is in man one single wisdom, and that from that unity proceed intelligence, memory, and genius. For genius," says he, "is the power of discovering what it has never been taught (the creative faculty); memory, that of not forgetting what has been learnt; intelligence, that of understanding what may be shown or taught. The second example is drawn from the three parts in the vine: the wood, the leaves, and the fruit; yet all three make but one and the same vine. His third

---

* See the Creed of St. Athanasius. Lactantius, as has been said, compresses this dogma into the following laconic words, "Deus trinus unus." The word "Trinity," which is even more compact, virtually comprehends the entire creed of St. Athanasius.

† Literally rendered by Chaucer—Troilus and Creseide—fifth book last stanza.

"Thou one, two, and three, eterne on live,
That raignest aie in three, two, and one,
Uncircumscript and all maist circumscrive."
  *   *   *   *   *   *
Thrice sang each spirit."

‡ This is to be found in the Apocryphal Book, entitled *Historia Cer-'aminis Apostolorum;* it is attributed to the first Bishop of Babylon, Abdias, who was contemporary with the Apostles.

example is, that the head is the seat of four senses; sight, taste, hearing and smelling; all these things are more than one, and yet form one single head * only."

DEFINITION OF THE DIVINE PERSONS.

It will be necessary here to complete what was said in the chapter on the Holy Ghost, relating to the properties peculiar to each of the three persons of the Divine Trinity. It was there observed, that this question had been pending throughout the entire course of the middle ages. Confounding the relations of the Divine persons between themselves, and with their relations towards men, the qualities of the Holy Ghost were attributed to the Son, those of the Father, but more particularly those of the Son, to the Spirit. With regard to ourselves, heaven has been distinguished from earth; things existent from all eternity have to us appeared different, in some respects, from those which have their origin in time. Theology, as may easily be supposed, is not always commensurate with history. It has consequently been stated, speaking of the Divine persons in their relation towards men, that the Father has manifested himself as the source of omnipotence; the Son, as the God of love; the Spirit, as the fountain of intelligence. Engravings have been given, in which each of the Divine persons is thus characterised. But it should be remembered that these engravings are exceptions; two examples only, out of several hundred subjects, have as yet come to our knowledge. Love

---

* This third example refers to plurality in general, not to triplicity. The following quotation is from the *Legenda Aurea* (De Sancto Thoma, Apostolo :)—" Tunc Apostolus cœpit eos docere et duodecim gradus virtutum assignare. Primus est ut in Deum crederent, qui est unus in essentia e trinus in personis. Deditque eis triplex exemplum sensibile, quomodo sint in una essentia tres personæ. Primum est quia una est in homine sapientia, e de illa una procedit intellectus, memoria et ingenium. Nam ingenium est inquit, ut quod non didicisti invenias; memoria, ut non obliviscaris quo didiceris; intellectus, ut intelligas quæ ostendi possunt vel doceri. Secundur est quia in una vinea tria sunt, scilicet; lignum, folia, et fructus; et omni tria unum sunt et una vinea sunt; Tertium est quia caput unum quatuo sensibus constat. In uno enim capite sunt visus, gustus, auditus, et odoratu et hæc plura sunt et unum caput sunt."

is habitually ascribed to the Holy Ghost, and intelligence to Jesus Christ, who is the "Word" made flesh; the Word of God incarnate, the λόγος of the Greek Church.

Saint Augustine adopts two opinions concerning the special definition appropriate to each of the three persons. "Man," says he, "was made in the image of God; there must therefore, be a Trinity in man, as there is in God. Thus in man we find the soul, its consciousness, and self-love.* Those three faculties reside also in God, but in infinite proportion." In the above theory, to which St. Augustine gives the preference, and which, probably, originated with him, the spiritual substance in man, his soul, is the image of the Father; intelligence, or the "Word," that of the Son; love, that of the Holy Ghost. "In the same manner," continues St. Augustine, "in which the mind and its love for itself, are two different things, so the mind, and its self-knowledge or consciousness, are also two distinct things. Therefore, the mind, its love, and its consciousness, form a triad; and that triad is, at the same time, an unity. When the three are perfect, they are equal." † According to a second opinion of St. Augustine, memory is the image of the Father; intelligence, of the Son; volition, of the Holy Ghost. In both theories, the Holy Ghost is love; and the Son, intelligence. In the first, the Father is substance; in the second, memory.

The doctrine taught by St. Ambrose is different. The soul of man (says the Archbishop of Milan) was made in the image of God; and the entire man is contained in the soul. Precisely as the Son is begotten by the Father, and as the Holy Ghost proceeds from the Father and the Son, so from the intelligence volition is engendered, and from those two powers proceeds memory. The soul, without that triad, is incomplete; one quality cannot be deficient, without rendering the others imperfect; and in the same manner, God the Father, God the Son, and God the Holy Ghost, are not three Gods, but one single God in three persons. Thus, too, the intelligence of the soul, its volition,

---

* "Mentem, notitiam qua se novit et dilectionem qua se diligit." St. August. *De Trinitate*, lib. ix., cap. vi.
† *De Trinitate*, lib. ix., cap. iv.

and its memory, are not three souls in one body, but one single soul possessed of three faculties.*

Thus, then, according to the theory of St. Ambrose, the Father is intelligence; the Son, love or volition; the Holy Ghost, memory. Love is here transferred from the Holy Ghost to the Son, and intelligence from the Son to the Father. The Holy Ghost becomes memory; and no allusion is made to that spiritual substance of the Divine soul spoken of by St. Augustine.

This formula, according to M. Buchez,† from whom the above series of facts is borrowed, is very far superior to that of St. Augustine.‡ In the formula of this great Doctor, it is shown that the Holy Ghost proceeds from the Father; but not that he proceeds also from the Son. Besides, it is erroneous to confound volition with love; to will is to act, to choose, but in neither case is it to desire.

Of these three opinions, St. Bernard adopts the second.§ St. Thomas Aquinas does not appear to adopt either, although, in admitting two-thirds of the first, he acknowledges the Son to be intelligence, and the Holy Ghost love.|| Bossuet takes the two first at the same time.¶ They are blended in one by M. L'Abbé Frère, and Bossuet and St. Augustine hesitate between the two.** M. Buchez adheres to the third opinion, which is the same as that held by St. Ambrose.††

The Abbess Herrade adopts the second opinion held by St. Augustine. She declares that memory belongs specially

---

* St. Ambrosii *Hexameron*, lib. vi., cap. vii., s. 43; ap. Opera. tom ii. Append. p. 612.

† *Traité Complet de Philosophie*, vol. iii., Ontologie, Chap. de la Trinité Humaine, pp. 374—377.

‡ We cannot acquiesce in this opinion, for memory being the offspring of intelligence and an immediate result of that faculty, it may be objected to the formula of St. Ambrose, that it attributes intelligence to two of the Divine persons; and besides, what, according to that theory, becomes of strength or power, which is, notwithstanding, a principal and important faculty?

§ St. Bernard, *Meditat. de Cognit. human. cond.* cap. i.

|| St. Thomæ *Summa*, pars. i., quest. 93, art. 8.

¶ Bossuet. *Élévations sur les Mystères*, 2ᵉ semaine, 6ᵉ élévat., édit. in 4º, tom. x., p. 33; 4ᵉ semaine, 7ᵉ élévat., tom. x., p. 71. Exorde du Sermon sur le Mystère de la Sainte Trinité.

** *L'homme connu par la Révélation*, tom. i.

†† Buchez, *Traité Complet de Philos.*, vol. iii., pp. 397—408.

to the Father; intelligence, to the Son; volition or love, to the Holy Ghost.* Richard de St. Victor, observing that, in all the above formularies, omnipotence, (which is, notwithstanding, the primordial and generative faculty,) had been forgotten, attributed to the Father power, but preserved to the Holy Ghost love, and to the Son intelligence.† In this arrangement, Richard conformed to the spirit of the times—it may indeed be said, to the spirit of the middle ages generally—and to the definition then prevailing,‡ which is almost universally interpreted by monumental images. In fact, the formularies suggested by St. Augustine and St. Ambrose, owe their origin rather to philosophy than to theology; naturally, therefore, they failed to make any great progress during the

---

* *Hortus Deliciarum.* " Divinitas consistit in Trinitate. Hujus imaginem tenet anima, quæ habet memoriam, per quam præterita et futura recolit; habet intellectum, quo præsentia et invisibilia intelligit; habet voluntatem, qua malum respicit et bonum eligit."

† Not to dwell longer on these points, the discussion of which is of far more importance to the future course of Christian Iconography, than to the Iconography of the middle ages, we shall content ourselves with quoting the Latin text of Richard. That profound theologian, in the *Tractatus Exceptionum*, lib. ii., cap. ii. (*Opp. Richardi S. Vict.*, in fo., Rouen, 1650), writes as follows :—" Invisibilia Dei a creatura mundi per ea quæ facta sunt intellecta conspiciuntur. Tria sunt invisibilia Dei: potentia, sapientia, benignitas. Ab his tribus procedunt omnia, in his tribus consistunt omnia, per hæc tria reguntur omnia. Potentia creat, sapientia gubernat, benignitas conservat. Quæ tamen tria sicut in Deo ineffabiliter unum sunt, ita in operatione separari non possunt. Potentia per benignitatem sapienter creat, sapientia per potentiam benigne gubernat, benignitas per sapientiam potenter conservat. Potentiam manifestat creaturarum immensitas, sapientiam decor, bonitatem utilitas." Afterwards, in a treatise addressed to S. Bernard, and entitled *De Tribus appropriatis personis in Trinitate*, lib. vi., p. 270, he considers "Cur attribuatur potentia Patri, sapientia Filio, bonitas Spiritui Sancto." Lastly, in his treatise *De Trinitate*, lib. vi., p. 264, he inquires, " Quare speciali, quodam decendi modo potentia attribuitur ingenito, sapientia genito, bonitas Spiritui Sancto." He concludes thus—" Quoniam ergo in potentia exprimitur proprietas ingeniti, speciali quodam considerationis modo merito adscribitur illi. Sed quoniam in sapientia exprimitur proprietas geniti, merito et illa juxta eundem modum adscribitur ipsi. Item quia in bonitate proprietas Spiritus Sancti invenitur, merito et ei bonitas specialiter assignatur."

‡ Dante, in the *Divina Commedia*, Paradiso, canto x., writes thus of the Trinity :—

" Guardando nel suo Figlio con l' Amore
Che l' uno e l' altro eternalmente spira,
Lo primo ed ineffabile Valore,

mediæval epoch; and men at that period, generally agreed in recognising omnipotence, as the characteristic of the Father; supreme wisdom, as that of the Son; and infinite love in the Holy Ghost. Abelard himself attributed omnipotence to the Father; to the Son, wisdom; and to the Holy Ghost, goodness; he merely repeated what nearly every one said. Abelard erred only in assigning to each Divine person one single quality, and refusing to acknowledge their possession of the other two. His doctrines were condemned from his having asserted that the Father possessed omnipotence, but without either wisdom or goodness; and that the Holy Ghost had wisdom, but not power.* The three persons were, by his theory, completely isolated in respect of their special attributes; and, with a singular inconsistency, he afterwards confounded them in a divine unity, so intimate and compact, that it was impossible to trace in it the three hypostases. This idea of the independence of the three persons on the one hand, combined on the other with a fusion so complete, led Abelard into a twofold error; still that celebrated representative of scholastic philosophy, admitted the speciality of the attributes, qualifying and applying them to the Divine persons, as had been

> Quanto per mente, o per occhio si gira,
>   Con tanto ordine fe' ch' esser non puote
>   Senza gustar di lui, chi ciò rimira."
> Looking into his first-born with the love
> Which breathes from both eternal, the first Might
> Ineffable, wherever eye or mind
> Can roam, hath in such order all disposed,
> As none may see and fail to enjoy.—*Cary's Dante.*, c. x. l. 1.

* Martenne and Durand, two Benedictine Monks, discovered in the Abbey des Prémontrés de Vigogne (diocese of Arras), a manuscript containing a treatise of St. Bernard against Abelard, which had been sent by the Abbot of Clairvaux to Pope Innocent II. At the conclusion of the manuscript, after the words "collegi et aliqua transmisi," the following propositions, extracted by St. Bernard from the writings of Abelard, are inserted:—" Quod Pater sit plena potentia, Filius quædam potentia, Spiritus Sanctus nulla potentia. Quod Spiritus Sanctus non sit de substantia Patris aut Filii. Quod Spiritus Sanctus sit anima mundi. Quod neque Deus est homo, neque hæc persona quæ Christus est, sit tertia persona in Trinitate. Quod in Christo non fuerit Spiritus timoris Domini. Quod ad Patrem, qui ab alio non est, proprie vel specialiter attineat omnipotentia, non etiam sapientia et benignitas. Quod adventus in fine sæculi possit attribui Patri." See *Le Voyage littéraire de deux Benedictins*, 11e partie, p. 213.

done by Richard de St. Victor, and most of the other theologians.

At all events, the reciprocal relation of the Divine persons was well explained by the above formula, but not their relation towards man. We have in consequence, been compelled to make the distinction alluded to in the previous chapter treating of the Holy Ghost, and to observe that it became necessary, while assigning omnipotence to the Father, to attribute love to the Son, and to the Holy Ghost intelligence.

The great Christian geniuses who have been named, St. Ambrose, St. Augustine, St. Thomas Aquinas, and others, preserved their orthodoxy, even while varying the terms, which to them appeared to designate the three Divine persons. We also desire to suggest a different arrangement of the Divine attributes, without departing from the creed.

Moreover the representations engraved and given in the previous volume, attribute to the Divine persons precisely the qualities to which attention has been particularly drawn. In the present day especially, the formula here adopted is in favour with everyone, and we may also repeat, that the following explanation of the sign of the cross as performed by the Greeks, was given by Daniel, bishop of Lacedemon, in the year 1839: "It is made by opening the three first fingers of the right hand, the thumb, the forefinger and the middle finger. The three fingers are here employed in honour of, and as symbolising, the Trinity. The thumb, being peculiarly active and strong, the only finger capable of offering resistance to the other four, and the instrument of manual action;—the thumb is the representative of the Father. The middle finger, which has the pre-eminence over the others, and which is on the right of the thumb when seen from the back of the hand, is the Son. The fore-finger, through which the middle finger is connected with the thumb, figures the Holy Ghost. The fore-finger (index) indeed directs the eye and points out the position of objects; it is the organ of intelligence, and the instrument of expression." The ingenuity and subtlety of this Byzantine interpretation is extremely striking.

Such was the general opinion in our own country, in the twelfth and thirteenth centuries, and the Liturgists, Durandus and Beleth amongst others, declared that the sign of the cross was made with three fingers in honour of the blessed Trinity. The fundamental idea is the same, whether it be of Latin or Byzantine origin. Nor is it by any means certain that the development of the idea does not belong equally to both churches, or even that it did not originate altogether in the West. According to the rituals of the twelfth, thirteenth and fourteenth centuries, in performing the marriage ceremony, the nuptial ring was placed successively on the first three fingers of the right hand of the husband as well as of the wife. When it was placed on the thumb, the following words were recited,—" In nomine Patris;" on the first finger—" et Filii;" and on the middle finger—" et Spiritûs Sancti." The fore-finger here is attributed to the Son, and not to the Holy Ghost, but this peculiarity is perhaps of but little consequence.*

To conclude, the Father is supreme power, and should be characterised by the globe, the universe, which was created by him: the Son is infinite love, and his symbol is the Cross. The Spirit is intelligence, and ought to have the book. In representations of this subject, the Father is usually drawn with the globe; the Son with the Cross or book, but more frequently with the globe, and the Holy Ghost without any attribute whatever. The Son thus absorbs in himself the three divine faculties, for the mediæval artists assigned to him as personal attributes, the globe, designating power; the book, symbolic of intelligence or wisdom; and love, symbolised by the Cross, while the Holy Ghost appears to be completely disinherited. In treating so grave a subject nothing should be left to the arbitrary decision of individual minds. Ideas and terms must be defined, in order that contemporary artists may not fall into error, but depict the three Divine persons, and their attributes, in strict conformity with the creed, and the dogmas of theology.

We must request forgiveness for having, in treating of archæology, thus invaded the province of theology and philosophy. Still Christian archæology may yet be called on to render important services to theology and philosophy.

* See in the " Bulletin Archéologique du comité historique des Arts et Monuments, vol. ii., pp. 498, 499," notices by M. l'Abbe Poquet and Lucien de Rosny, *correspondants historiques*, of two rituals formerly belonging to the Cathedral of Soissons (Aisne), and of the Abbey of Barbeau (Seine-et-Marne).

Archæology is not a mere science of names, neither is its nature purely descriptive; it is more properly "history," and embraces that part of history which has for its object the giving an interpretation of facts. Without venturing to give any positive solution, it must still be acknowledged that without some reference to theology, Christian archæology can never be made in any degree useful, nor will it be possible to comprehend the intention of the various figures, carved upon Christian monuments. It becomes absolutely indispensable, when viewing certain monuments, to dwell upon the principal questions and essential facts of ecclesiastical history. Theology is in truth a noble science, and has been far less deeply studied than it deserves. Long, and injuriously abandoned to ecclesiastics, as if the clergy alone were interested in the study, it ought now to be restored to its place of honour. Everything in the present day is in progress, and all sciences ought to be profoundly scrutinised, both in their doctrinal and in their historical bearing. Happy shall we esteem ourselves if the present work be in any degree instrumental in reviving a taste for this noble study, which disturbs, although only in order to solve them, questions the most difficult and profound.

THE MANIFESTATIONS OF THE TRINITY.

The Holy Trinity, that is to say, the union of the three Divine persons in one, is not once distinctly affirmed in the Old Testament. Certain texts of Holy Scripture lead us to infer its existence, but even those texts are in some measure liable to objections. In the book of Genesis, God speaks thus, "Let *Us* make man in our image, after our likeness." (Gen. i. 26.) He says, again, "Behold the man is become as one of *Us*." (Gen. iii. 22.) And a third time he says, "Let *Us* go down, and there confound their language." (Gen. xi. 7.)* Still these expressions do not necessarily imply the idea of the Trinity. God may have used the plural in speaking, simply because he was addressing an angel; or like a sovereign issuing a command, or an artist inciting himself to proceed with the work in which he is

* These two last texts have been before quoted, vol. i., page 441.

engaged. God may thus have used the plural number, without any reference to the other two Divine persons. The above objections have been refuted by theologians, but, nevertheless, seem to be of a certain importance. In one work on theology,* in use in the seminaries of France, it is declared that God cannot possibly have been addressing the angels, when he used the words "Let us make man in our image." But the doubts of modern theology had been anticipated in the thirteenth century, and an angel was then represented assisting the Creator to mould the clay of which the first man was fashioned. The following example, amongst others, is completely characteristic.

Fig. 131.—AN ANGEL ASSISTING THE CREATOR.†
Italian Miniature of the XIII cent.

God is here assimilated to an eminent artist, himself giving the last touch to a work that has been commenced by an inferior artist. The inferior artist, the practitioner, is

* "Theologia Dogmatica et Moralis," by Louis Bailly, tom ii. *Tractatus de S. Trinitate*, pp. 1—17.
† Psalterium cum figuris in fo., Bibl. Royale.

represented by the angel, who fashions the clay, giving it a rude outline only, and imparting to the mass the imperfect form and general lineaments of a man. This man is as yet merely clay; formless, motionless, senseless, and devoid of life. God Almighty is there present, the right hand raised in the attitude of benediction, blessing the statue which is to be Adam, and breathing into him the breath of life.* Thus the angel co-operates with God in the formation of Adam; the angel rudely frames what God completes and perfects. The "Let *Us* make," of Genesis, although implying that a plurality of beings assisted in the formation of Adam, does *not* intimate the plurality, much less the triplicity of the Divine persons.

The manuscript from which the drawing given above is extracted, is not a solitary instance of the language of the book of Genesis being thus interpreted. In the north porch of the Cathedral of Chartres, the exterior cordon of the voussoir of the central entrance is occupied by a series of figures representing the Creation. There, also, the Creator is assisted by an angel, with whom he appears to be in consultation. A manuscript in the Bibliothèque Royale† goes still further, and represents the angel as closely united with the Deity, and making with him one body only, as he makes but one mind or idea, while creating the earth, animals, and man. It must, however, be allowed, that this mode of interpreting the plural verb, employed in the book of Genesis, is an exception to the general practice; for, during the entire duration of the mediæval era, particularly in the Gothic period, artists depicted the three persons of the Trinity, creating and animating Adam: some examples of this have been already given, and others will presently follow. We merely desire to show that Socinians might have discovered in the religious Iconography of the middle ages, arguments in defence of their heresy, but we readily admit that Christian artists in general, and doctors of

---

* " Et inspiravit in faciem ejus spiraculum vitæ, et factus est homo in animam viventem." " And breathed into his nostrils the breath of life, and man became a living soul." (Gen. ii. 7.)

† Chronique d'Isidore de Seville, Bibl. Roy., 7135, close of the thirteenth century, " On voit dans le frontispiece du fo. 1. Dieu figuré avec deux têtes et des ailes."—*Catalogue des MSS. Franç.* Par. 1ᵉ, Paris, vol. v., p. 334.

theology, have agreed in recognising the presence of the Trinity, in the texts quoted above.

It has been already mentioned, (Fig. 19), that Abraham prostrated himself before one of the three angels, who met him in the valley of Mamre, and whom he invited to repose near his tent, beneath a tree. Abraham saw three angels, but addressed himself at first to one only amongst them, and spoke afterwards to all the three together. Commentators have thence inferred that the Divine Trinity appeared to the Father of the Patriarchs.* This interpretation of a dubious text, is rather ingenious than indisputable. However, the art has constantly ranged itself on the side of the commentators, and represented the three persons united, while Abraham falls prostrate before one of the three. Below the picture the following legend is sometimes placed, "*Tres vidit, unum adoravit.*"†

In the Psalms of David, the Divine persons are represented as speaking;—" The Lord hath said unto me,—thou art my Son; this day have I begotten thee." (Psalm ii. 7.) " The Lord said unto my Lord, sit thou at my right hand."

---

* Genesis xviii. 2—5. In a Latin MS. of Prudentius (Bibl. Roy. 8085), three angels, symbolic according to Prudentius, of the Trinity, appeared unto Abraham. One only has around his head a circle resembling a nimbus; the other two are without. [It is worthy of remark, that in most of the striking texts mentioned by Didron, there should be a great discrepancy between the versions. I particularly mention the fact that artists may be on their guard. I will instance that text, in particular, from Isaiah xl. 12, where the Vulgate has it, " Quis mensus est pugillo aquas, et cælos palmo ponderavit. Quis appendit *tribus digitis* molem terræ, et libravit in pondere montes, et colles in statere." And this term *tribus digitis* was used expressly by theologians in support of the argument that the Trinity had been foreshadowed in the Old Testament. These texts, where we find translations vary so much, must, therefore, be employed guardedly. Still, the *Vulgate* version should be always consulted and preferred when reference is made merely to the mode of representing the particular subject by the earlier mediæval artists, and as a guide we must constantly employ it in tracing the progress of mediæval iconology.—Ed.]

† See in the Church of St. Etienne-du-mont, in the south aisle, a painted window, belonging to the sixteenth century, on which the fact, and the legend explaining it, are represented. In the Bibl. de l'Arsenal a manuscript (*Missale parisienne*, Theol. lat. 182,) contains the three angels exactly resembling one another, and alike adored by Abraham. In Greece, at the foot of Mount Pentelicus, in a little chapel adjoining the monastery, is a picture representing Abraham entertaining the three angels at his table. These angels are completely equal, as in the *Hortus deliciarum* ; all three wear the same kind of nimbus, marked with the Divine cross, and with ὁ ὤν in the cross branches.

THE MANIFESTATIONS OF THE TRINITY. 17

(Psalm cx. 1.) "I begot thee in my bosom before Lucifer." (Psalm cx. 3.)*

These expressions have, consequently, been supposed to infer that allusion is here made to the Trinity; but this was going too far. Two Divine Persons may be there alluded to, but certainly not three. The very small number of texts relating to the Trinity, to be found in the Old Testament, has induced commentators to torture the sense of the language, and to wrest the meaning of facts. Artists, prompted by commentators, have introduced images of the Trinity into scenes in which they are highly inappropriate; thus in the following drawing they make three angels, figur-

Fig. 132.—THE TRINITY, IN COMBAT WITH BEHEMOTH AND LEVIATHAN.
From the same source, and bearing the same date, as Fig. 131.

ing the three Divine persons, in combat with Behemoth and Leviathan. One of the angels, that without wings, has a cruciform nimbus, which properly belongs only to Deity;

* Psalm cx. 3. The verse in our translation is as follows :—" In the beauties of holiness from the womb of the morning, thou hast the dew of thy
VOL. II. C

the nimbus worn by the two others being plain, there is but little doubt that the artist feared, or perhaps forgot to insert the cross.

A revelation of the Trinity has in like manner been discovered in the three companions of Daniel, Ananias, Misaël, and Azarias, who were thrown by command of Nebuchadnezzar into the fiery furnace. That in them may be traced an image, referring more or less obscurely to the Trinity, is very possible; but it is impossible to receive that image as a symbol of the doctrine. Besides, in a subject of such serious importance, a conjecture, a possibility, will not suffice; realities are needed, texts clear and precise in their nature.*

The Old Testament offers very few such texts; in that part of the Holy Scriptures, few real and confessedly indisputable manifestations of the Trinity are to be met with.

youth;" but in the version of the Prayer Book, the text is, "the dew of thy birth is of the womb of the morning." In the version of Tremellius it is "in decoris *locis* sanctitatis inde ab utero, ab aurora tibi aderit ros juventæ suæ;" and the Vulgate has " Tecum principium in die virtutis tue [*sic*] in splendoribus sanctorum : ex utero ante luciferum genui te."—ED.

* It may, however, be observed, that the angel commissioned by God to extinguish the flames of the furnace into which Nebuchadnezzar had commanded the three Hebrews to be thrown, appeared to the King of Babylon in form like the Son of God. The three Hebrews did, in a measure, symbolise the three Divine persons, who were united in one single God in a divine and living unity, in the person of an Angel. The story has been thus understood by numerous artists and commentators of the middle ages ; but it must always be confessed, that in this biblical history the Trinity is recognised through the medium of interpretation, and not as a necessary deduction. (See the Prophecy of Daniel, iii. 23, 24, 25, 26.) St. Cyprian recognised the Trinity, not merely in the three young Hebrews, but figured even in the distribution of the prayers which those young men offered up in conjunction with Daniel. (St. Cyprian, *De Oratione Dominica,* near the end. See the *Institutions Liturgiques* par Dom Gueranger, vol. i., pp. 49, 81.) It may also be remarked, that verse 51 of chap. iii.,* which describes the three children as praising God with one voice, only, has been claimed as an additional argument in support of the commentators, who, in the whole of that history, discover a representation of the Trinity. " Tunc hi TRES quasi ex UNO ore laudabant et glorificabant et benedicebant Deum in fornace."

M. Didron here refers to v. 28 of the Apocryphal book called the "Song of the Three Children." In Tremellius, the passage will be found in the " Adjectiones in Danielem," v. 51, among the Apocryphal books.—ED.

THE MANIFESTATIONS OF THE TRINITY. 19

Fig. 183.—THE TRINITY AT THE BAPTISM OF CHRIST.
Italian carving on wood, XIV cent.*

* The carving on wood from which the above engraving is copied, was

The New Testament is far more precise; it both name the Trinity and shows it in visible substance.

Jesus said to his Apostles, "Go ye therefore and teach al nations, baptising them in the name of the Father and c the Son, and of the Holy Ghost." (Matt. xxviii. 19.) Ou Saviour says to his disciples elsewhere, "And I will pray th Father and he shall give you another Comforter, that he ma abide with you for ever, even the spirit of truth." (S John xiv. 16, 17.) St. John, in his first Epistle, declare that there are three who bear record in heaven, "th Father, the Word, and the Holy Ghost; and these thre are one." (1 St. John v., 7.) These texts distinctl name the three Divine persons, uniting them in the sam phrase; but at the baptism of Jesus Christ the Trinity wa made visibly manifest, and in the same action. "An Jesus, when he was baptised, went up straightway out of the water: and lo, the heavens were opened unto him, an he saw the spirit of God descending like a dove and lightin upon him: and lo, a voice from heaven, saying, This is m beloved Son, in whom I am well pleased." (St. Matt. ii 16, 17.)

The doctrine of the Trinity, when its formula had on been clearly set forth and visibly demonstrated, soon toc possession of men's minds. The Old Testament was peruse and re-perused; men sought to find the truth unveiled i passages which were obscure or had hitherto been passe over unremarked. It was then that the plural numb used in the book of Genesis—the threefold acclamations the Seraphim—the three fingers of God, on which the wor is suspended*—the three Angels entertained by Abraha

brought from Italy by M. Paul Durand, to whom it belongs. It is a work the fourteenth century, and yet it will be seen that already, that is, in t fourteenth century, either from negligence, or perhaps pure forgetfulne neither the nimbus of the Father nor that of the Son, is cruciform. T Holy Ghost is surrounded by an aureole, and could not, therefore, have nimbus also. This example of the baptism of our Lord is one of the m perfect that has ever come to my knowledge; it has something of a Byzanti character and feature.

* Isaiah xl. 12 of the Vulgate: "Quis appendet *tribus digitis* mol terræ." In our version it is: "And comprehended the dust of the earth ir *measure*." The version of Tremellius and Junius: "Aut complexus *trientali* pulverem terræ?" In a French version published at Rochelle, 161 "Qui est celui qui a compris la poussière de la terre avec une *tierce?*"—E

—the three children thrown into the furnace—were regarded as allusions to the Trinity, as symbols or at least as figures of the three Divine persons.*

After making inquiry into history, men next interrogated the human soul, and in it they discovered a reflection of the Trinity. The soul, made in the image of God, was one in substance and triple in its attributes. The power of the Father, the goodness of the Son, the wisdom of the Holy Ghost were repeated in miniature in the will, the love, and the intelligence of the human soul.

The soul has the power of knowing, desiring, and doing evil, precisely in the same manner as it possesses that of learning, willing, and accomplishing good, with the faculties which it has at its disposal. This is a necessary consequence of the nature of man, and of the imperfect liberty of his condition. Complete evil, that is absolute evil in man, appears under three aspects, corresponding with the attributes of the soul. In the supernatural class—the class infinite—God is the absolute perfection of good, and Satan of evil. God is one person in three hypostases; Satan is one person in three, or rather with three faces. Theologians and artists of the middle ages thus understood and depicted the fulness of virtue and of vice. In some representations

---

* The following extract from the writings of the liturgist, Gulielmus Durandus, will illustrate the feeling with which the Trinity was regarded in the middle ages, and form the complement of the quotations already given : " Dicens Deum singulariter deorum fugit pluralitatem . . . . ' Audi Israel, Dominus Deus tuus, unus est.' (Deut. vi. 4.) Et Apostolus, ' Unus est Deus, una fides, unum baptisma.' (Eph. iv. 5.) Dicens vero Patrem incipit personas distinguere, de quibus Esaias, ' Quis appendet tribus digitis molem terræ.' (Esaias xl. 12.) Et alibi, ' Seraphim clamabant Sanctus, Sanctus, Sanctus.' (Esa. vi. 3.) Et Dominus, ' Baptisate omnes gentes in nomine Patris et Filii et Spiritus Sancti.' (Matt. 28, 19.) Et Joannes, ' Tres sunt qui testimonium dant in cœlo ; Pater, Verbum et Spiritus Sanctus.' (1 John, v. 7.) * Pater est prima, non tempore, sed auctoritate, in Trinitate personæ. Quod sequitur omnipotentem, nomen est essentiale, ideoque illud ad substantivum Deum, vel ad relativum Patrem, non sine ratione referimus, dicentes credo in Deum Patrem omnipotentem, vel credo in Patrem omnipotentem. Similiter et quod sequitur ; Creatorem cœli et terræ."—Gulielmus Durandus, *Rationale*, lib. iv., *De Symbolo*.

---

* This is the verse of the three heavenly witnesses so much contested by commentators. It is now universally considered to be an interpolation of the copyist.—ED.

God is exhibited under the aspect of a man with three faces, one for each person; and there are others which represent the Devil as a human being, with three faces on a single trunk, as in the drawing subjoined.

Let this diabolical Trinity be compared with several of the divine Trinities already given, or which will hereafter be inserted, and it will be seen that the idea by which artists were guided in the execution of these representations was in both cases the same. But evil is in some sort more wicked, than goodness is good. In the following design, the Satanic Trinity is depicted as exalted to the highest degree of power. Three heads in the lower part of the body—three or four heads on the breast—three heads or faces in the upper part of the body, fixed on the neck, and those faces surmounted by three stags' horns, thorn-like and sharp-pointed. In the right hand of this dread monarch of evil is a sceptre fleury, with three heads of monsters.

Fig. 134.—THE TRINITY OF EVIL.
From a French Miniature of the XIII cent.*

Time, which is the finite image of a boundless eternity, was regarded during the middle ages under the three aspects of the past, the present, and the future. The present was not recognised, or but imperfectly, by the Pagans.† But in the eyes of Christians it had more value than the past, and as much as the future. The Romans represented

---

* The above drawing is taken from a curious manuscript in the Bibliothèque Royale, entitled *Emblemata Biblica*, and belonging to the thirteenth century. Few manuscripts are equally rich in miniatures; it contains no less than three hundred.

† Delille, the poet, who was semi-pagan both in sentiment and language, strove to suppress the idea of the present when he wrote the following line:—
"Le moment où je parle est déjà loin de moi."

THE MANIFESTATIONS OF THE TRINITY. 23

Fig. 135.—THE TRINITY OF ABSOLUTE EVIL.
From a French Miniature of the xv cent.*

Janus, the genius or personification of Time, by a figure

* French manuscript in the Bibl. Royale, *Histoire du Saint-Graal.*

with one head and two faces. Their "Janus Bifrons" viewed the past with the face that looked backwards, and inspected the future with that placed in front; certain of the Christian artists, inserted between these two faces that of the present,* as in the engraving subjoined.

This little figure with three faces on one single trunk, eating and drinking to celebrate the commencement of a new year, is in effect a Janus; it is placed at the head of the calendar, forming a frontispiece to the month of January. But it is a Christian Janus or rather a perfected image of Time. What indeed is life without the present? The remembrance of the past, and anticipations of the future, apart from realities of the present, can be nothing more than vanished dreams, or reveries yet unreal and

No. 6770. This fearful image of Satan, is presiding over an assembly of demons who deliberate on the birth of Merlin, by whose means they proposed to repair the injury which the devil had sustained through Christ, by his death and descent into hell. I am indebted to the friendship of M. Paulin Paris, Membre of the Institute, and Conservateur of the Bibliothèque Royale, for my acquaintance with this remarkable miniature, which was communicated to me by him.

* We say, "certain of the Christian artists," because it must be confessed that the influence of the two-visaged Janus, the classic "Janus bifrons," continued in force during the whole middle ages. It is with two faces, no three, that he is constantly figured in various places; particularly in th western porches of the Cathedrals of Chartres, of Strasbourg, and of Amiens and in the Abbey of St. Denis. A man with two heads and one single body is seen seated at a table covered with food; one face is sad and bearded, th other gay, beardless, and youthful. The bearded head represents the yea which is about to close, the thirty-first of December; the youthful head is personification of the opening year, the first of January. The old head i placed next the empty side of the table; he has consumed all his provisions before the young head, on the contrary, are several loaves, and dishes, and th servant, a little child, appears to be bringing others. This child is an additions personification of the coming year; it completes the youthful head of Janus In fact, a child accompanies both the bearded and the beardless head; but, o the side of the old man, it appears to be dead, and the door of a little temple being closed upon the body; while that on the side of the young man issue joyously from a similar temple. The one is dying and retiring from th world, the other entering it, filled with life and animation. A complet monography of these Christian types of Janus would be highly interestin The elementary principles might be gathered from sculpture, painted window and more especially, the miniatures of illuminated manuscripts. The subje is extremely curious, and deserves to be recommended to the notice of suc young antiquaries as are about to commence the study of mediæval iconograph The present time, too, is favourable for such researches, as men's minds see at length disposed to take some interest in Christian symbolism.

undeveloped. The present alone wins pardon for the past and grace for the future.

The present, the offspring of the past, is, according to the profoundly Christian idea of Leibnitz, big with the future.

Fig. 136.—FIGURE OF TIME WITH THREE FACES.
From a French Miniature of the XIV cent.*

Thus then, in this instance, as in others, Christianity surpasses the limits of ancient civilisation. Christianity indeed, revived many antique ideas, but while preserving, it at the same time made it its glory, to exalt and enrich them with at least one new element.

The number three became more and more sacred. It was

* This personification of the year with three faces, is to be found in the Bibliothèque de l'Arsénal, MS. Théol. Lat., 133ᶜ, *Officium Ecclesiasticum*. It is placed at the commencement of the manuscript, below the month of January; the present is drinking and taking nourishment; the past and the future are content to meditate; one appears to remember, for the last time ; the other, perhaps, already begins to hope.

proclaimed by Christians to be pre-eminently the sovereign and truly divine number. Defining and circumscribing that Pagan axiom which had said, *Numero Deus impare gaudet*, it fixed the odd number at three. The doctrine of the Trinity having once been revealed, violence was often done to things the most compact, indivisible, and homogeneous in their nature, in order that they might be divided into three parts, and again recomposed into unity. An entire history of men and events, the History of the Celts of Great Britain, was compressed, either by its own tendency or by force, into divisions of three compartments each; it resembles a piece of music, regulated from beginning to end by the triple-time measure. These historical measures are called "triads."*

* It will suffice to give merely the heads of the chapters composing this extraordinary history, which is constantly falsified by symbolism and the ternary system.

"Triads of the Island of Britain, which are triads of memorable things, of recollections and sciences, relating to the famous men, and the deeds done in Britain, and concerning the circumstances and misfortunes which at several periods have desolated the nation of the Cambrians. These are the three names given to the Island of Britain—the three principal divisions of the Island of Britain—the three pillars of the nation in the Island of Britain—the three domestic tribes of the Island of Britain—the three refugee tribes—the three sedentary invaders—the three transitory invaders—the three cheating invaders—the three disappearings of the Island of Britain—the three terrible events of the Island of Britain—the three combined expeditions which started from the Island of Britain—the three treacherous rencounters which took place in the Island of Britain—the three notable traitors of the Island of Britain—the three contemptible traitors who enabled the Saxons to take the crown of the Island of Britain from the Cambrians—the three bards who committed the three 'benevolent assassinations' (*assassinats bienfaisants*) of the Island of Britain—the three frivolous causes of the combat in the Island of Britain—the three discoveries and concealments of the Island of Britain—the three governing energies of the Island of Britain—the three vigorous men of the Island of Britain—the three deeds that occasioned the reduction of Lloegrie, and wrested it from the Cambrians—the first three extraordinary works of the Island of Britain—the three lovers of the Island of Britain—the three first mistresses of Arthur—the three knights of the court of Arthur who guarded the Graal—the three men who wore golden shoes in the Island of Britain—the three royal domains established by Rhadri the Great in Cambria." "A king of Ireland, named Cormack," adds M. J. Michelet, "in the year 260, wrote De Triadibus. Certain triads are preserved in Irish tradition under the title of Fingal. The Irish marched to battle in threes: the Scotch Highlanders are ranged three deep." See *Histoire de France*, par M. Michelet, vol. i., pp. 461-71, edit. in 8vo.

With the studies of the middle ages, which are resumed in the present day, their mysticism also has revived. No longer content to recognise the number three, and the Trinity itself, in objects in which that symbol is evidently displayed, it is discovered where probably it has no actual existence. It has been asserted, for example, that mediæval artists composed a hymn in honour of the number three; and that in erecting the porches of the cathedrals which we are pleased to find consist of three stages in height, and intersected in breadth by three divisions, they constructed a geometrical figure of the Trinity. The trefoil again, so abundant in Gothic decorations, is supposed to have been adopted solely in honour of the Trinity; but as porches of four or five stages, and four or five divisions, are as numerous as floriations of four, five, six, and seven lobes, the idea of the Trinity can hardly have been so constantly present to the artist's mind, as in our day is supposed to have been the case.*

Whenever three objects are seen united, whether plants, animals, monsters, or men, the idea of the divine Trinity immediately presents itself to the minds of these mystics. If three fishes be sculptured on the baptismal font of Denmark, three hideous apes upon a similar vessel in France, or three fantastic personages carved in relief on the tympanum of a church door, those three strange or monstrous beings are immediately recognised as symbols of

* The learned and illustrious M. Boisserée, in his folio, *Déscription de la Cathédrale de Cologne*, published at Paris in 1825, writes thus—" The fundamental principles of ancient church architecture are based, firstly, upon the equilateral triangle originally adopted by the Pythagoreans as an emblem of Minerva or wisdom, and subsequently employed by our ancestors as the symbol of the Trinity; secondly, on the dodecagon, a figure resulting from the application of the triangle to a circle, a combination regarded by the ancients as well as by our own ancestors, as containing all musical and astronomical proportion." We regret that we cannot admit these theories, all ingenious as they are. In a work recently published (*Manuel de l'Histoire Générale de l'Architecture*, par M. Daniel Ramée, vol. ii., in 12mo, Paris, 1843,) the symbolic theory of numbers, and of the number three in particular, is again revived; but it is carried in this case to the most absurd lengths. Such imaginings are, in respect of truth, what dreams are in comparison with the clear waking thoughts of a man of sound and circumspect judgment. Architecture, even in its history, will lose more than it gains from dreams of such a nature. The clear and decisive judgment of French writers is shown by their treating all similar odd inventions simply as aberrations of the intellect.

God the Father, God the Son, and God the Holy Ghost. To endeavour to extract some new idea from every remarkable fact, is indeed a highly laudable attempt, but it requires to be guided and enlightened by reason.*

Objects in which the Trinity may be distinctly recognised both in intention and in reality, are found in sufficient number to make it unnecessary to seek or create fictitious resemblances. Many of these will be noticed in treating of the direct and indirect worship rendered to the dogma of the Trinity, that is, to God, revealing himself in his three hypostases.

THE WORSHIP OF THE TRINITY.

Eight days after the great feast of Pentecost, instituted in honour of the Holy Ghost, that of the Trinity is celebrated Christmas, we are told, is the festival of God the Father,† Easter that of the Son, and Pentecost of the Holy Ghost and eight days after Pentecost these three distinct solemni

---

* Frederick Münter, Bishop of Zealand, in Denmark, of whom we have already spoken, published, in 1825, at Altona, the first and second parts of a work in 4to., entitled *Sinnbilder und Kunstvorstellungen der alten Christen* (Symbolic and Figurative Representations of the early Christians). He then speaks of the three fishes on the baptismal font in the church of Beigetad, in Denmark, as symbolising the Trinity. All these singular and misty interpretations have their origin in Germany and the North of Europe. In a report addressed by M. Schmit to the "Comité Historique des Arts et Monuments," and which was published in 1842, under the title of *Souvenirs d'un Voyage Archéologique dans l'Ouest*, we read, page 33, "On the south side of the church of Notre-Dame-des-Neiges, at Brelevenez (Brittany), rise three pillars the lower parts forming buttresses to the side aisle; they then spring up, alone to the height (which however is very trifling,) of the ridge of the roof Those on the left and right, which are rather less elevated than that in the centre, are truncated, with square heads; the third, in the centre, has a sloped coping. The porch is semicircular, surmounted by a gable forming the summit of the two eaves; it is placed between the second and third pillars. Local traditions speak of this arrangement as emblematic of the Trinity, and adopted by the Knights Templars in the construction of their churches. I know not whether this fact be decisively proved; but if not, the three pillar might with equal probability be supposed to refer to Mount Calvary, especially as they are here erected on a lonely mountain, at an elevation of not less than 100 mètres. It seems more simple, and may possibly be more correct to consider these pillars merely as buttresses, raised to the intended elevation of the building, which is evidently unfinished." Our assent must be given to the last of these conjectures, as being more simple, more sensible, and consequently more likely to be correct.

† At the close of the middle ages, about the period of the Rénaissance, men

ties are combined in one. An entire office was composed in honour of the Trinity, but it seems singular that Christmas, Easter, and Pentecost, which hold the rank of grand annual feasts, that is, have the supreme grade in the hierarchy of festivals, should concentrate themselves in one feast inferior by three degrees, and descend into a minor solemnity. Still the Trinity has always received great honours and worship. At the conclusions of introits, prayers, *proses*, hymns, psalms, and responses, the doxology associates each of the three persons in the glories, and sometimes even blends them together in one phrase.*

first became anxious to assign to the Father a special festival. To create a new one would have been more simple, and would have shown a more proper feeling, but historical difficulties presented themselves. In fact, God the Father having never visibly manifested Himself, one could not with propriety consecrate the memory of an event which had never occurred. Liturgists therefore proposed to set apart Christmas Day to the Father. Yet to do so, was evidently violating the actual signification of events. The day on which Mary gave birth to the Infant Saviour ; on which the Word was made flesh, and born in a stable, ought undoubtedly to belong either to Jesus Christ or the Virgin Mary : the Father here acts only secondarily. Consequently, notwithstanding the devotional wish of certain theologians, and the efforts of numerous liturgists (See G. Durandus, *Rationale Div. Off.*), Christmas was dedicated as before to Jesus and the Virgin, and the Father had still no especial festival. A manuscript in the Bibliothèque Royale opens the festival of Christmas with a representation of the Father, and that of Easter, in like manner, with a picture of the Son ; but usually, it may almost be said always, we meet with the picture of the Nativity at Christmas, and the name of the Feast of the Nativity (in French *Noël*, Latin *Natalis*) still distinguishes the day of our Saviour's birth. The seventh volume of the works of St. Tommasi, edited by Bianchini, contains a note upon a supplication requiring the institution of a festival in honour of the Father Eternal.

* The " Gloria Patri, et Filio, et Spiritui Sancto," is attributed to St. Jerome, who is said to have sent it to Pope Damasus,* who directed it to be sung at the end of the Psalms. The hymns composed by Saint Ambrose, and which are sung at the " Hours," either on Sundays, or week-days terminate in a Gloria addressed to the three Divine persons :—

" Deo Patri sit gloria
Ejusque soli Filio
Cum Spiritu paraclito,
Nunc et per omne seculum."

Or else : — " Præsta, Pater piissime,
Patrique compar unice,
Cum Spiritu paraclito,
Regnans per omne sæculum."

* Elected Pope of Rome, A. D. 366, died A. D. 385. St. Jerome was his secretary.

The Trinity, like the Holy Ghost, gave the name to a religious order called the Trinitarians.*

Churches and monasteries were erected throughout Christendom in honour of the Holy Trinity. The Abbey of the Holy Trinity at Florence is famous from the fine paintings it contains, and which were executed, according to Vasari, by Giovanni Cimabue. Arezzo had, and probably has still, a convent of nuns of the Holy Ghost (di Santo Spirito). At Caen, Rouen, Fécamp, Poitiers, Vendôme, Angers, Lefay (in the diocese of Coutances), and in several other places, there were celebrated abbeys and churches dedicated to the Holy Trinity.

The name of Trisay-la-Sainte-Vierge, in the diocese of Luçon, is probably derived from the acclamation three times repeated by the celestial spirits in honour of the Trinity.† St. Williborde, bishop of Trèves, who died in 739, erected a monastery in honour of the Holy Trinity, in the basilica of which he was interred.‡

Not only were churches and convents erected in honour of the union of the three Divine persons, but the configuration

---

* The Trinitarians date from the year 1198. The Order was founded by St. John de Matha and Felix de Valois, for the repurchase or redemption of captives. The regulations of their order were approved by Pope Innocent III., who gave them, in 1199, a white mantle decorated with a red cross with double branches. This cross also surmounted the Holy Spirit, which was engraven on their seal. I am indebted for a copy of this seal to the courtesy of M. le Baron de Girardot, Conseiller de Préfecture et correspondant du Comité des Arts. One of the articles of the rules of the Trinitarians runs thus:— " Omnes ecclesiæ istius ordinis intitulentur nomine sanctæ Trinitatis et sint plani operis." This *planum opus*, imposed as an obligation on the Trinitarians, is a point of some importance in the history of architecture.

† In Greek, *Trisagion*, Latinised by *Trizaium*, *Trisagium*. The *Sanctus, Sanctus, Sanctus* (ἅγιος, ἅγιος, ἅγιος), was inserted by St. Ambrose and St. Augustine in the Te Deum, which is said to have been composed by them in common, both words and music. The two great doctors thus caused to be repeated upon earth the same hymn which St. John heard in heaven, and of which he speaks in the Apocalypse, iv. 8. In Greece, numerous angels painted in fresco or in mosaic, bear in their hands a kind of banner, on which is written, " ἅγιος, ἅγιος, ἅγιος." There was, near Mantes, a couvent of the Celestines, named the Trinity (See *Catalogue Joursanvault*, vol. ii., No. 1244); and at Beaulieu, in Touraine, there was also an Abbey of the Holy Trinity.

‡ The life of St. Williborde was written by Alcuin.

of those churches and convents, recalled by the number or form of certain parts, the idea of the Trinity. St. Benoît d'Aniane, the Carlovingian Apostle of the south of France, constructed a church which he dedicated, not to any saint, but to the Holy Trinity. To the high altar he annexed three subordinate altars, designing that the three persons should be symbolised by the latter, and the Divine unity by the former. The high altar, emblem of the two Testaments, was circular without, hollow within, and in the back a small door was inserted, affording access to shrines and relics of saints which were there kept on ordinary days.* One altar in that church was dedicated to St. Michael, another to the apostles St. Peter and St. Paul, a third to St. Stephen. Another church, dedicated to the Virgin, contained one altar, consecrated to St. Martin; another to St. Benedict, and the high altar belonged no doubt to the Virgin. Lastly, in the cemetery, a third church was erected and dedicated to St. John the Baptist. Thus in that convent there were three churches: one dedicated to the Virgin, with three altars; and another to the Trinity, having also three altars, but subordinate to the high altar.

At Fleury, now St. Benoît-sur-Loire, there were, not one, two, or three churches only, dedicated to the Trinity,

* See the original, which is not without value, in the *Act. SS. Ord. S. Bened.*, IV. Siècle Bénédictin, 1ᵉ partie, de l'an 800 à l'an 855. The life of St. Benoît d'Aniane was written by Ardon or Smaragdus, his disciple. At Munich is a church dedicated to the Holy Trinity. In that edifice the number three is inscribed upon the altars and in the ground-plan, which is a kind of trefoil. The church is covered with paintings of historical, psychological, and physical subjects, either natural or symbolical; making allusion to the number three and its divine properties. God is creating the sun, the moon, and the earth (three distinct worlds), and is represented with a nimbus of the triangular form. Jesus is transfigured in the presence of Moses and Elias, and St. Peter requests permission to erect three tents on the mountain. A hand performs a benediction with three fingers, in the name of the three divine persons. A large A shines resplendent with the following inscription: *Linea terna est unum alpha*. Beneath a hand, holding a candlestick with three branches, is seen, *Tenet una trinum*. Below a vessel with three sails is read, *Tribus his pellitur una*. An eye is shining in a triangle of flame, with three circles intertwined. Three mirrors reflect one single ray, emanating from the sun. Numerous other emblems adorn this curious church, which I should have described at length, did it not date from 1714, a period of no value in respect of religious archæology.

but the entire plan of the monastery bore inscribed upon its area, the idea of the Trinity. The ground plan was in the form of a delta, the mysterious triangle of the ancient alphabet. One point of this triangle turned towards France; another to Burgundy, while the third was in the direction of Aquitaine. "Fleury stood on the confines of three regions, like the present between the past and the future—like the perfect number between the imperfect and the pluperfect." *

Lastly, in a third instance, contemporaneous with the preceding, the emblematic idea of the Trinity will be seen carried even to a puerile excess, in the plan and arrangement of an immense monastery, that of Saint Riquier.† St. Angilbert, the son-in-law of Charlemagne, one of the companions and peers of that great Emperor, retired to Centula, and there re-built the monastery of Saint Riquier. He erected three churches, one dedicated to St. Riquier, one to the Virgin, and a third to St. Benedict. They were connected, one with the other, by a triangular cloister. Three smaller churches, at the entrance of the three gates of the monastery, were besides dedicated to St. Michael, St. Gabriel, and St. Raphael. In the church of St. Benedict there were three altars : there were three altars also in the churches of the angels, three ciboria, and three lectoria. The monks were three hundred in number—the children of the choir one hundred, divided into three sections—thirty-three children in the two last sections, and thirty-four in the

---

* The reader will remember what has been already said of the present, which in the middle ages was esteemed superior both to the past and the future, while classic antiquity, which appears to suppress it, gave to Janus, the personification of time, two faces only. The original quotation relating to Fleury is here transcribed, as it refers both to historical and mystical facts : " Situs loci Floriacensis monasterii * * * instar trigoni visitur sieti, et, ut expressius dicam, in modum litteræ proprio statu cernitur sidereum cornu occupare. Nam a septentrione Franciam, ab oriente Burgundiam, ab australi vero parte Aquitaniam tangit. Sicque in confinio trium regionum, velut præsens inter præteritum et futurum, naturali ordine obtinet primatum, et sicut perfectus numerus inter imperfectum et plusquam perfectum. Nam medietate vicem et locum possidet virtutum."—*Act. SS. Ord. S. Bened.*, IV. Siècle Bénédictin, " Histoire de l'Illation de St. Benoît," vers l'an 883.

† A long extract from this passage has been given verbatim, vol. i. pp. 61, 62. A further analysis of the same passage is here given : this repetition was rendered necessary by the subject at present under consideration.

first.* The whole body was divided into three choirs. One hundred monks and thirty-four children attended on the altar and formed the choir of the Holy Saviour: one hundred monks and thirty-three children belonged to the choir of St. Riquier, and an equal number to the choir of the Passion. These three choirs chanted the services in common; but afterwards, while two of the three divisions remained in the church, the third division rested.† In this puerile affectation of repeating the number three, the bias of men's minds in favour of the Trinity is easily perceptible.

The cloister of St. Riquier is no longer in existence, but at Planés in Roussillon, a little church is still standing, triangular in form, and surmounted by a cupola. The idea which prompted the construction of this curious edifice must have been analogous with that by which Angilbert's designs were governed.‡ In Rome, as it is said, the chevalier Bernin has distinguished by the triangular form the church of St. Sapienza which is dedicated to the Trinity. Wisdom in point of fact, is to the principal virtues, what God is to the Divine persons. Wisdom is the moral unity whence proceed Faith, Hope, and Charity, like daughters of one common mother. These three daughters of Wisdom, and Wisdom herself, the parent of the three, owed their existence to the lively imagination of the Byzantines. We meet in *legendary* history, with the life of Santa Sophia, the mother of three children of rare virtue and incomparable beauty, St. Faith, St. Hope, and St. Charity.

The mother and daughters having been converted to Christianity and baptised, preached the truth, and in their *turn* converted a countless number of Pagans, and became

* Thirty-three only would have been required by a strict attention to rule, n order to perfect the symbolism.

† *Act SS. Ord. S. Bened.*, 1ᵉ partie, du IVᵉ siécle bénéd., from the year 300 to 855. "Life of St. Angilbert." Angilbert, surnamed Homer in the Palatine Academy, as Charlemagne was there called David, united in his own mind, in their most brilliant and concentrated expression, the mystical deas prevalent during the reign of the Carlovingian race. At that period, owever, numerous discussions arose concerning the Trinity and the procession f the Holy Ghost.

‡ See the *Bulletin Archéologique*, published by the "Comité Historique es Arts et Monuments," vol. i, p. 133, for a description of this church, ritten by M. Jaubert de Passa, a non-resident member of the committee.

themselves subjected to persecution. Being led before the proconsul, they refused to offer sacrifices to false gods, and were therefore tortured and at length beheaded. The entire legend of this interesting family from their birth to their death, is painted on one of the walls of a convent on Mount Athos.* Among the relics of virgins, in the Cathedral at Canterbury, are preserved those of St. Sophia, and her daughters, Faith, Hope, and Charity.†

This personification and genealogy of Virtue, remind us of the personification and genealogy of Intelligence already mentioned, and which is figured in a manuscript bible in the public library at Rheims.‡ Philosophy engenders Physics, Logic, and Ethics, exactly as St. Sophia gives birth to Faith, Hope, and Charity.

CHRONOLOGICAL ICONOGRAPHY OF THE TRINITY.

A worship so solemn, so highly developed as that rendered to the Trinity, would naturally occasion numerous representations of the three Divine persons united in one group, and this is accordingly found to be the case.

* The great monastery of Chilandari. In the Byzantine manuscript which has already been quoted, instructions are given for painting St. Sophia and her three daughters, St. Faith, St. Hope, and St. Charity, who were all beheaded.

† "De reliquiis St. Sapientiæ et filiarum ejus, Fidei, Spei, et Charitatis" (*Vide* the *Monasticon Anglicanum*, by Dodsworth and Dugdale, vol i., p. 5). I discover from this singular fact, that a certain Byzantine influence was formerly in operation in England. It must be observed also, that the true Greek cross is not that with four equal limbs, since Procopius, a Greek writer, asserts that the foot of the cross ought to be longer than the arms or the top. Greek crosses are with double cross arms, like those engraved above, and which were brought from Athens and from Mount Athos. Some relics procured from Greece, and presented by the Kings of France to the Sainte Chapelle à Paris, were enclosed in cases made in the form of a cross with double arms. Now, it is precisely on this plan that several of the large English cathedrals are built, and in this fact also, I discover that England has been subjected to Byzantine influence, the traces of which deserve to be studied and investigated. Nothing analogous is to be found in France; Gothic or Christian art is with us "autochthone," except in a very few instances.

‡ In the Manuscript of Herrade, "*Hortus deliciarum*," Philosophy is represented sitting on a throne, and pouring from her bosom the sources of the liberal arts. The floriations of her diadem are formed by three human heads Ethics, Logic, and Physics, as saith the Legend.

The art eagerly took possession of a motive that addressed itself to the imagination with such singular force, and which was capable of being diversified to an almost unlimited extent. The centuries which elapsed between the first rise of Christianity and the Rénaissance, and during which Trinities were constantly designed, may be divided into four periods. The first division comprehends the eight first centuries; the second extends from the ninth to the twelfth; the third reaches to the fifteenth century; the last period comprehends the Rénaissance, that is to say, the fifteenth and more particularly the sixteenth century. With reference to architecture, the first period is called the Latin, because at that time, the basilicas of Constantine predominated; the second is the Romanesque, because the Latin style then began, amongst us more particularly, to be combined with indigenous elements; the third is the Gothic or ogival; the fourth, the Rénaissance.

During the eight first centuries Trinities were merely in a state of experimental preparation; various different modes of treatment were then attempted, which re-appeared in a more complete state of development in succeeding centuries. Not one really perfect group of the Trinity is to be found either in the catacombs, or upon ancient sarcophagi.

Jesus is frequently seen, but alone, or at most accompanied only by the dove, which symbolises the Holy Ghost. A hand is perceived, which ought to be intended for that of God the Father, holding a crown above the head of the Son, but in the absence of the Holy Ghost. The Cross and the Lamb, symbols of the Son, the hand revealing the presence of the Father, and Doves, sometimes symbolising the Holy Ghost,* are frequently seen in the fresco paintings, or on the sculptured marbles of the catacombs. But these symbols are almost always isolated; they are very rarely united in one spot, or upon the same monument, and never inked together and bound up in one.

Yet after the fourth century, in the time of Paulinus, bishop of Nola, who was born in 353, and died in 431,

---

* I say, *sometimes*, because the dove sculptured or painted in the catacombs most generally that bringing back the olive branch to Noah, and not the dove ! the Holy Ghost. See on this subject the " Roma Sotterranea" of Bosio.

groups of the Trinity made their appearance. In the apse of the basilica of St. Felix, erected by St. Paulinus himself at Nola, is a group of the Trinity executed in mosaic. St. Paulinus wrote the following lines in explanation of the subject:

> "Pleno coruscat Trinitas mysterio:
> Stat Christus agno, vox Patris cælo tonat,
> Et per columbam Spiritus-Sanctus fluit,
> Crucem corona lucido cingit globo;
> Cui coronæ sunt corona apostoli,
> Quorum figura est in columbarum choro.
> Pia Trinitatis unitas Christo coït."

Thus, in this Trinity, Christ is figured by a lamb, and the Holy Ghost by a dove. The Father is said to speak, but the poet does not say in what manner he was depicted.* In the same letter,—a little afterwards, when describing the painting which had been executed in the basilica of St. Felix at Fondi, in the interior of the apse,—St. Paulinus adds—

> "Sub cruce sanguineâ niveo stat Christus in agno,
> Agnus ut innocua injusto datus hostia leto.
> Alite quem placida sanctus perfundit hiantem
> Spiritus, et rutila genitor de nube coronat."

The lamb is here added to the Cross, in order to complete or to double the symbol of Christ. The Spirit is always in the form of a dove—it is the Divine bird; but the Father, if not represented entirely in the human form, must at least be figured by a hand holding a crown above the Saviour's head. The above are the earliest known indications of representations of the Trinity. It should be observed that these groups are mosaics, adorning the apses of basilicas. In fact, it is in mosaics and at the extreme end of Latin basilicas, that representations of the Trinity, resembling the second of

---

* See the works of St. Paulinus, *Epistola* 12ª *ad Severum*. A litl before the text just quoted, Paulinus had said—

"Atque ubi Christus ibi Spiritus et Pater est."

But that verse signified only, that in beholding Christ, the Father and the So also were consequently seen, and that each of the three persons was representu under a special figure.

those described by Paulinus, are most commonly seen. In the churches of St. Damien, and St. Cosmo at Rome, in 530; in St. Mark's, in the same city, in 774; in the Cathedral of Padua towards the close of the eighth century; in St. Prassede, in Rome, in 818, Trinities were executed in mosaic, which might be taken for copies of those of St. Paulinus.*

This theme remained in favour at Rome as late as the thirteenth and fourteenth centuries. Pope Nicholas IV., between the years 1288 and 1294, caused the apse of the Church of St. Giovanni in Laterano, to be decorated, and a large mosaic there, stands out in most resplendent brilliancy; it contains in the centre a representation of the Trinity. A Cross, covered with precious stones, is elevated on the summit of a mountain symbolic of Paradise. The Holy Ghost in the form of a dove, hovers above the Cross and envelopes it in a flood of radiance. Above all is the Father, emerging from the clouds, and with the bust and bare head alone visible; the latter encircled by a double nimbus, the square and the circular.†

Another type of the Trinity constantly to be met with in works of the fourteenth century, appears to have been in use, from the earliest Christian epoch.

The following history is given in " Jacobus de Voragine, at the Festival of the Exaltation of the Cross."

" In the year of our Lord 615, God permitted that his people should be scourged by the cruelty of the Pagans. Chosroes, king of the Persians, subjected to his empire all the kingdoms of the world. He visited Jerusalem, and quitted in awe the sepulchre of our Saviour; but carried away with him notwithstanding that portion of the Holy Cross, which had been deposited there by St. Helena. Chosroes, wishing to be adored by all mankind as a deity, commanded the erection of a tower of gold and silver, ornamented with glistening gems; there too, he placed images of the sun, the moon, and stars. By means of narrow and

---

* *Ciampini, Vetera Monimenta.* Engravings of these mosaics, and of many ther like designs, are given in that work. [See Tav., xvi., xlvii., lii., and v. The latter is a very fine example.—ED.]

† A description has already been given of this interesting mosaic, of which L. Tournal favoured me with a design.

hidden conduits he caused rain to fall as if he had indeed been God. Horses were placed on the top of the tower, round which they dragged chariots, thus shaking the building and producing sounds resembling thunder. Then relinquishing the kingdom to his son, the profane maniac retired into that pharos, and having commanded the Cross of our blessed Saviour to be placed near him, he desired all men to call him God. According to the account given in the book 'De Mitrali Officio,' * Chosroes seated on a throne like that of God the Father, placed the Cross on his right hand in the place assigned to God the Son, and a cock on his left, instead of the Holy Ghost; for himself, he commanded that he should be called God the Father."

The Emperor Heraclius made war on the son of Chosroes and defeated him; he entered his capital and penetrated to the apartment of the old king, who had then become insane. He found him seated in his tower of gold and silver, as in a sort of paradise, like the Father Almighty between the other two Divine persons. Chosroes refusing to become a Christian, Heraclius cut off his head with one stroke of the sword, in the presence of his painted angels and the cock.†

* This book, so frequently quoted by liturgists and legendaries, is attributed to a bishop of Cremona, Richard, who lived in 1195. The *Mitrale, vel Summa de Divinis Officiis* is still in manuscript. It is, however, a work well worthy of publication. Such books as the "Mitrale" would be of the greatest service to literati engaged in the study of Christian antiquities.

† The following is the original of this important passage, which has been here translated literally :—" Anno domini 615, permittente Domino flagellari populum suum per sævitiam paganorum. Cosdroe, rex Persarum, omnia regna terrarum suo imperio subjugavit. Hierusalem autem veniens, a sepulcro Domini territus rediit, sed tamen partem S. Crucis quam St. Helena ibidem reliquerat asportavit. Volens autem ab omnibus coli ut Deus, turrim et auro et argento et interlucentibus gemmis fecit, et ibidem solis, lunæ et stellarum imagines collocavit. Per subtiles etiam et occultos ductus, quasi Deus, aquam desuper infundebat, et in supremo specu equi quadrigas trahentes in circuitu ibant, ut quasi turrim moverent et tonitrua simularent. Filio igitur regno suo tradito, in tali phano prophanus residet, et juxta se crucem Domini collocans appellari ab omnibus se Deum jubet. Et, sicut legitur in libro ' Mitrali de Officio' ipso Cosdroe in throno residens, tanquam Pater, lignum Crucis sibi a dextris posuit loco Filii, et gallum a sinistris loco ' Spiritus-Sancti ;' se vero jussit Patrem nominari." The Emperor Heraclius made war on the son of Chosroes, destroyed his army, and entered his royal city. " Cosdroe autem ignorabat exitum belli, quia, cum ab omnibus odiretur, sibi a nemine intimatur.

In this description we have the living group of the Christian Trinity mocked, mimicked, dramatised by an old Pagan who had lost his senses. In this group the Father is an old man, the Son is represented by his cross, and the Holy Ghost by a cock, put in the place of the sacred dove. This motive resembles that described by S. Paulinus, and exhibited in the various mosaics that have been mentioned above: still it differs in certain points.

It is similar in regard to the symbols, showing forth the Divine persons; but different in the general arrangement of the group, and the disposition of the symbols of which it is composed. In the description given by S. Paulinus, and in the mosaics, the Trinity is vertical; in the Golden Legend it is horizontal.

S. Paulinus mentions the cross as placed below, and the Holy Ghost above the cross, and the Father surmounting the whole. In the legend the Father is in the centre, having the cross on his right, and the Holy Ghost on the left. Further, S. Paulinus and the Mosaicists place the Holy Ghost in the centre, while Chosroes as the Almighty Father, places himself in the midst, and gives the left to the cock, his Holy Ghost. As we proceed, the difference between these two types will be more fully illustrated by drawings.

During the second period, from the ninth to the twelfth century, the two anterior types continue in use,* but are

---

Heraclius autem ad eum pervenit et in throno aureo eum sedere reperiens, eidem dixit : ' Quia lignum S. Crucis secundum tuum modulum honorasti, si baptismum et fidem Christi susceperis, adhuc vitam et regnum, paucis a te acceptis obsidibus, obtinebis. Si autem hoc implere contempseris, gladio meo te feriam et caput tuum prescidam.' Cum igitur ille acquiescere nollet, extracto gladio, eum protinus decollavit, et, quia rex fuerat, sepeliri præcepit." (*Jacobus de Voragine, Legenda aurea, de Exaltatione S. Crucis.*)

* These types continue during the whole of the middle ages, even in France where men were less faithful to Latin tradition. In the voussure of the central door in the western porch of the collegiate church of Mantes, is a Trinity, represented by a cross, not carried merely, but exalted by two angels, by the Father who is of the same age and has the same features as the Son, and the Holy Ghost in the form of a dove, descending from heaven. The subjects are placed in vertical order, at the extremity of the three cordons. The Father is in the centre, the cross below, and the dove surmounting the whole. This sculpture dates from the twelfth century, or, perhaps, the close of the eleventh. This is a new and most interesting arrangement. I cannot speak of the Church of Mantes, without

enriched with two new motives, one borrowed from the human figure, the other from geometrical forms.

Anthropomorphism,* which was so repulsive to the first Christians, and had appeared to them like a revival of Paganism, did not meet with the same opposition during the middle ages, properly so called. Having attained the ninth century, Christianity had no longer anything to fear from Pagan ideas; the fall of Paganism had long been accomplished. The Almighty Father whose hand only had hitherto been shown or at most, his bust, was now represented at full length. Still no special form was assigned to him; he merely borrowed that of the Son, and from that time forward, it became difficult to distinguish the one from the other. The Son continued to appear, as he had been seen on earth, under the figure of a man of lofty stature, beautiful and solemn, of from thirty to thirty-five years of age. The dove of the Holy Ghost sometimes also threw off the veil of the bird-like form and assumed that of a man. Theology having positively declared that the three persons were not only similar, but equal amongst themselves, artists extended that similitude to their representations, and occasionally represented the three Divine hypostases as equal also.

Saint Dunstan, Archbishop of Canterbury, who died in 908, left behind him a manuscript in which the three persons are figured under the human form. The Father and the Son, clad in kingly apparel, with crowns on their heads and sceptres in their hands, both appear to be about thirty-five years of age. The Holy Ghost is younger, and scarcely more than eighteen or twenty-five. A similarity in person is apparent, but a difference in point of age. That latter difference finally disappears, and in the manuscript of Herrade, dating from the year 1180, it is replaced by absolute identity. The three Divine persons are of the same age, in the same attitude, and of the same temperament; all wearing

---

extolling M. de Wavrechin, the curé of that beautiful and ancient collegiate church, by whom it has been repaired and fitted up with truly archæological taste and science.

* By anthropomorphism must be understood, not the heresy to which that name has been given, but the figuring of Divine persons under the human form. It is the intention of the present work simply to state facts, not to test the soundness of doctrine.

also the same costume. Which is intended for the Father, which for the Son, and which for the Holy Ghost, in this anthropomorphic Trinity?

By comparison with other monuments, and bearing in mind the Scriptural texts already quoted, it may be supposed that the Father is in the centre, the Son on the right hand, and the Holy Ghost on the left, such being the most constant custom. But the miniaturist appears in this instance to have aimed at discomfiting both the antiquary and the theologian. On the feet of one of the Divine persons he has traced the stigmata, which, however, are scarcely visible in the original manuscript.* The stigmata, of course, can belong only to Christ the Saviour; yet it must be remembered that no similar marks are in the hands, and that even on the feet they are of singular form, that of a cross, which could not have been produced by nails. That form, however, is undoubtedly symbolic, and it must be supposed that the figure in the centre is that of Christ. Where then is the Father? It is impossible to determine, because impossible to decide whether the Holy Ghost is placed on the left hand or on the right. The identity of persons thus appears to be almost absolute.

The Trinity, in opposition to an anthropomorphism so peculiarly complete and material as the above, is sometimes figured under the driest and most abstract form; that of the triangle, which is borrowed from geometry. It was thence that the triangular form, in which the convent of Fleury is built, assumed its mystical signification; thence too, St. Angilbert erected the church of St. Riquier on a triangular plan, and in honour of the Trinity. The triangle, comprehending three angles in one single area, is a correct image of the three persons, resolving themselves into one single God.

The thirteenth century purchased to itself eternal glory, not merely by discovering and inventing new elements, that it threw into the crucible, wherein Christian and Catholic symbolism which had in former ages been elaborated, were then undergoing to a certain

* M. Durand, my designer, had not at first remarked them, and I found it necessary to point out to him this microscopic point, and request him to correct his drawing. A few errors of this nature have slipped into our engravings, but whenever it has been impossible to correct them, they have been mentioned

CHRISTIAN ICONOGRAPHY.

Fig. 157.—THE TRINITY IN THREE HUMAN PERSONS OF IDENTICAL FIGURE.
From a Manuscript of the XII cent.*

* "*Hortus deliciarum.*" The above Trinity is introduced in illustration

extent, the process of crystallisation, but rather by its having given full development to elements of which only the germ had existed in preceding centuries. It is the deathless glory of that epoch to have brought to maturity and formed into a flower what preceding periods had been content merely to sow. The little Latin bell or "sonnette" (squilla),* as has been elsewhere observed,† became in the Romanesque period the church bell; but after the thirteenth century it swelled into the "bourdon." The steeple became a bell turret, and in the thirteenth century a tower. The same may be observed with regard to Iconography. Trinities, which, during the first period were heteromorph, and the second alike in form, were still figured during the third; but they were then completed, multiplied, and brought to perfection. For one Latin Trinity, or two of the Romanesque period, we meet with perhaps twenty or thirty Gothic Trinities: they are found in the same relative proportion, starting even from the close of the twelfth century.

At that time, as in the earliest period, Trinities are seen, in which the Father is revealed by a hand only; the Son by the Cross, the Lamb, or the human form; and the Holy Ghost by the dove. The symbols of the three persons are grouped vertically or horizontally, as in the first period: there are also, as in the second period, geometric and anthropomorphic Trinities.

But the third period was not content to multiply, or to reproduce in considerable numbers, groups that had already been adopted; it modified and perfected them. To the cross of the Latin period the Divine figure of the crucified had

---

of the creation, at the moment when God, before creating man, says, " Faciamus hominem ad imaginem et similitudinem nostram et præsit cunctis animantibus terræ." The same text of Genesis is written on the scroll held by the three persons.

* And note, that there be six kinds of bells which be used in the church: namely, the *"squilla,* the *cymbalum,* the *nota,* the *nohila* (or double *campana*), the *signum,* and the *campana.* The *squilla* is rung in the *triclinium,* that is, in the refectory; the *cymbalum* in the cloister; the *nota* in the choir; the *nohila,* or double *campana,* in the clock; the *campana* in the campanile, the *signum* in the tower."—Durandus—first book of the *Rationale,* page 93.—*Trans.*

† *Monographie de Notre Dame de Brou,* in the Introduction.

44 CHRISTIAN ICONOGRAPHY.

been attached in the Romanesque epoch; so, too, the equality of the Divine persons, which owed its origin to the Romanesque period, was, during the Gothic, most energetically and distinctly expressed. In the manuscript of

Fig 138.—THE THREE DIVINE PERSONS FUSED ONE INTO THE OTHER.
From a Spanish Miniature of the XIII cent.*

Herrade, the three persons are depicted under the human form, and equal as far as was possible. Yet those persons,

* *Chronique d'Isidore de Seville*, MS. de la Bibl. Roy., 7135. The third head is not seen, because in plan the three heads would form a trefoil, and the

although sitting on one same throne—although supporting one single scroll, and all of the same age, are, nevertheless, very distinctly three bodies; they are drawn closely together, but still they are not in contact. Now, after the thirteenth century, not only do the divine figures *touch*, but they actually cohere. The three bodies form now one only, with three heads, which latter in their turn are completely welded together.

In anthropomorphic representations, one passes, so to speak, from similarity to identity. In geometrical figures, on the contrary, more distinction begins to be made between the three persons than in the preceding period.* The triangle, in fact, gives under a form the most compact, and with as little distinction as possible, the triplicity resolving itself into unity. The thirteenth century adds a new geometrical type, in which the triplicity is more visible and the unity less absolute. The circle is considered as emblematic of God, and three circles figure the three persons; but in order to mark the indissoluble union in which those three persons are linked together, the three circles are intertwined, one within the other, in such a manner that one could not be severed or removed without

third is consequently concealed by the two which are visible. If the manuscript from which the above design is taken be Spanish, like the text which it contains, mediæval art in Spain, it must be confessed, appears widely different from ours; it is far more original, or perhaps we should rather say abnormal. In a Spanish manuscript in the Bibliothèque d'Amiens, several singular particularities unknown amongst ourselves, are also to be found.

* After the eighth century, when it was desired to show the equality of the Divine persons, examples were taken which proved too much, the effect was a near approach to absolute identity. St. Odile, Abbess of the Convent of Hohenburg, in Alsace, which is known in the present day by the name of St. Odile, planted three linden trees in honour of the Trinity. The relation of this circumstance is curious enough to be worth transcribing. A man once came to seek the saint, and presented her with three branches, taken from one single linden tree; he desired her to plant them, that they might remain there in memory of her. "Et tulit (S. Odilia) unam in manu sua, et ait; 'In nomine Patris te planto.' Et accipiens alteram, dixit: 'Et in nomine Filii.' Et tertiam tulit dicens: 'Et in nomine Spiritus Sancti;' mysterium Trinitatis complens." The three branches took root, and became three large trees exactly alike, equal, and almost identical, beneath the shade of which the nuns enjoyed the air in summer.—See, in the *Act. SS. Ord. de S. Benedict*, vol. iv., "La Vie de Saint Odile," by an anonymous writer, apparently of about the eleventh century. Odile died about 720.

at the same time severing all the three. The word Trinity by a singular coincidence, may itself be divided into three syllables. One of each of these syllables is placed in each circle, but they have no perfect meaning, and will not form any word unless united. TRI-NI-TAS. In the space lef' vacant in the centre by the intersection of the three circles we read the word UNITAS. Thus, then, Unity is the centre from which radiates the Trinity.

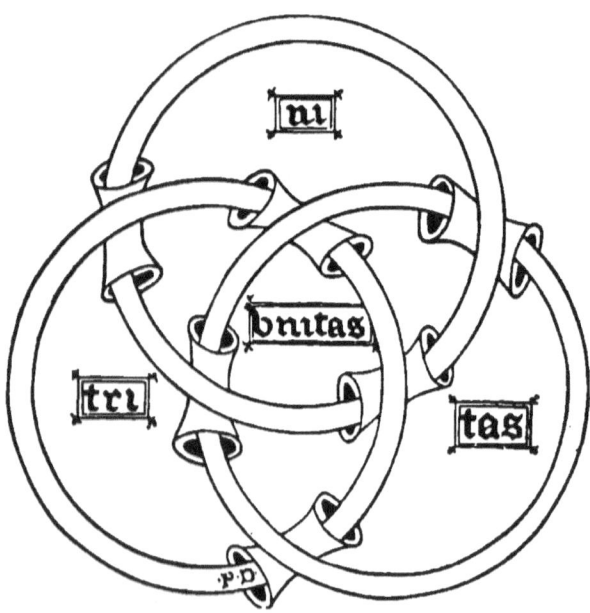

Fig. 139.—THE TRINITY UNDER THE FORM OF THREE CIRCLES.
From a French Miniature of the close of the XIII cent.*

In the same manuscript there are, besides the preceding three, other groups of three circles. One of these groups has the following words distributed equally throughout each of the three circles:—PATER—FILIUS—SPIRITUS—SANCTUS, all of which resolve themselves in the centre into VITA DEUS. In the second is VERBUM, LUX

* *Manuscript de la Bibl. Communale de Chartres*, No. 1355, end of the thirteenth century.

VITA, terminating in the centre in DEUS-EST.* In the third is, TRI-TRI, NI-NI, TAS-TATE; and in the centre, UNITATE—UNITAS. The Unity diverges into Trinity, the Trinity converges into Unity. Lastly, in the gloss we read, "Verbum, lux, vita Deus est,"—"Verbum, lux, vita Jesus-Christus est,"—"Verbum, lux, vita Spiritus-Sanctus est." Invert these three terms and displace the attributes, and the following dogma will be found to be the result. "Deus trinus unus." These figures, then, are merely the interpretation in a geometrical form of the Creed of St. Athanasius.

It might be expected of the subtle genius of Dante, that he would readily adopt such a geometrical formula. That great poet, in fact, closes the "Paradise" with the following strophes, in which the idea of both the Trinity and Unity is embodied in magnificent language.

"Nella profonda e chiara sussistenza,
Dell' alto lume parvemi tre giri,
Di tre colori e d'una contenenza;
E l' un dall' altro, come Iri da Iri,†
Parea riflesso; e'l terzo parea fuoco,‡
Che quinci e quindi igualmente si spiri.

* * * *

O luce eterna che sola in te sidi,
Sola t'intendi, e da te intelletta
Ed intendente te ami ed arridi!
Quella circulazion che sì concetta
Pareva in te, come lume riflesso,
Dagli occhi miei alquanto circonspetta,
Dentro da se del suo colore istesso
Mi parve pinta della nostra effige; §
Perche il mio viso in lei tutto era messo.

---

* In this group "Verbum" occupies the place which in the preceding is filled by the word "Pater;" "Filius" answers to "Lux," and "Spiritus Sanctus" to "Vita." Can this arrangement have been intentional? It seems scarcely possible to suppose so, for although the Son may be called Light, and the Holy Ghost Life, still the Father, most certainly, is not specially the Word. By attributing, on the other hand, the Word to the Son, Light to the Holy Ghost, and Life to the Father, the definition already given of the Divine persons is almost strictly adhered to.
† The Son by the Father; Lumen de lumine.
‡ The Holy Ghost: Qui ex Patre Filioque procedit.
§ The effigy of Jesus Christ. The Italian Poet has imagined a portrait in

Qual è 'l geometra che tutto s' affige
   Per misurar lo cerchio, e non ritruova
   Pensando, quel principio ond' egli indige;
Tale era io a quella vista nuova :
   Veder voleva come si convenne
   L' imago al cerchio, e come vi s' indova;
Ma non eran da ciò le proprie penne:
   Se non che la mia mente fu percossa
   Da un fulgore in che sua voglia venne.*
            Paradiso, Canto xxxiii., l. 115.

It has been frequently repeated that the genius of Dante was reproduced in the creations of Michelangelo. The painting of the Last Judgment, has with justice been regarded as an interpretation into line and colour of the gloomy and glorious poem written and sung by Dante. To us those illustrious Florentines appear like twin brothers in genius. The traits of similarity which mark them as belonging to one family have frequently been noticed, but one circumstance, elevating that similarity to the highest

---

the space, where the scholastic author of Chartres had written a word. The idea is analogous, but conveyed in two different languages.

* " In that abyss
Of radiance, clear and lofty, seem'd, methought,
Three orbs of triple hue, clipt in one bound ;
And, from another, one reflected seem'd,
As rainbow is from rainbow ; and the third
Seem'd fire, breathed equally from both.
   *   *   *   *
            O eternal light !
Sole in thyself thou dwell'st ; and of thyself
Sole understood, past, present, or to come ;
Thou smiledst, on that circling, which in thee
Seem'd as reflected splendour, while I mused ;
For I therein, methought, in its own hue
Beheld our image painted ; stedfastly
I therefore pored upon the view. As one
Who, versed in geometric lore, would fain
Measure the circle ; and, though pondering long
And deeply, that beginning, which he needs,
Finds not ; e'en such was I, intent to scan
The novel wonder, and trace out the form,
How to the circle fitted, and therein
How placed ; but the flight was not for my wing ;
Had not a flash darted athwart my mind,
And, in the spleen, unfolded what it sought.
      Cary's Dante, Paradise, Canto xxxiii., .. 136.

degree possible, has been completely overlooked, or rather, the fact has been observed, but not understood. Vasari, who lived on familiar terms with Michelangelo, was himself deceived; in fact, in his life of that sublime artist he writes thus: "Michelangelo, during the greater portion of his life, made use of a seal, bearing the emblem of three intertwined circles. He undoubtedly intended thereby to signify, that the union between painting, sculpture, and architecture, was so close and intimate, that the three ought never to be divided. The academicians,* judging him to have attained the highest rank in each of the three arts of design, changed the three circles into three crowns, and added to them the following legend: "TERGEMINIS TOLLIT HONORIBUS.'"†
I cannot subscribe to the opinion expressed by Vasari. It seems, in the first place, difficult to believe that Michelangelo indulged in the childish pride of carrying about with him a symbol of his excellence in the three arts of design; and, in the next, by comparing the above extract from Vasari with the language of Dante and the three circles of our own sculptor at Chartres, it is at once evident that the pretended seal, instead of being a monument of pride, was a symbol of faith. It was a ring, on which the creed of St. Athanasius had been traced with the compasses; a geometrical creed, in short. Both Vasari, and the Florentine academicians may have been alike deceived, but it is certain that the idea of the taciturn and impenetrable artist sprang from a source more elevated than, and very different from, that accorded to it by his countrymen and cotemporaries. Besides the seal just mentioned, Michelangelo had another; that famous engraved stone, a precious monument of antiquity, on which, in a very narrow field, were graven fifteen human figures, two animals, and a tree, surrounded by a vine and a curtain.

The three circles, an extension, and the complement of the triangle, were invented in the thirteenth century, and continued down to the sixteenth. During the period which commenced at the close of the fifteenth century and lasted

* Those of Florence, at the time of the pompous ceremony of Michelangelo's funeral.
† Vasari, "Life of Michelangelo." "Lives of the Painters," translated *Mrs. Foster.*—Bohn's Standard Library.

VOL. II.

till the seventeenth, embracing the whole era of the Rénaissance, nearly every type of anterior date was admitted to equality of rank, and treated with the same respect: it was an epoch of universal syncretism. Men were Pagans and Christians in the same degree,—monarchical and republican with equal intensity. In the plastic art, as well as in political and religious belief, everything that presented itself was accepted and received.

The Renaissance added some few novelties to the past, but its grand feature was, that it granted the rights of citizenship to everything that had been imagined or performed since the first creation of the world.* We find consequently in monuments of that period, instances of all the different types of the Trinity that have been mentioned. The Latin, Romanesque, and Gothic periods were eager to offer the types which they had created and modified, and the Rénaissance accepted all. The symbols invented in the earliest period, the hand of the Father, the cross of the Son, and the dove of the Holy Ghost, descended to the Rénaissance, but with additional details that had developed themselves between the ninth and twelfth centuries. The Father displays the head, the bust, or the entire body; the cross bears the crucified Saviour, and the dove is seen alighting on the head or hand of the Holy Ghost, whom it is employed to symbolise. This last addition belongs especially to the Rénaissance, while the others may be referred to the two preceding periods. It is, however, very rarel' that the Holy Ghost is represented at the same time under the human form, and that of a dove; nothing is so unusua as to see on the same monument the third person of th Trinity combine in himself the double symbol of man an

---

* The genius of the Rénaissance may be said to have drawn inspiration fro that of the Romans, whose civilisation it sought to revive. The Rom Emperors, in their universal toleration to all religious sects, granted the rigt of citizenship to deities of every nation, and it is well known that the Empei Alexander Severus kept in his Lararium images of Christ, of Apollonius Tyana, of Orpheus, and of Abraham, side by side with those of the b heathen princes, and most celebrated philosophers. To all these personag who doubtless marvelled to find themselves thus assembled, Severus p religious homage. The Rénaissance likewise treated with equal honour id the most discordant, and individuals the most dissimilar, and even the m at variance.

CHRONOLOGICAL ICONOGRAPHY OF THE TRINITY. 51

dove. We are at present aware of three examples only, two of which have been given in this work.*

Fig. 140.—THE DIVINE TRIPLICITY, CONTAINED WITHIN THE UNITY.
From a German Engraving of the XVI cent.†

Figs. 126 and 150. The third example was mentioned to me by Dusevel d'Amiens. In it the three Divine persons are represented in human , each holding on his knees his symbolic attribute. The Father with a gle, the Son with a cross, the Holy Ghost with a dove. This singular ›ct is painted in a manuscript of the fifteenth century, now in the possession I. Dusevel. I should have made an engraving of this design had I been r aware of its existence.

The above design is copied from an engraving belonging to the close of the

E 2

Just as to the dove of the Latin epoch, a man is annexed by the Romanesque school to complete the figure of the Holy Ghost; so also, in representing the entire Trinity, the Romanesque triangle is added to the Gothic circle, of which we have already spoken. These two geometrical figures are entwined one within the other, and the most complete formula imaginable, of the unity of substance circumscribing the triplicity of persons, is thus obtained. Further still, as if that figure did not give a sufficiently palpable idea of the divinity, it is placed in the hand of God himself. That aged man, measuring with his arms as with the branches of a compass, the diameter of the eternal circle, the area of that Divine unity in which the triangle of the three persons is inscribed, may be regarded in some sort, as the living interpretation of that geometrical abstraction.*

As to those Trinities in which all three of the Divine persons have the human form, a type which first appeared in the ninth century, and continued in use down to the close of the thirteenth, during the Romanesque period; its complete development is more particularly to be remarked in the fifteenth and sixteenth centuries.

Several examples have been already given, to which the reader is referred, and others will yet be added. The "Chronique d' Isidore de Seville," has furnished us with an anthropomorphic Trinity, representing the heads of the Divine persons, animating one single body; but those heads are distinct, although blended together.

In the following example, on the contrary, the heads are something more than a mere juxta-position, or even adherer or welded together; they are commingled, and so intimately blended, as to present one single skull only, with the faces.

sixteenth century, designed and engraved by Matheus Gruter; it belongs M. Guénebault, who pressingly invited me to make use of it. (See work of Gruter in the Bibl. Roy. in the Cabinet des Estampes.) The reader will remark the nimbus, its circumference radiating with teeth like those saw, which encircles the head of God, and the similar form of the aur surrounding a portion of His body.

* There is more of true dignity in figuring God the Father thus measur the world, than as holding in his hand a pair of compasses, as in Fig. The Rénaissance, whatever may be said of it, infused into ideas and the r of expressing them, a degree of nobleness rarely seen, especially in Fr during the middle ages.

Here the representation of the Trinity is as complete as possible. Besides the triple visage which supplies an

Fig. 141.—THE THREE FACES OF THE TRINITY, ON ONE SINGLE HEAD, AND ON ONE SINGLE BODY.
A French Example of the XVI cent.*

plication of the triangle cut off at the corners by the three cles symbolising the three Divine persons, a legend is ended, which serves for a gloss, and interprets at the same

The above representation may be seen in a volume of the *Hours*, ted on vellum at Paris, in 1524, by Simon Vostre. It is besides, very

time, both the difference and the equality of the three hypostases. The difference is read on the sides of the triangle, and the equality converges towards the centre, and meets in a circle resembling those in the corners. Upon the sides is written—" The Father is not the Son. The Father is not the Holy Ghost. The Holy Ghost is not the Son." But going from the corners towards the centre, we read—" The Father is God. The Son is God. The Holy Ghost is God."

This singular subject is transitionary, leading from purely geometrical images, to those which are human or anthropomorphic.

The Romanesque period first conceived this manner of representing the three persons under the human form, the Father as well as the Son, the Holy Ghost as well as the other two.

The manuscript of St. Dunstan has been already quoted and one miniature has been given from the manuscript of Herrade; but we should add that the three persons were regarded in this light by the philosopher Abelard, who had all the three sculptured in human form, in the Abbey of the Paraclete. "It deserves remark," says Father Mabillon "that Abelard had the three persons of the Trinity, to whom the Oratory in that place (the Paraclete) was dedi

commonly seen after the commencement of the fifteenth century. It ma be found sculptured at Bordeaux, on a house said to have been inhabite by Montaigne, in the "Rue des Bahutiers." This carving occupies tl exterior tympanum of the entrance door. The triangle and inscription are sti discernible, but the three faces and the four attributes of the Evangelists are longer in existence. The drawing given above is the most complete of th kind. Mr. Albert Way, director of the Antiquarian Society of London a correspondent of the "Comité des Arts et Monuments," informs me, that in t counties of Norfolk, Suffolk, and Essex, Geometrical Trinities resembling tl at Bordeaux, are constantly to be met with. These representations are to found on church portals, on funeral slabs, sometimes on painted windows. Th are all the work of the fifteenth and sixteenth centuries, and are traced up escutcheons in the manner of armorial bearings. We are assured that th occur in the eastern part of England alone, and have never been seen either the north or the west. This observation may be important, not only in bearing on archæology, but with regard also to history. Though frequ with us, it is uncommon in England, and found only in the counties nea France, and which were the first to be occupied by the Normans. [The sa triangle and cross-legends may be found in the arms of the monastery of Holy Trinity, or Christchurch, Aldgate. See *Tanner's Notitia Monasti* p. 46, fig. ci., and also in the centre of the large painted window of the nc transept of Canterbury Cathedral.]—ED.

cated, sculptured on a single stone. They are of human form and stature, an unusual mode of representation, and well worthy of a man who was original in everything."* The Father was in the centre, the Son on the right hand, the Holy Ghost on the left, holding his hands crossed upon his breast.

It was daring to represent as a man the Almighty Father, who had never been seen by man; but there seemed an excess of audacity in figuring as a man, and a man without wings, the Holy Ghost, who had never been seen except in the form of a dove. Consequently in the Gothic period properly so called, that which lasted from the close of the twelfth century to the end of the fourteenth, the type invented by Romanesque artists, was almost entirely abandoned; but at the time of the Gothic decline, at the dawn and throughout the entire duration of the Rénaissance, the same method of treating the hypostases was again resorted to.

With the exception of the miniature borrowed from the manuscript of Herrade, the drawings already given and those which we are about to give, are all of the fifteenth and sixteenth centuries; and it is a singular circumstance that even the Trinity sculptured by order of Abelard, as described by Mabillon, belongs to the sixteenth and not to the twelfth. It is possible that the group of which Mabillon speaks, may have been substituted in the place of one more ancient, and more or less resembling that which the learned Benedictine may have seen; but the monument he describes cannot have been contemporary with Abelard. In fact the Father was in the character of an Emperor, carrying the globe in one (the left) hand and having on his head a closed crown. He was clad in an alb, with a stole crossed upon the breast and confined by a girdle, and with a cope extending to the other two persons, whom it was intended to cover, thus typifying the Divine Unity. From the clasp (agrafe) of the mantle depended a scroll, on which was

---

* *Annales Benedict.*, vol. vi., p. 85, No. 14. Mabillon is mistaken; this manner of figuring the Trinity was not unusual, since, from the ninth century upwards, the divine persons are constantly thus represented on monuments; and in innumerable monuments of the fifteenth and sixteenth centuries, the same type is preserved. We shall return immediately to the writings of the illustrious Benedictine.

written "Thou art my Son." The Son was on the right hand of the Father, and wore a similar alb, but had no girdle. He held in his hand a cross, which he clasped to his bosom. On the left hung a scroll with the words "Thou art my Father." On the left of the Father was the Holy Ghost, having also a similar alb, his hands crossed upon his breast, and holding the following sentence—" I am the breath of both." The Son had a crown of thorns; the Holy Ghost a crown of olive. Both were looking towards the Father, who alone, of the three, wore shoes. All three had the same countenance, the same physiognomy, the same form.* With the exception of the crossed stole, which belongs to the Son, and not to the Father,† all the characteristics here given pertain to a monument of the sixteenth century, and not of the twelfth. The crown of thorns, in representations of the Trinity, the cross in the hands of the Son, the closed crown worn by the Father, the cope covering all the three persons at once, and the scroll hanging from it, are none of them earlier than the close of the fifteenth century. We have figures of the Trinity, cotemporary with Abelard, and not one among them agrees with the description

---

* "Videtur hic observare trium sanctissimæ Trinitatis cui dedicatum ejus loci oratorium est (the Paraclete), personarum extantes figuras ad humanam staturam, ex uno lapide fabrefactas, quas Abailardus ipse fabricari curavit, insolito, ut in omnibus insolitus erat, modo. Pater in medio positus est cum toga talari, stola et collo pendente et ad pectus decussata, atque ad cingulum adstricta: cum corona clausa in capite et globo in sinistra manu; pallio superindutus, quod ad duas hinc inde personas extenditur, cujus a fibula pendet lambus deauratus his verbis adscriptis: *Filius meus es tu.* Ad patris dexteram stat Filius cum simili toga, sed absque cingulo, habens in manibus crucem pectori appositam, et ad sinistram partem lambum cum his verbis: *Pater meus es tu.* Ad sinistram extat Spiritus Sanctus consimili toga indutus decussatus super pectus habens manus cum hoc dicto: *Ego utriusque spiraculam.* Filius coronam spineam, Spiritus Sanctus olearem gerit. Uterque respicit Patrem, qui calceatus est, non duæ aliæ personæ. Eadem in tribus vultus, species et forma."—*Annales Bened.,* vol. vi., p., 85, No. 14.

† The Son is a priest after the order of Melchisedeck; he is at the same time pontiff and victim. Hence it comes that he is sometimes represented performing the office of the Mass, often in bishop's robes, very frequently wearing above the alb a stole, crossed like that worn by priests under the chasuble. It is not thus with the Father. It is quite possible that Mabillon may have assigned to the Father attributes belonging properly to the Son, since he makes an error of four centuries in the date of the monument of which he is speaking.

CHRONOLOGICAL ICONOGRAPHY OF THE TRINITY. 57

given by Mabillon: we possess, and have given, copies of Trinities of the fifteenth and sixteenth centuries, and the characteristics by which they are distinguished range themselves amongst the number of those attributed to the Trinity of Abelard.

The anthropomorphic representation of the Trinity, appears then to have been in high favour at the Rénaissance, and the

Fig. 142.—THE THREE DIVINE FACES WITH TWO EYES AND ONE SINGLE BODY.
From a French Miniature of the XVI cent.*

* Manuscript of King Henry II., Bibl. Roy. The Trinity is here represented engaged in the creation of the world, as related in the Gospel of St. John; the Eagle of the Evangelist is placed upon a scroll-panel, on which is written, "In principio creavit cœlum et terram." The Eagle, as the attribute of an Apostle,

conclusion of the Gothic period. The type was greatly multiplied and as a necessary consequence, subjected to numerous modifications. To restrict ourselves to those changes affecting the three Divine heads, borne upon one single body, we may remark, in addition to what has been already said, that these heads, which at first were distinct and isolated, then placed in contact, then adhering, and next intimately united, ended by being confounded in one single skull.

The head then was single, but the three faces were distinct, because it was at least necessary to mark the triplicity of the faces. Still, four eyes at first, then three,* then two only were inserted in the three faces, and an almost absolute Unity was at length attained, even while the appearance of the Trinity was still maintained. Three faces, having two eyes only, one single forehead, and one sole body, give but a very feeble indication of the Trinity.

Ere long, artists fell into the monstrous. Allegorists, it is true, enjoy peculiar license, and they, like poets, are permitted to indulge in daring metaphors; still a metaphor has no more real authority in painting or sculpture, than a simple rhetorical figure. Meanwhile audacity knew no limits, and the more important the subject on which the imagination

---

has the nimbus; as symbolising an Evangelist, he bears a writing-horn in his beak. The Eagle is sometimes not content to hold a writing-horn merely, one of the material instruments employed to fix our thoughts. In ancient periods he is shown giving direct inspiration; he even dictates the idea, as do the Angel of St. Matthew, the Lion of St. Mark, and the Ox of St. Luke. But the manuscript here quoted belongs to the sixteenth century, and at that period the attributes of the Evangelists had become mere domestic attendants, and ceased to be regarded as the agents of inspiration.

* It appears that at St. Pol-de-Léon, in Brittany, there was a Trinity sculptured on the key of the vaulting, consisting of three faces, having only three eyes between them. It is easily seen that four, or even two, eyes might be placed naturally enough on three faces closely joined together; one of which would be seen in full face, while the other two would be in three-quarters only, or in profile; but it is more difficult to distribute three eyes between three faces. To do so it would be necessary, instead of exhibiting those faces vertically, or in their natural elevation, to place them horizontally, or "en plan." This is exactly what has been done at St. Pol-de-Léon. It should be observed that the three eyes, mouths, and noses, sculptured on the trefoil shaped boss which hangs from the vaulting of the Church of St. Pol, do indeed designate a triplicity, but the idea of God perhaps has little part in it. It was probably a mere caprice of the artist's fancy, who wished to unite three objects of any like kind in one single area.

exercised itself, the more serious the consequences which it involved.

St. Christopher carried the infant Saviour on his shoulder across a tempestuous arm of the sea, and it was Christ the second person of the Trinity, and not the Trinity itself, that the saint bore. But a piece of sculpture, executed in the fifteenth century, is still to be seen in the church of Sedgeford, in England, in which a gigantic St. Christopher is bearing the little Jesus, a child of three years of age, upon his shoulders: yet this child is not Jesus only; He is the impersonation of the Trinity, for three heads are seen on that one little body. Thus we have one instance of Christ in his own person comprehending the entire Trinity.*

The same idea has been carried still farther. The second person of the Trinity, the Son of God, descended alone into the bosom of Mary; neither the Father, nor the Holy Ghost, ever became incarnate in the womb of the Virgin. Yet in a certain manuscript of the end of the fourteenth century, there is a prayer addressed to the Virgin, the written character of which appears to belong to the

---

* I am indebted to the courtesy of Mr. Thomas Wright, an English antiquarian, who is also a correspondent of the Institute of France, and of the "Comité des Arts et des Monuments," for the communication of a very correct drawing of the St. Christopher above described, bearing on his shoulders the infant Jesus with three heads. One of the heads only has a nimbus; the other two are destitute of that distinctive ornament. It must be added, that these heads, having been covered with whitewash which has recently been removed, are at present somewhat indistinct. M. le Baron Taylor, to whom the drawing was communicated, believes, and with reason, that two of the three heads were probably abortive attempts of the painter. The artist may have made two or three different attempts to place a head on the body of the infant he had just drawn, and was not satisfied until the third attempt; hence the three heads. The above explanation seems plausible, and we willingly adopt it. Still it must be observed, that the definitive head, that wearing the nimbus, is even more indistinct than the others; in them the eyes and mouth, which in the first are not perceptible, are distinctly traced. Besides, the fact thus presented to us in the painting at Sedgeford, although irregular, is not unique, and we have a host of examples proving that Christ has been figured, absorbing in himself the three Divine persons. The most ancient St. Christopher in my recollection, is on a painted window in the south transept of the Cathedral of Strasbourg. It is Byzantine in design, and must date from the eleventh century. However, the little figure of Christ that he bears has but one single head.

fifteenth. In that prayer, which is rather remarkable, the following passage may be found. " Si vous souveigne, doulce dame, de la doulce annunciacion que le Sauveur de tout le monde vous envoya quand il se voulut tant humilier que il voulut en vous descendre et en vos précieulx flans prendre cher humaine pour nous povres pécheurs rachepter. Vuelliés ouvrir les oreilles de vostre très-grant doulceur à escouter les prières de moy povre pécheresse, quant pour les pécheurs se voust en vous herbergier le Père, le Filz et le Seint-Esperit. Pour quoy, doulce dame, à vous appartient estre advocate aux povres pécheurs, et par quoy vous estes la chambre de toute la Trinité." *

Thus then, as early as the close of the fourteenth century, or about the commencement of the fifteenth, the womb of Mary had been called the chamber of the whole Trinity, and the Chancellor Gerson, was unable to restrain his indignation at seeing in the church of the Carmelites, at Paris, a picture, in which the text of Troyes written one hundred years later, was pictorially represented. " On se doit bien garder" cried Gerson, "de paindre faulsement une histoire de la saincte Escripture, tant que bonnement se peut faire. Je le dy partie pour une ymage qui est aux Carmes et semblables, qui ont dedens leur ventre une Trinité, aussi comme toutte la Trinité, eust prins char humaine en la vierge Marie. Et, qui plus merveille est, il y a enfer dedens peint, et ne voy point pour quelle cause on œuvre ainsi; car, en mon jugement, il n'y a baulté ne dévocion en telles paintures; et ce doit estre cause d'erreur et de indignation ou indévocion."†

* "So remember, sweet lady, the sweet annunciation that the Saviour of all the world sent you, when he was pleased to humble himself so much as to descend into you, and in your sacred body to take upon himself human flesh, to redeem us poor sinners. Deign to open the ears of your great goodness, to hear the prayers offered by me, a poor sinner, inasmuch as for us sinners, the Father, the Son, and the Holy Ghost were pleased to take up their abode in you. Wherefore, sweet Lady, to you it belongs to be the advocate of poor sinners, and for that purpose you became the chamber of the Holy Trinity." This manuscript was communicated to M. Leon Aubineau, " Archiviste " at Tours, and correspondent of the " Comité des Arts," by M. l'Abbé Tridon, Professor of Archæology in the little seminary at Troyes.

† "We must guard as honestly as we can," exclaims Gerson, "against depicting falsely any story from the Holy Scriptures. I say this on account of a painting in the Carmelites, and others resembling it, which have within the

The cry of alarm, uttered with good reason by Gerson was echoed at Rome. There was indeed an impropriety, in exhibiting the Divine persons as enclosed within the womb of the Virgin, and to place Hell there also, was more unheard of still. It was a heresy to make the Trinity incarnate ;* it was audacious to depict the three hypostases fused and commingled in so monstrous a manner. Pope Urban VIII., on the 11th of August, 1628, prohibited representations of the Trinity under the figure of a man with three mouths, three noses, and four eyes; he proscribed also some other similar images. Disobedience to this command was threatened with the pope's anathema, and it was commanded that all Trinities of that description should be burned.†

womb a Trinity, as if the entire Trinity had been clothed with human flesh in the body of the Virgin Mary. And what is yet more surprising, Hell itself also is therein painted, and I see no reason why men should thus work; for, in my opinion, there is neither beauty nor devotion in such pictures, and they are likely rather to cause error and indignation, or a lack of devotion." Bibl. Roy., MS, 7282, fol, 60. I am indebted to M. B. Thomassy for the above extract, which is curious in several points, and which was found in a sermon preached on Christmas Day by the Chancellor Gerson. We have indeed seen pictures representing Jesus in the womb of Mary, and St. John in that of Elizabeth ; we have even given (Fig. 71) the copy of a painted window in which Jesus is represented naked, erect, and with joined hands, in the bosom of his mother. But the pictures described by Gerson, and which seem like reminiscences of the manuscript of Troyes, are at present unknown; it is probable that they have been destroyed. If found again, it would be proper to describe and carefully preserve them.

* In the present day men are equally heretical, although perhaps unconsciously and unintentionally so, when they place the triangle, the symbol of the Trinity, on the back of the modern chasuble, at the intersection of the arms of the cross; thereby indeed making it appear as if the entire Trinity had become incarnate and been crucified, when in truth Christ alone became man, and died upon the cross. Such chasubles, numbers of which may be seen, ought not to be worn in the sacred services, and yet they are advertised daily, and drawings of them are given in religious journals, and the clergy, who ought to be more scrupulous in regard to theological doctrines, daily purchase and wear them. The Reverend Father Dom Guéranger, who drew my attention to this involuntary error, deplored, and with just reason, that the designing of sacerdotal ornaments should be entrusted to ignorant or indifferent persons, and that the clergy should adopt without consideration whatever is offered them. It certainly seems an extraordinary thing, for a priest performing the ceremony of the Mass, to wear upon his back a flagrant heresy.

† Lucius Ferraris (*Prompta Bibliotheca Canonica*, in 4°, Rome, 1787) says, at the word " Imagines " : " Urbanus VIII. comburi jussit imaginem cum tribus buccis, tribus nasis et quatuor oculis, et alias si quæ invenirentur similes.

Benedict XIV., in a letter addressed in 1745 to the Bishop of Augsburg, repeats and confirms the condemnation promulgated by his predecessor.*

The Greeks, although of lively imagination, and strongly inclined to the living metaphor and personifications, have never more than once ventured, to our knowledge, to depict the Trinity as we have done. They adhered more closely to the Holy Scriptures, and did not permit themselves to wander into errors, such as we are sometimes betrayed into, when our reason is abandoned to the guidance of the imagination. The Trinity, having three human faces on one single body, is painted in fresco in the chapel of the cemetery of St. Gregory, in the convent of Mount Athos. The painting, however, was made in 1736; the three Divine faces have four eyes, three noses, three mouths, and one single nimbus: this last is cruciform, and bears engraven on the branches of the cross, the words "ὁ ὤν." One single example, belonging too to the eighteenth century, is of little moment. The Byzantine Manuscript so often quoted, and which is entitled "The Guide for Painting," prescribes the proper method both of representing Trinities, and each of the three Divine persons separately; it makes no allusion whatever to three heads or three faces upon one single body, but observes merely that, "Christ is represented in paintings under the human form, because he appeared upon earth, and conversed with men, being made in everything a mortal like ourselves, except in respect of sin. So also God the Father Eternal is figured as an aged man, because he so appeared to Daniel (Chap. vii.). The Holy Ghost is depicted as a dove, because he was seen under that form at the baptism of Christ in the Jordan." It must be acknowledged that the Greeks have carefully avoided the boldness and temerity into which the Latins have been betrayed.

Hæc enim nova inventio (new in Italy, but in France already old) repræsentandi sanctissimam Trinitatem tolerabilis non videtur."
* See the Bull of Benedict XIV. t. i., p. 166, § 28.

THE ATTRIBUTES OF THE TRINITY.

Some artists when they painted or sculptured the Trinity, preferred to represent the equality of the persons; and others, the distinction between them; and we thence obtain two different series, in groups of that description.

When it was the artist's intention to exhibit the Equality, or Divine Unity, the three persons were made as little distinguishable, the one from the other, as possible. These representations are marked by a total absence of character, or at least by the small number of attributes. The Trinity in the manuscript of Henry II., given above, (Fig. 142), is merely a figure supporting the sky.

If the figures be distinct, as they have been seen in the manuscript of Herrade (Fig. 137), their equality is still preserved, and all the three are very frequently covered with one single mantle, to figure the unity in which they are bound one with the other. This plan was that adopted by Abelard, according to Mabillon; nothing is more common in the figured monuments, sculpture, paintings, and miniatures of the fifteenth and sixteenth centuries.*

A diversity sometimes betrays itself by trifling characteristics, even in groups the intention of which is to throw out the unity in bold relief; the Holy Ghost is made younger, the Father more aged, and the Son of middle age; a book is given to the Holy Ghost, a cross to the Son, and a globe to the Father. Either the Papal or Imperial crown marks the Father, and a crown of thorns the Son, while the absence of either marks the Holy Ghost.

Between the two extreme points of an almost complete unity, and a nearly absolute diversity, some Trinities are seen in which the balance between the equality and individual distinction of the persons, is very well preserved.

In the following engraving the Father and Son are extremely alike. The same nimbus, the same tiara, and a similar style of hair; the same kind of alb, and one single mantle connecting the two Divine Persons: they are united by one

* Refer to Figs. 123 and 126, pp. 471 and 494, vol. i.

book, which they mutually support, and also by the Holy Ghost, linking them one with the other by the tips of his extended wings.

Fig. 143.—THE DIVINE PERSONS DISTINCT.
A French Miniature of the XVI cent.*

* The above drawing is taken from the celebrated *Cité de Dieu*, a magnificent folio manuscript of the sixteenth century, in the Bibliothèque de Saint Geneviève ; it will be found at folio 406. The nimbi are radiating, not cruciform. It belongs to an epoch when the cross of the divine nimbus and the nimbus itself had no longer any great value.

But here begins the difference. The Holy Ghost is not a man, like the other two persons, but a dove. The Father, too, is more aged than the Son; the beard of the first is forked, of the second round. The Father, not the Son, bears the globe of the world; the alb worn by the Father has no girdle, it is a robe. The Son, who is a priest, has an alb tightened by a girdle, and confined by a stole, which is crossed upon his breast.

In those Trinities, in which the distinction between the persons is made to predominate, distinctive characteristics abound. The most remarkable diversity possible is given by those Trinities of the Latin period, in which the Father is shown only by the hand or the bust, the Son by a cross or as a lamb, and the Holy Ghost by a dove. But between these types and others that tend towards the equality of the Divine persons, there are a thousand varieties, too many to particularise. It is, in fact, easy to arrive at the same ideas when the object aimed at, a representation of unity, is the same; but when distinction is to be marked, as many different types appear to have been invented as there have been representations executed.

It would be superfluous at this moment to enumerate the attributes which distinguish each of the three Divine persons, as they have been already fully detailed in preceding chapters devoted to the consideration of each of the Divine persons. It now therefore only remains to consider the attributes characterising the three Divine persons grouped, that is to say, the Unity into which their diversity resolves itself, or, in other words, the distinction between the hypostases converging into Divine equality, or substantial unity. The mode of grouping becomes, therefore, a point of some importance to establish, as the tendency which manifests itself more and more, to unite the three persons together, is there traceable.

The three persons were at first set apart at certain distances, isolated, as it were; they occupy the same tableau, but the group is distributed over the entire vaulting of apse. We thus find them in early Latin mosaics, and ancient frescos.*

* See Ciampini, *Vetera Monimenta.* That learned antiquary gives several gravings of these mosaics. See also Bosio, *Roma Sotteranea*, who has
VOL. II. ı ғ

During this first period, it is not so much the group of the Trinity that is depicted, as the casual meeting of the three persons.

The tendency towards a closer approximation is apparent about the ninth century. In the manuscript of St. Dunstan the three persons are in proximity. In the manuscript of Herrade, they are sitting on the same bench; they touch simultaneously the same scroll, which serves in some degree to unite them, though they are still at some distance from each other.

But in the twelfth century, the Father holds the cross to which the Son is attached, and the Holy Ghost hovers above them or descends like a breath from the mouth of the Father, and alights upon the head of the Son. The group is here perfectly defined. In the thirteenth and fourteenth centuries, an aureole frequently enframes the three persons; thus uniting them more closely still. The aureole follows the phases indicated in the chapter specially devoted to it, and which immediately succeeds that relating to the nimbus it is either circular, oval, triangular, almond-shaped, in trefoi or quatrefoil. In that aureole the three persons are united but not yet placed in juxta-position.

This juxta-position does not appear until the fourteentl century. In the celebrated manuscript of the Duke o Anjou,* the Divine persons are all three represented unde the human form, but one behind the other, and only abou to touch. In the fifteenth and sixteenth centuries, they ar actually in contact. The art was advancing by degrees, I d not say precisely to giving an absolute identity to all tl Divine persons, but towards a similitude closely allied 1 identity; an aggregation very much resembling fusion; Trinity, tending directly to Unity.†

---

given engravings of the ancient fresco paintings in the Catacombs. T mosaic decorating the apse in the Church of San Giovanni in Laterano, althou executed between the years 1288 and 1294, contains a picture of the Trini in which the three symbols are still placed at a distance apart; but this is Rome, where Christian Art long remained stationary. Even in the thirteer and fourteenth centuries, during the period of the greatest activity in Got art, Roman art always sought for inspiration, in the Catacombs, and ancient basilicas of the age of Constantine.

* Bibl. Roy., manuscript already quoted. Lavall, 127.
† It must then be observed, in completion of the indications and exam

After the close of the fifteenth century the union became still more complete. An attempt is made to absolutely identify in one the Father, Son, and Holy Ghost. They are at first connected only by the feet, so that with three heads and three bodies, they have two feet only. The connection or fusion next rises higher, and the three bodies are consolidated into one. Like a tree with three trunks springing from the same root, which enlarge day by day, and at last are united, interpenetrated, and absorbed one into the other, thus forming but one single stem, so the bodies of the three Divine Persons are likewise commingled. But the heads, as has been shown, remain as yet distinct.

A little later than this, in the sixteenth century more particularly, the heads themselves became blended one with the other, and the three faces were surmounted by a single forehead.* Faces, which had at first been seen in full or

lready given, that in a manuscript of the *Legenda Aurea*, of the Bibl. Roy., No. 6889, fifteenth century, vol. i., fol. 107, there is at the Annunciation a icture of the Trinity, in which the three persons are all of human form; they ppear to be three men, of from thirty to thirty-five years of age; all the hree are in the Papal costume, and a single cope serves to cover all. The Ioly Ghost bears a globe. At the Feast of Pentecost, fol. 158, is another 'rinity, also composed of three men covered with one and the same mantle. Iut, besides this, a second Holy Ghost, under the figure of a dove, detaches self from the three persons, to descend upon the Apostles. This dove innot, therefore, be intended either for that Divine person, nor for his symbol, it is rather the symbol and soul of the entire Trinity, the Spirit of God, :longing in common to the three persons. Here too, the Holy Ghost is)lding the globe, an attribute more especially appropriate to the Father. The)n, in the habit of a priest, has a stole crossed upon his breast. In vol. ii., l. 156, Jesus Christ may be seen as a Pope, wearing a stole, crossed, but bich the Father is without. In the MS. suppl., fol. 631, Jesus is represented icing a crown on the head of his mother; he is in Papal robes, and holds in ı hand the globe of the world: the drawing belongs to the fourteenth ntury. A copy of the *Legenda Aurea* (MS. de la Bibl. Roy., fourteenth itury, No. 6888) represents Jesus Christ as an emperor, crowning his)ther. The Father is simply an old man with a grey beard.

* See a beautiful painted window of the sixteenth century, in the north aisle the Church of Notre Dame at Châlons-sur-Marne. M. L'Abbé Jourdain, ar of the Cathedral of Amiens, found in the possession of a glazier at Amiens, I purchased, a plate of glass bearing date 1520, on which was painted a nity of very peculiar character. There are two heads on one single body. e heads are united one with the other, and have two noses and two eyes y, and wear one single crown. The third person is a dove, adhering to the of the head or face on the right, exactly like an ear. Equality and

three-quarters, afterwards became absorbed into the principal face which fills the centre. The manuscript of Henry II. has shown us three faces with one forehead, on one single body, so intimately blended that though there are indeed two profiles and one face, we can discern, not six nor even four eyes, but only two.

Each profile, when looked at separately, has its eye, and the face itself, which is in the centre, has two; but there is in fact but one head, but one entire face, and with two eyes only. These three figures, by a freak of pictorial Theology, (*i. e.*, Theology explained through the medium of design,) lend each other reciprocally the face and eye. It may be literally said of them, changing one word of a well-known text of scripture and inserting three in the place of two "Erunt tres in carne unâ."

Thus the different manner in which the Divine person are grouped may furnish good archæological characteristic for classifying such groups in chronological order. Th relative position occupied by these three persons is als deserving of observation. According to our creed God the Father begot the Son, and the Holy Ghos proceeded from both: it therefore became necessary, i accordance with hierarchical law, to represent the Son c the left hand of the Father, and the Holy Ghost betwee the two. This has been done in respect of the Holy Ghos who is frequently placed between the other two persons but in regard to the Son, the place assigned to him by tl dogma has been altered by the book of Psalms, in whi David says that the Father makes the Son to sit on H right hand instead of on His left. It is in fact on the rig hand of the Father that the Son, except in cases of error, always placed. But the right hand, and the text (*i. e.*, t text of the Psalms,) is here precise, is that of the Fath not of the spectator: it is the left of the person looking the picture. The same rule is observed in the treatme of pictures of the Trinity, as in blazoning, in which escutcheon of the husband is placed on the right of that

distinction appear in this singular example to be blended. The Spir distinct from the other two persons, who are positively equal. I since regret not having had time to get any engraving from this painted glas which M. Jourdain much wished to favour me with a sketch.

the wife. The emblazonment is supposed to be facing the spectator, and preserves its proper right or left, as in the case with the Trinity: the left and the right emanate from God, not from the spectator.

Still, whether by mistake, or from having imagined it correct to take the spectator's right and left, the Father has occasionally been placed on the right hand of the Son, instead of on the left. A most remarkable instance of this anomaly may be seen over the principal entrance of the Sainte Chapelle at Vincennes. The angelic hierarchy is ranged, tier above tier, on the voussure, and the Trinity sculptured at the top. The Father, in Papal robes, and grasping in his hand the ball of the world, is on the right of

Fig. 144.—THE HOLY GHOST, DESCENDING FROM THE FATHER UPON THE SON.

rom a French Miniature, MS. de duc d'Anjou, of the close of the xiii cent. Bibl. Royale.

e Son, who carries his cross. The Holy Ghost, in the m of a dove, hovers between them, uniting them one

70   CHRISTIAN ICONOGRAPHY.

with the other, by the extremity of the wings.* The same error is found in miniatures of manuscripts.

Fig. 145.—THE HOLY GHOST PROCEEDING FROM THE FATHER AND THE SON, AI
RE-ASCENDING FROM THE SON TO THE FATHER.
From a French Miniature, xii cent.†

* On the porch of a church at Etampes, the elect are seen ranged on left of the Saviour, and the damned upon his right, in a scene representing Last Judgment. This is contrary to the universal custom, and even to authority of Scripture, which places the sheep, or the elect, upon the 1 haud, and the goats, or the damned, upon the left. The sculptor of Etan like him of Vincennes, taking the spectator instead of God for his sta point, fixed the right and left by consideration of the person looking at picture, not of Christ the Judge.

† This manuscript, now belonging to the municipal library of Troyes,

The Father, in virtue of hierarchical law, is frequently placed in the centre, the Son on his right hand, and the Holy Ghost on his left. Examples of this arrangement have been given in the preceding chapters. (See especially Figs. 61, 111, 123, and 126, vol. I.) But when the artist desires to express the passing of the Holy Ghost from the Father to the Son, the Holy Spirit is placed in the centre, the Son on the right hand, and the Father on the left. This observation applies to Trinities disposed horizontally. In those which are in tiers or ranged in vertical order, the Son is below, the Father above, the Holy Spirit in the centre. The Spirit descends from the mouth of the Father, alights upon the head of the Son, and proceeds from both as in the preceding example, Fig. 144.

At other times the Holy Ghost, still occupying the centre between the Father and the Son, seems, on the contrary, to ascend from the Son to the Father. Instances of this peculiar arrangement are very rare, and the design opposite, Fig. 145, is copied from a Champenois manuscript, of which it forms the opening illustration.

In other representations the dogma of the Holy Ghost, proceeding from one to the other person, is less distinctly marked. The Holy Ghost, as in the following example, is in the presence of the Father and the Son, but he no longer unites them, nor does he appear to proceed from them.

The Father here holds the cross to which Jesus is attached, as in the two drawings given above; but the position of the Holy Ghost, who is placed upon, and walking on one of the arms of the cross, does not appear as if intended to signify

riginally from the Abbey of Notre Dame-aux-Nonnains. It dates from the welfth century. The design given above was traced in outline from the miniature itself, by M. Ch. Fichot, an artist of Troyes. The aureole surrounding the Trinity, which is of oval form, and of vegetable nature, deserves to be noticed. From the four outer ends of the leafy scrolls, issue the attributes of the Evangelists. M. Vallet de Viriville directs attention particularly to the manuscript of Notre Dame-aux-Nonnains. Even as late as the year 1840, the existence of this singular book was scarcely known. It may be remarked, that esus Christ is attached to the cross not by three nails, as was usual from the thirteenth century, and as is shown in the preceding drawing, but by four; and it may be likewise worth noting, that the attributes of the Evangelists have a nimbus like the persons symbolised by them.

his proceeding from the Father and the Son. The dove is added there simply to complete the Trinity. In some other instances a design of *not* interpreting the doctrine of Procession is even more evident, the Holy Ghost having been suppressed, as in the instances given above. (Fig. 63, vol. I.)

Fig. 146.—THE HOLY GHOST, NOT PROCEEDING EITHER FROM THE FATHER OR THE SON.
From a Woodcut or Engraving of the XII cent.†

In the Greek Church, which denies the doctrine of the Procession,* the Holy Ghost is never represented uniting the Divine persons by the extremity of his wings, or descending from the Father upon the Son, or ascending from the Son to the Father. The Greek Trinities have a certain resemblance to our own, as is evident from that given in the History of the Nimbus (Fig. 21, vol. I.); indeed, in groups representing the Trinity, the Greeks may, and in fact do, place the Holy Ghost between the Father and the Son, because, according both to the Greeks and the Latins, the third person in the Divine Trinity unites the other two; but he never appears to emanate from either; he never touches the mouths of the other two persons with his wings.

The nimbus, the aureole, and the glory characterise

---

* The Greek Church would anathematise any painter who should venture to design a Trinity resembling those given in Figs. 6 and 11.

† The Father is on a throne surmounted by a canopy; he wears the imperial costume. The design is copied from a wood engraving of the twelfth century, and various examples of a similar treatment of the subject are to be seen in books of " Hours" belonging to that period.

THE ATTRIBUTES OF THE TRINITY. 73

grouped Trinities, in the same manner as they distinguish each of the three persons when represented separated or isolated. The reader is therefore referred to the preceding volume, in which those subjects have been fully treated of. One word only in addition. The triangle being emblematic of the Trinity, the triangular nimbus seems especially to belong to the three persons grouped together. That form of the nimbus, is however very rare, and the following example is one of the most curious that can be offered.

Fig. 147.—THE THREE DIVINE HEADS WITHIN A SINGLE TRIANGLE.
From an Italian Wood Engraving of the xv cent.*

In this we have one single body with three heads; that in he centre figures the Father; it is older and larger than ie others—a twofold method of conveying materially the

* The above design, of which mention has been already made, is taken from copy of Dante printed at Florence in 1491, and illustrated with engravings. is taken from the *Paradiso*, folio cclxxviii.

idea of the Divine paternity. The head on the true right of the large head represents the Son; that on the left, which is beardless, younger, and smaller than either of the other two, the Holy Ghost. The three heads are encircled by one single triangular nimbus. They have but one body, two hands, and two feet: the left hand holds the globe, the symbol of power; the right hand is in the act of benediction, emblematic of grace or favour. This Trinity radiates within a circular aureole, the circumference of which is occupied by seraphim. We are in Paradise, and that Divine group, the centre of uncreated light, is placed upon a rainbow.

The head of the Trinity is adorned with a tiara, an imperial, or a regal crown, but in many instances also it is bare. In this peculiarity there are no characteristics, except those supplied by the form of the head-dress, which varies according to the age and country. The Italian tiara differs from the French. To take one example only: Pope Gregory the Great, a statue of whom adorns the north porch of the Cathedral of Chartres,* wears as a tiara a conical cap, ribbed and a tuft at the top. This was the French tiara of the thirteenth century.† In Italy, in the fourteenth century, great changes had taken place. The Pope then had a dome-shaped tiara, of elongated form, oval, and with the lower part ornamented with a crown.‡ The tiara of the present day is almost of the same form, but it is further encircled with two additional crowns.§ When

* It has been given in the chapter on the Holy Ghost, Vol. I., Fig. 114.

† M. le Comte de Montalembert (*Du Vandalisme et du Catholicisme dans l'Art*, in 8vo, Paris, 1839, p. 172) inveighs, and with much reason, against the cap still worn (1840) by the clergy in Paris, and which unfortunately continues in use in many dioceses; but it had not been remembered that that pointed cap was nothing more than the tiara of the thirteenth century, as drawn by the French, and perhaps, also, as it was worn in Italy by the Popes.

‡ See the Christ of Orcagna, given, Vol. I., Fig. 67.

§ It is said that the tiara with one crown was in use till 1298, that the tiara with two crowns continued predominant until 1334, and that after that period it had three crowns. Boniface VIII. added the second crown to the tiara, and Boniface XII.[1] or Urban V. tripled it. Monuments with figures

---

[1] Benedict XII. was Pope in 1334, and Urban V. in 1362; there does not appear to have been a Boniface after the ninth (1380) of that name. This must therefore be an accidental error. — EDITOR.

God the Father is in the costume of a Pope, he wears the pontifical robes and tiara in use at the period of representation. The most trifling details should be studied with attention, for in those details the most irrefragable archæological characteristics are frequently to be found.

The Holy Ghost is usually depicted with the head bare.* Christ, like the Father, takes indifferently the papal, imperial, or more especially the regal crown; but to it is added the crown of thorns. Frequently also his head is uncovered.

The globe of the world, or the volume of the Holy Scriptures, are frequently seen in the hands of the Trinity. God, the Trinity, having created the world, the globe, surmounted by a cross, is usually placed in his hands. Numerous instances of this have been given above.† We have seen the Trinity modelling and animating man.‡ From the manuscript of Henry II. we have produced a drawing of the Trinity supporting the heavens and the planets, which have just been created. § The following design presents the same subject, as treated by Buonamico Buffamalco.

The beautiful representation annexed, belonging to the earlier part of the fourteenth century, is unquestionably superior to that in the manuscript of Henry II. The Trinity is here concentrated in one single Person, in God, who holds the circles composing the universe, peopled by himself with beings of every nature. The exterior circles are animated by the nine choirs of angels,‖ the constellations roll in the intermediate circles, and in the centre is placed the earth, which was regarded as the heart or kernel of the world. ¶

are not completely in accordance with historical documents, and the latter, in general, are less to be relied on than monuments.

* The crown of olive mentioned by Mabillon, in his description of the Trinity said to have been sculptured by command of Abelard, at the Paraclete, we positively reject as of doubtful authenticity.
† See particularly, Figs. 113, 147.
‡ See Fig. 6.
§ See Fig. 142.
‖ They will be described in detail in the History of Angels.
¶ Instead of sketching out a description, I prefer giving the following extract from Vasari (*Vies des Peintres*, "Vie de Buffamalco"); the passage is

A subject closely resembling this, but treated in a very inferior manner, is to be seen in an illuminated manu-

Fig. 148.—THE TRINITY IN ONE GOD, SUPPORTING THE WORLD.
Fresco of the Campo Santo of Pisa, XIV cent.

not devoid of interest in itself: "Buonamico Buffamalco painted four frescoes in the Campo Santo. In these compositions we see represented the creation of the universe, in which the Father Almighty is depicted as five cubits in

script. God is the centre of nine concentric circles, seven of which are of flame: he holds in his right hand the compasses, with which he measures the extent of the world; and in his left the balance in which it is weighed. It answers to the well-known text in the Book of the Wisdom of Solomon, " Omnia in mensurâ, et numero, et pondere disposuisti " (chap. xi.).

Number is shown by the nine mystical circles surrounding God, measure by the compasses, and weight by the balance.

For these reasons the globe is constantly placed in the hands of the Trinity, and sometimes also beneath their feet, as in the admirable manuscript of Anne de Bretagne, preserved in the Bibliothèque Royale. At about two-thirds from the commencement of this beautiful book, is a picture of God the Father, in the habiliments of a Pope, with a long white beard, a disk-like nimbus encircling the head, a snow-white alb, green stole, and a red cope, adorned with orfray and historiated decorations with figures in gold, and the feet covered with golden slippers; the three fingers of the right hand are extended, in the act of benediction. On the left is Jesus Christ, in a brown robe, a red mantle, his head

height, raising the grand machine of the sky and the elements. Below this picture, two angles of which are occupied by St. Augustine and St. Thomas Aquinas, Buonamico wrote in capital letters (Majuscules) a sonnet explanatory of the subject, which is here inserted, as it will give some idea of the amount of scientific knowledge generally possessed at that period." Buffamalco died in 1340, aged 68. The following sonnet is that written below his painting :—

"Voi che avvisate questa dipintura
Di Dio piè, toso sommo creatore
Lo qual fe' tutte cose con amore,
Pesate, numerate ed in misura,

"In nove gradi angelica natura
In ello empirio ciel pien di splendore
Colui che non si muove ed è motore
Ciascuna cosa fece buona e pura.

"Levate gli occhi del vostro intelletto
Considerate quanto è ordinato,
Lo mondo universale ; e con affetto
Lodate lui che l' ha si ben creato:
Pensate di passare a tal diletto
Ira gli angeli, dove è ciascun beato.

Per questo mondo si vede la gloria,
Lo basso, ed il mezzo, e l' alto in questa storia."

bare, and crowned with thorns. He holds in his left hand the Cross of the Resurrection, the triumphal Cross, usually borne aloft in processions. His beard is red, and the nimbus

Fig. 149.—THE TRINITY IN ONE SINGLE GOD, HOLDING THE BALANCES AND THE COMPASSES.

From an Italian Miniature of the XIII cent.*

* The above drawing is taken from the *Psalterium cum Figuris*, a manuscript of the twelfth century, with Italian miniatures of the twelfth and thirteenth. The miniature from which this drawing is taken appears to be of the latter period.

resembles a disk : there are no wounds in the hands, and on the feet are shoes like those worn by the Father. The feet of both the Father and the Son rest upon a globe, in the upper part of which shine the sun, the moon, and the stars, while below undulate the waves of the sea, which is ploughed by vessels; in the intermediate space, rise towns surrounded by verdant meadows. Between the heads of the Father and the Son is the Holy Ghost, as a white dove with a red beak and outstretched wings: he wears a disk-like nimbus. This Holy Trinity is painted on a gold ground, and is enframed in an oval aureole completely bordered with clouds. In the four corners, on the outside of this luminous aureole, are the four evangelical attributes turning towards the Trinity, and each holding a scroll, on which is written, "Mattheus homo, Johannes avis, Marcus leo, Lucas vitulus." The symbols of the Evangelists are of azure, slashed with gold : all are winged, but without any nimbus. The Father and the Son support between them a large open book, on which is written—

"Ego sum alpha et O. principium et finis." *

In fact, next to the globe, the attribute most constantly seen in the hands of the Trinity, is the book of life, the Bible. The drawing copied from the "Cité de Dieu" (Fig. 143) has furnished an example of this description. On that book, in addition to the preceding inscription, which is that most commonly seen, are others of analogous signification. "Ego sum qui sum," "Rex regum,"

* In another manuscript in the Bibliothèque Royale (No. 886) also cotemporaneous with Anne de Bretagne, there is a Trinity resembling that described above. It is at about the middle of the manuscript; the Trinity is in an aureole of gold circumscribed by a circlet of blue clouds. The Father is represented as a Pope, with white hair and beard, and about sixty or seventy years of age, the "Ancient of Days." The Son, on his right hand, is in a violet-coloured robe with a reddish cope, his head uncovered, but crowned with thorns. Upon his feet are shoes resembling those worn by the Father, red slippers with golden ligatures; he is about thirty or thirty-five years of age. Between these two figures, and about on a level with their foreheads, is the Holy Ghost, in the form of a snow-white dove with wings outspread. The Father and Son hold between them an open book, on which is written : "Sancta Trinitas, Pater et Filius et Spiritus Sanctus. Ego sum alpha et O." The book has seven golden clasps, symbolising the seven Apocalyptic seals.

"Dominus dominantium." The greater number of those already given, as seen in the Book of Jesus Christ, are likewise inserted in the Book of the Trinity.* The Byzantine manuscript dedicates to these inscriptions an article as follows:—

INSCRIPTIONS FOR THE TRINITY.

The Father Eternal—The Ancient of Days.
The Co-eternal Son—The Word of God.
The Holy Ghost—He who proceeds from the Father.
The Holy Trinity—The only God of all things.

"In representing the Father and the Son with Scrolls, unrolled, write on the scroll of the Father, 'I begot thee before Lucifer;' or else, 'Sit thou on my right hand, until I make thine enemies thy footstool.' On the Gospel, in the hand of the Son, write, 'Oh Holy Father, I have glorified thee on the earth, I have declared thy name unto men;' or else, 'I and my Father are one; I am in the Father, and the Father in me.'"†

* A Romanesque enamel, of the twelfth century, in the collection of M. Didier Petit, of Lyons, represents God seated on a rainbow, and surrounded by an undulating edge of clouds. This figure of God performs, with the right hand, the gesture of benediction after the Latin manner; in the left he holds a long book, resembling the "Liber precum" in the Bibliothèque Royale. The book is open; on the recto and verso of two pages are the following letters, in small Roman minuscules, slightly uncial: a b c d e f g—h i k m n o p. These fourteen letters are thus arranged, seven on each page. I know not whether any signification can be assigned to the number and selection of these letters. In any case, this alphabet, which is nearly complete, and inscribed on the divine volume, is undoubtedly intended to signify that all knowledge comes from God, and that the book in his hand is that of the Holy Scriptures. This indication may be found at No. 184 of the Catalogue of M. Petit. I saw this enamelled plate in 1843, at the time of the sale, and myself made a copy of the alphabet, if so it may be called. We find in No. 204 of the same catalogue "Enamelled plate, the cover of a manuscript, representing Christ in the act of benediction, and holding in his left hand a tablet, on which are graven certain letters, in Roman and uncial characters." The letters are thus arranged, and placed within a frame The A only is uncertain.

A		I
O	F	X
M	S	N
M	E	M

† See the *Guide de la Peinture* (Ερμηνεία τῆς ζωγραφικῆς), nearly at the conclusion. The Holy Ghost is there said to proceed from the Father, but not from the Son. The inscription, taken from Psalm cix., is more complete than with us, who usually give the commencement only. The Greeks, les charitable, more harsh, and more Judaising in their ideas of Christianity, ad the words, "until I make thine enemies thy footstool."

THE ATTRIBUTES OF THE TRINITY. 81

The three persons of the Trinity are represented barefoot n Christian iconogiaphy, and the figures of the God in unity, with those of the Angels, of John the Baptist and of he Apostles, are also distinguishable from others by their are feet. However, examples may be found of Divine ersons having their feet clothed. We have described wo instances of such* and given an illustration of a hird.† When the Father or the Son appear in papal lress, then the footgear of the sovereign pontiff is given long with the pontifical vestments; but this is quite a eculiar instance, and even in such a case the feet of the)ivine persons are often left naked.

Fig. 150.—THE TRINITY IN HUMAN FORM, WITH CRUCIFORM NIMBUS AND AUREOLE OF FLAME.

The form of the nimbus, the crown and the aureole; ie form of the globe and its divisions, along with the bjects which fill these divisions; the form of the book id of the letters in the writing contained therein; the iape, number, nature, and colour of the robes furnish chæological characteristics by which the date of sculp-

* They occur in the manuscript of Anne of Brittany, and in another anuscript of the same period also in the Bibliothèque Nationale, Paris.). 886.
† Vol. I. page 226, Fig. 63.

tured, chiselled, and painted effigies of the Trinity may be determined.

It will be sufficient to give the accompanying illustration of the Trinity (Fig. 150), a work of the fifteenth century, which shows the three persons, each one in human form. Each has the cruciform nimbus, and is enveloped in an aureole of flame. The Divine Dove is seen seated on the head of the youth who personates the Holy Spirit. The Father, as Pope, carries the globe of the Almighty; the Son, as Christ, bears the Cross of infinite love; the two persons, Father and Son, are united by the Holy Spirit who is the central figure of the group.

Thus ends this portion of my task. I have felt it necessary in the first instance to give the history of an important archæological attribute, that is, the nimbus or glory; then that of the Being who presides over all images as over all Christian doctrine—the history of God. To enlarge in like manner on the rest of Christian iconography would be exaggeration; nor could one life suffice not only to bring forward, but even to gather the material for such a work. However, some very brief and purely technical information on the Angel, the Devil, on scenes from the Old Testament, the Gospels and the legendary or apocryphal writings will doubtless fulfil the object proposed by the Committee of Arts and Monuments.

ICONOGRAPHY OF
ANGELS, DEVILS, DEATH, THE SOUL,
AND THE
CHRISTIAN SCHEME OF SALVATION.

CONCLUDED AND EDITED BY

MARGARET STOKES.

EDITOR'S NOTE.

I HAVE been requested by the publishers of the English translation of this work by the late M. Didron to continue and complete it. No reason has been alleged to explain why the original scheme, as laid down in the Introduction to our first volume, was never carried out, but it is more than probable that its very magnitude prevented its completion, and that the labours undertaken by the author in the editorship of the 'Annales Archéologiques,' commenced in 1844, and only closing with his death in 1867, interfered with the completion o this special work. However, the history of the Iconography of Angel and Devils was in course of preparation at this period, and the 7(wood engravings from drawings by M. Durand executed to illustrate these subjects have ever since remained unpublished. Portions of the letterpress intended for this work appeared from time to time in th pages of the 'Révue Française' vol. x., and 'Annales Archéologiques, vols. i., xi., and xviii. The numerous engravings accompanying thes papers will now be reproduced here along with those hitherto un published.

I have been obliged reluctantly to curtail these contributions o M. Didron to the periodical literature of his day, in order to avoi printing much that, although new when it first appeared, is no' familiar to English readers. I have also occasionally been compelle to introduce passages explanatory of some of the illustrations prepare by the author for the continuation of this work, but for which r descriptive text could be found and the very *provenance* of which had to discover. It only remains to explain that the portions of th work translated from M. Didron's text may be recognised by th insertion of the initial D. at the top of every page, and by brackets the beginning and end of every interpolated paragraph.

I have to own myself responsible for all the text following c page 145, although the matter is mainly founded on the writings M. Didron, in whose footsteps, as a conscientious investigator of tl iconographical systems of the great French cathedrals, I have humb endeavoured to follow.

M. S.

CARRIG BRAEC, HOWTH,
March, 1885.

ICONOGRAPHY OF ANGELS.

The iconography of the Angels or Messengers of God naturally follows on that of the Deity Himself, since they —*beni Elohim*, sons of God—may be described as emanations from God and as powers fulfilling His will. While uniformly held to have been created beings, yet many and various have been the theories as to the period of creation at which they sprang to life. The generally accepted idea was, that as the incorporeal existed before the material, so angels were created before the world. Others have held that it was on the second day, and after the creation of the firmament, that angels came to life, and this view seems to have been adopted by the sculptor of the Creation of Angels in Chartres Cathedral, where their forms are seen emerging from the heavens. A third view is that God must have made the angels at the close of the sixth day, when the creation of all material things had been accomplished. Thus, according to this last theory, that principle of progress is maintained which is observable from the first to the sixth day in creation, rising from dead substances to living forms till Man is reached, and after him the still more perfect being, the Angel, is called into existence.

The creation of angels is a subject very rarely to be met with in art, still we may indicate three different methods of treating it. The first is in a manuscript of the close of the thirteenth century, where the Creator may be seen, in the form of God the Son, seated on a rainbow. Rays proceed from His mouth like a divine breath, from which nine groups of angels are born and over whom His left hand is raised in benediction. These rays are, as it were, the embodiment of the Word proceeding from God, the special fiat" at the utterance of which the angels were brought forth. An illustration of this has been already given in our first volume at page 240, where it will be seen that there are nine groups of angels, three in each group, but that all are identical. Thus the painter indicates the nine divisions of the heavenly host, but without ordering their ranks.

A second representation is afforded us by a carving in Chartres Cathedral. Here only two angels are seen instead of the nine united choirs. More materialistic, if one may say so, than the miniature painter, the sculptor of Chartres has endowed his angels with bodies, and bodies clothed in an upper and an under garment. These two angels open the first act of their life drama, the one in act of adoration, the other of service; the one with hands folded in prayer, the other with hands outspread in ministration.

A third representation, see Fig. 148, *supra*, p. 76, shows us the Creation of the Universe as arranged in concentric circles. The nine choirs of angels occupy nine of these circles. We may believe that the author of this picture, Buonamico Buffamalco, who painted it in the fourteenth century, on the wall of the Campo Santo of Pisa, held that angels were created after the material world. In fact, the nine external circles are filled by angels; the innermost circles, the kernel, by the earth; but between the angels and the earth, the signs of the zodiac, the constellations, the sun and moon, may be seen. Now, the stars having been created after the earth, from their intermediate position between the terrestrial globe at the centre, and the angelic circles which form the circumference, we must conclude that the order of creation indicated by this painting was from the centre to the circumference; that, according to Buffamalco, creation was perfected spiritually and enlarged materially from the little round point which is our globe to the immense outer circle filled by the most sublime of celestial beings—the Seraphim.

Thus, without straining the interpretation of these three figures too far, we may see in the first—the minia ture belonging to the close of the thirteenth century—the creation of angels before the creation of the world; in the second, which is a sculpture of the first half of the thirteenth century, the creation of angels on the second day, with the firmament; in the third, which is a mur painting of the first half of the fourteenth century, the creation of angels after that of the world.

It will be well to reflect on these three assumed epochs of the birth of angels. Nothing is unimportant in these Middle Age designs, which are often rigorous representations of theological doctrine.

St. John Damascene, in his treatise upon angels, thus expresses himself: "Some assert that angels were made before all other created substances; witness the words of Gregory the Theologian, who holds that intelligent nature was created first and that of sense followed, and that thus man, who is composed of both, was finally created."* At first God conceived the idea of angelic and heavenly virtues, and then the idea was translated into being. Others admit, in preference, that angels were created after the first heaven. But all agree that they were made before man.

St. Jerome shared this opinion; but he placed the creation of angels at an epoch infinitely long before that of the world of sense. He carried it back to several thousands of centuries before the age of the world. Dante, on the contrary, thought that this creation of the angels had scarcely preceded that of the world, and perhaps even had followed it. Indeed, he says that angels are the motors of the sensible universe; but the motor may very well come after the substance that he sets in motion. The passage from Dante, which forms, as it were, a summary of our chapter, may be quoted here:†—

> ". . . Not for increase to himself
> Of good, which may not be increased, but forth
> To manifest his glory by its beams;
> Inhabiting his own eternity,
> Beyond time's limit or what bound soe'er
> To circumscribe his being; as he willed,
> Into new natures, like unto himself,
> Eternal love unfolded: nor before,
> As if in dull inaction, torpid, lay,
> For, not in process of before or aft,
> Upon these waters moved the spirit of God.
> Simple and mix'd, both form and substance, forth

---

* St. Gregory Nazianzen, *Oratio Secunda*.
† Dante, *Paradiso*, translated by Cary, cant. xxix.

> To perfect being started, like three darts
> Shot from a bow three-corded. And as ray
> In crystal, glass and amber, shines entire,
> E'en at the moment of its issuing; thus
> Did, from the eternal Sov'ran, beam entire
> His threefold operation, at one act
> Produced coeval. Yet, in order, each
> Created his due station new; those highest,
> Who pure intelligence were made; mere power,
> The lowest; in the midst, bound with strict league,
> Intelligence and power, unsevered bond.
> Long tract of ages by the angels past,
> E'er the creating of another world,
> Described on Jerome's pages, thou hast seen.
> But that what I disclose to thee is true,
> Those penmen, whom the Holy Spirit moved,
> In many a passage of their sacred book,
> Attest; as thou by diligent search shalt find:
> And reason, in some sort, discerns the same,
> Who scarce would grant the heavenly ministers,
> Of their perfection void, so long a space.
> Thus, when and where these spirits of love were made,
> Thou know'st, and how: and knowing, hast allay'd
> Thy thirst, which from the triple question rose."

The angel is conceived as a being at once intelligent, immortal and incorporeal, therefore practically invisible to mortal eyes. However, in poetry and art the angel, as the Deity Himself, has been endowed of necessity with form and body. Words can present images less formally than line and colour, and they have resources which allow the poet to rest in an abstraction forbidden to the designer or the painter. So, in poetry, the angel's body is more ethereal, more immaterial than in pictures. Ezekiel presents his angels, not only by comparing them to brilliant stones, to crystal, molten brass, burning coal flame, sparks, rainbows, clouds, lightning, breaths, glimmerings, but also to apparitions and even to visions of apparitions of these images. It is impossible to attenuate or to spiritualise a substance farther. There is nothing perceptible to eye or ear beyond such visions of light and air. Light, that swiftest, least weighty, least material of all bodies, is the substance to which angels have been likened. They are said to be made of light—or, as by St. John of Damascus, held to have been a reverberation of uncreated light, a reflection of the Divinity. An angel with Christian and Middle Age artists, is a multiform focus of light, the varieties of which we shall have to mention hereafter.

In Ezekiel, this angel form is that of a circle or of a winged wheel covered with eyes. The wheel and wings to express the constant mobility with which angels are endowed; the eyes to symbolise the wakefulness of their intelligence. "Angelus itaque est substantia intelligens, perpetuo motu, nec non arbitrii libertate prædita, corporis expers,"* &c.

[These wheels are united, in the prophet's vision, with the body of a living being having hands, feet, with the face of a man or a lion, an ox or an eagle, but all with two or three pairs of wings, which are indeed the principal feature in these descriptions, being instruments of locomotion and symbols of swiftness. From the time of Ezekiel we find that the winged human form, resplendent in light and colour, is the most usual representation of the angel offered to us by poetry and art. Dante, having in the 31st canto of *Paradise* shown us the luminous home in which these multitudes of celestial beings shine and shimmer, thus goes on to describe them (Purg. c. ii., translated by H. F. Cary):—

"A light, so swiftly coming through the sea,
No winged course might equal its career.
From which when for a space I had withdrawn
Mine eyes, to make inquiry of my guide,
Again I looked, and saw it grown in size
And brightness: then on either side appear'd
Something, but what I knew not, of bright hue,
Then by degrees from underneath it came
Another. My preceptor silent yet
Stood, while the brightness, that we first discerned,
Open'd the form of wings: Then when he knew
The pilot, cried aloud, 'Down, down; bend low
Thy knees; behold God's angel; fold thy hands:
Now shalt thou see true ministers indeed.
Lo! how all human means he sets at nought;
So that nor oar he needs, nor other sail
Except his wings, between such distant shores.
Lo! how straight up to heaven he holds them rear'd,
Winnowing the air with those eternal plumes,
That not like mortal hairs fall off or change,

---

* Opp. S. Joh. Damasceni, tom. i. *de Angelis*, cap. iii.; Ezekiel i. 15-21; x. 9-14.

As more and more toward us came, more bright
Appear'd the bird of God, nor could the eye
Endure his splendour near: I mine bent down."

In canto xii. of *Purgatory*, Dante adds some details
his picture:
"Behold,
That way an angel hasting towards us . . .
The goodly shape approach'd us, snowy white
In vesture, and with visage casting streams
Of tremulous lustre like the matin star.
His arms he opened, then his wings; and spake."

Whoever has seen the mural paintings of Italy, t]
mosaics of Greece, the Byzantine enamels scattered throug
out Europe, will recognize that the angels of Giotto a1

Fig. 151.—SERAPH OF ST. FRANCIS.

of Orcagna, of Fra Angelico and of Perugino, the ang
of St. Luke in Livadia, and Santa Sophia of Salonica,
well as the angels on that priceless work,* the Byzanti

* This reliquary, made to enshrine a portion of the true cross, is
considerable value and unparalleled beauty. It is held to date from t
tenth century, and originally belonged to the Cathedral of Trèves.

eliquary of Limbourg, are only another expression in art
f such angels as Dante has described. The same forms,
he same wings, the same light; poetry and painting have
ranslated an absolutely identical thought into two
anguages, the one through words, the other through line
nd colour. Unfortunately we can only place our poor
ngravings by the side of the splendid text of Ezekiel and
f Dante; but they suffice, however, to fill the eye with
he principal lineaments of these celestial forms.

In light and colour, this seraph, taken from a miniature
f St. Francis receiving the Stigmata (Fig. 151) forcibly
ecalls the imagery of Dante. Wings, head, and body are
ne starlike flame, appearing like a meteor in the deepest
lue of an Italian sky. St. Francis kneels in ecstasy upon
ie ground below, while five rays dart from the seraphic
ymbol and pierce his hands and feet and side as he listens
o its salutation:—

"Salve! sancte Pater patrie lux forma."*]

The following (Fig. 152) is the most complete illustra-
on that we are acquainted with of the winged and fiery

Fig. 152.—THRONES.—FIERY TWO-WINGED WHEELS.

* These words are written in the fly-leaf opposite. This illustration, which
aken from the illuminated Hours of Anne of France, daughter of Louis
., was executed by Loys de Laval de Chastillon, and afterwards belonging
Henri IV. Bibl. Nat. No. 920 (formerly 4299), fol. 284a.

wheels spoken of by the prophet Ezekiel, "full of eyes round about."* It comes from a little church at Athens, now probably destroyed, but which, at the date of our journey in Greece in 1839, possessed very remarkable mural paintings of the thirteenth century.

In a representation on the imperial dalmatic now preserved in the treasury of St. Peter at Rome, the feet of Jesus Christ rest on two wheels which exactly resemble these. This magnificent vestment is of Byzantine origin, and indeed throughout all the ancient empire of Byzantium, angels are found of this wheel form, intended to bear the figure of God the Father or of Jesus Christ.† These wheels, specially assigned to the order of Thrones by the Byzantines, but attributed by Ezekiel to all angels in general, are of various forms. At Chartres, they have neither flames, nor wings, nor eyes; they rather affect the more material form of a chariot wheel. This is less symbolic, less poetic, and more commonplace. True, this wheel is only the footstool, as it were, of the angel with the six wings and eyes of the wheel in Greece.

Fig. 153.—SCULPTURED ANGEL, CHARTRES, XIII. CENT.

On an ivory in the museum of the Barberini Palace, engraved by Gori, we find, not a wheel, but a circle without eyes and stripped of flames and wings. In the place of wings, an interlaced ribbon passes into the circle and forms a kind of quatrefoil. This is far —very far indeed—from the mysterious poetry of Ezekiel.

The Latins, more rational than the Easterns, have preferred representing angels under the human form. As regards the ideal, Latin nations are divisible into two classes: ultramontane or Italian, and western. Italians nearest to that Greece who planted her foot among them at Venice, at Ravenna, and throughout all Sicily

* "Et omne corpus earum (rotarum), et colla, et manus, et pennae, et circuli plena erant oculis, in circuitu quatuor rotarum. Et rotas illas vocavit volubiles." *Prophetia Ezechielis*, cap. **I.**, v. 12 et 13.

† *Ann. Archéo'.* vol. i. p. 152.

love to spiritualise the angels. They often leave them nothing more of the human form than the head, that is, the seat of intelligence. Nothing is more common, even in the paintings of Perugino, at the dawn of the materialist

Fig. 154.—ANGELS. (Piero della Francesca.)

enaissance, than to see angels figured by infant heads, rrrounded by six wings. Sometimes Italian artists like furnish these angels with a body. and in doing so they it off the body below the bust.* The lower portion of the unk being intended for locomotion, they replace it by

* *Annales Arché logiques*, vol. i. 157.

a pair of wings. These wings fulfil the function of the limbs.

The number of monuments is very great in which angels are thus represented without bodies or limbs, and we refer our readers to those portions of our first volume

Fig. 155.—ANGEL WITHOUT FEET OR LEGS.
Italian painting, XIV. cent.

in which they are illustrated. Thus, at page 452, one of these angels, " disembodied souls," may be seen. The seal of the university of Avignon, a thoroughly Italian university, founded in 1303, shows an infant head surrounded by six wings. Indeed this is the form allotted to Cherubim, of whom intelligence, that legitimate aim of all universities, is the especial attribute as compared with other orders of angels.

In the West, where symbolism has least taken root, and where the ideal always gives way to the real, the angel is no longer a mere child such as the Italians give us, but a full grown, almost aged man, such as may be seen in many German, French and English manuscripts. This (Fig. 156) is one drawn from a miniature probably executed by a French hand, which dates from the twelfth

:entury. It has wings and nimbus, it is true, but is upwards of forty or fifty years of age, with robe, mantle, and a sceptre that rather resembles an alpenstock than a symbol of power or authority; with feet shod as if those

Fig. 156.—ANGEL from MS.

an angel accustomed to fly with strong wings, and therefore protected from sharp stones of earth.*
Of all the angels we have ever noted, this is the most material, the most human, the least celestial spirit. We all perceive, in the course of our study, that the Western

* This figure represents the angel announcing the Ascension of Christ the Women at His tomb. It is drawn from a MS. in the Bibl. Nat. ris, the number of which had escaped M. Didron's memory.—[ED.]

nations have an invincible tendency to humanise, and to give an ordinary, every-day character to their angelic beings.

In Ezekiel the angel is particularly described as covered, and, as it were, clothed, by feathers. "And their wings were stretched upward; two wings of every one were joined one to another, and two covered their bodies.... Every one had two which covered on this side, and every one had two which covered on that side, their bodies." Ezek. i. 11, 23. A scarf is knotted round the neck, like that borne by the angel of Chartres; see Fig. 153. This scarf we find adopted by six of the nine choirs of angels painted on the glass windows of the chapel of New College, Oxford. But these Oxford angels have also a girdle bound round their loins.

Generally, where angels are given three pairs of wings, the addition of a scarf for the neck is sometimes thought sufficient, and more rarely still the waist scarf is introduced, but it is superfluous to endow them with robe and mantle besides. Two wings, crossed on the breast, two wings enclosing the body and limbs, is certainly sufficient. Nevertheless, the Middle-Age miniaturists, painters and sculptors, have arrayed their angels, already clothed with six wings, in robe and mantle. Such is the following angel taken from a manuscript Bible of the tenth century, or perhaps the ninth, with miniatures, which, though very ugly in execution, are most curious as drawings.*

Finally, to complete the costume or signs of the angels, it must be remarked, that, after the fifth century, all without exception bear a circular nimbus on the head, but before that date they are without this adornment. After God the angel is the most sublime of beings; if apostles and saints of every order are adorned with the nimbus how much rather should the angel carry this sign. And further the angel by ordination of God sometimes represents the Divinity himself. Thus one of the three angels or three persons whom the patriarch Abraham adored in the valley of Mamre bears a cruciform nimbus, and this is the one who

* Bibliothèque Nationale, 'Biblia Sacra,' Lat. 6, fol. 7a. This Bible with its outline drawings, appears to have been executed in the north of Spain. In the 12th century it belonged to the Abbey of St. Pierre d Rosas in Catalonia. It afterwards formed part of the library of th Maréchal de Noailles.

directly represents the unity of God. Thus in the combat of the three angels with the demon, he who attacked Behemoth and who, being alone, would seem to require exceeding strength and almost divine power, if he is to prove victorious, bears a cruciform nimbus, while the two antagonists of Leviathan have only a plain nimbus (see Fig. 132, *supra*, p. 17).

Fig. 157.—SIX-WINGED ANGEL HOLDING LANCE, WINGS CROSSED ON BREAST, ARRAYED IN ROBE AND MANTLE.

We see almost always among the Byzantines, and occasionally with the Italians also, a small horn upon the angel's brow, or an elongated triangle or sometimes a cross, besides the often richly decorated nimbus which surrounds the head. Is this simply a head ornament, a jewel, and as it were part of the dress, or rather a symbolic attribute? It may be both. We see, if we look back to Vol. I. p. 282, the archangels Raphael, Michael, and Gabriel wearing this little triangle on the forehead, or a reversed crescent such as that which forms the diadem of one of the enamelled Byzantine angels on the so-called cross of Samur. Perhaps this reversed crescent, this little horn, as St. Veronica calls it, is the sign of flame or star-like fire, placed by pagans on the brow of their genius to express that sublimity of mind which burns as light and comes from heaven. This Italian St. Veronica, who died in 1497, often saw angels who came to visit and converse with her. She gives a description of one of them in the following passage : "She saw that the angel re a little horn on the middle of his forehead, that a ole hung from his neck, and that he had wings, like as Christian painters habitually represent the angels."*

This little horn is the jewel or the flame we have just

* *Annales Archéol.* vol. xi. p. 361

mentioned; the stole is probably the scarf of the neck to which we referred in a previous passage. As to our French angels, they wear the nimbus on the head and that is all; no jewel, no flame, no star and no cross. Van Eyck and Hemling, Master Stephan and Albert Dürer, afford examples of the cross borne on the angel's brow, examples which also occur in the miniatures of such manuscripts of the sixteenth century as are executed under an Italian or German influence.

In order to complete the subject of the signs of angels we should enumerate and describe the attributes which characterise them, and the objects or divers instruments which they bear in their hands. But these attributes and instruments are given them according to the functions they fulfil as laid down by Dionysius the Areopagite,[*] who, following the passages in St. Paul's epistles to the Ephesians (ch. i. 20) and Colossians (ch. i. 16), made the following classification of the angelic hierarchy and their symbols:—

Counsellors	Seraphim. Cherubim. Thrones.	Six wings and flabellum; head and tw wings; fiery wheels; eyed wings.
Governors	Dominations. Virtues. Powers.	Wear long albs, golden girdles; and gree stoles. A golden staff in right han the seal of God in the left.
Ministers	Principalities. Archangels. Angels.	In soldier's garb, golden belts; holdin lance-headed javelins; and hatchets i their hands.

The saint then proceeds to enumerate other attribute with which they are endowed. They wear rings symbols of royal authority and of the rectitude with whic they work; their lances and hatchets express the facult they possess of discerning right from wrong, and t sagacity, vivacity, and power of this discernment. The instruments of geometry and different arts shew that the know how to lay the foundation, to build up, and to fini their work, and that they possess all the powers of th secondary providence which guides inferior natures a conducts them to their goal. Sometimes also the emblematic objects carried by these holy intelligenc

[*] See Œuvres de St. Denys l'Aréopagite, traduites du grec par M. l'A Darboy. Paris, 1845, in-8vo. ch. i. de la Hiérarchie Céleste, p. 242.

announce God's judgments upon man, the severity of His chastisements, the vengeance of His judgments. It may be also deliverance from peril, the fulfilment of the chastisement, the restoration of the lost treasure, and the increase of corporeal and spiritual graces.
In the ordinary preface of the mass, which is very ancient, the Angels, Archangels, Thrones, Dominations, Powers, Virtues, Seraphim, are mentioned. Neither the Cherubim nor Principalities are present, and the hierarchical order is not well observed. In the "Te Deum" the Cherubim are named with Seraphim, the Powers, the Angels, and the Heavens (Thrones), but neither the Dominations, Virtues, Principalities nor Archangels figure there. Thus out of nine, four and perhaps five classes are absent. Therefore it is to St. Dionysius that not only the complete nomenclature of the nine choirs of celestial spirits belongs, but also their systematic hierarchy.

St. Dionysius was a Greek, consequently it is in the Greek and in the Byzantine church that we should meet with the most frequent and most complete representation in art of the nine choirs of angels. In the Latin church it is a little more rare, as we shall see, to find a hierarchy, painted or carved.

The Cathedral of Chartres offers one example sculptured on the southern porch, and another painted on glass in the south transept. The hierarchy occupies the cordon of the voussoir of the port of the Sainte-Chapelle of Vincennes, which gives two examples drawn from each of the nine groups, so that the whole of the order is clearly characterised. In a south chapel of the cathedral at Cahors, the whole celestial army is sculptured in detail. That of Chartres belongs to the thirteenth century, Vincennes to the fourteenth, and Cahors to the fifteenth. In Fig. 158 we show one of four seraphim which stand in the bay of the south porch of Chartres, in the first row of the hierarchy of angels in the Last Judgment. This form is six-winged, holding flames, while the next, Fig. 159, holds globes upon which the monogram of Christ is inscribed. This last is one of four cherubim on the left side of the row on the same porch. Figs. 160 and 161 are two angels enthroned, one holding a sword, the other with crown and sceptre. There are three of these throned figures, sceptred, crowned, and with feet shod. Fig. 162 is an Angel of Judgment sounding the trumpet. There are four of these, two to the right and two to the left. Fig. 163 is an angel wearing a dalmatic and holding a book of the Gospel, " Liber scriptus proferetur." There are nine of these in a line to the left of the spectator.*

Greece, the country of St. Dionysius, is richer than

Fig. 158.   Fig. 159.

France in such complete representations of the hierarch:

* M. Didron adds in a note to the Guide to Painting, p. 77 : "D l'Iconographie Chrétienne, Histoire de l'Ange, nous décrirons en détail l(différents chœurs des anges sculptés et peints à la Sainte-Chapelle de Vii cennes, à la cathédrale de Chartres, à celle de Cahors, à celles d'Albi et (Reims." We shall give a definition of their names and functions wit respect to God and man. Hitherto we have only given the generic, not tl individual nomenclature. See *Annales Archéologiques*, tom. xviii. p. 72.

of angels. One of the finest examples we can bring forward is to be seen in the great convent of Ivirôn on Mount Athos, in the cupola of a church dedicated to the archangels. The Pantocrator presides in the centre of the cupola; the nine choirs of angels are arranged around him in nine ranks. An inscription runs under each telling the name and function of each order. The Creator

Fig. 160.

Fig. 161.

faces the west, to his right are the three orders of Counsellors, to the left, of Governors, and above his head the Ministers. Each choir is represented by a vast multitude of angels receding and ascending, step by step, till they are finally lost in the blue of heaven. Commencing with (I.) COUNSELLORS, we see first a little figure holding a scroll on which we read ΣΕΡΑΦΙΜ (seraphim), and this being is further described in the Greek inscription which occupies the entire length of the compartment,

πύρινοι ὄντες οἱ σεραφὶμ τὸ εἶδος
πυροῦσι βροτοὺς πρὸς ἀγάπησιν θείαν.

"The seraphim being fiery in appearance, inflame mortals towards divine love."

They are altogether red like flame. Their bodies and their three pairs of wings all red; a red and flaming sword

Fig. 162.

Fig. 163.

in the right hand. Their feet are bare. Thus, accordin to the etymology of their names, they are living flame that burn with and enkindle Divine love.

II.—CHERUBIM.

The little angel who introduces them bears on i scroll: XEP.

The inscription on the compartment runs thus:—

χύσιν σοφίας χερυβὶμ κεκτημένοι
χύδην κινοῦσι τε ἡμῖν ἐκεῖθεν.

"The cherubim, possessors of the pouring forth of wisdom, pour it forth in floods from that source into us."

A single pair of wings, variegated, but whose general aspect is blue. A robe surmounted by a mantle, and below the mantle, a short tunic descending to the knees, slightly resembling that worn by our bishops. Feet shod. The robe, the mantle, the tunic, and the foot-gear all very rich.

III.—THRONES.

Upon the scroll held by the little angel we read: ΘΡΟΝ
The inscription in the compartment reads:—

ὑπερίδρυνται ἐσχατίας ἁπάσης
οἱ ἀμφὶ τὸν ὕψιστον ὑψηλοὶ θρόνοι.

"Above all limit are set the high thrones around the Most High."

Two fiery wheels, winged with four wings filled with eyes. An angel's head with aureole appears below each of these wheels and rises towards the centre. The Virgin appears below near these thrones, in that choir of which she forms a part, according to Byzantine theology. She is praying, her hands raised towards heaven. Near her this inscription may be read:—

ἐξαίρει θρονοὺς τοῦ θεοῦ ὄντως θρόνος θεοῦ.

"True Throne of God, she exalts the thrones of God."

IV.—DOMINATIONS.

On the scroll of the little angel here: ΚΥΡ.
Inscription on the compartment:—

πρὸς τὴν ὄντως φέρουσι κυριαρχίαν
αὐτοκρατόρου κυριότητες νεύσιν.*

"The dominations direct their will in accordance with the truly supreme power of the absolute Master."

It would appear that this motto has been incorrectly copied from the fresco painting.

Angels with two wings, robe, mantle and clothing for the feet. In the right hand, the seal of God, a disc marked by the Greek monogram of Jesus Christ I͞C X͞C. In the left hand, a long staff surmounted by a cross. The Holy Virgin belongs to the Thrones; St. John the Baptist is among the Dominations. This is a human domination, a dignity due to him, according to Byzantine theology, because of his virtue and his title as Harbinger of Jesus Christ. St. John is winged, exactly because he was the angel and the messenger of God. His robe is of skin, and mantle of stuff. He has naked feet, like an apostle and Jesus Christ himself, although the dominations, to whom he is allied, have feet shod.

V.—POWERS.

Upon the scroll of this little angel: ΔΥΝ̄.
The inscription on the compartment:—

ἀκατάσειστον ἀνδρείαν αἱ δυνάμεις
φέρουσι τὰς σφαίρας τε πόλου κινοῦσι.

"The Powers possess invincible courage and put the spheres of heaven in motion."

Angels with two wings, robe, and mantle, above which is a short tunic descending to the knees. Embroidered border at the bottom of robe and tunic and round the collar of the mantle. The feet are bare. In the right hand, the seal of God, or the globe, marked by the monogram of Jesus Christ; in the left hand a long staff terminated by a cross.

VI.—AUTHORITIES.

On the scroll of the little angel: ΕΞΟΥΣ̄.
The inscription on this compartment:—

ἡ ἐξουσιῶν ἔξοχος ἐξουσία
ὅλη νένευκε τῇ ἐξουσιαρχίᾳ.

"The authority that excels authorities has wholly bowed to the arch-authority."

Angel with two wings, a robe and mantle, but without ornaments, and with bare feet. In the right hand, the seal of God stamped with the monogram of Jesus Christ; in the left hand, a long staff ending in a cross.

VII.—PRINCIPALITIES.

On the scroll of the little angel: APXĀI.
Inscription :—

τὸ θεοειδὲς ἀρχικὸν ἐκτυποῦσι
πλεῖστα θαύματ' αἱ ἀρχαὶ ἐνεργοῦσαι.

"Principalities, many wonder working, figure the essence of Divine rule."

Angels with two wings, robe, mantle covered by a tunic descending to the knees. Feet shod. Great richness of dress. In the right hand the seal of God engraved with the monogram of Christ; in the left, a lily branch, instead of the baton expanded into a cross.

VIII.—ARCHANGELS.

On the scroll of this little angel: APXAΓ̄.
Inscription :—

ἀρχαγγελικὴ ἀρχαγγέλων τάξις
μέση ταῖς ἀρχαῖς κοινωνεῖ καὶ ἀγγέλοις.

"The archangelic order of archangels combines with the principalities and the angels, being between them."

Soldiers winged with two wings: no helmet, but a breastplate and buskins. In the left hand a globe marked by the monogram of Jesus Christ. In the right hand a naked sword, point upwards. This is the type so constantly presented in the archangel Michael.

IX.—ANGELS.

On the scroll of the little angel: AΓΓĒ.
Inscription :—

τὸ λειτουργικὸν ὄντως ἀγγέλοις πρέπει
ἄνω κάτω τρέχουσιν ἕνεκ' ἀνθρώπων.

"The work of ministry is the true office of angels who ascend and descend in the service of men."

A multitude of two-winged angels richly clothed. Dressed like deacons in alb and dalmatic. In the right hand, the Divine seal marked by the monogram of Jesus Christ. In the left hand, a long staff terminating in a little cross. Feet richly shod, like those of angels on the reliquary of Limbourg.

The following inscription runs all round this cupola, from base to frontal. It is, in a manner, a résumé of that which has been already given in detail:—

οἱ ἀμφὶ τὸν πρώτιστον νοῦν τὴν τριάδα νόες δεύτεροι
τριαδικῶς τελοῦντες ἐκ τριῶν πάτων τὸ τριμερὲς
νόος μου λῦσαι ὡς θέμις τοῖς λειτουργοῖς τριάδος.

"May the secondary spirits which surround the primary Spirit, the Trinity, working in a threefold manner, deliver the triple part of my spirit from the three passions, as is right for those who adore the Trinity."

At the same Monastery of Ivirôn, in the church of the Παναγία Πορταίτισσα, that is to say, of the Virgin Portress, or virgin guardian of the door, the angels who surround this Virgin are, on the one hand, Seraphim with six wings, named Ἐξαπτέρες, but without feet; on the other Πολυόμματα, Thrones, circles of five with four wings filled with eyes.

In the great church of the same Convent of Ivirôn, named Παναγίας Κοίμησις, "Death of the Virgin," the porch, which is entirely painted over, shows in the vault the nine choirs of angels surrounding Jesus Christ, whose golden and cruciform nimbus is marked with O ΩN Their names not being inscribed and their attributes being almost the same in all, it is not possible to define them. There are only two choirs more clearly defined than in the Church of the Archangels, the one being that of the Thrones, the other that of the Angels, properly so called. The Thrones are crowned as kings; they are clothed in long robe and mantle. They hold in the left hand a long sceptre or baton, with floriate termination in the right hand a staff, with a cartel, banner, square, and flat, on which may be read: "Holy, holy, holy, Lord God of Sabaoth; heaven and earth are full of Thy glory." As to the angelic choir, it is represented by a crowd of two-winged angels, in soldiers' dress, with casque, cuirass and shod in buskins, holding a floriate sceptre, and in the left, a staff with square banner on which we may read "Holy, holy, holy!"

We seem now to have said enough upon all these Greek

angels, still so imperfectly defined, notwithstanding the laws laid down by St. Dionysius the Areopagite; endowed with attributes too similar to allow of our distinguishing one from another without risk of error; baptised by names which have synonymous names, and which are borne by diverse choirs. In addition we still have to treat of the hierarchy of Latin angels and enlarge on this subject, but before doing so we must pass in review those angels executed in Latin churches under evidently Byzantine influence, and our remarks on this Romano-Byzantine hierarchy will serve to clear up what is still obscure about the nine choirs of the Greeks.*

["In his character of Messenger," writes Mrs. Jameson, "the Greeks represented John with large wings, of which there are many examples in Byzantine art. For instance, in a Greek ivory diptych, in which he stands thus winged, with his head in a dish (charger) at his feet. In another instance, a picture half-length, he has large wings, and holds his own head in his hand." A somewhat similar representation of this figure is given at page 70, Vol. I. of this work, from a fresco painting in the Convent of Kaisariani on Mount Hymettus. The Greek Church translates literally the words of St. Mark: "Behold I send my angel before thy face (i. 2). In the West, where the spirit is more regarded than the letter, St. John has a nimbus, but the wings are dispensed with. In this illustration the angel-saint holds his cross and scroll in the left hand while giving benediction with the right, and on the scroll is written:—

ποιήσατε κάρπους ἀξίους μετανοίας.
"Bring forth fruits worthy of repentance.

The place of John in the hierarchy of angels is among the Dominations, as has been indicated in the extract from St. Dionysius given above (see p. 104) in the description of the Hierarchy in the church of Ivirôn.

Wingless angels with feet firmly planted on the ground are seen occasionally in Western art. Thus in a manu-

* M. Didron did not live to carry out this portion of his work, and the following account of the Iconography of Angels is extracted and condensed from his essays on the subject in the *Annales Archéologiques*, vol. xi. pp. 346, 362; xii. p. 168; xviii. p. 72.

script of the eleventh century, in the Bibliothèque Nationale, M. C. Bayet* has found an illustration of the Repose of Christ, where the Saviour is represented reclining on a couch, with fifty-seven angels and seraphs

Fig. 164.

standing in serried ranks behind, none of whom have wings. Piero della Francesca also, in his Presepio, in the National Gallery of London, paints the noble forms of five wingless angels, who have walked across the hills to sing their simple hymn in the stable at Bethlehem (see Fig. 154).†]

* See *L'Art Byzantin.* C. Bayet, p. 163.
† N.B. The portions of this work enclosed in brackets are by the Editor.

ICONOGRAPHY OF DEVILS.

The Iconography of Lucifer and the rebellious angels should follow that of the Hierarchy of Heaven. The origin of these images is traceable to the Hebrew Scriptures. Thus in Isaiah we read, "How art thou fallen from heaven, O Lucifer, son of the Morning! how art thou cut down to the ground, which didst weaken the nations! For thou hast said in thine heart, I will ascend into heaven, I will exalt my throne above the stars of God: I will sit upon the Mount of the Congregation" (xiv. 12, 13).

"The following illustration," says M. de Challemel, "shows

Fig. 165.—LUCIFER BEFORE THE FALL.

Lucifer before his fall.* It is drawn from the MS. entitled Hortus deliciarum,' formerly in the library of Strasurg, which was written and painted for the Convent of

* See *La France Littéraire*, vols. ii., iii. "Hist. du Diable."

St. Odilius in Alsace. Strength and pride are the characteristics of this figure, standing with globe and sceptre, as one who would make himself equal to God. In another manuscript,* 'Bible historiée of the 13th century,' Lucifer is represented as irreverently seated in the presence of God, in illustration of the words 'I will *sit also upon the Mount of the Congregation.*' These are the only instance we have met with as yet of Lucifer before the fall."

There is a manuscript in the Bibliothèque de l'Arsenal, in Paris, No. 1186, called the Breviary of St. Louis on the fly-leaf of which is inscribed, "C'est le psautier Monseigneur Saint Loys . . . lequel fu à sa mère.' The following illustration of the fall of Lucifer is taken from this breviary, and it adds no little to the interes of this miniature that it is found in a prayer-book of the celebrated Queen Blanche of Castille (A.D. 1220 to 1252) and was possibly given by her to St. Louis of France when a youth under her careful guardianship. The painter of this miniature appears to have closely followed the instructions of the Byzantine painter's guide:—

"Heaven. Christ seated as King on a throne, holding the Gospel open at the words: 'I have seen Satan like lightning fall from heaven.' A multitude of angels stand around in great fear. Michael is in the midst; on his scroll is written, 'Let us stand in awe and here adore th King our God.' Mountains are beneath, and a great gul in which is written: TARTARUS. Lucifer and all his army fall from heaven. Above the forms [of his angels] ar very beautiful; at a lower point they change to angel of darkness; lower still they are darker and blacker below that again they are half demons, half angels; an finally they are all black and hideous demons. At th bottom, and under all the others, in the midst of the abys —Lucifer, blackest and most terrible of all, lies prostrat on the ground, looking upwards."

Thus in this illustration the forms of Lucifer's army just falling out of heaven where the Lord is seated amids His adoring host, are angelic still. They have the nimbus wings and robes of prismatic colours, red, blue, green etc., on a golden ground. But the features are already

* See *History of Our Lord in Art*, Introd. vol. i. p. 56, where Lad Eastlake gives engraved facsimile of this figure.

undergoing a transformation, the mouth changing to an

Fig. 166.

open throat, the nose to a beak. When they enter the gulf they have neither nimbus nor robe; a tail projects behind, feet and hands are changed to paws, nails become as claws, and all the skin resembles that of a monkey; the face is no longer human, but bestial and monstrous.

In the Italian Speculum Humanae Salvationis (Bibl. de l'Arsenal, No. 593), the illustrations in which are held to belong to the school of Giotto, we have the following repre-entation of the Fall of the Angels: The Almighty, partially seen through the clouds, drives them downward with a motion of His hand.

Fig. 167.—FALL OF LUCIFER.

Lucifer, emperor of demons, as he is called in a MS. preserved in the Bibliothèque Nat. Paris, is represented under the most hideous aspects. He has frequently three heads each one of which devours a soul of the damned. Even before the time of Dante, these three-headed demons have been painted in France, and before the birth of the artist who has depicted them upon the walls of the Campo Santo of Pisa. This is one proof amongst many that Dante visited France, and having seen Paradise, Purgatory, and Hell sculptured in the voussoirs and painted on the glass of our reat cathedrals, he loves to describe them in poetry.* Fig. 68 represents a four-headed Satan, engraved by Didron, the *rovenance* of which we have not been able to ascertain.

Fig. 168.

<pre>   *   Yet in the abyss,
        That Lucifer with Judas low engulphs,
        Lightly he placed us.
                            The emperor who sways
        The realm of sorrow, at mid-breast from the ice
        Stood forth; and I in stature am more like
        A giant than the giant are his arms.
        Mark now how great that whole must be which suits
        With such a part.   If he were beautiful
        As he is hideous now, and yet did dare
        To scowl upon his Maker, well from him
        May all our misery flow.   Oh, what a sight!
        How passing strange it seemed when I did spy
        Upon his head three faces: one in front
        Of hue vermilion, the other two with this
        Midway each shoulder joined and at the crest;
        The right twixt wan and yellow seemed; the left
        To look on, such as come from whence old Nile
        Stoops to the lowlands.   Under each shot forth
        Two mighty wings, enormous as became
        A bird so vast.   No plumes had they,</pre>

We have also seen a three-headed devil, devouring three figures, at St. Basile d'Étampes.]

Satan is alive wherever evil and suffering exist, so that to write a complete history of the Devil we should de: with a great part of the history of the universe; therefor we must confine ourselves to a certain limited treatmer of the subject. It is with archæology, positive, exper mental, anatomical, if we may so say, that we are here co cerned—not with philosophy; our business is to record ar describe, but not to seek to interpret.

Evil is either physical or moral; it gnaws and consum the body or the soul of man, it demands his life or b virtue. <u>The personification that has been made of ev through help of metaphor, concentrates these two kinds evil in itself.</u> Among the ancients, as among Christia at a la'er age, physical evils are personified in natural pl nomena, such as convulsions of nature, precipices, gulfs ever open to devour mankind. Thus, in the gulf betwe Messina and Reggio there was a horrible monster; t Greeks represented it as a beast with six long necks, a enormous heads, twelve claws to grasp its prey, a six throats ready to devour it. A host of dogs bark in its belly, and issuing forth from its body, though tied its waist, by their continual yelling terrified all th passed by. When the monster, who had been, before fall, a lovely nymph, a kind of pagan angel, beheld metamorphosis, it was so terrified that it threw itself ir the sea, in the very strait that bears its name and wh it still inhabits. If Etna almost perpetually growls, a

---

but were in texture like a bat, and these
He flapped in the air, that from him issued still
Three winds wherewith Cocytus to its depth
Was frozen. At six eyes he wept: the tears
Adown three chains distilled with bloody foam.
At every mouth his teeth a sinner champed,
Bruised as with ponderous engine; so that three
Were in this guise tormented.

In the systems of infernal government constructed by later wri Lucifer was either placed at the head of all the devils, or reckoned as of the seven chief infernal potentates under the supremacy of Belial. Marlowe's *Faustus* (sc. iii.) he is "Arch-regent and commander of spirits," "Chief Lord and regent of perpetual night!... Prince of the E: (sc. v. 104). He reigns in the Orient, while Beelzebub rules in the So

shakes from base to summit, if it vomits masses of rock and floods of burning lava, it is a giant thunderstruck by Jupiter and chained within its caverns, if it quakes it is the giant within who strikes the mountains, if it groans he howls in echo. The mournful and angry sigh of Enceladus tears the rocks, and tosses them to the sky with flaming breath, as if to attack triumphant Jupiter again.

Among the Scandinavians these earthquakes were in like manner personified as gods: such as the evil god, or demon, named Loki. After having scattered sin throughout all Scandinavia, as a sower sows his grain, Loki was at last chained to pointed rocks. When he turns himself,

Fig. 169.—PERSONIFICATION OF RIVER.*

like a sick man upon the sharp stones, the earth trembles, when he foams at mouth and drops his poisonous spittle on the ground, his nerves are convulsed, and the earth quakes. Among Christians, the ardent southern imagination of France personifies the inundations and caverns of the Rhone in the monster of the Tarasque.† So when Christianity expelled Vulcan, the Cyclops, and the Giants from Etna and the Lipari islands, it was only to make room for

* It is to be regretted that the *provenance* of this illustration has not been ascertained.—[ED.]
† On the River Symbols of Antiquity, see *Annales Archéol.* tom. ix. 107-8.

demons in their stead. Indeed, Odilon, abbot of Cluny, instituted the Fête des Morts in order to release a multitude of suffering souls from purgatory, and to place them in paradise. He freed these souls, purified by the prayers of the living, from the demons who tormented them, to give them to the care of angels. "Then," as a holy hermit relates, "frightful sounds were heard in Etna, and deafening explosions in the neighbouring isles." This uproar was caused by Satan and all his court, Satan and all his demoniacal retinue, who howled in despair, and with loud cries demanded back the souls lost to them since the day of the new Festival.

The history of these imaginary monsters is much the same in the end, although they are called by different names thus, the Serpent is called Graouilli at Metz; Gargouille at Rouen;* Clair Sallé at Troyes; Grand Gueule at Poitiers Tarasque at Arles.† "In France," says M. Alfred de Maury "these legends do not date very far back, and the oldest that of the Tarasque of Arles, is first mentioned by Gerva of Tilbury, an English writer, marshal of the kingdom of Arles, who lived in the beginning of the 13th century

I now have to treat of the authors of conflagration (incendiaries) in the history of the Devil.

"One day," writes Frodoard, an historian, born at Epernay in 894, and who wrote the history of the Church of Rheims—"one day St. Remi, Archbishop of Rheims was absorbed in prayer inside a little church in his beloved town. He thanked God for having been able to save from the snares of the demon all the most beautiful souls in his diocese, when some one announced to him that the town was on fire. Then the lamb turned to a lion; and inflamed the face of the saint, who stamped on the flagstones of the church with terrible energy, and cried out 'Satan, I detect thee. After all I am not yet rid of thee and thy wickedness.' The footprints where St. Remi

* Gargouille, from Low Latin *gargola*, which means a shout.
† Tarasque is derived from the name of a French town, Tarascon n Arles, where it was the custom on holidays to carry round the effigy of monster or dragon. *Légendes picuses au Moyen Age*, Maury, p. 147, n
‡ "Les miracles que Frodoard attribue aux premiers archevêques Rheims ne sont pas racontés avec le génie d'Homère; cependant ils aussi excité l'enthousiasme populaire, ils ont aussi été admis et trans de bouche en bouche avec une foi fervente; et le tableau de St. Remi ch

furiously stamped on the flagstones at the door are still shown. Then the saint armed himself with his crosier and his cope, as a warrior with his sword and his cuirass, and flew to meet the enemy. He had scarcely advanced a few steps when he perceived the wreaths of fire and flames devouring, with irresistible fury, the wooden houses of which the city was built, and their thatched roofs. At sight of the saint the fire seemed to lessen and grow pale. Remi, who knew the enemy with whom he had to do, made the sign of the cross, and the fire retreated as the saint advanced. The fire slackened its hold and fled as if subjugated by the power of the bishop, or like some intelligent being that understood its own weakness. Some-

Fig. 170. FIRE DEMON.*

times it bore up again, took courage, and attempted to encircle the saint in fire, to blind him, and reduce him to cinders, but with the sign of the cross he parried the attacks and defeated its purpose. Thus forced back, and retreating from the houses, one after another, that had been enveloped in flame, the fire demon sank at the bishop's feet like a conquered animal, let itself be taken and led at the will of the saint, outside the town, into the moat by which Rheims is still fortified, and Remi opened a door leading to a subterranean chamber, and there thrust down the flames as a malefactor might be thrown into a pit; he made fast the door and forbade its ever being opened again under pain of anathema, —of ruin of body and death of the soul. Once an imprudent, curious, and perhaps sceptical man, wanting to brave this

---

unt devant lui, de rue en rue, l'incendie qui consumait la ville de Rheims, 'est dépourvu ni d'énergie ni d'éclat." For legend see Frodoard, Hist. de Eglise de Rheims; Guizot, Mémoires relatifs à l'Histoire de France, p. 35.
* It is to be regretted that the *provenance* of this illustration has not been ascertained.—[Ed.]

prohibition, and to force his way into the abyss, was driven forth by rolling masses of flame, scorched, and then retreated finally of themselves into the cave where the deathless will of the saint held them enchained."*

In the Missal of Poitiers we see the Devil as at once the ruler and the guardian of hell (see Fig. 171).

He is chained to its mouth as a dog to its kennel, and yet wields his trident sceptre as if monarch of the Hell he guards. Cerberus and Pluto in one, he is yet a Cerberus of Christian art, a demon more hideous and more filled with energy than Pagan art has offered. Mounted above the monkey demon whom we see here caught in the jaws of Hell and Death, this image figures the various aspects of infernal sin by its many faces, having a face on the breast as well as the head, a face on each shoulder and a face at each hip. How many more behind? With long ears like those of a hound, thick short horns of a bull, his legs and arms are covered with scales, and seem to issue from the mouths of the faces at his joints. He has a lion's head with tusks, and hands like the claws of a bear. His body, open at the waist, reveals a nest of serpents darting forth and hissing. In this monster we find all the elements of a dragon, leviathan, lion, fox, viper, bear, bull, and wild boar. It is a compound of each evil quality in these animals, embodied in a human form.

One of the most extraordinary conceptions of Satan that has come down to us from the Middle Ages is that figure seated in the midst of the Hell which forms one of the four "Novissima" on the walls of the Campo Santo at Pisa, said to have been painted by Orcagna in conjunction with his brother Bernardo.† A vast rib or arch in the walls of pandemonium admits one into the gulf of Hell, in which Satan sits in the midst, in gigantic terror, cased in armour and crunching sinners. The punishments of the wicked are

* See *La France Littéraire*, vol. iv. p. 174. (1841.)

† In another of the same series of frescoes in the Campo Santo, on the wall between the first and second entrance, demons are represented torturing St. Ranieri, which certainly date from the period when ideas and types belonging to the East begin to invade the West. These demons all have human faces, however. These scenes from the life of St. Ranieri, the patron of Pisa, were formerly held to have been painted by Simon Martino of Siena, but this is contradicted by Kugler, who holds them be the work of some unknown artist about the date 1360.

Fig. 171.—SATAN IN MISSAL OF POITIERS.

portrayed in numberless circles around him. Although

Fig. 172.—DEVIL IN CAMPO SANTO, PISA.

according to Vasari, Orcagna in this work drew much
his inspiration from Dante, yet his is not the thre

faced monster of the poet's *Inferno*, canto xxxiv. [M. Didron discovers a great resemblance between this Pisan devil and the great Satan in the Last Judgment on the west wall of the principal church in the Convent of St. Gregory at Mount Athos. The latter is naked, and carries the enormous key of hell hanging to his waist. A human form, fat and gross, but with a long and powerful tail. His feet and hands have eagle's claws, an ox head and horns, and a goat's beard. Flames issue from the eyes and mouth. He holds a little naked being (one of the damned) in his left hand, squeezing him against his side till fire gushes from his mouth; with his right hand he directs another little devil to carry a basket full of the scrolls in which the evil deeds of men are chronicled, to deliver to the angel who weighs men's souls in the balance. For ears he has dogs' heads; and on each shoulder a monstrous head stretches open its throat and vomits flame. At each knee another head also vomits flame. This Satan of Mount Athos again bears a singular resemblance to a chief Satan which appears in a fifteenth century MS. in the Bibliothèque Nationale, Paris. It would be deeply interesting to establish the Greek origin of the Satan of the Campo Santo and of that of the illuminator.]

The Oriental Devil is the personification of a rank and exuberant nature, mother and cruel step-dame, creatrix and homicide all in one. In the first ages there was understood to be but one primary Cause of all—this Cause both good and evil : one sole God himself the author of evil as of good. Later on the start was made, the Cause bifurcated : on one side was God, the source of all good ; on the other the Devil, who engenders all evil. But God and the Devil are clothed in monstrous forms—the Devil especially. His intellectual and varied powers are designated by many heads on one trunk. The intelligence that can embrace all things and penetrate everywhere is symbolised by a number of arms and legs. As the animal life is stronger than other created life, more intelligent and more formidable, and as each animal is endowed with some particular quality, this symbol of the evil genius was composed of all these predominant attributes without any secondary characteristic, and the Devil became an epitome of all hideous forms in zoological nature. A Persian Devil

122   CHRISTIAN ICONOGRAPHY.   [D.]

appears in an engraving in the Didron collection in the form of a man, clothed and wearing necklets, bracelets, and anklets, but with claws on his heels and toes, and horns on his head. He is named Ahriman, Spirit of Darkness, the Iranian enemy of Ormuzd, second-born of the Eternal One, like Ormuzd, an emanation from the Primal Light; equally pure, but ambitious and full of pride, he had become jealous of the first-born of God. He created three series of evil spirits—male and female (see Fig. 20).

An Egyptian Devil, engraved from *Montfaucon*, see Fig. 174, has a human head from which project the heads of six animals, one that of an ox, one of a bird, and four others apparently those of serpents. Typhôeus, the whirlwind, or Typhoon, has a hundred serpent heads in Greek mythology. This extravagant and monstrous image cited by Montfaucon has a human body with large wings and four arms. With one of his hands he holds an object described by Montfaucon as the tail of some animal.*

A hideous representation of another such monster is to be found in a Turkish manuscript in the Bibl. Nationale, Paris, S.C. 242. This book was obtained by Napoleon I. at Cairo, and presented to the National Library of Paris. On the fly-leaf we read " Livre qui contient la figure d'Aftree," and below the author's name is given, " Saïaidi Mahammed ebn emer Hassan esseoudi," 990^AD. The flesh of this monster is olive, his eyes are green with red pupils, and his tongue is also red. He wears a green

Fig. 173.—PERSIAN DEVIL.

* See Montfaucon, *Antiquité Expliquée*, vol. ii. plate facing p. 197, Fig. 6.

scarf round his loins, pale purple trousers lined with blue, and necklets and armlets of gold. (See Fig. 175.)

The Devil was also endowed with the features of a lion, of a tiger, an eagle, a man, or a bull, to show that evil was angry as one, cruel as another, swift as a third, intelligent as a fourth, strong and indomitable as the last. Out of this combination and multiplicity of bizarre, heterogeneous, and impossible forms, a monstrous being was developed.*

Monstrosity is, in fact, the character of the Genius of Evil in the East. Therefore it is that in the Apocalypse, which is a work altogether Eastern both in conception and in execution, so much stress is laid upon the monstrous forms of its demons. There we find, Rev. xii. 2, the dragon with seven heads and ten horns, and a tail so mighty that with it he can cast the stars of heaven to the earth with one blow. And there is the beast of the sea, Rev. xiii. 1, with a body like a leopard, feet as the feet of a bear, mouth like the mouth of a lion.

Fig. 174.—EGYPTIAN DEVIL.

In Egypt, Typhon, who is the personification of brute matter and of purely animal life, is hideous. His head is enormous, like a flattened ball in front, with gigantic ears; he has a large, fat, squat body, pendant flabby belly, legs swollen and formless as those of an elephant. The Behemoth of Job (Job xl. 15) eats grass like an ox.† He is armed with a tail long and thick as a cedar tree. Now the book of Job, like the vision of St. John, is an eminently Oriental poem. Such infernal genii as are there described may be seen on the beautiful vases of China and Japan. They

* See Fig. 47, vol. i. p. 162.
† Didron adds, "Il est tout couvert d'écailles," but scales are an attri bute of Leviathan in chap. xli. 15, not Behemoth, xl. 15.

are hideous fabulous beasts covered with extravagant excrescences, and formed out of all known proportions.

Such is, then, the physiognomy attributed to the Genius of Evil in the East. A gigantic, monstrous, composite, incoherent animal, covered with excrescences.

This is not so in the West. Here we find less extra-

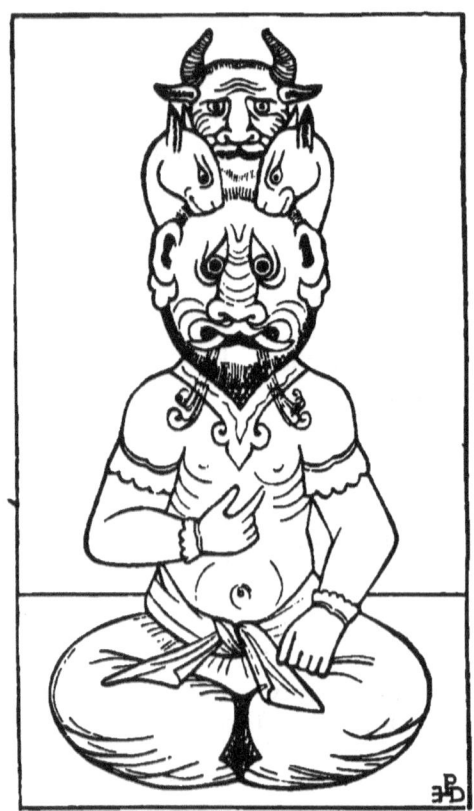

Fig. 175.—TURKISH DEVIL.

vagance. Men are more self-contained, more reasonable. Nature is less powerful for good as for evil; it is unproductive except under the hand of man. The soil must be broken by the plough or by the spade, must be moistened by the sweat of the labourer, be pruned and trimmed every season, that it may bring forth plants flowers, fruits or grain. It is man, on the contrary, who is everything. It is he who does well or ill. Satan is almost completely transformed into man; these monstrous Eastern forms would have rather excited laughter than fear in our cold, rational, and mocking regions. Greece, owing to the proximity of India, still preserved some hideous forms of the Devil, but she embellishes them with her passionate genius for beauty. Cerberus has three heads, but he is in every way a dog. Harpies are unclean birds, fetid, hideous, but not monstrous. Medusa is frightful, and yet hers is a woman's head, round which, instead of hair, serpents grow and hiss. And still this Medusa becomes singularly more human in her passage from Greece to Sicily (see the bas-reliefs in Selinunte), where Pluto, Proserpine, the infernal divinities, and the pagan divinities, clothed in reasonable human form, take the place of the monstrous images of the East.

Fig. 176.—SATAN WITH SERPENT HORNS.*

The West is not so imaginative; its birds are smaller and less coloured, its flowers and trees more pale and feeble, its mammiferæ less developed and formed in better proportions. The elephant and camel thrive badly among us, where the horse and the ox do well. The Devil of the West was also smaller, less exaggerated, less monstrous. The seven-headed devil is out of place in our churches, where the devil with one head swarms, breeds, and thrives wonderfully.

Before any constant communication between the East and West took place, and from primitive times down to the twelfth and thirteenth centuries, the Christian devil constantly assumed the human form. These forms varied, but not in any vital point, and sometimes the devil was only a very ugly man. Indeed, he presents himself on our most ancient monuments with a physiognomy shrunken, lank, degraded both morally and physically. There are no devils properly so called in the catacombs either in frescoes or on

* MS. circ. 13th century. Coll. of Duke of Anjou. Bibl. Nat. Paris.

sarcophagi; there are no devils in the basilicas, or among the mosaics and capitals, but the old manuscripts show them, though rarely.* In the Sacramentaire of Drogon, Bishop of Metz, preserved in the Bibliothèque Nationale, we see a devil in human form entirely clothed. He is a beggar, whose unkempt, long, sparse hairs seem bristling up. Rags and shreds of clothing fall round his body; this is the devil that tempted Jesus Christ in the desert.†

During the Roman period the genius of personification seems to have been more active than in the Gothic, or than that from the close of the twelfth to the end of the fifteenth century. There is a Latin Bible in the Bibliothèque Nationale held to be of the tenth century.‡ Numerous rough miniatures accompany the text. When the abyss is mentioned, a little conical mound is represented divided by spiral zones, like a winding path. The first zone at the base is occupied by birds, the next by fish, the higher by vegetables. Finally, the summit of this cone is hollowed like a crater, and from this species of volcano emerges a great bare, savage, human head. This hideous being, of ferocious aspect, figures the Abyss (see Fig. 177).

Art has translated and, as it were, commented upon the first words of Genesis; thus God, seated upon Chaos, which is in the semblance of clouds rolling beneath His uncovered feet—or like diluent mud, undulating in swelling waves or like heavy clouds. The Almighty crushes this Chaos beneath his feet as the enemy of Creation, just as Michael crushes Satan the enemy of Virtue. God looks forward and somewhat upward, as if seeing in the future the earth and heaven He predestinates.

M. Alfred de Maury (p. 136) observes: "The oldest representation of the Devil in a human form that we know of is found upon an ivory diptych which covers the manuscript entitled the Evangélistaire de Charles-le-Chauve." Here the Spirit of darkness turns his head and

---

* In the mosaics at Torcello, Hell, at the foot of the picture of the Last Judgment, is thronged with devils.
† On the ancient sarcophagi and the old fresco paintings the Genius of Evil is only seen under the form of a serpent: this is the serpent who seduced Eve.
‡ Biblia Sacra, Bibliothèque Nat. Paris, Lat. 6.

howls against the God-man. His brow is armed with horns, a kind of crook may be seen under his arm instead of a sceptre; with one hand he directs a serpent which is coiled round his body; with the other he holds a vase whence issues a poison that blackens the ground.* It was only at the close of the thirteenth century that Satan was endowed with the hideous form which artists have ever since adhered to. In the first representations given of him in a man's figure, they confined themselves to impressing a cruel character on his face, and making his hair to stand on end.†

Lucas van Leyden, in his series of prints from the New Testament, represents Satan in the guise of a monk or learned professor in robe and cowl, as he is indeed often

Fig. 177.—ABYSS.

represented in the art of the sixteenth century, and even early in the fourteenth. In the following illustration taken from the Speculum Humanae Salvationis of the school of Giotto, now preserved in the Bibliothèque de l'Arsenal, Paris (No. 593, fol. 15), and on the curious tapestries of Chaise Dieu, he is also a doctor clad in the ample robes of his profession. In the last instance he shows a countenance wan and wasted by long vigil, study and books; his forehead large and high, his chin sharp and

* As Tennyson describes the shadow of the fallen queen,
  "Broadening from her feet,
  And, blackening, swallow all the land."

† See for such representations, Missal of Worms; MSS. of the tenth century. Bibl. de l'Arsenal, Paris. MSS. in Bibl. Nat. Paris, in 4°, No. 75. Cf. MSS. Bibl. Nat. 6829, in 4°. MSS. Bibl. de l'Arsenal in fo. 34. p. 40.

pointed, his eyes black and piercing. [Thus also has the English poet Giles Fletcher, at the close of the sixteenth century, conceived the tempter in his poem of *Christ's Victorie on Earth*:—

"At length an aged Syre far off he sawe
Come slowely footing; everie step he guest
One of his feete he from the grave did drawe
  *   *   *   *   *

A good old hermit he might seem to be,
That for devotion had the world forsaken,
And now was travailing some Saint to see."]
  *   *   *   *   *

The Behemoth of Job, described in the text as a terrible and monstrous form, is illustrated in Bible Lat. No. 6, in the Bibliothèque Nationale. In this manuscript, which is an example of Western art in the eleventh century, we find this demon curiously modified and embellished. We behold him completely under the form of a man, and, what is more, of an angel. He even wears a nimbus as significant of power, and he has a bird's wings upon his shoulders (see Vol. I. p. 158, Fig. 46).

Fig. 178.—CHRIST TEMPTED.

Here Behemoth is exactly similar to the angel, illustrated in the same Bible, that accompanies Elias when transported to heaven in his chariot of fire; indeed, they might be taken for two brothers, and in a scriptural sense they are two brothers of whom one has fallen, the other risen; however, the fallen angel is distinguished from the other by his claws, which project from the fingers and toes of his hands and feet, but there the difference ends, and the good angel, who is the living symbol of light, and the evil angel, who is the symbol of darkness, are painted in the same colours. The evil angel ought to be black as soot, and to fly with a bat's wings like a bird of darkness as it is, and yet it has a bright aspect and eagle's wings, as of one that loved the sun and the noonday.

[But more striking still is 'Le Diable en femme,' where the tempter is disguised as a splendidly dressed, grandly developed woman, from whose seductions the Anchorite of the Thebaid is turning away. He kneels before a furnace,

Fig. 179.—TEMPTATION OF ST. PAPHNUTIUS, CAMPO SANTO, PISA.

holding his hands in the flame, while his face is upturned in prayer.

The Devil may also assume the disguise of a holy angel, as we see in the following illustration from the life of St. Juliana.*

* Julienne (S**te**), vierge et martyr à Nicomédée au V* siècle. Honorée l**e** 16 février à Cume en Campanie. AA. SS. Boll. Feb. ii. p. 875. Représentée

The Devil, willing to tempt St. Juliana, a young Roman virgin imprisoned by the Prefect because she would not deny Jesus Christ, transformed himself into an angel with white clothing and fair young face. Still

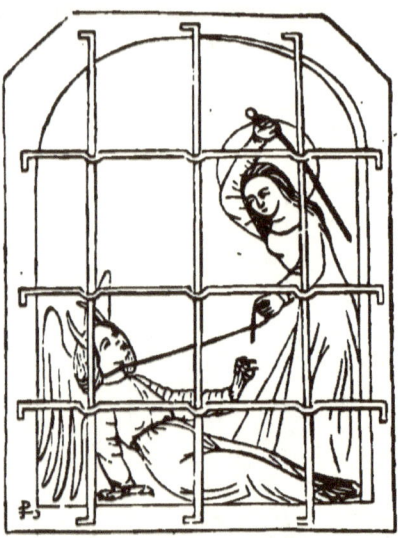

Fig. 180.—ST. JULIANA AND THE DEVIL.

horns projected from his forehead, and the nails on his feet and hands were prolonged into claws. Entering her prison he said, "Juliana, frightful torments are prepared for thee: sacrifice to idols and thou shalt be saved." " Oh, God of heaven and earth!" cried she, "who art thou that speaketh thus to me?" She then seized Belial by the throat and fastened a rope round his neck. "Declare to me," she said in anger, "who thou art, whence comest thou, and who hath sent thee." Satan, captured, answered her: " I am the devil! I have done wickedly in desiring to tempt you: but free me, I pray you, I will do so no

---

en prison, visitée par Satan sous la forme d'un ange, qui vient pour ébranler sa foi et l'engager à apostasier. Quatre pièces signées de Th. de Leu, Sadeler, Adrien Collaert, et une copie. Folio 89 du IVe volume de la Collection des Saintes, Cabinet des Estampes de Paris. W. No. 236 et 1024 en rouge, Bibl. Ste Geneviève, Paris, Cabinet des MSS. et des livres à figures.

more." Then Juliana, strong in the Spirit of God, whipped the demon with a rod till he was heard to cry,

Fig. 181.—DEMONS ON THE TOMB OF DAGOBERT.

"Lady Juliana! friend of angels, I entreat thee by the passion of Jesus Christ the Lord, pity my misfortune, have pity upon me!" But Juliana only struck him the more. On this, the prefect sent for the saint, and she approached, dragging Satan after her; thus she passed into the public court, displaying the humbled demon to the people; till, having reached the mouth of a pit, she threw him in.*

The demons on the tomb of Dagobert have the human form, but with animals' heads. This monument stands to the right of the high altar in the Church of St. Denys near Paris. The subject of the bas-relief illustrates a legend connected with the death of Dagobert (A.D. 628–638). "A hermit on an island in the Mediterranean was warned in a vision to pray for the Frankish King's soul. He then saw Dagobert in chains, hurried along by a troop of fiends, who were about to cast him into a volcano. At last his cries to St. Denys, St. Michael, and St. Martin, brought to his assistance those three venerable and glorious persons, who drove off the devils, and with songs of triumph conveyed the rescued soul to Abraham's bosom."†

The legend says nothing of the boat, like Charon's, crossing the river. The beautiful monument on which this bas-relief appears was erected by St. Louis at St. Denys.

In the Cathedral of Chartres we have the following group of devils in human form, only distinguishable from the men they drag down by their horns, and winged, cloven feet. (Fig. 182.)

This group is found on the rose window, west transept, Chartres Cathedral, towards the bottom on the left.]

In general, the Oriental devil is a monstrous and gigantic animal; the Western devil is human and of ordinary size; but it is necessary to fix the date of these two so different types, that we may say how and at what time they remained intact, independent one of another, and when and how they were commingled and modified, the one by the other. Christian architecture throughout every country and period, may be divided into five

---

* Life of St. Juliana. *Acta* SS. of the Bollandists, vol. ii. February.
† Gesta Dagob. (cc. 23, 44). Baronius (647. 5). D. Bouquet. Rec. des histoires de France, t. ii. p. 593.

branches, which, while issuing from one common trunk, present themselves under different aspects. In some places Byzantine or Oriental styles will be found modified in Latin or Western architecture. While, in Roman architecture, which is a combination of both styles, the Western element predominates, Gothic architecture was a new

Fig. 162.—CHARTRES. THE DEMON IN MAN.

type developed in their midst, wherein some forms may be distinguished which, though not distinctly Oriental in origin, yet betray an Eastern influence. Finally, we have the architecture of the Renaissance, which honours first principles, and the forms of paganism as well as of Roman Christianity. The devil has his phases according to the style of the architecture to which he belongs: he is Byzantine or monstrous at Constantinople and Jerusalem; ugly but human in Rome, among the Latins; animal, yet his brute form modified by his human form among the Romans; human, but taking the forms of the beast among the Goths; and finally, with

Fig. 183.—THE DEMON AS SATYR.

the Renaissance, returning to an ancient Satyr, which has the feet and horns of a goat, but the body and head of a man. [" A time came," says M. Réville,* "when the idea that the devil had a distinct bodily shape became settled; and this form was that of the ancient fauns and satyrs, with hoofs, protruding legs, hairy skin, tail, cloven

* *History of the Devil:* M. Réville.

foot or horse's hoof." The foregoing illustration is drawn from a panel of the ivory case of the flabellum or fan of Tournus, described in the Benedictine Annals (No. LXIII.).

This case is believed by some antiquaries to have been originally intended to contain a copy of the works of Virgil, and to date from the fifth century. It is the opinion of M. Charles le Normand that in the twelfth century the monks of Tournus used it as a box for the flabellum.* The designs carved in the compartments are apparently illustrations of the Eclogues of Virgil.]

Excepting the miniatures of Byzantine and Latin manuscripts, we have very few monuments from which to derive our types. On one side we have the Apocalypse and Apocryphal gospels, on the other the writings of the fathers of the Latin Church. The latter, St. Martin especially, scarcely saw the Devil in any form but that of pagan gods, of Jupiter, Mercury and Venus. The manuscripts supply us with very curious Roman devils. The Gothic devils merit a long examination, and we find the devils of the Renaissance principally in the works of Michael Angelo and Raphael; thus one may divine the country and epoch of a monument from the type of demon without much difficulty, as we tell the age and country of a building by its architectural forms.

We now pass on to the nomenclature of the Devil. The genius of evil has a multitude of names. Satan simply means Adversary. Among the Persians he is called Ahriman; Typhon among the Egyptians; Leviathan and Behemoth in the Bible; Beelzebub, Béhérit, Baal, Bel, Bélus, Dagon, Dragon, Astaroth, Astarté. Moloch, Militta, Asmodeus, Salmanasar, Semiramis, in Palestine and Babylonia—the angel or king of the bottomless pit whose name in the Hebrew tongue is Abaddon, but in the Greek tongue his name is Apollyon.

---

* *Flabellum*, or fan, is a kind of fly-brush used in the celebration of the Lord's Supper. The use of this implement is one of the oldest and least known of ecclesiastical rites. In the East, where food may be covered with swarms of flies in a moment, it was natural that the bread and wine should be guarded from them. It continued in use from the first to the thirteenth century. See Du Sommerard, *Les Arts du Moyen Age*, text, vol. ii. p. 195; iii. p. 251; v. p. 231, note.

In the West, the names given to the Devil are less monstrous, just as the forms under which he is shown are less repulsive. The name Dragon is preserved, and to it have been added those of Satan, Demon, Devil, Serpent, Asmodeus, Prince of the World, Zabulus or Zabolus; he has even been endowed with the glorious title Lucifer, or Lightbearer, just as the Greeks called their furies Eumenides, or well-doers. The opposite phrase also applies to Satan, for he is Ahriman, or the god of night. The name that seems to have prevailed everywhere is that of Demon, though, like that of tyrant, which at first simply signified king, it was not meant to express either good or evil. The evil has triumphed, and demon, which only means genius, has been used to signify, and still signifies, a wicked spirit; tyrant also now means nothing more than a wicked king.*

We must make a selection among all these names in order to avoid confusion. However, as among Christians the Devil is not a single being, but extraordinarily multiform—as multitudinous as the angel—we must try to distinguish him in the midst of this crowd. In the Gospel describing the man possessed, Jesus Christ asks his name while exorcising him. "My name is Legion," he answered. This response signifies the number to which demons may attain; for here is one who in himself alone is the personification and aggregate of a multitude of others. Mary Magdalene, whom Jesus Christ also exorcised, possessed seven demons who were driven in succession from her body.

We have been enabled by the help of St. Denis the Areopagite to indicate the ranks in the hierarchy of angels; but such a hierarchy could not exist among demons, because of the discord and confusion in which they live, disorder being their sovereign order. Milton gives us a picture of a revolt of demons, but if the attempt were now made to introduce order among the diabolic crowd it would prove labour in vain. As the Apocalypse bears the same relation to devils that the Divine hierarchy of the Areopagite holds to angels, it is through its pages

---

* In Friar Bacon, ix. 144, and xi. 109, the titles of "guider" and "ruler of the north" are given to Asmenoth.

we must seek for any light upon the present question. When we carefully reperuse the Apostolic vision, this is the order which we believe may be traced throughout.

First there is a devil called the Old Serpent [Rev. xii. 9], the great Dragon Satan, the Devil properly so-called, the king of the bottomless pit, the Exterminator. This, in the Apocalypse, is the great red dragon, having seven

Fig. 184.—BEAST WITH SEVEN HEADS.
Painting on glass, St. Nisier, Troyes.*

heads and ten horns, and seven crowns upon his heads, and a tail which drew the third part of the stars of heaven. This is the chief devil, the master of all those we shall see afterwards pass before us in succession.

Satan has two lieutenants, if we may so say: one on the earth and one on the sea; for, master of the whole world, his power extends over seas and continents. His repre-

See Ann. Arch. vol. i. p. 77.

sentative on the sea has, like himself, seven heads and ten horns,* but he carries ten crowns, three more than his master, and upon his heads the name of Blasphemy; and the beast is like unto a leopard, and his feet were as the feet of a bear, and his mouth as the mouth of a lion which vomits blasphemy.

Then coming out of the earth [Rev. xiii. 11], the agent of Satan is a beast with two horns, which speaks the language of the dragon. This is the third great symbol of the Genius of Evil. This dragon holds the whole world, the sea and the earth in his hands; he gives the leopard the empire over the floods, and the beast over the earth. Here we have the Satanic Trinity. It shares the sovereignty of evil just as the Divine Trinity shares that of good.

But the diabolical trinity, as the Divine Trinity, has its ministers, its inferior agents who execute his orders. From the mouth of these monsters three impure spirits not named in the Apocalypse come forth; they have the form of frogs. They are the ministers of these three great demons. They are the agents who summon the kings of the earth to fight against God.

The army that these chiefs command is composed of grasshoppers who come forth from wells in the bottomless pit like the smoke which exhales from a great furnace. The beasts that follow in the Apocalypse resemble horses ready for the battle. Their face is as the face of a man, on their heads are crowns as of gold, they have hair as women, lions' teeth, iron cuirasses, scorpions' tails pointed like barbed darts, wings that resound like horses and chariots rushing to the combat. Such is the infantry of the Devil. As to the riders, they have breastplates of fire, of jacinth, and of brimstone. Their horses, which vomit brimstone, fire and smoke, have heads like lions, tails like serpents, armed at the end by heads which poison and slay.

This diabolical company is very monstrous. It is conceived in such proportions as to furnish forms of horror for all demons engendered from it and represented in images of plastic art.

On the ancient sarcophagi and in the old frescoes the

* Rev. ii. 3, 4, 9.

Genius of Evil is seen under the form of a serpent; this is the serpent who seduced Eve, and the being in the Apoca-

Fig. 185.*

lypse called the Old Serpent, the Great Dragon Satan, the Devil properly so called, the king of the bottomless pit, the Exterminator.

Fig. 186.—ON SARCOPHAGUS, VATICAN MUSEUM.

In Christian iconography the serpent appears, as might be expected, most frequently in the temptation of Adam

* This illustration is taken from the Biblia cum Figuris, MS., Bibl. Nat. Paris, No. 9561, fol. 8a.

and Eve. We see it represented simply with its mere zoological character on a sarcophagus of the first Christian period in the Vatican; and again it is represented as borrowing the head and arms of a human being, a treatment which Raphael has not feared to adopt in his turn from the thirteenth century. The serpent has occasionally two heads, one female with which to address the man, the other male with which to address the woman.

He also assumes the form of the ancient hydra, which

Fig. 187.
French MS., XIII. cent., Bibl. Nat., Paris.

is only a multiform serpent, and it is converted into the seven-headed beast of the Apocalypse, transforming the hydra into the dragon.

Each of the horned heads in this seven-headed beast which is represented in the stained-glass window of the sixteenth century at St. Nizier at Troyes, is surrounded by an aureole.* In the East, the nimbus is given as a symbol of power; therefore at Troyes, where certain

* See Vol. I. *supra*, p. 163.

riental influences are traceable, the formidable beast of he Apocalypse is found with this attribute.

Art falls into the grotesque when, endeavouring to igure the demon, it endows him with a serpent's tail (see Fig. 70, Vol. I. p. 277), or when it paints serpents proceeding from the head of the Devil, like horns, as is shown n a MS. of the Duke of Anjou, Bibl. Nat., thirteenth century.*

In the frescoes of the Campo Santo, the serpent becomes igain the emblem of life, but only of material life. He becomes the medium through which the demon drinks the blood, or rather absorbs the soul, of his victim. That is to say, Life in the demon's hands is the siphon with which he sucks out the soul and substance of those who fall beneath his sway.

We have dwelt at some length on all these details; for it is important, when we study a cathedral door, a sculptured voussoir, a Last Judgment, or a Hell, painted on glass, that we should be able to distinguish Satan the chief from his two principal agents, and these again from the crowd of lesser demons. The detailed description in the Apocalypse furnishes all the data for this distinction. We have there a complete, complex, monstrous, multitude of these demons. A chief named Satan or Dragon; a demon of the sea named Leopard, a demon of the land called the Beast: the three composing a trinity. Three principal ministers of this trinity are frogs and locusts, an army of foot soldiers composed of monstrous frogs, and a cavalry more monstrous still.

Fig. 188.—VAMPIRE, CAMPO SANTO, PISA.

Such are all the horrible forms which characterise the devils of the thirteenth and fourteenth centuries, as they appear sculptured and painted in our churches. In the following pages the term demon or devil will be used in-

* See Ann. Arch. I. 75.

differently to designate all evil spirits; it is a generic term, that of Satan being reserved for the prince of the infernal regions.

[In Byzantine art, the demons of the New Testament who tempt Jesus, who are cast into hell, who are driven into the herd of swine, and whom we meet with again in the Last Judgment, are of all varieties of form and colour However, as is the case with our Latin demons also their usual colour is black and blue, the form mon-

Fig. 180.—DEMON ON THE CASQUE OF GOLIATH.

strous and composite, made up from parts of different animals; bats' wings attached to the shoulders; a tail sticking out below the spine; limbs and arms hideously thin; the trunk fat and flaccid, or dried up like that of a skeleton; eyes flaming (see Fig. 173); vomiting flames at every issue; wrinkles and boils on the skin; the face twisted into grimaces and the limbs contorted. We would refer back to Fig. 135, ii. p. 23, the Trinity of absolute Evil, as an instance of one of the most curious demons we have seen. He here presides over an assembly of demons who deliberate on the birth of Merlin, who is to assist them to repair the injury sustained by the Devil in the death of Christ and his descent into Hell.*

Satan is represented as wearing a cap of flame on the casque of Goliath in Fig. 189, which would appear to be an initial P taken from some mediæval MS. David with his sling and bag of pebbles confronts the giant, and the

Fig. 190.—AMIENS CATHEDRAL, WEST FRONT.

hand of the Father appears from Heaven to protect the young warrior.

We have seen that the Gospel, while on the one hand it seemed to banish the Devil to regions of symbolism, on the other, by identifying him with the natural man, showing the heart of man as his seat, brought him into closer and more intimate relationship with man than

* French MS. in Bibl. Nat. Histoire du *Saint-Graal*, No. 6770.

before. Only in this way can we explain the fact that in the earliest ages of Christianity his domination was extended, his interventions in human affairs were multiplied. Heathen gods, institutions, empires, all belonged to his kingdom. The Græco-Roman gods became demons who had usurped Divine rank. From the close of the second century, the antagonism of these forces of Satan and the kingdom of the Messiah was summed up in a grand drama, whose climax was the Descent into Hell, the victory of that Power that had been obedient unto death.

The absorbing nature of the belief in the Devil during the Middle Ages must be clearly recognised if we would understand Mediæval art. It was the one fixed idea with every one, particularly from the thirteenth to the fifteenth century. The sense of humour which is always allied to powerful character becomes manifest.* Diabolism had its humorous side, especially when a prominent part came to be assigned to Satan in the Mediæval religious plays; scenes in which the Devil is cheated, outdone, and castigated, formed the comic element of the Sacred Drama, and the miniature painters of sacred books are not wanting here either, as we may see by looking at Figs. 180, 190, 191, and 192.

Fig. 191.

In the fifteenth century, Innocent VIII. issued his famous bull *Summis desiderantes*, by which he not only confirmed and enlarged the powers of the Inquisition

---

* As instances of such humorous subjects, I now recall a picture of a devil blowing a bellows in the face of a terrified angel in the Book of Hours belonging to Anne of France, daughter of Louis XI., No. 920, fol. 316a, Bibl. Nat. Paris. In a MS. in the Bibl. de l'Arsenal, the reference to which I have lost, I saw a miniature illustration of the good Shepherd, who, having rescued the Lamb, is bearing him on his shoulder into the fold, here symbolised by a church. A well-shaven and rather repulsive-looking priest stands at the door with open arms ready to receive the Lamb, who peers round from the back of Christ's head with a comically doleful expression, as much as to say he would far rather stay where he was

against diabolism and witchcraft, but prescribed all manner of recipes by which the devil might be exorcised, such as the sign of the cross, holy water, the judicious use of salt, the name of the Holy Trinity. In Fig. 192 we have an example of exorcism by sprinkling with holy water, the priest who drives the offending demon being armed with an aspergillum, the brush or twig used for sprinkling holy water. This implement was occasionally

Fig. 192.—EXORCISM.

a fox's brush, as is indicated by the modern French name *goupillon*, but was anciently made of hyssop, a plant supposed to possess cleansing virtues (see Psalm li. 7.) This illustration is taken from a manuscript in the Bibliothèque de Chartres, No. 1380.]

In the thirteenth century it was even thought possible that men might be begotten of the Devil in a literal sense. Mussato, a Paduan historian and poet, A.D. 1261–1330, attributes an infernal origin to Ezzelino, adopting a tradition of the house of Este, that a devil clothed with a human body supplied his father's place when he was begotten.*

The demon is thus described by the unhappy woman in the play :—

> "Haud tauro minor
> Hirsuta aduncis cornibus cervix riget,
> Setis coronant hispidis illum jubæ,
> Sanguinea binis orbibus manat lues,
> Ignemque nares flatibus crebris vomunt.
> Favilla patulis auribus surgens salit
> Ab ore spirans. Os quoque eructat levem
> Flammam, perennis lambit et barbam focus."

Lucifer's address to the infernal host in the mystery play of the Passion of St. Quentin, performed about the year 1350 in the body of the collegiate church of that town, is a curious example of diabolic poetry.

> "*Lucifer.* Diables courants, diables cornus,
> Diables fallans, diables formis,
> Diables tondus, diables tondis,
> Diables touffus, diables maudis,
> Diables farcis, diables senglos,
> Diables, diablesses et diablos,
> Diaboliques poulleries,
> Sallés hors de vos diableries,
> Diables, plus tost que vint soulcil.
> *Sathan.* Quels tous diables vous faut-il
> Que vous diabliés en ce point ?
> Dictes quel grant diable vous point
> Et quel grant diable vous avés."†

The Devil is represented in the following figure upon a seal which we suppose to have been attached to one of those curious documents used, it may be, in the mystery plays of the fifteenth and following centuries, such as the Lawsuits of Paradise; episodes in the history of the rebel angels, which were given under many various forms either in recitation or upon the stage. The allegory c

---

* Hist. of the House of Este, Lond. 1681, p. 138. This Ezzelino was the most cruel tyrant in the Marca Trivigiana, Lord of Padua, Vicenza Verona, and Brescia, who died in 1260. Note on translation of Ariosto Orl. Fur., by Sir John Harington, 1634, cant. 3, st. 33. Dante translated by Cary, Inf., cant. xii. l. 109, note 3.

† Ann. Archéol. tom. xv. p. 29.

the Lawsuit of Paradise is found among the writings of Hugo de St. Victor, who died in 1140, and was first suggested by the 10th verse of the 85th Psalm. "Mercy and Truth are met together—Justice and Peace have kissed each other." The subject is entitled, 'The Lawsuit that Mercy opened against Justice for the Redemption of Man.' In like manner we have lawsuits of Christ and Lucifer, and this seal would be affixed to some such document as the brief of the master of hell in defence of his claim on the human soul.*

In Fig. 193 we have Lucifer throned as king, and

Fig. 193.—SEAL OF LUCIFER.

wielding a prong with which he catches sinners, instead of a crosier, whilst his hands are clawed like those of a beast of prey. The inscription running round the figure may be deciphered as follows:—

"Seel Lucifer Mâtre de l'abisme d'Enfer."

---

* See *Les Mystères*, Petit de Julleville, tom. ii. p. 359; *Histoire du Théâtre François*, Parfait, tom. ii. p 301. Among the different early translations of the *Procès de Miséricorde et Justice*, that contained in the MS. at the Bibl. Nat. Paris (12th cent., 2560) is, at least, mainly attributed Guillaume Herman. Finally, another translation, which is in the Bibl. Nat. (13th cent. in 4° vellum, 172 ff.), is attributed by M. P. Paris b Robert of Lincoln. M. F. Michel has published the *Procès de Miséricorde* at the close of the *Libri Psalmorum versio antiqua Gallica*, Oxford, 1860, pp. 364, 368.

The artist who made this drawing has perhaps mistaken the fifth letter U for D, and omitted to notice the mark of contraction over the a of Matre—which stands for Maistre—thus the whole may be translated

"Seal of Lucifer, Master of the abyss of Hell."

Fig. 194 shows the signature of the demon Asmodeus

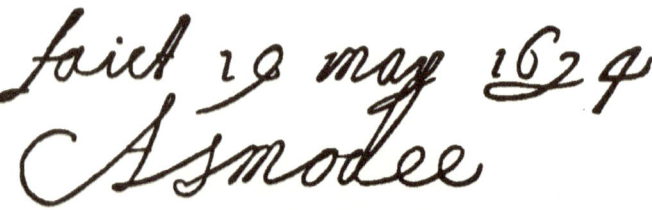

Fig. 194.—WRITING OF ASMODEUS.

probably appended to a document of a similar nature, Asmodeus being a name for the Devil.

This chapter on the iconography of the Devil may fitly close with two allegorical female figures, one symbolising Impiety, and the other Covetousness. In Fig. 195 we see Impiety as spoken of by the prophet Zechariah, ch. v. 7 seated in an ephah and borne to Shinar by two women with stork's wings. This image is carved upon a sculptured medallion in the great porch of Amiens Cathedral. It forms the last of a series of subjects illustrating the prophetical writings and opposed to another series of Gospel subjects so arranged that this image of Impiety contrasts with that of Holiness as embodied in the Virgin's form.*

Our second allegorical figure is an image of Covetousness taken from a MS. copy of *Le Romant des trois*

---

* The Virgin with the Holy Child on her lap seated in a font is of mediæval type of the source of living waters, the Fountain of Life. S. *Caractéristiques des Saints*, Ch. Cahier, tom. ii. p. 544. Marie.

Zechariah v. 7 :

"And behold there was lifted up a talent [or weighty piece] of lead—and this is a woman that sitteth in the midst of the ephah. And he said, This is wickedness. And he cast it into the midst of the ephah; and he cast the weight of the lead upon the mouth thereof. Then lifted I mine eyes, and looked, and, behold, there came out two women, and the wind was in their wings; for they had wings like the wings of a stork: and they lifted up the ephah between the earth and the heaven. Then said I to the angel that

ALLEGORICAL FIGURES. 149

Pèlerinages, which dates circ. 1330.* (See Fig. 196.) One of these pilgrimages is the allegory of the *Life of Manhood*, an old English translation of which may be seen in

Fig. 195.

manuscript in the University Library, Cambridge.† The original text was composed by Guillaume de Guillauille (fols. 5, 30), prior of the Cistercian Abbey of Chaulis, in the diocese of Senlis, founded by St. Louis in the twelfth

---

talked with me, Whither do these bear the ephah? And he said unto me, To build it an house in the land of Shinar: and it shall be established and set there upon her own base."

Explanation of figs. in great door of Amiens Cathedral. See *Bulletin Monum.* xi. and xii., by MM. Jourdain and Duval, the medallions explained by M. de Caumont, ibid. vol. xx.

* This manuscript is preserved in the library of St. Geneviève in Paris, and the figure of Covetousness occurs on fol. 61, verso.

† See Roxburgh ed. of *The Pilgrimage of the Lyf of the Manhode*, ed. Aldis Wright, pt. iii. cap. i. p. 137.

century. The pilgrim is met by Covetousness as he descends a deep valley, and we learn from the description,

Fig. 196.—COVETOUSNESS.

which is too long to be given here in full, the meaning of this image.

The idol worn upon her head is "the peny of gold or

of silver whereon is emprinted the figure of the hye Lord of the cuntree." The false God that blindeth him that turneth his eyes towards him and maketh fools to bend their eyes downwards. This God by whom she hath been disfigured and defamed is Avarice. The hands behind like griffin's claws are to symbolise "Rapine, Coutteburse, and Latrosynie."

In the next pair of hands she holds a bowl for alms, or for the money she extorts through beggary, and a hook, with which she enters the house of Christ and seizes his servants. Taking their croziers and shepherds' crooks, she furnishes them with this devil's prong instead, fished up by her out of the darkness of Hell, and this hand is named Simony. In the next hands she holds a yard-measure, purse, and scales. With the measure she deals out false lengths, with the balances she weighs false measure, and into the purse she puts the ill-won gains of her treachery, gambling, and dishonesty. Round her neck hangs a bag, and nothing that is put therein can ever come out again; all things remain there to rot.

We may here insert the following extract from the old English translation of the passage in which this apparition is described:

"... Disgised shrewedliche* she was ... Boystows she was and wrong shapen and enbosed and clothed with an old gret bultel † clouted with cloutes of old cloth and of lether. A sak she hadde honged at hire nekke. Wel it seemed that make flight wold she nouht for she putte ther inere bras and yren and sakked it. Hire tonge whiche she hadde‡ ... out halp hire ther to faste. Hire tunge was mesel and foule defaced. Sixe hondes she hadde and tweyne stumpes the tweyne hondes hadden nailes of griffouns, of whiche that oon was bihynde in strangie manere.

"In oon of that oother handes she heeld a fyle as thouh she shulde fyle brideles. And a balaunce wherinne she peisede the zodiac and the sunne in gret entente to putte hem to sale. A disch in that oother hande she heeld and a poket with bred. In the fifte she hadde a crochet and

* Rough, churlish.
† A bolting cloth.
‡ Gap in MSS. suppie drawen sa langue qoe hors traicte auoit.

upon hire hed a mawmett* shee bar which made hire eyen biholde downward. The sixte hand she hadde lenynge upon hire brokene haunche and sum time she haf it hye to hire tunge and touchede it.

"The hondes of my yivinge ben kilte and doon from here stumpes† ... Sixe hondes i haue for to gripe with in sixe maneres ... for to sakke in my sak to peise me and charge me with to that ende that if i falle adoun i mowe no more ryse aygen."

* Mawmet, *i.e.* idol.
† *i.e.* for giving with were out.

ICONOGRAPHY OF DEATH.

RELIGIONS do not develop suddenly and fitfully any more than physical nature in its creations. They are connected by links and chains so gradually modified that no one faith can refuse to acknowledge that which it has inherited from its predecessor. Such links are often most distinctly perceptible in the iconography of different religious systems. Thus, when Christianity had recourse to images to propagate its lessons and to awaken the popular mind to a faith in its dogmas, it endued Death with an individual existence, a language, action, form, special physiognomy. Such a form was not borrowed from the Jews, but from Græco-Latin polytheism, whose figures and plastic images it adapted to newly formed ideas. Neophytes borrowed their images of Death from Greek and Latin Art, not the grand ideal art inspired by Poetry and Philosophy, but only the crude and popular art which was confined to the reproduction of the coarse ideas of the populace, in whose imaginations all evil things were identified with spectres, larvæ, lemures, whose figures they transferred to Death.

Such images form a strong contrast to the winged Thanatos on the column of the temple of the Ephesian Artemis, now in the British Museum, which, of all the figures we have met with, best embodies the classic Greek conception of Death, and which has been thus described by Sir Frederic Burton.* "A youth faces us with long drooping wings; his head, with heavy parted hair, inclines to his left with a pathetic expression, and his left hand is raised, as if beckoning. A weighty sheathed sword hangs

* See *Saturday Review*, No. 897, vol. xxxv. p. 50.

by his left haunch. . . . The pathetic character [of this nude winged youthful figure] points to the new Attic school, no less than the almost feminine softness of the forms. . . . The workmanship of this figure is not careful. It is a mag-

Fig. 197.

nificent sketch by a practised and fearless hand; the object being the expression of the whole rather than any careful individualizing of parts. . . . This mysterious figure, from wings and bodily type, has been thought to represent Erōs; we should venture to call it Thanatos. The attribute held in the now destroyed right hand was probably the inverted torch.

"But it is the head which most strongly answers to the character of the genius of Death, as conceived by the Greek imagination. A dreamy *sehnsucht* pervades the almost sexless face; a sadness as if Death himself felt that he too was but the victim of an inexorable fate, whose behests he must execute; and the lax, unwavy hair is drawn back behind the ears as if carelessly confined there. The ambrosial locks of Erōs* are, on the contrary, curly and rippled, and hang in tresses on the shoulders, or are knotted in clusters behind the head. We think, however, that the presence of the sword decides the question, and we recall the passage in the *Alkestis* of Euripides, where Thanatos appears, armed with a sword, ready, as 'Priest of the Dying,' to sever the lock from the victim sacred to Persephone":—

Death.—" This woman will descend to the mansions of Hades; and I am advancing against her that I may perform the initiatory rites with my sword; for that man is sacred to the gods beneath the earth, the hair of whose head this sword may have hallowed."

The Etruscans have their exterminating angel, who has been designated as the Etruscan Charon. His figure is constantly shown upon funereal monuments armed with a hammer. His face is repulsive, his hair and beard jagged, serpents crown his brow, his ears are pointed like those of a satyr. He watches at the entrance to Hell, and with another genius he accompanies Death. On one sarcophagus, two genii of the spirit-world assist at the deathbed of a wife. On one side a winged genius in female form seeks to draw the dying woman towards her gently while she addresses her last words to her husband; on the other side Charon, or rather the evil angel, holding a pincers in one hand and a torch in the other, prepares to accompany the dying woman into the dominions of the Shades.†

Christians had to seek in the ancient iconology for a more fitting representative of the offspring and avenger of

---

* Two images of Death hardly to be distinguished from Erōs are mentioned by Mr. King, one on a Roman gem, the other on a fresco in the catacomb of Prætextatus. See King's *Gnostics and their Remains*, p. 155. n. 2.

† See Micali, *Storia degli antichi popoli Italiani* Atlas, pl. text, vol. iii. p. 10, lx.

transgression, something that should be ghastly and awe-inspiring—and such a representative they found ready to hand in the old way of picturing the Larva, or bad man's ghost. This had always been depicted as a skeleton.* To the Christian, Life, here and hereafter, is the fulfilment of divine law. Death, here and hereafter, was the consequence of original sin and the infraction, not fulfilment, of law. Thus such images of horror as they found in these countries, where Helleno-Latin polytheism flourished, were adopted by them in place of the gentle and peaceful Thanatos of Greek allegory, coming like evening of a

Fig. 199.†

beautiful day; and, through a series of links in the development of religion, and of impressions of one religion upon another, Death has become a living skeleton among Christians. The portraits of Satan in early Christian legend represent him as a hideous, fleshless being, a soot-black skeleton; thus in the apocryphal book of the martyrdom of the Apostle Bartholomew, the Death demon whom he overcame is described as "like an Ethiopian, black as soot; his face sharp like a dog's, thin-cheeked, with hair down to his feet, eyes like fire, sparks

* The Etruscan image passed down into the belief of the mediæval Florentines, for Dante, Inferno c. iii. l. 110, introduces—
 "Charon dimonio con occhi di bragia."

† See *Symbols and Emblems of Early Christian Art.* By Louise Twining. Pl. LXIX.

coming out of his mouth; and out of his nostrils came forth smoke like sulphur, with wings spined like a porcupine."

Thus we believe we may trace the causes of the transposition of the features of the corpse to the genius of evil, the association of Death, and the skeleton, and the Devil, in mediæval art,*—Death which had been painted by the artists of antiquity under forms so different. This iconological revolution was brought about by the effect of the association of pagan and oriental ideas. But this metamorphosis, once accomplished, did not end here; the person of the demon having drawn to himself the figure of a skeleton, soon effaced this to make room for a pure abstract personification from which all thought of Satan had disappeared, and round which a crowd of ancient traditions soon gathered."†

Soon Andrea Orcagna had, according to some writers, completed the great paintings of Paradise and Hell, in the church of Sta. Maria Novella at Florence; the Pisans commenced the decoration of the Campo Santo, the cemetery of Pisa, the Triumph of Death being included in the series. As Vasari says, "Andrea left a universal judgment there." It has been said that he followed his contemporary Petrarch in his conception of Death; that he was inspired by the poet's grand and solemn song, 'Il Trionfo della Morte,' where Death appears in female form:

"Ed una donna involta in vesta negra,
Con un furor qual io non so se mai
Al tempo de' Giganti fosse a Fegra."

Fierce, inveterate, deaf and blind, with sword in hand she slays and stabs and cuts. Greece, Troy, the Roman empire, barbarian and foreigner, all fall before her. The plain beneath her is heaped with dead, from India, from Cathay, Morocco, Spain, lying in numbers inconceivable. Sovereigns, Pontiffs, Emperors reduced to naked, poor and miserable corpses. A noble company of prayerful women next appear who strive by their petitions to stay the hand

---

* See *Mémoire sur l'évangile de Nicodème* in the *Revue de Philologie*, tom. ii. p. 443. A. de Maury.

† See *Personnage de la Mort* (A. de Maury): *Revue Archéol.* iv. pt. i. pp. 306, 6E6, 737, 784; v. p. 286.

of Death, but she shears one golden head of the fairest in their band as she sweeps along.

> "Allor di quella bionda testa svelse
> Morte con la sua mano un aureo crine.
> Così del mondo il più bel fiore scelse;"

Although Orcagna's treatment of this scene in many points bears a strong resemblance to the poem of Petrarch, yet in the form of Death herself he seems to have followed quite another tradition. His Genius of Death resembles the Parcæ,* the Keres,† black-winged beings with cloven feet corresponding to the Norns, Valkyrie of the

Fig. 199.

Scandinavians. Fury-like she advances with rapid flight,

* Quoique les Parques commissent les Kères au soin de frapper les hommes du coup mortel, elles s'acquittaient parfois elles-mêmes de ce ministère.... C'est encore par ce motif qu'elles sont les assistantes de Proserpine, qu'elles conduisent des enfers au ciel, et qu'elles apparaissent dans le sombre séjour près de Pluton et de Charon. Les héritiers des anciens Grecs continuent à attribuer aux Moîrai ou Mîres ce rôle léthifère : 'Ce sont ces trois femmes, disent les modernes Hellènes, qui produisent la peste.'" Ib. p. 700.

† The *Ker*—black-robed—of Homer. The Furies that pursue Orestes on the painted vases described by Pausanias as well as Aeschylus were old women brandishing serpents or scythes.—King, *Gnostics and their Remains*, p. 162.

a fearful-looking woman, with wild streaming hair, claws instead of nails swooping from the sky on large bat's wings, and swinging a scythe in her hand, prepares to mow down the happy forms of those who are seen seated under trees listening to music.* Petrarch's Death is indeed

Fig. 200.—DEATH AS A WOMAN.

also a woman, but a woman who may occasionally soften and lead the dying, without fear or sorrow, to the grave, while in the Pisan fresco she flits in the sky above her doomed victim like some fearful bat that will drop and fix itself in

* In the allegories of the life of the true monk, given in the *Manual of Panselinos*, p. 404, Death appears in like manner armed with a *scythe* and a *dial plate* worn on the head, as if Time, her work accomplished, had yielded up her attribute to form a crown for her Destroyer. The *trident* is another attribute of Death in the Greek Manual, reminding us that we are in the country of Neptune. Death pierces the hypocrite's heart with a trident, or drives a flaming trident into the body of a sinner.

hate upon his brow. Petrarch's Death carries a sword, the painter's wields a scythe. Fig. 200 is one of the Didron collection of illustrations, the provenance of which we have not yet ascertained, which gives another female bat-winged Death, probably taken from a quattrocento manuscript. Her clawed fingers and pendant breasts add to

Fig. 201.—TRIUMPH OF DEATH.

the horror of this image. Death—Mors—was amongst the Latin Christians the queen of Hell, the spouse of Satan. Thus in the apostolic history of St. Bartholomew, a demon is made to say: "But He (Jesus) has made prisoner Death herself, who is our queen, and even our king, the husband of Death, hath He also bound in chains of fire." *

* Fabricius, Codex pseudepigraphus Novi Testamenti, t. i. pt. ii. pp. 679, 680.

Death, as a rider whose horse leaps forth from the mouth of Hell, is shown in the two Figs. 201 and 202, also probably taken from quattrocento MSS., but illustrating the subject of the Triumph of Death,* one of the finest representations of which was painted by the first painter

Fig. 202.—TRIUMPH OF DEATH.

of Sicily, Crescenzio, on the wall of the courtyard of the Hospital at Palermo. Instead of the yawning mouth of Hell to the left, we have the most beautiful group in the

* The reader who wishes to study the treatment of the Triumph of Death in Mediæval Art more fully should read a paper in the *Cornhill Magazine*, September, 1879, by Miss Clerke, where she alludes to the following illustrations of the subject:—Titian's Triumph of Death; where the skeleton victor is seen leaning on his scythe enthroned on a funeral car drawn by oxen preceded by the Parcæ. A painting in San Giacomo Maggiore at Bologna. Here a vision of the last judgment represented in an oval forms part of the composition. Didron, *Ann. Arch.* tom. xvi. p. 170, describes the riders in the Apocalypse on the tomb of Jean de Langheac at Limoges. In the same paper this writer describes the sculptures on the Hôtel Bourgtheroulde, at Rouen, in which the six Triumphs of Petrarch are represented. Here Death takes a third place; it precedes the form of Religion, and the wheels of the Chariot of Death are crushing the representatives of human power in the persons of kings, pontiffs, etc.

VOL. II.   M

whole composition, composed of the figures of those who have escaped Death. One woman, who weeps as she contemplates the scene of havoc before her, is said to be especially fine.

The horse, a skeleton form, bounds through the air, while his wild rider, also a skeleton, draws his bow and with his arrows strikes princes, pontiffs, and all the great ones of the earth, while the wretched and diseased call on him for deliverance. The bolt will not fall upon them, but amid a merry group on the left, where some dancing girls surround a zither player, and who, while yet in the fulness of life, are smitten by mortal pallor, the precursor

Fig. 203.

of dissolution. Above these again are a company of youths and maidens seated by a fountain in happy ignorance of the approaching gloom.

The framework of the Divine Comedy was not without its parallels in antiquity. Poetry in all time has been occupied with the immutable destiny of man, and the walls of the Campo Santo of Pisa, on which the Lorenzetti and their colleagues painted the soul's drama, resemble those of the Lesche, painted by Polygnotus, in this, that both are expressions of the faith of the day in which they were executed, as regards the condition of the soul after death.

The series, of which the Triumph of Death was only one chapter, should be considered in the following order: 1. The Crucifixion. 2. The Resurrection. 3. The Ascension. The Triumph of Death. Judgment. Hell. The Angelic

Life. This last scene, the climax of the whole, must be held in view if one would understand the author's drift throughout all the previous scenes. The quiet mountain side, the hermit life of solitude and sanctity, one old man reading, another resting on his crutches, a third milking his doe, while squirrels play at his feet, the monastery in which they pass their ordered life, all rise in contrast with the life of the world, its vanity and madness and sin. The following verses are written on a scroll, held by two angels :*—

"Ischermo di savere e di ricchezza
Di nobilitate ancora e di prodezza
Vale niente ai colpi di costei.
Ed ancor non ʍi truova contra lei,

"O lettore, niuno argomento,
Eh! non avere lo'ntelletto spento
Di stare sempre in apparecchiato
Che non ti giunga in mortale peccato." †

The whole upper half of the fresco on one side is filled with angels and demons snatching away the souls of the dead, and bearing them to their destinations. The angels are graceful and tender in their care of the pure souls entrusted to them, while the wicked souls are snatched off by the bat-winged scaly demons who, flying or flitting through the air, throw them headlong into the mouths of Hell—the craters of volcanoes belching out flames. Fig. 204. The fresco is filled with such mottoes as this:—

"Dacche prosperitade ci ha lasciati,
O morte, medicina d' ogni pena,
Deh vieni a darne ormai l' ultima cena."

"Since nought of happiness to us remains,
Come, then, O Death!—the cure for every grief—
Give our last supper, and relief from pain."‡

---

* See *Vasari*, vol. i. p. 207. Ed. Bohn.
† "Nor wisdom's aid, nor riches may avail,
Nor proud nobility, nor valour's arm,
To make thee shelter from the stroke of death;
Nor shall thine arguments, O reader saye,
Have force to change her purpose: wherefore, turn
Thy wealth of thought to its best use—be thine
The watch unsleeping, ever well prepared
That so she find thee not in mortal sin."
‡ See *Revue Archéol.* 1844, p. 461, for ancient figure of Death. See *Catal. de la Bibl. du duc de Luoullière*, 1783, tom. ii. p. 285, No; 2736.

Near the subject of the Triumph of Death, Orcagna has illustrated an older mediæval poem, 'Three Deaths and Three Lives,' * a poem which gave rise to many representations of which his is the best known.

Le dit des Trois Morts et des Trois Vifs first appears in the thirteenth century as one of a collection of moralities. The earliest existing copy, that of Baudouin de Condé, was written about the beginning of the fourteenth century. This manuscript is preserved in the Bibl. de l'Arsenal (No.

Fig. 204.

175, Fonds Français) and is adorned with a miniature of that date showing three youths of noble countenance and great beauty of form, but whose hearts were filled with pride. God, to abate this pride, sends them a fearful apparition of three corpses, fleshless, worm-eaten, who confront the three fair youths, and the second speaking, tells them to behold in him a mirror sent by God of their future state. "Behold what we are, such will you be."

---

* This poem has been analysed by M. Paulin Paris, *MS. Français*, tom. vii. p. 340. Another MS. copy is preserved in the Bibl. Nat. Fonds, 7292.

THREE DEATHS AND THREE LIVES. 165

".... Vées quel sommes,
Tel serez vous. Et tel com ore
Estes, fumes...."

This subject, which is a not uncommon one in mediæval art, is thus treated on the walls of the Campo Santo.* Three uncovered tombs in the foreground contain corpses eaten by enormous worms, before which three knights,

Fig. 205.—FRANCESCO DA VOLTERRA, CAMPO SANTO, PISA.

one carrying a falcon on his wrist, pause in astonishment. They are accompanied by squires and huntsmen. On

* See *La Danse des Morts* dessinée par Hans Holbein, &c. expliquée par Hippolyte Fortoul, Paris, 1842, p. 33. This "Morality" is represented in a miniature of the middle of the fourteenth century, the prayer-book of Margaret of Flanders, wife of Philip the Bold, duke of Burgundy. Here the three knights are on horseback as in the fresco of the Campo Santo. The subject appears in sculptures on the south door of the church of the Holy Innocents at Paris, *Ann. Archéol.* vol. xvi. p. 165. Since the invention of printing the subject appears constantly as a sequel to the Dance of Death (*Recherches Hist. et Litt. sur la Danse des Morts*, Dijon, 1826). Neither Lasinio nor Giovanni Rosini in his *Descrizione delle pitture del Campo Santo* (Pisa, 1837, p. 25) appear to have heard of the *Moralité Française*, which may have been carried by Dante from France to Tuscany and afterwards suggested this scene to the painter

the second floor a hermit reading the following scroll may be seen:—

"Se nostra mente fia ben accorta,
Tenendo fisa qui la vista afflitta,
La vana gloria ci sarà sconfitta
E la superbia ci sarà ben morta."

The scene next to this in the series of frescoes is that of the Anchorites of the Thebaid, and it is possible that Orcagna introduced the hermit, who does not appear in the original poem—a transition from one scene to the other, from the fall of human pride and glory to the poverty of the Anchorites in the desert.

Il Carro della Morte (the chariot of Death) was a pageant which would seem to have been the production of a genius not less gloomy and sublime than that of Dante. "In the carnival, and in the night of its greatest festivity, the citizens gazed in silence on this frightful scene as it passed along the streets. It consisted of a black funeral car, on which were painted white crosses, and dead men's bones. It was drawn by four buffaloes, and a ghastly figure with a scythe sat upon it. This figure represented Death, and had at its feet graves opening, out of which skeletons were continually issuing. Many hundred persons, clothed in black, with masks resembling deaths' heads, marched before and after it with lighted torches in their hands. The lights were so well arranged that they fell exactly on the car and the procession, so that the whole appeared very natural. Numbers of other masks, not less frightful, mounted on the poorest horses that could be found, with black housings trailing the ground, carried standards of black taffety, embroidered with crossed bones and tears. The skeletons, in trembling and mournful voices, sung penitential psalms, with the Miserere; and the instrumental music, corresponding to the vocal, added to the melancholy and petrifying spectacle."*

The Death of man is figured in the allegory of the Ladder of the Soul's Salvation, and the way of Heaven. The method in which this subject should be treated is laid

---

* *Vasari*, tom. iii. pp. 76, 78; translated by Sir Richard Clayton. Walker, *Drama in Italy*, App. p. 25.

down in the Manual of Panselinos, and the accompanying illustration has probably been suggested by this Byzantine model. The ladder of salvation rests against the *Arbor peccati*, whose branches are haunted by birds, and in which a crowned and sceptred figure inscribed *Vita mundi* sits enthroned. The soul having escaped from the grave, inscribed *Mors humana*, climbs the ladder, which is so firmly planted against the tree of life that the efforts of the Devil to drag him down are all in vain.

Fig. 208.

The Moral Ladder appeared in miniature in a manuscript now destroyed, entitled *Hortus deliciarum*, in the public library of Strasburg (circ. 1160), accompanied by an explanatory text of the scenes following.

A great ladder is placed standing on end, and rising from earth to heaven. On the last and highest round of the ladder the hand of God issues from the clouds and holds the crown of life for those who mount without falling. Below, on the first round, the Devil, under the form of a dragon, may be seen, holding snares for those who wish to scale the ladder. Two demons draw their bows to shoot those who mount; but two angels, armed with sword and buckler, ward off their arrows, and prevent them piercing those who would rise. First in order comes a soldier accompanied by a woman. The soldier is overthrown, he falls upon the horses and bucklers in which his delight has been. The woman of the world is also overthrown, and falls among the luxuries of the city towards which her desire has been.

A series of examples of such efforts and failures follows until we reach the thirteenth round, where Virtue [Virtus id est Caritas] appears as a young woman with long fair hair and bare head, who advances to take the crown that God holds out to her. On one side-post of the ladder we read: "Hos omnes, periculose ab alto cadentes, potest Dominus medicina penitentiæ verum ad virtutum culmen restituere." "These all who fall with danger from on high, the Lord is able by the salve of penitence to restore to the true height of virtue."

Christ appears as the Conqueror of Death, in the Missal of Worms, a MS. of the eleventh century in the Bibl. de l'Arsenal. Death, the enemy of Christ, is here represented as a demon in chains.* Christ, a kingly form with nimbed head, holds His cross in one hand, and in the other the end of the heavy chain with which His foe is bound.† In the refectory of the monastery of Vatopedi on Mount Athos, Death is represented as crushing Intemperance, personified under the image of a man who has fallen near a tomb. This Death is horrible; a human form black as night, a skeleton merely covered by a shrunken skin dried to the bones. There is a dreadful power in this figure; it holds a sickle in the right hand, and a sharp scythe in the left which it brandishes in the air and with which it cuts short the life of the drunkard; those escaping from him slay one another. This subject is accompanied by inscriptions such as, "Fear the grave; Death approaches; Behold Charon." The Death is in fact not Christian Death, which is either a crowned skeleton, or black woman with her tombstone, or frantic horseman armed with a deadly

---

* See vol. i. Fig. 77, p. 300.
† See Miss L. Twining, *Symbols and Emblems in Christian Art*, p. xxix. See *La France*, Tillenain.

shaft passing in full gallop on his wild horse; or human form with bandaged eyes and spear which he blindly casts at all that cross his path. All these Deaths are drawn from the Apocalypse or from the mystic writers of the middle ages. But at Mount Athos we are in Greece, and pagan mythology, which held undisputed sway throughout this country, could not at once be ousted by Christianity. Charon therefore holds his place by right in the refectory of Vatopedi, as in the works of Dante and of Michael Angelo.

The crowned skeleton occurs in the frescoes of Giotto, at Assisi, where, to the right of the door, St. Francis, facing the spectator, points to such an image. Fig. 207 is a fair example of a figure of a dead king rising from his tomb at the sound of the last trumpet, such as often occurs in quattro-cento representations of the Last Judgment.

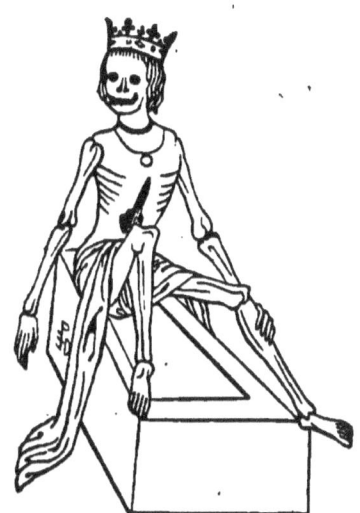

Fig. 207.—DEATH A CROWNED SKELETON ON TOMB.

The spectacles or performances of the Dance of Death, so common in the middle ages, were often relieved of their gloom by the introduction of interludes in which the Fool took a prominent part. Such scenes when illustrated formed part of the series of subjects of engravings of the "Danse Macabre." The Fool is seen at strife with his adversary Death, and hitting him with a bladder full of peas or pebbles.*

Fig. 208.—DEATH AS ECCE HOMO.

We frequently meet with allusions

---

* See Crowe and Cavalcaselle, *Hist. Painting in Italy*, vol. i. p. 249.

to Death's fool in Shakespeare. Thus in 'Measure for Measure' the Duke says to Claudio (Act iii. sc. 1) :—

"Merely, thou art Death's fool;
For him thou labour'st by thy flight to shun,
And yet runn'st toward him still."

And again in 'Pericles,' Act. iii. sc. 2, where Cerimon upholds the pursuit of philosophy and virtue above that of rank and wealth, says:—

". . . . which doth give me
A more content in course of true delight
Than to be thirsty after tottering honour,
Or tie my treasure up in silken bags,
To please the fool and death."

M. Langlois is of opinion that Death and the Fool were introduced as agents into all the dramatic representations of France, Italy, and England, acting as mutes, and of whose performance that of the modern harlequin is an imperfect reproduction.* In the mortuary chapel in the Augustinian church of Vienna, the figure of Harlequin making grimaces at Death may be seen in the wall paintings of the "Danse Macabre." Is not this the Fool of the middle ages reproduced in he costume of the stage harlequin?†

Fig. 209.

* Death and the Fool appear in Holbein's *Imagines*, Cologne, 1566.
† See H. Green, *Emblems*, p. 472. Didron's illustration is taken from a "Danse Macabre" of the fifteenth century. The oldest edition of the "Danse Macabre" cited by bibliographers is that of Paris, 1484; but more than a century previous to this date French miniaturists had already figured Dances of Death in the marginal borders of their MS. Books of Hours in a similar manner to those of Simon Vostre. A magnificent MS. of the second half of the fourteenth century affords a remarkable instance. It was enriched with numerous miniatures, and was presented by Louis XV. to Dr. Mead, from whose collection it came into that of M. Ambr. Firmin

Although the Danse Macabre,* with its long sequence of scenes in which Death is seen dancing away with his victims irrespective of age or condition, seems to date from the fourteenth and fifteenth centuries, yet occasional instances occur of similar scenes on ancient gems. M. de Maury publishes a curious engraved stone from the collection of M. Badeigts de Laborde, which represents Death as a skeleton dancing before a shepherd and laying hold of him as he sits playing on a double flute. The shepherd's foot rests upon a ball, while two butterflies, emblems of the soul, flutter above his head. This intaglio is held by Mr. S. S. Lewis to be about the time of Hadrian, when such conceits had supplanted the truth and simplicity of earlier art; the engraver was doubtless a Greek, who had gone to seek fame

Fig. 210.

Didot. See *Essai sur les Danses des Morts*, C. H. Langlois, tom. i. 139, 140, 253–261; Douce's *Dance of Death*, fig. xliii.; Woltmann's *Holbein and his Times*, vol. ii. p. 121.

* As to the Dance of Death or "Danse Macabre," it does not appear before the end of the fourteenth century. The oldest is believed to have been executed at Minden in Westphalia in 1383. Fabricius, *Biblioth. Med. Ætut.* tom. iv. p. 1. In 1407, Guillebert of Metz indicate- the artists of the cemetery of the "Innocents" at Paris as "notable painters of the Dance of Death and other works." These paintings must have been at that time twenty-four years in existence. In 1424, the Dance of Death was played in the cemetery of the Innocents. We know how universal this strange subject became in the fifteenth century, though unfitted to inspire any delicate art. This particular illustration of Death's Fool has been already published by M. Challemel (who borrowed the block from Didron) in *La France Littéraire*, iii. p. 182, but he gives no reference further than that it is taken from a MS. Danse Macabre of the fifteenth century. In Stowe's *Survey of London*, 1618, is a contest between Death and the Fool copied into Knight's *Shakespeare*, vol. viii. p. 303. The fool was a kind of satiric figure under whose garb all humanity was occasionally figured. An instance of this may be seen in the *Stultifera Navis* of Sebastian Brandt, a gothic publication of the close of the fifteenth century, containing numerous engravings on wood, originally printed in Germany; at Basle and Nuremberg in 1494.

and fortune in the Eternal City* like those described by Juvenal in the early part of his third satire.†

Two similar representations of Death on onyx gems are engraved in Mr. King's edition of Horace illustrated from ancient gems, pp. 20 and 253. Cupid, hovering above, throws the light of his torch into the depths of an immense Corinthian *crater*, out of which a skeleton, terrified at the hateful light, casts himself headlong on

Fig. 211.

the opposite side. The skeleton can only represent a ghost; Ovid's "ossea larva," Seneca's "larvarum nudis ossibus cohærentium figuræ." The ghosts of the wicked became larvæ, but those of the good were elevated into Lares.‡

The second, a sardoine gem, executed with great finish in the Roman manner, shows a skeleton, emerging from an urn decorated with cross torches in

* *Revue Archéol.* vol. v. pt. i. p. 295.
† ".... Non possum ferre, Quirites,
Græcam urbem, quamvis quota portio fæcis Achææ?
* * * * * *
Ingenium velox, audacia perdita, sermo
Promptus, et Isæo torrentior: ede, quid illum
Esse putes? quemvis hominem secum attulit ad nos,
Grammaticus, rhetor, geometres, pictor, aliptes,
Augur, schœnobates, medicus, magus; omnia novit:
Græculus esuriens, in cœlum, jusseris, ibit."

"I cannot, Romans, stand a Grecised Rome; and yet, after all, what a fraction of our *canaille* are Achaia's sons. ... Their wits are all alive; their effrontery desperate; and readiness of speech is theirs—a flood of words that beats Isæus. Say now, what think you, is his line? Why he puts himself at our service a Jack-of-all-trades—a critic, a rhetorician, geometer, painter, trainer, prophet, rope-dancer, doctor, sorcerer. The starveling Greek knows all the sciences." D. J. Juvenalis *Satyra* iii. v. 60, 61, 73 78. The Thirteen Satires of Juvenal, translated into English by H. A. Strong and Alex. Leeper, 1882.

‡ This mysterious scene may be supposed to envelope a moral similar to that conveyed in the concluding verses of this ode:

"Sapias, vina liques et spatio brevi
Spem longam reseces. Dum loquimur fugerit invida
Ætas: carpe diem, quam minimum credula postero."

"Be wise, strain clear the wine; and since our span is short cut off a length of hope. While we are speaking, envious Time will have fled; snatch to-day, and utterly mistrust to-morrow." Hor. *Od.* i. 11.

allusion to the Eleusinian mysteries, and plucking a brand from a palm-tree. This remarkable design obviously and ingeniously expresses the winning of unfading glory *after* death, for the arms of the defunct hero are seen piled at the foot of his urn.*

ICONOGRAPHY OF THE SOUL.

THE images of the soul which Art in all ages has bequeathed to us may be divided into two classes—symbols and mere emblems.

The nature of the emblems of the soul among the Egyptians is known from a compilation made about the beginning of the fifth century by Horapollo, an Egyptian scribe who endeavoured to collect in a volume the symbols upon the monuments of his country. "How," he asks, "do the Egyptians represent a soul passing a long time here? They paint a phœnix, since of all creatures this bird has by far the longest life. Again, the soul departing is represented as a hawk sitting on a mummy." The hawk is put for the soul from the signification of its name, for it is called Baieth: Bai, soul, and eth, heart, the heart being the shrine of the soul.

The ancients held that in death the soul was delivered with the last breath through the mouth;† thus Homer,

* ". . . . diram qui contudit hydram
Notaque fatali portenta labore subegit,
Comperit invidiam supremo fine domari.
Urit enim fulgore suo, qui prægravat artes
Infra se positas: extinctus amabitur idem."

"He who crushed the dreadful hydra and subdued the well-known monsters by the labours which fate ordained, by experience found that envy was a monster not to be conquered till the hour of his death. He who depresses the merits of others who are inferior to himself, blasts them by his own brilliancy. When his light is quenched his memory will be loved."

† In Byzantine art the soul of a hypocrite is figured as a serpent issuing from his mouth as he lies on his death-bed. See *Manual of Panselinos*, or *Byzantine Guide to Painting*, p. 107. A very common Gnostic emblem of the soul in death is the butterfly crushed by the winged foot. King's *Gnostics and their Remains*, p. 159.

Iliad 9, speaks of the soul after it has passed the barrier of the teeth, and can never by any means return. At what time an image of the soul thus passing forth was first given we do not know, but the butterfly escaping from the chrysalis seems to have been the oldest as well as most common emblem. The iconography of the butterfly has been so exhaustively treated by Max Collignon in his *Essai sur les Monuments Grecs et Romains relatifs au Mythe de Psyché*, that little more need be added here.

At first the fable of Psyche appeared merely as a graceful allegory springing from the Greek poetic imagination. The name signifies both soul and a night butterfly; thus, by a natural association, the one came to stand for the other, and the allegory was developed. At a later period philosophy laid hold of it as a symbol in which ideas of renovation and futurity found expression. But the figure was in use as a funereal emblem before Christianity.

Fig. 212.—PSYCHE IN DESPAIR SEATED ON A ROCK AND BEWAILING THE FLIGHT OF CUPID.

M. Langlois remarks, "Souvent la figure d'un papillon exprimait la fuite et la légèreté de cette *animula vagula* qu'en l'interpellant en ces termes, Hadrien mourant interrogeait en lui. Cette jolie allégorie se trouve dans la gravure d'un monument fort curieux donnée par Spon (*Miscellanea Eruditæ Antiquitatis*, pl. vii.); l'on y voit étendu par terre un corps, de la bouche duquel s'échappe un papillon." We give an illustration of this curious monument in Fig. 213.

On the wall, the wreaths and flowers and vase of ointment, hung there by the mother of the dead, may be seen. This is taken from a marble sculpture which formed part of the collection of Petrus Antonius Rascasius de Bagarris, and a very remarkable funeral inscription found in Spain seems to illustrate the meaning of the whole, where the dying man prays for loving service at his grave that so his liberated soul may linger near: "Also I therefore command my heirs to entomb my bones so that the drunken butterfly may flutter upon my ashes." *

According to M. Gerhard, the genius of death may also be an image of the genius that personifies the divine or immortal part of the human soul. This close and mystic alliance of the human soul and divine genius reunited by a kind of hypostatic union, was allegorically represented in the tale of Eros and Psyche—Eros being the vital form,

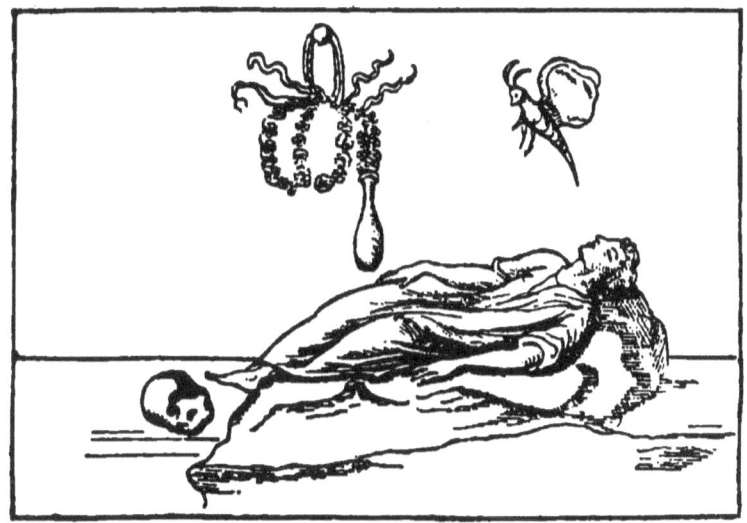

Fig. 213.

the loving and divine principle spread throughout the universe and animating each being—Eros the mysterious link between humanity and divinity. The soul is seen as Psyche led by Hermes, while the genius νοῦς stays

* *Spon. Miscell. Erud.* p. 8, Tabula iv.

"Cur animam figurâ papilionis fingerent diximus supra. Credebatur ea per os reddi : unde Homerus Iliad. 9, dicit animam postquam efflata est, vel septum dentium, ut loquitur transivit remeare aequaquam posse. Papilio igitur hic expressus viri defuncti anima est quæ avolat. Uxor autem aut mater filium adstantem monere videtur, ut vivat, monstrans ei corollas et unguenta. Vinum enim, rosæ et unguenta complectebantur omnem vitæ voluptatem et delicias. Extat talis inscriptio in Hispania quæ habetur apud Moralem, p. 31.

"Haeredibus meis mando etiam cinere ut meo volitet ebrius papilio ossa ipsa tegant mea."

beside the body weeping for the dead, upon a bas-relief of Prometheus in the Capitol.*

M. Collignon enumerates twelve instances of the figure of Psyche represented as an emblem of the soul upon Christian monuments of an early date; eight on sarcophagi; one on the bottom of a painted cup found in the catacomb of Flavia Domitilla; one in a mosaic in Santa Costanza, near Rome; and two paintings in the catacomb of Flavia Domitilla. He has failed to notice that remarkable subject—the infusion of the living soul into the

Fig. 214.

human body, in the mosaics of St. Mark's at Venice, which is illustrated by Lady Eastlake in the *History of our Lord in Art*, page 90; where the Creator, or the Saviour, for he wears the cruciform nimbus, lays the Soul on Adam's breast, still holding it by one wing.

In Byzantine art the soul has been occasionally represented in the likeness of a human form, a white child without the Psyche wings, but translucent and surrounded by a luminous aureole white as snow, or, as it were, a mass of light solidified, suggesting a material substance

* *Essai sur les Danses de Mort*, vol. i. p. 66.

transmitted into immaterial. In the subjects of the death of the Virgin, and of the death of St. Anthony, in the Greek churches, painted after the directions given in the *Manual of Panselinos*, the soul thus appears in size as a little child, naked, sexless. In the Martyrdom of St. Stephen sculptured on the porch of St. Trophimus of Arles, the martyr's soul is seen in human form as it passes from his dying mouth into the arms of two angels, who bear it up to God.

In the Martyrdom of St. Lawrence,* as represented on a small medal or plaque in the Christian Museum of the Vatican, the soul of the saint stands with outspread arms above the body stretched upon red-hot irons; a hand ready to descend upon the head of the rising soul appears above, holding a crown between the signs Alpha and Omega.

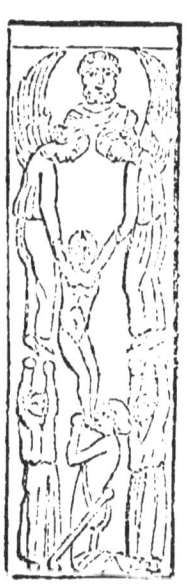

Fig. 215. — MARTYR-DOM OF ST. STEPHEN, SCULPTURE ON PORCH OF ST. TROPHIMUS AT ARLES.

The conception of the soul as an infant form is of earlier date than the beginning of the Christian era. Various instances are recorded in which Mercury and Iris † —the divine messengers or angels of the ancients—are seen bearing souls wrapped in small bands, just as the souls of St Amoun or St. Alexander are painted in the Greek Menologium of the emperor Basil.

Mrs. Jameson illustrates this subject by many fine examples in Christian art, to which we may add that it appears in a bas-relief on the façade of the church of St. Trophimus at Arles. And we have seen this subject in the illuminated Psalter given to St. Louis of France by his mother, Blanche of Castille.‡

* *Dict. Christian Antiq.*, Money.
† Cf. Inghirami, *Vasi fittili*, tab. lxv.; Stackelberg, *die Graeber der Hellenen*, taf. xxi. Cf. sur le génie de la naissance, R. Rochette, *Orcsteïde*, par. 8, p. 2. Pausan. i. 83. Cf. Ed. Gerhard, *Aus. griech. Vasenbilder*, taf. lxxxiii. t. ii. p. 15. Iris était aussi une divinité psychopompe comme Mercure. Voyez *l'Enéide*, iv. 693. C'était comme ce dieu un véritable ange. Cf. Platon, iv. Leg. 717. See *Museum Capitolinum*, iii. tab. 25.
‡ The struggles of angels and demons for the soul of the departed is a

The weighing of souls in the balance at the Judgment Day is the office of Michael in Christian, as it was that of Hermes in Pagan art, when the fortunes of gods and heroes were at stake.

Fig. 216.—SOUL BORNE TO HEAVEN BY ANGELS.

In a MS. circ. 1300, formerly in the collection of M. Dupasquier at Lyons, St. Michael is represented as slaying the Dragon, and, at the same moment, weighing

---

frequent subject in mediæval art and legend. One such tale occurs in *Faits et miracles de Notre Dame*, MSS. franç. fonds Lancelot, f. 34, also in the *Life of St. Anthony*—*Vies des Pères du désert*, trad. d'Arnauld d'Andilly. See also dissertation of M. Labitte, entitled *La divine comédie avant Dante* p. 89 *de la traduction de l'épopée de Dante*, par M. Brizeux. St. Fursey St. Vettin, St. Jean de Pulsani, St. Columba in the island of Iona—all were witnesses of like struggles till we come down to the scenes in the *Inferno* of Dante, c. xxvii. line 120, and *Purgat.* c. v. line 100, in which Dante describes St. Francis and a demon contending for the soul of Guido da Montefeltro, and the demon is victorious. Again, a like contest is described over the soul of Buonconte da Montefeltro, who says:

"Me God's angel took,
Whilst he of hell exclaimed: O thou of heaven!
Say wherefore hast thou robbed me?"

the souls of the good and evil man, where a demon catches hold of the scale in which the soul of the good man is rising.*

M. de Maury, in his treatise on the origin of the subject of psychostasis, has shown that St. Michael of Christian iconography takes the place of Mercury in ancient representations of the weighing of souls. He endeavours to show the linking of those beliefs that bound together the

Fig. 217.

doctrines of an attendant genius and an angel shade leader and weigher of souls. How almost inconceivable at first sight it appears that the messenger of Olympus should become chief of the legions of Jehovah: that Mercury, Hermes, Thoth, of expiring religions, should enter Christian mythology. With the Mussulmans also the functions

* See D'Agincourt, *Hist. de l'Art*, pt. i. pp. 94, 196. There is no allusion to this subject, however, in the *Byzantine Manual*.

of Michael are said to be fulfilled by Azrael, and with the Persians by Mordad.

The following figure of the weighing of souls in the balance is taken from a vase which forms part of the collection of the Duke de Luynes, and is believed to represent the scene in the twenty-second book of the Iliad, where the gods deliberate upon the fate of Achilles and Hector.* The combat of the gods, described towards the end of the twenty-first book, was painted on the reverse. Here Hermes, bearded, may be recognised by the caduceus which

Fig. 218.

he raises above his head in his left hand, while he holds the balances in the right, in which are the tiny figures of two soldiers wielding lances. These are coloured violet. The balances are steady and equal, showing that the fate of the warriors in the scale is as yet undecided. Jupiter, armed with a thunderbolt and leaning on a knotted staff, stands on the left; a crown of yew leaves surrounds his head. A goddess, probably either Athene or Thetis, for

* See *Monuments inédits de l'Inst. Arch.* t. ii. pl. x. b.; *Annales de l'Inst. Arch.* t. vi. p. 296.

there is no attribute here by which she may be distinguished, stands on the right side; she lifts her tunic with the left hand, while she waves the right in sign of deliverance and victory.

A gem engraved by Chifflet shows Mercury seated upon a rock, as he is constantly represented on ancient engraved stones. He holds a great caduceus and wears a winged petasus; before him stands a cock, crowing. The name MICHAEL is engraved upon this stone.* Two Hebrew letters traced upon the field form the word *Ath*, signifying *time*. This word appears to be an allusion to future judgment. The cock figures as the usual symbol of Mercury; thus Mercury standing for Michael, the cock is doubtless represented as an emblem of the Last Judgment, of the day when the trumpet call shall awaken man from the tomb as the bird of dawning recalls him from sleep to activity.

Fig. 219.

As Mercury was also shade-leader, so Michael leads souls into the presence of God. On an agate onyx in the collection of the Duke of Orleans published by Abbés de la Chaud and le Blond, vol 1. fig. 23, Hermes, holding the caduceus in one hand, is seen to lift the soul from the tomb in the other. Again, on gems in the Uzielli collection published by C. W. King, Hermes leads souls to Charon, or, by virtue of his wand, raises souls from the Shades.† Figs. 219, 220.

Fig. 220.

The dedication of rocks and high places to St. Michael

* Tab. xxi. fig. 85, and in *Cabinet des Pierres gravées de Gorlée*, t. ii. pl. ccxviii. No. 435; Gori, *Inscript. Antiqs.* i. p. l. tab. iii. 1.
† *Antique Gems and Rings*, C. W. King, vol. ii. p. 53, pl. xxi.

182   CHRISTIAN ICONOGRAPHY.

is a practice we have before alluded to. The Skelig Michel off the west coast of Ireland, St. Michael's Rock off the shore of Cornwall, Mont St. Michael off the coast of Brittany, are instances of this custom, and it is a notable fact, as bearing upon our subject, that certain temples of Mercury have been replaced in Gaul by churches under the invocation of

Fig. 221.

St. Michael. Thus, near Puy en Velay, the church of St. Michael (built in the year 965, on the top of one of its sharpest peaks, the Aiguille), has been erected on the ruins of a temple of Mercury, some remains of which may still be seen.

The numerous apparitions and miracles of Michael may be read in the 'Golden Legend' (*De Santo Michaele Archangelo*).* He indeed plays a great part in the Christian drama as in the Hebrew religion. Jacobus de Voragine has said : " Ipse olim princeps fuit synagogæ, sed nunc constitutus est a Domino in principem ecclesiæ." In the *Manual of Panselinos* it is Michael who appears to Hagar in the wilderness and directs her to the well; it is Michael who stays the hand of Abraham when about to sacrifice his son ; it is Michael who protects the body of Moses from Satan at his burial; it is Michael who appears to Gideon and strengthens him against Midian; it is Michael who appears to Joshua before Jericho, saying, " Loose thy shoes from off thy foot, for the place whereon thou standest is holy" (Josh. v. 15); it is Michael who appears to Manoah and announces the birth of Samson ; it is Michael who, when exterminating the people, stays his hand because of the sacrifice of David; it is Michael who descends to the three children in the furnace; Michael who brings food to Daniel through the mediation of Habakkuk ; Michael who protects Constantinople against the Persians, and saves the church from inundation, and Michael who appears with Gabriel in the midst of a boat in which three monks are seen about to drown a little child, which he rescues and conveys to the abbot of a monastery on the neighbouring shore.

In the scene where he appears to Joshua as prince of the heavenly army he is always attired as a warrior in armour, with a naked sword, his costume in Greek paintings being generally that of the Roman emperors. He is clad in a complete suit of mail in the accompanying illustration (Fig. 221) from a MS. at Amiens, of the date 1197, and we give another illustration (Fig. 222) from the Book of Hours of Henry II., A.D. 990. This manuscript is a Gradual of the Abbey of Prume, and was executed in the lifetime of Abbot Hilderic, who died in 993, and Abbot Stephen, who died A.D. 1001.† Above the figure of Michael the following inscription may be read : " Magnum Te Michiale."

* See *La Légende Dorée par Jacques de Voragine*, traduite par M. G. B. Paris, 1843, vol. ii. p. 151.
† See *Codex*, fol. 48. Bibl. Nat. Paris, Lat. 9448.

184   CHRISTIAN ICONOGRAPHY.

The book is also entitled, *Liber precum cum Notis Canticis et Figuris.*

Mrs. Jameson remarks, in a thoughtful passage on this Archangel, that the glorification of St. Michael may be traced back to that primitive Eastern dogma, the perpetual antagonism between the Spirit of Good and the Spirit of Evil, mixed up with the Chaldaic belief in

Fig. 222.

angels and their influence over the destinies of Man." All tales of the wars and wrestlings of divine beings and heroes, with dragons, lions, and composite animals, may be held to signify the struggle of mind with brute force, of good and evil, of life and death, the divine strife, man's capacity for which and deathless persistence in which distinguishes him from the animal creation, and is pledge

ST. MICHAEL AND THE DRAGON.

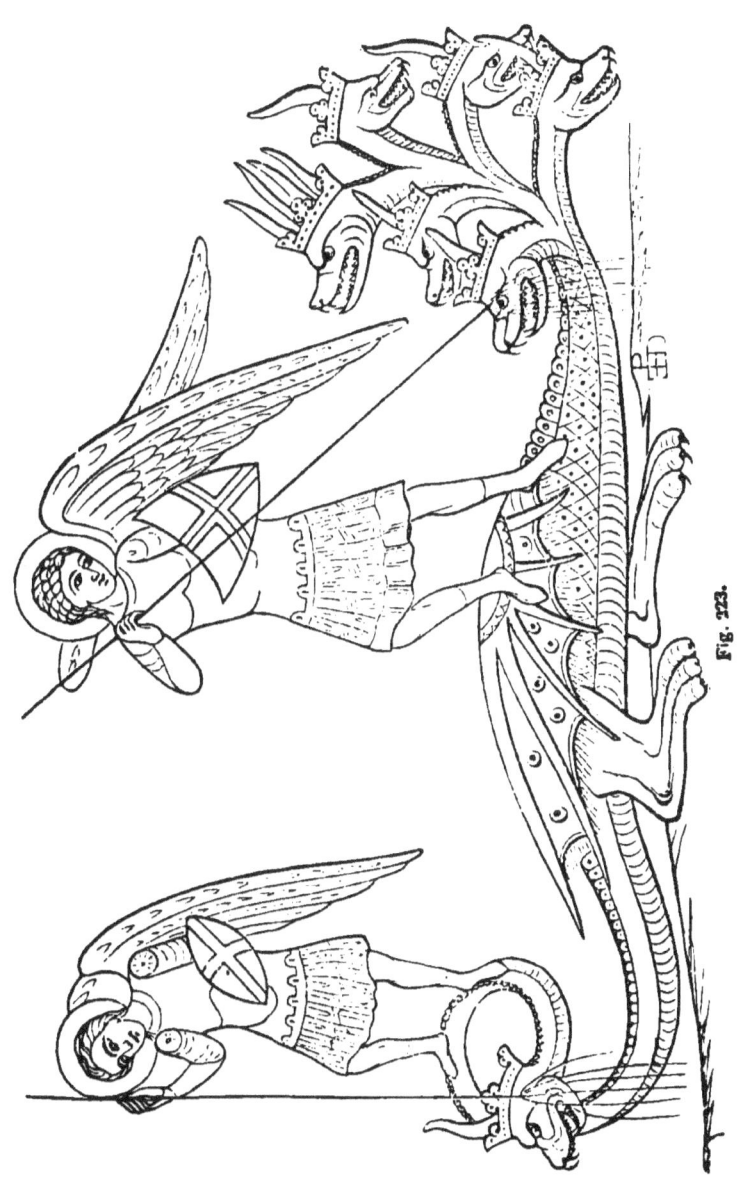

Fig. 223.

of his soul's divinity. The final triumph of Michael and his angels as related in the book of the Revelation of St. John, is our next illustration (Fig. 293). "And there was war in heaven: Michael and his angels fought against the dragon; and the dragon fought, and his angels, and prevailed not; neither was their place found any more in heaven. And the great dragon was cast out, that old serpent, called the Devil and Satan, which deceiveth the whole world." This monster is the great red dragon [Rev. xii. 3] having seven heads and ten horns, and seven crowns upon his heads, another representation of which is given in our first volume, Fig. 47, page 163. Both are taken from the same manuscript, Psalterium cum figuris, No. 8846, Bibl. Nat., Paris. This monster resembles the Lernean hydra, having one body from which ten necks project, each terminating in a head. As to the ten horns, they are generally distributed, two upon each of the three first heads, and one on each of the others. The form of the body is that of a dragon with or without wings, with paws of lion, body of a crocodile, tail and neck of a serpent. The heads are either those of a lion or a serpent.*

One of the grandest conceptions of the struggle of St. Michael and the Dragon was a scene only known to us now through an engraving, painted by Spinello at Arezzo on the façade of the great altar in the church of St. Agnolo, or the Archangel Michael. The fresco itself and its fate have been well described by Lord Lindsay. "The composition, embracing Heaven and Chaos, was divided into three great masses; God the Father sat enthroned on the summit, in the centre Michael engaged in personal conflict with Satan, 'that old serpent,' the seven-headed dragon of the Apocalypse, while the angel host precipitated his demon proselytes over the ramparts of heaven into the lower world, in which, lowest of all, Satan was a second time represented in his new shape, horribly transformed, reclining on a rock, the monarch of the dreary region." Vasari† has described this altar,

---

* Examples were seen by M. Didron in the *Hortus Deliciarum;* the west window of the Sainte-Chapelle in Paris, the painted glass, and St. Martin-ès-Vignes, and St. Nizier at Troyes.
† See Vasari, *Lives of the Painters*, vol. i. p. 268. Ed. Bohn.

whereon was represented Lucifer fixing his seat in the North, with the fall of the angels, who are changed into devils as they descend to the earth.* In the air appears St. Michael in combat with the old serpent of seven heads and ten horns, while beneath and in the centre of the picture is Lucifer, already changed into a most hideous beast. And so anxious was the artist to make him frightful and horrible, that it is said—such is sometimes the power of imagination—that the figure he had painted appeared to him in his sleep, demanding to know where the painter had seen him looking so ugly as that, and wherefore he permitted his pencil to offer him, the said Lucifer, so mortifying an affront? The artist awoke in such extremity of terror, that he was unable to cry out, but shook and trembled so violently, that his wife, awakening, hastened to his assistance. But the shock was so great that he was on the point of expiring suddenly from this accident, and did not in fact survive it beyond a very short time, during which he remained in a dispirited condition, with eyes from which all intelligence had departed. It was thus that Spinello closed his career, leaving his friends in heavy sorrow for his death. He died in his ninety-second year. "When last at Arezzo," writes Lord Lindsay, "I made anxious search after this memorable fresco. The church has long since been desecrated, but part of it, including the altar-wall, still exists, partitioned and commuted into a contadina's cottage, and known by the name of "Casa de' Diavoli." Some remnants of the fresco are just traceable on the wall of the good woman's bed-room, and in the dark passage beneath it; in the former several of the angels, with their fiery swords striking down the devils, are full of spirit, and even grace, and Luca Signorelli has evidently remembered them while painting at Orvieto.

* See Fall of Lucifer, supra, p. 111, where the same metamorphosis is represented as occurring.

ICONOGRAPHY OF THE CHRISTIAN SCHEME.

It was the great merit of Didron when commencing the history of Christian iconography that he not only worked with method and system himself, but that he aimed at discovering and mastering the secrets of the method and system under which the great artists of the Middle Ages developed their art. Dying before even the first portion of his vast scheme, as laid down in the preface to this work, was accomplished, the task of carrying it on after the lapse of thirty years seemed at first a bewildering one; the labours of writers in the same field, the Abbé Crosnier, Alfred de Maury, Mrs. Jameson, Lady Eastlake, Miss Twining, instead of exhausting the subject, only threw the portals wider and revealed an ever-increasing multitude of images to be surveyed. A clue to the labyrinth could only be found by closely following Didron's lead and investigating the system, searching for the framework by aid of which the fathers of great art pursued their aim. The Christian Epos was their subject. This was the theme for many centuries of Poetry, the Drama and Art, but no epic is perfect without a plot. The plot is the bone and marrow of the composition, the framework on which the structure may be raised in symmetry and beauty. In the following pages we hope to show what was the nature of this framework of the Christian iconographic system, to trace its origin and development. Hitherto the reader of this work may have learned something of the nature of those images in which men clothed the Deity and his attributes, as of Satan and his diabolic company, along with the various personifications of Death and the Soul. However, here the author was but reviewing singly and in succession the motors and instruments in the great drama of the Soul's history. We have seen how men seemed unconscious that the imagery of the prophets and singers of old, however sublime in words, may produce a very different effect when literally translated into form and colour, and they carved in monstrous shapes the seven-headed, many-tailed creatures of the prophets until the multitudinous mass of images in Christian mythography becomes bewildering to contemplate. The company seems ever increasing in number and variety from century to century as apocryphal legends creep in, and Christian mythology borrows its imagery from various polytheistic religions. A system, a scheme was required, and as it now presents itself to us we seem to see that the history of Christian iconography is a history of the gradual development and evolution of an art inspired by a religion and philosophy advancing steadily within the bounds of order and of system, slowly revealing a scheme which, though capable of condensation in such a framework as that of the series of symbols in the paintings of the Sistine ceiling, or the statuary of Chartres Cathedral, could yet embrace all creation, all natural and spiritual law.

The conception of this scheme, gradually developed as Christians laid hold of the mysterious connection between the facts of the Old and New Testament, was based on certain passages in the New, where Christ and St. Paul point to the Old as the foundation of the New dispensation. The restoration of fallen humanity in the person of Christ was found to be pre-ordained, to have formed part of the divine plan as revealed from Genesis, and a necessary result of belief in the overruling providence and beneficent Will of a Being who conceives and carries forward a scheme for the perfecting of His work to a result without flaw or speck.

The treatment of the religious drama founded on this scheme varied according to time and place. Five different systems of iconography were developed in illustration of it, which we propose to consider in the present chapter. The first, as presented to us in the Byzantine Guide to Painting, is chronological, the second sacramental, the other three are typical and philosophic as well as historic.

The date of the original copy of this Byzantine guide is unknown. That which M. Didron found at Esphigmenou was held by the monks of Mount Athos to belong to the tenth or eleventh century, but was probably not older than the fifteenth or sixteenth. It is a copy of an older manuscript compiled by the monk Dionysius from the works of " the celebrated and illustrious master Manuel Panselinos of Thessalonica, a painter who," says Didron, "was the Giotto of the Byzantine school," and who flourished in the twelfth century, during the reign of the emperor Andronicus the First. Frescoes, said to be from his hand, are still shown in the churches of Kares and Vatopedi on Mount Athos. One of his pupils, "wishing to propagate the art of painting which, with much pains, he had learnt at Thessalonica,* among those who are willing to devote themselves to it," points out the sequence of subjects to be chosen from the Old and New Testament so as to epitomize the Divine Scheme of Salvation, and the manner in which the historical events, as well as the miracles of the New Testament and parables of our Lord, should be represented. He also adds the scrolls and inscriptions belonging to each prophet in his turn, and the names and physiognomy of the principal saints, following the order of the calendar as to their martyrdoms and miracles, and points out how these subjects should be distributed on the walls and in the cupolas of the Greek churches.

However, in this iconographical system laid down in the Manual of Dionysius, little more is attempted than to present an abstract of the history of the Christian scheme, by illustrating the successive events which mark the progress of religion, from Genesis to the death and ascension of Christ, and the Apocalypse.

In the systems next to be discussed, of Western Art, history and chronology were subservient to the idea of the symbolism of certain events recorded; and the cycle of subjects chosen was very much smaller than the Byzantine. The copy of the Manual of Dionysius first seen by Didron was in the hands of Joasaph, a monkish painter at Esphigmenou. The work, the date of which in its original form is unknown, had been extended and completed in successive centuries—but the copy in the hands of Joasaph

* *i.e.* Salonica, formerly a great school of painting at the gate of Mount Athos.

was not three hundred years old : it had been loaded with
notes written by himself and his master, which notes, in
due course of time, would be incorporated with the book
when recopied, just as those earlier ones found by the
painters of the fifteenth and sixteenth centuries on the
margins of their books had been incorporated in the work
by them. And so this book grew from century to century
and year to year. A transcript of this guide is to be found
in every atelier on Mount Athos. Macarios, a monkish
painter, only second to Joasaph, possessed a fine copy of it.
This bible of his art was laid open in his workshop, and
his pupils read from it by turns in a loud voice, as the
others painted in obedience to its directions. This recalls
a similar incident connected with the early history of
church decoration in Western Art, recorded by Gregory
of Tours, who wrote at the close of the sixth century,*
where Namatia, the aged wife of Namatius, bishop of
Auvergne, A.D. 423, reads to the painter deco a ing the
walls of the church she had raised over her husband's
tomb the scenes he is to depict.

" In the suburb of the town the wife of bishop Namatius
built the basilica of St. Stephen.† And, as she would fain
adorn it with pictures, she used to hold a book on her
knees, reading thereout stories of the deeds of the men of
old and pointing out to the painters what they should
set forth on the walls. Now on a certain day it came to
pass that as she sat in the church and read, a poor man
drew nigh to pray. And beholding a woman robed in
black raiment, and already stricken in years, he took her
for one of the needy, and drawing forth a cake of bread,
he placed it in her lap and went away. But she, despising
not the gift of the poor man, who had not recognised her
rank, accepted the bread, and thanked him. And she
placed it before her on her table, and every day she used
it for the prayer of benediction, until no more thereof
remained."‡

* Hodie ecclesia S. Eutropii Suburbicarii ; in ea sepultus fuit S. Namatius
cum aliis sanctis, ut indicat libellus de Sanctis Claromont. cap. 13. S. Greg.
Turon. *Hist. Franc.*, ii. 17. (Migne's note.)

† Sic Regm. Picturas in ecclesiis memorat passim Gregorius ut lib. vii.
cap. 36, lib. x. cap. ult., &c.

‡ The church of St. Stephen, in which the incident related above

It is probable that the book used on this occasion by Namatia was a manual somewhat like that of the monk Dionysius in its original form, and may very possibly have been of Byzantine origin.* In the early miniature paintings of France sacred subjects are constantly treated in accordance with the directions given in this Greek Manual. This is especially manifest in the Menologium of Basil II. Even were the miniatures herein contained

---

occurred, was built by the widow over the tomb of Bishop Namatius A.D. 423, and he in his day had erected the cathedral of Clermont in which to enshrine the relics of St. Vitalis and Agricola, which he had conveyed from Ravenna. It is not improbable that Byzantine art penetrated, even at this early date, through Ravenna to France; and we read in Didron's notes on his visit to Athens that he found in the ancient cathedral or church of the Transfiguration there, many points in common with the cathedral of Clermont, as well as Sta. Sophia at Constantinople.

773. Cap. xliv. De Agricola et Vitali martyribus. Horum reliquias Namatius, Arvernorum episcopus, devote expediit, ut scilicet eas in ecclesia quam ipse construxerat collocaret: derexitque unum illuc presbyterum, qui, abiens cum Dei gratia, quæ patierat detulit.

69. xvi. Sanctus vero Namatius, post obitum Rustici episcopi, apud Arvernos in diebus illis octavus erat episcopus. Hic ecclesiam quæ nunc constat, et senior infra muros civitatis habetur, suo studio fabricavit, habentem in longum pedes centum quinquaginta, in latum pedes sexaginta, in altum infra capsum usque cameram, pedes quinquaginta: inante absidem rotundam habens, ab utroque latere ascellas eleganti constructas opere, totumque ædificium in modum crucis habetur expositum. Habet fenestras quadraginta duas, columnas septuaginta, ostia octo. Terror namque ibidem Dei, et claritas magna conspicitur; et vere plerumque inibi odor quasi aromatum suavissimus advenire a religiosis sentitur. Parietis ad altarium, opere sarsurio, ex multo marmorum genere exornatos habet. Exacto ergo in duodecimo anno beatus pontifex ædificio, Bononiam civitatem Italiæ sacerdotes dirigit, ut ei reliquias SS. Vitalis et Agricolæ exhibeant, quos pro nomine Christi Dei nostri, manifestissime crucifixos esse cognovimus." (on which Migne's editor remarks in a note as follows:) "Haec est ecclesia cathedralis, de qua Savaro multa observat in notis ad cap. i. libri de ecclesiis Claromontensibus. Unde senior in Mor. s. et Regm. dicitur, pro qua voce editi habent veterrima. Opus sarsurium idem esse observat Altaserra ac opus tectorium, quod varium est et multiplex, sic dictum a verbo sarcire. Parietes autem templorum et publicorum ædificiorum marmore tegebantur seu incrustabantur, qualiter hic describitur templum a S Namatio constructum. Et quidem reliquias horum martyrum obtinuit, ut narrat ipse Gregor. lib. i. de Gloria Mart., cap. 44. Eorumdem martyrum passionem describit S. Ambrosius in lib. de Exhortatione virginit., cap. 1 & 2.

* *Hist. Eccles. Francorum.* lib. ii. cap. xvii.; *Patrologia Lat.* t. lxxi. col. 215, cap. 36.

only reductions from mural paintings of a much earlier date, as some have held, still the correspondence of the subjects with the Manual would go far to showing that they both belong to an iconographical system that endured for many centuries.

The scheme in the Byzantine Manual in question commences with the Prologue in Heaven; the Assembly of the Heavenly Host and Fall of Lucifer.

Scenes 1-14. The Fall of Lucifer to the Murder of Abel.
Scenes 15-20. Life of Noah to the Sin of Ham.
Scenes 21 to 30. Life of Abraham to the Sacrifice of Isaac.
31-33. History of Jacob.
34-43. „ of Joseph.
44-59. „ of Moses.
60-62. „ of Joshua.
63. „ of Gideon.
64-70. „ of Samson.
71-75. History of Samuel.
76-81. „ of David.
82-84. „ of Solomon.
85-96. „ of Elijah.
97-103. „ of Elisha.
104-106. „ of Isaiah.
107-108. „ of Jeremiah.
109. First Capture of Jerusalem.
119. Life of Daniel.
123. „ of Jonas.
126. „ of Job.

Following these scenes are nine subjects illustrating the Patriarchs, Holy Women, Prophets and Philosophers of Greece, who were said to have declared the Mystery of the Incarnation of Christ.

Thus the " Wonders of the Ancient Law " are set forth in 136 scenes, to be followed by 151 scenes representing the Wonders of the Gospel; 76 relating the Life and Miracles of Christ; 35, the Passion of Christ; and 40, the Parables.

These 208 scenes are followed by three mystic subjects generally reserved for the cupolas of the Byzantine churches, those of the Divine Liturgy, the Communion of Christ's body and blood, the Communion of Spirits. They are followed by the Apocalypse, and Second Coming of Christ, and the Final Judgment.

In the 35 following scenes the feasts of the Blessed Virgin, and figures of the Apostles, Evangelists, Martyrs, Anchorites, Poets, Myrrhophoræ—are given with the subjects of the Exaltation of the Cross, the Œcumenical Councils, and Holy Images. In eight scenes more the Miracles of Michael, of John the Precursor, of Peter,

Paul, Nicolas, George, Catherine, and Anthony, are added. These are followed by the Calendar of the Year, and Allegories of the Life of the Monk, the Ladder of Salvation, the Death of the Hypocrite, the Death of the Sinner, and the Deceitfulness of Life.

And the work closes with directions as to how these subjects should be distributed on the walls and in the cupolas of the Byzantine churches.

In this Manual it is evident, as we have already observed, that the scenes from Biblical history were merely arranged in chronological order; that, in their selection, the primary object was historic and prophetic, and that the key to the arrangement and choice of subjects is found in the fulfilment of Old Testament prophecy in the historical events of the New. In the West the Christian painters in the Catacombs limited themselves to a smaller cycle of subjects, and, setting history and chronology aside, treated these subjects solely with reference to some hidden, moral, or devotional truth which they were known to signify. Thus the events recorded were turned to symbols; a system of such symbols was developed, which was expressive of the salient points in religion. A hieratic cycle of subjects came into use, not necessarily for doctrinal purposes, but as expressive of religious faith.

The cardinal points of the religion thus symbolised were the belief in the Eternity of Life and the miraculous power represented in the Sacraments which should transmute the Material and the Mortal to the Immaterial and the Immortal. Added to these were certain ethical ideas realised in the persons of the Christ as the Good Shepherd, of Daniel and the Children in the Furnace, and in the Call of the Magi. By arranging these symbols in the following order we arrive at the framework of the Christian scheme as first conceived in Western Christian Art:—

Immortality
- Baptism .. {Noah in the Ark. / Moses striking rock.}
- Lord's Supper . {Assembly at table. / Miracle of loaves and fishes. / Water changed to wine.}
- Resurrection . {Raising of Lazarus. / Deliverance of Jonah.}

Triumph over Suffering { Daniel in Lion's den.
Three children in furnace.
Call of the Gentiles { Call of the Magi.
The woman of Samaria.
Christ and the Church { Good Shepherd.
Orante.*

These subjects may still be seen repeated with little variety on the walls of the Catacombs of SS. Nereus and Achilles, St. Calixtus, St. Prætextatus, St. Priscilla, St. Agnes, St. Petrus, St. Marcellinus; and their symbolic meaning can be demonstrated by written tradition as well as supported by the testimony of contemporary monuments, by comparison of various paintings and other monuments one with another, as also with the language of the Hebrew Scripture and the holy Fathers.† St. Augustine, speaking of the interpretation of Scriptural figures, insists that when we find anything represented which does not correspond with the truth either of history or of nature, it must be taken to be a symbol, intended to suggest some further idea beyond itself.

It is on the walls of these catacombs that we are to seek the origins of Western Christian Art, and the first image-writing of our religion. These images are held to date from, or to have been copied from works of, the second to the eighth century. They closely resemble antique painting in form and mode of conception, and follow the heathen art of Rome gradually, as it degenerates into stiffness and want of form. The painting on the walls of Pagan buildings and tombs, as we learn from Maitland,‡ is subservient to decorative purposes, and the whole is subordinated to a particular colour on the walls. Landscapes, for instance, are painted brown on brown, green

* It is probable that the type so common in the Catacombs which has been named Orante—a figure standing upright with arms outspread—is of Eastern origin, and this seems borne out by the legend of the figure of a Madonna Orante sculptured in bas-relief at Santa Maria in Porto, Ravenna. This figure is said to have been miraculously transported from Greece into Italy at an early date, and the characters giving the Virgin's name as well as the whole style of the work leave no doubt as to the origin of this sculpture. It must have been carried into Ravenna from the East at the time of the Crusades.

† *Roma Sotteranea*, J. S. Northcote and W. R. Brownlow, part. ii. p. 48.

‡ *Church in the Catacombs*, C. Maitland, M.D., p. 156.

on green, and greenish white on a red wall. The olive alone retains a certain character, and where garlands and leaf-work appear as part of the decoration, only the most necessary part of the special form of the leaf is indicated with bold effect.

It appears desirable to enter into all these details if we would be in a position to form a fair judgment on the first images of Christian Art. The scheme to which they belong was, as it were, the nucleus from which the larger framework grew of such mediæval mystic poems as the *Speculum Humanæ Salvationis* and the *Biblia Pauperum*, and *Speculum Sanctæ Mariæ Virginis*, where we find, in addition to the primitive symbols of faith in the immortality of the soul and triumph over suffering, those of the worship of Mary, the divine strife with evil, transfiguration, penitence, and the adoration of the Cross.

The earliest image hitherto found of this last subject occurs upon a gem,* lately brought from Alexandria, of the purest lapis-lazuli, oval in form, with surface slightly convex—a woman kneeling in prayer and with both hands holding up a Latin cross, at which she gazes fervently. Behind her is the tree of life. "Much attention," writes Mr. King, "has been bestowed upon the head and features, the part of the composition always the first to fail in the works of the Decline."

Fig. 224.

The Mirror of human salvation is usually illustrated by one hundred and eight subjects, arranged in groups of four—three types to an antitype—or twenty-seven scenes from the life and passion of Christ, with eighty-one drawn from the Old Testament and heathen mythology. A certain chrono-

---

* See *Report Cambridge Antiquarian Society*, vol. v. No. 2, p. 75, 1884. "On two unpublished Christian Gem Types." Rev. C. W. King. The author of *Ecclesiasticus*, most probably a resident at Alexandria, speaks of the seal-cutter's art in the following passage: "Every craftsman and workmaster that labours night and day, he who hath graven seals, and by his continuous diligence varieth the figure: he shall give his mind to the resemblance of the picture, and by his watching shall finish the work ... Without these a city is not built." *Ecclesiasticus* xxxviii. 28, 36.

logical sequence is preserved in the events of our Lord's life, chosen for antitypes, which is quite absent in the selection of the types, the arrangement of which is entirely subservient to their moral significance and prophetic character. In the selection of these subjects the idea of presenting religion as a divine scheme is well thought out. The types of fallen, suffering, and redeemed humanity are pictures painted, as it were, on the background of the life of Christ, and the first scene in the drama, the type behind all types, is the Fall of Lucifer and the rebel angels; just as in Milton's poem the origin of evil is removed into the dim vista of pre-Adamite ages. The New Testament history supplies the main features of the plot to which the Old Testament events are merely subsidiary.

The first six scenes are devoted to the story of the miraculous conception and birth of Christ and the message to the Magi, proclaiming the breadth and universality of the scheme of redemption. Next comes the act in the Virgin's life that signifies her humility and obedience to law. In the scenes selected from the life of Christ after baptism, we have a sequence of symbolic acts that correspond with the phases through which the Christian soul passes in the warfare with evil, and the extension of its power, as one victory after another is gained, till life eternal is restored. Close following on the dedication of his life to His Father's cause * comes the divine strife of the moral and spiritual with the physical man; † and, consequent on the victory gained, is the power to bid the dead ‡ become a living soul—the power to transfigure the thought of death itself to joy.§ Penitence sits in peace at those feet she has bathed in her tears,‖ and the temple is cleansed.¶ These are the five acts into which the mission of Christ is condensed. Then the narrative is resumed; the passion, death, and resurrection—the conspiracy, betrayal, distrust, judgment, profanation, self-offering, sacrifice, and the

* The Baptism of Christ.
† The Temptation of Christ.
‡ The Raising of Lazarus.
§ The Transfiguration.
‖ Mary Magdalene at the feet of Christ.
¶ Christ driving out the money-changers from the temple.

198 CHRISTIAN ICONOGRAPHY.

Fig. 225

individual death by which is purchased the release of the human soul from hell and its restoration to eternal life. The spirit is caught up in the mantle of God, and the pure woman, into whose own soul also the sword had entered, is crowned by the Saviour's hand.

We have considered these facts in the life of Christ, which became the leading subjects in Christian Art, as a series of symbolic acts, the true intention and meaning of which is in many instances helped out and explained by the types chosen as their background—each group thus arranged in skeleton form, by the author of the text, to be hereafter thought out and worked out by the painter who has to handle it. These selected scenes became the special themes of mediæval dramatists and painters, and in cases where a question may arise at the present day as to the significance of a particular subject or symbol in Christian Art, a clue to its solution may often be found by reference to the types in the *Biblia Pauperum*, and the text that accompanies these types. Thus it has been asked of the crown of thorns, Was it significant of physical torture, or was it placed in mere mockery upon the sacred head? Had it been the former, then some instance of violence would have formed the type for this subject which is the antitype; but, on the contrary, the types chosen are cases of mockery and profanity, the sin of Ham, and the mockery of the prophet Elisha by the children. It is true that no more forcible types of torture could be found than that of a father profaned, or the hate of a child, but it is moral, not physical torture. Again, in the Descent of Christ into Hell, the moral significance of the subject is only pointed out by the types. (Fig. 225.) The spirits that await the Christ are in the jaws of Death. The Saviour, bearing His bannered cross with one hand, lifts them upwards with the other. Death is represented as a monster with a lion's head. The type to the right is Samson struggling with the Lion, that to the left, David slaying Goliath—subjects signifying the redemption of Israel, often used as types of Christ's victory over Satan in the Temptation, and His final conquest in death. Here, then, the moral significance of the subject is indicated by the types chosen, which correspond to those tales of heathen mythologies of the wars and wrestlings of man with animals real or imaginary, signifying the strife of mind with brute force, of good and evil, of moral life and moral death—the divine strife, which, once seen in a human face, once read in a human heart, is the revelation of all that is deepest in human nature. Here the author points to the event upon the cross as the climax of this divine strife, the crucial test, as it is also the pledge of the soul's divinity, the evidence of divine grace that gives warrant of immortality.*

The coincidence of the types in the background of the Temptation of Christ and those of the Descent into Hell is a remarkable feature in these works. In the first, the types are Daniel and the Dragon, David and Goliath, Theseus and the Minotaur. In the second, Samson and the Lion, Banaias and the Lion, David and Goliath. In this we are reminded of Milton's selection of the Temptation rather than the Crucifixion as the climax of his great poem—the event which marked *the* victory and death, of which the physical death on the cross was the final symbol. In the Angels' Anthem at the close of Milton's poem we find the clue to this poet's Paradise Lost and Regained.

---

* These mystic and ascetic poems seem to be drawn from the Bible Historiale and *livres de clergie*, *i.e.* science, of the middle ages, which formed a class of sacred and doctrinal encyclopædias. A few words on the bibliography of these texts must be added here to show their claim to be considered as the foundation of the mediæval Christian drama. The text of the Mirror of Human Salvation is a poem of much greater length than that of the *Biblia Pauperum*.

Brunet, speaking of the *Speculum Hum. Sal.*, says, " Poème ascétique, en vers rimés, d'une latinité barbare, sur les sujets bibliques. *Plusieurs MSS. portent la date de* 1324, qui est peut-être aussi celle de la composition de l'ouvrage lequel, dans les manuscrits cités, est divisé en 45 chapitres et orné de 192 figures. *Manuel du Libraire*, tom. 5me, 1re partie, Paris, 1863.

Three MSS. of the *Speculum* are preserved in the library of Vienna, held by M. Denis to belong to the fourteenth century. See Denis, *Codices Manuscripti Theologici Bibliothecæ Palatinæ Vindobonenses*, col. 439, 2218, 2322. Vindobonae, 1793–95. In fol.

The British Museum possesses four MSS. of the *Speculum*, 1st, Vesp. E. 1, Cotton; 2nd, Arundel, No. 120; 3rd, Harleian, No. 26; 4th, No. 16,578 Add. MSS.

... "Now thou hast avenged
Supplanted Adam, and, by vanquishing
Temptation, hast regained lost Paradise,
And frustrated the conquest fraudulent.
He never more henceforth will dare set foot
In Paradise to tempt; his snares are broke.
For, though that seat of earthly bliss be failed,
A fairer Paradise is founded now
For Adam and his chosen sons, whom thou,
A Saviour, art come down to reinstal:
Where they shall dwell secure, when time shall be,
Of tempter and temptation without fear.

*   *   *   *

Thus they the Son of God, our Saviour meek,
Sung victor, and, from heavenly feast refresh'd,
Brought on his way with joy. He, unobserved,
Home to his mother's house private returned."

The correspondence of these Christian types with heathen is curiously illustrated by a gem and coin, the one representing Christ, the other, a tetradrachm, Hercules struggling with a human-headed serpent (Fig. 227-8). In the first, Christ, as the Good Shepherd, is about to bruise

Fig. 226.

the serpent's head with a staff, tipped with the sacred monogram. In the second, Hercules firmly plants his foot on the human-headed hydra's tail, just as Christ does on the serpent's, which curls up into the field behind him and terminates as a barbed arrow-head.* See Fig. 228.

* See Report of Cambridge Antiquarian Society, vol. v. No. 2, p. 82:
"On two unpublished Christian Gem-types." Rev. C. W. King, M.A.

The text of the *Biblia Pauperum** consists of passages in prose and verse, with quotations from the prophets and psalmists relating to the types and antitypes of Holy Scripture represented in each triptych. A Leonine verse †

Fig. 227-8.

accompanies each picture. The author who conceived this book and wrote these verses is unknown, although St. Ansgar, the Apostle of the North, is believed by many to have originated it.‡ He was a monk in the monastery

* The text of the *Biblia Pauperum* was copied, and the scenes drawn therein were represented on the convent windows of Hirschau A.D. 1085, when the new cloister with its forty windows was erected. In the year 1180, a manuscript of the *Biblia Pauperum* was extant in the Convent of Tegernsee illustrated with figures drawn by the hand of some unknown artist. Another manuscript is referred to by C. B. J. Hugo, the keeper of the library of Wolfenbüttel :—" Certum hic liber qui dudum ante invek tam typographiam in MS. extitit, olim appellabatur *Biblia Pauperum* ut constat e codice seculi xii. vel xiii., sed 38 modo figuras continenti, bibliothecæ Guelpherbitanæ."

It is certain that this book, which appeared in MS. long before the invention of printing, was formerly called *Biblia Pauperum*, as it consists of a codex of the twelfth or thirteenth century, but containing only 38 figures, in the library of Wolfenbüttel.

† A measure much used by writers in the middle ages. It consists of a Latin hexameter, of which the last foot rhymes with the end of the first hemistich.

‡ In an old copy of the xylographic *Biblia Pauperum* at Florence, there is a Latin entry to the effect that St. Ansgar wrote this book for the conversion of pagans, and that it was entirely composed of signs. The first manuscript copy of which there is any authentic description was written in the old Saxon-Danish tongue. Bircherodius had seen a part of this MS. and thus describes it : " I was recently told that a certain man living in the country had a refectory hung with elegantly figured parchments. I sent thither and obtained the same to the number of eleven and in the form of full folio. The leaves were adorned on each side with figures satisfactorily large, and most beautiful Bible stories in all colours in every page, types from the Old Testament of several subjects, with the antitypes out of the New, and the prophecies relating to them : in this order, above are seen two, and below also are two prophets of the Old

of Corbey in Germany, born A.D. 801, who, in the reign of the emperor Louis the Pious was sent on a mission to the Danes.

The texts referred to accompany the drawings of the subjects, which are arranged in three compartments on each page, the pictures being set in an architectural framework. The subject taken from the Life of Christ, i.e. the antitype, being in the centre, the types from the Old Testament are placed at each side, with two figures of prophets and psalmists above and below. The Leonine verses on scrolls winding through the composition explain the subjects. The architectural disposition of the triptych containing these designs suggests the idea that they were intended for pattern books for the painters of church windows or decorators of cloistered walls. When Ugolino da Sienna and Pisano worked in the Duomo d'Orvieto it is very plain that they followed the general plan laid out for them in some such works, as well as did the sculptors in San Miniato in Florence, and Santa Maria, a small and now disused basilica erected in the sixth century at Toscanella, N.W. of Rome.

Manuscript copies with original paintings in miniature f these two works—the *Bible of the Poor*, and the *Mirror*

Testament, as it were in converse one with another, painted uncommonly well, and showing their prophecies one to another.

"At the sides of these are seen pairs of stories of the Old Testament written beautifully and accurately in the ancient Saxon-Danish tongue, with a picture of the same portrayed in vivid and pleasing colours, and in the middle of the page is seen a certain story of the New Testament, or the antitype of the rest, depicted with no slight skill; *e.g.* one page has, above, David and Isaiah, below Job and Anna showing each to the other by turns their sayings or prophecies concerning the resurrection of the dead; on the right side is the story of the dead boy raised to life by Elijah, written down as elegantly as it is painted; on the left the story of the boy restored to life by Elisha is represented as well by letters (i.e. in writing) as in pleasing colours. In the middle of the page Christ calling forth Lazarus from the dead, with a crowd of men and women standing round, is set forth with like skill. So another page treats of the remission of sins, with the most beautiful figures of Nathan absolving David from his sin, of Moses absolving Miriam, and of Christ absolving Mary Magdalene, with written stories subjoined." *De Deperditis Septentrionalium Antiquitatibus et maxime Gotho-cimbricis.* See Westphalen, *Monum. inedit. rerum Germanicarum.* Folio. Lipsiæ, 1739, tom. iii. p. 698. See Fiorillo, *Geschichte der Zeichnenden Künste in Deutschland*, Hanover, 1815, 8vo. Meerman, *Origines Typographicæ*, Hagæ Comit. 1765, 4to.

of Human Salvation—are extremely rare. Of the first, one beautiful example, with miniatures of the early Dutch school, is preserved in the British Museum, King's MS. 5. A. 1, d. 12.

Two Italian manuscripts of the *Mirror* with miniature paintings of the school of Giotto may be seen in Paris. The first, which dates circ. 1300, is preserved in Paris in the Bibliothèque Nationale, Suppl. Lat. 9584. Examples of the miniatures in this MS. have appeared in the present work. The Christ in an elliptical aureole;* God the Father;† Jesus‡ showing his wounds to the Father.

The second, equally beautiful if not more so, is also in Paris in the Bibliothèque de l'Arsenal (*Theol.* Lat. 593); it contains 150 miniatures and 590 figures. Two illustrations from this work appear in the preceding pages, one being a portion of the painting of the Fall of Lucifer, the other a scene in the Temptation of our Lord, where the Devil appears in the garb of a professor (Fig. 178 *supra*). This manuscript bears the date 1324, and the miniatures, two of which appear at the head of each page, have been attributed to Taddeo Gaddi by some, and to Giotto by others. We translate the passage at the opening of this book :—

" Here begins the proem of a certain new compilation brought out in the year of the Lord 1324, but the author is in humility silent as to his name. The title or name of the work is *Speculum Humanæ Salvationis*." § Then follows an epitome of the contents, in which we noticed one curious error. In place of " Jephtha sacrifices his daughter," we read, " Joseph sacrifices his son," fol. 7 verso. at fol. 8 verso. Type 3 has been erased, and a different subject, painted in a very inferior manner, inserted. The MS.‖ is a small folio, of forty-two folios of two columns in

---

* Vol. i. p. 24, fig. 2.   † *Ib.* p. 64, fig. 42.   ‡ *Ib.* p. 304, fig. 79.

§ " Incipit phemium cui°dam nove 3pilationis edite s͡b anno d͠ni mcccxxiv., no͞m uó autoris hūilitate sil̄etur. S꜀ titulus siue no͞m opis est Speculm̄ hūmane saluationis." Renouvier has copied the first lines of this Italian manuscript very well. See *Hist. de l'origine de la Gravure dans les Pays-bas et en Allemande*, p. 88, *n.* 2. A second *Speculum Humanæ Salvationis* is preserved in the Bibliothèque de l'Arsenal, No. 40, but this is only copied by hand from a block book.

‖ " Le plus ancien MS. que j'ai vu," says Heineken, "me paroit être du douzième siècle." This, with two other MSS. of the *Speculum*, is preserved

vellum, two miniatures at the head of each page, so that, as the volume lies open, four scriptural subjects are displayed, the first being the antitype, the following three the types. In *Les Arts Somptuaires* of Louandre and Seré, coloured drawings on an enlarged scale are given from three of these miniatures. The first is one of the types for the adoration of the three Kings—the three warriors bringing the water of the cistern to David.* Here one figure is clothed in complete armour of wrought iron, while the other two warriors are clothed in mail covered by a tight jerkin; the water-vases, as well as the steel helmet with broad leaf, are peculiar to Italy. The next subject copied by Louandre is the chastisement of Heliodorus, one of the types of Christ driving out the money-changers from the temple. Heliodorus, who is being flogged with a whip of three knotted lashes, lies prostrate on the ground. The angels sent to execute his punishment are represented as wingless and in merely human forms: one wears a Tuscan head-dress. The next subject is the escape of Lot and his family from Sodom, one of the three types of the release of the souls from Hell. The two girls walk with virginal serenity by the side of their aged father; their character, added to that of severe majesty in the angel behind, certainly recalls the mural paintings of Giotto. Everything tends to confirm the belief that in these miniatures we have examples of the most beautiful thirteenth or fourteenth century art of Italy, the same elegance and simplicity of outline, the same profound yet *naif* sentiment, and we may well be correct in our supposition that these beautiful compositions are from the hand of Giotto, b. 1276, d. 1337, or Taddeo Gaddi, b. 1300, d. 1366.

Thus far we have dealt with the authorship of these texts, it now remains to be seen to what schools the miniature paintings (varying in number from 100 to 160) which illustrate them may be attributed; and this

---

in the Vienna library. See M. Denis, *Codices Manuscripti Theologici Bibliothecæ Palatinæ Vindobonensis*, coll. 439, 2218, 2322; Vindobonæ, 1793-95, in fol. Four MSS. of the *Speculum* are preserved in the British Museum, one of which, written in 1370 by Conradus de Alzeya, has been published by M. Berjeau.

* 1 Chron. xi. 15. This subject has been misnamed Esther Enthroned.

question is of no little weight in the history of Christian iconography, when we reflect that these books were followed in the mural paintings, the stained glass windows, the sculpture and the religious drama of the Middle Ages. The natural result of adherence to such a system of illustration as this laid down in the *Speculum* was the development of certain established symbols, sacred types of phases in the history of the moral strife and victory of humanity, of the mysteries of birth and death, and of the fall and redemption of man. For they offered a series of scenes from the history of the Jews as a nation, such as should serve as examples to mankind as individuals; these types all finding their fulfilment in the person of Christ, all again to be reflected in the spiritual experiences of each and all of His followers. Yet, while in these books we have scriptural subjects, thus selected and grouped according to a certain preconceived plan, yet the treatment of such was left to the knowledge and individual power of the painter. There is much evidence of the fact that it was owing to the number and variety of such books that Italy and France succeeded in shaking themselves free of the paralysing traditions of Byzantinism and developing what of original thought lay in the mind of the artist, who we may imagine could with comparative freedom best work out his own conceptions at first in the quiet of his chamber and at his desk.*

In France, as in Italy, mural painters sought in manuscript miniatures for their designs.† In Pisa, whence the

* The art of miniature painting was practised at a very early period in Italy, as we know from the beautiful examples of the third and fourth century in the Vatican Virgil. It was especially encouraged by the Carlovingian emperors,* and also much cultivated in Paris before the thirteenth century, as we know from Dante, "quell' arte ch' alluminare è chiamata in Parisi." (*Purg.* c. xi. 81.) Indeed, the French excel the Italian miniaturists as colourists.

† Jean Costa in France was favourite painter of King John. He began to work in 1349. He worked alone, leaving nothing to his pupils. He sought in manuscript miniatures for models for his mural paintings. Miniatures were too often taken as models by mural painters, hence a dryness and minute detail in these life-size subjects which should only characterise miniatures. France was especially the home of miniature painting. Dante

* Kugler, *Handbook*, p. 20, refers to the Bible of St. Paolo fuori le mure, preserved in San Calisto in Trastevere See D'Agincourt, *Peinture*, pp. 40–45.

art spread over Tuscany, were miniature painters, who, "transferring their art from small to large works," like Franco of Bologna, "betook themselves to painting on walls and panels" (see Lanzi, *Painting in Italy*, vol. i. p. 37, ed. Bohn). This Franco, founder of the Bolognese school, was himself the pupil of the miniature painter Oderigi of Gubbio, who worked long at Bologna. He whom Dante hails in *Purgatory:*—

"'Art thou not Oderigi? Art not thou
Agobbio's glory, glory of that art
Which they of Paris call the limner's skill?
'Brother!' said he, 'with tints, that gayer smile,
Bolognian Franco's pencil lines the leaves.'"

Some Italian schools took their origin, without any Byzantine aid or example, from such miniature painters, who in the twelfth century formed a very distinct class. Treviso and other minor cities gave birth to a style which may be termed national, and which owed much of its originality to the miniature painters who improved their talent by drawing from the life and not from any Greek or Italian master, whether Panselinos or Giotto. To this class belong M. Paolo,* the earliest painter in this national manner, circ. 1300. Giotto† himself was a miniature painter

---

makes illumination an entirely Parisian art. However, there is very noble design in some Italian illuminated books. It is probable that Dante was familiar with some such text as that of the *Biblia Pauperum*, since in the series of sculptures described by him among the bas-relief on the second cornice of Purgatory were the subjects forming part of that series. The Annunciation, The Ark drawn to the house of Obed-edom, David dancing before the Ark, Michal deriding David, which he tells us were

"so exactly wrought
With quaintest sculpture, that not there alone
Had Polycletus, but e'en nature's self
Been shamed."

* A record of this painter exists in a parchment dated 1346, and examples of his work may be seen on the front of the great altar of St. Mark's and in the Sacristy of the Padri Conventuali at Vicenza, dated 1333. See Lanzi, vol. ii. p. 77.

† Giotto began by studying the art *di minio*, i.e. the art of painting with a peculiar red colour early applied to the ornamenting and illuminating of MSS., hence the derivation of the word miniature, and one of the minor peculiarities which differentiates his work from that of the Byzantine schools is the adoption of this delicate pale red in place of the darker tints of the former school.

who gave a great impetus to his art as well as Taddeo Gaddi, after whose death the fraternity of the Camaldulites furnished some remarkable miniaturists such as D. Silvestro. But it was in Mantua* that this method reached its highest perfection, and in the school of Giulio Romano where Clovio was trained and whence the art spread throughout Lombardy.

Among the artists of Italy who imitated or copied the subjects in the *Speculum Humanæ Salvationis* are Ugolino di Prete Ilario, G. Pisano, Orcagna, and Taddeo Gaddi.†

The frescoes of the Capello del Corporale at Orvieto and some scenes painted on the wall of the tribune in the same cathedral, the bas-reliefs of Giovanni Pisano, framed in by Tuscan pillars like those that enclose the subjects in the *Biblia Pauperum*, all correspond with these books of types and antitypes. They were probably begun in 1290. The story of the Creation, the Fall and Expulsion, the fratricide of Cain, are ably told and well contrasted with the scenes of Mercy and of Judgment in the new. Our Lord is seen attended by two angels throughout the work of Creation, and their floating attitudes may have suggested to Ghiberti his exquisite amplification of this idea on one of the Gates of the Florence Baptistery.‡

A volume containing a hundred miniatures, examples of Italian Art in the thirteenth century, was secured some years ago by the late Sir William Boxall, who presented it to Lord Coleridge. This is a fragment of an original copy of the *Speculum Sancte Marie Virginis* and *Speculum Humanæ Salvationis*, the text of which was written by Joannes Andreas de Bologna (circ. 1270–1348). The miniatures appear to belong to the same early date, and their origin may perhaps be traced to some painter of the school of Siena.

In Germany the number of artists whose names are said to be connected with the *Speculum* and *Biblia*

---

* See the Anthem Book preserved at S. Benedetto in Mantua, one of the most ancient remains of this art existing.

† See in the Sacristy of the Vatican the representation in miniature of the Acts of St. Peter and St. Paul, with some representations of the lives of our Saviour and various saints.

‡ Lord Lindsay, vol. ii. p. 121.

Pauperum are very numerous: Van Liesborn, Quentin Matsys, Lucas van Leyden, Joachim Patenier, Albert Dürer, Hans Schæuffelein, Joh. Memlinc, Martin Schoen. The Annunciation painted in 1465 for Liesborn, the former convent near Münster, the Presentation in the Temple, and the Virgin and Child accompanied by seven figures of mystic meaning from the Old Testament, may be seen in an altar-piece painted by Quentin Matsys for the church of S. Donatus at Bruges; the Crucifixion by Cornelius Engelbrechtsen of Leyden, flanked by the Sacrifice of Isaac and the uplifting of the Brazen Serpent; the Tree of Jesse below. The subject most frequently copied is that of Christ on the Judgment Day, seated on a rainbow, His feet resting on the globe, a sword and lily at either side of His head, and the graves below giving up their dead. In a triptych of Lucas van Leyden some of the subjects of the Passion are treated as in the block book *Biblia Pauperum*. Albert Dürer in his treatment of the Ascension, the Entry into Jerusalem, and Apotheosis of Christ, followed the same work.[*]

The Duomo of Orvieto, circ. 1300, with its ornamented gables, windows divided by a single pillar, reminds us of the framework of the *Biblia Pauperum*. The Coronation of the Virgin, the Creation of Eve, &c., seem as if derived from the same origin as the windows of Hirschau Abbey in the Black Forest, painted in the year 1085, after tho subjects in the *Biblia Pauperum*.

Another class of miniature painting besides that on vellum are such Byzantine miniatures on wood as may be seen in numbers in the Vatican museum; the subjects generally resemble those in mosaic and mural painting. We see there a subject exactly corresponding to the fresco in the Pisan Campo Santo, illustrating the ascetic life in the desert, aged men seated in mountain caves, some reading, some plaiting straw for baskets. At one side the death of St. Ephraim and his soul borne aloft by an angel—at the other St. Simeon Stylites. Emmanuel Tyanfurnari was the author of this painting, and there is

---

[*] The Passion of Christ, with types of the successive scenes, is shown in the painted windows of Bourges Cathedral. Also the Resurrection of our Lord, with Elisha raising the widow's child, and the Lion-cub legend, which latter also occurs at Tours as type of the Resurrection.

210   CHRISTIAN ICONOGRAPHY.

a tradition that the work was brought into Italy by
Squarcione, master of Mantegna.

In all such works we still find evidence of the double
current flowing through art, the feeling for the antique
side by side with the ascetic type; and in these manuals and
texts we have been dealing with it is interesting to find
many types of events in the Christian life drawn from
Classic and Pagan mythologies. On this subject we hope
to enlarge in the following chapter.

Fig. 229.—DANIEL AMONG LIONS; HABAKKUK AND THE ANGEL.

MYTHOLOGICAL LEGENDS IN THE SPECULUM HUMANÆ SALVATIONIS.

WE find that nine legends from Pagan mythology have been included in the Mirror of Human Salvation as types for events in the life of Christ and of the Virgin.

1. The myth of Cyrus and the vision of his grandfather Astyages before his birth, became a type of the prediction of the Virgin's birth to Joachim. The king dreams that he sees a vine rise from his daughter's womb and grow into a great tree that overshadowed the earth, and learns from his interpreter that this foreshadows that the babe to be born of Mandane will reign in his stead.

2. The legend of the offering of the golden table in the temple of the sun-god is taken as a type of the Presentation of the Virgin in the temple. The story is as follows: Three fishers threw their net into the sea in the hope of catching fish, but when they drew in the net again they found, intead of fish, a golden table of wondrous beauty and splendour. Close by the sea-shore stood a temple built by the neighbouring people in honour of the sun whom they worshipped as a god, and the fishermen brought their table here and offered it to the sun-god, so that it has since been called of all people the Table of the kingdom of the sun. The author of the *Bible Historiée* adds that this table of the sun-god (on which the image of the sun-god stood in the temple) prefigures the Virgin Mary, on whom the God of Paradise descended: but the golden table was offered in the temple of a corruptible sun, Mary in an incorruptible; and while food for man's body was held by the one, so the bread of life was laid upon the other.

3. Another type of the Virgin and her presentation in

P 2

the temple is found in the person of Semiramis. In the myth of this Queen of the East we have many of the same elements as occur in the story of Cyrus, which we have had already as a type of the Nativity of Christ, and which these tales again have in common with the legends of Romulus, Oidipous, Telephos, and others. Like them, she is exposed in her infancy, saved by doves, and brought up by a shepherd. "Semiramis is simply," writes Mr. Cox,* "the Dawn Goddess, the daughter of the Fish-god Derketo, the lover of Tammuz, the counterpart of Aphroditê with the boy Adonis. Semiramis is sometimes replaced by Esther in later copies of the *Spec. Hum. Sal.* Both were patriot queens—the one built numerous cities and wonderful temples, such as the great tomb of Ninus, her husband, and she planned the hanging gardens of her people's city, on the highest point of which she is often represented as standing, by the oldest miniature painters."†

4. The Sibyl showing Augustus a vision of the Virgin with infant Christ is the third figure for the Nativity following on the vision of Pharaoh's cup-bearer and the blossoming of Aaron's rod.‡ The legend is already so familiar to the readers of Mrs. Jameson and Lady Eastlake's *History of Our Lord in Art*, that it is unnecessary to repeat it now.

5. The subject of the child Moses breaking Pharaoh's crown, or, as it has been sometimes called, "Moses' Choice,"§ forms one of the three figures that accompany the Sojourn of Christ in Egypt. The legend appears in Bartolocci, *Biblioth. Magna Rabbinica*, pt. iv. p. 115, and is as follows :—

"It is related in Medrasc that Moses, whom, when he was three years old, Bathiah, the daughter of Pharaoh, had taken from among the rushes, in the presence of Pharaoh and the Magi, took the crown from Pharaoh's head and

---

* See Cox, *Aryan Myth.*, i. 223, note, ii. 84; *Dictionary of Literature, Science, and Art*, s. v. (Brande and Cox).

† Mr. Sayce observes in a note to the editor, "It is very curious to find Semiramis representing the Virgin. In the Pseudo-Lucian's treatise *De Dea Syria*, Semiramis is given as the name of the Syrian Venus worshipped in the great temple of Hierapolis (the town which succeeded to Carchemish)."

‡ See *Mirabilia Romæ*. Scholastic History.

§ Moses' Choice is the subject of a fine painting by Giorgione in the Uffizi.

placed it upon his own head, and all wondered, but Pharaoh feared. Balaam his Councillor gave this counsel to Pharaoh—that Moses should be slain. And [it is related] that God sent the angel Gabriel in the likeness of one of the Magi of Pharaoh, and he gave him the counsel that two vessels should be brought; in one vessel should be placed *Daisies*, and in a second live burning coals, and both should be shown to the boy; but if the boy should take from the *Daisies*, it would be a sign that he had done this thing with intent and out of malice, and so the boy should be guilty of death; but if he should stretch out his hand to the burning coals, it would be a sign that this thing had been done not with design and with intent, and so the boy should be free. And so it was done. However the angel saw them, but they did not see the angel; and he raised the hand of Moses, and he took the burning coal, and he put it to his mouth, and the edge of his lips was burnt, and Moses became stammering and slow of speech, and he went out free."

We find a slightly different version of this tale in the *Bible Historiée*. "The daughter of Pharaoh brought the child Moses to a feast before her father, who, when he saw the beauty of the child, placed his crown upon his head, in which crown was fixed an image of the idol Haman. And when Moses had the crown upon his head, he took it and threw it so rudely on the ground, that both the crown and the idol were broken. Then the high priest who was present said that it was he by whom the kingdom of Egypt should be destroyed, and that he must die. But another answered that he had done it through childishness, and he brought red charcoal and placed them before the child, and Moses took one up burning and put it in his mouth, and it burned him so that he cried. Therefore he escaped from death. Herein is a figure of Christ; for as Moses was born for the deliverance of Israel, so Christ was born to deliver us from Satan; as Moses broke one idol, so Christ broke all idols; and as Moses escaped while all the other infants of Israel were destroyed by Pharaoh, so the infant Christ was saved from Herod."

6. Two of the figures which accompany the subject of the Flight into Egypt are mythological, but the first is

chosen from Christian mythology, being the Fall of the Egyptian Idols before the child Christ; the legend is given in the apocryphal gospels of the Infancy of Christ. "And they came into the borders of Hermopolis and entered into a certain city of Egypt, which is called Sotinen; and because there was no one known in it from whom they could have requested hospitality, they went into a temple which was called the Capitol of Egypt, in which temple three hundred and fifty-five idols were placed, to which the honour of Deity was rendered in sacrilegious rites. Now it came to pass that when the most blessed Mary, with her little Infant had entered the temple, all the idols were prostrate on the earth, so that they all lay upon their faces wholly shattered and broken, and so they showed evidently that they were nothing. Then was fulfilled what was spoken by the prophet Isaiah: Behold the Lord shall come upon a light cloud, and shall enter Egypt, and all the handiworks of the Egyptians shall be moved at his presence (Isa. xix. 1)."*

7. The voluntary sacrifice of Codrus, king of Athens, is one of the three types of the Crucifixion of Christ. It is a tradition connected with the expedition of the Peloponnesians against Athens after the conquest of Peloponnesus by the Dorians. When the good king saw his city surrounded by the enemy, he took counsel of the god Apollo as to how his city might be saved, and the answer given by the oracle was that he, the king, must die for the city. This he resolved to do, and he rode forth alone so that the enemy might see him and slay him. But the Dorians had heard of the oracle, and knew that if they slew the king, the city would be lost to them. Therefore they allowed Codrus to pass on and return through the gates unhurt. Then Codrus divested himself of his kingly garments, and put on poor and vile clothing. He then issued forth from the city again, and his enemies, not recognising the king, thus disguised as a beggar, attacked and slew him before the city walls.†

* See *Gospel of the Infancy*, cap. 10 ; *Codex Apocr. N. Test.* tom. i. p. 75; also *Apocryphal Gospels*, B. H. Cooper, p. 63, 15th ed.

† See Pausanias, vii. 25, English translation, ed. 1794, vol. ii. 366, chap. lii., vol. iv. 5, chap. lvii. 2; see Lycophr. 1388, and Tzetzes' note; Herod. v. 76; Leoc. 20, sect;. 194, 196; Vell. Pat, i. 2; Justin, lib. ii 5, &c.; Strab. xiv. p. 633.

LEGEND OF THE OSTRICH. 215

8. One of the types for Christ in Hades is the myth of the ostrich who delivers her young one imprisoned in a vase.* This is represented in early art by an ostrich which stands

Fig. 230.

with a worm in its mouth by the side of a high glass vessel, in which the young bird is imprisoned. The legend is thus given by Petrus Comestor :—

* See *Bible Historiée* ; Petr. Comestor, *Hist. Schol.* lib. Regum iii. cap. 8 ; Baring-Gould, *Curious Myths*, second series; Cox, *Aryan Mythology*, vol. i. p. 216.

"The Jews said that for the purpose of cutting stones more quickly, Solomon had the blood of a worm called tamir, by which marble was easily split by sprinkling, which he discovered after this manner: Solomon had an ostrich with a chick, which the King had shut up in a glass vessel. When the ostrich saw it, but could not get at it, she brought from the desert a worm, with whose blood she smeared the vessel, and it broke."

Mr. Cox classes this legend with similar stories of swans and eagles which carry stones capable of splitting the hardest substance—all of which he holds to symbolise the cloud charged with lightning till the moment to use the mighty weapon comes. "Finally," he says, "the stone becomes a worm, and thus we have the framework of a large family of stories, which, if they have their origin among Aryan tribes, have been extended far beyond the limits of that race. In all the Hebrew versions of this legend the cloud is a bird, the lightning either a stone or a worm. Thus Benaiah, the son of Jehoiada, discovers the wonder-working pebble Schamir, by watching a moor-hen, which, finding a piece of glass laid over her nest, flies away, and, fetching a worm, splits the cover; or Solomon obtains it in the form of a stone from the raven, of which he has been informed by the demon Sackar.

In similar stories told by Ælian and Pliny of the wood-pecker or the hoopoe, the instrument by which the bird gets at her young is a grass; and thus we reach the family of plants, whose power of splitting rocks has won for them the name of Saxifrage * or Sassafras. This grass or plant will either reveal treasures, as they are revealed by the blinding glare of the electric fluid, or it will restore life, as lightning in splitting a rock sets free the waters on a parched-up soil.

Following Baring-Gould, we find this worm in his chapter on Schamir is a talisman, that in the legends of some countries is represented as about the size of a barley-corn; and as entrusted to the keeping of a moor-hen or a sea-god. The bird may also be a raven, an eagle, a hoopoe (the woodpecker of the Greeks), a swallow, or an

* Saxifrage : Isaiah vii. 2, 3; ix. 17; x. 17; xxxii. 13. The spell at sound of which the doors of Aladdin's cave fly open. *Sesamum Orientale*, an Eastern plant. "Open Sesame."

ostrich. But among some nations this talismanic power is said to lie not in the worm but in a stone. In Normandy we find a legend of this stone as in the keeping of a swallow. In Iceland it is a pebble kept by a raven. In all cases it is a talisman bringing deliverance from death and imprisonment. Occasionally we meet it as a red flower, *Lactua agrestis*, purple stained, and then it is the blue "Forget-me-not."

9. The legend of the vengeance of Queen Tomyris on the dead body of Cyrus is one of the three types for the subject of the Virgin Mary when she quells Satan by holding before him the emblems of the Passion. Judith and Jael are the other two types. The author of the *Speculum* has probably taken the story from Justin, who quotes from Herodotus. This is one of the subjects wrought on Dante's pavement in Purgatory.*

"Where is shown the scath and cruel mangling made
By Tomyris on Cyrus, when she cried,
'Blood thou didst thirst for: take thy fill of blood.'"

Herodotus (Book i. cap. 214), Justin (Book i. cap. 8), and Valerius Maximus (Book ix. cap. 10), said that Cyrus met his death in a battle against the Massagetæ. According to Herodotus, Tomyris their queen, having beheaded him, plunged the head in a skin filled with blood, saying: "Though living and victorious, thou hast lost me in destroying my son, who has fallen into thy snares; but I will satiate thee with blood as I have threatened thee."†

10. The last purely legendary incident in the subsidiary pictures of the *Speculum Humanæ Salvationis* is that of the footprints of Christ on the Mount of Olives. When Christ ascended it was held that the prints of His sacred feet remained upon the rock on which He was last seen to stand. "A similar form of relic worship," writes Mr. King, "manifests itself in the very metropolis of Christianity; for the prints of Christ's feet on a slab of basalt, a paving-stone of the Via Appia, have been worshipped from time immemorial in the church of Domine quo vadis, built over

* See Dante, translated by H. T. Cary. *Purg.* c. xii. l. 51.
† See Herod., bk. i. Clio. Cox, *Myth. Aryan Nations*, vol. i. pp. 260, 309 · vol. ii. pp. 74, 83.

the consecrated spot."* Moor notices the existence of the impressions of a pair of feet cut upon a flat stone about many Hindoo temples, and the tradition that they commemorated Satís, marking the place whence the widow stepped from earth upon the funeral pile, or into the gate of Heaven.

This custom bears upon the Buddhist veneration for the print of Adam's foot upon the summit of the peak called after him in Ceylon, held by the Mahommedans to be the footprints of Adam. "In the Christian period of Egypt," writes Mr. Sayce,† "pilgrims in Upper Egypt used to cut representations of their feet on stones of the old temples which had been converted into Christian shrines."

We have already shown that the miniature paintings illustrating these Italian Mirrors of Salvation and of the Holy Virgin, are characterised by the same simplicity an human interest which distinguish the mural painting c the school of Giotto. Touches of nature appear in these works, indicating the awakening of human and kindly sympathies, through the influence of which Western Art freed itself at last from the trammels of Byzantinism. The slavish adherence of the later Greek Church painters to the methods laid down in their Manual, resulted in a stony stiffening of forms which were only copies fr m copies, and faces whose original wistful sadness was replaced in the copyist's hands for a vacant stare. The system of the thirteenth century in Italy led to very different results, for, while it still prescribed the choice and grouping of subjects, so as to subserve to a great religious dramatic scheme, yet it left the artist free to turn to nature for his models. And, only intent on the moral significance of the sacred story he was to relate, he sought for his models and backgrounds amid the daily life and scenery of his own home, just as he found the inner realities he was to symbolize by introspection of his own means, an introspection which it is the peculiarity of the artistic nature to indulge in, even in moments of all bu the most disturbing passion, and to draw thence material for art.‡ So it was the habit with our old English poets

* See King, *Gnostics and their Remains*, p. 159.
† In a letter to the Editor.
‡ These remarks, as I learn from my friend Dr. Waldstein, may als apply to the days of great art in Greece. There the heroes of Homer as

also, who were not at pains to associate the scenes and acts of Christ's life solely with the hills and trees of Palestine, but sought to bring home His passion, strife, and victory to the very walls of their old towns, or by their shores and river-banks, amid the primroses and hawthorns of their own island.

Thus in his opening scene of Christ's Temptation, Giles Fletcher shows us the Prince of Peace when found by the demon in the wilderness:

> "Upon a grassie hillock he was laid
> With woodie primroses befreckelled.

In the same poem we find it is the hawthorn that is pulled in honour, and afterwards plaited in *dis*honour, of the Sacred Head:

> "It was but now they gathered blooming May,
> And of his arms disrobed the branching tree,
> To strow with boughs and blossoms all thy way;
> And now the branchlesse trunck a crosse for thee,
> And May, dismaid, thy coronet must be."

With violets and primroses and the song of English birds he celebrates the resurrection, when:

> "Every bush lay deeply purpured
> With violets; the wood's late wintry head
> Wide flaming primroses set all on fire,
> And the bald trees put on their green attire,
> Among whose infant leaves the joyous birds conspire."

The true instinct followed by painters and poets in the Middle Ages in such matters has found a warm defender in a poet of our own day, who in the following lines corrects some pedant critic for carping at the method of Paul Veronese in his treatment of sacred subjects.

> "They err who say this long-withdrawing line
> Of palace-fronts Palladian, this brocade
> From looms of Genoa, this gold inlaid
> Resplendent plate of Milan, that combine
> To spread soft lustre through the grand design,
> Show but in fond factitious masquerade
> The actual feast by leper Simon made

---

conceived as being armed and acting like people of the time of Pheidias, and we find the groups of Lapiths against Centaurs and Amazons as well as gods against giants represented like Athenians of his own age.

> To that great Guest, of old, in Palestine.
> Christ walks amongst us still; at liberal table
> Scorns not to sit: no sorrowing Magdalene
> But of these dear feet kindly gets her kiss
> Now, even as then; and thou, be honorable,
> Who, by the might of thy majestic scene,
> Bringest down that age, and minglest it with this."*

The great book of Nature once opened, a wider and still more magnificent Iconographical system of symbols was developed than those we have dealt with as yet, which only owe their origin to the Hebrew Scriptures and a few mythological legends. Christian philosophy and her handmaidens, Poetry and Art, with their transforming power, naturally grew out of the study of the Bible as the word of God. The expressions of his thought, found by the philosopher in words, become images in the artist's mind. Such images, if bearing a faithful analogy or affinity to the idea represented, become symbols holding the same relation to the idea as the bird of dawning does to sunrise. And such symbols may become parts of the harmonies of nature with which poetry has to do. "So," writes Ozanam, "it was in the study of Scripture; the events recorded have both a figurative and a real signification; the figures moving on this stage have a prophetic and symbolic, as well as historic part to fill. They are Ideas incarnate; Contemplation, Action, Hope, Charity, Faith, Penitence, as well as brute force in man, are embodied in such forms as those of Rachel, Leah, or Mary and Martha, of Peter, James, John, of David, the Magdalene, and Goliath.

As Science and History grew with Philosophy, so the necessity of arrangement of these branches of human ideas led to the great encyclopædias of the Middle Ages which embraced the whole scheme of Nature. The work, compendium, or abstract in which this scheme was epitomized, was still termed a mirror—in allusion, doubtless, to that image of St. Paul, when he says, "We now see in a mirror darkly." Hugo de St. Victor writes on this (A.D. 1150): "For now we see in a mirror darkly † [in an enigma], but then face to face. To see in a glass is to see an

---

* Poems, by Sir Samuel Ferguson, 1880, p. 157.

† We must remember, if we would understand this passage, that the mirrors of the ancients were of bronze or polished metal.

image; to see face to face is to see the thing. That which we see in an image is a sacrament, that which is seen in the thing is the thing (the reality) of the sacrament. But what is the enigma in which the image is seen darkly until the thing itself may be seen? The enigma is the Sacred Scripture. And the mirror is your heart, if so be it be pure, and cleansed, and clarified. If the highest good for a man is the contemplation of his Creator, that faith by which he begins, in some way, to see Him who is absent, is rightly spoken of as the initial good, the beginning of his restoration. Faith is the initial good. This work of restoration will be continued till we all, with unveiled face reflecting as a mirror the glory of the Lord, are transformed into the same image from glory to glory." We read of the Mirror of Human Salvation, the Universal Mirror, the Historical Mirror, the Moral Mirror, the Doctrinal Mirror, and the Mirror of Nature. The first shows how God's Being is reflected in the whole order of the Universe, in the wonders of Nature, in the providences of life, in the written Word, the dispensations of His grace, in the sacramental system of the Church. Hugo distinguishes three kinds of works, the work of God, the work of Nature, the work of the artificer imitating Nature, "whose business," he adds, "is to unite things which are separate and to distinguish things that are joined;" and this is only done through contemplation. "The statue," he says, "comes from the contemplation of a man," and the contemplation of Nature is the contemplation of that which is the archetype of all things in the eternal mind.

In France Vincent de Beauvais, when in his *Speculum Universale* he showed as in a mirror the order of God's Universe, was followed by the architect and sculptors of Chartres Cathedral, who, personifying each heading in his philosophy, theological, doctrinal, historical, or natural, covered its walls with icons that symbolized this universal scheme. Eighteen hundred and forty figures in stone, eight feet eight inches high, compose the icons of Chartres Cathedral on the outside, while within, the statues and bas-reliefs comprise not less than two thousand figures. The order of their arrangement is in obedience to the scheme of Vincent de Peauvais, an expression in stone of the Christian philosophy as classified by this great writer of the Middle Ages, the friend of St. Louis and tutor of his children. The *Speculum Majus* was divided under three heads: *Speculum Naturale*, *Speculum Doctrinale*, and *Speculum Historiale;* Mirror of Nature, Science, and History. The Natural Mirror deals with God as Creator of the Universe and of Man,* God as reflected in His works; and the six days of creation are treated in succession, beginning with that of the pure Spirits or Angels; of the Heavens and Stars, Meteorology, Geognosy, Mineralogy, Botany, Zoology, as sciences commencing on each successive day, and closing with the creation of Man, soul and body. This portion of the work is illustrated in thirty-six bas-reliefs and seventy-five statues. The series opens with the form of the Creator as He comes forth from His eternal rest to create the Heavens and the Earth, and closes with the awful climax of The Fall of Man.

In the second division of the philosopher's scheme the labours and arts of man are treated, and Agriculture here holds a prominent place, as also the Industries of the Farm, of the Manufacturer, of Commerce and Art. Chapters are devoted to the nature of seeds, plants, medicinal herbs, cultivation of trees, and all things are shown to have their fitting use, either through the good we extract from them, or the functions they fulfil in nature. Twelve subjects in bas-relief correspond to the chapters on the agricultural labours of man, while the liberal arts are symbolized elsewhere. The labours of the country form a calendar: thus January is shown by an interior where a man is seen seated at table laden with vessels and wine; February, a figure warming himself before the fire, a large roll on the mantelpiece; March, digging the vineyard; April, vine-dresser trimming his vine; May, a youth giving an opening flower to his betrothed, whose hand he holds in his; June, a horseman gallops to the chase; July, mowers in the meadow; August, reapers in the cornfield; September, thrashing the corn; October, filling measures with new wine;

---

* "Man," says Vincent, "that epitome of the wonders of creation, that little world, that universal creature made in the image and likeness of God, should be himself, in thought and wisdom, the living image of the universe—the universal mirror in which God, the world, and humanity are reflected."

November, storing faggots for winter use; December, killing the fattened pig.

The *Speculum Doctrinale* of the philosopher offers a mirror of the arts and sciences of human learning: Grammar, Morals, Jurisprudence, Physics, Literature, Politics, Mathematics, Medicine. Two hundred and fifty-one figures symbolise the various subdivisions of these sections. Thus Grammar is symbolised by an aged woman wearing a Roman mantle, who holds a round ivory box divided into compartments like a medicine chest, whence she draws forth her implements, such as knife, pens, ruler, mill hammer, and waxen tablets; she holds a file also, marked by eight golden divisions for the eight portions of her discourse.

Dialectic is symbolized by a thin spare female figure holding a serpent as an attribute, or two serpents in one hand; sometimes her robe is confined at the waist by a serpent as by a belt or girdle. She presides over a struggle between a dragon and a serpent. A monkey, symbol of malice, is at her side.

Rhetoric: an upright figure holding a small cross on high with the action of a preacher.

Arithmetic: figure of a man counting on his fingers.

Music: figure playing on a harp.

After the chapters on moral philosophy the virtues and vices of man are discussed in this Mirror of Human Doctrine, and these sections are symbolized by one hundred and forty-eight effigies. A few examples will suffice to show how this portion of the book was carried out. Faith, a kneeling figure at an altar, is opposed to Idolatry; Hope, a little girlish figure as if springing towards Heaven, which she gazes on with love, is opposed to Despair, a famished woman with dishevelled hair and bosom bared for the knife with which she is ready to slay herself. Charity, a woman giving alms, is opposed to Avarice, who stores her money in a safe. Chastity, a woman in long flowing robes and mantle, holding a prayer-book in the left hand, is opposed to Impurity, a female figure walking lightly through a wood, her clothes raised so as to lay bare her person. Humility, a wise virgin, seated, calm and veiled, holding an open book on her knee, and a phial of sweet perfume in her hand, is opposed to Pride, a rider splendidly equipped and mounted, who encounters a hurricane of wind, rain, and flame, vomited forth from the throats of three dragons by which he is driven into Hell among the damned. The Christian religion, symbolized by a vigorous large-breasted woman, is opposed to the Jewish, a spare woman blindfold, having closed her eyes to truth. And Wisdom, a grand and temperate female form, is opposed to Madness, a woman in rags, with naked breast, legs and feet.

The public virtues are symbolized by fourteen queenly figures with crowns and bucklers, which are ranged along the upper bay of the face of the North Porch. The first, leaning on a shield and holding what seems to have been either a cross or a banner, has not been identified; the second, crowned and nimbed, with standard and shield, is Liberty; the third, Honour, holds a shield with two crowns; the fourth, Prayer, holds a cross and shield on which an angel is seen among clouds; the fifth, Adoration, holds a shield with an angel swinging a censer; the sixth, Swiftness, has three arrows on her shield; the seventh, Fortitude, has a lion rampant on her shield; the eighth, Concord, shield with turtle-doves; the ninth, Friendship, shield with a flock of birds on wing; the tenth, Power, shield with a bird holding a sceptre; the eleventh [subject unknown], three sceptres on a shield and cross in her hand; the twelfth, Health, holds standard, and the fish of Tobias * is represented on her shield; the thirteenth, Security, holds a standard in her right hand, and a fortalice is represented on her shield; the fourteenth is a figure not identified, who bears a dragon on her shield.

All these virtues are represented as women, sainted and queenly forms wearing crown and nimbus, but true women, fitted for counsel, support, and comfort. All are standing upright, ready for action at the first sign; indeed, Swiftness seems by the motion of her head to have already received her mission. They are young and in full vigour, for virtue is the youth of the soul, as youth is the strength of the body. All carry shield and spear with cross and standard. Robed in long mantles, their drapery falls around them in grand folds; large-

* The fish drawn from the Euphrates by the young Tobias, whose gall restored sight to the blind old man.

breasted women in noble attitudes, the expression of each face proud or sweet according to the character symbolized.

The Historical Mirror of the philosopher, which is illustrated at Chartres by fourteen hundred and eighty-eight figures, embraces ancient history, sacred and profane, and modern history, civil and ecclesiastical. In the first thirty-one books the history of Man is given in that of the world, divided into six ages; the first from the Creation to the Deluge; the second from the Deluge to Abraham ; the third from Abraham to David ; the fourth from David to the capture of Jerusalem ; the fifth from the fall of Jerusalem to the coming of Christ; the sixth from Christ to the thirteenth century. The north and south porches of Chartres are encrusted with the images which translate this history into plastic art.

From the date at which Vincent de Beauvais wrote, i.e. from about the year 1244, the Historic Mirror becomes prophetic, and Art brings her thousand symbols to prophesy the Future, as before she has striven to revivify the Past. The philosopher foresees the accomplishment of Time, the end of the Universe, the Last Judgment of man, and foretells that, through the agency of fire and water, the world will end its days. The artist finds in the writings of the Prophets and the Apocalypse all the symbols he requires for figuring this portion of the philosopher's work, and these groups, the last of the series, fill the three recesses of the north porch and all the great southern porch with its three bays.

Thus Didron [*] has found the clue to the labyrinthine scheme of Christian Iconography in the Middle Ages, though, as he states in the introduction to this work, some one chapter of this Mirror of the Universe may be more fully treated than another in certain places. The Life of Christ and scenes from the Apocalypse are more extended in Rheims Cathedral than in Chartres. The Life of Christ follows that of His mother. The temptation is here given as the leading and principal event in a series which closes with the Crucifixion. In another place, to

[*] *Annales Arch.* vol. vi. pp. 35, 39; vol. ix. pp. 41, 99, 175, 232. Rheims, *Ann. Arch.* xiii. pp. 289, 299.

the right, the scenes after death and the history of the Invention of the Cross are given.*

Before passing on to the iconographical systems illustrating the Christian scheme followed by the artists of the culminating period in Christian Art, it will be well to look back on the ground we have trodden, and where we have striven to indicate the origins of much in the highest period of Art, the history of whose development we have hitherto neglected. We have found in the first instance that the scheme of the Byzantine painter was a chronological abstract of the Hebrew Scriptures and New Tes'ament; secondly, that the Catacomb Christian painters' scheme was symbolic and sacramental; thirdly, that the texts of the *Biblia Pauperum*, and Mirror of Human Salvation, were a complete series of scenes from the life of Christ, selected for their symbolic signification, which was explained by types from antiquity; fourthly, that the artists of the French cathedrals enlarged their horizon, and their scheme was, to present a Mirror of the Universe, of Nature, Science, and Human History. The final scheme was that attempted in the Vatican, and most fully worked out on the walls and in the ceiling of the Sixtine Chapel by Michael Angelo and his predecessors. On the north and south walls of this building the wonders of the Old and New Law were to be displayed in eighteen scenes. Moses being the embodiment of the Old, Jesus Christ of the New. On the ceiling, the Mirror of Human Salvation was displayed, the scheme which we may say formed the plot of the Divina Commedia of Michael Angelo.†

* Daunou (*Hist. Litt. de la France*, Académie Royale des Inscriptions et Belles-Lettres, vol. xviii. pp. 471, 503, where an abstract of the Historic Mirror is given) states that the portion of this work of Vincent de Beauvais called the Historic Mirror has been translated from Latin to French by Jean de Vignay, head of the hospital of St. Jacques du Haut-Pas, in the reign of Philip de Valois. This translation was printed in 1495 at Paris, and a fine example is preserved in the Bibl. de Ste. Geneviève, Paris. An index to the *Speculum* was made in the fourteenth century by a priest named Jean de Hautfumy; it is preserved in the Bibl. Nat. Paris, N. 490–6, Catal. MSS. t. iv. p. 16.

† The artists employed on the scheme of the Old and New Law were Perugino, Luca Signorelli, Sandro Botticelli, Cosimo Roselli, D. Ghirlandaio, and Cecchino Salviati.

THE OLD LAW.	THE NEW LAW.
Moses found in the bulrushes.*	Christ in the Manger.
Circumcision — Moses and Zipporah.	Baptism of Christ.
Moses overcomes the Egyptians. Defence of daughters of Jethro.	Temptation, Conquest of Satan.
Call of the Israelites,† after passage of Red Sea.	Call of the Apostles.
Moses on the Mount.‡	Christ's Sermon on the Mount.
The Priesthood (Korah, Dathan, Abiram).	Sacrament of Holy Orders. Christ gives keys to Peter.
Moses' last commands to Joshua.	Christ's Last Supper.
Moses' body upborne by Michael.	Resurrection of Christ.

With Michael Angelo the Mirror of Human Salvation is treated as a drama in five acts, the Prologue to which is

THE FALL OF LUCIFER.

ACT I.—CREATION.

Scene I.—Creator rising from Chaos.
II.—Division of Light and Darkness.
III.—Division of Land and Water.
IV.—Creation of Man.
V.—Creation of Woman.

FALL OF MAN AND ITS RESULTS.

VI.—Temptation; Fall, Expulsion from Paradise.
VII.—The Deluge.
VIII.—Sacrifice and Covenant of the Rainbow.
IX.—Inebriety of Noah and Sin of Ham.

ACT II.—REDEMPTION.

Scene I.—The Raising of the Serpent in the Wilderness.
II.—Punishment of Haman.
III.—David slaying Goliath.
IV.—Judith and Holofernes' Head.

ACT III.—COMING OF CHRIST.

PROPHETS OF HEBREWS.	PROPHETESSES OF GENTILES.
Jeremiah.	Persian Sibyl.
Ezekiel.	Erythrean Sibyl.
Joel.	Delphic Sibyl.
Zacharias.	Cumæan Sibyl.
Isaiah.	Libyan Sibyl.
Daniel.	

---

* This subject is in the Byzantine Manual series.
† In the Byzantine Manual series. ‡ In the Byzantine Manual.

Act IV.—God in Man.
The Genealogy of Christ.

Act V.—Resurrection.
Jonah raised from the Monster.

THE LAST JUDGMENT.

Assumption of the Virgin.   Coronation of the Virgin.

It is now manifest that each one of the pictures comprised in this cycle has its long train of forerunners in Art. The great painters, like the great architects of old, rose upon the shoulders of their predecessors, entered into their labours and carried them on, worked on their lines, and were the expounders of the same vast scheme, old as Eternity itself, in which each individual soul was but an instrument. The crowd of figures outside these subjects, of recumbent athletes and children, in this great composition, are all mere accessories subordinate to the principal themes—statues in the temple where Michael Angelo enshrined his Mirror of Salvation—yet forms of men listening and deeply stirred by the message borne on the wind that fills the temple and swells the folds of their drapery. They are moved by the sound, though not upborne in that passion of rapture or of sorrow which fills the Prophets and the Sibyls at its voice of thunder. Are they not types of Humanity first awakening from its long slumber in the dawn of a new revelation?

The expectancy of Christ to come is shown in the grand figures of the Prophets and Sibyls who sit enthroned all down each side of these paintings. They are eleven living forms, all animated by the expression of a higher inspiration, raised by a superhuman power above time and the world. The human and divine united in a generation of Titans, who, dwelling in deep caverns of the past, have been wakened by an angel's voice. All are represented seated, employed with books or rolled manuscripts; mighty souls, pensive, meditative, inquiring, or looking upwards with inspired countenances. Their forms and movements, indicated by the grand lines and masses of the drapery, are majestic and dignified. We see in them beings who, while they feel the sorrow of life, are upborne by the revelation vouchsafed to them, and see consolation in the future. In all these figures, in the absence of any attribute by which to identify them, the name of each is written on a slab. In the art of former days their individuality was indicated by texts written on scrolls held in the hands of the figures. Michael Angelo discards such aid, and gives in the expression of each face and figure an abstract of the thought or passion uttered by the text.

The ancestors of Christ are represented in the lunettes and in the triangular spaces above the windows. In Byzantine art they are illustrated in the genealogical tree of Jesse—and in older art generally they are given as a series of kings or heroes, in costumes appertaining to their high estate, and in the performance of royal acts or deeds. But how infinitely greater is Michael Angelo's treatment of this part of his subject! He simply seeks in Scripture for what indication he may find there as to the true condition of those very ancestors of our Lord; and, from the lowly life of Joseph and of Mary amid their humble labours, he brings us back to the shepherd kings of old. Taking for his models such family groups as he might meet with in the peasant life he saw in his daily walks, he consecrates their poverty and toil by showing that such was the lowly birth and ancestry of Christ. He gives us a long series of pastoral scenes; the poetry of calm seclusion, of a dignified yet humble domestic life, pervades them all; and the playful children, the thoughtful, loving fathers, and the tender mothers we meet with in these groups, show us how rich in human sympathy was the great heart of Michael Angelo. The series commences with Joseph, the reputed father of our Lord, and Jacob, the father of the Virgin Mary, and works backward, showing the royal pedigree of Christ among the kings of Judah, as given in the Gospel of St. Matthew, until we reach Aram and Aminadab.

At the same time in which Michael Angelo unveiled the first half of the vault in the Sistine Chapel, Raphael finished his great frescoes in the Camera della Segnatura of the Vatican; Jurisprudence, Philosophy, Poetry and Theology, scenes in the Tribune, the atrium of the Temple, on Mount Parnassus, and in the Courts of Heaven. This last has been named the Dispute of the Sacrament.

There are two subjects in early Byzantine art from which this composition of Raphael's seems to have been evolved. One is named The Mystagogia, the other, the Spirits' Reunion. It is directed in the Manual of Dionysius, that one or other of these subjects is to be allotted to the cupola of the church. In both paintings the scene is laid in Heaven. The finest examples of the Mystagogia are to be found in the Catholicon of Vatopedi, in the cupola of Chilandari, in the mosaic of St. John Lateran, and on the front of the Imperial dalmatic preserved in the Sacristy of St. Peter's in Rome. In the Byzantine churches the subject is accompanied by the following inscription: "Oh! bright Heaven! Church open to all the faithful who have entered into thee, we here inscribe these words: Oh Lord, confirm Thy house!"

The subject is treated as follows: In the centre, above, God the Father is seen enthroned, and giving the sign of benediction with His hand, saying, "I engendered thee in my bosom before Lucifer." The Dove, symbol of the Holy Ghost, is seen below, and then the Lord's table. Christ stands at the table as the High Priest, attended by angels attired as deacons carrying for Him the utensils for the Mass, and the instruments of His passion. He takes, as at Vatopedi, the disc from an angel's head, which will serve Him as a paten, or, as on the dalmatic, He stands amid the stars and gives the bread and wine to the reverent crowd around Him.

The second subject is named the Spirit's Reunion, or the Communion in Heaven. Here Christ is shown seated among the stars, beneath the sun and moon; the Virgin Mother to the right, and John the Baptist to the left. Around stand the nine choirs of Angels, Thrones, Cherubim and Seraphim, the four evangelical symbols, and the twelve signs of the Zodiac, beneath which the 148th Psalm is inscribed. Below appear the company of Saints, Patriarchs, Prophets, Apostles, Prelates, Anchorites, Kings, holy women; and in the distance, mountains, trees and birds, with animals both wild and tame.

This subject is found in the cupola of the portico at Iviron on Mount Athos; it is sculptured on a side porch of Chartres Cathedral, and west porch of Notre Dame,

Paris; painted and sculptured on the rose window of Rheims, as also in a triptych illustrated by D'Agincourt, where it is accompanied by the following inscription:
"Thou art a perfect Saviour, Thou art all we long for, all our infinite desire; all peerless beauty and goodness—then let it be Thy will that we be translated unto Thee, cleansed by Thy loftiness and worthy Thy divine perfection."

It would appear that this is the subject of Raphael's early fresco at Perugia, and thus a link is given between Raphael's later work, hitherto known as the Disputà del S. Sacramento, but which we should simply term the Communion in Heaven. Instead of representing a congress on earth before whose astonished eyes the clouds have burst asunder and the glory of the revealed God is suddenly perceived, we hold that the whole is a scene in heaven, and the redeemed are seated in the courts of heaven to whom Christ has manifested Himself in His eternal manhood. This is borne out by the scroll held over the picture by the figure of Theology containing these words "Rerum divinarum notitia"—the knowledge of things divine—as by the description given by the first engraver of the work, Giorgio Chisi, in the year 1552. "The principal men of Holy Church with all the inhabitants of Heaven praise and adore the Holy Trinity and the Majesty of of God. Who should not be incited to piety by their example?" and Vasari, soon afterwards, describes it as "HEAVEN with Christ and the Holy Virgin, John the Baptist, the Apostles, Evangelists and Martyrs in the clouds, with God the Father sending down His Holy Spirit upon all, and with an endless number of the Saints." The painter's meaning is also helped out by the subsidiary paintings in the series to which it belongs. In the accessory to the scene on the mountain sacred to the Muses symbolising Poetry, the figures of the poets are contrasted with that of Marsyas punished. In the picture which accompanies that of which we treat, redeemed humanity is contrasted with the fallen Adam. The Fathers Jerome, Augustine, Ambrose, and Gregory, with St. Dominic, Francis, and Nicholas, Dante, Savonarola, Thomas Aquinas, Bonaventura, Duns Scotus, and others having entered into the courts of the heavenly city, contemplate the Mystery of the Eucharist, before which they have bowed, and by which they have lived.

We are keenly aware of the fact that in this chapter on the Iconographical schemes of the Middle Ages, and in these bald classifications we have been obliged to resort to, we lay ourselves open to the charge of attempting to reduce Art and Poetry to a bare skeleton where all is mapped out with scientific precision; but Art in its wider sense can bear the test of analysis as surely as any great epic such as those of Milton or Dante. Now that we have attempted to reveal the framework of the Christian Epos in the Middle Ages, we hope to add in our following chapters some remarks on the vivifying influence of the Drama, and of Poetry in the opening life of Religious Art. The result of these Mirrors and Bibles of the Poor was to offer the painter in a certain sequence a vast gallery of symbols associated with the primitive emotions of humanity, while the actor, using the same texts, makes these emotions intelligible through look, gesture, and action. Thus, in the Mystery Plays and Sacred Drama of the Middle Age, the early painters may have first conceived their spellbound Byzantine forms awakening to life and motion, as they beheld their Nativities or Passion scenes enacted by groups in their native valleys lit by the solemn light of sunset.

The Portico of Ivirôn resembles in every way that of St. Germain l'Auxerrois. The porch is open and the whole vault is covered by the figures belonging to this subject. In the centre Jesus Christ is seated, His right hand raised in benediction, and holding a globe with the left, which also rests upon His knee. Beneath His feet are fiery-winged wheels, full of eyes, the thrones of the hierarchy of angels. His golden nimbus is circular, cruciform, and inscribed with the Alpha and Omega, IC and XC. Eight choirs of angels surround Him, singing "Holy, holy, holy, Lord God of Sabaoth!" many of whom carry either a globe or round shield. The evangelical symbols are placed at the four corners of this group.

INFLUENCE OF THE DRAMA ON ICONOGRAPHY.

ABOUT the year 1204, St. Francis, as we learn from Bonaventura, wishing to arouse the public devotion, resolved to celebrate the Nativity of Christ with all possible solemnity in the town of Grecio. Having obtained the necessary licence from the reigning Pontiff, he had a crèche prepared and furnished with straw, and an ox and an ass led in. The fraternity are assembled, the people crowd in; the forest resounds with canticles, and the solemn night grows melodious with music and resplendent with light. The Man of God stands before the crèche, devout, in tearful joy. Mass is celebrated, and Francis, as deacon, chants the holy Gospel. He then preaches to the assembled multitude, announcing the birth of this King among the poor, whom, in the tenderness of his heart, he loved to call the little child of Bethlehem. Now a worthy knight, Sire Jean de Grecio, who, later on, abandoned the profession of arms for love of Christ, attests that he saw a little child of extreme beauty sleeping in the crèche, and that the blessed Father Francis pressed it in his arms as if to awaken it.[*]

That the dramatic representations of the Biblical epos in the Middle Ages, thus so simply inaugurated, had a powerful effect in the quickening and development of the painter's and the sculptor's art, is a point that has not been sufficiently appreciated by historians.

It is when we find religion neither theoretical, dogmatic or theological, but the simple story of man's daily life, that we can look to find its spirit reflected in his art. Religious types (stereotyped and lifeless in Byzantine art) had to be brought before the senses of the people in a

[*] St. Bonaventure, *Legenda S. Francisci*, cap. x.

living and still artistic form. We find this thorough blending, this active intermingling of art and life in the Christian drama of the Middle Ages to have its parallel in Greece, where the artistic was also thus brought face to face with Nature and with life in the palæstra, and where the plastic attitudes of actors in the great Greek dramas must have trained the eyes of the Greek sculptors and painters. Moreover we have an analogous case in the development of Greek painting. It was in the second half of the fifth century B.C. that real illusiveness was given to painting by the introduction of foreshortening and perspective, for purposes of scene paintings first developed by Apollodorus.

We have learned from Dr. Waldstein how much Greek art seems to owe to the athletic games and the scenes in the palæstra, if not of religious emotion, yet of knowledge of the human form in action inspired by a noble intention and for a lofty purpose. He begins by saying truly, that so long as the sculptor's art is entirely in the service of religious worship there is small chance of its freeing itself from conventional imperfections; the sculptor must be brought face to face with man, and then he may reconstruct his work out of the ideal combination of the most perfect forms which he has studied in man, but has never found together in one man. The first great task was that of bringing the artist down from conventionality and abstract symbols of gods, to nature and to man. The next was to lead the artist through nature to the ideal. In the first and earliest stages of the palæstra, the athletic games are a class of religious institutions without human interest. In the highest period this institution had a real national aim, to provide and encourage perfect physical education for the youths and men who were to form the strength of the nation. Here then it would seem that the institution shook itself free from all religious associations, if such ever did form any integral portion of its being. If it did not, we must look beyond the athletic games for the source of certain attitudes as of certain expressions of the human countenance in Greek art, which have a distinctly religious character; the bowed head of the patient Psyche, the sublime submission of the Cnidian Demeter.

In the early mediæval period, and in the twelfth and thirteenth centuries, art may have gained much from the mysteries and plays of the time which were pressed into the service of religion, and have been affected in much the same manner as Greek art was by the athletic games; but the action in the Christian drama was concentrated on, and only bore relation to, the religious idea. And it belonged to a religion which includes faith in such transfiguration and transmutation, or, at all events, transformation, of the human and the physical, which is the aim of art in its highest manifestations. This unity of dramatic action and art with a religion based on the ideas of self-offering, transfiguration and renewal, had never before been seen.

At every turn the same drama was offered to the eye and ear, whether by carver, sculptor, painter, architect, musician, actor, or poet. The Mirror of Human Salvation was the framework of the divine comedy, whatever form of language men chose to work it out in. It was the source of the text, or, if we may use the word, the libretto, for such performances as the dramatic processions of Bethune, for the shows and passion plays of France, Italy, and Germany, and we find it to be so still in the Ammergau mystery play. Thus in the scene of The Last Supper, this, which forms the central subject of the group in one page of the *Biblia Pauperum*, is the scene enacted by the Bavarian peasants. The two wings of the triptych, or pictures at each side on the page, are the types from the Old Testament. At Ammergau these are given as tableaux-vivants, forming the background, displaying the Israelites gathering manna in the wilderness, and Melchisedek offering bread and wine, while the explanatory and illustrative texts on the scrolls in the pictures, are chanted by the chorus and its leader. 1st chant: "Man did eat angels' food." 2nd chant: "Come eat of my bread, and drink of the wine which I have mingled." 3rd chant: "Thou gavest them bread from Heaven for their hunger."

The very costumes worn agree in many instances with the mediæval paintings, the man who personates the Christ appearing exactly as Van Eyck represents Him in his pictures, with papal tiara, and rich tunic studded with pearls, stole and pastoral staff. The dramatic processions of Bethune were also this very series of scenes from the life of Christ, with the difference that both type and antitype were enacted and not mere tableaux-vivants. Here the performers belonged to the various guilds of the city, by whom scaffolds were erected in lines to right and left of the street, those on the left to form stages for the types, those on the right for the antitypes.

Universally as these texts seem to have been used, we do not mean that they supplied the only framework for dramatic representation.

The mother standing by the Cross, and the mother weeping over the body of her son, with the archetypal pictures of parental love and sorrow taken from Genesis in the background, are subjects descending to us from the earliest ages of Christian worship. In the East, 'Mary's Lament; or, the 'Threnodia,' was represented at Constantinople in the fourth century. It was one of the earliest and simplest of the German mystery plays. We find it represented in a Book of the Gospels of the year 1100, preserved in the Convent of Vatopedi. It always forms one of the scenes of the Passion, painted in fresco on the left wall of the apse, in the churches of Mount Athos; till at length all the sorrow and the passion of these subjects is taken up and uttered in the words of the hymn, 'Stabat Mater dolorosa,' and finally it descends to us in the dramatic music of Rossini and Dvorjak.

Indeed it would appear that the origin of the sacred Christian drama may date as far back as to the very dawn of Christianity, and that the pagan drama, though it had fallen low, had never quite died out before the Christian arose. We read that Gregory Nazianzen, archbishop and poet,* hoping to banish profane plays from the theatre of

---

* In the following verse translated from a poem of his by Newman, there is more knowledge of art than in any passage we know of in Christian literature of this date:
"As when the hand some mimic form would paint
It marks its purpose first in shadows faint,
And next its store of varied hues applies
Till outlines fade and the full limbs arise."

Mrs. Barrett Browning in her too short sketch of this poet, writes: "A noble and tender man was this Gregory, and so tender, because so noble. . . . Half apostolical he was, and half scholastical; and while he

Constantinople, had composed many sacred dramas which he intended to substitute for them, with hymns taking the place of the chorus in the Greek dramas. Chrysostom also wrote the dying Christ in Greek, between the years 347 and 407, which was represented, with the addition of tableaux-vivants, at Constantinople. Among other Christian fathers who dramatised sacred subjects was St. Avitus in the sixth century, who prepared a play on the fall of Adam, entitled *De Origine Mundi, de Originali Peccato et de Sententiâ Dei*. A similar effort was made about the year 990, when Theophylact, another patriarch, invented or adapted to the stage certain plays called *Fête des Fous, Fête de l'Ane*,* *Fête des Innocents*, which were acted in silence, the performers appearing as mutes. This innovation is said to have originated in the desire of weaning the people from Bacchanalian and calendary rites and other pagan ceremonies, by the substitution of Christian spectacles. The mystery plays of France and England appear to have arisen out of these performances. Frederic Barbarossa is known to have presided at the performance of a drama entitled 'The Arrival and Destruction of Antichrist' at Tegernsee, not very far from the present Ammergau. 'The Harrowing of Hell' is the first English mystery play that has come down to us; † and in 1174 William Fitz-Stephen, Monk of Canterbury, says, "London, for its theatrical exhibitions has religious plays, either the

---

mused, on his bishop's throne, upon the mystic tree of twelve fruits, and the shining of the river of life, he carried, as Milton did, both hands full of green trailing branches from the banks of the Cephissus, nay, from the very plane tree which Socrates sat under with Phædius, when they two talked about beauty to the rising and falling of its leaves." See *Greek Christian Poets*, p. 29, Elizabeth Barrett Browning.

* The Prose de l'Ane is preserved with many other remarkable pieces, in a manuscript at Sens. This work is not of the nature or character that the antiquaries, following Voltaire, have deemed it. They have either wilfully or involuntarily mistaken the parody for the original piece coming from the pen of the author, the learned and pious archbishop of Sens, Pierre de Corbeil. The writer is dealing with the important place occupied by this animal in Scripture from the Jewish ass first seen on the hills of Sichem and beyond Jordan and then at Bethlehem where it is associated with the Christian beast of burthen, who showed the triumph of the New Dispensation, bearing his Master in the gates of Jerusalem. *Annales Archéol.* vi. p. 304 ; Fête de l'Ane, *ib.* vol. vii. p. 28.

† Hallam, *Literature of Europe*, p. 105.

representations of miracles wrought by holy confessors or the sufferings of martyrs;" and Geoffrey, afterwards Abbot of St. Albans, while teaching a school at Dunstable caused the legend of St. Catherine to be acted there, Geoffrey taking part in the performance. The first dramatic writer of note in Italy was Albertino Mussato, who was born at Padua in 1260; but St. Francis, as we have seen, had some years before initiated the sacred drama at the town of Grecio.*

A comparison of the dates marking distinct epochs in the history of the arts of the drama and of painting and sculpture goes far to prove that their growth was contemporaneous; and here we are reminded of Mr. Watkiss Lloyd's interesting remarks on the relation of the masterpieces of Greek drama to contemporary graphic and plastic art. It was the same in Greece as in the Italy of the Middle Ages, at the period when the drama both assumed its systematic form and sprung at once to its perfection. Celebrations, in which the entire State was represented in procession, and recitations of the Homeric poems and musical performances, gave moving and audible expression to the general enthusiasm. Thus, it is characteristic of certain epochs of development of genius, that the arts are found to advance concurrently, and the passion grows for combining them. When, as in the following instances (Figs. 229 and 230), we see distinct evidence of the illustration of the symbols of one art in those of another, the interest of such objects is much enhanced by these considerations.

In a series of lectures delivered in La Sorbonne by M. Magnin (1834–5), this author referred to various illustrations of the drama, both pagan and Christian, to be found among the sculptured and painted monuments of mediæval art in the south of France.† At Autun, M. Didron found a representation of a scene in a tragedy of Terence on the front porch of a building in that town.

* The tragedy of the Ten Virgins, dramatised by the Dominicans, was produced at Eisenach in 1322. A high and healthy morality belongs to this tragedy, and the drama may be taken as a fair index of the moral and religious conditions of the time in which it arose. See *The Ober-Ammergau Passion Play*, M'Coll, p. 22, 1880.

† See *Annales Arch.* vol. vii. p. 303.

In the following illustration we have a scene from the mystery play of the "Acts of the Apostles and of Dionysius the Areopagite," performed in the Roman amphitheatre formerly standing in Bourges.* This is one of a series of miniatures illustrating the Life and Passion of St. Dionysius the Areopagite, which has been proved

Fig. 231.—MINIATURE XIV. CENT., BIBL. NAT. PARIS, FONDS LATIN NO. 5086.

by M. Didron to correspond in a remarkable manner with the directions for the *mise en scène* of the drama itself given in another ancient MS. found by M. le Baron de Girardot.† It illustrates the following incident in the drama. Dionysius has suffered martyrdom in company with his friends Rusticus and Eleutherius, and angels have borne their souls in a mantle up to Heaven. Regulus,

* The old Roman amphitheatre of Avaricum was standing in the sixteenth century, but destroyed in the seventeenth. See *Ann. Archéol.* xiii. pp. 16, 62, 134, 185; xiv. pp. 14, 73.

† Bibl. Nat. No. 5286, Ancien fonds Latin, folio 51. *Ann. Arch.* xiv. 16.

whom Dionysius had consecrated Bishop of Arles, was saying mass one day, attended by a deacon and sub-deacon. When he had pronounced the Missa Est, he beheld the souls of the three martyrs, under the form of three doves, descend and rest upon the crucifix before which he stood. This miniature is most curious as an illustration of the Sacrifice of the Mass and the drama in one. The three saints, Denis, Eleutherius, and Rusticus, have come down in the form of birds, and are lighting upon the crucifix. Each holds a scroll in his beak, on which the name is written by which the Bishop of Arles may recognise them. All the minor details are of interest; the flabellum formed of peacock's-eyed feathers; the great patina upheld in the air. The altar, covered by a large cloth with nothing on it but the crucifix, the missal, and the chalice covered by the napkin.*

This mystery play of the 'Acts of the Apostles and St. Dionysius' should be studied by all who are interested in Christian iconography. Many of the mosaics at St. Mark's, in Venice, would seem to be reproductions of scenes in this drama, such as those in which Gondoforus, the Indian king, and Abanes, his provost-marshal, take a part; and the lists of Jews and members of the Synagogue named in the manuscripts of the *dramatis personæ* may guide us towards the identification of many hitherto anonymous figures in our churches.

Another scene, corresponding to one in the drama of the Acts of the Apostles, is represented in sculpture on the outer wall of the Cathedral of Paris, between the southern transept and the apse. The subject is an incident occurring at the funeral of the Virgin, and is explained in a remarkable manner by the directions for the *mise en scène* of this incident in the MS. of M. le Baron de Girardot.

The directions to the stage-manager are as follows:—

"Fault quelque bar pour porter le corps de ladicte dame au monument.

"Fault le monument. . . .

"Bellezeray, prince des Juifs, et autres se meetent en chemin pour

---

* "Miniature extrêmement curieuse sous le rapport symbolique et liturgique," writes M. Didron. Note the flabellum made of peacock's feathers, the patina held by the sub-deacon, the chalice covered with a napkin, and the scrolls marking the name of each down.

ILLUSTRATIONS OF MYSTERY PLAYS. 241

aller empescher que le corps de lad[icte] dame ne soit mis au monument. Les Juifs s'efforcent mectre la main au corps de la Vierge Marie pour l'oster aux apostres, et incontinant les mains leurs demeurent seiches et sont aveuglez par le feu que leur gectent les anges. Belzeray meetant les mains à la lectiere où l'on porte la Vierge Marie et ses mains demeurent atachées a lad[icte] lectiere, et se geetent sur eulx force feu en maniere de fouldre, et doivent cheoir à terre les Juifs aveuglés.

"Les mains de Bellezeray doivent estre detachees et rejoinctes a ses bras, puis luy est baillée la palme qu'il porte aux autres dont ceulx qui voulurent croire furent illuminez, puis rapporta lad[icte] palme."*

Fig. 232—BAS-RELIEF OF THE XIII. CENT. AT NOTRE DAME, PARIS.

In the sculptured panel from Notre Dame (Fig. 230) we see the figure of the Jewish prince represented, first as

* See *Annales Archéol.* vol. xiii. p. 135. The costumes were generally those of the period in which the play was enacted. The Christ was dressed as a pontiff in papal tiara, wearing a rich tunic studded with

VOL. II   R

laying hands on the Virgin's coffin; and, again, as maimed and prostrate, while his hands are seen fastened to the pall.—Such examples of the mutual relations of the drama and sculpture of the Middle Ages are of extreme interest. We should study such works as these mediæval stage directions, published by Didron and his friends in the *Annales Archéologiques*,* scene by scene, to compare the details of each furnished by them with the representations of similar subjects in painting and sculpture, if we would learn how far the grouping, scenic effect, and dramatic action of the whole scene may have been influenced by these performances, which had descended from the Greek to the mediæval stage. Also, when examining as to what were the influences at work that aroused Italian art, in the time of Giotto, and his school, from the death sleep of Byzantine formalism, may we not attribute much of the inspiration of the thirteenth and following centuries to the drama. The artists who witnessed at Florence the performance of the "Electra" of Sophocles by Alessandra Scala,† may have felt in this embodiment of noble womanhood, much as did the scholars and artists of Ireland in 1835, when the "Antigone" of Sophocles was represented for them by Helen Faucit. Their scholarship received an impetus, and their genius was warmed at sight of living passion infused into forms which before had but faintly been associated with the idea of life. " With the writings," they said, " of the Grecian dramatists, it is true, we have long been familiar; but their power and their beauty have come down to us through books alone. 'Mute and motionless' that drama has heretofore stood before us; you, madam, have given it voice, gesture, life; you have

---

pearls, and with stole and pastoral staff, while in the scenes of the Nativity the Magi wore the costly dress of the knights and merchants of the time, rare foreign stuffs and velvet coats trimmed with fur, while the ordinary wore the costumes of citizens and peasants with pointed shoes and head-circlets of tinkling bells, all of which details are to be seen repeated in the miniatures of the early French and Italian MSS.

* *Annales Archéol.* vol. viii. pp. 272, 274.

† See Walker, *Drama in Italy*, p. 49. In the person of Leo Baptista Alberti we find one who was dramatist, painter, sculptor and architect. His comedy of " Philodoxeos " appeared in his twentieth year. See Walker, ib. p. 32.

realized the genius and embodied the inspirations of the authors and of the artists of early Greece, and have thus encouraged and instructed the youth of Ireland in the study of their immortal works." *

So, mute and motionless, stood the Christian drama also, and its long lines of angels, saints and martyrs, had for centuries looked out with their fixed gaze from the walls and domes of their solemn basilicas, till a like vivifying and invigorating influence was brought to bear upon its art.

* See *Essays on the Drama* Theodore Martin, p. 26.

MEDIÆVAL ART AND THE ANTIQUE.

IN the discussions carried on by some writers in the present day as to the attitude of mediæval Christian art in the presence of the antique, it has been asked whether the study of nature and of the antique, which were two factors in the art of the Renaissance, were not opposing influences in the beginning, however they may have, in the end, combined to produce great results; whether, at first, the studies of nature and the antique were not as rival forces confusing the artist and marring his work. When we follow the history of the gradual development of art, the signs of such opposition between the two styles seem to disappear; and the more we learn of art before Dante, the less reason we have for believing in the existence of these hard and fast lines between heathen and Christian mythography. We have seen in the course of this work how, in the texts of the *Speculum Humanæ Salvationis* and *Biblia Pauperum*, tales from heathen mythology were taken as types of Christian virtues—contemplation, fortitube, moral strife, and self-sacrifice. Christ Himself borrows the image of the Good Shepherd from a heathen writer, and St. Paul finds in the Isthmian games an image of the Christian course. So it was with the iconography of the first Christian period. In the lives of the four sculptor-saints, Claude, Castory, Symphorian, Nicostratus, we find them working at genii, amorini, victories, &c. In early Christian places of worship, Orpheus, Psyche, Deucalion, Hermes, Ulysses, are seen side by side with Christian symbols and figures. In fact, one system of iconography appeared to dovetail into the other, and the use of certain heathen images was never wholly abandoned, even down to the time of Dante.

In the illuminated manuscripts, even of the tenth

century, classic influences are seen to linger, and the miniature painter will dwell as fondly as Mantegna himself, on antique bas-reliefs, sarcophagi, and architecture, and occasionally caryatide, or figures of naked warriors; but these are always treated as accessories, and kept in the background. In an illuminated manuscript of the eleventh century, "Sermons on the Festivals of the Virgin," mythological personifications of rivers are constantly occurring; in fact, such images never disappeared from Byzantine art.

Lingering traditions of pagan mythology are constantly appearing on the church walls in the monasteries of Mount Athos, and elsewhere in Greece, as well as in Ravenna. Thus, in the refectory of Vatopédi, we see the name Charon inscribed under the image of Death: the figure resembles a skeleton, although the bones are still covered by a shrunken skin. He holds a sickle in his right hand, and a scythe in the left. We have seen an illustration of a portion of mosaic, dating, according to Ciampini, from the year 314, which formed part of the pavement above referred to, in the Church at Pavia, dedicated by Constantine to St. Michael in Ticino, and thus described by Ciampini (Vet. Mon. Tab. 11, fig. 2).

"In this part, then, another tesselated work is seen, and it is seen in the pavement of the church of St. Michael Ticinus, in Ticino; an example of it has been made known to us by the most illustrious and reverend Don Franciscus Bellisomus, which he says he received from Don Marcellinus, ruler of the church of St. Nicolas, Moneta. To these men I acknowledge my obligation for their singular desire to enrich this collection of mine, a desire made known to me by such proofs. At what time this mosaic was made it is hard to find out.

"Carolus Sigonius, a celebrated writer of the last century, in the third book of his *History of the Western Empire to the Year* 314, says that by popular report the Emperor Constantine the Great, after gaining a victory over the Franks, built that temple. Accordingly by this simple disclosure of a report, the time of the building of the temple is made doubtful. It is certain, however, that there is to be seen there a tesselated pavement made in a rude fashion, in which we see images both sacred and profane. In the midst of it are circles of various sizes, which form the middle part of the labyrinth, in the centre of which the well-known story of Theseus* slaying the Minotaur is represented, as the writing itself makes known, which says:—

---

* See Ciampini, *Veter. Mon.* tom. ii. pl. ii. See *Ann. Archéol.* vol. xv. p. 231; vol. xvii. pp. 69-193.

"(1st Inscr.) 'Theseus entered, and slew the biform monster.'
"(2nd Inscr.) 'Savage am I, and fain would deal death-wounds to the brave.'
"(3rd Inscr.) 'The proud one is laid low; the gentle one stands raised on high.'"

M. Durand is of opinion that the church in which this mosaic was found is of the eleventh century (see *Ann. Archéol.* vol. xv. p. 231, note). Another such mosaic pavement was found in the lower church of St. Savin at Piacenza,* and another, held by some antiquarians to date from the fifth century, in the choir of the cathedral at Aosta.† Another belonged to the cathedral of Acqui, a portion of which is now in the Museum of Turin.

In the association of this subject with that of Goliath and David, a parallel is clearly drawn in early Christian art, between the deeds of the hero of Hebrew Scripture and that of the Greek mythology; and the study of a pavement such as this, along with the records we possess of those of Sta. Maria Maggiore at Vercelli (Lalande, *Voyage en Italie*, vol. i., p. 265), of the year 1040, and San Miniato, A.D. 1207, is interesting as pointing to the origin of that passage in the "Purgatorio" of Dante, canto xii., where the poet treads a pavement wrought with like symbolic forms, both pagan and Christian. Didron was the first writer we know of who drew attention to the resemblance between this description of Dante's and the older portion of the pavement of Siena cathedral.‡ The path of Dante leads from the purgatorial gate, up the Mountain of Healing, on the summit of which is the celestial Paradise, where he is met by Beatrice; and this portion of the pavement he describes, is at the turn in the way leading from the first to the second ledge, or cornice by which the steps in his ascent are marked. The path of the mosaic master on the floor of Siena cathedral, leads up the nave of the building from the porch to the gate of the sanctuary, where the pilgrim is met by the female form,

* *Descrizione dei monumenti e delle pitture di Piacenza*, p. 6. Parma, 1828.
† *St. Savin.* Sur le pavé, une mosaïque de pierres blanches et noirs offre les signes du zodiaque avec les inscriptions latines et en caractères romains, mais que les archéologues et quelques mosaïstes savants attribuent aux artistes grecs venus à Venise dans vii°. siècle. Valéry, *Voyages en Italie*, ed. de Bruxelles, vol. i. liv. ii. ch. x. p. 27.
‡ See Vasari, ed. Bohn, i. 241-244; iv. 137, and note.

symbolising Mercy and Gentleness, inscribed " Mansuetudo-Misericordia."

The pavement of the first mountain level of Dante's vision corresponds to the fourth triforium or bay in the mosaic floor of the cathedral, the images visible on both pavements signifying Natural Law and Human Morality, being drawn from pagan mythology. Here, as in the cathedral at Ulm, and as in the monastery church of Ivirôn on Mount Athos, we have the forms of Greek philosophers, side by side with the sages and heroes of the Hebrew Scriptures: Socrates, Crates, Epictetus, Aristotle, Seneca, and Euripides, along with the heathen allegory of the Wheel of Fortune, the four phases of which are symbolised by the form of a youth on the wheel—aspiring, throned, dethroned, and fallen.* The sibyls, pagan prophetesses of Christ, are also here, though whether they belong to the later portion of this pavement or not, Didron does not say.

In the cathedral pavement the heathen subjects form the background to the Hebraic. In that of Dante they alternate, or the poet may intend that they are placed to left and right, and so strike his eye as he advances, as it were, up the imaginary nave, looking to the left and right aisle:—

Left Aisle.—Heathen.	Right Aisle.—Hebraic.
1. Briareus.	1. Lucifer.
2. Niobe.	2. Nimrod.
3. Arachne.	3. Saul.
4. Eriphyle.	4. Sennacherib.
5. Tomyris.	5. Judith.
6. Troy.	6. Jerusalem sacked.

Here Briareus, who had seated himself next to Jove, is punished as Lucifer, who would have equalled himself to God; Niobe, who would have exalted herself above Latona,

---

* See *Annales Arch.* vol. xvi. p. 337, engraving of Fortune's Wheel. The drawings of this pavement by Signor Leopoldo Maccari, Scultore dell' opera del duomo at Siena, have been acquired by the Fitzwilliam Museum, Cambridge. Mr. Sidney Colvin, following Signor L. Maccari, has given a history of this pavement in the *Fortnightly Review*; Mr. J. A. Symonds (*Sketches in Italy and Greece*, p. 49) also alludes to it.

is punished as Nimrod, the ambitious builder of Babel. Arachne, who in her pride destroys herself, is compared to Saul, who will die rather than fall into the Philistines' hands; Eriphyle, slain by her sons for greed and treachery, to Sennacherib, slain for like reasons by his sons; Tomyris and Cyrus, Judith and Holofernes.

Such was the pavement, wrought with warnings of Heaven's judgments on evil, pride, treachery, greed and cruelty, which the poet bade Dante bend his gaze upon:—

"To ruminate the bed beneath his feet."

And all these images, he tells us, were with most " curious skill of portraiture o'erwrought:"—

"What master of the pencil or the style
Had traced the shades and lines, that might have made
The subtlest workman wonder? Dead, the dead;
The living seemed alive: with clearer view,
His eye beheld not, who beheld the truth,
Than mine what I did tread on, while I went
Low bending."

It is important just at this time to show that even before the age of Dante both poets and artists drew their images from the classic as well as from the Hebrew writings, since an erroneous opinion appears to be gaining ground that art had to wait for the great antiquarian movement of the Renaissance at the close of the fifteenth century to show any knowledge of or sympathy with the wisdom and learning of the ancients. Some writers, indeed, would seem to trace the origin of the system of parallelism between heathen and Hebraic history to Dante, with whom it certainly did not originate, however characteristic of his broad nature his adoption of it may seem. It has been thought that Dante gave the idea to the mosaic workers of Siena on the one hand, and, on the other, that he derived it from them; but we have seen that long before, at Pavia, at Vercelli, and at Florence, the same system of parallelism was pursued, and in each instance the moral significance of the images chosen was of the same lofty nature. And the divine strife with evil is equally symbolised by Theseus and the Minotaur, and

David with Goliath; types, of which the Temptation of Christ in the Wilderness, was the antitype.*

In order that we may possibly follow out this system of parallelism between heathen and Christian symbols, Didron, in a remarkable passage on the wheel windows of the French cathedrals, compares the symbolism in them with that of Homer in the shield of Achilles, and of Dante in the vision of the snow-white rose which concludes his Divina Commedia. "These rose windows of France, at Rheims, or Paris, Chartres, Laon, Soissons, or Strasbourg, are compared by him to a luminous star shining in the vast space of the cathedral, or to a large eye, reflecting heaven on the face of the sanctuary. Painted in the glass, and sculptured on the mullions of such windows, may be found the summing up of all the story, given in detail, throughout the building: the Communion of Spirits, the Hierarchy of Heaven, the Assembly of Saints, the Triumph of Christ, the Courts of Paradise, back to the wheel of human destiny and the Creation of Man."†

Thus, he continues, the shield of Achilles, in Homer's 18th book of the Iliad, is but a rose of concentric circles, filled with subjects forged upon the anvil of a god. The outer circle is formed by the river of Ocean. Between the outer and the inner zones there is a space, set, as we may say, with medallions. In one we have the City of Peace, with marriage feast and bridal song, music and dancing, and elders seated in the sacred circle, holding in their hands staves from the loud-voiced heralds.

In another, the City of War, which is besieged by two armies, "on the wall there stood, to guard it, the dear wives and children, and with these the old men, but the rest went forth, and their leaders were Ares and Pallas Athene, both wrought in gold, and golden was the vesture they had on." They lie in ambush, and presently come the cattle, and with them two herdsmen, playing on pipes, that took no thought of guile. The assailants fly to arms. A battle ensues, and strife. Tumult and fell Death

* The drawings by Signor Leopoldo Maccari, Scultore dell' opera del duomo at Siena, have been acquired by the Fitzwilliam Museum, Cambridge.
† See *Annales Arch.* vol. x. pp. 2, 16.

appear, and the raiment on her shoulders was red with the blood of men.

In a third medallion we see, as it were, a vintage where dark purple grapes hang on silver poles, and maidens and striplings in childish glee bear the sweet fruit in plaited baskets. And a dancing place was there like unto that which once in wide Knosos, Daidalos wrought for Ariadne of the lovely tresses.

If, says Didron, we turn from this passage in Homer to that of Dante at the close of the *Paradiso* where the elect are ranged, circle within circle, we find this poet using the rose as his symbol. " Then she " (i.e. Beatrice) " showed me all the sacred host of those whom Christ espoused in His blood ranged in the form of a snow-white rose."* Thus both poets have framed their symbols in a wheel or circle, just as the architect of the Middle Ages framed his in the round window. As the poet's gaze was fixed on the river of the water of life, and as he bathes his eyes in its refining wave, he beholds its course turning to a circle, with which the petals of his rose unfold, which correspond to the mullions and foliate traceries of the cathedral window. This river's banks are painted with spring flowers, which are gradually transformed to angels, ranged around the courts of heaven, and Beatrice draws him on, as one who is silent and yet fain would speak, that he may behold how vast this white-robed company, how great the circuit of this heavenly city, how filled its seats that few are left to need them.

We have dwelt thus long on the system of parallelisms between the images of mediæval and antique art, because we hold that it was not out of discord and enmity, but rather in the recognition of such harmonies, such broad unity of moral significance, that the greatness of Renaissance Art derived its origin; certainly no sign of the rivalry, alluded to above, can be found in the writing of Dante. In the first awakening of the poetic spirit it is impossible to over-estimate the influence that genius such as that of Dante must have exercised upon the art of his own date and the years immediately succeeding him.

* See Dante, *Paradiso*, canto xxx. l. 61, 85, 90, 100, 105, 114, 125; xxxi. l 1, 45, 95, 125.

We may bring forward an instance in Venice in illustration of this. A few years after Dante died at Ravenna, the noble capital symbolising Justice was carved in the Ducal Palace of Venice. And M. Didron has shown how closely in this instance the poet was followed by the sculptor.

In canto x. of *Purgatory*, Dante, mounting to the second cornice or story of his ascent, perceives a bas-relief carved in white marble, representing the incident of Trajan and the widow. The emperor, riding forth from the city gates, is stopped by a widow who, seizing his horse by the bridle, demands justice on the murderers of her son, and Trajan, yielding to her prayer, stops in the midst of his royal progress and administers justice forthwith.[*] Again, Dante shows Trajan, seated beneath the brows of the symbolic eagle (image of imperial justice), having won his seat in Paradise by this act of mercy. Dante has also named as the great representative of law and justice the emperor Justinian, chief of that band of spirits whom Beatrice desired him to "trust as gods." Turning to the capital of the Ducal Palace, sculptured with the figures symbolising Justice, we find the inscription Justinia[n] beneath a figure representing the great Byzantine emperor as an angel of justice, winged and crowned, seated on two lions, and among the other figures that surround the capital we find those of Trajan on horseback, armed and holding weapons in his right hand, while the widow is seen on her knees before him, and below is the inscription: TRAIANO IPERADORE CHE FE JUSTITIA A LA VEDOVA.

But this is not the only instance in which these *bassirilievi* imagined by the poet on the border of the second rock in Purgatory were wrought into form by mediæval art. The Annunciation, painted by Marcello Venusti from Michael Angelo's design in the Sacristy of San Giovanni Laterano, was also a development of the poet's conception. His genius foresaw that which the genius of two centuries later was able to fulfil.

We must now draw to a close this imperfect sketch of the Mediæval systems of Image writing, in which we

[*] See *Ann. Archéol.* vol. xxii. p. 207. Two pictures of the Veronese School, illustrating this subject, have been lately added to the National Gallery of London, Nos. 1135, 1136.

have endeavoured to show that the composer's aim in his treatment of the Christian epos in Western art was neither historical, chronological, or dogmatic. His aim was symbolism, and in the successive schemes we have indicated as existing from that of the Catacomb paintings in Rome to the mediæval Mirrors of Man's Salvation, and of Universal Nature down to that of Michael Angelo in the Sistine Chapel, we find a consecutive series of symbols resting on the plot of the great story of divine strife in Man and his redemption.

The system was a fertile and a long enduring one, because it belonged to a religion not only of ideals and theories but of facts and deeds. The events, recorded in the Bible and in the art of this religion, formed a chain of symbols corresponding with experiences in the soul's history of each individual, but they still remained real events and real experiences in the physical and material history of humanity, as well as in the moral and spiritual life. The death upon the Cross was a fact, but one that would have lost its aim had it not ever since been mirrored in the inner life of Man.

But when at the present day we approach such subjects we are met at every turn by the danger of falling into platitude and cant, and it would seem as if an entirely novel phraseology must be invented for the religious poetry and art of the future. Yet the sorrow is the same, and the hope the same, which mediæval art symbolised by the archetypal forms of Genesis as by those beloved of Christ, and we do but wait for some sincere religious movement for a noble iconography to be again evolved, believing that Christianity is a storehouse, inexhaustible, of germs which it does but take successive intellectual atmospheres to develop.

APPENDIX I.

ADDITIONAL NOTES.

APPENDIX I.

ADDITIONAL NOTES.

I.

"ATTRIBUTES OF THE TRINITY," p. 69, vol. ii.

THE Trinity painted by Francesco di Pesello or Pesellino is altogether the most magnificent symbol of this mystery we have seen. This painting, the masterpiece of a great artist, and perhaps the finest work of its time, now hangs in room xiii. of the National Gallery, London—No. 727. The Father, surrounded by cherubim and flaming seraphim, supports a crucifix above the clouds. A dove upon His breast seems to hover over the Saviour's head. A solemn landscape with level bands of dark cloud along the sky completes the sublime composition. The arrangement of the figures corresponds with fig. 144, p. 69, supra, taken from a French miniature in a 13th century MS. in the collection of the Duke of Anjou, in the National Library, Paris.

FIG. 150. THE TRINITY, THREE PERSONS, EACH IN HUMAN FORM, p. 81.

Two interesting examples of this treatment of the symbol have been brought before my notice since this work went to press, by Sir Frederic Burton, who has kindly given me the following information as to their origin. They are miniatures, painted by Jehan Foucquet, from a Prayer-book made for Maître Etienne Chevalier, Treasurer under Charles VII. and Louis XI., belonging to Herr Ludwig Brentano, in the Taunus Platz,* Frankfort-on-the-Maine, and are said to be the finest of his productions. Foucquet visited Italy, and was in Rome in 1445. But his works show no

* On Jean Foucquet, see *Renaissance des Arts à la Cour de France*, vol. i. pp. 155, 691. Paulin Paris, MSS. françaia de la Bibl. du Roi, vol. ii. p. 260.

sign of Italian influence in any respect. He painted Eugenius IV. in a portrait once in the Minerva at Rome. In the Bibliothèque Nationale in Paris is a Josephus illuminated by him at least in part, and in the Royal Library at Munich a Boccaccio, done for the same Maître Etienne.

II.
WINGLESS ANGELS, p. 93.

Mrs. Jameson (*Sac. and Leg. Art*, i. p. 58) gives a wingless angel by Francia, singing the Virgin's praise to a mandola. The angels who visit Abraham in Raphael's painting of this subject are without wings.

Mrs. Jameson observes: "Raphael, here as elsewhere a true poet, has succeeded in conveying, with exquisite felicity, the sentiment of power, of a heavenly presence, and of a mysterious significance. The three youths, who stand linked together hand in hand before the patriarch, with such an air of benign and superior grace, want no wings to show us that they belong to the courts of heaven, and have but just descended to earth. Murillo (in his painting in the Sutherland Gallery) gives us merely three young men travellers, and has set aside wholly both the angelic and the mystic character of the visitants."

The angels of Michael Angelo, in the "Last Judgment," are also without wings.

III.
ANGELS OF BOTTICELLI.

THE ALLEGED HERESY IN THE "ASSUMPTION OF THE VIRGIN."

Since much interest has been expressed about the angels once condemned as heretical in the painting known as the Palmieri Botticelli, now in the National Gallery, London, we venture to offer a short account of its curious history, as well as of the life of the learned Florentine for whom the work was executed.

Matteo Palmieri was a distinguished citizen in Florence, holding a high position there about the year 1470. He was ambassador from the Florentine Republic to King Alfonzo of Naples, also deputy in the name of the Republic to the Fathers of the General Council held under Eugenius IV. The house of his family stood near the Spezieria delle Rondini, in Florence; and a shield bearing his arms—a palm-tree between two lions rampant—was inserted in the wall. As an author, Palmieri seems to have been much esteemed. He wrote—(1) *La Vita di Niccolo Acciajuoli*; (2) *Trattato della Vita Civile*; (3) *De Captivitate Pisarum Historia*; (4) *Chronicon seu de Temporibus, Cronica dalla Creazione del Mondo fin all' anno* 1449. In addition to these published works, Matteo held another in reserve, the story of which recalls that of the little book bequeathed by our own George Herbert to "his dear brother Ferrar," with a message telling him that in it he should find "a picture of the many spiritual conflicts" that had passed betwixt God and his soul before he could subject it to his Master's will, and adding that "if he can think it may turn to the advantage of any poor dejected soul, let it be made public; if not let him burn it." Matteo's work was a poem of three cantos written after the manner of Dante in *terza rima*, and entitled " La Città di Vita." It was kept secret while he lived, and laid upon his bosom in the grave. Another copy had been left by Matteo in the Medicean Library under the Proconsul's care, with directions that the codex should not be read by any one during the writer's lifetime. In it the author relates how a Sibyl appears to him in middle life, and, winning his soul by speech of all things beautiful, and showing him a vision of the Elysian Fields, she draws him on to follow her through Hell to Heaven. She reads for him the book of Nature and the Past, and declares the order of the stars and planets, and the way of Life.

"Se è mi vien gratia infusa dal Eterno
  Per darmi Lume da la sancta luce
In Ciel mi guidi, et mostrimi lo 'nferno;
  La gran Città di Vita che conduce
Ciò che creò quel Padre la governa
  Canto col male ben vi si riduce
Et certo facil fiame, se superna
  Virtù mi chiama ad sì degno lavoro
Et senza quella in van convien si cerna.

"Come mi fu di cosi fare offerto
  Vidi ad gli stremi d'una selva oscura
Grato splendor da Ciel di nuovo aperto
  Levami gli occhi ad quella luce pura.

> Et chiari gli affisai nello splendore
> Et più non m' era selva sepultura
> Parlando quella con divin fervore
> La luce dixe tutti vi conduce
> Per la via mena, sempre senza errore."

The fate of the poem after publication was not so happy as might have been hoped. Misnamed by some "The Sibyl of Palmieri," by others a "Treatise on Angels," the author was condemned by one party for holding the philosophy of Pythagoras, while by others he was accused of Arianism.

Palmieri died in 1475; and the painter Sandro Botticelli was at the zenith of his power in the year 1470, about which time it would appear that he was commissioned by Palmieri to paint the altarpiece for his family chapel in the church of S. Pietro Maggiore, in Florence, the subject of which was to be drawn from the "Città di Vita." Such was the origin of this picture of the Assumption of the Virgin, in which are shown the three circles composed of divine forms of prophets, saints, martyrs, angels, and all the heavenly host, while below, the towns of Florence and Pistoia lie in the calm sunlight, and Matteo and his wife are seen kneeling in the foreground.

Among other accusations of heresy brought against the poem which inspired this work, Richa states that Palmieri followed the condemned opinion of Origen more by poetic licence than from theological sentiment, feigning that our bodies are animated by the angels—by those, that is to say, whom he falsely supposes to have remained neutral when Lucifer fell, and whom the Almighty, willing to prove them once more, compelled to unite themselves to human bodies here below. And, further, his accusers suspected that Palmieri, in displaying, by means of the picture, his erroneous opinions over the most sacred spot in his chapel, had desired to give—or to usurp—the sanction of the Church to those opinions; in fact, to palm off upon the devout his heretical views as consistent with the Canons of the Church. The result was that for many years this great painting of Sandro Botticelli was interdicted and kept covered from view.

Both Palmieri and Botticelli doubtless owed much to the inspiration of Dante. About the year 1481, Botticelli not only commented on Dante, but, with Baldini, executed in the then new art of engraving a series of illustrations of the "Divina Commedia."

It is impossible to contemplate the painting in question without recalling Canto xxx. in the "Paradiso," where the Poet enters the Empyrean, and first beholds the Court of Heaven. In these three circles, "which seem as if encompassing the light, but are indeed encompassed by it," those saintly bands are seen "in fashion like a snow-white rose," while angels mingle with the crowd of saints and martyrs "whispering the peace and ardour which they won from that soft winnowing."

Standing before this picture the lines rise to our memory—

> "And as a pilgrim when he rests
> Within the temple of his vow, looks round
> In breathless awe, and hopes some time to tell
> Of all its goodly state; e'en so mine eyes
> Coursed up and down along the living light—
> Now low, and now aloft, and now around,
> Visiting every step. Looks I beheld,
> Where charity in soft persuasion sat;
> Smiles from within and radiance from above,
> And in each gesture, grace and honour high."

IV.

DEMONS OF FLOODS, p. 116.

In the old rituals of Provence the dragon, carried in the rogation processions as a symbol of heresy, bore the name of Gargouille; it is now applied to chimæras, dragons, and monsters, wrought into waterspouts; first appearing in England in the early English architecture. One of these figures, at Lincoln, is called the "Devil looking over Lincoln." Alexandre Dumas, in his novel of "Le Comte de Monte Christo" (vol. ii. p. 47, ed. 1873), alludes to the procession of Tarasque.

V.

DEVIL AS A LEARNED PROFESSOR, p. 128.

Among the stage directions for the performance of the Mystery play of the Acts of the Apostles we read: "Fault des lunettes pour Sathan." "This," writes M. Didron, "is a curious detail of the

* Dante, Paradiso, canto xxxi. l. 39. (Translated by Cary.)

costume of Satan as represented in the sixteenth century, when every old man wore spectacles."

At Bourges in 1536 we read of the performance of the Holy Acts of the Apostles within the old Roman theatre. The performance lasted forty days. The amphitheatre was covered in and veiled over, so as to protect the spectators from weather and sun, and painted excellently in gold, silver, azure, and other rich colours. The Chapters of the Cathedral and St. Chapelle have lent from their stores rich costumes and vestments.

The performance (monstre) commenced with furies, who issued from the fire like a plague of flies. Then four little demons with gilded bells and wings always in motion. Following them six devils clothed in velvet of divers colours, little serpents, lizards, snakes, and other beasts—" faictes di broderie et bien enrichies"; others followed with fire issuing from their nostrils and ears. Then came a great dragon, twelve feet long, ever-moving head, eyes, and tail, and spurting fire from his mouth.

As regards the history of the Devil, nothing can be more curious than the information to be gained from these texts of the "Mystery of the Acts of the Apostles," including the tenth book, which contains the history of the martyrdom of St. Dionysius; and M. Didron stated it to have been his intention to transcribe and annotate them in his "History of Demons." In the mystery play of St. Quentin, enacted in the collegiate church of St. Quentin, the Hell scenes must have been very striking. The choir of this church in the north of France, west of Caen, is the only original portion of the building which still remains; it dates from the year 1257. The play was enacted there about the year 1350. At the tidings of the birth of Christ, which reach the ear of the parents of St. Quentin at the moment of his birth, and at the time when Diocletian, sinking under the weight of authority, calls on Maximian to share his throne, the depths of Hell are roused; Lucifer, Satan, Ashtaroth, Leviathan, Beelzebub, Cerberus, and a less familiar devil, Berith, meet in counsel. They determine to tempt Maximian, and whisper hatred of Christianity in his ear. (See "Annales Archéologiques," vol. xv. p. 29.)

VI.

THE TEMPTATION OF ST. PAPHNUTIUS, p. 129, vol. ii.

This episode in the scenes of the Hermitage in the Thebaid has been illustrated by Lasinio, *Pitture a Fresco del Campo Santo*, plate c., and explained by Rosini in the text that accompanies the work.

The painter, he tells us, would shew that the Tempter, whether disguised as learned professor, or in the form of a woman, may follow man even into the wilderness, and there, either through terrors or enticements, seek to divert the best from their sacred occupations. The figure kneeling to the right, and thrusting his hands into the flames, is shown to be the blessed Paphnutius, who adopts this expedient rather than yield to the attractions of the graceful woman who kneels behind. She, in the second scene, stricken by the judgment of heaven, falls senseless to the ground; but (in the third scene) revived through the prayers of the Saint, she renounces her evil life, and, kneeling, commends herself to God, that He may pardon her sin and receive her among His followers consecrated to His service.

VII.

FRESCOES—CAMPO SANTO, p. 165, vol. ii.

In the early part of the fourteenth century, the Lorenzetti illustrated hermit life on the walls of the Campo Santo. In 1370 the frescoes of the trials of Job were executed by Francesco of Volterra.

The three upper scenes in the series illustrating the life of St. Raniero are now found to have been executed by Andrea da Florentia, and the three lower to have been by Simone of Siena, and continued by Antonio Veniziano in 1386. In 1391 Spinello Aretino laboured at the scenes from the lives of SS. Ephesus and Pontus. Buffalmacco, or, as he is now called, Buonamico Cristofani painted the Passion, Crucifixion, Resurrection, and Ascension. It is now held that the figures of Macarius and the hermits, formerly assigned to Orcagna, are the work of the Lorenzetti. (Crowe and Cavalcaselle, Hist. Painting, vol. i., p. 445.)

By many authorities the name of Orcagna is now dismissed from the honours of the Campo Santo, because it is held that the style of these frescoes evinces a Sienese rather than Florentine character.

VIII

"MERCURY AND MICHAEL," p. 181, vol. ii.

Gem. Chalcedony, carved, ring collection of the Grand Duke of Tuscany. Latin inscription. Michael—i.e., Like unto God. Gori remarks upon this gem :—
" Mercury sitting on a heap of stones with the caduceus, and his astronomical sign representing the caduceus and two marks. A cock is standing beside him, the symbol of watchfulness. This gem was inscribed by the Basilidian heretics, or the followers of Priscillianus, who added names of holy angels to those of the impure idols of gods, Jupiter, Diana, Mercury, Serapis, as one may see in ch. v. of Chifflet, tab. xxi., who has brought forward this one also among the Abraxa gems, seeing that on this gem Mercury is represented, not standing upright as is frequently seen on coins, gems, and old seals, but sitting down on heaped stones. I think it means Mercury of the roads, or the guardian of the roads, such as Pausanias has described in bronze. sitting among the Corinthians on the road leading to Lachæum, with a ram helping him; because one special office of Mercury was believed to be to guard and increase the flocks. The ancients used to put on their roads a Mercury as the god who ruled over commerce, in order that in business they might obtain prosperous journey and return. Who also, when they went on a journey, used to heap up stones and crown the heaps; to which Tibullus has borne witness in these lines :

" 'For I adore whether a deserted heap in the fields
   Or an old stone on the cross-roads which holds the flower-wreaths.'

Moreover old monuments shew Hercules the companion of Mercury as guide and guardian of journeys." (See Gori, Inscript. Antiqs. 1, p. l. tab. iii. 1.)

APPENDIX II.

"BYZANTINE GUIDE TO PAINTING."

TRANSLATED INTO FRENCH FROM A GREEK MANUSCRIPT

BY DR. PAUL DURAND;

AND FROM FRENCH INTO ENGLISH

BY MARGARET STOKES.

M. Durand's translation of this work from the Greek was enriched with many interesting notes by M. Didron. They appear here only in an abridged form, for the editor found that the substance of many of them was worked into other printed writings of his, which have been incorporated in this volume, so that to have printed them in extenso would have been needless repetition.

[265]

APPENDIX II.

(*See pp.* 189-191.)

"BYZANTINE GUIDE TO PAINTING."

SECOND PART.*

HOW THE WONDERS OF THE ANCIENT LAW ARE REPRESENTED.

ON THE NINE CHOIRS OF ANGELS.

The choirs of holy angels are nine in number, according to St. Dionysius the Areopagite, and are divided into three orders :—

First Order.—Thrones, Cherubim, Seraphim.

The Thrones are represented as fiery wheels surrounded by wings. These wings are filled with eyes: the whole figure symbolises a royal Throne.†

The Cherubim are represented with a head only, and two wings.

The Seraphim with six wings, two of which rise towards the head, two descend to the feet, two are outspread for flight; they bear the flabellum (see note, p. 135 *supra*) in each hand, with this inscription: " Holy, holy, holy." Thus they appear to the prophet Isaiah.

How to represent the Tetramorph.—They have six wings, angel's face and head surrounded by nimbus; in their hands they hold the Gospels against their breast. There is an eagle between the two

---

* The first part only refers to the *technique* of the painter's art, and has therefore been omitted from this work.—ED.

† In the convent church of Cesariani on Mount Hymettus the Trinity is represented in fresco. The Father, an aged man; the Son, a man of thirty-five years; the Spirit as a dove. The bare feet of the Father and Son rest on a fiery circle with wings of fire, just as the Greek figure the choir of angels surnamed Thrones. This winged and flaming wheel is as it were the throne of the Divine feet. Ezek. x. 12, 13. See pp. 91, 98, *supra*.

wings that rise above their head, and a lion by the right wing, and an ox by the left. These three symbolic animals look upwards, and hold the Gospels between their feet. Thus the Tetramorphs appear to the prophet Ezekiel.

Second Order, surnamed Government.—Dominations, Virtues, Powers.

They wear albs down to the feet, golden girdles and green stoles. They wear rings of gold upon the right hand, and hold this seal in the left : (X)

Third Order.—Principalities, Archangels, Angels.

They are represented in soldiers' dress with golden girdles. They hold javelins with hatchets in their hands. The javelins end in lance-heads.

Fall of Lucifer.*

Heaven. Christ seated like a king upon His throne, holding the Gospel open at these words : " I beheld Satan as lightning fall from heaven." All around are choirs of angels filled with profound dread. Michael stands in the midst holding a scroll on which is written, " Let us stand in fear ; let us here adore the King our God." Below are seen mountains, a vast crater beneath which is inscribed the word " Tartarus." Lucifer and all his army fall from heaven. The angels above are full of beauty ; those below are angels of darkness ; lower still they are darker and blacker ; still lower, they are half angels, half demons ; finally they are altogether black and hideous demons. At the bottom and in the midst of the abyss Lucifer, most fearful and blackest of all, lies forward on the ground, looking upward.

Creation of Adam.

Adam, young, beardless, naked, upright. The Eternal Father, surrounded by dazzling light, stands before him, sustaining him by the left hand. Trees and divers animals around. Above, the sky with sun and moon.

* Lady Eastlake remarks that the Greek Church, according to the 'Guide,' gives in greater detail the process of " brutification." She quotes the whole of the scene of the " Fall of Lucifer."

Adam gives names to the Animals.

Paradise, with various trees and little flowers. Adam seated in the midst; one hand outstretched the other across his knees. Before him the cattle and the creatures of the earth, who gaze upon him.

Formation of Eve.

Paradise as above. Adam, naked, asleep, his head resting upon his hand. Eve comes forth from Adam's side, her arms outstretched in the air. Before her, the Eternal Father resplendent in light; He sustains her with His left hand and blesses her with the right.

Fall of Adam and Eve.

Paradise as above. Adam and Eve below, and naked. Before them a great tree like a fig-tree covered with fruit; a serpent entwined around it, with head turned towards Eve. Eve gathers the fruit with one hand, and with the other offers it to Adam, who accepts it.

Adam and Eve cast out.

Paradise as above. Adam and Eve naked; they have twined the leaves of a fig-tree round their waists. They fly, looking backwards. A fiery angel, with six wings and flaming sword, pursues them.*

Lamentation of Adam and Eve.

Paradise closed. A fiery sword before the door. Adam and Eve are seated close by, wailing and tearing their hair.

Adam digs the ground.

Adam, armed by a double-toothed pickaxe, digs the soil; Eve, seated opposite. holds a distaff and winds thread on her spindle.

Birth of Cain.

A grotto. Eve within, laid upon her mantle. Adam, the first father, seated; he holds Cain, an infant in swaddling clothes.

Birth of Abel.

A grotto. Eve, laid upon her mantle. Adam washes Abel in a basin. Cain pours water out of a vase.

---

* This is a seraph. Sometimes St. Michael himself is represented here, as guardian of Paradise.

Cain ploughs the ground.

Cain, young, beardless, in a field with two oxen under a yoke and plough. With one hand he holds the plough, and with the other he goads the oxen. He may also be seen reaping the corn.

Abel with his sheep at pasture.

Abel, young, beardless, carrying a staff; a flock of sheep before him.

Sacrifice of Cain and Abel.

An altar. Above, a sheep burning; the flame rises to the sky. The righteous Abel close by, raising his hands and eyes to heaven. Another altar at the side, on which a sheaf of corn is burning; Cain before it with his hands covering his face; the altar-flame bends round towards him like an arch.

Cain killing Abel.

Mountains. Abel, wounded and stretched upon the ground; Cain, farther on, holds a dagger.

Adam and Eve weep for Abel.

Abel thrown down upon the ground; blood flows from his head. Adam, with grey hair, and Eve weep for their son. An angel says to Adam on a scroll: " Weep not; he will revive at the last day."

Noah receives from God the order to build the Ark.

Noah, below, looks upwards. Above, the sky. A ray falls on Noah; in the midst of this ray there are these words: " Build thee an ark of gopher wood, for I am going to send the deluge. For, behold, I, even I, do bring a flood of waters upon the earth."

Noah builds the Ark.

A great ship; Noah, in front, holding a vase, lays a coat of pitch upon this wooden vessel. His sons calk it, others square it with the hatchet. The women are in the ark; the men outside: some eat, drink, and sing with the women, others are mocking at Noah. Fallow beasts, birds, and all kinds of animals enter the ark.

The Deluge.

A great sheet of water; many drowned men. In the midst of

the waters the tops of mountains may be seen; the ark rests on one of them. Noah opens a window, and holds a dove in one hand.

Sacrifice of Noah.

Mountains. The Ark on a height; fallow beasts, domestic animals, birds coming out of the ark. Outside is an altar upon which a sheep, with other unblemished animals, clean beasts and clean fowl and birds are laid. Noah with his sons and their wives stand round, their hands raised to Heaven.

Noah plants the Vine.

Some men are digging, others turn up the earth with a hoe. Noah, behind, holds the stock of the vine with one hand while he plants several with the other.*

The Intoxication of Noah

Houses. Noah, seated, holds a jug and drinks the sweet wine. Further on, he is again seen asleep and naked. Two of his sons, Seth (sic: Shem?) and Japhet, bear a garment on their shoulders and walk towards him backward. Behind, Ham looks at Noah, and points him out to the two brethren.

Building of the Tower of Babel.

A fortified city and a very lofty tower, on which men are engaged in building. Some have hammers, others divers utensils; others carry bricks; others water; others mortar; others burn the bricks. Many clouds are above the tower. Fiery tongues fall separately on each of the workmen.

Abraham receives God's command to quit his country.

Abraham, standing below, looks upwards. Above is the sky. A ray descends towards the patriarch. In the midst of this ray these words are written: "Get thee out of thy country and from thy kindred, unto a land that I will shew thee."

Abraham going into Egypt.

Abraham riding, Sarah behind him. Before them is a city, at the gate of which are men watching them.

* This is a favourite subject in the vine districts. It appears on the fine stained glass windows of the sixteenth century, in the church of Epernay in Champagne.

Pharaoh, having taken Sarah, Abraham's wife, is reproached by God.

The palace. King Pharaoh asleep on a golden bed; above, an angel, bearing a sword, fills him with terror. Sarah in a corner praying.

Abraham, leading away his wife, whom Pharaoh has respected, turns towards the desert.

The palace. Pharaoh seated upon a throne; soldiers around. Abraham, holding Sarah by the hand, stands before him; the king shows her to him. Farther on, Abraham riding, with Sarah behind him. Lot and his slaves eating with him. Sheep and other animals.

Abraham having conquered Chedorlaomer and his companions, delivers Lot.

Soldiers are seen pursuing other soldiers and a king: they cut them in pieces. Abraham, armed in the midst of them, holds Lot with one hand. Behind them horses, sheep, oxen.

Melchisedek comes before Abraham.

The righteous Melchisedek, arrayed in a sacerdotal vestment, holds plates containing three loaves and a flask of wine; Abraham, dressed as a warrior, stands before him, with Lot. Other soldiers, horses and oxen.

Hospitality of Abraham.

Houses. Three angels * seated at table, having on a plate before them, an ox's head, loaves, besides meats in other dishes, with flasks of wine and cups. On their right, Abraham with a covered dish; on the left Sarah brings another with a dressed fowl.

Burning of Sodom.

Three angels look down on the earth out of the midst of clouds; flames descend from these clouds. Below are houses, burnt and in ruins; men's dead bodies seen among them. Upon a mountain Lot is seen flying with his two daughters. Behind is his wife, white as salt, turned back.

* See vol. I. of this work, p. 52, and fig. 19, p. 54.

Sacrifice of Abraham.

Abraham, on the summit of a mountain, ties his young son Isaac on the wood; he holds the sacrificial knife. Above, an angel points to the lamb caught in the bush by the horns, and says to him: "Abraham, Abraham, lay not thine hand upon thy child!" At the foot of the mountain two youths hold an ass harnessed.

Isaac blessing Jacob.

Houses. Isaac, very aged, on a bed; near him a table covered with viands. Jacob, young, on his knees before him. Isaac holds Jacob by one hand and blesses him with the other. Esau may be seen in the distance on a mountain, holding his bow and hunting animals.

Jacob's Ladder.

The patriarch Jacob, asleep. Above him a ladder reaching to heaven. The angels of the Lord ascend and descend upon this ladder.

Joseph's Dream.

Joseph, a beardless youth, is sleeping. Above him shine sun and moon and eleven stars. Before him twelve sheaves; one is upright, the others make obeisance to it as if in worship.

Joseph sold by his brothers to the Ishmaelites.

A pit; inside of it the beardless Joseph. Two of his brothers hold him by the arms and lift him up out of the pit. The other brothers and the sheep stand close by. The Ishmaelites, with the camels, count out money on a stone, which the others take.

Joseph leaves his garment and flies from sin

A palace. A woman on a couch, seizing Joseph by his garment. Joseph escapes and leaves his garment in her hands.

Joseph in prison explains the dreams of the Chief Cupbearer and the Baker.

A prison. In the midst, Joseph; two men, kneeling before him, seem to address him. The one carries a tray on his head full of eatables; birds fly above and feed upon them. The second bears a cup in one hand; in the other he crushes a bunch of grapes.

Joseph explaining Pharaoh's dreams.

A palace. The king asleep upon a golden bed. Mountains and river outside the palace. Near the river seven kine, well-favoured and fat-fleshed, feed in a meadow; seven black and lean kine come up out of the river. Near that seven ears of corn ripe and good, and seven others thin and blasted. Further on still the king seated on his throne and Joseph before him, saying on a scroll: " The seven well-favoured and fat-fleshed kine are seven fruitful years; the seven thin kine are years of famine."

Joseph established by Pharaoh as master of the land of Egypt.

Pharaoh seated on a throne surrounded by soldiers; before him, Joseph seated on a golden chariot drawn by two horses. A man sounds a trumpet before him; behind him a troop of soldiers bearing lances, accompanied by a multitudinous crowd.

Joseph adored by his Brethren.

A palace. Joseph the patriarch, seated like a king upon his throne; his ten brothers kneel before him. Beneath the palace are beasts of burthen loaded with sacks.

Joseph making himself known to his Brothers.

A palace. Within, Joseph embraces his brethren. Outside is seen the desolation of Joseph's brethren; beasts of burthen; sacks overturned on the ground; soldiers seizing them. One of these soldiers draws a silver cup from Benjamin's sack.

Joseph sets forth to meet his father Jacob and his brethren.

A city. Outside, soldiers, officers, knights; in f ont a horse, with gold-embroidered saddle and golden bridle, is led by two soldiers in raiment of wrought gold; before them Joseph, on foot, embraces his father Jacob. The brethren are behind Jacob. Beasts of burthen laden. Chariots with women carrying children.

Jacob blesses the sons of Joseph, Ephraim and Manasses, and prefigures the Cross of the Lord.

Jacob seated up in bed. Manasses before him to the right; Ephraim to the left. Jacob, having his hands upon their heads, makes the form of the cross by placing his right hand on Ephraim, and his left on Manasses.* Joseph, astonished, behind his sons.

Jacob blesses his twelve Sons.

Jacob, seated up in bed, spreads out his hands in blessing; his children are all on their knees before him.

Moses found by Pharaoh's daughter in an ark of bulrushes.

Mountains and river. In the middle, on the river bank, a little ark, the king's daughter seated on a throne. On her right and left two younger girls hold garments; one young maiden opens the ark before her and draws forth the infant.

Moses feeding his flocks, beholds the burning bush.

Moses untying his sandals. Sheep stand round. Before him a burning bush, in the middle and on the top of which is the Virgin holding her Child; close to her an angel looks towards Moses. At another side of the bush, Moses appears again, one hand outstretched and holding a rod in the other. See vol. i. p. 172.

Moses announcing their redemption to the Hebrews.

Moses standing upright. Aaron at his side. In front a crowd of Jews do him homage.

Moses warns Pharaoh to let the Hebrews depart.

A palace. Pharaoh seated on his throne; Moses and Aaron stand before him; in front, a great serpent who swallows up the other little serpents. The people stand near; they wear high headdresses and great furred hats, and they hold papers. The Hebrews stand outside the palace, some mix the mortar and some the straw, while others mould the bricks and others bake them. Others are being flogged by the Egyptians.

The Ten Plagues of Egypt.

1. Aaron, with his rod, changes the rivers and waters into blood. Rivers and fountains turned to blood. Moses stands upright, Aaron before him, stretches his rod towards the river. The

* See Lady Eastlake, *Hist. of our Lord in Art*, vol. i., p. 169. Martin et Cahier, *Vitraux de St. Étienne de Bourges*, Atlas, pls. i., iv. G. Durandus, *Rationale Divin. Offic.*, lib. v. cap. ii.

Egyptians, in consternation and bewildered, cannot slake their thirst.

2. Aaron and Moses, having stretched out their rod towards the river, make frogs appear.

3. Aaron and Moses, having struck the earth with their wands, gnats appear.

4. The Egyptians are devoured by a swarm of rats.

5. Murrain of the beasts of Egypt.

6. Moses and Aaron, having stetched forth their rod in the presence of Pharoah, bring boils upon the Egyptians.

7. Moses, having stretched forth his hand to heaven, hail and fire destroy the plants and animals of Egypt.

8. Moses, having stretched his rod towards heaven, draws down locusts.

9. Moses, raising his hands towards heaven, draws down a fog of extraordinary thickness.

10. An angel passes over; he strikes the firstborn of Egypt dead, from man to animals.

Moses eating the Passover with the Hebrews.

Houses. A table, upon which a roast lamb and large loaves around it. Moses, Aaron, with other Hebrews, eat, standing and carrying a knapsack and a staff.[*]

Moses, having led the Hebrews across the Red Sea, submerges the Egyptians.

The sea. Women dance upon the shore. A crowd of Hebrews, men and women, having children in their arms and on their shoulders. Moses strikes the sea with his rod. Soldiers are seen in the midst of the sea, some on horseback, some in chariots, covered by the water to the middle of the body or to the head.[†]

Moses with his rod sweetens the bitter waters of Mara.

Mountains. A space filled with water. Moses smites the water with his rod. Near him Hur and Aaron, with a crowd of Hebrews behind them and children, who drink the water.

[*] On many ancient sarcophagi, especially those in the museum at Arles, the Hebrews who depart from Egypt are represented as carrying children or clothes on their shoulders, exactly as here indicated.

[†] In certain Greek manuscripts in the Bibliothèque Nationale, Paris, the Red Sea is personified by a vigorous man, who, seizing Pharaoh, drags him, his chariot and all his army down into the abyss.

Moses and the people arrive at Elim, at the twelve fountains and the seventy palm-trees.

Mountains; twelve wells spring forth, shaded by three-score and ten palm-trees. Moses and the Hebrews stand in the foreground.

Moses on the mountain; he holds his hands outstretched and triumphs over Amalek.

Moses upon a mountain; he is seated on a rock. At each side Hur and Aaron support his hands in the air. At the foot of the mountain, Joshua, son of Nun, and the Hebrews pursue their enemies; they cut them to pieces.

Moses receiving the Law.

A high mountain. On the summit Moses, on his knees, holds the tables of the law. Above, many clouds, fire and lightnings. Angels blowing the trumpet. Lower down upon the mountain, Moses is seen breaking the tables of the law. At the foot of the mountain, the Hebrews feast and dance. In their midst a lofty column supports the golden calf. Aaron stands apart in sorrow.

Moses and Aaron celebrating in the Tabernacle of Witness.

Four golden columns support a tent shining with gold angels with six wings outspread. Below is the Ark of the Covenant, on which rests a golden vase, a seven-branched candlestick and five loaves. Above the ark, and just in the middle, the Holy Virgin is seen with her Child; on one side of the ark we see Moses with his rod and the tables of the law; on the other Aaron in his sacerdotal dress and with a tiara on his head. Aaron holds his golden censer in the one hand and his blossoming rod in the other. Below the arch, Nadab and Abihu, sons of Aaron, with their sacerdotal vestments and censers, are lying dead upon the ground. Outside the tabernacle a crowd of people, an altar covered with victims, sheep and birds, consumed by fire.

Moses, having struck the rock angrily, makes the water gush forth.

Moses, standing up, strikes the stone with his rod. The water gushes forth; the children draw it in vases. A crowd of Hebrews men and women, near Moses. At the top of the rock we read these words: " The waters of strife." *

Balaam goes to curse the Hebrews; he is prevented by an angel.

Two vines. Between the hedges of the vine Balaam mounted on a mule, which he strikes with a staff. The mule kneels and turns his head towards Balaam. The Archangel Michael stands forward with an unsheathed sword. The king's officers and knights appear between the two mountains.

Balaam, called by Balak to curse the Hebrews, blesses them.

Moses, with the Hebrews, fights the Moabites. Upon the mountain are seven altars, on each of which is a bull and a ram. King Balak surrounded by his officers. Before him Balaam looks down on the Hebrews; he blesses them, saying on his scroll: " A star shall come out of Jacob, and a sceptre shall rise out of Israel, and shall smite the chiefs of Moab."

Death of Moses.

Moses lies outstretched in death upon a mountain. The demon stoops towards his feet, an archangel stands at his head, stretches his hands out toward the demon, and threatens him with his sword.

Twelve priests bear the ark into the middle of the Jordan, while Joshua, son of Nun, makes the Hebrews cross the Jordan with dry feet.

Twelve priests carry the Ark of the Covenant upon their shoulders; they stop in the middle of the Jordan, which is dried up behind them. The chariot, drawn by two oxen, is guided by a driver. A multitude with Joshua, son of Nun, crossing the Jordan.

Joshua, son of Nun, sees the leader of the heavenly hosts.

The Archangel Michael, clothed in warrior's garb,† holds a naked sword. Joshua, son of Nun, with grey hair; he is on his knees before Michael, and unties the strings of his shoes, while gazing at Michael.

---

* The water issuing from the rock which Moses struck is an image of Christ. This subject appears on the painted windows of Bourges, Tours and Du Mans, where the Passion of Christ is represented as prefigured in the Old Testament.

† The military costume worn by the archangel Michael and the warrior saints is always that of the Roman emperors.

The Angel of the Lord appears to Gideon while he gathers in the harvest, and encourages him to strive against the Midianites.

Fields. Men gathering in the wheat harvest. An altar blazing. The Archangel Michael holds a rod in his hand, with which he touches the altar. Gideon, on his knees, stretches out his hand towards him; a scythe lies on the ground beside him.

Gideon wrings out the fleece, water streams from it and fills a vase.

A mountain. A threshing-floor. Gideon in the midst at prayer. Before him a lamb's skin with wool; rain falls from the sky upon the fleece. A second time Gideon, outside the threshing-floor, wrings out the fleece over a basin.*

An angel announces the birth of Samson to Manoah and his wife.

Manoah, an aged, bald-headed man; near him his wife. They kneel, their hands and eyes raised to Heaven. Before them an altar with a kid burning. An archangel surrounded by light appears at the same moment in the sky.

Samson kills a lion.

Samson, standing up, tramples a lion at his feet. He turns his head backwards and tears it open.

Samson, having fastened firebrands to the tails of three hundred foxes, sets fire to his enemies' corn.

Corn in great plenty, vines and olives; fields burnt. In the midst, foxes with torches tied to the tail. Samson, holding a fox, fastens a torch to his tail.

Samson, with the jaw-bone of an ass, exterminates ten thousand enemies.

Samson, with the jaw-bone of an ass, strikes the enemies that are before him. Behind him a great number of the slain.

Samson, having carried away the gates of the city of Gaza, brings them up on a mountain.

A city, open and without gates. Samson, bearing the gates upon his shoulders, scales the mountain.

* This event figures the virginity of Mary. In the narthex of the great church of the monastery of Chilandari, on Mt. Athos, this event is represented, and on the fleece may be seen a little image of the Virgin, white as the fleece itself.

Samson blinded by his enemies.

Samson bound in chains; before him, his enemies, who put out his eyes. The woman Delilah stands behind, watching him.*

Samson, having seized two pillars of a house, causes its downfall and the death of his enemies.

Houses ruined, men dead. In the midst of them, Samson himself is dead, still holding the two pillars between his arms.

Samuel assisting at the sacrifice in the temple of the Lord.

A temple and an altar. In the front the prophet Samuel, as a little child, clothed in alb and holding a censer; before him the prophet Elias, who blesses him. His mother Hannah and father Elkanah watch him.

God relates to Samuel the death of the priest Eli and his sons.

The temple. The aged Eli, high-priest, in a deep sleep. The prophet Samuel, a little child, stands near, stretching one hand out and speaking to him. Farther on, Samuel, seated on a bed and looking up; an angel blesses him out of heaven.

Death of Eli and of his sons.

A city. The high-priest, Eli, an old man, is stretched upon his couch with his head broken; a youth stands before him astonished. Outside, the Hebrews pursued by foreigners. The ark is also borne away by enemies. Near at hand, Hophni and Phineas, the sons of Eli, clothed in their sacerdotal robes, lie dead upon the ground.

The enemy tormented in various ways by reason of the Ark of the Covenant; they send it back to the Hebrews.

Two oxen draw a chariot upon which the ark rests. Behind the ark the enemy is seen watching it from a distance; in front, fields and reapers. Priests receive the ark.

* This subject was a common one in the time of the Rennissance, and is represented frequently on capitals, pilasters, stalls, glass and tapestry. Adam listening to Eve, Samson sleeping at the knee of Delilah, Aristotle, as a beast of burthen, carrying the mistress of Alexander, Vergil (a magician) in a panier, Hercules at the feet of Omphale, Pyramus and Thisbe dying by their own hand, are all famous historic, legendary, and mythologic examples of the triumph of love.

THE WONDERS OF THE ANCIENT LAW. 279

The prophet David consecrated king by Samuel.

The child David. The aged Samuel pours oil from a horn on his forehead. Behind David his father Jesse is seen, an aged man, with his seven brethren standing in wonder.

David, playing the harp before Saul, drives the demon from the king.

King Saul, an aged man, seated on a throne, his two hands outstretched towards David; soldiers stand near him. The youth David holds a harp, on which he plays before Saul.

David slays Goliath.

David, beardless, having a sling hung from his belt and a pouch on his right shoulder. He holds a head in his left hand and a sword in the right. Before him, the headless body of his enemy Goliath lies on the ground in armour. Further on, the Hebrews pursuing their enemies; at a still greater distance, choirs of maidens with harps and dulcimers.

David and the people bear the Ark into Jerusalem.

Two oxen draw a chariot, on which the Ark, formed like a golden shrine, is placed; it is surmounted by golden cherubim. Before it, David, in white vestments, plays the harp; he is accompanied by priests, some with dulcimers, others with cithara, others with trumpets. Near the arch, Uzzah lies dead; in the background the people follow in a crowd.

David repents of his sin after the rebuke of the prophet Nathan.

A palace. A golden throne before which David kneels. The prophet Nathan stands up before him, and says to him upon a scroll: "May the Lord pardon thy sin." An angel stands near him.

David having numbered the people, the Lord, displeased, sends his angel, who destroys 70,000, and does not rest till they are exterminated.—1 Chron. xxi. 1–19.

A vast square. An angel in the midst of it stretches out his sword. In the fields around a great number of dead men are seen. At one end of this square stands an altar upon which are the remains of charcoal, corn, and two burnt oxen. David kneels before the altar, his face turned towards the angel. Two soldiers are on the other side. The prophet Gad, between the angel and David, turns toward David and shows him the angel. The city of Jerusalem is seen a little further on.

Solomon consecrated king.

David seated on a throne; before him, the child Solomon is consecrated by a priest who pours oil from a horn.* Further on Solomon is seen mounted on a horse with a golden bridle. Behind him, priests and people playing on divers instruments. The prophet Nathan stands before Solomon.

Solomon building a temple to God

A great temple with cupolas. Builders at work; some carry lime, others cut wood and stones. Near at hand Solomon with his soldiers and officers; he holds a closed book.

Solomon having built temples for idols, his wives come to worship them.

A temple with idols and altars. Women prostrate themselves, Solomon in the midst of them.

The prophet Elijah fed in a cave by a raven.

A cave. The prophet Elias seated within, his elbow on his knees. his chin resting on his hand. Above the cave, a raven watches the prophet and brings him bread in his beak.

Elijah blessing the widow's meal and oil.

A house. A woman holds two vases; the prophet Elijah stands before her and blesses them.

Elijah raises the widow's son.

A high house. On the top a bed in which a child is laid. The prophet Elijah holds the child by its hand and breathes into its mouth; the mother stands behind him.

---

* The consecration of Saul, David or Solomon is thus represented in our Latin monuments also. In the cathedral of Rheims, the above subject occurs among the remarkable sculptures on the outer cordon of the archivolt enclosing the western rose window.

THE WONDERS OF THE ANCIENT LAW. 281

King Ahab goes before Elijah.

Mountains. King Ahab, an old man, mounted on a horse in golden harness; soldiers behind him. In front the prophet Elijah seems to speak to him.

Elijah, by his prayers, causes fire to descend from heaven and consume the sacrifice.

The prophet Elijah stands upright, his hands upraised to heaven; he says on a scroll: "O Lord God, answer me to-day in fire." Before him is an altar upon which an ox is laid. Fire falls from heaven and consumes the sacrifice. A crowd of men lie prostrate on the ground.

Elijah puts the priests to shame and slays them.

A river. On its bank men are seen, bound and led by soldiers; the prophet, armed with a sword, cuts off their heads.*

Elijah asleep under a tree. An angel awakens him and commands him to eat.

A great tree. Under it, Elijah sleeping; near his head a cake and a cruse. An angel comes to touch him by the hand.

Elijah consecrates Elisha the prophet.

A field. Men at work with twelve pairs of oxen. Elisha on his knees holding the mantle of Elijah. Elijah, standing, blesses his disciple. Further on Elijah is seen again, and several altars are before him. Upon these altars, fire consumes the oxen and the broken ploughs.

Elijah draws down fire to destroy two captains.

A high mountain; the prophet Elijah, on the top, looks down around him. At the foot of the mountain are a multitude of dead

* In the art of the Latin Church, Elias is never represented as himself beheading the Jewish priests, as here directed. At Mount Athos, in the convent of St. Laura, Christ, in like manner, is represented in an ancient mosaic as holding an open book with His left hand, and in His right a naked sword, point upwards. In France the right hand is raised in blessing, not in menace. In Italy, the Christ is sometimes armed as in Greece. An Italian MS. in the Bibl. Nationale, 'Psalterium cum Figuris,' shows Christ holding a bow and arrows in the left hand, and a naked sword in the right.

soldiers; the fire from Heaven descends upon them. Further on other soldiers, prostrated on their knees, implore the prophet's protection.

Elijah, walking on his mantle, crosses the Jordan.

The prophet Elijah strikes the Jordan with his mantle. Elisha near him. Fifty sons of the prophets watch them from a distance

The prophet Elijah taken up in a chariot of fire.

A fiery chariot; Elijah, in the centre of the chariot, taken up in heaven.* Elisha, below, receives the mantle that Elijah lets fa towards him; with the other hand he holds a scroll upon whic may be read: "Oh, father, you are the arm that defends Israe You are his champion!" †

The prophet Elisha takes the mantle of Elijah; he strikes the water and crosses with dry feet.

Elisha holds in one hand the folded mantle of Elijah; he strike the Jordan. With the other hand he holds a scroll, on which w read: "Where is the Lord God of Elijah?"

Elisha purifies with salt the poisoned waters.

Elisha throws salt into the middle of the river, and holds a scro on which may be read, "This is the word of the Lord: I purify thes waters." ‡ Near him a crowd of men; some members of the crow drink of the waters.

Elisha curses the children who have insulted him; the bears com out and devour them.

A forest of great trees. Two bears devour a number of children some escape up the trees. The prophet Elisha, below, looks up a them angrily.

Elisha blesses the widow's oil.

A great number of jars. A woman holds a little pot of oil and pours it into the jars; Elisha, standing, blesses the oil. Two youth carry other jars.

* Elijah, borne to heaven on a fiery chariot, is a figure of Christ's Ascension with a red banner in His hand. It occurs frequently on the Christian sarcophagi in the museums of Arles, Marseilles and Paris.

† "My father, my father, the chariot of Israel, and the horsemer thereof!" (2 Kings ii. 12.)

‡ "I have healed these waters. (2 Kings ii. 21.)

Elisha raises the Shunammite's child.

A high house; a bed on the top. On the bed, the prophet Elisha embracing the little child, his mouth upon his mouth, his eyes upon his eyes, his hands upon his hands; outside, a woman in great affliction.

Elisha commands Naaman to go and wash. He washes in the Jordan and is healed.

Naaman, naked, in the midst of the Jordan. On the shore, the soldiers with horses and chariots. His clothes are on the shore.

Gehazi is covered with leprosy, Elisha having cursed him.

Elisha standing with a wrathful look, says on his scroll: "The leprosy of Naaman shall cleave unto thee and to thy race." Gehazi stands before the prophet in consternation.

Sennacherib besieges Jerusalem; the Angel of the Lord descends and slays one hundred four-score and five thousand men.

A city on a mountain. Below the city walls, a multitude of soldiers, some of whom are dead, others being dragged off by their horses; others take flight, looking backwards in terror. Above, an archangel on the clouds surrounded by a great light; he holds a fiery sword in his hand.

Vision of the Prophet Isaiah.*

A cave. Within it clouds and a great light; Christ in the midst seated as a king upon a lofty throne of fire. Christ blesses with the right hand; He holds a scroll in the left, on which may be read: "Whom shall I send, or who will go forth to these people?" Around Him a circle of six-winged seraphim crying and saying, "Holy, holy, holy, Lord God of Sabaoth! All the earth is full of His glory." On the right the prophet Isaiah, filled with a great fear, says upon a scroll, "Woe is me, for I am a man of unclean lips! I have seen with mine eyes the King and Lord of Sabaoth!" A seraph before him holds a live coal with tongs; he places the coal on the prophet's lips.† He holds in his left hand a scroll with these words: "This hath touched thy lips, and hath purged thy

---

* Isaiah, vi. 1. See vol. i. p. 178.

† This subject is sculptured on the west porch of Amiens Cathedral, at the base of a colossal statue of Isaiah. Attributes of Seraph, see p. 102 *supra*.

sins." On the left hand, the prophet Isaiah is again seen in front of Christ; he stands in awe before Him, saying on his scroll: "Here am I; send me."

Martyrdom of Isaiah.

The prophet Isaiah tied to a tree. Two soldiers saw him asunder with a wooden saw. Before him, King Manasses on a throne; near him a crowd of Jews, idols and altars.

The prophet Jeremiah.

A cistern. The Hebrews seizes the prophet Jeremiah by the feet, and throw him head-foremost into the cistern.

The Prophet Jeremiah drawn forth from the cistern by Abimelech.

A cistern. The prophet Jeremiah being gradually raised; at the top of the well, men draw him out with ropes. Abimelech takes Jeremiah by the hand.

Jerusalem taken the second time.

A city burned and in ruins; outside, a crowd of soldiers seize the Jews and King Zedekias. Near the town, Jeremiah and Baruch above, in the midst of the desolation.

Daniel and the three children, only living on pulse, appear fairer and fatter in flesh than they that eat of the king's meat.*

Men eating meat and drinking wine. In the distance Daniel and the three children eat cakes of the pulse and grain. Farther back still is a palace, and King Nebuchadnezzar seated on a high throne. Near him, many satellites; before him, the three children, the prophet Daniel and the others. An officer points them out to Nebuchadnezzar.

Daniel defends Susannah.†

The prophet Daniel, a youth, stands upright. Susannah before him, her hands tied behind her back. Two elders, in ample robes and with their heads covered, show Susannah to Daniel; near her stands Joachim her husband. In the distance the two elders are again seen. The people stone them.

* Daniel i. 15. † Susannah vv. 46, 62.

Daniel interprets the first dream of Nebuchadnezzar.[*]

A palace; the king asleep upon a golden couch. Outside of the palace, a mountain; at its foot an idol with a golden head, breast and arms of silver, body and thighs of copper, legs of iron, feet half iron, half clay. A stone falls from the top of the mountain on the head of the idol. Further on, the king seated upon his throne; Daniel before him points out to him the idol.

The three children refuse to worship an idol; they are thrown into the furnace, where an angel comes to refresh them.

A furnace. Within, the three children, clothed, with hands and face raised to heaven; the archangel Michael in their midst Outside the furnace the soldiers are devoured by the flames. Close by there stands a statue of the king.

Daniel interpreting his dream.

A great and lofty tree. Many birds among its branches; animals feeding at its root. An angel strikes the tree with his hatchet. The king asleep in his palace, on a bed. Further on, the king seated on a throne; Daniel, near the king, shows him the vision.

Daniel interpreting the handwriting on the wall of the palace of King Balthazar.

A palace. A hand, seen as far as the wrist, traces these words upon the wall: "Mene, tekel, upharsin." The king standing struck with terror; before him is Daniel, who shows him this inscription; near them the Magi and wise men. A table prepared for a feast; women in the background.

Vision of the prophet Daniel.[†]

A house. The prophet Daniel asleep upon a bed. Outside of the house, the sea. The four winds blow from the four parts of the sea, whence issue four beasts. The first beast is a lion with eagle's wings; Nebuchadnezzar, king of Babylon, seated above, holding a sceptre in his hand. The second is a bear armed with three rows of teeth; above him, Darius, king of Persia. The third, a leopard with four wings and four heads; above him, Alexander, the king of Macedon, armed with a javelin. The fourth like a black lion,

[*] Daniel iv. 20.   [†] Daniel vii.

with teeth of iron and ten horns upon his head. Three horns are broken; but in the midst of the others there arose a little horn with eyes and a mouth as a man. Above, Augustus, king of the Romans, bearing his sceptre. What remains of the vision is given below at the Second Coming (*i.e.* the Last Judgment).

Daniel, having exposed the deceitfulness of the priests, burns the temple and breaks the statue of Baal.

A temple with a great idol, before which is a table covered with bread and viands. Outside the temple, the king with his satellites. Near the door, Daniel holds a sieve and scatters the ashes before the idol. Further on, Daniel is seen burning the temple and breaking the idol. Soldiers putting priests, with their wives and children, to death.

Daniel destroys the dragon.

A cave. Within, an enormous dragon with gaping mouth; Daniel stands in front and throws black bread down its throat. Behind Daniel, the king and a crowd of people.

Daniel in the den of lions; he is fed by Habakkuk, sent by the angel of the Lord from Jerusalem.

Daniel in the midst of a dark pit, his hands and eyes raised to Heaven; he is surrounded by seven lions. Above him, the archangel Michael, holding the prophet Habakkuk by the hair. This prophet carries a basket filled with bread and viands, which he presents to Daniel.*

The prophet Jonah, flying before the face of the Lord, is thrown into the sea.

A furious sea; enormous waves. In the midst, a ship and sailors throwing Jonah head-foremost into the sea. A monstrous fish receives the prophet in his jaws.

Jonah delivered up by the fish on the bank near Nineveh.

A town; the sea below. A sea-monster casts Jonah on the bank Jonah holds a scroll on which is written: "I cried out of my affliction to the Lord."

* Apocrypha: Bel and the Dragon, vv. 31–42.

Jonah preaching to the Ninevites.

A city; a multitude. Jonah holds a scroll with these words: "Yet three days and Nineveh will be destroyed." Before him are men, women, and children; some crying, others praying. The king, prostrate on the ground, covered with ashes and clothed in sackcloth, tears his hair; his regal robes and crown are cast upon the earth. Behind him rises a royal throne.

Jonah afflicted by the sight of a withered gourd

A stem of gourd withered to the top of its branches. Below, Jonah in distress, one hand extended towards heaven, and holding with the other a scroll containing these words: " I shall mourn for this gourd till death." On high, a ray descends from heaven towards Jonah. Upon this ray we read: "Thou pitiest this gourd; and I, should I not be touched with compassion for the great city of Nineveh?" Below the head of Jonah the sun shoots rays which burn him.

Job, bereft of his children and his goods, blesses God.

A palace. Job, seated upon a throne, looks down and rends his garments; at his side, three men converse with him. Outside of the palace is a dilapidated house. The sons and daughters of Job are destroyed. Farther on, fields, sheep, and oxen; robbers arrive and kill the shepherds. Farther still, horses and camels, whose conductors have also been killed by robbers.

Job sits among the ashes.

A city. Outside, Job, covered with sores, stretched on a heap of ashes; at his side stand three kings who speak to him. His wife says to him: "Curse God and die." Job looks at her with an angered face, and says to her, " Why hast thou spoken as a foolish woman? We have received good at the hand of God, why should we not also receive evil? It is the Lord's will that hath happened. 'Blessed be the name of the Lord.'"

Job, because of his humility, receives twofold for what he had lost.

A temple. An altar upon which an ox and a sheep are burning. Before the altar, Job is seen in prayer, clothed in regal robes. At his side are his wife, seven sons and three daughters, with garments embroidered in gold. Further on, outside, on the mountains and in the fields, are a great number of oxen, sheep, horses and camels, with shepherds and servants.

The righteous Judith slays Holofernes.

A lofty city. Below it many tents are visible within which soldiers are asleep. In the midst is one tent decorated with ornaments of gold. Within it is a golden bed, on which lies Holofernes, beheaded, his body enveloped in a gold embroidered quilt. Judith, clad in sumptuous apparel, stands before him bearing in one hand a bloody sword, while with the other she places the head of Holofernes in a wallet which her servant holds for her. The same city is again seen further on. Men upon its walls hold banners and carry the head of Holofernes on the end of a pike. Outside the town, the Jews pursue their enemies.*

The Holy Patriarchs according to the genealogy.

The first father, Adam : an old man, long hair, white beard.
The righteous Abel, son of Adam : young, beardless.
The righteous Seth, son of Adam : an old man, brown beard.
The righteous Enos, son of Seth : an old man, beard bifurcated.
The righteous Cainan, son of Enos : an old man, large beard.
The righteous Mahalaleel, son of Cainan : an old man, bald.
The righteous Jared, son of Mahalaleel: an old man, beard trifurcated.
The righteous Enoch, son of Jared : an old man, beard pointed.
The righteous Methuselah, son of Enoch : an old man, bald.
The righteous Lamech, son of Methuselah: an old man, beard rounded.
The righteous Noah, son of Lamech: an old man, beard pointed, long hair; he holds the Ark.
The righteous Shem (Gen. xi. 10), son of Noah : an old man, beard bifurcated.
The righteous Japhet, son of Noah: an old man, crisp curly hair, beard round.
The righteous Arphaxad, son of Japhet: an old man, beard large.

* Here end the scenes and pictures, properly so-called, from the Old Testament. Now we shall see single figures at full length. The pictures occupy the highest portion of the walls; the separate figures are ranged below immediately above the casement. This arrangement is followed in the Greek church paintings.

The righteous Cainan, son of Arphaxad: an old man, great brown beard.
The righteous Salah, son of Cainan: an old man, five-pointed beard.
The righteous Eber (from whom the Jews draw their name Ebrews), son of Sala: an old man, beard pointed.
The righteous Peleg, son of Eber: an old man, bald, beard pointed.
The righteous Reu, son of Peleg: an old man, beard bifurcated.
The righteous Serug, son of Reu: an old man, beard large.
The righteous Nahor, son of Serug: an old man, beard trifurcated.
The righteous Terah, son of Nahor: an old man, beard pointed.
The patriarch Abraham, son of Terah: an old man, long hair, beard descending to his waist.
The patriarch Isaac, son of Abraham: an old man, pointed beard, long hair.
The patriarch Jacob, son of Isaac: an old man, long hair, a great beard bifurcated.

The twelve sons of Jacob.

The patriarch Ruben: old man, bald, beard pointed.
The patriarch Simeon: old man, beard bifurcated.
The patriarch Levi: old man, beard rounded.
The patriarch Judah: old man, beard large.
The patriarch Zabulon: old man, beard long.
The patriarch Issachar: old man, beard jonciform.
The patriarch Dan: old man, beard bristly.
The patriarch Gad: old man, beard and hair curled.
The patriarch Aser: old man, fine pointed beard.
The patriarch Nephtali: old man, beard long and full.
The patriarch Joseph: old man, beard long; he carries a mitre.*
The patriarch Benjamin: old man, beard brown, curly hair.
The righteous Zarah, son of Judah: an old man, beard small.
The righteous Pharez, son of Judah: an old man, beard large.
The righteous Hezron, son of Pharez: old man, bald, beard round.
The righteous Aram, son of Hezron: old man, beard pointed.
The righteous Aminadab, son of Aram: greyhaired.
The righteous Naashon: old man, beard bifurcated.
The righteous Salmon, son of Naashon: old man, beard large.
The righteous Booz, son of Salmon: old man, beard round.

* The mitre, or tiara, a sign of sovereign power in Egypt.

The righteous Obed, son of Booz and Ruth : old man, bald.
The righteous Jesse, son of Obed : old man, beard pointed.
The prophet King David, son of Jesse: old man, beard rounded.
The prophet King Solomon, son of David : young, beardless.
The king Roboam, son of Solomon : beard commencing.
The king Abias, son of Roboam : young, beard rounded.
King Asa, son of Abias : old man, pointed beard.
King Josaphat, son of Asa: old man, rounded beard.
King Joram, son of Josaphat : old man, pointed beard.
King Ozias, son of Joram : grey hair, rounded beard.
King Joatham, son of Ozias : young, beard bifurcated.
King Ahaz, son of Joatham : old man, large beard.
King Hezekias, son of Ahaz: old man, pointed beard.
King Manasses, son of Hezekias : old man, large beard, bifurcated.
King Ammon, son of Manasses : old man, grey hair.
King Josias, son of Ammon : old man, beard fine pointed.
King Jeconiah, son of Josias : young, rounded beard.
The righteous Salathiel, son of Jeconiah : young, beard commencing.
The righteous Zorobabel, son of Salathiel : grey hair.
The righteous Abiud, son of Zorobabel: old man, bald.
The righteous Eliakim, son of Abiud : old man, beard bifurcated.
The righteous Azor, son of Eliakim : old man, large beard, coloured brown.
The righteous Sadoch, son of Azor : grey hair, beard bifurcated.
The righteous Achim, son of Sadoch : young, beard commencing.
The righteous Eliud, son of Achim : old man, bald, beard round.
The righteous Eleazar, son of Eliud : old man, large beard.
The righteous Matthan, son of Eleazar : old man, beard trifurcated.
The righteous Jacob, son of Matthan : old man, beard pointed
The righteous Joseph, son of Jacob: betrothed to Mary, of whom was born Jesus, who is called Christ. (Matt. i. 16.)

Other ancestors outside the genealogy.

The righteous Melchisedech: an old man, with large beard, adorned in sacerdotal vestments, a mitre on his head; he carries three loaves on a disk.

The righteous Job: an old man with rounded beard and crown upon his head; he holds a scroll containing these words: " Blessed be the name of the Lord, from this time forth for evermore!"

The prophet Moses: grey hair, very little beard; he wears a sacerdotal dress, a mitre and a veil, and holds the two tables of the law.

The prophet Aaron: an old man with a large beard; he is clothed in a sacerdotal garment, and wears the mitre (or tiara); he holds a golden censer and a blossoming rod.

The prophet Hur: an old man, his beard bifurcated; he wears a sacerdotal vestment, and holds a scroll unopened.

The righteous Joshua, son of Nun: an old man with a rounded beard; he wears a crown and a military dress, and holds a sceptre.

The prophet Samuel: an old man with a great beard; he wears a sacerdotal vestment and a mitre, he holds a horn of oil and a censer.

The righteous Tobias: a large beard bifurcated; he says upon his scroll: " Many nations will come from afar in the name of the Lord God, bearing presents in their hands."

The righteous Tobias, his son: an old man with curly hair; he says upon a scroll: " May the God of our fathers be blessed! May His sacred and glorious name be blessed throughout all ages!"

The three children, Ananias, Azarias and Misaël: young, beardless.

The righteous Joachim, father of Mary of whom was born Jesus, who is called Christ: grey hair, round beard.

The righteous Simeon, who received the Lord in his arms: an old man, great beard.

Holy Women of the Old Testament.

The first mother Eve: old, with white hair.
The righteous Sarah, wife of Abraham: aged.
The righteous Rebecca, wife of Isaac: aged.
The righteous Leah, first wife of Jacob: the same.
The righteous Rachel, second wife of Jacob: young.

The righteous Asenath, wife of Joseph: young.
The righteous Miriam, sister of Moses: aged.
The righteous Deborah, who judged Israel: aged; she wears a crown.
The righteous Ruth: young.
The prophetess Huldah: aged. (2 Kings xxii. 15.)
The righteous widow of Sarepta to whom Elijah was sent: aged.
The righteous Shunamite, who showed hospitality to Elisha: aged.
The righteous Judith, who cut off the head of Holofernes: young.
The righteous Esther, who saved the people of Israel: young.
The righteous Hannah, mother of the prophet Samuel: aged.
The righteous Susanna: young.
The righteous Anna, mother of Mary: aged.

The Holy Prophets, their characteristics and epigraphs.

The prophet Moses: grey hair, very little beard; he says, "May the heavens rejoice with Him, and may all the angels adore Him!"

The prophet King David: an old man, rounded beard; he says, "O Lord, how great are Thy works; in wisdom hast Thou made them all."

The prophet King Solomon: young, beardless; he says, "Wisdom has built itself a dwelling."

The prophet Elijah: an old man, white beard; he says, "May the Lord, the Almighty God, the God of Israel, live!"

The prophet Elisha: young, bald, shaggy beard; he says, "The Lord liveth; He hath given life to thy soul, and He will not forsake thee."

The prophet Isaiah: an old man, a great beard; he says, "Listen O ye heavens, give ear, O ye earth, for the Lord hath spoken the sons ..."

The prophet Jeremiah: an old man with short spare beard: "An it has happened that the word of the Lord hath said unto me Before I formed the ..."

The prophet Baruch: an old man, rounded beard; he says, "O Lord, look down upon Thy holy house, and incline Thine ea towards ..."

The prophet Ezekiel: an old man, pointed beard; he says, "T Lord says: Behold I will Myself search out My sheep ..."

The prophet Daniel: young, beardless; he says, "The God

heaven will raise up a kingdom which will remain indestructible for centuries . . . "

The prophet Hosea: an old man, round beard; he says, " I will have mercy and not sacrifice, and the knowledge of God is better than burnt offerings, saith the Lord . . . "

The prophet Joel: a black beard, bifurcate; he says, "And the Lord will shout from Mount Zion, and He will raise His voice in the midst of Jerusalem."

The prophet Amos: old man, round beard; he says, "Woe unto them that desire the day."

The prophet Abdias: grey hair; he says, " In this day shall I lose the sages of Idumæa."

The prophet Jonah: a bald old man; he says, " Out of my trouble have I cried unto the Lord, and He has heard me."

The prophet Micah: old man, pointed beard; he says, "In this day, saith the Lord, I shall unite that which was broken . . . "

The prophet Nahum: an old man, short beard; he says, " Who can endure the face of His anger, and who can resist His indignation?"

The prophet Habakkuk: young, beardless; he says, "O Lord, I have heard Thy voice. Give life to Thy work and . . . ".

The prophet Zephaniah: an old man, white-haired; he says, " The day of the Lord is near; it is near and rapid."

The prophet Haggai: an old man, round beard; he says, " Behold what the Almighty Lord sayeth: Place your hearts . . . "

The prophet Zacharias: young, beardless; he says, " Such are the words of the Lord: Behold, I shall save My people out of the east . . . "

The prophet Malachi: grey hair, round beard; he says, " Thus hath the Lord spoken: ' From the rising of the sun to the going down thereof . . .'"

The prophet Gideon: old man, bald, round beard; he says, "If the dew has only fallen on the fleece, and that the dryness . . . "

The prophet Zechariah, father of the Baptist (the Harbinger): old man, large beard, sacerdotal dress; says, " Blessed be the Lord God of Israel, for He hath visited and redeemed His people."

The prophet Nathan: a bald old man, round beard.

The prophet Achias: old man, long and large beard.

The prophet Sameas: old man, round beard.

The prophet Joad, whom a lion had torn; strong beard.

The prophet Azarias, son of Adeo: old man, hair curly.
The prophet Ananias: old man, beard bifurcate.

Other prophecies on the Festivals of the Lord, on the Miracles, Passion, and Birth of Christ.

The patriarch Jacob: "The sceptre shall not depart from Judah, nor the government from his descendants, until He who should be sent (the Messenger) cometh, who is the desire of all nations." (Gen. xlix. 10.)

David: "He shall descend as rain upon a fleece, and as the dew which moistens the ground."

Isaiah: "Unto us a Child is born, unto us a Son is given, and He shall be called by His name, the Angel of the Mighty Will." *

Habakkuk: "God will come from the south, and the Holy One from a mountain covered with thick cloud."

Micah: "And thou, Bethlehem, land of Judah, are not least among the cities of Judah, for out of thee shall come forth a Governor that shall rule My people." (Micah v. 2.)

Malachi: "He will arise, for you who fear my name, a Son of Righteousness, with healing in His wings." (Mal. iv. 2.)

Baruch: "He is our God; no other God can stand beside Him." Afterwards: "He hath appeared upon the earth, and He hath talked with men."

Moses says upon the Circumcision: "And on the eighth day ye shall circumcise the child." (Lev. xii. 3.)

Moses says on the Presentation: "Every male coming forth from his mother's breast (that openeth the womb) shall be sanctified to the Lord." (Luke ii. 23.) Another prophecy: "Consecrate unto me every first-born—every first male child." (Ex. xiii. 2.)

On the flight into Egypt: "Behold, the Lord rideth upon a swift cloud; He shall come into Egypt, and the idols of Egypt shall be moved at His presence." (Is. xix. 1.)

Hosea: "I have called My Son out of Egypt." (Hosea xi. 1.)

On the massacre of the Innocents, Jeremiah: "A voice was heard in Rama, lamentation and bitter weeping." (Jer. xxxi. 15.)

On the baptism of Jesus Christ, David: "The waters saw, O God,

* Further on we shall speak of the Angel of the Mighty Will or Counsellor, a wonderful creation of Greek art almost unknown to us. (Isaiah x. 6.)

the waters saw, they were afraid; the depths also were troubled." (Psalm lxxvii. 16.) (See p. 302, *note.*)

Isaiah: "Wash you, make you clean, put away the evil of your doings." (Is. i. 16.)

Jeremiah: "Oh, Jerusalem, wash thine heart from wickedness, that thou mayest be saved." (Jer. iv. 14.)

Ezekiel: "Behold, thus saith the Lord: I will sprinkle clean water upon you, and you shall be clean." (Ezek. xxxvi. 25.)

Nahum: "Behold, thus saith the Lord, who ruleth the great waters." (Nahum 1. 4.)

Malachi: "Behold, I shall send My messenger, and he shall prepare My way before Me." (Mal. iii. 1.)

Zechariah: "And it shall be in that day that living waters shall go out from Jerusalem." (Zech. xiv. 8.)

On the miracles of Christ, Isaiah says, "Surely He hath borne our griefs and carried our sorrows." (Is. liii. 4.)

On the parables, David saith, "Behold, I will open My mouth in a parable." (Ps. lxxxiii. 2.)

On the Transfiguration, David: "Thabor and Hermon shall rejoice in Thy name." (Ps. lxxviii. 12.)

On the resurrection of Lazarus, Hosea: "I will ransom them from the power of the grave, I will redeem them from death." (Hosea xiii. 14.)

On the Festival of (Palm) Branches, David: "Out of the mouth of babes and sucklings Thou hast perfected praise." (Matt. xxi. 16.)

Zechariah: "Rejoice greatly, O daughter of Zion, for behold thy King cometh unto thee, meek, and sitting upon an ass, and a colt, the foal of an ass." (Matt. xxi. 5.)

Jesus driving out the salesmen: "My house, saith the Lord, shall be called the house of prayer for all people." (Matt. xxi. 13; Is. lvi. 7.)

Upon the mystic supper, Jeremiah: "Behold, the days come that I will make a new covenant with the house of Israel." (Jer. xxxi. 31.)

Upon the covenant of Judas, Zechariah: "So they weighed for My price thirty pieces of silver." (Zech. xi. 12.)

On the betrayal, David: "He who did eat of My bread hath practised treason against Me." (Ps. xli. 9.)

Upon the judgment of Annas and Caiaphas, David: "False

witnesses did rise up; they questioned Me on things that they knew not. (Ps. xxxv. 11.)

On the repentance of Judas, Zechariah: "And they took the thirty pieces of silver, the price of the honourable." (Zech. xi. 12; Matt. xxvii. 9.)

Upon the judgment of Pilate, David: "Why do the heathen rage, and the people imagine a vain thing?" (Ps. ii. 1.)

Upon the flagellation, Isaiah: "I gave My back to the smiters, and My cheek to blows." (Isa. l. 6.)

Upon the mockery, David: "I am become a mockery for all My enemies." (Ps. xxii.)

Upon the Bearing of the Cross, Jeremiah: "I was like a lamb that is brought to the slaughter." (Jer. xi. 19.)

Upon the elevation of the Cross, Isaiah: "He is brought as a lamb to the slaughter; and as a sheep before her shearers is dumb, so He openeth not His mouth." (Isa. liii. 7.)

Upon the Crucifixion, Moses: "Look upon your life hung before your eyes." (This refers to Numb. xxi. 8, 9, and John iii. 14.)

David: "They have pierced My hands and My feet." (Ps. xxii. 16.)

Isaiah: "He hath poured out His soul unto death; and He was numbered with the transgressors." (Isa. liii. 12.)

Isaiah: "The righteous have been taken away from the evil." Isaiah, lvii. 1.

"He stooped down, he couched as a lion and as an old lion; who shall rouse him up?" (Gen. xlix. 9.) (See vol. i., p. 341.)

David: "Awake! Why sleepest thou?" (Ps. xliv. 23.)

Solomon: "I sleep, but my heart waketh." (Cant. v. 2.)

Isaiah: "Your tomb shall be in peace."

Isaiah: On the Descent into Hell: "Hell from beneath is moved for thee to meet thee at thy coming" (Isa. xiv. 9.)

Hosea: "In the third day He will raise us up." (Hos. vi. 2.)

David: "Let God arise; let His enemies be scattered." (Ps. lxviii. 1.)

Zephaniah: "Therefore wait ye upon Me, saith the Lord, until the day that I rise up." (Zeph. iii. 8.)

Upon the women bearing perfumes, Isaiah: "Women sent of God shall come here."

Upon the Ascension, David: "God has gone up with a shout, the Lord with a sound of a trumpet." (Ps. xlvii. 5.)

Zechariah: "And His feet shall stand in that day upon the Mount of Olives, which is before Jerusalem." (Zech. xiv. 4.)

Upon the Pentecost, Joel: "And it shall come to pass afterward that I will pour out my spirit upon all flesh, and your sons and your daughters shall prophesy." (Joel ii. 28.)

Zechariah: "In that day, saith the Lord, I will pour upon the house of David and upon the inhabitants of Jerusalem, the spirit of grace and of supplication." (Zech. xii. 10.)

Other prophecies at the Festival of the Mother of Christ.

Upon the Nativity of the Mother of Christ, Ezekiel: "This gate shall be shut, it shall not be opened, and no man shall enter in by it." (Ezek. xliv. 2.)

Upon the Presentation, David: "The virgins, her companions that follow her, shall be brought to the King."

Upon the Annunciation, David: "Hearken, O daughter, and consider; incline thine ear and forget also thine own people." (Ps. xlv. 10.)

Solomon: "Many daughters have done virtuously, but thou excellest them all." (Prov. xxxi. 29.)

Isaiah: "Behold: A virgin shall conceive and bear a Son, and shall call His name Jesus." (Isa. vii. 14.)

Upon the death of the Virgin: "Arise, O Lord, into Thy rest; Thou, and the ark of thy strength." (Ps. cxxxii. 8.)

How to represent the Philosophers of Greece who have spoken of the Incarnation of Christ.

APOLLONIUS.—An old man: large beard, bifurcate, wearing a veil on his head; he says upon a scroll: "I, even I, announce one God alone in a Trinity, reigning above all things. His incorruptible Word will be conceived in the bosom of a young Virgin. Like a fiery ark He will swiftly shoot through space. He will seize on all the living universe and bear it as an offering to His Father."

SOLON, the Athenian.—An old man: beard rounded. He says, "When He overruns this transitory world, He will set there a throne without blemish. The unwearied object of the Godhead is to annihilate incurable passions. He will be hated of all faithless men. He will be hung upon a mountain, and will endure all these things willingly and with sweetness."

THUCYDIDES.—Grey hair: beard trifurcate. He says, "God is a visible light, praise be unto Him. All things proceed from His intelligence, resolve again in His sole unity! There is no other God, neither Angel, nor Wisdom, nor Spirit, nor Substance; but He is the only Lord, the Creator of all that exists, the perfect Word, fruitful above all. Letting Himself fall upon a fertile nature, He has caused fountains to spring from nothing."

PLUTARCH.—An old man: bald, beard pointed. He says, "Nothing can be imagined above Him who surpasses all things: it is from Him and not another that the Word emanates. It is proved immutably that Wisdom and the Word of God embrace the ends of the earth."

PLATO.—An old man: tall, with a large beard. He says, "The old is made new and the new is old. The Father is in the Son, and the Son is in the Father. Unity is divided into three, and trinity is reunited into unity." (See vol. i. p. 2.)

ARISTOTLE.—An old man: shaggy beard. He says, "The generation of God is inexhaustible, for the Word itself derives its essence from Him."

PHILO the Alexandrian.—An old man: bald, large beard, bifurcate. He says, "Behold Him who walketh upon the heaven, that exceeds in brightness the imperishable flame. All tremble before Him, both the heavens, the earth, the sea, the abyss (Chaos), hell and all demons. He is the Father of fathers, and has no Father. He is thrice blessed.

SOPHOCLES.—An old man: bald, beard with five points. He says, "There is but one eternal God—in His nature simple; He hath created heaven and earth."

THOULIS, King of Egypt.—Old man: large beard. He says, "The Father is the Son and the Son is the Father; without flesh and incarnate, God Almighty."

THE DIVINE BALAAM.—Old man: round beard, a veiled head. He says, "There shall come a Star out of," etc.

THE WISE SIBYL:—" There will come from heaven an eternal King, who will judge all flesh and all the universe. From a virgin, a spotless bride, the only Son of God should come. Eternal, unfathomable, the only Word of God. It makes the heaven shake and the human soul to tremble."

How to represent the tree of Jesse.

The righteous Jesse sleeps. Out of the lower part of his breast spring three branches; the two smaller ones surround him, the third and larger one rises erect and entwines round the figures of

Hebrew kings from David to Christ. The first is David; he holds a harp. Then comes Solomon, and after him, the other kings following in their order and holding sceptres. At the top of the stem, the birth of Christ. On each side, in the midst of the branches, are the prophets with their prophetic scrolls; they point out Christ, and gaze upon Him. Below the prophets, the sages of Greece and the soothsayer Balaam, each holding their scrolls. They look upwards and point towards the Nativity of Christ. (See vol. i. p. 475.)

HOW TO REPRESENT THE FESTIVALS OF THE LORD, AND THE OTHER WORKS AND MIRACLES OF CHRIST ACCORDING TO THE HOLY GOSPEL.

The Annunciation of the Mother of God.

Houses. The Holy Virgin standing before a seat, her head a little bent. In her left hand she holds a spindle with silk rolled on it; her right hand is stretched out open towards the Archangel. St. Michael is before her; he salutes her with the right hand, and holds a bâton (long as a lance) in his left. The sky above the house. The Holy Spirit descends from it upon a ray which reaches to the Virgin's head.

Joseph reproaches Mary.

Houses. The Holy Virgin, pregnant; Elizabeth astonished. In front stands Joseph, leaning with one hand upon a staff; he extends the other towards the Virgin, whom he looks at angrily.

The Salutation of the Virgin Mother and Elizabeth.

A house. Inside Mary and Elizabeth embrace. Further on Joseph and Zachariah converse. Behind them a little child with a stick upon his shoulder, at the end of which a basket is hanging. On the other side is a stable. A mule is tied to it and feeds.

The Call of the Magi.

A palace. King Herod seated in a hall, upon his throne. Before him, the three Magi stretch out their hands to him; behind, Jews, Scribes, and Pharisees, converse.

The Nativity of Christ.

A grotto.* Within, upon the right, the Virgin kneeling; she lays

---

* In the East the scene of the Nativity is always laid in a grotto or cave, whereas, in the West, it is in a poor cabin or stable covered with thatch.

Christ, an infant in swaddling clothes, in a cradle. To the left Joseph upon his knees, his hands crossed upon his breast. Behind the cradle, an ox and an ass are watching Christ. Behind Joseph, Christ and the holy Virgin, the shepherds, each holding his staff, watch with astonishment. Outside the cave sheep and shepherds; one of them playing on the flute, the others look upwards in fear. Above them an angel blessing them. On the other side, the Magi, on horseback and in regal robes, point to the star. Above the grotto a multitude of angels in the clouds carrying a roll with these words: " Glory to God in the highest, and on earth peace, goodwill towards men!" A great ray of light descends upon Christ's head.

Adoration of the Magi.

A house. The holy Virgin seated, holding the infant Christ, who blesses. Before her, the Magi present their gifts in golden shrines. One of the kings, an old man with a great beard, and head uncovered, kneels, and gazes on the Christ; with one hand he proffers Him his gift, and, with the other holds his crown. The second king has very little beard, the third none at all.* They look at one another and point to Christ. Joseph stands in wonder behind the holy Virgin. Outside the grotto, a youth holds the three horses by the bridle. In the background, the three Magi are again seen returning to their country; an angel goes before to show the way.

Candlemas.†

A temple and cupola. Underneath the cupola, a table on which a golden censer is standing. St. Simeon Theotokos ‡ takes the little infant Christ in his arms and blesses it. On the other side of the table the holy Virgin stretches out her open arms to the Babe. Behind her Joseph carrying two doves in his robe. Near her the prophetess Anna says upon her scroll: "This Child is the Creator of heaven and of earth."

The Flight into Egypt.

Mountains. The holy Virgin seated on an ass with the child,

* The aged king was named Gaspar; he of middle age is Melchior; Balthazar is the young king; he is beardless, and generally represented like a negro, with thick lips, flat nose and curly hair.
† The Purification Festival, Feb. 2, when lights were carried in procession, in allusion to the words, "a Light to enlighten the Gentiles"— a custom still practised in London in 1548.
‡ He who has received God.

looks behind her at Joseph, who carries a staff and his cloak thrown over his shoulder. A young man leads the ass and carries a rush basket.* He looks behind him at the Virgin. Before them a city and idols falling from its walls.

Massacre of the Innocents.

A city. Herod seated on a throne; two soldiers are near him. In the foreground, many other soldiers with a standard. Other towns upon the mountains with women in them carrying infants; others fly hiding them behind them, and striving with their hands to save them from the soldiers. Other women are seen seated in lamentation by the dead bodies of their children. In other parts soldiers tear the children from their mothers' arms, others stab them with their swords or hew them in pieces, or cut off their heads. A crowd of children stretched bleeding upon the earth. Some in their swaddling clothes, others with their dresses. Elizabeth carries the Harbinger,† a little infant, and flies, looking behind her; she is pursued by a soldier with drawn sword. A rock, mighty as a mountain, splits open to receive her.‡

Christ, when twelve years old seated, among the doctors.

A temple. Within Christ seated on a throne; with one hand He holds a roll, and He stretches out the other. The Scribes and Pharisees seated at each side look at Him in great astonishment. Behind the throne stand Joseph and the Virgin, pointing Christ out to him.

Christ comes to the Jordan to be baptised.

Mountains. Below, the river Jordan. Christ advances; the Harbinger shows Him to the people, and says upon his scroll: § "Behold the Lamb of God, who taketh away the sins of the world." Christ is at a distance standing on the banks of the Jordan. The Harbinger says to Jesus on his scroll! "It is I that should be baptised of Thee, and comest Thou to me." But Christ, blessing him, says: "Prophet, suffer it to be so now, for thus it becometh us to fulfil all righteousness."

* The youth here introduced comes from a now forgotten legend. In Italy, and sometimes in France, he has been replaced by an angel who guides the divine exiles.
† Or Precursor: title of John the Baptist
‡ Apocryphal Gospel.
§ See note, vol. i., page 336, of this work.

Baptism of Christ.

Christ standing naked in the midst of the Jordan. The Harbinger, on the river bank to the right of Christ, looks upward; his right hand rests upon the head of Christ, he raises the left towards heaven. Above, the sky is seen, whence issues the Holy Spirit, descending on a ray which rests upon the head of Christ. In the midst of the ray we read the words: " This is My beloved Son, in whom I am well pleased." On the left angels stand in reverence with arms outspread. Clothes lie on the ground. Below the Harbinger, and across the Jordan, a naked man reclines, who looks behind him at Christ, as if in terror. He holds a vase whence he pours water.* Fish surround Christ.

Christ tempted by the Devil.

The desert and trees. Christ standing, and the devil showing Him some stones, says to Him: " If Thou art the Son of God, command that these stones be made bread." Christ answers upon a scroll: " Man shall not live by bread alone." Near at hand the temple is seen, and on the pinnacle stands Christ, the devil in front of Him, saying: " If Thou be the Son of God, cast Thyself down from hence." And Christ answers him upon a scroll: " Thou shalt not tempt the Lord thy God." Near that, a very high mountain, Christ upon the summit, and the devil standing before Him, showing

---

* This naked man, who looks with fear at Christ, is only another Jordan, a personification of the river, leaning on his urn. It is in accordance with the prophecy of David, as given above, that Jordan is represented as in fear (pp. 294, 295). In the West, the Jordan is sometimes personified at the time of the Baptism. Our thirteenth-century glass windows and miniatures of the eleventh and twelfth centuries afford us many examples. And even more than this: the name Jordan has been divided into two syllables (Jor—Danus), and the baptism is represented as taking place at the meeting of two waters, the Jor and the Danus, being shown as two small human figures, each holding an urn from which they pour water into one bed. See MS., Bibl. Nat. Suppl. Lat. 641. ninth cent. Two rivers of Jordan are represented on a glass window in the sanctuary of Chartres. I have seen, perhaps twenty times in Greece, the baptism in the Jordan thus represented. Jesus stands naked in the middle of the river, His feet placed on a squared stone which rises between two streams; out of the four corners of this stone issue four serpents, who dart body, neck and tongue, out towards Christ with great, though impotent, fury. A similar representation occurs in the cupola of the baptistry of St. Laura at Mount. Athos. Here the sea is also personified, but by a woman's form.

Him all the kingdoms of the world, and saying: "All these things will I give, if You fall at my feet and worship me." Christ says to him upon a scroll, "Get thee behind Me, Satan; for it is written, You shall worship the Lord your God." At the base of the mountain may be seen cities and fortresses; kings seated at table, soldiers, with standards standing round. Further still, Christ and the angels around Him, some on their knees, others holding fans, and the devil in flight, looking backwards. (See vol. i. p. 277.)

The Harbinger testifies for Christ before His disciples.

The Harbinger points out the Christ to John and Andrew. Near at hand are Andrew leading Peter, and Philip leading Nathaniel up to Christ.

Christ calls His disciples, who give up fishing for fish.

The sea. Two ships in the midst of it; in the one Christ, Peter kneeling before Him. Andrew draws the net. In another ship, John and James, with their father Zebedee, draw the same net. There are so many fish to be seen in it that the net breaks.

Christ changes water to wine at the marriage at Cana

A table; Scribes and Pharisees seated near. The chief personage in the company holds a cup filled with wine, and looks astonished. The bridegroom with grey hair, and round beard, is in the midst of the group; the bride stands near him. They wear crowns of flowers on their heads. Behind them a youth carrying a large vast and pouring wine into a cup. Under the table six jars, which two youths fill from leathern bags. Christ, seated at the head of the table, blesses them. The Holy Virgin and Joseph are near Him, and the Apostles behind.

Christ questioned by Nicodemus.

Christ seated. Behind Him the apostles. Nicodemus seated before Him, questioning Him.

Christ talketh with a woman of Samaria.

Christ seated on a stone, and the apostles behind Him astonished. A well in the foreground, near which is a woman holding a pitcher in her left hand, and stretching out her right towards Christ. Christ blesses her. There is an urn at this woman's side.

Christ heals the nobleman's son.

A city. Christ blessing. Behind Him the apostles. In front a man with fur bonnet and magnificent dress speaks to Him. Behind this man, three soldiers watch him, and point to a great palace in the background, in the midst of which is a bed; upon this bed is a youth holding his belt.

Christ teaching in the Synagogue.

The temple. Christ, standing up in the midst, holds a book in two hands, and reads these words: " The spirit of the Lord is upon Me, therefore I preach the gospel to the poor." Near Him a youth stretches out his hand eagerly to receive the book. The Scribes and Pharisees seated round Him point Him out to one another. A number of people regard him with astonishment.

Christ healing the possessed man.

The temple. Within it Christ and His apostles. Before Him is a young man laid upon the ground and foaming at mouth. Scribes, Pharisees, and people stand round in admiration.

Christ cleanses the leper.

A mountain. Christ at the foot of it, with His apostles; before Him, a naked man, all covered with sores, kneels at His feet. Christ lays His hand upon the head of the leprous man, from whose mouth fall scales like the scales of a fish.

Christ heals the centurion's servant.

Christ with His apostles. A man in military costume kneels before Him. In the distance, a palace and a youth rising from his bed. Around him stand men and women. A man, near the centurion, points to the palace.

Christ raises the widow's son.*

A city. Outside the gates, a crowd of men. In the midst, four of them place a bed upon the ground, on which a young man, covered with a winding sheet, is laid. He raises himself a little and looks at Christ. Christ touches the bier with one hand, and with the other blesses the young man. Behind Christ are the Apostles. At His feet, a woman weeps and tears her hair.

* Luke vii. 11-16.

*Christ healeth Simon's wife's mother.**

A house. The mother-in-law of Peter, an old woman, laid upon a bed. Christ raises her by the hand. The apostles behind.

Christ heals different sicknesses.

Christ standing, blessing. The apostles behind Him. A crowd of sick people before Him: some laid on their beds, some upon crutches, some carried on other men's shoulders; the blind, the lame, the paralysed.

Christ stilling the winds and the sea.†

A furious sea, and a little vessel sailing in the midst. Christ asleep, at the prow. Peter and John, filled with fear, stretch out their hands to Him. Andrew holds the helm; Philip and Thomas make fast the sails. Christ is seen a second time in the midst of the ship raising His hands before the winds and rebuking them. Clouds above; winds blowing through the sails.‡

The demoniacs in the country of the Gadarenes; Christ heals them and drives the demons into the swine.§

A city. Mountains and a great number of tombs around. Two demoniacs come forth; they lean with one hand upon the ground, and stretch out the other towards Christ. Christ, surrounded by His disciples, blesses them. A multitude of demons issue from the mouths of the demoniacs, and are driven towards a herd of swine grazing close by. Some ride astride on the backs of the swine, others run down their throats. The swine throw themselves into the sea, and the herdsmen fly towards the city, looking backwards.

Christ heals the man sick of the palsy in a house.‖

A house. Christ with his disciples. Pharisees seated. Above

* Matt. viii. 14; Mark i. 29; Luke iv.
† Matt. viii. 23; Mark iv. 35; Luke viii. 22.
‡ The Greeks, powerful in imagination, and ready to embrace the images of heathen mythology, personify the winds. In the great convent of Vatopedi, on Mt. Athos, the four cardinal winds are figured on the walls of the porch of the principal church. They are represented as heads without bodies, with inflated cheeks, and two great wings, with mouths wide open they blow upon the sea. Near their bristled hair may be read "Zephyrus"—"Boreas"—"Notus." Notus alone is young and beardless; the others are old and bearded. See *Annales Arch.*, vol. i., pp. 38, 40.
§ Matt. viii. 28; Mark v. 1; Luke viii. 26.
‖ Matt. ix. 1–8; Mark ii. 1–12; Luke v. 17–26.

Christ are two men upon the roof; they hold a bed suspended by means of cords; before Christ a man, half sitting up, is on the bed. This man is seen again in the midst of the crowd; he is walking, and carries his bed on his shoulders.

Christ calling Matthew from the receipt of custom.

Christ standing with His apostles; before Him, Matthew on his knees. Behind Him, a house with boxes, account-books and writing materials. Above them a pair of scales.

Christ eating with publicans.

Houses and table. Christ seated. Men, some with fur hats, others with turbans, others with bare heads. Matthew and two female attendants serve the food. A youth carries a vase and serves the wine. The disciples are outside the house. The Pharisees talk to them and point at Christ.

Christ cures the woman with an issue of blood.*

Christ, standing, turns His face backwards towards His disciples. A woman on her knees holds the hem of Christ's garment and raises her eyes towards Him. He blesses her. A crowd of people stand around.

Christ raises the daughter of Jairus.†

A house. A young girl seated on a gilded bed. Christ standing before her, takes her by the left hand, while He blesses her with the right. Behind Christ, Peter, James, and John. On one side of the bed is a man with a fur robe, and a veiled head; on the other side, a woman weeping. A great crowd is seen outside the house.

Christ cures two blind men.‡

Christ. The apostles behind Him. Two blind men in front with their sticks. Christ touches their eyes with His hands.

Christ cures the man possessed by a deaf and dumb spirit.∥

Christ with the apostles. Before Him a man, out of whose mouth a demon issues. Christ touches the ear of the deaf man

---

* Matt. ix. 20–22; Mark v. 25–34; Luke viii. 43–48.
† Matt. ix. 18; Mark v. 22; Luke viii. 41. ‡ Matt. xx. 30.
∥ Matt. ix. 32; Luke ii. 14; "a dumb spirit;" deafness not mentioned. St. Mark vii. 32: "a deaf and dumb spirit:" devil not mentioned.

with His right hand. Scribes and Pharisees, and a crowd around Him.

Christ questioned by the disciples of the Harbinger.*

Christ with ten disciples; He blesses them, and says upon a scroll which He holds : " Tell to John that which you have heard and seen." Before Him stand the blind, the lepers, and the demoniacs, demons issuing from their mouths. Opposite Christ, John and Andrew, holding a scroll on which we read : " Art thou He that should come, or do we look for another ? "

Christ crossing the fields at harvest-tide.†

A fortified town. Outside, a field of corn in ear; the disciples pluck the ears of corn; some rub them in their hands, and others eat them. At the far end of the field Christ is seen, holding a scroll, and saying : " Have ye not read what David did when he was an hungered?" Before the gates of the town the Pharisees stand watching Him; one of them holds a scroll with these words : " Why do they on the Sabbath day that which is not lawful?"

Christ cures a man with a withered hand.‡

The temple. Christ in the midst with His apostles ; He gives His benediction. A man before Him holds up his withered hand with the other, which is healthy, and shows it to Christ. The Jews in the background.

Christ cures the blind and dumb demoniac.

Christ with His apostles; He gives His blessing. Before Him a blind man, holding his crutch in one hand, and touching his ear with the other ; a demon issues from his mouth.

Christ sought out by His Mother and His brethren.

A house. Christ in the midst of it with His apostles, and teaching. Outside the gate, the Holy Virgin, and James Adelphothéos, and Simeon his brother, with two other men and women. A man at Christ's side; he points to the Virgin outside.

* Matt. xi. 1. † Mark ii. 23.
‡ Matt. xii. 10; Mark iii. 1; Luke vi. 6.

Christ cures the paralysed in the Piscina probatica.[*]

The pool. Below, five arches. An angel plunges his hands in the waters of the pool. To the right, Christ with the apostles; He gives His benediction. Before Him, a man with a rounded beard, and dress cut short at the knees and elbows. Near Him are other sick people stretched on their beds.

Christ blessing the five loaves.[†]

Mountains. A child carries a basket containing five loaves and two fish. Christ, standing looking up to heaven, holds the basket with the left hand and blesses with the right. Near Him, Philip and Andrew; a multitude seated in five different places. Three apostles, bending down a little, carry baskets on their shoulders; three take pieces of bread in the baskets placed before the men who are sitting down. Others carry the baskets and distribute the portions among the people.

Christ walking on the sea.

The sea, with frightful and furious waves. In the milst of it, a little vessel, in which are the apostles, terrified. Outside the vessel, Peter has sunk up to his knees in the sea, stretching out his arms. Christ, walking on the waves, takes him by the hand.

Christ heals many sick who touch the hem of His garment.

Christ blessing, and surrounded by the apostles. A great number of persons all around afflicted by divers maladies. They touch the fringe of the Saviour's garments.

---

[*] Bethesda: John v. 2. "According to apocryphal legend it was into this piscina that the colossal beam was thrown of which the Saviour's cross was made. The story is as follows: It is related in scholastic history that the Queen of Sheba saw this wood in the temple, and she said to Solomon, on her return to the palace, that He who would one day hang upon that tree would by His death bring about the destruction of the Jewish empire. Solomon therefore caused the tree to be taken and ordered it to be buried in the bowels of the earth. Thus in the spot where it was buried the *Piscina probatica* was hollowed out, and it was not only because of the descent of the angel, but also because of the virtue of the wood, that the waters were moved which restored health to the sick. When the time of the Passion of Christ drew near, this beam arose from beneath the waters; and the Jews, on beholding it, begged for it, and fashioned the cross of the Lord therefrom."—See *Légende Dorée*, vol. ii., p. 109.

[†] Matt. xiv. 15.

Christ heals the daughter of the woman of Canaan.[*]

Christ blessing, surrounded by apostles; a woman prostrate at His feet. A little further on, behind this woman, a young girl laid upon a bed. A demon issues from her mouth.

Christ healing a stammerer.

The same as the dumb demoniac. (See p. 306.)

Christ blessing the seven loaves.†

Seven loaves and some little fishes in a basket. Christ, looking up to heaven, blesses them. The apostles, two by two, carry baskets filled with bread to be divided among the crowd. The others distribute them.

Christ curing the blind man at Bethsaida.‡

A town. Christ outside the town. Before Christ a blind man holding a staff; the Saviour touches his eyes with the right hand. The apostles stand near.

The Transfiguration.

A mountain with three summits and peaks. Christ stands in white garments upon the middle one; He blesses. A radiating light surrounds Him. On the peak to the right, Moses appears, holding the tables of the Law. The prophet Elias on that to the left. Both are standing, and gaze supplicatingly at Christ. Below Christ, Peter, James, and John lie prostrate, with heads upturned; they appear lost in ecstasy. Behind, on the mountain side, Christ is again seen mounting with the three apostles, and showing them the top of the mountain. On the other side the disciples are seen descending in fear, and looking behind. Christ, coming after them, blesses them. (See vol. i. p. 117, fig. 39.)

Christ heals the lunatic child of the archon.§

Christ, standing, with the apostles. Before him, at his feet, a youth, chained and laid on his back, as if dead. With the foam proceeding from his mouth, a demon issues also. The father is on his knees, holding out his hands towards Christ.

* Matt. xv. 22. † Matt. xv. 36.
‡ Mark viii. 22. § Matt. xvii. 14.

Christ, with Peter, paying the didrachma (tribute-money).*

The sea-shore. Peter, with bare feet, and almost without clothing, is seated on a stone, and holds a fish attached to a sprig of straw. A little further on, Christ and Peter may be seen giving the silver to a soldier.

Christ blessing a little child.†

Christ, seated, holds a little child with one hand; He blesses it with the other, and, showing it to the apostles, He says: " Whosoever shall humble himself as this little child, the same is greatest in the kingdom of heaven." The apostles look at one another in astonishment.

Christ questioned by a doctor of law.‡

Christ seated; the disciples stand behind Him. A doctor of law, an old man with veiled head, holds a closed book in his hand; he stands before Christ and questions Him.

Christ received into the home of Martha and Mary.

A house. Within it, Christ seated upon a chair; behind Him, the apostles. Mary, seated at His feet, gazes up to Him and listens eagerly. Opposite to Him, a table laid. Martha brings a plate to this table with more viands; she looks at Christ.

Christ, in the synagogue, cures the woman with the spirit of infirmity.§

The temple. A woman, quite bent down, leans upon a stick. Christ stands before her; He places His hand upon the head of this woman; He stretches out the other towards the Pharisees, looking at them. The chief of the synagogue points out Christ in the crowd, towards whom He turns His face. The apostles, standing behind Christ, are in astonishment.

Christ heals the dropsical man.

A house. Within, Christ with the apostles. Before Him, a dropsical man, naked, only wearing drawers. He is much swollen; he leans on two crutches and looks at Christ. All around, a crowd of Jews.

* Matt. xvii. 24. † Matt. xviii. 4.
‡ Luke x. 25–28. § Luke xiii. 11.

Christ healing the ten lepers.

The enclosure of a town. Christ with His disciples. Before Him ten lepers, naked, only wearing calicon, their bodies all covered with wounds. Christ blesses them.

Christ blessing little children.

Christ seated. Women lead little children before Him. The apostles wish to repulse them, but Christ gives them His benediction.

Christ questioned by the rich youth.*

Houses. Christ seated. Behind Him the apostles; before Him the rich youth, respectfully questioning Him.

Christ teaching the sons of Zebedee.

Christ standing. Before Him, James and John, their hands stretched out towards Him; their mother near them, kneeling, her hands and eyes raised towards Christ. He stretches out one hand, and holds a scroll in the other: "You know not what you ask." Behind Him, the other apostles regard James and John with indignation.

Christ enters into Jericho.

The walls of a city. Outside the gates, Christ standing; the apostles behind Him. Before Him, a blind man holding a staff; Christ blesses him.

Christ calling Zacchæus.†

A city and a numerous company; a sycamore-tree in the midst, on the top of which is a man of small stature, with grey hair. He wears a short and narrow dress; his head is covered with a handkerchief, and his eyes are fixed on Christ. Christ and His apostles look at him from below; He blesses him with one hand; with the other He holds a scroll, on which is written: "Zacchæus, haste thee to descend."

Christ leaving Jericho.

The same as above, only that the faces of the blind men should be different, for the sake of variety.

Christ absolves the adulterous woman.

The temple. Christ is seated writing on the ground, and says: "Let him who is without sin among you throw the first stone."

* Mark x. 21.   † Luke xix. 5.

Behind Jesus, the apostles; before Him, a woman, standing, her hands crossed upon her breast. Scribes and Pharisees fly, looking behind.

Christ on the point of being stoned by the Jews.

Christ teaching. The apostles hear Him; all round, the Jews holding stones.

Christ cures the man born blind.

The streets of the city of Jerusalem. A blind youth kneeling upon a stick with a knapsack slung upon his shoulders; his toes outside his shoes. He is standing before Christ. Near Him the blind youth is again seen washing his eyes in the water of a pool.

Christ a second time in danger of being stoned.

The same as before.

The resurrection of Lazarus.

A mountain with two peaks; behind the walls of a city of considerable size. The Hebrews in tears issue from the gates and advance towards the centre of the mountain in the background. Before this mountain is a tomb; a man has raised a stone by which it is covered. Lazarus stands upright in tne midst of the tomb; another man takes off his winding-sheet. Christ blesses him with one hand; in the other He holds a scroll, and says, "Lazarus come forth." Behind Him are the apostles. Martha and Mary prostrate themselves in adoration at the feet of Jesus.

Mary, sister of Lazarus.

A house. Within, a table, before which Christ is seated, with the apostles, with Lazarus and Simon, his father. Mary, on her knees before the Saviour, dries His feet with her hair and embraces them near her, a glass vase with narrow neck. Opposite, Martha carries a reed in her hand and looks at Christ with astonishment. Judas indignant, points out the vase of myrrh to the others.

The Festival of Palms.

The walls of a city. A mountain outside. Christ, seated on an ass, gives his benediction. Behind Him, the apostles; before Him. a tree upon a mountain. Children with hatchets cut branches from this tree, and strew them on the ground. Another child, having climbed a tree, looks down at Christ from the branches. Below, several children near the ass. Some carry branches, others throng round Him, others spread garments, others throw armfuls of branches under His feet. Outside the city gate stand Jews, men and women, carrying children in their arms, upon their shoulders, and holding branches; others watch Christ from the summits of the walls and the city gates.

Christ drives the salesmen and the merchants from the Temple.

The temple. Inside, tables and hanging cases, pieces of money scattered, here and there, upon the ground. Some men dragging oxen, others sheep, others asses; others carry doves. They wear fur caps upon their heads or veils or hats. They take flight, looking behind them frightened. Christ, armed with a whip, pursues them in anger. The apostles follow Him.

Christ heals the blind and the lame in the Temple.

The temple. Christ inside. The apostles are behind Him, the blind and the lame, before Him. Some lean on crutches, others hold staff. Christ blesses them.

Christ curses a fig-tree.

A fortified city. Outside are mountains and a fig-tree, barren, and with withered leaves. Christ, looking at it, stretches His hand towards it. Behind, the apostles astonished.

Christ questioned by a lawyer.

Christ seated with the apostles. Before Him, a crowd of scribes and pharisees, who converse; one among them turns his face towards Christ and speaks to Him.

Christ commends the widow's pennies.

The temple. A box into which Pharisees and archontes throw coins, some of gold and some of silver. In the midst of them a widow throws in two pennies. Christ seated opposite points out the widow to the disciples, and says on His scroll: " Verily I say unto you, this woman hath cast in more than they all.

Christ in the house of Simon ; a woman anoints his head with myrrh.

A house. Christ seated at the table with Simon and the apostles. A young servant. Behind Christ a woman carrying a glass vase, which she breaks above the head of Jesus.

THE HOLY PASSION.
The compact of Judas with the Jews.

A house. Within, Annas and Caiaphas seated on thrones; the scribes and Pharisees seated around them. In front, a chest, on which one among them counts out the silver. Judas before the chest; he extends his hands towards the silver which Annas shows him.

The holy ablution.

A house. Peter, seated upon a seat, points to his feet with one hand; he places the other upon his head.* Christ kneeling before him, His robe raised and fastened with a towel for a girdle; He takes the foot of Peter with one hand and stretches out the other towards him. Before the knees of Christ stands a basin of water and a ewer. The other apostles seated behind talk to each other; many of them fasten their shoes.

In another place Christ is again seen seated and again dressed He extends one hand to His disciples, and with the other He holds a scroll, on which He says: "Verily I say unto you, one of you shal betray Me." The apostles, behind Him, look at Him alarmed, and speak to one another.

The mystic meal.

A house. Inside a table with bread and plates full of viands; a cup and a large flask of wine. Christ seated at this table with Hi apostles. John at His left side leaning on His breast; Judas † to th right stretches out his hand towards a dish and looks at Christ.

The prayer of Christ.

A garden with trees. In the middle, Christ on His knees, Hi hands and eyes raised to heaven; drops of blood fall from His fac

---

* By this action signifying the disciple's words: "Not my feet only, bu also my hands and my head." This treatment of the subject is foun among the sculptures in the cloister of the cathedral of Notre Dame, Pari

† Judas is represented with a dark nimbus. *See* vol. i., p. 157.

upon the ground. An angel above, surrounded by a great light, stretches out his hands towards Him. A little behind Christ, Peter, James, and John asleep. Above, Christ may be seen again taking Peter by his mantle and holding a scroll with these words: " Is it thus that you have strength to watch with me ? "

The treason of Judas.

A garden. Judas in the midst embracing Christ, who gives him the kiss of peace. Behind Judas, Peter, and, below him, a young soldier * on his knees, whose ear he strikes with his sword. Soldiers stand round Christ, some with naked swords, others with lances, others with lanterns and torches; others seize Christ and strike Him.

Judgment of Christ.

A palace. An old man with a great beard, in ample robes and with a large mitre-shaped hat,† stands upon his throne and rends his garments. Caiaphas, grey-haired and with a long beard, is at his side, filled with indignation. Before them Christ, bound. A servant strikes Him; other soldiers maltreat Him. Scribes and Pharisees. Two men, standing up before Christ, point Him out to Annas.

The third denial of Peter.

Below the palace of Annas, where Christ is condemned, Peter is standing on a slight eminence. Before him, a fire may be seen and two soldiers warming themselves at it and questioning Peter. Further on, Peter near the gate of the palace, much terrified and stretching out his arms; a young girl shows him Christ. Above, upon a window, a cock crows. Peter is again seen in another place, weeping.

Christ condemned.

A palace. Pilate, young, with a large beard and splendid vestments; his head-dress embroidered with gold. He is seated upon a throne. Before him, Christ bound, led by soldiers. A crowd of scribes and Pharisees point out Jesus to Pilate.

Judas detests his crime and hangs himself.

The temple. Annas and Caiaphas, scribes and Pharisees seated before them. A chest. Judas, standing a little bent down, with

* Malchus.
† A kind of mitre with two points; the hat of the high priest.

his two hands throws the pieces of silver down upon the chest. The others with one hand on their breast stretch out the other to Judas. Outside the temple are mountains, Judas hanging to a tree so that the branches bend beneath his weight till his toes touch the ground.

Christ condemned by Herod.

A palace. Herod, an old man with round beard, in regal robes, is seated upon a throne. Behind him are soldiers; Christ is before him, and two soldiers clothe him in white. Behind, a crowd of Jews are seen.

Pilate washes his hands.

A palace. Pilate seated on a throne, his eyes turned towards the Jews. One man before him, carrying a basin and ewer, pours out the water and washes his hands. Behind him a youth whispers in his ear. Near the throne another youth writes these words on a scroll: "Lead out this Jesus of Nazareth to the public place of execution and fasten Him to a cross, between two thieves, for He hath corrupted the people, insulted Cæsar, and, as witnessed by the wise men of the people, He hath falsely proclaimed Himself to be Messiah." The Christ stands before him, soldiers seize upon Him. Annas, Caiaphas and other Jews lay their hands upon the heads of a group of children who stand before them, look towards Pilate and approve his sentence.

The Flagellation.

The Christ, his hands tied behind Him, is fastened to a column; His body is covered with stripes. Two soldiers flog Him.

Christ mocked.*

Christ stripped, only clothed in the purple chlamys, a crown of thorns upon His head, and a reed in His right hand. Soldiers stand around laughing at Him: some kneel, others strike Him on the head with a rod.

Christ bearing His Cross.

Mountains. Soldiers, on foot and on horseback, surround Christ some among them carry a standard. Christ, exhausted, falls to the earth and supports Himself with one hand. Standing before Him Simon the Cyrenian may be seen, grey-haired and with a round

* Matt. xxvii. 25.

beard, wearing a short dress. He takes the cross upon His own shoulders. Behind Him may be seen the Holy Virgin, John Theologos, and other women weeping. A soldier pushes them back with his baton.

Christ nailed to the Cross.

A crowd of Jews and soldiers seen upon a mountain. A cross laid upon the ground in their midst. The body of Christ upon it. Three soldiers hold it by ropes at the arms and foot. Other soldiers bring nails and drive them with a hammer through His feet and hands. In another place Christ is seen standing before the cross. A soldier holds a cup of wine to His mouth; but Christ turns away His head and refuses to drink.

The Crucifixion of Christ.

Christ upon the cross on a mountain. At each side of Him the thieves are to be seen, crucified. The thief to the right, a grey-haired man with round beard, says to Christ, "Lord, remember me when thou comest into Thy kingdom." He to the left, young and beardless, turns back and says to Him: "If thou art the Christ, save Thyself and us." A tablet may be seen, nailed to the top of the cross of Christ, on which are these characters, I.N.R.I. Below and to the right, a soldier on horseback pierces the right side of Christ; water and blood flow forth. Behind Him, the mother of Christ may be seen insensible; other women, carrying myrrh, support her. Near her John Theologos stands in sorrow, his cheek resting on his hand.* St. Longinus the centurion looks at Christ; he raises his hand and blesses God. A soldier on horseback to the left holds a sponge attached to the end of a rod, which he reaches to the mouth of Christ. Near at hand are other soldiers, scribes, pharisees, and a crowd of people. Some speak to each other and point to Christ; others look at Him terrified; others contemptuously; others stretch out their hands to Him, saying, "He saved others, Himself He cannot save." Three soldiers are seated and parting His garments among them. The central figure in this group has his eyes shut, and is stretching out his hands towards those of the others on the right and left. At the foot of the cross is

---

* This gesture is very common in the Latin Crucifixions, especially of the Roman period. *See* vol. i. *supra*, fig. 3, p. 29.

a little hollow, inside which may be seen the skull of Adam and two cross-bones stained by the blood that falls from the feet of Christ.*

Joseph demanding the Lord's body.

A palace. Pilate within, seated on a throne. A soldier at his back holds a sword in its sheath. Joseph, an old man, bent, stands before Pilate stretching out his hands towards him. The centurion between Joseph and Pilate speaks to the latter.

The Descent from the Cross.

Mountains. The cross fixed in the ground with a ladder placed against it. Joseph mounts to the top of the ladder, clasps Christ round the waist, and lets Him down. Below is the Holy Virgin, standing. She receives the body in her arms, and kisses the face. Behind her, women † may be seen carrying perfumes, Mary Magdalene takes the left hand of Christ and kisses it. Behind Joseph stands John Theologos, and kisses the right hand of Christ. Nicodemus is bending down, extracting the nails from the feet of Christ with the help of pincers; a basket at His side. Below the cross the head of Adam may be seen, as in the Crucifixion.

The Lamentation at the tomb.‡

A great square tomb. Below it a winding-sheet unfolded, upon which the body of Christ is laid, naked. The Holy Virgin, kneeling, bends over Him and kisses His face. Joseph kisses His feet, and the Theologos,§ His right hand. Behind Joseph, Nicodemus, leaning upon the ladder, gazes at Christ. Near the Virgin, Mary Magdalene throwing up her arms to heaven and weeping; the other women, who carried spices, tear their hair. Behind them the cross with its inscription may be seen. Above Christ, the basket of Nicodemus, containing nails, pincers, and hammer; near that a vase in the form of a small bottle.

---

* *See* vol. i., page 271: note on the nails and the chalice in the Crucifixion; also fig. 68, p. 269.

† These women are the myrrhophoræ of whom mention will be made further on.

‡ We have an echo, as it were, from the funeral rites of antiquity in this term, "the lamentation."

§ St. John the Evangelist. The Greeks surnamed him the Theologian because he spoke more clearly than the other evangelists about God and the divinity of the Word.

Christ laid in the tomb.

A mountain, and a stone tomb on the side. Nicodemus carries the body of Christ in its shroud. He supports the head. Outside the tomb the Holy Virgin clasps the body in her arms, and covers it with kisses. Joseph supports the knees, and John, bending down a little, holds the feet. The women who carry the myrrh weep. The cross may be seen behind the mountain.

The soldiers watching the tomb.

A marble tomb, sealed with four seals. The soldiers sleep around: some lean against their bucklers, others are on their knees, others on their hands. St. Longinus, the centurion, seated in their midst in perplexity. Before the tomb the women bearing myrrh, seated and weeping. One holds a small case in her hands; another, a small glass vase.

The Descent into Hell.

Hell, like a dark cave, beneath the mountains. Radiant angels chain Beelzebub, the Prince of Darkness; they strike at other demons, and pursue others with their lances. Several men, naked and fettered, look upwards. A large number of broken locks may be seen. The gates of hell are cast down; Christ tramples them beneath His feet. The Saviour takes Adam by the right hand, and Eve by the left. To the left of the Saviour; the Harbinger points to Him with his forefinger. David is near Him, as well as other righteous kings, with crowns and aureoles. To the left the Prophets Jonas, Isaiah, and Jeremiah; the righteous Abel, and many others with aureoles. A brilliant light and crowd of angels all around.

The Resurrection of Christ.

The tomb half open; two angels, clothed in white, seated at each end. Christ tramples on the stone which covered the tomb. He blesses with the right hand, while He holds the banner with the golden cross in the left. Some of the soldiers below take flight; others lie, as if dead, upon the ground. In the distance are the women carrying myrrh.

An angel appears to the women carrying myrrh, and announces the Resurrection to them.

The open tomb. Angel clothed in white is seated on the lid; he holds a lance with one hand, and with the other points to he shroud and winding-sheet in the bottom of the tomb. The women bearing myrrh; they hold vases in their hands.

Christ appears to the myrrh-bearers, saying " Rejoice ye."

Christ standing, His two hands raised in blessing. The Holy Virgin on His right; Mary Magdalene on His left. They fall on their knees and embrace His feet.

Peter and John, arriving at the Tomb, believe in the Resurrection.

The tomb. Peter stoops to look within, and touches the shroud with his hands. John standing outside, looks on with astonishment. Near him, Mary Magdalene weeping.

Christ appearing to Mary Magdalene.*

The tomb; two angels in white are seated above it. Before the tomb, Christ, standing, holds His mantle in one hand; in the other He carries a scroll, on which is written: " Mary, touch Me not!" Mary, kneeling before Him, prays that she may touch His feet.

Christ, at Emmaus, recognised by Luke and Cleophas in the breaking of bread.

A house. A table and viands inside. Luke and Cleophas seated near. Christ seated between them; He holds the bread and blesses it.

Christ, appearing to the two Apostles, eats before them.

A house. The apostles inside, and Christ among them. Peter stands before Him, holding a plate, on which is half a fish and a honeycomb. Christ with the right hand blesses the plate; He takes the fish and honey with the left.

The touch of Thomas.

A house; Christ within. Raising His right hand in the air, He lifts His garment with the left, and reveals the wound in His right side. Thomas standing near Him in fear puts one hand into the

---

* This subject has been sculptured, about the end of the thirteenth century, in the cloister of the choir of Notre Dame de Paris, on the south side. In the Cathedral of Autun, a "Noli me Tangere" of the Renaissance period is one of the most gracious images we know of. The perfection with which the draperies are executed is especially to be noticed.

hollow of the wound, and holds a scroll in the other, whereon he says: "My Lord and my God!" The other apostles stand round in wonder.

Christ appearing to the Apostles on the shore of the Lake of Tiberias.

The lake. In the midst a vessel, on which ten of the apostles are seen drawing in a net filled with fish. Christ, standing on the shore of the sea, blesses the apostles. Peter, naked, plunges into the sea and approaches Him. Behind Christ, fish on a fire of charcoal.

Christ's threefold question to Peter.

The sea. A ship drawn up on shore. The apostles have left it Christ, standing, looks at Peter, and holds a scroll, on which he says: "Simon, son of Jonas, lovest thou me?" Peter, before him standing awe-stricken, says upon his scroll: "Lord, Thou knowest all things: Thou knowest that I love Thee."

Christ appears to the Apostles upon the Mount of Galilee.

A mountain. Christ, standing, blesses with two hands. Before Him Peter and the other apostles, their hands stretched out towards Him.

The Ascension of Christ.

A mountain with a grove of olive-trees. Above, the apostles, astonished, with hands outstretched, gaze up to heaven. The Virgin Mother in their midst also gazes upwards. Two angels clothed in white at her side point out the rising Christ to the apostles. The angels hold scrolls. The angel on the right says: "Ye men of Galilee, why stand ye gazing up into heaven?" The other saith: "This same Jesus, which is taken up from you into heaven, shall so come in like manner as ye have seen Him go into heaven."

Above them, the Christ seated upon clouds, arises into heaven; He is received by a multitude of angels, with trumpets and cymbals and many instruments of music.

The Descent of the Holy Spirit.

A house.* Twelve apostles seated in a circle. Under them a little vault, in the midst of which an aged man holds, in both hands

* This is the guest-chamber.

before him, a sheet containing twelve scrolls rolled up; he wears a crown upon his head. Above him this inscription: "The World." Above the house the Holy Spirit is seen in the form of a dove; a great light all around. Twelve tongues of fire escape from this dove and rest upon the apostles.[*]

HOW TO REPRESENT THE PARABLES.

The Parable of the Seed.[†]

The subject is painted in this manner: Christ stands teaching; He holds the gospel. Four orders of men stand before Him. The first, those who pass along the wayside talking to one another, regardless of Christ; demons hold them in a leash. The second order, those on stony ground: men appearing to listen gladly. Idols are behind them; they turn and worship them. A tyrant and his soldiers menace them with naked swords. The third order, those among thorns: men carousing and eating with women: demons standing near them. The fourth order, those who are on good ground: monks at prayer in grottoes before images of Christ and the Virgin, surrounded by lights. Others appear as deacons, priests, or laity, at prayer in churches or monasteries.

The Parable of the Tares.[‡]

Christ with the gospel. Before Him a great crowd, some of whom appear to be patriarchs, some martyrs, and others saints, with nimbi round their heads. Angels stand near them. Heretics with

---

[*] The personification of the World under the figure of an old man, crowned, is introduced here to indicate that, after the descent of the Holy Spirit, the apostles will be dispersed throughout all the earth to teach, convert and baptise all nations. The twelve rolls that the World holds in his lap, are the Gospels, written in twelve different languages, and each apostle takes his own. This personification of the World on the day of Pentecost is quite peculiar to the Byzantines; it does not exist with us. In the catholicon of Chilandari at Mount Athos, the World is replaced by the prophet Joel. He is crowned as a king, and he holds twelve rolls upon a sheet. His name is painted near his head. The reason this prophet is chosen to fill the office of the World at Pentecost is that he said: "I will pour out My Spirit upon all flesh, and your sons and your daughters will prophecy; your old men shall dream dreams, your young men shall see visions, and also upon the servants and upon the handmaids in those days will I pour out My Spirit."

[†] "A sower went forth to sow his seed." (Mark iv. 2.)

[‡] "The kingdom of heaven is like unto a man which sowed good seed." (Matt. xiii. 24.)

demons on their shoulders are in the middle. Hell and paradise appear at the side. Angels lead the orthodox into paradise; the demons bind the heretics in chains and drag them into hell.

*Parable of the Mustard Seed.**

Description.—Christ in a tomb. A tree issues from His mouth; the apostles among its branches with open scrolls. Below, men are looking up to the apostles.

Parable of the Leaven.†

Description.—Christ holds the gospel, and says: "Go teach all people." Before Him, the apostles baptise; some preach to others. An innumerable multitude assembled before them.

Parable of the Treasure.‡

Description.—St. Paul saying upon a scroll: "We speak the hidden wisdom."§ Men and women stand around; precious objects, books, and silver are scattered on the ground behind. Others are seen to shatter idols.

The Parable of the Searcher for Goodly Pearls.∥

Description.—Christ stands upright in the act of blessing. Before Him the holy King of India, Josaphat,¶ clad in ecclesiastical robes, stands respectfully. Near the king stands St. Parlaam,** who points with his finger to Christ, saying on his scroll: "Behold the goodly pearl." Behind him lie a crown, kingly robes, riches and fragments of shattered idols cast upon the ground. The Greek sages stand near, holding their scrolls. These words may be read above the figure of Christ: "Jesus Christ, the pearl of great price."

* "The kingdom of heaven is like to a grain of mustard seed." (Matt. xiii. 31.)
† "The kingdom of heaven is like unto leaven." (Matt. xiii. 33.)
‡ "The kingdom of heaven is like unto a treasure hid in a field." (Matt. xiii. 44.)
§ "Which God ordained before the world unto our glory." (1 Cor. ii. 7.)
∥ Matt. xiii. 45.
¶ See the *Légende Dorée*: De Sanctis Barlaam et Josaphet.
** This is in allusion to the legend of Barlaam the Saint, who dwelt in the desert of Sennaar, and who possessed a pearl of such wondrous virtue that, if a man approached it whose eye was not single or heart pure, he would become powerless.

The Parable of the Net.*

Description.—A crowd of people belonging to different nations. The apostles stand around. To the right, behind the apostles, paradise may be seen, and Peter in the midst surrounded by a great crowd. To the left, hell may be seen, and men being chastised by demons.

The Parable of the Hundred Sheep.†

Description.—The heavens. Nine orders of angels in the highest heaven, with an empty throne in the centre. Below, the Descent of Christ into Hell may be seen. (See above, page 98.)

The Parable of the Drachm.‡

Description.—Christ crucified; a great light surrounds Him. A number of men are breaking their idols; others are being baptised; others, like the Greek monks, are praying in grottoes. Others, on their knees, prostrate themselves before the cross. Heaven is seen above the cross, with the nine orders of angels holding harps and trumpets. Christ is seen throned in their midst. He holds Adam with one hand, and a scroll with the other, on which He says: "Rejoice with Me, for I have found the piece which I had lost."

Parable of the Debtor for ten thousand talents.§

Description.—Christ seated as a king upon His throne, blessing. He is surrounded by angels. Before Him a man kneels, saying: "Have patience with me, and I will pay Thee all." Demons are behind Him, carrying a number of written papers. Further on the same man may be seen behind Christ, and dragging another man to prison, saying these words, "Pay me that thou owest." Again, we see Christ in another place seated; two angels look at Him and point out this man. The man subsequently appears before Christ and is dragged away by demons, who bind him in hell.

Parable of the Labourers hired for the day.‖

Description.—Christ standing. The holy patriarchs are seen

---

* "The kingdom of heaven is like unto a net." (Matt. xiii. 47.)
† "What man of you having a hundred sheep." (Luke xv. 4.)
‡ "What woman having ten pieces of silver." (Luke xv. 8.)
§ "The kingdom of heaven is likened unto a certain king which would take account of his servants." (Matt. xviii. 23.)
‖ "The kingdom of heaven is like unto a man that is an householder which went out early in the morning to hire labourers." (Matt. xx. i.)

behind the Saviour, divided into four companies or orders. Enoch offering sacrifice, Noah carrying an ark, and other aged men at prayer with him, compose the first order. Above them is written, "The labourers of the first hour." To the second order belong Abraham sacrificing Isaac, Isaac blessing Jacob, Jacob blessing his twelve sons. Above them is written, "The labourers of the third hour." To the third order belong Moses holding his tables and teaching the Hebrews; Aaron and other righteous men stand near him. Above them is written: "The labourers of the eighth hour." In the fourth order are the prophets, some stoned, some sawn asunder, some in chains. Above them is written, "The labourers of the ninth hour." The apostles and the multitude kneel be.ore Christ. Above them is written, "The labourers of the eleventh hour." Christ again appears in another part of the composition, in paradise, with a crowd of angels and the orders of the saints. The apostles are seated near. The righteous Enoch and those belonging to his order hold crowns in their hands; they say to Christ, pointing out the apostles to Him: "These last have wrought but one hour, and Thou hast made them equal unto us, which have borne the burden and heat of the day." Christ answers gently: "My friend, I do thee no wrong; didst not thou agree with Me for a penny? Take that thine is, and go thy way."

*The Parable of the Two Sons.**

Description.—Christ standing. At one side of Him are seen the Jews, scribes and pharisees. The scribes turn from Him, despising his words. On the other side publicans, fallen women, and heathens prostrate themselves before Him.

Parable of the wicked Husbandmen.†

Description.—A town. The temple and sanctuary. The doctors holding papers and teaching; a crowd of Hebrews before them. In the midst of the sanctuary the Prophet Zecharias may be seen, with a soldier cutting his throat. Outside the temple, a king strikes the Prophet Micah in the face. Close by, men stone the Prophet Zachariah, son of Judas. Outside the town, the Crucifixion of Christ upon a mountain may be seen.

* "A certain man had two sons; and he came to the first, and said, 'Son, go work to-day in my vineyard.'" (Matt. xxi. 28.)
† "There was a certain householder which planted a vineyard.' " (Matt. xxi. 33.)

The Parable of the Corner-stone.*

Description.—A church. The apostles, patriarchs and saints are inside, teaching and baptising. Greeks and Hebrews embrace. Christ is above, blessing them. Close at hand is Jerusalem on fire; soldiers issuing forth in pursuit of the Jews. The Prophet Isaiah points to Christ, and says upon his scroll: "Behold I lay in Zion for a foundation a stone, a tried stone, a precious corner-stone, a sure foundation: he that believeth shall not be deceived."

Parable of the Marriage Feast of the King's Son.†

Description.—A church. Outside, at one side, Jews are seen counting money; oxen and other animals before them. Elsewhere, women amuse themselves with music and dancing. In another part of the composition Isaiah suffers martyrdom—is being sawn in two. Again, Jeremiah is seen thrown by the people into a pit full of filth. At the other side of the church the apostles are represented as teaching. Before them stand heathen, publicans, fallen women, all casting themselves at their feet, and breaking their idols. A table stands in the midst of the church, on which a cup and plate are placed. The orders of the angels and choir of saints, all clothed in white and bearing lamps, are ranged in circles round. In the midst a man in squalid garments may be seen. Demons bind his feet and hands, and drag him towards hell. Christ, clothed in a regal and patriarchial costume, standing near him, says upon a scroll: "Friend, how comest thou in hither, not having a wedding garment?"

Parable of the Great Supper.‡

Description.—Christ standing, in the act of blessing, surrounded by the apostles. Jews, doctors, and pharisees are to His left. Some are eating and drinking, others carry on their business. The monks prostrate themselves at the feet of Christ. On the other side the apostles are teaching the heathen, who also kneel before Him.

Parable of the Talents.§

Description.—Paradise.—Outside, Christ seated like a king upon

---

* "The stone which the builders rejected," &c. (Matt. xxi. 42.)
† "The kingdom of heaven is likened unto a certain king." (Matt. xxii. i. 14.)
‡ "A certain man made a great supper, and bade many." (Luke xiv. 16.)
§ "A man travelling into a far country, called his servants and gave them his goods." (Matt. xxv. v. 14.)

a throne; angels placed in a circle around Him. To His right, a holy high priest, and a holy priest holding the gospels, gaze upon Christ and draw His attention to a crowd of holy men and women in the background. Christ blesses them. On the left-hand side, presents the gospel to him with one hand, and points to it with the other hand, saying, "Lo there, that is thine." Demons behind force him down to hell.

*Parable of the houses builded on a rock, or on the sand.**

Description.—Christ. The apostles behind Him; before Him are two men, one old and the other young, both of whom are listening eagerly to His words. Further on, the old man is seen praying in a grotto. Fallen women and demons surround him and fire darts at him. Other men pull him by his garments. In another part of the composition the young man is seen eating and drinking at table with women, while demons watch him—laughing.

Parable of the blind leader.†

Description.—High priests, Pharisees, and doctors are seen teaching. Demons on their shoulders are bandaging their eyes. Jesus stands before them and appears to listen. Demons cover their eyes also. Other demons, having cast a cord around them, drag them into hell. Christ, standing in the distance, points them out to His disciples, and says to them, on His scroll, "If a blind man lead another blind man, both shall fall into the ditch."

The Parable of the Ten Virgins.‡

Description.—Paradise. Christ looks out from the interior. The five wise virgins carrying lighted lamps are behind Him. The five foolish virgins are outside, holding their lamps, which have gone out; they knock at the door of Paradise, saying: "Lord, Lord, open unto us." But Christ answers, "Verily I say unto you I know you

---
* "Every one that heareth these sayings of mine, and doeth them." (Matt. vii. 26.)
† "If the blind lead the blind, both shall fall into the ditch." (Matt. xv. 14.)
‡ "The kingdom of heaven shall be likened unto ten virgins." (Matt. xxv. 1.)

not." Tombs may be seen further on. Above an angel sounds a trumpet.*

The Parable of the Man who fell among Thieves.†

Description.—Paradise. A fiery sword at the gate: Adam and Eve outside, naked and weeping. Further on a crowd of men, some worshipping idols, cats and dogs; others sacrificing oxen; others sacrificing men to idols; others eating and drinking with women. Moses on one side, with the Tables of the Law, and Aaron turn to look at them. The prophet Isaiah also, on the other side, turns back to look at them. Further on a church may be seen, in which the apostles are baptising some, teaching others, or administering the Communion. Christ in front presents the Tables of the Law and the Book of St. Paul with one hand, and with the other carries His cross upon His shoulders, and points at the aforesaid persons behind Him.

The parable of the Unjust Judge.‡

Description.—Christ above in heaven. Below Him an ecclesiastic

---

* This subject is one of the most common in our Gothic and Romanesque sculpture. The ten virgins appear as statues larger than life in the cathedral of Strasburg; as statues, half life-size, in the cathedral of Rheims; as statuettes in the churches of St. Denis and St. Germain l'Auxerrois. The same subject occurs three times in the side porches of the cathedral of Chartres; twice in the cathedral of Paris, and also at Amiens. The wise virgins, generally dressed as nuns, with long robes and wearing veils, carry their lamps lighted, and carefully trim them; the foolish, generally women of the world, with bare heads, or wearing circular fluted hats and clothes clinging tightly to the figure, hold their lamps upside down, and without wicks or oil. The calm faces of the wise, and the troubled faces of the foolish reveal the nature of their souls. A withered olive-tree, without fruit or leaves, grows at the side of the foolish, and a healthy olive-tree, laden with ripe fruit and ready with abundance of oil, is beside the wise, in the cathedral of Amiens. At Strasburg, and on a glass window in the cathedral of Troyes, Christ leads the wise, and Satan the foolish, virgins. At St. Germain l'Auxerrois, in the top of a voussoir, Christ leans out of heaven holding a scroll in each hand; the one for the foolish is inscribed: " I know you not;" that for the wise: " Watch and pray." In Freiburg-in-Breisgau, where they are seen as statues at each side within the porch, a little angel holds a scroll on which we read: " Watch and pray." At the cathedral of Rheims a temple with closed doors is seen near the foolish and beside the wise, a church with folding doors thrown open, which is a figure of Paradise. Occasionally, as in the cathedrals of Rheims and Laon, the foolish virgins wear the nimbus as well as the wise: we have pointed out and tried to explain this curious point at p. 136, vol. i. of this work.

† Luke x. 30.

‡ "There was in a city a judge who feared not God," &c. (Luke xviii. 1.)

is praying, but tormented by heretics, who in their turn are pursued by an angel armed with a sword. Farther on a young saint may be seen in the midst of the fire. Water falls from heaven to refresh her. Two angels stand near her. In another part a saint is kneeling at prayer. He is surrounded by demons who shoot arrows at him; the angel of the Lord puts them to flight.

*The Parable of the Prodigal Son.**

Description.—The temple and the altar. Near the temple the elder son at prayer. Close at hand the younger son is shown eating and drinking with low women. This prodigal son is again seen in the midst of the temple. Christ administers the Communion to him. The apostles anoint him with myrrh and give him a cross. Choirs of angels around the altar sing their joy with harps and trumpets, and other instruments of music. Outside the temple, Christ is again seen taking the prodigal son in His arms, and kissing his face. In another place, again, Christ calls the elder son to Him, and says upon His scroll: "My son, thou art ever with Me, and all that I have is thine." The son looks at Him and turns away.†

Parable of the Rich Man who had great Possessions.‡

Description.—Houses. A man wearing a purple robe and fur hat looks much embarrassed. Before him lie heaps of corn. Men overturn his granaries and rebuild others. A little farther on the same man is seen again, reclining on his couch of gold. Demons, with three-pronged forks, stand around him, preying on his soul.

Parable of the wicked Rich Man and Lazarus the beggar.§

Description.—A palace. Inside, a table is seen, set out with a variety of dishes. A man arrayed in rich and splendid dress is

---

* "A certain man had two sons; the younger of them said to his father . . ." (Luke xv.)

† The parable of the prodigal son is one of the most common subjects in Gothic art, especially in stained glass. It is found treated with elaborate detail on the windows of the cathedrals of Chartres and Bourges. But, in Western art, the parable itself is literally represented, not its interpretation, as with the Greeks, and as prescribed in our Guide. [See *Monographie de la Cathédrale de Chartres*, publiée par le Ministère de l'Instruction publique, 1ière livraison; et *Les Vitraux Peints de Bourges*, par MM. Arthur Martin et Charles Cahier, 5ième livraison.]

‡ Luke xii. 16.

§ "There was a certain rich man, which was clothed in fine linen . . ." (Luke xvi.)

seated at this table, holding a cup in his hand. He is served by a crowd of slaves, who offer him divers dainties. In another place he is seen again, in bed, demons preying on his soul; women and children weeping around him. Below the palace gate, a naked man, full of sores, is laid upon the ground. Dogs lick his sores. David appears above him with a harp, and the ranks of angels, who receive his soul with music of divers instruments. Hell is farther on in the composition. Here the rich man is seen in flames, and saying: "Father Abraham, have mercy on me." Opposite to him is Abraham in Paradise, with Lazarus in his bosom. Abraham answers the rich man: "Son, remember that thou in thy lifetime receivedst thy good things."*

Parable of the Strong Man.†

Description.—Christ stands in the act of blessing. Matthew, the publican, the apostle Paul, Mary Magdalene, a fallen woman, and many other converted sinners throw themselves before His feet. In another part, angels bind the devil and cast him into hell.

The Parable of the Candle.‡

Description.—The temple. A holy high priest preaching in a chair; an angel speaks into his ear, and he is surrounded by a bright light. Men are seen below him, listening eagerly, and with raised hands. Christ blesses them from above, and says in His gospel: "Let your light so shine before men that they may see."

Parable of the Barren Fig-tree.§

Description.—The temple. In the midst, a man on a grey horse, his arms crossed upon his breast. Near him, Death, carrying a scythe.‖ Christ orders the man to be slain. The guardian angel of this man's life kneels before Christ, praying to Him, and saying, "Lord, grant him yet a while."

* This subject is a common one in France. Generally, as at St. Lazare at Autun, or St. Saturnin at Toulouse, it is found at the church door and at the side porch through which the poor are admitted, and where the rich pass by, whose aid they solicit.
† "No man can enter into a strong man's house," &c. (Mark iii. 27).
‡ "Neither do men light a candle," &c. (Matt. v. 15.)
§ "A certain man had a fig-tree planted in his vineyard." (Luke xiii. 6.)
‖ This is an instance of the lingering traditions of pagan mythology among the Greeks. In the refectory of Vatopédi, Death, a skeleton still covered by its skin, carries a scythe in his left hand and a sickle in his right. This image of Death is inscribed "Charon."

HOW TO REPRESENT THE PARABLES. 331

*Parable of him who would build a tower.**

Description.—St. Paul, preaching, and saying upon his scroll: "I have laid the foundation, which is Jesus Christ." He is surrounded by men, who listen attentively. In another part, men are seen eating and drinking and working. They are seized by demons, and above them these words are written: "These are they which thrive yet cannot accomplish."

Parable of the Publican and the Pharisee.†

Description.—The temple, with a flight of steps. The Pharisee in front of the sanctuary; an old man, with a great beard and full robes, his head veiled, stands gazing up to heaven. He lifts one hand; with the other he points at the publican. The demon of pride is seated on his head.‡ The publican opposite to him, with eyes fixed on the ground, strikes his breast. An angel blesses him from above.

Parable of the Faithful and Wise Servants.§

Description.—The temple. Inside, a venerable old man; the high priest is preaching. A holy priest holds a cup in his hand. A holy deacon carries a disc upon his head. Others hold lamps and censers. Other disciples and a crowd of people at prayer. Christ blesses them from above.

Parable of the Evil Servants.‖

Description.—Houses. Inside of them are Christian men—ecclesiastics, monks, laity—eating and drinking to the sound of dances and drums, and some quarrelling. Death is in their midst, mowing them down with his scythe. Christ is above them; angels, also holding scythes,¶ form a circle round Him. The impious and heretics are devoured by the flames of hell close by the houses.

* " Which of you, intending to build a tower," &c. (Luke xiv. 28.)
† " Two men went up into the temple to pray." (Luke xviii. 10.)
‡ This method of presenting a visible translation of evil thoughts is common in the middle ages: it is not unusual to see demons on the head or at the ear of Herod, ordering the massacre of the Innocents (see the cloister of the choir of Notre Dame de Paris.) This evil spirit is sometimes represented as a black emaciated bird (see vol. i. of this work, p. 465, fig. 120; p. 466, fig. 121; vol. ii. p. 142, fig. 189: Goliath).
§ " Who then is the faithful and wise servant?" (Matt. xxiv. 45.)
‖ " If the evil servant shall say in his heart . . . " (Matt. xxiv. 48.)
¶ In France, as in the Last Judgment of Jean Cousin, these angels hold sickles.

Demons seize upon the men in these houses, in order to drag the[m] down into hell.

Parable of the Salt of the Earth.*

Description.—The temple. High priests, priests, disciples. Som[e] are teaching from their chairs, others from their thrones, othe[rs] studying their books. St. Paul, holding a scroll, says: "Let yo[u] speech be always with grace, seasoned with salt."†

The Parable of Light and Darkness.‡

Description.—Christ on one side surrounded by a great light; H[e] holds the gospel, and says: "I am the light of the world." Th[e] Apostles stand near Him. On the other side, the Prince of Dar[k]ness, the devil, surrounded by gloom; § near him the doctors of th[e] Pharisees, and a crowd of impious persons form a circle around hi[m] turning and moving away from Christ.

The Parable of the Meat.||

Description.—A house. Men eating and drinking inside. Th[e] temple near at hand, in which other persons are seen to partake [of] the divine mysteries of the Communion. Others preach, and othe[rs] pray. Christ points them out to His disciples, saying on His scroll "Labour not for the meat which perisheth, but for that meat whic[h] endureth unto everlasting life."

Parable of the Door and the Sheepfold.¶

Description.—A church. At the gate outside, Christ holds th[e] open gospel, saying, "I am the Door; he that entereth in throug[h] Me shall be saved." Moses is behind the gate, holding the tables o[f]

---

* "If the salt have lost his savour, wherewith shall it be salted.'
(Matt. v. 13.)
† Coloss. iv. 6.
‡ "Light is come unto the world, and men love darkness rather tha[n] light." (John iii. 19.)
§ Satan is not only enveloped by darkness himself, but he causes it b[y] extinguishing the light wherever he passes; he is black, smoky, dark a[s] thickest night. In the legends of France he is constantly called the soot[y] spirit, the Ethiopian, his body covered with black skin and hair. We fee[l] him to be the parent of Arihman, the god or the spirit of night, a[s] Ormuzd is the god of day. Satan extinguishes the lamp of the deaco[n] Paul, the wax light of St. Geneviève. (See vol. i. p. 464.)
|| "Labour not for the meat that perisheth." (John vi. 27.)
¶ "He that entereth by the door into the sheepfold is the shepherd.'
(John x. 1.)

he Law. Outside the gate the holy prelates stand before Christ, olding the gospels and teaching. These words are written above hem: "Those who have entered in by the Door" (which is Christ). iefore them a crowd of Christians attentively listening. Behind he Christians, Arius and other heresiarchs torment them. Above hem is written: "Those who entered not by the Door, but who ave climbed up some other way."

The Parable of the Vine.*

Christ, carrying the gospel upon His breast, and raising both His ands in blessing, saith: "I am the Vinestock, and ye are the ranches." The apostles are encircled by the branches of the vine, vhich spring from His body.†

The Parable of the Hypocrite.‡

Description.—A man standing up with a little piece of stick in us eye. Before him stands a Pharisee with a large beam of wood n his eye; he is saying to him: "My brother, let me pull the straw ut of your eye." Christ is above them, watching the Pharisee n displeasure. He says upon His scroll: "Thou hypocrite, first ast out the beam out of thine own eye."

The Parable of the Good and the Corrupt Trees.§

Description.—Men standing on one side. From the mouth of ne the Holy Spirit issues, an angel falls from the mouth of mother, a gentle flame from another, a rose and various other precious things from the mouths of the others. Opposite to them stand another group of men, from whose mouths fall demons, serpents, swine, thorns, and other evil things. Christ, pointing them out from a distance, says upon His scroll: "Every tree shall be known by its fruits."

---

* "I am the Vine, ye are the branches." (John xv. 5.)
† This subject, as we have already stated, is painted in the little convent of Cesariani on Mount Hymettus, in the church-porch against the east wall. To the left of the door we have the material genealogy of Christ, his ancestry from Jesse to St. Joseph; on the right his spiritual posterity, the apostles. This subject of Christ as the vine, of which the apostles are branches and fruit, is painted upon glass in the cathedral of Troyes.
‡ "Why beholdest thou the straw that is in thy brother's eye?" (Matt. vii. 3.)
§ "A good tree cannot bring forth evil fruit." (Matt. vii. 18.)

The Parable of the Strait Gate.*

Description.—Mountains and caverns. Saints are seen at prayer, demons tempting them. Farther on, martyrs enduring all manner of torment at the hands of tyrants. Christ appears above in the clouds, blessing them. He carries the Gospel open upon His breast, and says: "Strive to enter in at the strait gate."

The Divine liturgy.

A cupola. Below, a table on which the holy gospel is laid. Above, the Holy Spirit. Close by, the Eternal Father seated on a throne; He raises His sacred hands in blessing, and says upon a scroll: "I have engendered thee in My bosom before Lucifer." Christ, in the act of blessing, is at the right side of the table in a patriarch's robe. Before Him, all the ranks of angels, clad in sacerdotal robes, and filled with awe, form a circle extending to the left side of the table. Christ takes a disc from the head of an angel in a deacon's dress. Four other angels stand near; two swing incense before Christ, and two carry great candles. Others come behind, also carrying—one a little spoon, another a lance, another a sponge, another a cross, and others tapers.†

The Apostles receive the Body and Blood of our Lord.

Houses. A table, on which a plate is laid with bread cut up in pieces. In the middle, behind this table, the form of Christ is half visible, His hands stretched out. He holds the bread in the right hand, and the chalice in the left. Before Him the gospel lies open. On the right page is written: "Take, eat; this is My body." On the left, "Drink ye all of this, for this is My blood;" at each side the apostles, bending slightly forward, fix their gaze on Christ. Peter, foremost of the five apostles to the right, places his hand under the bread given him by Christ. John, foremost of the five apostles to

---

* "Enter ye in at the straight gate; for wide is the gate and broad is the way," &c. (Matt. vii. 13.)

† These are both the instruments of the Passion and the articles used in the service of the Mass. The Greeks have retained the memorials of the Passion in their Mass, more than we have in the Western Church. Besides the body and blood of the sacred Victim, they have the lance, with which they still pierce the Saviour's side as Longinus did on Calvary; the sponge, the reed, and the cross; and thus the sacred drama is less effaced in the Greek than in the Western rite.

the left, with one hand on his breast, stretches out the other; his mouth approaches the edge of the chalice. Judas is behind them, and turns away; a demon enters his mouth.

The Spirits' reunion

Heaven, with sun, moon and stars. Christ in the midst, seated, holding a scroll, on which is written: "The Lord hath established me as the beginning of His ways; He hath founded me before the centuries." The four evangelists appear at the corners in the forms of a man, an ox, a lion, and an eagle. The Holy Virgin and the Harbinger stand at each side of Christ, saluting Him with reverence. A circle formed of the nine choirs of angels surrounds Him; thrones, cherubim, seraphim, saying: "Holy, holy, holy." The other orders carry scrolls with inscriptions. Thus the Dominations speak of "Glory to dominions, beauty uncreate!"—Virtues: "Glory exceeding, of virtues all-powerful"—the Powers of "Glory unattainable; light of dazzling power!"—Principalities, "Glory; shining light of wonderful principalities! Glory! the ineffable Light of archangels!"—Angels, "Glory, divine beauty of angels!" Heaven is encircled by the mottoes, "May every spirit praise the Lord!" "May the Lord of heaven be praised!" "Praise ye the Lord of heaven!" "Praise Him in the highest heaven!" "To you, O Lord, be all praise given!" *

Underneath, the orders of the saints are seen seated on the clouds and holding scrolls. The holy patriarchs are before them. Adam says, " Glory of the patriarchs; transport and joy." Moses, foremost of the prophets, says, " Glory of the prophets, perfected of law." Peter, foremost of the apostles, says, " Glory of the apostles; infinite praise." Chrysostom, foremost of the prelates, " Glory of the holy chieftains; beauty and sublimity." George, foremost of the martyrs, " Glory of the persecuted! strength and power." Anthony, foremost of the solitaries: " Glory of the holy hermits and ascetics; praise ineffable!" Constantine, foremost of the righteous kings: " Glory of the orthodox; kingly strength." Catherine, foremost of the martyred women: " Glory of virgins; heavenly spouse." Euphraxia, foremost of the heavenly saints: " Glory be to Thee, eternal joy of all the lonely!"

Under the saints, mountains may be seen with trees, laden with

* A Te Deum sung in Paradise to Christ, by all nature, saints and angels.

fruit and flowers, and at their base all the anim[
and tame.*

HOW TO REPRESENT THE APOCALYP[

"I was in the isle that is called Patmos, for the word behind me a great voice as of a trumpet, saying, I am . what thou seest write in a book." (Rev. i. 9.)

The picture.—A grotto; St. John Theologos se[
ing behind him; he is wrapped in ecstasy. He see
the clouds, clothed with a white garment, and g[
girdle; He has in His right hand seven stars, and [
comes a sharp two-edged sword. Seven golden
Him, and a great radiance issues from His person.†

"After this I looked, and, behold, a door was opene[
a voice said, Come up hither, and I will shew thee thin
hereafter. And immediately I was in the spirit; and, be
set in heaven, and round about the throne were four-and·
And I saw in the right hand of Him that sat upon [
. . sealed with seven seals." (Rev. iv. 1.)

Picture [of the vision: ch. iv. 1].—Clouds. [
Eternal Father, seated, holding a closed book, s[
seals, in His right hand. A lamb having seven horn
sustains, by two pedestals, the book held by the
Seven lighted candlesticks are before the thr[
glass like unto crystal] and the tetramorphs [eva

---

* The most complete painting of this magnificent sul
decorates the external porch of the great church of Ivirč
See p. 230, *supra*.

† Scenes from the Apocalypse are very common in W
cathedral of Rheims, the right door of the great po
statues representing the figures in the Apocalypse. Of
and forty-six figures that ornament this door within
hundred and sixty-five are consecrated to this mysteri
tomb of Jean de Langheac, bishop of Limoges, who died
tured with bas-reliefs representing scenes in the Apoca
of the cathedral of Auxerre was painted in fresco with [
the Apocalypse, two of which only now remain. They
of the thirteenth century, and have been engraved
vol. i. p. 108, fig. 36; p. 509, fig. 81). Glass-painters lo
The western rose-window of the Ste. Chapelle of Paris
subject—it is also given in a great window in the south[
Martin-ès-Vignes at Troyes.

HOW TO REPRESENT THE APOCALYPSE. 337

and'ng round. Four-and-twenty elders,* on either side, seated on their golden thrones, clothed in white raiment, and having crowns of gold upon their heads. They hold golden vials full of odours in the right hand, and harps in the left. A winged angel, with hands outstretched on either side, stands below the Eternal Father, open-armed and ready to receive the prayers of the holy.

"And I saw when the Lamb opened one of the seals, and I heard one of the four beasts saying with a voice as it were of thunder, Come and see. And I saw, and behold a white horse: he that sat on him had a bow—and a crown was given unto him." (Chapter vi. 1, 2.)

Picture.—Mountains. Men lying prone on the ground, some dead, others, living, filled with terror. Above them a rider on a white horse : he wears a crown. He holds a bow and shoots his arrows among men. Behind him a rider on another horse that is red. *He holds a great sword. Behind him is a third rider, he is on a black horse ;*† he carries a pair of balances in his hand. Behind him is Death again, mounted on a pale horse, and carrying a great scythe. (See page 160, *supra.*)

"And when he had opened the fifth seal, I saw, under the altar, the souls of them that were slain for the Word of God." (Chapter vi. 9.)

Picture.—An altar. Beneath it the souls of the holy martyrs clothed in white with uplifted hands and eyes. Angels at each side in converse with them.

"And when he had opened the sixth seal, lo! there was a great earthquake: the sun became black as sackcloth of hair, the moon became as blood, and the stars of heaven fell into the earth, and the heavens departed as a scroll when it is rolled together." (Chapter vi. 12, 14.)

Picture.—Gloomy mountains. A great multitude, some royal, others noble, others commoners, hide themselves in dens and rocks in the mountains. The sky above them like a closed parchment roll; the sun black and the moon blood-red; the stars falling on the ground.

"After these things, I saw four angels standing on the four corners of the earth, holding the four winds of the earth, that they should not blow

---

* The four-and-twenty elders are thus sculptured on the southern porch of Chartres cathedral, on the west door of the church of St. Denis and the cathedral of Rheims, and on a glass window in St. Stéphen du Mont. These figures have in their hands either a violin or some other stringed instrument, such as a harp.

† The words in italics were introduced by the copyist of the manuscript.

VOL. II. z

on the earth nor on the sea, nor on any tree. And I
ascending from the east, having the seal of the living God

Picture.—The earth and the sea. The winds ↋
of the earth. Four angels, armed with swords,
winds that they should not blow: one angel
another Notus, another Zephyrus, another Sanu
east an angel rises on the clouds; he holds the se
living God in one hand, and stretches out the oth
four angels. Below him another angel anoints t
great multitude.

"After this I beheld, and, lo, a great multitude, w
number, of all nations and people, and tongues, stood
(Chapter vii. 9.)

Picture.—Masses of clouds. The Eternal Fath
throne in the midst; the four evangelical tetramc
corners of the throne. The orders of angels fo:
The Lamb opens the gospel held by the Father on ⁚
the throne a great multitude clothed in white, and
their hands; the twenty-four elders beside the t
near them, to whom one in the crowd shows th
white robes. (See vol. i. pp. 318–337.)

"And when he had opened the seventh seal, there w
about the space of half an hour. And I saw the seven
before God; and to them were given seven trumpe
came and stood at the altar, having a golden cense
sounded the trumpet." (Chapter viii. 1.)

Picture.—Heaven. Above, the Eternal Father
seated on a throne. Around are seven angels wi
prostrate themselves in adoration before Him. Be
angel holding a golden censer, whence a smoke is⸱
at His feet. Four angels look down out of them
trumpets. Below, another angel may be seen
stretched out; he holds a scroll in the other, on
"Woe, woe, woe to the inhabiters of the earth
other voices of the trumpets of the three angels
sound." On one side the blackened sun appears
moon, a third of which has turned to blood. A r
the third of which are black, also appear. Und
glass mingled with fire. A mountain devoured by

* See *Annales Archéologiques*, vol. i. pt. ii.: Personi

nidst of the sea. Ships and wrecks blown down and engulfed. ↨eyond the sea a multitude of trees and plants consumed by fire; a iver beyond, in the midst of which a large radiant star is seen to hine. Men drink on the bank of this river, others lie prostrate in ↨eath upon the ground.

"The fifth angel sounded, and I saw a star fall from heaven unto the ↨rth, and to him was given the key of the bottomless pit. And he opened he bottomless pit, and there arose a smoke out of the pit, as the smoke f a great furnace. And there came out of the smoke locusts upon the ↨rth." (Chapter ix.)

Picture.—Clouds. An angel is above them, looking downward ↨d sounding a trumpet; he holds a key in his hand. Below him vast pit is seen; a thick smoke issues from this, which obscures he sky and sun. In the midst of this smoke an awful star shines orth. Locusts come forth out of this smoke, with faces of men, and ↨air of women, and teeth as the teeth of lions; on their heads they ↨ave crowns of gold, and breastplates of iron on their breasts; they ↨ave tails like scorpions, and stings in their tails, and their wings ↨semble bucklers. At each side of the pit men hide themselves ↨mongst the mountains.

"And the sixth angel sounded the trumpet; and I heard a voice from he four horns of the golden altar, which is before God, saying to the ↨ngel which had the trumpet, Loose the four angels which are bound." C↨apter ix. 13.)

Picture.—Heaven. Above, the Eternal Father, seated on a throne, ↨nd clothed in white raiment; a golden altar before Him. An ↨ngel on His right sounds a trumpet and looks down. Below, mountains are seen, and four angels hewing men in pieces. In the midst f these angels, a crowd of soldiers wearing iron breastplates, red, ↨lear, flame-like; they have iron helmets; they ride upon horses ↨ith lions' heads and scorpions' tails; and stings are in their tails, ↨nd out of their mouths issue fire and smoke and brimstone. ↨nder their feet, and before them, are a crowd of men, slain; and ↨thers take flight, looking backwards in terror.

"And I saw another mighty angel come down from heaven, clothed with cloud; and a rainbow was upon his head, and his face was as it were the un, and his feet as pillars of fire. He set his right foot upon the sea, ↨d his left foot upon the earth; and he had in his hand a little book." Chapter x. 12.)

Picture.—The sky, the sea and the earth below. An angel, ↨lothed like a cloud, with face resplendent as the sun in all its

brightness. His feet as fire, the right foot resti[ng]
the left on land. A little book is in his hand, w[ith]
out towards heaven. St. John kneels at his sid[e]
the little book from his hand.

"And there was given me a reed like unto a rod;[*]
me, Measure the temple of God, and the altar, and
therein, but the court which is without the temple lea[ve]
it not, for it is given unto the Gentiles, and the holy ci[ty]
under foot for forty and two months." (Chapter xi.)

Picture.—The temple. An altar within. Joh[n]
a reed. Below, a savage winged beast, carrying [a]
head. Enoch and Elias are seen rising in the sky
the temple are houses falling into ruins. Dead m[en]
their hands and eyes towards heaven.

"And the seventh angel sounded; and there we[re]
heaven, saying, The kingdoms of this world are beco[me]
the Lord, and of His Christ; and he shall reign for ever
(Chapter xi. 15.)

Picture.—Our Lord Jesus Christ above the c[louds]
high throne. The orders of the angels form a c[ircle]
The twenty-four elders bend their knees before
Him. A temple stands at His right hand, in the
a golden ark. A multitude of people are below it.
great hailstones fall from heaven.

"And there appeared a great wonder in heaven: a [woman]
the sun, and the moon under her feet, and on her head
stars." (Chapter xii. 1.)

Picture.—The Holy Virgin upon clouds, with [a]
angel's wings. Twelve stars around her crown. F[iery]
rays surround her from her head to her feet. Th[e]
feet. A red dragon, with seven heads and ten hor[ns]
the dragon casts out of his mouth water as of a
opens and swallows up the flood. Behind the dra[gon]
of stars. The Holy Virgin is seen below, borne b[y]
veil. Christ in her lap; clouds innumerable surro[und]

---

* This rod or measure is the geometrical rod or
middle ages was put in the hands of architects. It [is]
a sculpture in Rheims Cathedral. *Ann. Archéol.* vol. [.]

† See vol. i. p. 162, fig. 47; fig. 184, p. 137, *supr[a]*
supra.

HOW TO REPRESENT THE APOCALYPSE. 341

"And I saw a beast that was like unto a leopard: his feet were as the feet of a bear; his mouth as the mouth of a lion. It had seven heads and ten horns." (Chapter xiii. 2.)

Picture.—The earth and sea. The beast with seven heads coming out of the sea. It is worshipped by men of power. Another smaller beast, with two horns, like a lamb. Fire and hail fall from heaven.

"And I looked, and, lo! a Lamb stood on Mount Zion, and with Him a hundred and forty and four thousand, having His Father's name written in their foreheads. These are they which were not defiled with women; for they are virgins, and follow the Lamb whithersoever He goeth." (Chapter xiv. 1.)

Picture.—A high mountain, the Lamb standing on the summit; He wears a crown upon His head, a sceptre in one of His paws—that is to say, a small red flag with a cross at the end.* The evangelical tetramorphs stand at the four corners of the throne. The twenty-four elders, and a number of angels holding harps, are to the right and left. Close by, a crowd of virgins clad in white, their hands and eyes turned towards the Lamb. Numbers of clouds below, from the tops of which four angels are looking down. One of them carries the gospel open, saying: "Fear God and give glory to Him, for the hour of His judgment is come." On His right, another angel points to the ground with one hand, and holds a scroll in the other, on which is written: "Babylon is fallen—is fallen, that great city." Another angel to her left, with hand stretched out, and another holding a scroll, with these words: "If any man worship the beast, and receive his mark in his forehead, or in his hand, he shall drink of the wine of the wrath of God." Under them, the city of Babylon in ruins.

"And I looked, and behold a white cloud, and upon the cloud one sat like unto the Son of Man, having on His head a golden crown, and in His hand a sharp scythe." (Chapter xiv. 14.)

Picture.—Clouds. Christ above, crowned and holding a scythe, with which He reaps as He passes over the earth. Another angel also holds a sickle, and cuts the grapes, which are afterwards crushed in a wine-press; blood flows from it instead of wine (v. 20). Above the heaven is a temple, in which an altar stands. An angel comes forth from the gate of the temple; looking at Christ, he stretches out one hand towards Him, and carries a scroll in the

* See vol. i. p. 43, fig. 13; p. 67, fig. 23.

other, on which is written: "Thrust in thy sharp ⸱
the clusters of the vine of the earth, for the time is
reap." Another angel comes forth from the sanct
at the angel who gathers in the grapes, and points ⸱
hand, while holding a scroll in the other, on which ⸱
in thy sharp sickle, and gather the clusters of
earth."

"And I saw another sign in heaven, great and marvel
having the seven plagues, for in them is filled up tl
(Chapter xv. 1.)

Picture.—Mountains. A multitude of men: s⸱
the ground. Others, faces upwards, insensible a⸱
sores. Christ seated upon a throne in their midst.
and crowned, and a seven-headed dragon. Thre⸱
come out of the dragon's mouths, resembling frogs.
is in ruins. The sea and waves are as blood. Eu⸱
river, is dried up. The sun in the midst of the ⸱
its great rays across the heavens. Hail falls fron
tabernacle of witness is at the top of the sky. S⸱
forth from it clothed in white and wearing gold
first angel pours forth his vial upon the earth an⸱
The second pours forth his vial on the sea. The
his vial upon the rivers. The fourth pours fortb
sun. The fifth pours forth his vial on the thro⸱
The sixth pours forth his vial on the Euphrate
pours forth his vial on the air.

"And I saw a woman sit upon a scarlet coloured beas
blasphemy, having seven heads and ten oorns." (Chapt⸱

Picture.—Seven tops of mountains. Above, a
heads and ten horns. A woman is seated on it
crown and apparel gleaming with gold. She hold⸱
her right hand, which she offers to the kings. T⸱
of the beast turn to gaze upon her. Behind the l
tude of people and chieftains and nobles. Abov
written: "Babylon the great, the mother of the
the earth." *

* This personification of Babylon is very often repr
The monks of Mount Athos have childishly destroyed t
woman which was painted on the wall of the porch of tl
the convent of Coutloumousi, near Kares. A fine e⸱

"And after that I saw another angel come down from heaven, having great power; and the earth was lightened with his glory, and he cried mightily with a strong voice." (Chapter xviii.)

Description.—The earth, mountains, sea and a city; all enveloped in fire and flame rising in the air. Kings stand far off, and merchants wail and lament: some tear their hair, others strike their breasts. Others raise their hands and eyes to heaven. A crowd of other personages. The sky above. An angel descends, surrounded by a dazzling aureole. With the right hand he points out the city, while in the left he holds a scroll: "Babylon the great is fallen, is fallen!" Another angel near, upon the clouds, casts a stone like a great millstone into the sea, holding a scroll and saying: "Thus with violence shall that great city Babylon be thrown down, and shall be found no more at all." Above the angels other dark clouds, vomiting hail and fire on the sea and earth. Above the sky the Eternal Father seated on a throne. Near the throne two angels holding scrolls. The angel to the right says, "Praise our God, all ye His servants." He to the left continues, "All ye that fear Him. both small and great." The evangelic tetramorphs and the orders of the angels form a circle round the throne. A great multitude clothed in white sing, "Alleluia! Salvation and glory and honour and power unto the Lord our God, for He hath judged her who did corrupt the earth, and He hath avenged the blood of His servants at her hand." The twenty-four elders worship Him, saying, "Amen! Alleluia!"

"And I saw heaven opened, and behold a white horse; and he that sat upon him was called Faithful and True, and his name is called the Word of God." (Chapter xix. 11, 13, 18.)

Painting.—The heavens are opened. Christ issues forth on clouds; He rides upon a white horse. He is clothed in a crimson vesture and wears a crown upon His head, and out of His mouth issues a sharp sword. Above Him these words are inscribed: "Jesus Christ, the Word of God, King of kings, Lord of lords." He is followed by armies of men, all riding upon white horses, clothed in white linen. Their helmets and their girdles are of gold.

---

seen in the MS. destroyed in the burning of Strasburg Library, the *Hortus Deliciarum*. Fortunately M. le Comte Auguste de Bastard has published a reproduction of this Babylon in his great work: *Peintures et Ornéments des Manuscrits.*

They are armed with sharp swords. Kings and n
soldiers riding on high horses go before. They
heralds of a victory; they fly looking backwa
stretched dead upon the earth; others have beer
their horses, and birds of prey devour their f
watching these birds stands beneath the sun, a
scroll: "Gather yourselves together here, that ye
of kings, the flesh of captains, the flesh of mighty
vanquished is hell and a river of fire. Two an
beast with seven heads and Antichrist; whom the
the river of fire.*

"And I saw an angel come down from heaven, hav
bottomless pit and a great chain." (Chapter xx. 1.)

Painting.—Heaven. An angel holding a key i
a demon chained in the other. The angel casts
devouring flames.

"And I saw a great white throne, and Him that sat
face the earth and the heaven fled away, and there w
for them. And I saw the dead, small and great, stand
the books were opened." (Chapter xx. 11.)

Painting.—Christ seated upon a white throne
angels encircle Him, and the rest of the picture i
Second Coming (p. 345, *infra*).

"And I John saw the holy city, new Jerusalem, comi
out of heaven, prepared as a bride adorned for her husb
great voice out of heaven, saying, Behold the tabernac
men, and He will dwell with them, and they shall be H
Himself shall be with them, and be their God." (Chapt

Painting.—The city of Jerusalem, adorned with
stones. It has twelve gates: on the east three
north three gates, on the south three gates, and o
gates. An angel stands at each gate holding
the right hand and the seal of the living God
John stands upon a high mountain and con-
city. Heaven is opened above, and Christ is revea
throne, whose wonderful radiance is shed abroad ov
the orders of the saints and angels, with the twe
form a circle round the throne of Christ. One an

* See vol. i. fig. 81, p. 308.

of heaven points the city out to St. John, saying to him on the scroll: "Behold the tabernacle of God!" Another angel, holding a reed, measures the city of Jerusalem.*

How to represent the Second Coming of the Lord.

Christ, clothed in white, seated on cherubim and flaming angels. He flings abroad His thunderbolts on sun, and moon, and stars. Before Him appears the symbol of His manifestation: that is to say, the cross. On His left is she, the queen-like Mother, who gave Him birth, a Virgin evermore. Christ advances on the clouds of heaven, to the sound of psalms, and hymns, and innumerable instruments by which the heavenly hosts celebrate His glory. He raises His Almighty hands in blessing; He holds the gospel open, on which these words may be read: "Come unto Me, ye blessed of My Father; inherit the kingdom that I have prepared for you!" And also He saith: "Depart from Me, ye cursed."

Above Him are these words: "Jesus Christ, the joy and the glory of the righteous." All the saints prepare to meet Him according to the order in which, through help of divine grace, they have arisen from earth to heaven; they are all seated upon clouds. First come the choir of apostles. 2nd, the choir of our first parents. 3rd, the choir of patriarchs. 4th, the choir of prophets. 5th, the choir of bishops. 6th, the choir of martyrs. 7th, the choir of saints. 8th, the choir of righteous kings. 9th, the choir of martyred or solitary women. All carry branches in their hands to signify their virtues. An angel flies in the air and sounds the last trumpet. The earth is below with its cities and wealth; then the sea, with its ships and its boats, gives up the dead it has destroyed.† The dead

* In the great convent of Xeropotamou on Mount Athos the Apocalypse is painted in much detail. It occupies the entire of the external porch of the great church, and concludes with the Last Judgment. Here we feel we are in the region of Greek mythology : the dragons that have sat for the painter here belong to the land of the hydra, and tradition has transmitted them from mythology to Christianity. So is it also with the Babylon; she is a sort of female Bacchus. This grand symbolic woman is clothed in very rich vestments; her breast is covered with gold pieces, one of which adorns her brow like the young brides in Greece at the present day. Corn-blades are woven through her hair, she holds a cup in her right hand. She advances seated on a beast, which, were it not for the seven heads springing from its neck, would be a tiger.

† The Greeks in their representations of the Second Coming personify the earth and the sea. In the convent of Vatopédi on Mount Athos, the Last Judgment is painted in fresco on the western wall of the church on

awaken either in their tombs or in the sea ; th
fear, and their expressions vary strongly. All
clouds ; but some come before Christ, while sinne
the place of vengeance. Farther on stand the
scrolls with inscriptions as follows :—
 Isaiah : "The Lord will come to judge."
 Joel : " All nations shall awaken and will come
 Daniel : " And many that sleep in the dust shall

The righteous and universal Judgment of our Lo
Christ on high, seated on a fiery throne. Clot
casts His thunderbolts upon the sun. All the mi<
with terror, tremble at His presence. With His
He blesses the saints, with the left He shows th.
tation and woe. He is encircled by a great light,
written : " Jesus Christ, the righteous Judge." A
the Holy Virgin and the Harbinger bending in reve
and the twelve apostles are seated on twelve thro
saints are also present; they stand to the righ1
branches, signs of their power, in their hands.
into three orders: in the first are the choir of
patriarchs and prophets; in the second the choir o
and solitaires; in the third, the choir of righ1
women or martyrs. On the left hand of Christ ɾ
out of His presence, and condemned, along with the
all demons, tyrant kings, idolators, antichrists, he
traitors, thieves, robbers, those who refuse to gi
misers, liars, sorcerers, drunkards, the self-indul; en

---

the outside of the porch, where the same subject is ɾ
the French cathedrals. Earth is a vigorous woman ric
crowned with flowers, and she holds a bunch of brancl
in her right hand ; in her left a serpent, whose body sh
seated on two lions, and borne aloft by two eagles.
personification of strength, and the allegory is a curio
the antique Cybele. The Sea is a less robust and mor
floats along between two marine monsters who serve
to whom two great wheels, like those of antique chariot
the convent of St. Gregory on Mount Athos this figure
Last Judgment painted on the western wall of the prin
 * For illustrations of this subject see vol. i. of this w
Arch. i. 165, pl. 12.). Mortuary chapel, St. Gregory
mosaic in church of Torcello, Murano, near Venice. Se<

the ungrateful Jews, scribes and Pharisees. All utter great cries and wailings. Some tear their beards, others rend their garments. They look towards Jesus, and the saints and the prophet Moses, who points to Christ and says upon his scroll: "The Lord will raise up a Prophet from among their brethren like unto me; unto Him ye shall hearken."* The symbol of the cross is before the throne with the ark of the testament of the Lord, with the witnesses of the law and the prophets, and with the gospel open between two scrolls. Upon the scroll to the right is written: "And the dead were judged every man according to their works." On that to the left is written: "And whosoever was not found written in the book of life was cast into the lake of fire." A river of fire flows beneath Christ's feet, demons cast the wicked and uncharitable into it, and torture them horribly with divers instruments of torture, with harpoons and lances. Others drive them into the flames with pikes, others encircle their bodies like fiery serpents, and drag them into caverns and outer darkness, where there is weeping and gnashing of teeth, and the worm dieth not and the fire is not quenched. Hell is seen through rents in the rocks, where men are chained with iron in the darkness, gnashing their teeth and consumed by the fire that cannot be quenched, and the worm that dieth not. The rich man, who has been uncharitable, looks out into the faces of those who in Abraham's bosom rest in paradise among the blessed saints. Paradise is surrounded by a wall of crystal and pure gold, adorned with trees filled with bright birds. To right and left stand the prophets holding scrolls thus inscribed:—

Daniel: "I beheld till the thrones were cast down, and the Ancient of Days did sit." (vii. 9.)

Malachi: "And the day that cometh shall burn them up." (iv. 1).

The righteous Judith: "The Lord Almighty will take vengeance" (xvi. 17).

THE FEASTS OF THE DIVINE MOTHER.

The Conception.†

Houses and gardens planted with various trees. St. Anna in the garden at prayer. Above her is an angel blessing her. A mountain

* Deut. xviii. 15.

† Called Annunciation to St. Anna in " Legends of the Madonna," pp. 137, 143-4. Mrs. Jameson enumerates the following illustrations of this subject: Annunciation to St. Anna, Luini, in the Brera, Milan ; Vision of the Virgin by St. Anna, Cesi, Bologna.

is seen outside the garden, where Joachim is seen
angel blessing him also.

The Nativity of the Divine Mother.
Houses. St. Anna lying on a bed under a coverl
ing on a pillow. Two attendants support her from
stirs the air with a fan. Other women, carrying di
the door. Under them are others, seated, who was
basin. Another, again, rocks the infant in the crac

The Divine Mother blessed by the prie
Houses. A table furnished with food. Joach
holding the little infant, the Holy Virgin, in his
behind him. Three priests, seated at the table,
Virgin and bless her.

Presentation of the Divine Mother in the
The temple. A staircase leading up to the porch
Zacharias stands at the gate, clothed in pontifical ro
his arms open. The Holy Virgin, three years old,
before him. She holds out one hand and carries
other; Joachim and Anna, behind, point her ou
virgins carrying tapers, who stand near.§

The temple is crowned by a magnificent cupola
seated beneath the centre of the dome; she takes
to her with a benediction by the archangel Gabriel.

Joseph leading the Divine Mother into the Ho
Within the temple. The prophet Zacharias
benediction. Behind, other priests point out the
to another. In front, Joseph takes the Holy Virg
Other persons stand behind.¶

* Birth of Virgin, D'Agincourt, Greco-Italian; Birth
Tadeo Gaddi, Baroncelli Chapel, Florence.
† Two scenes or acts are comprised under this heading
the rocking to sleep.
‡ "Now there were around the temple, according to
of degrees, fifteen steps to go up."— *Apoc. Gosp. Nat. of*
§ Bas-relief, Orcagna, San Michele, Florence. Fres
Baroncelli Chapel, Florence. Painting, Carpaccio, Acca
‖ Gabriel thus ministering to the child Mary is carve
Amiens Cathedral. The Virgin spinning with an angel
presented in Office of the Virgin: Bodleian, 1408, Oxfor
¶ Virgin and Joseph, Luini, the Brera, Milan. The
Virgin is omitted in the Greek manual.

Death of the Virgin.*

A house. The Holy Virgin within lies dead upon a couch, her arms crossed upon her breast, torches and lighted tapers at each side of the bed. Beside the bed stands an angel with a naked sword, and a Hebrew, whose hands are cut off and fastened to the bed. St. Peter incenses the feet of the Holy Virgin with a censer. At her head stand St. Paul and St. John Theologos, who kisses her. Other apostles and bishops stand round. Dionysius the Areopagite, Hierotheus and Timotheus holding the gospels. Women in tears. Christ is above, holding in His arms the soul of the Blessed Virgin, clad in white. She is surrounded by a great light and a crowd of angels. The twelve apostles advance on clouds in the air. On the top of the house to the right John of Damascus holds a scroll with these words: "You indeed, O heavenly Virgin, merit that you should be received still living into heaven, tabernacle of the divine." St. Cosmas, the poet, on the left, holding a scroll with these words: "You appear to be a mortal woman, but your apostles see you truly, O immaculate Divine Mother."

The Divine Mother laid in the Tomb.†

A tomb. Within it the apostle Peter supports the head of the Holy Virgin; outside Paul supports her feet; John Theologos embraces her. The other apostles stand round, holding wax tapers and uttering lamentations.

The Assumption of the Divine Mother.‡

An open and empty tomb. The apostles astonished. Thomas, in their midst, shows them the Virgin's girdle which he holds. Above them in the air the Holy Virgin ascends to heaven on clouds. Thomas is again seen upon the clouds at the side of the Holy Virgin, and receives the girdle from her hands.§

---

* Mrs. Jameson remarks that this scene, in those examples derived from the Greek school, is always represented with a mystical and solemn simplicity, adhering closely to the formula laid down in the Greek manuals. See sculpture of Death of the Virgin in the abbey church of Solernes.

† Mrs. Jameson mentions painting of this scene by Angelico, engraved in "Etruria Pittrice" (see "Leg. of Madonna," p. 317). Taddeo Bartoli (Siena, Pal. Publico), Parmigiano, and Fra Angelico, treated this subject.

‡ A. Orcagna, sculpture in San Michele. See Mrs. Jameson, "Leg. Madonna," pl. xxvii. Agnolo Gaddi, fresco in Chapel della Sacratissima Cintola, Prato. Taddeo Bartoli, Palazzo Publico, Siena.

§ Two scenes under this heading.

Fountain of Life.

A golden fountain. The Divine Mother in the midst with upraised. Christ in front of her (see vol. i. p. 486), blessing to and left, the gospel open on His breast at these words: "I a living Water." Two angels hold, each with one hand, a crown the Holy Virgin's head, while carrying scrolls in the other, on is written: "Hail, fountain of life and purity!" "Hail, pure of the Divinity!" Under the fountain is a large basin with At each side patriarchs, kings, queens, princes, princesses bat and drink of the water from cups and vases. A crowd of sic] paralysed come there also; and a priest holding a cross them. A man possessed by a devil. The baptism of a Thes by a captain of a vessel, who pours water over him, is also repres here.*

The prophets on high.†

The Holy Virgin seated on a throne, holding the infant C Underneath her pedestal are these words: "Prophets have claimed your name from on high." The prophets stand rou follows:—

The patriarch Jacob, holding a ladder. He says upon his s "I beheld you in a dream as a ladder planted upon earth reaching to the heights of heaven."

Moses holding a bush, says upon a scroll: "I have called tree, O Divine Virgin Mother; for in a bush have I beheld a mystery!" ‡

Aaron, holding a blossoming rod, says upon his scroll: "Th has foreshown to me, O spotless Virgin, that you have given to the Creator, even as a plant to a flower!"

Gideon holding a fleece says upon his scroll: "O pure V this fleece has foreshown you to me; for by this fleece I hav the miracle of your deliverance!"

David, holding an ark, says upon his scroll: "Gazing o

---

* The origin and history of this incident of the Thessalian is for even by the painters of Mount Athos.

† The Virgin enthroned and honoured by prophets and patria illustrated at Chartres, Rheims, Amiens, Laon, and Mans Cathedral also in mosaic, cath., Capua. Virgin enthroned with Isaiah and Jer Ste. Maria della Navicella, Rome.

‡ Moses was said to have seen a vision of the Virgin and Child the burning bush. See p. 273, *supra*.

eauty of the temple, O young Virgin, I have forenamed you, Virgin, the holy ark."

Solomon holding a bed, says upon his scroll: "I have named you 1e royal couch, predicting your prodigious wonders."

Isaiah, holding a ladle, says upon his scroll: "O spotless Virgin, have foreshown you, in this lamp of burning charcoal, the name : the kingly throne."

Jeremiah, pointing to the Divine Mother, says upon a scroll: "I ave seen you, O Maiden, Virgin of Israel, led forth to tribulation."

Ezekiel (xliv. 2), holding a gate, says upon a scroll: "I have :held you, closed gate of God! by which the sole God of the niverse hath gone forth."

Daniel (ii. 34), holding a mountain, says upon a scroll: "I have 'renamed thee as a spiritual mountain, whence a stone was cut 1t,* O spotless Virgin Mother!"

Habakkuk, holding a shady mountain, says upon a scroll: "Being 1 the spirit and filled with prophetic joy, I have beheld you as a lountain covered in impenetrable shade."

Zachariah (iv. 2), holding a seven-branched candlestick, says pon his scroll: "I have looked, and behold a candlestick of gold, and is seven lamps thereon, O Spiritual Light, to enlighten the world."

The Salutations.

Heaven with sun and moon. The Holy Virgin above seated on a 1rone with the Infant Christ. The following inscription surrounds er: "Rejoice, Queen of Angels, O full of grace!" Above her 1 1ultitude of holy angels to right and left. Four of them hold :rolls; on the first is written: "Rejoice, Glory of Angels, protectress ! men." On the second: "Rejoice, Temple Divine, Throne of the ord." On the third to the left: "Rejoice, Paradise of Delight! !joice, Tree of Life!" On the fourth: "Rejoice, Palace and Throne : the great King!" Beneath the angels come all the orders of the ints upon clouds, each band preceded by a leader holding a scroll)ntaining his verse of the litany :—

John, first of prophets, saith: "Rejoice, you that fulfilled the :pectation of the prophets!"

* Dan. ii. 34: "A stone was cut out without hands, which smote the 1age upon his feet, that were of iron and clay, and brake them in pieces .. and the stone that smote the image became a great mountain and .led the whole earth."

Peter, first of the apostles, saith: "Rejoice, O laudable eloqu of apostles!"

Chrysostom, first of the bishops, saith: "Rejoice, glory (priests, reward of bishops!"

George, first of martyrs, saith: "Rejoice, glory of martyrs, str(of warlike men!"

Anthony, first of solitaries, saith: "Rejoice, famous a solitaries, glory of monks; religious!"

Constantine, first of righteous kings, saith: "Rejoice, O V strength and diadem of kings!"

Catherine, first of female martyrs, saith: "Rejoice, glor virgins: their fortress and their citadel!"

Euphraxia, first of female solitaries, saith: "Rejoice, consol sweet of women who live in solitude!"

The Paradise of Eden is seen above these figures, adorne birds of various plumage and animals, by flowers and varied sl and magnificent trees, and surrounded by a wall built of s precious as pure gold. The patriarch Abraham stands in the n Around him a number of little innocent children. All the patria righteous men, with women and children, in contemplation transport of joy. The saints and the penitent thief, bearing the on his shoulders, are also with them.

How to Represent the Twenty-four Stations of the Div Mother.

The Angel appears for the first time. . . .*

Houses. The Holy Virgin, sitting on a throne and spinnin(silk. Above, the sky. An angel descends upon clouds; he bl the Virgin with the right hand, and holds in the left a blosso rod.†

The Holy Virgin looking. . . .‡

Houses. The holy Virgin astonished. She holds a scroll saith: "How shall this be, seeing I know not a man?"

* This title and those which follow are the opening words of a sei prayers in constant use among the Greeks.

† None of the examples quoted by Mrs. Jameson in the "Legends (Madonna" quite correspond with this subject.

‡ Cimabue. The mystery of the Annunciation and Incarnatio Conception—is represented in four different scenes in the Greek man

archangel Gabriel, standing before her, blesses her with the right hand; in the left he holds a scroll and saith: "Rejoice, thou much graced; the Lord is with you!"

Third Station.

Houses. The archangel, standing reverentially, points with the right hand to heaven; in the left he holds a scroll and says: "Behold the handmaid of the Lord: be it unto me according to thy word."

The Power from on high. . . .

The Holy Virgin seated on a throne. An angel at each side lifts a great veil behind her, which stretches from the head to the feet. Above her the Holy Spirit appears, surrounded by clouds and a great light.

She who possesses God. . . .

Houses. Within the holy Virgin and Elizabeth, embracing. At a little distance Joseph and Zacharias speak together. Behind them a little child in short dress holds a stick upon his shoulder, from which a basket hangs.* Below the house, a stable: a mule tied to it eats from a manger.

Having a storm within. . . .

Houses. The Holy Virgin in ecstasy. Joseph before her, supported by his staff, extends his right hand towards the Holy Virgin, and looks at her with a troubled countenance.†

The shepherds have heard. . . .

The arrangement is identical with that of the Nativity of Christ; only here the Magi are not represented. (See above.)

The star, the road of God. . . .

The sky. A brilliant star comes forth in the midst of a ray. Beneath are mountains. The Magi, on horseback, point out this star to one another.

---

* "The old Italians," says Mrs. Jameson, "seldom omit this attendant. Michael Angelo, in the picture in the possession of Mr. Bromley, substitutes a maiden for the boy."

† See Mrs. Jameson, "Legends of the Madonna," p. 194, on this trouble and the repentance of Joseph.

The children of the Chaldæans have seen. . . .

Houses. The Holy Virgin, seated on a throne, and holdin little Infant Christ in her arms. The Magi, kneeling before offer gifts. Joseph stands behind her. Above, a star. O the house, a youth holding the horses of the Magi by a bridle.

The heralds of God. . . .

A city. Before the city gates, the watchman, looking outv At the extreme end of the city are mountains, and the Ma horseback. An angel guides the Magi.

His splendour in Egypt.

See above: The Flight into Egypt.

The expectation of Simeon.

The arrangement here quite the same as that for Candl (See above.)

He has revealed a new creation. . . .

Christ upon a cloud, blessing with both hands. The four c of the cloud, the four evangelical tetramorphs. Above, and at side of them are the apostles, the martyrs, the bishops, an other orders of all the saints.

They behold a wonderful birth. . . .

The sky. The Holy Virgin and Child throned on high. I the multitude of saints, their eyes raised to heaven.

He took heed of the things here below. . . .

The sky. Christ on high, surrounded by a circle of infinit and the orders of angels. Above, heaven; Christ is seen bl with both hands. Apostles and a great multitude on either si

All the angelic host. . . .

Christ seated on a throne, blessing. Above, heaven ar orders of the angels in wonder. They ascend and descend to Jesus.

The rhetors in various tongues. . . .

The Holy Virgin and Child enthroned. To her right and l young men and aged, wearing hats of fur or veils upon their

They are all astonished. Books, both open and closed, lie upon the ground at their feet.*

Christ has willed the salvation of the world. . . .

The sky, with sun, moon, and stars. Two angels descend from heaven. Below, mountains covered and beautified by trees, flowers, and houses. Christ walking on foot; the apostles following Him reverently.

The protection of virgins. . . .

Houses. The Holy Virgin standing in the midst, holding the Lord, a little infant, in her arms. A crowd of virgins surround her.

A universal hymn. . . .

The sky. Christ throned and blessing. A multitude of angels surround Him; bishops and saints stand below Him, holding open books.

Shining lamp. . . .

The Holy Virgin standing on a cloud; she carries the Lord, a little infant, in her arms. She is surrounded by a great light, whose rays strike downwards. A dark grotto below, in which men, kneeling, raise their eyes towards the Holy Virgin.

Christ willing to grant grace. . . .

Houses. Christ standing inside. He bears papers in His hands, covered with Hebrew characters. At the close of these papers are the words: "The Chirograph of Adam." Youths and old men kneel at each side of Christ.

Chorus of praise to the Son. . .

Houses. The Holy Virgin on a throne; she holds the Lord, an infant, in her arms. Bishops and priests are before the houses; one carries the gospel, the other a censer. Behind them, musicians singing; some wear hats, others great white bonnets. Deacons in their midst, with open rolls, lead the singing.†

O Mother, famed throughout the universe! . . .

The Holy Virgin seated on a high throne, a footboard beneath her

* These books are meant to figure human knowledge, which, when matured, does homage to divine wisdom symbolised in a child.
† At the present day, in Mount Athos, the deacons give the note and direct the singing.

feet with three steps. Kings, priests, bishops, and solitaries before it, some standing, others kneeling. They hold scrolls inscriptions.

The character of the faces of the twelve holy apostles.

St. Peter: an old man with a round beard; he holds an epist which is written: "Peter, apostle of Jesus Christ."

St. Paul: bald, beard grey and stubbly; he holds his twelve e tied together in a roll.

St. John Theologos: an old man bald; large, not very thick, t he holds the Gospel.*

St. Luke, Evangelist: young, curled hair, small beard; painting the Divine Mother.

St. Mark, Evangelist: grey hair, round beard; he holds the G

St. Andrew: an old man, frizzled hair, double-pointed bear holds a cross and closed scroll.

St. Simon Zelotes: an old man, bald, round beard.

St. James: young, beard beginning.

St. Bartholomew; young, beard beginning.

St. Thomas: young, beardless.

St. Philip: young, beardless.

All these personages hold closed scrolls.

The four evangelists seated at their desks, writing.

St Matthew, Evangelist, writing: "The book of the genera! Jesus Christ, the son of David, the son of," &c.

St. Mark, Evangelist, writing: "The beginning of the go Jesus Christ, the Son of God, as it is written," &c.

St. Luke, Evangelist, writing: "Forasmuch as many have ta hand," &c.

St. John Theologos, Evangelist, seated in a grotto, in ecstasy turns his head backwards towards heaven; his right hand

* In Western art, St. John has been, from the earliest times, repr without a beard; in the East, on the contrary, he is bearded. The Church represents him young, as he was at the time of the Last ! when he leaned on the breast of Christ; the Greek Church paints the time when he wrote the Apocalypse, in the island of Patmos— to say at a very advanced age, sixty-three years after the death of and in the year of the assassination of Domitian. St. John is repr thus in a MS. of the eleventh century in the Bibl. Nat. Paris (se p. 269, fig. 68), in the gospel of Charles the Bald (Bibl. Nat. N and in another MS. (Suppl. Lat. No. 641). In such instances we in a Byzantine origin.

upon his knee, the left is extended towards St. Prochoros.*
Prochoros is seated before St. John, who writes these words:
"In the beginning was the Word, and the Word was with
God..."

Before the evangelists, the tetramorph, winged beasts, each
carrying the gospel. They turn their gaze towards the four
evangelists in the following order: a man at the side of St Matthew,
a lion at the side of St. Mark, an ox at the side of St. Luke, an
eagle at the side of St. John. Interpretation: That with the
semblance of a man signifies the Incarnation;† that with the
semblance of a lion signifies strength, royalty;‡ that with the
semblance of an ox indicates the priesthood and sacrifices; that
with the semblance of an eagle indicates the inspiration of the
Holy Ghost. It must be remembered that St. Matthew, St. Mark,
and St. Luke are represented in houses when writing, whereas
St. John is represented in a grotto with Prochoros.

* * * * *

Here we omit the long catalogue of mere names which occupies
seventy-five pages of the translation of the Byzantine Guide, as likely to
be of little use to English readers: Apostles, Bishops, Deacons, Martyrs,
Solitaries, Stylites, or saints who lived on columns (Simon Stilites, Simeon
the wonderful orator, Daniel Stylites, Alypius Stylites and Luke Neo-
stylites); the Poets; the Righteous; the Myrrhophoræ or women carrying
myrrh, Mary Magdalen, Salome, Joanna, Mary, Martha, Mary sister of
Cleophas, Sosane; Female Martyrs; Female Solitaries; Righteous Women.

The exaltation of the holy and life-giving cross.

A temple. Within, St. Macarius, Patriarch of Jerusalem, upon
an ambo, holding the revered cross of Christ. The empress St.

---

* Mrs. Jameson does not mention Prochoros the deacon, who in Greek
art always accompanies John, and often is represented as writing under
his dictation. This deacon is scarcely known in the Latin Church.

† Because he begins his gospel with the human generations of Christ.

‡ Because he has set forth the royal dignity of Christ. The Latin
Church attributes the same symbols to the evangelists, and interprets
them in like manner. A gospel in folio, coming from the Sainte-Chapelle
in Paris, to which church it had been given in 1379 by Charles V., contains these lines, summing up all the explanations given at different times
in the Middle Ages for these mysterious attributes:—

"Quatuor haec Dominum signant animalia Christum;
Est homo nascendo, vitulusque sacer moriendo,
Et leo surgendo, cœlos aquilaque petendo.
Nec minus hos scribas animalia et ipsa figurant."

Helena standing below the ambo; with her a number of princes, a a multitude of people gazing upwards with raised hands.*

THE SEVEN HOLY SYNODS.

The first Œcumenical Holy Synod at Nicœa, under Constantine Great, in the year 325, against Arius (318 holy fathers of Church).

Houses. The Holy Spirit above. St. Constantine throned in midst. The following holy bishops are seated in pontifical dr to the right and left: Silvester of Rome, Alexander of Alexand Eustathius of Jerusalem, St. Paphnutius the Confessor, St. Jame Nisibia, St. Paul of Neocesarea; other bishops and fathers seated around in three ranks. A philosopher in their mi astonished. St. Spiridon, standing before him, stretches out hand towards him, and clasps a brick, whence fire and water issu The fire escapes and rises, the water flows between his fingers to ground. Arius standing, also in pontifical robes. St. Nich stretches out his hand to blow upon it.† Heretics of the Arian are seated together below. St. Athanasius, a young beard deacon, is seated, and writes: "I believe in one God," down "and I believe in the Holy Ghost."

The second Holy Œcumenical Synod at Constantinople, un Theodosius the Great, in the year 381, against Macedoni (with 150 fathers of the Church).

Houses. The Holy Ghost above. The great Theodosius thro in the midst. The following saints are to be seen seated at e side: St. Timotheus of Alexandria, Meletius of Antioch, Cyril Jerusalem. Gregory Theologos, Patriarch of Constantinople, wr

---

* This subject, which is one of the most imposing in Greek paintin, not sufficiently dealt with here. It is described more fully in the volume of this work, at pages 414–417.

† St. Nicho'as, an ardent defender of the Trinity, is particul venerated by the Russians, who represent him as holding three perfe equal balls in his hands. To cause water and fire to issue from ba clay is the figure of the Trinity which includes a God in three person the brick contains three elements in one substance. The creed of Ath sius proclaimed at this Council is devoted to the development of the do of the Trinity.

‡ Macedonius disputed the divinity of the Holy Spirit.

the portion of the Creed from the words, "And in the Holy Ghost," to the end. Near them are seated other bishops and priests conversing.

The third Holy Œcumenical Synod, at Ephesus, under Theodosius the Younger, in the year 431, against Nestorius (200 fathers of the Church).

Houses. The Holy Ghost above. King Theodosius the Younger in the midst. He is seated on a throne, young, and with beard commencing. Seated at each side of him are St. Cyril of Alexandria, Juvenal of Jerusalem, and other fathers and archbishops. Before them, Nestorius, an old man in archbishop's robes; he disputes with them. Near him are heretical sectarians, with demons on their shoulders.

The fourth Œcumenical Synod at Chalcedon, under King Marcian, in the year 451 (630 fathers of the Church), against Eutyches and Dioscuros.*

Houses. The Holy Ghost above. King Marcian, an aged man, seated upon a throne. Near him, princes with fur head-dresses and crimson hats, embroidered with gold. Seated on either side are St. Anatolius of Constantinople, Maximus of Antioch, Juvenal of Jerusalem, and the bishops Paschasinus and Lucensius, representatives of Leo, Pope of Rome, with other bishops and priests. Dioscuros in front, in pontifical robes, and Eutyches near him; they converse together. Devils are on the shoulders of the heretics, whom they bind in chains. (See vol. i. pp. 465, 466.)

The fifth Œcumenical Synod at Constantinople, under Justinian the Great, in the year 553 (151 fathers of the Church), against Origen.

Houses. The Holy Ghost above. The king enthroned; seated to his right and left are Vigilus, Pope of Rome, Eutychius of Constantinople, and other priests and archbishops. In front, Origen, an old man, addresses them. A demon, seated on his shoulder, holds his eyes shut.

* Eutyches and Dioscuros maintained that there was only one nature in Christ.

360   APPENDIX II.

*The sixth Holy Œcumenical Synod at Constantinople, under
stantine Pogonatus,* in the year 680 (160 fathers (
Church), against Honorius, Sergius and Pyrrhus.†*

Houses. The Holy Ghost above. The king, a grey-haire(
with forked beard, is seated on a throne. Behind him, the
phoroi (lance-bearers), and the saints seated on each side
George of Constantinople, Theodore and George, representati
the Pope at Rome, with other priests and bishops. The h(
speak to one another.

*The seventh Œcumenical Synod at Nicœa, under Constantin
Irene, in the year 787 (350 fathers of the Church), agai}
Iconoclasts.*

Houses. The Holy Ghost above. King Constantine, a
child, and his mother Irene, seated upon thrones. Const
holds the image of Christ in his hands, and Irene the image
Virgin. At their sides are St. Tarasius of Constantinople, tł
bishops, Peter, representative of the Pope, and other pontif
priests, all seated and holding images. A bishop writes]
midst of them : " He that revereth not these holy images a}
venerated cross, let him be anathema."

The exaltation of holy images.

A temple. St. Methodius, patriarch, is outside in archbi
robes, and holding a cross. Behind him, other archbishops b
images. Before them, deacons hold the image of Christ
others carry the image of the Holy Virgin, called the Condu
whose feet are shod with gold. Behind the patriarch,
Theodore, and king Michael his son, still a child, also carry i}
Behind them, priests with censers and lamps. The ascetic
John, Arsakios, and Isaiah, and a crowd of hermits. Near
Saint Cassia, and with her a crowd of female religious soli
A vast number of others of the laity—men, women, and chil(
bearing crosses and tapers.

* The bearded.
† These are the Monothelites, who only admit a single will i}
Christ.

HOW TO REPRESENT THE MIRACLES OF THE PRINCIPAL SAINTS.

MIRACLES OF THE ARCHANGEL MICHAEL.

Michael showing water to Hagar.

A house. Abraham at the door; Hagar before him holding the child Ishmael by the hand. She carries a leathern bottle of water, and a basket of bread upon her shoulder. Farther on, a mountain. Ishmael laid upon his back under a tree. Hagar near at hand, as well as the archangel, who points to water upon the ground.

Michael prevents Abraham sacrificing Isaac. (See p. 271, supra.)

Michael forbids the demon to enter the body of Moses. (See p. 276.)

Michael appears to Joshua, son of Nun, and orders him to unfasten his shoes. (See p. 276.)

Michael appears to Gideon, and strengthens him against Midian. (See p. 277.)

Michael appears to Manòah, and announces the birth of Samuel. (See p. 277.)

Michael appears to David, and ceases to exterminate the people because of his sacrifice. (See p. 279.)

Michael descends to the Three Children. (See p. 285.)

Michael, owing to the mediation of Habakkuk, brings nourishment to Daniel. (See p. 286.)

Michael preserves the city of Constantinople, and prevents its being taken by the Persians.

A fortified town, spacious and beautiful. Below, tents. A crowd of soldiers, on foot and on horseback, speak together; others place ladders against the walls. Michael is above upon the clouds. A great light surrounds him, and he holds a fiery sword.

Michael prevents his church from being destroyed in an inundation.

A church. Inside, Saint Archippos, an old man with a pointed beard, is at prayer. Michael standing before him; he strikes the

foundations of the church with a lance, and splits a stone. In
distance, two torrents, descending from the mountains, unite be
the church, and pass through the broken stone. Above, upon
mountains, are men armed with pickaxes and other tools, who t
the course of the torrents.

*The archangels Michael and Gabriel save a child from being
engulfed in the sea.*

The sea. In the midst, three monks in a caïque with sails.
of them holds the rudder, the two others have fastened a st
round a child's neck, and throw it head-foremost into the
Winged archangels take up the child at either side. On the
shore a monastery and church, in the midst of which the s
child is seen asleep, with the stone round its neck. The higoumen
of the monastery, standing before him, touches him with a r
Behind the higoumenos, a crowd of monks are to be seen in adm
tion and astonishment.

THE MIRACLES OF THE HARBINGER.

*The prophet Zacharias warned by the archangel of the concepti
of the Precursor.*

The temple and altar. Zacharias, standing before the altar, h
a censer in his right hand; he raises his eyes to heaven,
stretches out his left hand. Above the altar, Gabriel says to h
"Fear not, Zacharias, for your prayer is granted." Outside
temple a multitude of Jews, both men and women, at prayer.

The nativity of the Harbinger.

Houses. Elizabeth laid upon a mattress in the bed. A ser
stands before her, fanning her; other servants, coming into
house, carry food to Saint Elizabeth, and offer it to her. O
servants, at the bedside, wash the infant in a basin. Zacha
seated, writes upon a scroll: "His name will be John."

Elizabeth takes John, and flies into the desert.

Mountains. Elizabeth carrying the infant John in her ar
she flies, looking behind her. There is a great rock before her,

---

* The higoumenos is the abbot, the director of the Greek monaster

from top to bottom, in which she is already partly hidden; a soldier, armed with a sword, pursues her from behind.*

The Harbinger preaches the baptism of repentance, on the shore of the Jordan.

A multitude of men and women carrying little infants on their shoulders, and in their arms. The Harbinger, standing in their midst, says upon a scroll: " Repent, for the kingdom of heaven is at hand."

The Harbinger teaches the Jews and Pharisees on the banks of the Jordan.

A multitude of people; doctors and Pharisees. Near them, great trees, and an axe buried in the root of the tree. The Harbinger, showing the hatchet with one hand, and holding a scroll in the other, saying: " O generation of vipers, who hath warned you?" Near the tree where the axe is laid, the words, " But now the axe is laid," &c.†

The Harbinger baptising the people.

A crowd of men, women, and children. Some are undressing; others step into the water. The Harbinger baptises a man, and says upon his scroll: " I indeed baptise you with water; but there cometh " &c.

The Harbinger points out Christ.

[This picture is omitted in the manuscript; but it is known to every one. John points out Jesus, passing in the distance, to the astonished crowd. John points with the forefinger of his right hand, saying, " Behold the Lamb of God!" John is frequently represented among us using this gesture.—*Didron.*]

The Harbinger reproves Herod because of Herodias, his brother Philip's wife.

A palace. Within, King Herod, an old man, seated upon a throne; Herodias near him, also seated upon a throne. A circle of

---

* This rather a common subject in France. It may be seen carved in ivory on the magnificent triptych of Poissy, now in the museum of the Louvre. This work, of Italian origin, belongs to the close of the thirteenth century.

† This subject is carved in the cathedral of Rheims, on the western wall. inside.

soldiers surround them. The Harbinger, standing befo-e H shows him Herodias, saying, "It is not lawful for thee to hav(woman." Two soldiers seize John.

The Harbinger imprisoned.

A dark prison. A soldier in front holds by one hanc Harbinger bound. With the other hand he opens a door v key. Behind the Harbinger stand other soldiers, who hold hi force.

The Harbinger beheaded. (*Four scenes.*)

A palace. Within, a table at which Herod, with his pi and nobles, is seated. Two servants take plates from the l of another, visible outside the window as far as his shou and arms. In front of the table a young girl, richly at dances.

Near the table is a room at one side, in which Herodias in robes is seated; before her, a young girl holds the Harbir head in a charger.

In the distance, some way from the palace, the prison, wit iron-barred window, is visible. The Harbinger, beheaded stretched upon the ground outside. The executioner, holding head in his hands, places it upon the charger held by the y maiden.

At a little distance the apostles Andrew and John carry body to the tomb.*

The first invention† of the venerated head of the Harbinger

A house with a door. Outside the door, a little staircase; a foot of the stair, an open tomb, in which the head of the Harb is laid. A hermit with a pickaxe removes the stone that c the tomb; another, in front of him, holds a box.

Farther on the two hermits appear again; one carries his cl in a roll hung at the end of a crook; the second, in front of gives another man the Harbinger's head in the box. A

---

* This subject of the entombment of John the Baptist by St. An and his brother arises from a tradition peculiar to the East, and r represented by the Latins.

† Invention, meaning discovery; Latin *inveniens*, to come upon or on anything; hence to find, to discover.

stands before them, bearing this inscription: "The potter receives the head of the Harbinger from the hands of two hermits." *

The second invention.

A grotto. A terra-cotta urn is seen within, containing the Harbinger's head. Rays of light fall from the roof of the grotto upon the head. A priest, carrying lamp and censer, incenses the head. A monk, slightly bent, holds a taper with one hand in front of him; with the other he points out the head. There is a little house behind the grotto.

Behind the grotto there is a small house. A hermit, an aged man with long beard, is escaping, and looks behind him. Two of the laity pursue him and beat him with sticks. This inscription is over their heads: "Eustace the Arian pursued by the orthodox because he denies the truth of the miracles wrought by means of the sacred head of the Harbinger."

The third invention of the venerated head of the Harbinger.

A church. The venerated head, in a golden shrine, stands in the midst. A chandelier and lighted lamps before it. On each side of the shrine two deacons hold candelabra and tapers; a bishop incenses it with a censer. At his side a king, with an incipient beard, remains standing respectfully.† Behind the king his governor and other nobles. On the other side are priests and two musicians playing the harp. A deacon, standing in the midst, conducts the music. Another singer at the king's side. A crowd of people form a circle round. This inscription is above: "The venerated head of the Harbinger revered by the king and his people."‡

---

* This potter was from Emessa, in Syria. The story is as follows: "As the two monks were returning from the palace of Herod, where they had found the head of St. John the Baptist, they were joined on the road by a native of Emessa, who had left that city because of his great poverty. He carried their packages as well as the saint's head. At night, St. John having appeared to him and having directed him, he left the monks and carried off the head to Emessa. Then, having hidden it in a cavern, and always treating it with the greatest veneration, he prospered greatly. There it lay concealed for many generations, till a star guided Marcellus to the place where it lay." (See *Légende Dorée*, vol. i. p. 283.)

† This monarch is the Emperor Theodosius the Great, who brought the head of St. John the Baptist from Chalcedon to Constantinople. In the reign of Pepin this head is said to have passed from Constantinople to Poitiers, where numerous miracles were wrought by it.

‡ The whole legend of the beheading of John the Baptist is given in bas-relief in the cloister of the choir of Amiens cathedral, southern side.

APPENDIX II.

THE MIRACLES OF THE APOSTLE PETER.

Peter cures the man lame from his birth.

The temple with steps. A man seated, his head covered a veil, on the highest step at the temple gate; a wallet is from his shoulders. His hands and eyes are raised towards At his side two crutches hang against the temple wall. standing before him, blesses him with one hand; he holds a scroll in the other. John Theologos is behind him, y beardless.

Peter destroys Ananias and Sapphira.

Houses. Peter, standing in front, one hand outstret Sapphira stretched dead at his feet. At a little distance men carry away the body of Ananias, her husband. The ap and a great crowd stand behind Peter.

Peter restores Tabitha to life.

A high house. A woman laid upon a bed at the top c house. Peter, taking her by the left hand, blesses her wit right. Women, widowed and infirm, are showing him the gan and tunics she had given them.

Peter baptises the centurion Cornelius and them that are with

The water. In the midst of this water stands Cornelius, naked, grey-haired and with a long beard. Five other pe Peter, his right hand upon the head of Cornelius. Outsid water a crowd of men and women.

Peter withdrawn by an angel from the house of Herod.†

A prison. In the midst of it Peter seated between two sc who sleep; he has shoes upon his feet, and two chains are near him upon the ground. An angel with outstretched stands before him.

* In the church of St. Bartholomew, at Liège, baptismal fonts of may be seen, executed in the twelfth century by Lambart Pat celebrated jeweller of Dinant). It is a choice example of the pr works in metal so renowned in the middle ages. These fonts wei cuted for the church of Notre Dame des Fonts, now quite destroyed. are shaped like a vat, or the brazen sea executed by Solomon, whic supported by twelve oxen. Scenes of baptism are represented on t of the vessel, such as that of Jesus by John the baptist, of the philo Crato by St. John the Evangelist, and of Cornelius by St. Peter.

† This subject is generally called St. Peter in chains.

THE MIRACLES OF THE SAINTS. 367

Peter destroys Simon the magician.

Houses; the temple. Two winged demons in the air. Simon the magician stretched upon the ground, his skull broken. Peter stretches out his hand and threatens the demons. A crowd of men surround him.

The apostle Peter crucified head downwards and put to death.

A cross planted in the earth. St. Peter crucified upside down, his head down, his feet upwards. A crowd of soldiers encircle him; some nail his hands, others his feet.*

THE MIRACLES OF THE APOSTLE PAUL.

Paul called by the Lord on the road to Damascus.

St. Paul prostrate on his face upon the ground; his hands are over his eyes. Heaven above; Christ is therein. A vivid light, composed of several rays, issues from heaven, and rests upon St. Paul's head. In the midst of these rays, we read: "Saul! Saul! why persecutest thou Me?" Near him are four men with fur hats and turbans; they stand upright and are dumb with amazement.

Paul baptised by Ananias.

Paul, naked, standing in the midst of the water. Ananias lays his hand upon his head; scales, like fish-scales, fall from the eyes of Paul.

Paul blinding the magician Bar-Jesus.†

An archon seated upon a throne. A diadem upon his head. Before him, the magician, covering his eyes with his hands. Paul, in front of him, stretches out his hand towards the eyes of the magician. Barnabas is behind Paul. A crowd of men and women stand round, astonished.

Paul shaking off the viper into the fire that had bitten his hand.

A fire of faggots and brushwood. Paul standing, holding his

* Although upside down, St. Peter was crucified vertically, like Jesus Christ. St. Andrew was crucified horizontally. It was not till the fifteenth century that St. Andrew was represented fastened vertically to a cross saltire. Before that he is shown on an ordinary cross, the cross of Jesus—but fixed sideways—on the cross-bar—horizontally.

† Acts xiii. 6.

hands open over the fire. A viper bites his finger in the π
and hangs to it. St. Luke is near him; other soldiers and
seated in a circle, warming themselves.

St. Paul beheaded.

St. Paul kneeling, his eyes covered with a veil. The execut
raises his sword above the head of St. Paul. Other soldiers
round. A little further on a woman, blind of one eye, looks ‹
Paul.*

THE MIRACLES OF ST. NICHOLAS.

St. Nicholas throwing money into a house.

A high house. Inside, a man asleep; his three daughters
little distance. St. Nicholas, young, standing under the h
holds a handkerchief full of money; he throws it through a wi
into the house.†

St. Nicholas ordained deacon.

A church; the sanctuary and the table.‡ The saint, young,
round beard, bends a little forward before the holy table.
archbishop—an old man with a large beard—lays his hand
the saint's head, his hypogonation and the end of his homoph
The Holy Spirit is above, surrounded by rays. Two deacor
each side, carrying three-branched candlesticks. Torches
lamps, illuminated, are outside the temple. A crowd of people

St. Nicholas ordained priest.

The same composition.

St. Nicholas, in a ship, restores a dead sailor to life.

The sea. A vessel, in the midst of which the saint is se‹
prayer. A dead sailor lies stretched before him. Other s‹
stand round astonished.

* This woman is Plantilla, Platilla or Lemobia, for she is known 1
three names, disciple of St. Paul. She gave the veil to St. Paul,
which he covers his eyes before the execution. See *Légende Dorée*, ›
p. 307.
† See Mrs. Jameson, *Sacred and Legendary Art*, vol. ii. p. 452.
‡ i.e., the altar, which in the Greek church is a table, and in the
a tomb.
§ The hypogonation is a little lozenge-shaped ornament, falling ‹
the knee of the bishop and originally intended to hold his handker
The homophore corresponds to our stole.

St. Nicholas consecrated bishop.

The same as above, only there are three bishops.

St. Nicholas in prison; he receives the gospel from Christ, and a stole from the Mother of God.

A prison. The saint inside. To his right, Christ holding the gospel; to his left, the Mother of God carrying a stole: they present these things to him.

St. Nicholas delivers the innocent men from death.

A city. Mountains outside, and three men condemned to death, kneeling, their eyes covered with a veil, and their hands tied behind their backs. The executioner behind them, holding a naked sword; the saint, behind him, snatches it angrily from him. Three men are near the saint with furred hats and pelisses. Prince Eustatius humbles himself to the earth before the saint, and repents. Behind him a horse with gilded harness.

St Nicholas appears in a dream to the Emperor Constantine and to Eularius; he delivers the soldiers.

Palace. Constantine the Great, asleep upon a golden bed. He is covered to his breast with coverlets shining with gold. The saint appears to him at his head, and fills him with terror.

At a little distance is another palace, and the saint in like manner frightening the sleeping Eularius.

The death of St. Nicholas.

The saint laid dead upon his bed, in pontifical robes. Bishops holding open gospels stand around him; one of them embraces the saint. Deacons with censers, torches, and open books. A crowd of people, monks and laity. A monk, clothed in a mantle, strikes a simander,* and makes it resound.

THE MIRACLES OF ST. GEORGE.

St. George speaks boldly to Diocletian.

A palace. The emperor Diocletian seated on a throne. Near him his *epitrope* (vice-emperor), Magnentius, seated upon a lower throne. Behind the emperor two soldiers with lances. Near them

* A kind of wooden instrument like a gong.

other archons and soldiers. The saint, standing before the em
extends his right hand towards him. Two soldiers pierce hin
two javelins.

The saint thrown into prison.

A prison. In the midst, the saint laid upon his back, b
fastened in a wooden instrument. A soldier closes this instr
with a key; two other soldiers lay a great stone upon the
breast.

The saint placed upon a wheel.

A square beam, covered with iron spikes, and surmounte
wheel. The saint fastened by his feet and hands to this
Two executioners, holding cords, turn the wheel. The empe
seated opposite upon a throne. Magnentius, before him, poin
the saint. Above the wheel, an angel sits on the cloud ne
saint, whom he comes to unbind. Outside the town, two a
and a great number of soldiers are beheaded by executioners.

The saint with his feet tied up in shoes of red-hot iron.

The saint seated, his hands tied. A soldier fastens his fee
red-hot iron shoe. Behind them, a coal fire, upon which is a
shoe.

The saint drinks a mortal poison.

The emperor seated on a throne, as well as Magnentius.
raise their hands towards the saint. He, standing before
drinks the poison from a narrow-necked terra-cotta vase.
magician Athanasius is standing in front of him; he holds a
vase in his left hand, while with the finger of his right ha
points out the saint to the emperor. Near at hand, a great cr
soldiers.

The saint restores the dead to life.

The emperor and Magnentius seated upon thrones. The ma
Athanasius is near them, astonished. In front and at a
distance, the saint prays before an open tomb, in which th
rises, standing upright and full of life. Near that, a cro
admiration.

Further on, the magician Athanasius and the restored
beheaded by an executioner.

The saint restores a peasant's ox to life.

The saint, seated in a prison and blessing. Before him, o

the prison, and near his master, is the revived ox The peasant, on his knees, turns his hands and eyes towards the saint.

The beheading of St. George.

The saint kneeling. Before him, the executioner, with a sword. At a little distance, Queen Alexandrina, seated on a stone; she breathes a last sigh, and an angel receives her soul.

THE MIRACLES OF ST. CATHERINE.

The saint learning from her confessor.

A grotto. Inside, a hermit confessor, seated on a stool; he lays his hands upon the saint. She is before him, fixed in astonishment. Her mother is near her.

Christ averts His face from St. Catherine because she is not baptised.

A grotto. The saint bears herself humbly before the Mother of God, who is holding the Christ in her arms as a little infant is held. He turns His face away so that St. Catherine may not see Him.

The saint baptised by her confessor.

A grotto. Within, the same hermit as above; he baptises the saint. Near her, her mother holds a lighted taper.

The saint receives a token of betrothal from Christ.

A grotto. The saint standing within, her right hand extended open. Before her, the Holy Virgin, holding Christ, as a little child, by one hand, taking the saint's right hand with the other. The Lord puts a ring upon the little finger of her right hand; He holds a scroll in the other hand, with these words: " Behold, I take thee to-day for mine inviolable spouse." *

The saint speaking boldly to the king.

A temple. Within are idols; before these idols is an altar with animals burning thereon. Men: some strangle oxen and sheep with cords; others carry birds; others sacrifice. The king enthroned, surrounded by his guards. The saint stands forward and addresses them.

* The four first subjects in St. Catherine's life are not often seen in Western art. In France her life commences at the Mystic Marriage.

The saint disputes with fifty philosophers.

A palace. The king within, seated on a throne. Fift[y] sophers seated at once, some on one side and some the other. heads are veiled.* The oldest of these philosophers, standi[ng] the king's throne, disputes with the saint, pointing out th[e] philosophers to her. All are astonished. Some hold their in their hands; some talk to one another, and point out the

The saint fastened to wheels.

Four wheels, armed with iron blades, crossed by a sing[le] The saint below, stretched upon the earth, her hands tie[d] angel, standing near, loosens her cords. Several soldiers r[ound] wheels are dead or cut to pieces; the king on his throne is o[ne] The queen, coming out of the door of a house, reproaches h[im] great crowd of men stand round.

A little farther on, the queen is again seen, beheaded executioner. A number of other soldiers beheaded by exec[utioner] because they believed in Jesus Christ.

The beheading of St. Catherine.

The saint kneeling; the executioner lifts a sword over [her] multitude of men and women shed tears. †

THE MIRACLES OF ST. ANTHONY.

The saint beaten by demons.

A tomb. The saint is laid in it at the bottom. Demons s[trike] him, and strike him with a stick. Other demons drag off t[he] of the tomb.

The saint, taking refuge in the desert, finds a disc of silver gold upon the road.

Mountains and highway. In the midst of the highway,

* The veil is always part of the philosopher's costume in B[yzantine] art. The philosopher is likened to a priest, and even at the pre[sent] the monks of Mount Athos wear a black veil—the veil being a s[ort of] head-dress.

† At Athens, in a half-ruined church near the temple of Ju[piter] legend of St. Catherine is painted in six pictures. The saint is [in her] form, standing, nimbed, covered with long black hair in which p[earls] shining. She wears a radiated crown adorned with pearls. A[t] her right hand and wheel to the left. The legend of St. Eustace [may] be seen at Athens in the church of the Great Virgin.

disc of silver falls to the ground; a little further on, a great lump of gold. The saint carries staff and knapsack upon his shoulders; he quits the highway on seeing these objects. *

St. Anthony tills the ground.

A little vegetable garden; a grotto at the end. The saint, armed with a pickaxe, is busy weeding his vegetables.

The saint confounds the philosophers, and cures those who are possessed by demons.

The saint, standing. Three of the possessed lie on their backs before him; demons issue from their mouths. At the side are three philosophers, wearing veils on their heads; they appear astonished and embarrassed.

The saint led by a lion into the grotto of St. Paul.

The desert. The saint walks behind a lion. At a distance before them the grotto of St. Paul appears across the trees and mountains.

St. Anthony, having found St. Paul, embraces him.

A grotto. Outside, St. Paul the Theban, wearing a hair mat which covers him from his shoulders to his knees. He and St. Anthony embrace. A raven perched on the top of a tree holds bread in his beak.†

St. Anthony burying the body of St. Paul.

St. Paul stretched dead upon the ground; St. Anthony covering him with a winding-sheet. Close by, two lions tear up the earth with their fore-paws.

Death of St. Anthony.

A pit dug. Two brethren carry the saint enveloped in a shroud; one has gone down into the pit, the other is outside. Near them, an axe and a shovel thrown on the ground. Above the saint, a crowd

* He knew the devil could transform himself into silver and gold. (See the life of St. Anthony, written by St. Athanasius.)
† This subject of the meeting of Paul and Anthony is sculptured on the Ruthwell cross. See Stephens' *Runic Monuments*, vol. ii. pt. 1

of angels having tapers and censers, carrying his soul, cloth(white, and raising him to heaven.*

HOW TO REPRESENT THE MARTYRS OF THE YEAR.

Month of September.

1. The holy brothers Evodos, Callixtus, and Hermogenes headed.

Description.—St. Evodos and St. Hermogenes extended o1 ground and beheaded; the one young, the other old. Their Callixta near them; at her side the executioner with a sword.

2. St. Mamas perishing, his entrails torn out.

Description.—Mountains, with a grotto. St. Mamas, y beardless, laid upon his back. Above him, a soldier armed v three-pronged fork, which he buries in the saint's body.

3. The holy martyr of Anthymos, decapitated.

Description.—A city. Outside the city is the saint wit incipient beard, young, clad in pontifical robes, kneeling, wit head cut off. Above him is the executioner, holding a b sword. Before him, another executioner holds the head tha been cut off.

4. St. Babylas, with three children, beheaded.

Description.—St. Babylas, in episcopal dress, an old man large beard, his head cut off. Near him are three children, low their heads. Above them, the executioner, with a sword.

5. The prophet Zacharias, father of the Harbinger, slain bel the temple and the sanctuary.

Description.—The temple. Inside, a cupola, beneath whicl table. The saint is in front of it, an old man with a large 1 dressed as a Jewish high-priest, his hands and eyes raised to he A soldier seizes his head by the hair, and buries his sword throat.

6. SS. Eudoxia, Zeno, Romulus, and Macarius, beheaded.

Description.—St. Eudoxia and St. Zeno, young, incipient 1 kneeling, their hands raised to heaven and their heads lying ‹ ground in front of them. Above them an executioner, puttir sword in his sheath. At his side, St. Romulus, an old man, beh

* See chapter on Iconography of the Soul, p. 177, *supra.*

by another executioner. St. Macarius, a youth, kneeling; an executioner plunges his sword in his throat.

7. St. Soson, beaten by a club.
Description.—The saint stretched on the earth; two soldiers strike him with stakes of wood.

8. St. Severianus hung at a wall, a stone attached to his feet.
Description.—A city. Two soldiers upon walls, where the saint is hung. A great stone fastened to his feet.

9. St. Menodora, St. Metrodora, and St. Nymphodora perish under the rock.
Description.—The saints stretched upon the ground, naked to the middle of their bodies; veils cover their heads. Three soldiers strike them with sticks.

10. SS. Diodorus, Diomed, and Didymus, beaten to death.
Description.—St. Diodorus, an old man, St. Diomed and St. Didymus, young, with incipient beards, laid on the ground, their bodies covered with wounds; three soldiers flog them.

11. St. Autonomous, flogged and stoned, perishes.
Description.—The saint, young, with round beard, is kneeling, his hands raised to heaven; above him are four soldiers, some with stones, others with sticks, beating the body.

12. SS. Cronides, Macrobius, Leontius, Serapion, cast into the sea, perish.
Description.—The sea; in the midst a small ship, in which are soldiers, who cast the saints into the sea. St. Macrobius, an old man, is half in the boat and half outside. St. Cronides, a youthful deacon; the others are grey-headed.

13. St. Nicetas perishes in the fire.
Description—A great fire, in which is the saint, young, with an incipient beard, eyes and hands raised to heaven. Two soldiers fan the flames.

14. St. Euphemia, delivered up a prey to bears and lions, remains unharmed and renders up his soul to God.
Description.—Lions and bears; in their midst the saint upon his knees, his hands and eyes raised to heaven.

376   APPENDIX II.

15. St. Sophia beheaded with her three daughters, Faith, and Charity.

Description.—Mountains and houses; the saints are near Both stretched upon the ground with their heads cut off, t] others, kneeling, bow their heads. The executioner raises his over them.*

16. SS. Trophimus and Dorymedon beheaded, St. Sabl flogged to death.

Description.—St. Trophimus, with incipient beard, is str upon the earth beheaded. St. Dorymedon, beardless, knee hands tied behind his back; the executioner cuts his throat sword. St. Sabbaticus, stretched on his back, is covered with w Two soldiers with sticks are above him; one strikes, the brandishes his stick in the air.

20. St. Eustatius and his family are thrown into a red-hot bull.

Description.—A brazen bull; with the saint, grey-haired, a beard, with his son and his wife. Under the bull, two soldier up a great fire.

21. St. Codrates dies by the sword.

Description.—St. Codrates, an old man, beard stubbly, kn stretching out his hands towards the sky. The executione is over him, strikes him with a sword.

22. St. Phocas, beheaded.

Description.—The saint, an old man, with pontifical stretched on the ground, his head cut; fire behind his feet. executioner looks backwards.

24. St. Thecla enters a rock, which lacerates her, and peris

Description.—Mountains and a grotto; a little before the is a great stone split open. The saint is hidden in it, an

---

* The whole legend of the Holy Wisdom, or Sophia and her daughters, is painted on the walls of Chilandari on Mount Athos. cathedral of Canterbury the relics of the holy Wisdom and her dau are to be found. (See *Monasticon Anglicanum*, Dodsworth and D vol. i. p. 5.) This personification and genealogy recalls the genealo personification of Intelligence figured in a MS. Bible in the public of Rheims, where the daughters of Philosophy are Physics, Log Ethics. (See p. 34, *supra*.)

appears again. Christ upon a cloud above; He blesses the saint with His right hand, and with the left he shows the stone.

25. St. Paul; his mother and children die in tortures.
Description.—Houses and mountains. In front St. Paul, an elderly man, and his mother, very aged. The family: Savinien, young, beard round; Maximian, incipient beard; Rufus, young, beardless; Eugenius, a child. All are naked, covered with wounds, and dying. Two soldiers hold the little child, one by the head, the other by the feet, and they torture it.

26. St. John Theologos dies at Ephesus, where he is buried by his disciples.
Description.—The ground and a pit. Before the pit seven of the saint's disciples. Some hold pickaxes, others hatchets and shovels. The saint is buried in a ditch, and two other disciples cover his eyes with a veil.*

27. St. Callistratus and his companions, beheaded.
Description.—A vessel; inside hang broken idols. The saints, old and young, some beheaded, others kneeling, ready for the executioner's sword. St. Callistratus is near them; he is an old man, kneeling, his hands tied behind his back. Close to him, the executioner with his sword.

28. St. Mark, Alexander, Zosimus and Alpheus die, crushed upon a stone.
Description.—Mountains; the saints above. St. Alexander, grey-haired; St. Zosimus and Alpheus,† with incipient beards. They are crushed on stones, and dead. St. Mark, whose white hair descends almost to his feet, is also crushed upon a stone. He still breathes. Above him the executioner with a sword.

29. St. Gobdeleas, fastened by his feet to a horse; St. Dadas, cut in pieces; St. Casdoa, in a king's gardens, renders up her spirit in peace to the Lord.
Description.—Mountains; at the top, St. Gobdeleas, young, beardless, tied by the feet with cords to a horse, who drags him over the rocks; St. Dadas, an old man with a large beard and very richly dressed; he is stretched upon the earth, beheaded. Soldiers with

* This is represented on a glass window in the south side aisle of Chartres cathedral.
† Strange to give to a saint the name of a river.

their swords stand round him. St. Casdoa receives tne sacrament in a garden ; a priest and an angel are near her.

30. St. Mardonius dies, his body covered with burning charcoal. Description.—Houses ; the saint, grey-haired, with stubbly beard, is stretched upon his back on the ground in one of them. A soldier takes charcoal with a spade, and lays it on the saint's breast.

So far we have expounded the martyrs belonging to one month; the remaining martyrs throughout the year are represented in like manner as described in their lives and legends. Seek in the tables (of the martyrology) for the character of face belonging to the saints individually, as also the sayings on their scrolls.

[Here follows the martyrology for the months of the year following, but, as it is nothing more than a list of names, we have thought it better to omit this portion of the work, which occupies sixteen pages. M. Didron in a note observes, " I do not know why our Greek manuscript commences at the month of September, and why it does not in preference describe the saints of January, which begins the civil year, or still more December or April, the leading months of the religious year." The outer porch of Chilandari, on Mount Athos, is painted with the martyrdoms of the principal saints.]

ALLEGORIES AND MORALITIES.*

How to represent the life of the true monk.

Draw a monk† embracing a cross, wearing his priestly robe, on his head a calimafki ;‡ he should be barefoot, and his feet should rest upon the footboard of the cross, his eyes being cast down and his mouth closed. The following epigraph on the top of the cross near his head : " Lord, Son of God, set a seal upon my mouth, and a door upon my lips." He holds lighted wax-lights in his hands ; this epigraph is close to the wax-lights : " Let your light so shine before men, that they may see your good works, and glorify your Father which is in heaven." He has a lozenge-shaped scroll upon his breast, with these words : "Give me a pure heart, O God, and renew a right spirit within me." Upon his waist another scroll like a standard, with these words : " O monk, be not deceived by the appetites of the body." Below that again another scroll says :

* This title, added here by M. Didron, does not appear in the original MS.
† In French *caloyer*, meaning a Greek monk, of the order of St. Basil.
‡ A head-dress like an advocate's cap, worn by monks.

" Mortify your members here upon earth." And lower still another scroll saying : " Make ready your feet for the way of the gospel of peace." Above, on the highest portion of the cross, nail a title with the words : " Glory not because of me, if it be not in the cross of my Lord." Put seals at the other three ends of the cross. On that to the right inscribe: " He who endures to the end shall be saved." To the left : " He that renounces not all that he hath, cannot be a disciple of Christ." Upon the seal which is below the footboard write : " Narrow is the way, and filled with affliction, that leadeth unto life." On the right side of the cross, represent a dark cave with a dragon hidden in its midst, and write : " All-devouring hell." Above the dragon's mouth, a naked youth with his eyes bandaged, and holding a bow, fires an arrow at the monk. A scroll is tied to this arrow with these words : " Be sinful." Above that again : " The passion of love." Draw a crowd of serpents above the cave, and write : " Remorse." Close to hell make a demon dragging the cross with a cord, and saying : " The flesh is weak, and cannot withstand." At the right hand of the footboard make a lance, with a cross and standard, and write above it : " I can do all things through Christ who strengtheneth me." To the left of the cross, make a tower with a gate; issuing from it a man mounted on a white horse. This personage wears a furred hat, and garments glistening with gold and trimmed with fur. He holds a vase of wine in his right hand, and in his left a lance, to the end of which a sponge is attached. A scroll is attached to this lance saying : " Partake of all the world's delights." Write this inscription over the man : " The mad world." Place Death below him as if proceeding from him ; he carries a large scythe upon his shoulders, and a dial on his head ; he looks at the monk. Above him the inscription : " Death and the tomb." Below, at each side of the hands of the monk, make two angels holding scrolls. On that to the right is written : " The Lord hath sent me to your assistance." On that to the left : " Do well, and fear naught." Above the cross, paint heaven, with Christ holding the gospel open on His breast at these words : " He that will be My disciple must renounce himself, take up his cross and follow Me." He holds a royal crown in His right hand and a crown of flowers in the left ; an angel at each side below looks at the monk and points to Christ ; they hold between them both a great scroll with the words : " Labour for the crown of righteousness, and the Lord will give unto you a crown of precious stones." Then write this inscription: "The life of the true monk."*

The ladder of salvation and the heavenward way.

A monastery. A crowd of young and old monks outside the gate. In front a very great and high ladder, reaching to the sky. Monks are upon it, some starting to climb, others grasping the foot of the ladder, in order to rise higher. Above, winged angels appear to assist them. Higher still, in heaven, the Christ. An aged monk is before Him, upon the last step of the ladder; he stretches out his hands and looks towards heaven like a priest. The Lord takes him by one hand; with the other He lays a crown of flowers on his head, saying to him: "Come unto Me, all ye that labour and are heavy laden, and I will refresh you." Underneath the ladder a great crowd of winged demons seize the monks by their dress; they pull at some, but cannot cause them to fall. With others they have succeeded in drawing them a little way from the ladder, some with only one hand, others with two. Finally other monks are quite withdrawn from the ladder, and demons seize them by the waist and drag them away. The all-devouring hell is beneath them, under the form of an enormous and terrible dragon; a monk, whose feet only are now visible, has fallen backwards into his jaw. Write this sentence: "Behold the ladder that leans upon heaven, and reflect well upon the foundations of virtue. With what speed this fragile life is borne away! Approach the ladder and mount with courage. You have the choirs of angels as your defenders; you will surmount the snares of evil demons. Reaching the gates of heaven, you will receive the crown from the hand of the Lord."†

How to represent the death of a hypocrite.

A monk wrapped in bedclothes; a great serpent issues from his mouth. A demon over him buries a trident in his heart.

How to represent the death of the righteous.

A man with an incipient beard, laid in a decent and modest manner upon an humble bed, his eyes closed and hands crossed

---

* There is a fine example of this subject in a fresco painting in the porch of the principal church of the convent of Philotheou at Mount Athos.
† See Fig. 206, page 167, *supra*.

upon his breast. An angel above looks at him with joy, and receives his soul in veneration and respect

The death of the sinner.

An aged man, naked, laid upon a bed, half concealed by a magnificent covering, turns away his eyes in horror, moving his feet and throwing his arms from one side to another. A demon, above him, buries a trident in his heart; he torments him with all manner of atrocities and tears away his soul by force.

How to represent the illusive seasons of this life.

Describe a little circle; within it put an aged man, with rounded beard, in regal robes, and wearing a crown, seated on a throne, his hands stretched out at either side, and holding the same object as is held by the World,* who is figured above the apostles in Pentecost. Around the circle, write: " The mad, deceitful, and seductive world."

Outside the first circle make another still larger. Between these two circles, inscribe four semicircles, placed crosswise; in the midst of them represent the four seasons of the year: spring, summer, autumn and winter. At the top, spring, like this: a man seated in the midst of flowers and verdant fields; he carries a crown of flowers upon his head, and strikes a harp that he holds in his hand.† To the right, represent summer in this way: a man, with a hat, holds a sickle, and reaps a field. At the bottom, represent autumn thus: a man beats a tree and shakes down its flowers and fruits. To the left, represent winter thus: a man seated, wearing a pelisse and cowl, warms himself before a blazing fire. (See p. 222, *supra*.)

Outside this second circle, describe another still larger; divide it into twelve compartments, and put the twelve signs of the twelve months inside. Take care to place each sign near the season that corresponds with it. Thus, near spring, put the ram, the bull and the twins; near summer, put cancer, the lion, the virgin; near autumn, the balance, the scorpion, the archer; near winter, capricorn, aquarius, and the fish. Then arrange these signs according to their order, and be careful to write its name above each, as well

---

* The World is personified in the form of an aged man, crowned, holding twelve rolls in his lap (p. 322).

† In Western art, musical instruments are very rarely given to the Seasons.

as the names of the months, in the following manner. Above the ram, write March; above the bull, April; above the twins, May; above cancer, June; above the lion, July; above the virgin, August; above the scales, September; above the scorpion, October; above sagittarius, November; above capricorn, December; above aquarius, January; above pisces, February.

Outside the third and largest circle, make the seven ages of man in the following manner. Below, upon the right side, place a little child climbing; write before him on the circle, " child of seven years." Above this make another child more grown, and write, "child of fourteen years." Higher still, draw a youth with hair upon his face, and write, " youth of twenty-one." Above, on the top of the wheel put another man, with incipient beard, seated on a throne, his feet upon a cushion, his hand stretched out on either side, holding a sceptre in his right hand, and a purse full of money in his left; he is clad in regal robes, and wears a crown upon his head. Under him, upon the wheel, write: " youth of twenty-eight years." Under him to the left, make another man, with pointed beard, with head bent down, but looking up; " man of forty-eight years." Under him another man with grey hair, laid upon his back, and write : " mature man of fifty-six years." Under him, place a bald man, with white beard, bowed head, and arms hanging down, and write " aged man of seventy-five years." Then under him place a tomb, in which is a great dragon, holding in his jaws a man upon his back the half of whose body only is visible. In the tomb close by is Death, armed with a great scythe, which he buries in the throat o the old man, and mows him down.

Outside the circle write the following inscriptions, near the mouths of each individual:—

Near the little child : " When then, having climbed, shall arrive on high ? "

Near the child : " O Time, turn quickly, that I may reach th heights."

Near the youth : " Behold, I approach the point when I may b seated on my throne."

Near the young man: " Who is a king like unto me ? Who i above me ? "

Near the mature man, write: " Unhappy that I am. O Time how thou has deceived me!"

Near the aged man : " Alas! alas! O Death, who can escape thee ?

DISTRIBUTION OF PAINTINGS IN CHURCHES. 383

Near the tomb, these words: "Death and all-consuming hell."
Near the man devoured by the dragon: "Alas! who will save me from the all-devouring hell?"
Then to the right and left of the wheel put two angels under each half of the seasons, and turning the wheel with cords. Above the angel to the right, inscribe: "Day;" above that to the left: "Night." Above the wheel write this epigraph: "The senseless life of the deceitful world."*

THIRD PART.

DISTRIBUTION OF SUBJECTS.

How to paint the different elevations of the walls of a church.

[Here the Guide distributes the pictures according to the order in which the artist ought to execute them from top to bottom in succession. He begins at the cupola, then proceeds to the sanctuary, and works down from the highest point of the summit of the apse, from the fifth zone, to the ground-floor. The paintings on the walls of a moderately high church are arranged in five bands, dividing them into five storeys, reaching from the ground-floor to the vault. The cupola forms a sixth storey. A special series of paintings is attached to each of these elevations, and each band is, besides, divided into three or four sections, each containing its particular subject.]

When you desire to paint the walls of a church, first draw, near the summit of the cupola, a circle of different colours, like a rainbow seen on clouds in rainy weather. In the centre represent Christ, blessing; He bears the Gospel on His breast. Paint this inscription: "Jesus Christ, the Almighty." (See vol. i. p. 174.)

---

* In the church of Sophades, a village in Thessaly on the Peneus, this subject is painted in fresco on the western wall. The wheel is set in a great square, in the four corners of which we have the sun, the moon, day and night. This painting has supplied the key to the figures on the great rose window of the cathedral of St. Stephen of Beauvais, now proved to be the wheel of fortune. The same subject may be seen on the walls of the Refectory at Ivirôn on Mount Athos. It is on the southern rose window of Rheims, on the rose of the south porch of Amiens. The allegory is given in another form on a painted window in the church of St. Nizier at Troyes; and again, in the cathedral of Canterbury, on a painted window in the nave, the ages of human life are given.

Around the circle place a multitude of cherubim and thrones, and write this inscription: "See now that I, even I, am He, and there is no God with Me. I have made the earth and created man upon it. I have stretched out the heavens." (Deut. xxxii. 39; Isaiah xlv. 12.)

Above the Almighty draw the orders of angels around, and in the midst of the eastern side place the holy Virgin, her hands stretched out right and left. Above the Virgin write this inscription: "The mother of God and queen of angels."

Opposite to her and at the western side of the cupola draw the Harbinger, and underneath these figures put the prophets. Beneath the prophets inscribe this verse in a circle round the cupola: "Establish Thy church, O Lord, formed by the reunion of those who hope in Thee, and whose foundations are laid in Thy holy blood." Lower down in the pendentives of the vaults, represent the four evangelists. Between these evangelists, and at the summit of the archivaults of these vaults, draw the holy Veil to the east; opposite to it the holy Cup; Jesus Christ on the right hand holding the Gospel and saying: "I am the Vine and ye are the branches;" Emmanuel, on the left hand, holding a scroll with these words: "The spirit of the Lord is upon Me, therefore He hath anointed Me."

Make the stems of the vine go forth from these four subjects,[*] dividing at the bottom where the evangelists are placed, and rising to the angles of the pendentives, entwining their branches around the apostles. Within the vault of the cupola, and at the top of each of the arcades in the vault, put three prophets with scrolls containing the prophecies relating to the festivals represented below the prophets; each prophet points out with his finger to the festival he has foretold. (See above.)[†]

Beginning of the first and highest storey in the sanctuary.—
[This topmost zone or band of paintings goes all round the church starting from and ending with the form of the Virgin. Commencing at the north, which is always at the left hand looking towards the sanctuary, we come round to the right, thus having included all tha portion of the building allotted to the paintings of the principa gospel events.]

[*] Emmanuel; Jesus the Vine; the Cup; and the Veil. These fou subjects belong to the later period of fresco-painting in Greece
[†] In the cupola of the great church of the convent of St. Luke ii Livadia, A.D. 920, the subjects of the mosaics are, with a few exceptions arranged in accordance with the directions of the Guide.

Inside the sanctuary, at the centre of the eastern end of the vault, below the prophets, which are at the summit, draw the Virgin seated on a throne, and holding Christ as a little child. Place this inscription above her: "The Mother of God, the Queen of Heaven."

At each side put the archangels Michael and Gabriel bending reverently. Then to the left hand commence the representation of the twelve principal festivals, the Holy Passion, and the miracles following on the Resurrection; represent them below the prophets, this band going all round the church and returning to the right (or southern side) of the summit. Thus the first band of pictures should be placed.

Beginning of the second storey.

Under this topmost band, represent the divine liturgy or Mystagogia.* (See pp. 334, 335, *supra*.) Finally, and commencing at the left (the north side), represent the divine works and miracles of Christ, in succession, round the church up to the right (south) side of the liturgy. Thus the second band of subjects should terminate.

In the two small hemispherical cupolas of the sanctuary, on the side of the offerings, represent Christ in episcopal robes, seated on a cloud and giving His benediction. He holds the Gospel open and says: "I am the good shepherd." Above Him is this inscription: "Jesus Christ, the great patriarch."

In a circle round Him, represent the Cherubim and Thrones, and, underneath, a line of bishops to be selected according to your own judgment. Lower down represent the sacrifice of Cain and Abel (see p. 268); the sacrifice of Manoah (see p. 277). Upon the vault of the offerings, the descent from the cross.

In the cupola at the opposite side represent the Holy Virgin, with the child Jesus in the midst of a circular aureole, with arms outstretched on both sides. Write this inscription: "The Mother of God, the greatest in heaven."

Underneath, a circular band of bishops, selected at will. Under them Moses looking at the burning bush (see p. 273); the three children in the furnace (see p. 285); Daniel in the den of lions (see p. 286); the hospitality of Abraham, (see p. 270).

Beyond the sanctuary, in the highest part of the first of the four

* Services for the administration of the Eucharist were specifically called liturgies. (See p. 230, *supra*.)

niches or little apses,* above the deacons' seats, represent the Angel of the great Will. He is on a cloud supported by four angels; He holds a scroll and says: "I Myself, I come from God and I return to Him, for I am not come of Myself, it is He that sent Me." Write this inscription: "Jesus Christ the Angel of the great Will." In the second vault represent Emmanuel upon a cloud, saying on a scroll: "The Spirit of God is upon Me; because He hath anointed Me, etc." . . . At the four ends of the cloud, represent the tetramorphs of the evangelists. In the third vault show the archangel Michael, holding a sword in his right hand, and a scroll in his left on which is written: "They who enter the holy and divine house of God with impure hearts, shall I strike with mine inexorable sword." In the fourth vault represent the Harbinger; let him be seated on a cloud, giving his benediction with his right hand and holding a cross and scroll in his left, with these words written thereon: "Repent, for the kingdom of heaven is at hand."

In the lower part of the first niche (under the Angel of the Will) represent Moses holding the tables of the law, and Aaron holding a golden vase and flowering rod. Both are clothed in archiepiscopal robes, and they each carry a mitre. Then draw Noah, holding the ark in his hand, and Daniel holding a scroll.

In the second niche (beneath the form of Emmanuel) paint th prophet Samuel, holding a horn of oil and a censer; Melchisedek holding three loaves upon a disc (plate); the prophet Zachariah father of the Harbinger, with a censer. They also wear sacerdota vestments. Add the righteous Job, wearing a crown upon his head and holding a scroll with these words: "May the name of the Lor be blessed now and evermore."

In the third and fourth niches (under Michael and the Harbinger represent the twelve apostles as they are described above.

2. On the eastern side, above the two columns, represent th annunciation of the angel to the Mother of God. Behind th Virgin, the prophet-king David, holding a scroll with these word "Hearken, O daughter, and attend with thine ear!" Behind th

---

* These niches in the wall of the apse are divided into two parts—tl vault, and the sides reaching to the floor. The deacons gain admissi by the southern apse. In the church of the convent of Daphne, on t sacred way from Athens to Eleusis, inscriptions placed at the entrance two small side apses indicate that the northern apse is destined for sacred vessels—the south for the utensils and robes of the officiat ministers. (See vol. i. p. 293, note.)

ingel, Isaiah points with his finger to the Holy Virgin; he says upon a scroll: "Behold a virgin shall conceive and bear a Son, and they shall call His name Emmanuel."

On the four capitals of the columns* (supporting the central cupola) inscribe:—

On the first: "This house is the house that the Father hath built."
On the second: "This house is that which the Son hath founded."
On the third: "This house is that which the Holy Spirit hath renewed."
On the fourth: "Holy Trinity, glory be unto Thee!"

Beginning of the third band.—Within the sanctuary, underneath the divine liturgy (the Mystagogia) represent the distribution of the Lord's body and blood to the apostles (see p. 334). To the right of this communion, turning towards the church (i.e. to the north of the church), represent the following subjects:

The Presentation of the Holy Virgin (see p. 348).
Moses and Aaron celebrating the sacrifice in the tabernacle (see p. 275).

At the left side of the communion, also turning towards the church (on the south side), represent:—

The ladder of Jacob (see p. 271).
The ark borne into Jerusalem (see p. 279).

Outside the sanctuary, all round the temple, on the right and left sides represent a selection of parables (see pp. 322 et seq.); and also the exaltation of the cross and the triumph of images. At the west end, above the church door, represent the death of the Mother of God and her other festivals. Thus the third band of paintings concludes.†

Beginning of the fourth band.—Underneath the third order, and round the church and sanctuary, represent the saints in medallions and circles. Put the bishops inside the sanctuary, and the martyrs outside, and choose certain ecclesiastics and poets to place at the west end.

Beginning of the fifth band.—Under the fourth order, the sainted

---

* The inscriptions defining the offices of the Trinity call to mind this inscription on a window in the church of St. Andrew at Rheims, "Pater plantavit, Filius rigavit, sed Spiritus Sanctus fructum dedit," where the Father is seen planting a tree, the apostles watering, and the Holy Ghost causing it to bear fruit.

† In the east end Mary is alive and holding Christ. In the west she lies; living in the sunrise, she dies at sunset.

bishops seated round the holy table: to the right, the great S
Basil; to the left, St. Chrysostom, along with the rest of the mo⟨
renowned bishops, with their scrolls and their inscriptions. Nea
the apse of offering, represent St. Peter of Alexandria, holding
scroll with these words: "Oh Saviour, who is it that thus hat
rent Thy garments?" Before him, represent Christ as a littl
child, standing upon the holy table, and clothed in a torn tunic; H
blesses the saint with His right hand, and holds a scroll in the le⟨
containing these words: "Peter, it is Arius the hateful one, th
madman!" [who hath done this].* Beneath the vaults, put th
holy deacons. Outside, towards the singers' choir, represent th
principal martyrs (p. 374): St. George on the right; St. Demetriu
on the left, and the rest in order (see above). Then represent th
holy Anargyres (Ascetics); then St. Constantine, and St. Helen
holding up the venerated cross of the Lord.

To the west, place St. Anthony on the right, and St. Euthymiu
on the left; and the other holy men and poets with their scroll
and inscriptions (see the different pages in which they are described⟩
Inside the temple door, place the archangel Michael to the right
he holds a sword and a scroll with these words: "I am the soldie
of God, and am armed with a sword. I defend, I preserve,
protect, I watch over all who enter into this place with awe; bu
those who come with impure heart, I pitilessly smite with thi
sword."

On the left side, Gabriel holds a scroll, and traces these words i
it with a reed: "With this reed I write the inmost thoughts ⟨
those who enter here; I take care of the good, but I quick⟨
destroy the wicked." Above the door represent Christ, under t⟨
form of a little child of three years, asleep, and lying on a carp⟨
with His head resting upon His hand.† The Holy Virgin stan⟨
respectfully in front of Him. Angels, holding fans, stand round
a circle; they refresh the infant Jesus by the motion of their fa⟨
Under Him, write a title with this inscription: "The present a⟨
most holy church of the divine and sacred monastery of . .

* In the great church of the Meteores, a monastery in Thessaly, t⟨
subject is painted.

† This subject of the sleep of Jesus has been already described as rep⟨
sented in the convent of Philotheou on Mount Athos. (See vol. i. p. 3⟨
A lion sleeps at the child's feet, and there is an inscription taken fr⟨
Gen. xlix. 9: "From the prey, my son, thou art gone up; he stooped do⟨
he couched as a lion."

has been painted with the concurrence, and at the expense of ...
in the year ...."

*How the narthex should be painted.**

In such a case as that in which the narthex, you desire to decorate with painting, is capped by two cupolas, represent the Reunion of Spirits in one of them, after the following manner: Describe a circle, and place Christ in the middle, with the orders of the angels; and a little lower down, upon three zones, the orders of the saints (see preceding pages). In the other cupola, put the prophets at the top. Describe a circle for heaven. Draw the Holy Virgin with the infant Jesus in the middle. She is upborne by angels, and the prophets are a little below her, all around (see above).

Below, in the pendentives, are the poets, seated writing. At the right, where the Reunion of all the spirits is represented :—

St. John Damascene, writing these words: "He who is engendered by His Father before all ages, the God-Word made flesh in the bosom of the Virgin Mary."

St. Cosmas writing: "Matchless image of Him that is the seal immovable, unchangeable; Son and Word of God; the arm, the right hand, the strength of the Most High. We glorify Thee, with Thy Father and Thy Holy Spirit."

St. Anatolius, writing: "Rejoice, ye heavens! Ring, ye foundations of the earth! Ye mountains, resound with joy; for behold Emmanuel!"

St. Cyprian, writing: "How wonderful art Thou, O our God! How marvellous are Thy works, and Thy ways past finding out; for Thou art the wisdom of God, the perfect hypostasis, the power co-infinite and co-eternal."

On the left hand, where the prophets are represented on high, paint the following personages :—

St. Metrophanius writing: "The prophets have foretold, O immaculate Virgin, thine ineffable and inexplicable child-bearing, learned by us as the mystery of a triune Godhead!"

St. Joseph writing: "He who hath unfolded the heavens by His will alone, hath formed of you another earthly heaven, O immaculate Mother of God, and hath manifested Himself through being born of you!"

* The porch—one, and constantly two, sometimes even three of which precede the church properly so-called.

St. Theophanius writing: "Informed by the words of the divine orators, O thou spotless one, we know thy divine child-bearing, for thou hast engendered a God made flesh!"

St. Andrew writing: "O inexplicable birth of an immaculate conception!"

Lower upon the vaults of the lesser apses, represent a certain number of the martyrs of the year; as many as the space admits (see p. 374). Represent the twenty-four stations of the Mother of God in symmetrical arrangement (see p. 352). Lower down towards the east, and above the door (leading from the narthex into the church), represent Christ throned, with the gospel open at these words: "I am the Door, by Me if any man enter in, he shall be saved." At each side show the Holy Virgin and the Harbinger, bending forward in reverence.

To the west place the saints of the [seven] Œcumenical Councils (see p. 358). Give the tree of Jesse (p. 208), the sin and banishment of Adam (p. 267), and other subjects from the Old Testament near the right hand side of the choir, and, near the left, represent the parables and the celestial ladder. Lower down give examples of poets and holy men according to your own judgment.

*How the Fountain should be painted.**

In the cupola above, paint the sky, with sun, moon and stars. Outside of the circle where the sun is, make a glory with a multitude of angels. Underneath the angels, and in a circle, represent on the first line, the incident of the Harbinger in the Jordan. On the eastern side, give the baptism of Christ, and (see p. 301) the Holy Spirit descending out of heaven at the end of a ray. These words run down the middle of the ray, from top to bottom: "This is My beloved Son, in whom I am well pleased." Below this, make a second band, showing those miracles in the Old Testament which prefigure the divine baptism:—

Moses saved by the waters (see p. 273). (Ex. ii. 3.)

The Egyptians swallowed up in the sea (see p. 274). (Ex xiv. 27.)

Moses sweetening the bitter waters (see p. 274). (Ex. xv. 23.)

The twelve wells of water, &c. (see p. 275). (Ex. xv. 27.)

* The fountain is a building of diminutive size, opposite to the entrance but distinct from the church: a marble basin supplied by a natural spring, in which the people washed hands and faces before entering th church. It was also used for baptism; hence the origin of the baptistry

The water of strife (see p. 276). (Ex. xvii. 7 ; 1 Cor. x.)
The ark of the covenant crossing the Jordan (see p. 276). (Josh. iii. 15.)
The dew on Gideon's fleece (see p. 277). (Judg. vi. 37.)
The sacrifice of Elijah (see p. 281). (1 Kings xviii.)
Elijah crossing the Jordan (see p. 282). (2 Kings ii. 8.)
Elisha purifying the waters (see p. 282). (2 Kings ii. 20, 21.)
Naaman washed in the Jordan (see p. 283). (2 Kings v.)
The fountain of life (see p. 350).
Represent the prophets upon the capitals, and all that they have prophesied concerning baptism.*

How to paint the refectory.

When you desire to adorn a refectory with paintings, first put in the vault over the table of the higoumenos (the abbot) the Mystic Supper. On the side walls, beyond the vault, put the Annunciation of the Mother of God, and, all around, the following acts of Jesus Christ :—

Christ eating with the publicans (see p. 306).
The apostles rubbing the corn in their hands (see p. 307).
Christ blessing the five loaves (see p. 308).
The hospitality of Martha (see p. 310).
Christ at Emmaus, and the breaking of bread (see p. 320).
Christ upon the Lake of Tiberias (see p. 321).
Christ eating the broiled fish and the honey (see p. 320).

Also represent a selection of such of the parables as bear upon the subject ; and paint the miracles of the patron saint of the monastery and the Fall of Lucifer.†

Commencement of the second band.—Place, underneath the

* The most beautiful examples of such fountains are to be found on Mount Athos, in the convents of St. Laura and of Vatopédi. There is another at Chilandari. The fountains at Xerapotamou and St. Laura have two zones of paintings running round the cupola ; the pendentives are also painted in fresco; and at the time of M. Didron's visit to Greece, the painter Joasaph at Esphigmenou was preparing to paint the fountain, then in process of erection, exactly in accordance with the instructions handed down from the time of Panselinos, the twelfth-century painter at Mount Athos, in this Byzantine Guide to Painting.

† In the refectory of Vatopédi, the Gospel King may be seen casting into hell the unbidden guest. In the Fall of Lucifer those vices that follow on gluttony are shown forth, such as luxury, idleness, and gluttony itself.

subject of the mystic supper, the chief bishops in their pontifical vestments and with their appropriate legends.

St. Basil, to the right, saying upon his scroll: "The beauty of the soul should be preserved with great care; God will seek for it in our sobriety."

St. Gregory, the theologian, saying: "Let the wise shepherd of a flock be simple, humble, merciful and sweet; since by this means you will grow in the Lord."

St. Nicholas, saying: "There is but one sole God, the Father of the Word and the beginning of wisdom."

To the left, St. Chrysostom saying: "Let each man that would be saved, sincerely promise to forsake those sins that have already soiled him."

St. Athanasius saying: "We worship one God in trinity, and trinity in unity."

St. Cyril saying: "Those who refuse the armour of abstinence, fall into the offence of gluttony, and perish in the madness of excess."

Outside the vault, place St. Anthony to the right, turning to the table and saying on a scroll: "Oh! monk; may you never be seduced by fleshly appetites; obedience and abstinence overcome demons!"

St. Ephraim on the left, turning towards the table, and saying: "A silent and well-ordered table, giving glory to God, wins praise from the angels; but a fastidious table, with frivolous talk, is vilified by demons."

Choose a number of holy men with inscriptions to place round the table. At the end of the refectory represent the anchorite life* (see above), and the mad life of the world † (see p. 378–380).

If the refectory be an apartment of considerable size, and in the form of a cross, then add the Apocalypse of St. John Theologos, and choose some other subject. Outside the refectory, above the door, represent the patron of the monastery.‡

---

* This subject may be seen in the refectory of St. Laura on Mount Athos.
† This subject is painted in the great convent of Ivirôn on Mount Athos.
‡ The refectory is the most richly adorned portion of the monastery next to the church, the western door of which it faces. The church is entered from the west, the refectory from the east. It is a rectangular building terminating with an apse, and crossed by transepts. The nave, choir, transepts and apse are furnished with marble tables. The apse is the

How a cruciform church with four vaults should be decorated.

When you wish to paint a cruciform church, put the Pantocrator[*] in the centre; surrounding Him, the orders of angels, the four evangelists in the pendentives. Place, over the arches below, such of the patriarchs and prophets as you think fit to select. But if the church be a large building with five cupolas, then place the form of the Pantocrator in the great central cupola, as described above. For the remaining four, place in one, the angel of the Great Will; in another, Emmanuel; in the third, the Holy Virgin with the Child; in the fourth, the Harbinger. Upon the arches underneath, put the evangelists, prophets, and patriarchs. Represent the principal festivals symmetrically upon the walls, the Holy Passion, the miracles of the patron of the monastery, and the other subjects treated of above.

How to paint a church roofed with a barrel vault.[†]

It may happen that you have to decorate a church with a barrel vault. Place the figure of the Pantocrator, surrounded by a circle, above in the middle of the vault. Then the Holy Virgin at the eastern summit of the temple; the Harbinger being at the western. From the Holy Virgin to Christ, and from Christ to the Harbinger, put heaven and a multitude of angels therein. To the north and south, at each side of heaven, put the prophets and patriarchs. Under them, put the first line of the principal festivals; the holy Baptism, and the miracles following on the Resurrection. Represent the Queen of Heaven in the roof of the sanctuary. Underneath this first line of paintings, place the second as indicated above. Outside the sanctuary the evangelists and the miracles of the patron of the monastery. For the remainder follow the directions already given.

---

place of honour for the abbot and his vicars, and from it the fountain is visible which stands between the refectory and the church. The refectory is intended to be the terrestrial reflection of a celestial ideal, which is the church, in which the bread and wine of heaven are given. Its paintings are all on a golden background.
   [*] The Almighty.
   [†] There are two types of churches in Greece. The first is cruciform, with branches of equal length, roofed with cupolas, five in all, like St. Mark's in Venice. The second type is long, like a basilica, without cupola or cross, like that of St. Demetrius of Salonica, and most of the basilicas of Constantine at Rome.

Appendix.
The method by which we have learned to paint the holy images.

We have learned not only from the holy fathers, but even from the apostles, and, I might venture to say, from Christ Himself, as has been shown at the beginning of this book, how holy images should be represented. Christ is painted in the human form because He has appeared on earth conversing with men, and He has made Himself a mortal man, like unto us, yet without sin (Baruch iv.). In the same way we represent the Eternal Father as an aged man, because it is thus that Daniel hath seen Him (ch. vii.). We represent the Holy Spirit as a dove, because it is thus He hath been seen in the Jordan. We also represent the features of the Virgin and of the saints, and, though we reverently honour them, we do not adore them. Thus we do not affirm such or such a representation in painting to be veritably the Christ, or Holy Virgin or saint; but when we bow before an image, we mean to tender such homage to the prototype represented in this image. When, for example, the image we salute and embrace represents Christ, that respect we pay the figure is connected with Christ Himself, the Son of God made man for us. We do not adore the colours and the art, but the type of Christ—the real person of Christ—who is in the heavens; for, saith St. Basil, the homage rendered to an image belongs to the model of that image. In like manner, when we regard the image of the Holy Virgin respectfully, or that of any other saint, it is the prototype we honour. If we represent them, it is to remind us of their virtues, their labours, and to raise our souls to their level. We do wisely therefore in representing and in honouring holy images. Anathema on all blasphemers and calumniators.*

On the character of the face and body of our Lord, as we have learned it from those who have seen Him with their eyes.

The body, at once human and divine, of our Saviour, is three cubits in height. The head slightly bent. Sweetness is the characteristic expression of the face. Fine eyebrows, meeting; beautiful eyes and finely formed nose. Complexion the colour of wheat. Hair curled and inclining to golden; a dark beard. The

---

* We need hardly observe that this anathema and these reflections on the worship of images may well come from the Greek painters, who had suffered so much from iconoclasts. On the Trinity, see p. 62, *supra.*

fingers of His pure hands, are very long and finely proportioned. His character is simple, like that of His mother, from whom He hath received life and the human form.*

On the character of the physiognomy of the Mother of God.

The most Holy Virgin is in her middle age. Many have asserted that her height also was three cubits; her complexion the colour of wheat; her hair and eyes are brown. Grand eyebrows and beautiful eyes; a middle-sized nose and long fingers. Clad in beautiful clothing—humble, beautiful and faultless; liking her garments to be (undyed) of their native colour, as is seen in her homophore (stole) preserved in the temple dedicated to her.

How to represent the hand in blessing.†

When you represent the hand in blessing do not join the three fingers together; but cross the thumb by the fourth finger, so that the second, named the index, remaining upright, and the third being slightly bent, they may both form the name of Jesus (IHCOYC) IC. Indeed, the second, remaining open, indicates an I (*iōta*), and the third, when curved, forms a C (*sigma*). The thumb is placed across the fourth finger; the fifth is also a little bent, so as to indicate the word (XPICTOC), XC; for the junction of the thumb and the fourth finger forms a X (*chi*), and the little finger by its curvature forms a C (*sigma*). These two letters are the abridgment of Christos. So, by the divine providence of the Creator, the fingers of a man's hand, whether they be long or short, are so placed that it is possible for them to figure the name of Christ.

Inscriptions for the Holy Trinity.

The Eternal Father—Ancient of days. (Dan. vii. 9.)
The Co-eternal Son—The Word of God. (John i. 1.)
The Holy Spirit—He which proceedeth from the Father. (John xv. 26.)
The Holy Trinity—Sole God of all things.

Within the cross marked upon the crowns (nimbi) of these three persons, Father, Son, and Holy Spirit, write these letters, OωN (He

* See vol. i. of this work, pp. 242, 278.
† In the Cathedral of Puy, M. Aug. Aymard, *Correspondant de Comite Historique des Arts et Monuments*, has found, in an ancient wall-painting, the divine hand represented in this Greek form of benediction. This cathedral is vaulted, with cupolas like a Byzantine church. (See vol. i. p. 407.)

who is); for thus it is that God spoke to Moses when He appeared to him in the burning bush ("I am (:at I am"). Arrange the letters thus: let the omicron (O) be on the right side of the nimbus the omega (ω) on the top, the *nu* (N) upon the left side (of the divine head).*

Inscriptions for the Holy Trinity where the Father and the Son are represented with the scrolls unfolded.

On the scroll of the Father.—" I have engendered Thee before Lucifer": Psa. cx. 3. (See p. 17, *supra.*)

Or this.—" Sit Thou at My right hand, until I make Thine enemies Thy footstool": Psa. cx. 1 (" Sede a dextris meis: donec ponam inimicos Tuos," &c.).

On the Gospel of the Son.—John xvii. 6: "O holy Father, I have glorified Thee on the earth, and I have manifested Thy name unto the men which Thou gavest Me."

Or this.—" I and My Father are one; I am in the Father, and the Father in Me ": John x. 30. (See p. 80, *supra.*)

The epithets that should be inscribed upon the images of Christ.

IC. XC (*Jesus Christ*).—The Pantocrator.—The Giver of Life. —The Saviour of the World.—The Merciful.—The Angel of the Great Will.—The Emmanuel.

When you represent the Second Coming or Last Judgment.—The righteous Judge.

When you represent Christ as bishop.—The King of Kings, the great Patriarch.

When you represent the Crucifixion.—The King of Glory.

Jesus bearing His cross.—The Lamb of God, that taketh away the sins of the world.

The Holy Veil.

The Holy Cup.

Epithets inscribed upon images of the Mother of God.

MHP.ΘY (Mother of God)—The Merciful.—The Guide.†—The

---

* Here the right and left refer to the divine Person bearing the nimbus, and not to the spectator. For all relating to the nimbus see vol. i. of this work, pp. 148, 163; also fig. 15, p. 46.

† Or Conductress. This inscription ὁδηγήτρια may be seen on a Byzantine painting on wood of the Madonna in the treasury of St. Paul of Liège.

Virgin, 'Η Γοργοϋπήχοος.*—The Queen of Angels.—The Queen of Creation.—The Spotless Mistress.—Highest in the Heavens.—Fountain of Life.—Sweet Friend.—Nursing Mother.—Dread Protectress.†—Sinner's Salvation.—Consolation of the Afflicted.—Joy of All.—Guardian of the Gate of Ivirôn.—Virgin of the Grotto.—Virgin of the Third Hand of John Damascene.‡

Inscriptions on the Gospel of Christ, according to the different places where it is represented.

When held by the Pantocrator.—" I am the Light of the World; he that followeth Me shall not walk in darkness, but shall have the light of life." (John viii. 12.)

By the Saviour of the World.—" Learn of Me, for I am meek and lowly of heart; and you shall find rest unto your souls." (Matt. xi. 29.)

By the Giver of Life.—" I am the living bread which came down from heaven; if any man eat of this bread he shall live for ever." (John vi. 21.)

By the angel of the Great Will.—" I am come from God, and I return to Him; for I am not come of Myself, but He . . ."

By Emmanuel.—" The Spirit of the Lord is upon Me; because He hath anointed Me to preach the gospel to the poor." (Luke iv. 18; Isaiah lxi. 1.)

When you represent Christ as bishop.—" I am the Good Shepherd. The good shepherd giveth his life for the sheep; but he that is an hireling and not the shepherd, whose own the sheep are not . . . ." (John x. 11.)

When you represent Christ with the angels.—" I beheld Satan as lightning fall from heaven." (Luke x. 18.)

When you represent Christ with the prophets.—" He that receiveth

* M. Durand found this word untransleateable, but suggests that it may mean the " very obedient."

† Or the Formidable, as in the legend of the miracle of Theophilus, when she forces the devil to resign his contract.

‡ This title refers to a legend of St. John Damascene, the great defender of images, whose hand was cut off by the iconoclasts, and who, approaching a picture of the Virgin, pressed the maimed stump to her lips, and hit hand sprang up like a plant. The picture by which this miracle was worked was preserved at Mount Athos in the convent of Chilandari in 1839. It had been brought from Jerusalem to Servia, and thence carried to Chilandari, which is filled with Servian monks.

a prophet in My name [? in the name of a prophet] shall receive a prophet's reward." (Matt. x. 41.)

When you represent Him with the apostles.—" Behold I give unto you power to tread on serpents and scorpions . . . " (Luke x. 19.)

When you represent Him with the bishops.—" Ye are the light of the world; a city that is set on a hill cannot be hid." (Matt. v. 14.)

When you represent Him with the martyrs.—" Whosoever therefore shall confess Me before men, him will I confess also before My Father which is in heaven." (Matt. x. 32.)

When you represent Him with the solitaries.—" Come unto Me, all ye that labour and are heavy laden, and I will give you rest. Take My yoke upon you, and learn of Me, for I am meek and lowly of heart; and ye shall find rest unto your souls."

When you represent Him with the anargyres.—" Heal the sick, cleanse the lepers, [raise the dead,] cast out devils; freely ye have received, freely give." (Matt. x. 8.)

When you represent Him over a door.—" I am the Door; by Me if any man enter in, he shall be saved." (John x. 9.)

When you represent Him in a cemetery.—" He that believeth in me, though he were dead yet shall he live." (John xi. 25.)

When you represent Him as the great pontiff.—" Lord, Lord, look down from heaven, and behold and visit this vine and the vineyard which Thy right hand hath planted." (Ps. lxxx. 14.)

Inscriptions for the scrolls carried by angels, in the picture of the Nativity called The Rose.

On the scroll of St. Michael: "Bright star! Hail, peerless woman!"
On the scroll of Gabriel: "Hail, mother of the Divine!"
On the scroll which they hold together: "O pure rose—peerless flower!"

Inscriptions held by the Harbinger and the Mother of God when you represent the Trinity.

On the scroll of the Holy Virgin: "Eternal Son! word of the living God, born of the Father, yet not divided from Him, always united to Him; you who in the fulness of time art incarnate in my bosom, spiritual seed fallen from above, judge not the sinful, but hearken to Thy mother's supplication."

On the scroll of the Harbinger: "And I, even I, join Thy mother's supplication, oh, my Master! with that voice that was blest in proclaiming Thy coming. Oh, Word of God! Those Thou hast redeemed in Thy precious blood, the unrighteous who hung Thee on the Cross and slew Thee, grant them grace to become reconciled anew! Oh, merciful Word, Thou who lovest all men!"

On the special scroll of the Harbinger: "Repent ye, for the kingdom of heaven is at hand."

On the gospels held by archbishops and bishops: "He who entereth not the sheepfold by the gate . . ." or rather: "Let your light so shine before men that they may see your good works, and glorify your Father which is in heaven."

Inscriptions for the festivals of the Church.

The Annunciation of the Mother of God.—The nativity of Christ. —Candlemas.— Baptism of Christ.— The Transfiguration.— The Resurrection of Lazarus.—The Palm-branches.—The Crucifixion of Christ.—The Descent from the Cross.—The Tears upon the Tomb.— The Resurrection of Christ.—The Incredulity of Thomas.—The Ascension.—The Descent of the Holy Spirit.—The Death of the Holy Virgin.

Always be careful to place the Crucifixion in the centre of the festivals represented in the tops of the churches. If the edifice be one of considerable size, and you wish to introduce other subjects, select them from among the miracles and sufferings of Christ, as well as His acts after His Resurrection. You will find in them all that you can desire.

Inscriptions for the other feasts and holy images.

The conception of the Mother of God.—The nativity of the Mother of God.—The presentation of the Mother of God.—The nine orders of angels.—The reunion of all spirits.—All Saints' Day.

APPENDIX III.

TEXT OF THE BIBLIA PAUPERUM.

TRANSLATED FROM THE LATIN.

See pages 196, 199, 202.

APPENDIX III.

TEXT OF THE BIBLIA PAUPERUM.

TRANSLATED FROM THE LATIN.

The Annunciation.

Vs. 1.—The serpent loses his power: for the Virgin bears a son.
Vs. 2.—The fleece is wet with dew: the earth remaineth dry.
Vs. 3.—The Virgin is saluted: though unwedded she conceives.

Gen. iii. 14, 15.—It may be read in the third chapter of Genesis
that the Lord said unto the serpent: "Prone upon the ground thou
shalt go." And after, in the same place, it is said of the serpent and
the woman: "She shall bruise thy head, and thou shalt ensnare her
heel." Now this is fulfilled in the annunciation of the glorious
Virgin, the Blessed Mary.
Isa. vii. 14.—"Behold a Virgin shall conceive and bear a Son."
Ezek. xliv. 2.—"This gate shall be shut, and it shall not be
opened."
Judg. vi. 36.—It may be read in the sixth chapter of Judges
that Gideon prayed for a sign of victory through the fleece being
wet with dew; which figured the glorious Virgin Mary without
sin impregnate with the infusion of the Holy Spirit.
David: Psa. cxxxiii. 3.—"The Lord shall descend like dew upon
the fleece."
Jer. xxxi. 22.—"The Lord hath created a new thing in the earth:
a woman shall compass a man."

Central subject: the Annunciation. On the right: the serpent,
Eve, and God the Father. On the left: Gideon and his fleece
Above: Isaiah and David. Below: Ezekiel and Jeremiah.

The Nativity.

Vs. 1.—It glows and kindles: but the bush is not consum[ed] by fire.

Vs. 2.—This is contrary to nature: a rod bears a flower.

Vs. 3.—Without pain thou bearest a son, O Virgin Mary!

Ex. iii. 2.—It may be read in Exodus (chap. iii.) that Moses s[aw] the bush burning with fire, and the bush was not consumed, a[nd] heard the Lord speaking thus from the bush. This bush th[at] burned, and which yet did not consume, figures the blessed Virg[in] Mary, who, bearing a Son without touching the purity of her bod[y] because a virgin, gave birth and remained uncorrupted.

Dan. ii. 34, 35.—"A stone, rugged, was cut out, without han[ds] from the mountain."

Hab. iii. 2.—"O Lord, I have heard Thy speech, and was afrai[d]"

Num. xvii. 8.—It may be read, in the book of Numbers, that one night the rod of Aaron brought forth buds and blosson[s] whereby is figured the Virgin Mary, who miraculously broug[ht] forth the ever-blessed Jesus Christ.

Isa. ix. 6.—"Unto us a Child is born, unto us a Son is given."

Micah v. 2.—"Thou, Bethlehem, in the land of Judah, shalt n[ot] be least among the princes of Judah."

Adoration of the Magi.

Vs. 1.—The multitude here typify the nations longing to joined to Christ.

Vs. 2.—This typifies the Gentiles, to whom the coming of Ch[rist] was known.

Vs. 3.—Christ is adored; gold, frankincense, and myrrh are l[aid] before Him.

2 Sam. iii. 10.—It may be read in the second book of Ki[ngs] (chap iii.) that Abner, chief captain of the armies of Saul, came [to] David in Jerusalem, offering to subdue all the people of Israel [to] him which then followed the house of Saul. Which thing p[re]figures the coming of the Magi to Christ, who adored, offering my[stic] gifts.

David: Ps. lxxii. 10.—"The kings of Tharsis and the i[sles] bringing gifts."

Isa. ii. 2.—"And all nations shall flow unto Him, and many peo[ple] shall go up unto the Lord's house."

1 Kings x. 1.—It may be read in the first book of Kings that the Queen of Sheba heard of the fame of Solomon, and came into Jerusalem with great gifts, in adoration for him; which queen was a Gentile; which will typify the Gentiles who came from afar to worship with gifts.

Isa. lx. 14.—"And they shall worship Thy footsteps." *

Num. xxiv. 17—" There shall come a star out of Jacob, and a rod shall arise out of the root of Israel."

The Purification

Vs. 1.—Here the first-born is presented, that he may be redeemed.

Vs. 2.—Samuel prefigures Thee, O Christ, when Thou wast presented.

Vs. 3.—The Virgin receives back Christ from Simeon.

Lev. xii. 6.—It may be read in the twelfth chapter of Leviticus that every woman, when the days of her purifying are fulfilled, shall present (after the birth of her first-born) a lamb; and if she be not able (in her poverty) to bring a lamb, then she shall bring two turtle-doves or two young pigeons, and this for her sin-offering; and she shall be clean: which the glorious Virgin fulfilled, although not requiring to be cleansed.

David xi. 4.—" The Lord is in His holy temple."

Zech. ii. 10.—" Lo, I come, and I will dwell in the midst of thee, saith the Lord."

1 Sam. i.—We read in the first book of Samuel (chap. i.) that Hannah, the mother of Samuel, offered him to the priest Eli in the temple: which offering prefigures the offering of the Lord made to Simeon in the temple.

Mal. iii. 1.—" And the Lord whom ye seek shall suddenly come to His holy temple."

Zeph. iii. 15.—" The King of Israel, the Lord, is in the midst of thee."

The flight into Egypt.

Vs. 1.—Jacob fled from his father's roof through fear of his brother.

Vs. 2.—Daniel escaped from the snares of Saul by Michal's aid.

Vs. 3.—The child Christ fled from the cruel wrath of Herod.

* " They shall bow themselves down at the soles of Thy feet." (Authorised Version.)

Gen. xxvii. 42, 43.—It may be read in Genesis (chap. xxvii.) that when Rebecca, mother of Esau and Jacob, heard what would in time come to pass, and that Jacob would be killed, she herself sent her son Jacob from his own land. Which thing prefigures well the flight of Christ into Egypt, whom Herod sought to destroy after His birth.

Isa. xix. 1.—" Behold, the Lord shall come into Egypt, and the idols of Egypt shall be moved at His presence."

Jer. xii. 7.—" I have forsaken mine house, and I have left mine heritage."

1 Sam. xix. 12.—We read in the first book of Samuel that when king Saul sent messengers to seek David and to kill him, that the wife of David, by name Michal, let him down through a window with a rope, and he thus escaped from his pursuers. In this view the same king Saul prefigures Herod, who sought Christ to destroy him, when Joseph led him with Mary into Egypt, and so they escaped from the hands of the pursuers.

Ps. lv. 7.—Lo ! then would I wander afar off; I would lodge in the wilderness.

Hosea v. 6.—" They shall go to seek the Lord, and shall not find Him."

The Holy Family in Egypt.

- Vs. 1.—By Moses the sacred image of the calf was destroyed.
Vs. 2.—The ark is made the cause of the sudden ruin of Dagon.
Vs. 3.—The idols fell swiftly when Christ was present.

We read in the thirty-first and thirty-third chapters of Exodus that when Moses had come to the foot of Mount Sinai, he alone ascended the mountain to receive the law; and when he had done this, and was descending, he saw the molten calf which Aaron had made of gold. Moses himself, having thrown away the tables destroyed the calf, and broke it up : which well figured the idols falling in a heap when Christ entered Egypt.

Hosea x. 2.—" He shall break down [their altars]."

Zech. xiii. 2.—" I will cut off the names of the idols out of the earth."

We read in the first book of Samuel (chap. v.) that the Philistines had placed the ark of the Lord, that they had taken in war, near Dagon, their god. Those who entered the temple in the morning found Dagon lying on the ground, and both his hands broken off: which figure was truly fulfilled when the Blessed Virgin came with Christ, her child, into Egypt; then the idols of Egypt fell in a heap; and it figures the Virgin, who, with Christ, enters the state of trial, into which infidels, through error, have collapsed.

Nahum i. 14.—" Out of the house of thy gods will I cut off the graven image and the molten image."

Zeph. ii. 11.—" The Lord will famish all the gods of the earth."

Murder of the Innocents.

Vs. 1.—Saul for David: so the anointed of the Lord were overthrown and slain.

Vs. 2.—Our child being taken off by stealth, the royal seed was given.

Vs. 3.—These children, instead of Christ, are taken away from the world.

We read in the first book of Samuel (chap. xxii.) that King Saul caused all the priests of the Lord in Nob to be slain, because they had received the fugitive David, and had given him the holy bread. Saul figures Herod, for David typifies Christ, and the priests the children whom Herod, in their innocence, caused to be slain on account of Christ.

David: Psa. lxx. 10.—"Avenge, O Lord, the blood of Thy priests!"

Jer. xxxi. 15.—" A voice is heard in Rama—lamentation."

2 Kings xi. 1.—We read in the second book of Kings (chap. iv.) that Athaliah the queen, seeing her son dead, caused to be slain all the sons of the king, lest they should reign instead of her offspring; but from her the sister of the king withdrew his younger son, who afterwards was made king. The cruel queen figures Herod, who ordered the children to be slain on account of Christ, whereas the child, withdrawn from death, figures Christ furtively taken away from the massacre of King Herod.

Prov. xxviii. 15.—" As a roaring lion and a hungry bear, so is the wicked ruler over the poor people."

Hosea viii. 4.—" Kings have reigned, and not by me." *

* In the Biblia Pauperum this verse is rendered " Cristi regnaverunt et non ex me."

Return from Egypt.

Vs. 1.—When Saul was dead, David returned to his country.
Vs. 2.—Jacob fears his brother, [but] longs to see his father.
Vs. 3.—Jesus, who had withdrawn to Egypt, returns to the holy places.

We read in the second book of Samuel (chap. ii.) that on the death of king Saul, David consulted the Lord, who answered him that he should return to the land of Judah. Now David signifies Christ, who on the death of Herod returned to the land of Judah, for thus the Gospel testifies, saying, " The angel of the Lord said: Arise, and take the young Child and His mother," &c.

David: Psa. cvi. 4.—" O visit me with Thy salvation."

Hosea xi. 1; Matt. ii. 15.—" Out of Egypt have I called my Son."

We read in Gen. xxxi. 17—that Jacob, returning into his own country, from which he had fled on account of the fury of his brother Esau, sent before him his sheep and his oxen, his camels and his asses, and he himself followed, with his wives and children. Jacob, who had fled from his brother, signifies Christ, who fled from King Herod, whom Esau signifies; but, on Herod's death, Christ returned from the land of Judah.

Hosea.—" Egypt, weep not, for the Lord hath grieved for thee!"*
Zech. i. 16.—" I am returned to Jerusalem with mercies."

John baptising Christ.

Vs. 1.—Their foes are drowned; they walk through the path of the sea.
Vs. 2.—The river is crossed, and the land of honey reached.
Vs. 3.—While he is baptising, Christ sanctifies baptism.

We read in the fourteenth chapter of Exodus (v. 23), that Pharaoh, when he was pursuing the children of Israel with chariots and horsemen, entered the Red Sea after the children of Israel, and the Lord closed the waters upon them, and thus liberated his people from the hand of those who were following. Likewise, through the water of baptism, sanctified by Christ, He has freed Christian men from sin.

Isa. xii. 3.—" Therefore with joy shall ye draw water out of the wells of salvation."

* This verse has not been identified with any passage in Hosea.

Ezek. xxxvi. 25.—" Then will I sprinkle clean water upon you."
We read in the thirteenth chapter of the book of Numbers that the messengers who were sent to explore the Land of Promise, when they returned, brought a cluster of grapes on a staff; and when they had crossed the Jordan, they brought it as a proof of the fruitfulness of the land: which signifies that, if we wish to enter the heavenly kingdom, we must first pass through the waters of baptism.

Ps. lxviii. 26.—" Bless ye God in the congregations, even the Lord from the fountain of Israel."

Zech. xiii. 1.—" In that day there shall be a fountain opened to the house of David."

Temptation of Christ.

Vs. 1.—In his desire for lentils, he shamefully loses his honour (birthright).

Vs. 2.—The serpent conquered Adam so that he should eat of the forbidden fruit.

Vs. 3.—Satan tempted Christ that he might overcome Him.

Gen. xxv. 29-34.—We read in the twenty-fifth chapter of Genesis that Esau, after he had sold his birthright for the pottage which Jacob had sod—that is, he lost the honour due to the first-born, and the blessing of the father: so the devil deceived our first parents by gluttony and pride, saying, " Ye shall be as gods, knowing good from evil."

Ps. xxxv. 16.—" They mocked me, and gnashed upon me with their teeth."

2 Sam. vii. 9.—" I have cut off all thine enemies out of thy sight."

Gen. iii.—We read in the third chapter of Genesis that Adam and Eve were deceived by the serpent, who tempted them through their appetites, because the devil, like an instrument, seduces by deceiving: which well figured the temptation which the devil laid before Christ when he tempted Christ, saying, " If Thou be the Son of God, command these stones that they be made bread," which temptation involved appetite.

Isa. xxix. 16.—" Surely your turning things upside down shall be esteemed as the potter's clay ?" *

---

* Perverse thoughts, like clay against a brick. This cogitation of yours is perverse, as if the clay should contrive against the brick.

Job xvi. 9, 10.—"They have gathered themselves together against me. Mine enemy hath beheld me with terrifying eyes."

The raising of Lazarus.

Vs. 1.—The widow's son was restored to life by Elijah.
Vs. 2.—By Thy gifts, O God, Elisha gave him life.
Vs. 3.—By Thee, O Christ, Lazarus became restored to life.

We read in the third [first] book of Kings (chap. xvii.) that the prophet Elias bore the dead child up to the top of a mountain, praying, and saying, "I beseech that the soul of the child may return;" and so it was done, and he restored the child alive to his mother: which well figured the raising of Lazarus, whom the Lord raised from the dead and restored to his sisters, Mary Magdalene and Martha.

Deut. xxxii. 39.—"I will kill and make alive; I will smite and will heal."

Job xiv. 14.—"If a man dies, shall he live again?"

We read in the third book of Kings (chap xvii.) that the prophet Elisha saw the child of the widow with whom he used to lodge, dead, and prostrated himself upon the child, and the flesh of the child became warm, and the child revived. Elisha figures Christ, but the child who rose from the dead represents Lazarus, whom He restored to life in the face of the Jews.

Ps. xxxiii. 19.—"Lord, Thou hast delivered my soul from death."
1 Samuel ii. 6.—"The Lord killeth and maketh alive."

The Transfiguration.

Vs. 1.—Abraham contemplates three, but only worships one.
Vs. 2.—In that sight the glory of Christ is revealed to the Gentiles.
Vs. 3.—Lo, the three disciples behold the Son of God glorified!"

We read in the eighteenth of Genesis that Abraham saw three youths, or angels, who had come to his dwelling. He saw three, and he worships one; the three angels signified the Trinity of persons— i.e. as regards the man who adored one whom he understands to signify the unity of the essence. Thus Christ, in His transfiguration, reveals Himself the true God, one in essence, triple in person.

David (Ps. xlv. 2).—"Beautiful in form beyond the sons of men."

Mal. iv. 2.—" But unto you that fear My name shall the Sun of righteousness arise."

In the third chapter of Daniel, we read that Nebuchadnezzar, king of Babylon, sent three youths into a fiery furnace; and when he came to the furnace that he might look at them in the fire, he saw with them a fourth, like the Son of God: the three youths signify the Trinity of persons; the fourth reveals the unity of essence of Christ in His transfiguration, and reveals Him truly one in essence, triple in person.

Isaiah lx. 1.—" Jerusalem! Thy light is come, and the glory of the Lord is risen upon thee."

Habakkuk iii. 4.—" And His brightness shall be as the light; He shall have horns coming out of His hands, or bright beams out of His side."

Mary Magdalene at the feet of Christ.

Vs. 1.—Nathan, by his word moving the heart of the king, corrects his wicked deeds.

Vs. 2.—She (Miriam), made leprous, by penance is made clean again.

Vs. 3.—So, the fount of goodness absolves this woman from her sins!

2 Sam. xii.—We read in the second book of Kings [Samuel] (chap. xii.) that Nathan the prophet had been sent to David to reprove him; but David himself, the king, led by penitence, obtained mercy from God. David, in his penitence, typified Mary Magdalene in her penitence, who won the pardon of all her sins.

Ezek. xviii. 22.—" All his transgressions that he hath committed, they shall not be mentioned unto him."

Zech. i. 3.—" Turn thee unto Me (saith the Lord of Hosts), and I will turn unto you."

We read in Numbers xii. that Miriam, the sister of Moses and Aaron, became leprous for her sin, and was healed from her uncleanness by Moses. Moses is a type of Christ, who cleansed Mary Magdalene from all the uncleanness of her sins, as Himself testifies in St. Luke, saying, " Thy sins are forgiven thee."

Ps. li. 17.—" A broken and a contrite heart, O Lord, Thou wilt not despise."

2 Sam. vii. 22.—" For there is none like Thee, neither is there any God besides Thee."

Christ's entry into Jerusalem.

Vs. 1.—As David, who overthrew his foes, is praised in song.

Vs. 2.—The glory of Elisha typifies Thy glory, Thou Son of God.

Vs. 3.—The song of the good Hebrews is raised in Thy praise, O Christ!

1 Sam. xvii. 51, xviii. 6.—We read in the first book of Kings [Samuel] that when David smote Goliath, he cut off his head and brought it in his own hand. When coming from the Philistines, the women came rejoicing, and received him into Jerusalem with great glory. David thus typifies Christ, whom the children of the Hebrews received into Jerusalem, shouting with loud voice, and uttering blessings on Him who came in the name of the Lord.

Ps. cxlix. 2.—" Let the children of Zion rejoice in their King."

Zech. ix. 9.—" Behold, thy King cometh unto thee, meek, just, and having salvation."

We read in the second book of Kings (i. 15) that when Elisha would return into his city, there met him sons of the prophets, receiving him with great glory and honour, and praising him. Elisha signifies Christ, who, coming into Jerusalem, the sons of the Hebrews received with great glory and honour.

Cant. iii. 11.—" Go forth, O ye daughters of Zion, and behold your King!"

Zech. ix. 9.—" He Himself, meek, and riding on an ass, and a colt, the foal of an ass."

Christ driving the money-changers out of the Temple.

Vs. 1.—He (Daniel) orders the temple to be cleansed and a feast proclaimed.

Vs. 2.—Maccabæus sets himself to purify Thy sacred places, O God!

Vs. 3.—Christ drives out those who bought and sold in the temple.

Esdras iv. 17.—The king Darius gave orders to Esdras, the scribe, to go to Jerusalem and himself to cleanse the temple. King Darius signifies Christ, who drove out from the temple buyers and sellers. Thus he cleansed the temple of the Lord from unlawful practices, giving by this to understand that the temple of the Lord is a house of prayer, and not a place of merchandise.

Hosea ix. 15.—" I will cast all out of My house."

Amos v. 10.—" They held in hatred Him who hastened in at the gate."

1 Macc. iv. 41-57.—We read in the fourth chapter of the first book of Maccabees that Judas Maccabæus ordered the Jews to cleanse and sanctify the temple because it had been polluted against the law. Maccabæus himself signifies Christ, who, having made a scourge of small cords, cast out . . . and forced them out, saying, "Make not the house of My Father a house of merchandise."

Psalm lxix. 9.—" The zeal of Thine house hath eaten me up."

Zechariah xiv. 21.—" There was no longer any merchant in the house of the Lord."

Judas Iscariot betrays Christ.

Vs. 1.—The band of brothers wickedly conspire against the boy Joseph.

Vs. 2.—The accursed son (Absalom) conspires against his father's fortune.

Vs. 3.—So these men plotted together the death of Christ

We read in the thirty-seventh chapter of Genesis that the brothers of Joseph said to their father Jacob that a very evil beast had devoured his son. This they did, fraudulently conspiring towards the death of their brother. Joseph fraudulently sold by his brother signifies Christ, without fault, fraudulently sold by Judas into death.

Gen. xlix. 6.—" O my soul, come not thou into their secret!"

Prov. xxi. 30.—" There is no wisdom nor understanding nor counsel against the Lord."

We read in the Second Book of Kings (ch. xv.) that Absalom, the son of David, stood at the entry of the gate of the city of Jerusalem, and spoke to the people coming in, saying, " Who will make me judge?" and the hearts of the men who were conspiring with him against his father inclined to constitute him king instead of David, and afterwards they pursued his father, whom he intended to kill. This Absalom signifies Judas the traitor, who conspired with the Jews towards the death of Christ.

Ps. xxxi. 13.—" They took counsel together against me to take away my life."

Jer. xi. 19.—" They devised devices against me."

Judas receiving the thirty pieces of silver.

Vs. 1.—That boy (Joseph) who was sold typifies Thee, O Christ.
Vs. 2.—Whatever is done against Joseph applies to Christ.
Vs. 3.—Judas, thou who sellest Christ, wendest thy way to hell.

We read in the thirty-seventh chapter of Genesis that the brothers of Joseph sold him to the Ishmaelites for thirty pieces of silver. This Joseph, a just man, was sold by his brothers, though innocent, and is a type of Christ, who, though innocent, was sold by Judas (who sold Christ Himself to the Jews) for thirty pieces of silver; and these are the thirty pence for which Joseph was sold, one of which is worth ten ordinary pence.

David : Ps. cix. 8.—" Let his days be few, and let another take his bishopric."

Hag. i. 6.—" He that earneth wages, earneth wages to put it into a bag with holes."

We read in the thirty-ninth chapter of Genesis that when the Ishmaelites who had bought Joseph came into their own country with Joseph, they sold him in Egypt to the captain of the king's guard, whose name was Potiphar: this boy Joseph is a type of Christ, who was sold by the impious Judas.

Prov. xvi. 30.—" He shutteth his eyes to devise froward things."

Zech. xi. 12.—" So they weighed for My price thirty pieces of silver."

The Last Supper.

Vs. 1.—They mark the sacred things of Christ which Melchizedek gave to them.

Vs. 2.—He holds himself in His hands; the food partakes of itself.

Vs. 3.—The King sits at supper, surrounded by a company of twelve.

We read in the fourteenth chapter of Genesis that when Abraham returned from the slaughter of his enemies, bringing with him much spoil which he had wrested from his enemies, then Melchizedek, the high priest of God, brought him bread and wine. Melchizedek is a type of Christ, who at supper gave to His disciples bread and wine—that is, His body and blood—to eat and drink.

Ps. lxxviii. 25.—" Man did eat angels' food."

Isa. lv. 2.—" Hearken, ye that hear me, and eat ye that which is good."

We read in the sixteenth chapter of Exodus that the Lord commanded Moses to tell the people each of them to gather of the manna from heaven enough for himself for the day. Now this manna from heaven which the Lord gave the Israelites is a type of the holy bread, to wit, of His most sacred body, which He Himself gave to His disciples when He said, " Take of this, all . . . " &c.

Prov. ix. 5.—" Come, eat of my bread, and drink of the wine which I have mingled."

Wisdom vi. 20.—" Thou didst send them from heaven bread prepared without their labour."

Christ leaving His disciples in Gethsemane.

Vs. 1.—They leave Michaiah, the prophet, who do not believe him.

Vs. 2.—They do not believe Elisha when he prophesies to the people.

Vs. 3.—Jesus passes through Gethsemane, and then says farewell to His disciples.

We read in the first book of Kings and twenty-second chapter that the king of Samaria and king Jehoshaphat, being prepared for war, consulted four hundred false prophets, and that a lying spirit spake in the mouth of all those prophets speaking peace : " Go in peace." Micaiah, a true prophet of the Lord, prophesied that the king should not return in peace, which came to pass. So the king commanded that there should be given him the bread of affliction. This Michaiah is a type of Christ, who for His truth was given the bread of affliction—to wit, His suffering even to death.

Micah ii. 10.--" Arise ye, and depart, for this is not your rest."

Jonah iv. 3.—" It is better for me to die than to live."

We read in the sixth chapter of the second book of Kings that, so great was the famine in Samaria, that a woman boiled her son and ate him ; the king wished to kill Elisha, the prophet of the Lord ; but Elisha said, " To-morrow a measure of fine flour shall be sold for a shekel." The king would not believe as the prophet had spoken ; wherefore Elisha said, " Thou shall see it, but shall not eat thereof." On the day after the king was trodden to death in the gate of Samaria by those who brought the fine flour. This Elisha is a type of Christ, who spake truth to the Jews which they believed not; and they killed the good and innocent Jesus.

Baruch iv. 25.—" Oh, children, suffer patiently the wrath that is come upon you from God!"

Tobias xii. 20.—" For I go up to Him that sent me."

Christ in the Garden of Olives.

Vs. 1.—The hope given to the wise is taken away from the foolish virgins.

Vs. 2.—The old serpent fell, driven backward from his throne.

Vs. 3.—Thus they who would seize Christ fell back to the ground.

Matt. xxv. 2, 3.—We read in the twenty-fifth chapter of St. Matthew that those foolish virgins who had no oil with their lamps found the door—to wit, the gate of eternal salvation—shut upon them. These virgins mean the Jews, who fell back when asked by the Lord on the Mount of Olives, " Whom seek ye?" That is, they fell back into foolishness and hardness of heart, and are therefore already in hell for that they believed not.

Lamentations ii. 16.—"So we have found it; this is the day that we looked for."

Jer. xiv. 3.—" They returned with their vessels empty."

We read in the Apocalypse (twelfth chapter) and in Isaiah (fourteenth chapter) that Lucifer fell by his pride from heaven, with all his angels. These proud devils signify the Jews, who feared to lose their habitation and their land, and therefore killed the lowly good Jesus, and crucified Him, and themselves fell into the pit which they had made—to wit, into a living hell, as it is written in the psalm.

Isa. liii. 2, 3.—" There is no beauty that we should desire Him." " He is despised and rejected of men."

Baruch vi. 27.—" For if they fall to the ground at any time, they cannot rise up again of themselves."

Judas betraying Christ with a kiss.

Vs. 1.—Joab speaks kindly to him [Abner], but kills him basely.

Vs. 2.—Tryphon prepares treacherous arms underneath his smooth words.

Vs. 3.—Through peace, O Christ, that traitor betrays Thee to these men!

We read in the second book of Samuel, and third chapter, that Joab, the captain of King David's guard, came in guile to Abner to talk with him, and, while speaking to him with crafty sweetness, pierced him with a sword. Joab, who spoke deceitfully to Abner, is a type of Judas, who with guilt kissed Christ, and gave Him over to the impious Jews to be crucified.

Ps. xli. 9.—" Yea, mine own familiar friend in whom I trusted."

Isa. iii. 11.—" Woe to the wicked man: an evil retribution shall be given unto his hand."

We read in the first book of the Maccabees, and twelfth chapter, that Tryphon came to the men of Judah and Israel to speak with them craftily and capture them. This Tryphon is a type of Judas the traitor, who came with guile to Christ and kissed Him deceitfully, and so gave Him over to the impious Jews to be killed.

Prov. xvii. 20.—" He that hath a perverse tongue falleth into mischief."

Jer. ix. 8.—" With his mouth he speaketh peace to his friend."

Pilate washing his hands.

Vs. 1.—So the fierce multitude dared to condemn Jesus without cause.

Vs. 2.—The fierce woman would fain slay the prophet, so the wicked condemn Christ.

Vs. 3.—This cruel race would do Daniel to death.

We read in the nineteenth chapter of the first book of Kings that Queen Jezebel, when she had slain the prophets of the Lord, would then have slain the prophet Elijah. This wicked queen is a type of the Jews, who meant cruelly to slay the true Elijah—that is Christ—through envy, because by His preaching He showed them their wickedness.

Isa. v. 20.—" Woe unto them that call evil good and good evil."

Job xxxvi. 17.—" Thou hast fulfilled the judgment of the wicked."

We read in Daniel (sixth chapter) that the wicked people of Babylon came to king Nebuchadnezzar and said, " Deliver unto us Daniel," who was innocent. This people is a type of the Jews, who cried out eagerly again and again to Pilate: " Crucify Him, crucify Him ; " and again : " If thou let Him go thou art not Cæsar's friend." And that king signifies Pilate, who, fearing the Jews, handed over to them the innocent Christ.

Ps. i. 5.—" It is not good to take part in the counsel of the ungodly."*

Amos v. 7.—" Who turn judgment to wormwood, and (leave off) justice."

Christ crowned with thorns.

Vs. 1.—As Ham profaned his father when he saw his nakedness.

Vs. 2.—They who mocked Elisha were smitten by the wrath of God.

Vs. 3.—So for us, Christ, Thou Holy One, dost suffer grievous wrong.

We read in the ninth chapter of Genesis that Noah was sleeping within his tent, lying naked upon the ground; when his son Ham saw him he laughed him to scorn, but his other sons would not behold him, but covered their eyes. Noah is a type of Christ when the Jews laughed Him to scorn, and crowned Him and stripped Him; thus those faithless sons mocked him as though he were a fool.

David (Ps. xxii. 7).—" All they that see Me laugh Me to scorn."

Lamentations iii. 14.—" I was a derision to all My people."

We read in the second book of Kings, and the second chapter that when the prophet Elisha was going up into Mount Bethel there met him some children who cried out and mocked him, and laughed him to scorn saying, " Go up, thou bald-head; go up, thou bald-head!" Elisha is a type of Christ, whom His children—that is, the Jews—mocked in His crowning and passion.

Prov. xix. 29.—" Judgments are prepared for scorners, and stripes for the back of fools."

Isa. i. —" They have blasphemed the Holy One of Israel."

Christ bearing His cross.

Vs. 1.—That boy, bearing the wood, foreshadows Thee, O Christ

Vs. 2.—The widow's crossed pieces of wood are mystic signs.

Vs. 3.—Christ bears the tree of the cross, thinking it a worthy burden for Himself.

We read in Gen. xxii. 6, that when Abraham and Isaac set out together, Abraham carried the sword and the fire, but Isaac carrie

---

* The reference given to this verse in the Biblia Pauperum is Ps. xvii This is evidently a mistake.

the wood by which he was himself to be sacrificed; this Isaac who carried the wood is a type of Christ, who carried on His own body the wood of the cross on which He meant to be sacrificed for us.

Isa. liii. 7.—" He is brought as a lamb to the slaughter."

Psalms.—" Run, hasten to save the victim."

We read in 1 Kings xvii. 10, that Elijah cried out to a woman who was going into the field to collect wood, and make food for herself, and she, answering him, said: " Lo, I gather two sticks, and with them will I dress food for me and my son." The two sticks which the woman gathered were types of the wood of the cross which Christ took to carry on His own body.

Jer. xi. 19.—" Come, let us destroy the stalk with his bread."

Jer. xi. 19.—" I was like a lamb or an ox that is brought to the daughter."

Christ on the Cross.

Vs. 1.—The father sacrifices his son, who typifies Christ.

Vs. 2.—The wounded are healed when they behold the serpent raised.

Vs. 3.—The Passion of Christ snatches us from the gloomy byss.

Gen. xxii. 10.—We read in Gen. xxii. that when Abraham had stretched forth his hand to slay his son, the angel of the Lord from heaven prevented him, saying, "Stretch not forth thine hand against the child." Abraham signifies the Heavenly Father, who sacrificed His Son, to wit, Christ, for us all, on the Cross, that thus He might show us a sign of His fatherly love.

Ps. xxii. 16.—" They pierced My hands and My feet."

Job xli. 1.—" Canst thou draw out Leviathan with a hook."

Num. xxi. 9.—We read in Numbers xxi. 9, that when the Lord willed to save the people from the serpents which had bitten them, he commanded Moses to make a brazen serpent and to hang it from a tree, so that whosoever looked upon it should be saved from the serpents. The serpent which was hung up and beheld by the people signifies Christ on the cross, whom all should behold who would be saved from the serpent, that is, the devil.

Isa. liii. 7.—" He was oppressed and He was afflicted; and the Lord hath laid on Him the iniquity of us all."

Hab. iii. 4.—" He had horns coming out of his hand, and there was the hiding of his power."

APPENDIX III.

The Crucifixion and the soldier with a spear.

Vs. 1.—As the first woman proceeded from the side of the man:
Vs. 2.—As water from the rock struck by Moses signifies Christ:
Vs. 3.—So hence water came forth with blood from the side of Christ.

Gen. ii. 21.—We read in Gen. ii. 21, that while Adam was asleep the Lord took a rib from out of his side and with it made a woman; Adam, asleep, is a type of Christ already dead upon the cross, from whose side flowed for us the sacraments when the soldier with a lance, pierced the side of Christ.

David (Ps. lxix. 26).—" And they talk to the grief of those whom Thou hast wounded."

Lam. i. 12.—" O you who pass by, behold and see if there b any sorrow like unto My sorrow."

We read in Exodus xvii. 6, that when Moses led the peopl through the desert and they were thirsy from the lack of water Moses with the rod which he held in his hand smote a rock and there gushed water in great abundance as if from an abys This unavenged rock or stone signifies Christ, who for us poure forth healing waters—to wit, the sacraments—from His side whe on the cross He suffered it to be pierced by the soldier's lance.

Zech. xiii. 6.—" What are these wounds in Thy hands?"

Amos viii. 9.—" In that day I will cause the sun to go down noon; I will darken the earth in the clear day."

Entombment of Christ.

Vs. 1.—He is thrust into that ancient tomb.
Vs. 2.—Jonah is swallowed, yet found again unhurt.
Vs. 3.—Myrrh is brought: and Christ is buried by these.

We read in Gen. xxxvii. 24, that when the brothers of Jose wished to sell him to the Ishmaelites, they stripped him of his co and threw him into an old pit. This Joseph is a type of Christ, w was thrown into a pit—that is, the tomb—when His friends to Him from the cross and laid Him in it.

David (Ps. lxxviii. 65).—" The Lord awaketh as one out sleep, and like a mighty man that shouteth by reason of wine."

Isa. xi. 10.—" And His rest shall be glorious."

We read in the book of Jonah, chapter ii., that when Jon himself took ship to go to a place called Tharys, a great storm ar in the sea, and those who were in the ship cast lots among themselves; and the lot fell upon Jonah, whom they seized and threw into the sea; and a mighty fish straightway swallowed him, in whose belly he was three days and three nights. Jonah typifies Christ, who was three days and three nights in the belly of the earth.

Song of Solomon v. 2.—" I sleep, but my heart waketh."
Gen. xlix. 9.—" He stooped down, he couched as a lion."

The descent into Hell.

Vs. 1.—Typifying Thee, O Christ, he (David) subdued Goliath.
Vs. 2.—And as Samson's strength that destroyed the lion's mouth :-
Vs. 3.—So the death of Christ destroyed the gates of Hell.

We read in the first book of Samuel, chapter xvii., that David smote the giant Goliath with his own sword and slew him, and cut off his head; so Christ, who rose from the dead, freed men from hell, and saved them from the power of the devil, and weakened the devil himself in his power.

Psa. cvii. 16.—" For He hath broken the gates of brass, and cut the bars of iron in sunder."

Zech. ix. 11.—" By the blood of Thy covenant I have sent forth Thy prisoners out of the pit where there is no water."

We read in the first book of Judges, chapter xiv., concerning Samson, that when a lion roared against him, he seized the lion and slew him; Samson is a type of Christ, who slew the lion, that is the devil, when He freed men from his power.

Hosea xiii. 14.—" O Death, I will be thy plagues; O grave, I will be thy destruction."

Gen. xlix. 9.—" From the prey, my son, thou art gone up."

The Resurrection.

Vs. 1.—Samson carried off the gates of the city.
Vs. 2.—The man (Jonah) rising up, denotes Thee, O Christ.
Vs. 3.—Christ comes forth, bursting the tomb covered by a stone.

We read in the 16th chapter of the book of Judges, concerning Samson, that in the middle of the night he arose, and of his own might cast down both the brazen gates of the city, and, going out from the city, carried them with him. Samson is a type of Christ, who, rising from the grave in the middle of the night, cast down the gates of the tomb and left it in freedom and power.

David lxxviii. 65.—" Then the Lord awaked as one out of sleep.'

Hosea vi. 2, 3.—" In the third day He will raise us up, and we shall know and follow Him."

We read, in the second chapter of the book of the prophet Jonah that when Jonah himself had been in the belly of the whale three days and three nights, afterwards the fish vomited out Jonah on dry land. Jonah, who after three days came out from the fish, is a type of Christ, who after three days came out, or arose, from the grave.

Gen. xlix. 9.—" Judah, my son, is a lion's whelp."

Zeph. iii. 8.—" [Wait] until the day of My resurrection. I will gather the nations."

The three Maries and the Angel at the tomb.

Vs. 1.—As Reuben fears that the lost boy is killed.

Vs. 2.—As she (the daughter of Zion) with holy zeal seeketh her lost spouse.

Vs. 3.—So they, seeking Thee, O Christ, learnt from the angel that Thou livest.

We read, in the 37th chapter of Genesis, that Reuben came and sought his brother Joseph in the well; and when he found it he was greatly troubled, and said to his brethren, " The child is not there and I, whither shall I go?" This Reuben signifies Mary Magdalene who with sorrow and devotion sought for Christ in the tomb, and received from the angel the answer that He had risen from the dead she herself was afterwards found worthy to see Him.

Isa. lv. 6.—" Seek ye the Lord while He may be found: call y upon Him while He is near."

Micah vii. 7.—" Therefore I will look unto the Lord; I will wa for the God of my salvation."

We read in Solomon's Song, third chapter, concerning that bric who, while seeking for her beloved spouse, saith, " I have sougl him whom my soul loveth, and I have not found him." Th bride is a type of Mary Magdalene, who sought her Beloved in th tomb, and afterwards, when He had risen, found Him.

David cv. 3—" Let the heart of them rejoice that seek the Lord.

Gen. xlix. 18.—" I have waited for Thy salvation."

Christ appearing to Mary Magdalene in the Garden.

Vs. 1.—The king rejoices when he sees (Daniel) alive.

Vs. 2.—The loved bride now rejoices over her spouse whom she sought.

Vs. 3.—Showing Thyself, O Christ, Thou comfortest the holy Mary.

We read in Daniel vi. that when the prophet Daniel was cast into the lions' den, that the lions might slay him, in the morning the king came to the lions' den, and to Daniel to see if he still lived, and when he saw him alive he rejoiced greatly. Now this king signifies Mary Magdalene, when she came to the tomb after seeing her Lord, and rejoiced greatly because He had risen from the dead.

David ix. 10.—" Thou, Lord, hast not forsaken them that seek Thee."

Isa. lxi. 10.—" I will greatly rejoice in the Lord; my soul shall be joyful in my God."

We read in the Song of Solomon, chap. iii., that when the bride had found her beloved she said, " I have found him whom my soul loveth, and I will again hold him and will not let him go." This bride is a type of Mary Magdalene, who, seeing her spouse, that is Christ, would fain have held Him; but He answered thus: " Touch me not, for I have not yet ascended to my Father."

1 Sam. ii. 1; Cant. iii. 4.—" My heart rejoiceth in the Lord." "I held him; I would not let him go."

Hosea ii. 14.—" I will bring her into the wilderness, and there speak unto her heart."

Christ appearing to His disciples.

Vs. 1.—He (Joseph) who formerly vexed his brethren, now embraces them.

Vs. 2.—The father in tears embraces his son, now recovered.

Vs. 3.—Jesus appears to these (disciples); His risen glory is revealed.

We read in Genesis xlv. that Joseph saw his brethren smitten with fear and afraid of the multitude, and knowing not that it was Joseph; and he said to them: " I am your brother Joseph: touch me not," and thus he consoled them. Joseph signifies Christ, who after His resurrection appeared to His disciples who were in the flesh, and spake to them and comforted them, saying, " Fear not, I am. . ."

David (Ps. xvi. 11).—" In Thy presence is fulness of joy."
Isaiah li. 1.—" Look unto the Rock whence ye are hewn."
We read in the 15th chapter of the gospel of St. Luke that the son of a certain rich man said unto his father, " Give me my portion of the inheritance ;" and when he had given it unto him he departed into a far country and squandered all his substance, and then returned to his father, who received him kindly and comforted him. Now this good father signifies that Heavenly Father who, coming to His disciples after His death, comforted them and showed them His resurrection.

Wisd. i. 2.—" He sheweth Himself unto such as do not distrust Him."

Ezek. xxxiv. 11.—" Behold I, even I, will both search My sheep and seek them out."

The incredulity of Thomas.

Vs. 1.—The Angel exhorts Gideon not to fear.
Vs. 2.—Jacob, when he wrestled, was named Israel and blessed.
Vs. 3.—Thou dost suffer Thyself to be touched, that he may give in.

Judges vi. 12.—We read in the sixth chapter of Judges that the angel of the Lord came to Gideon and said unto him, " The Lord is with thee, thou mighty man of valour, wherefore thou thyself shalt deliver the people,"—which came to pass. Now Gideon signifies Thomas, to whom there came an angel, a wonderful Counsellor, to wit, Christ, to strengthen him in his faith, saying unto him, " Thrust thine hand into My side, and behold the marks of the nails ; and be not faithless, but believing."

Isa. lvii. 18.—" I have sent him away and I have brought him back. I have seen him and will heal him. I will lead him also and restore comforts unto him and to his mourners." *

David.—" Make glad, O Lord, the heart of Thy servant."

Gen. xxxii.—We read in the thirty-second chapter of Genesis that when an angel of the Lord came to Jacob, he seized the angel and wrestled with him, and did not let him go until he blessed him. Jacob signifies Thomas the apostle, who by touching an angel, to wit, Christ, was deemed worthy to get a blessing—that is an assurance of Christ's resurrection.

* In the Vulgate : " Vias ejus vidi, et sanavi eum, et redux ; eum et reddidi consolationis ipsi, et lugentibus ejus."

Jer. xxxi. 18.—" Turn Thou me and I shall be turned, for Thou art the Lord my God."
Zeph. iii. 7.—" Surely thou wilt fear Me; thou wilt receive instruction."

The Ascension.

Vs. 1.—Enoch, translated, is joined to the company of heaven.
Vs. 2.—Elias was translated into heaven, carried through the air.
Vs. 3.—Saint of saints: Christ seeks the stars of heaven.

Gen. v. 24.—We read in the fifth chapter of Genesis that Enoch pleased God, and was translated into Paradise; Enoch, who pleased God, is a type of Christ, who pleased the Father on high, and was therefore thought worthy to ascend to the heavenly Paradise —that is, heaven—for, in the day of His ascension, He exalted Him above all the choirs of angels.

David (Ps. xlvii. 5).—" God is gone up with a shout: the Lord with the sound of a trumpet."

Deut. xxxii. 11.—" As an eagle stirreth up her nest, fluttereth over her young." *

2 Kings ii. 9.—We read in the second book of Kings, second chapter, that when Elijah the prophet was raised into heaven in a fiery chariot, Elisha cried out, " My father, my father, the chariot of Israel and the horsemen thereof." Elijah is a type of Christ, whom His apostles, typified by Elisha, saw ascending into heaven, and wondered when Christ said unto them, " I go unto My Father."

Isa. lxiii. 1.—" Who is this that cometh from Edom, with dyed garments from Bozrah ?"

Micah ii. 13.—" The Breaker is come up before them."

Descent of the Holy Ghost.

Vs. 1.—The Divine Law was given to Moses from the top of Sinai.
Vs. 2.—The celestial flame comes to soften the hearts of men.
Vs. 3.—The gentle Spirit fills the hearts of the faithful.

Exod. xxiv. 12; xxxi. 18.—We read in the twenty-fourth chapter of Exodus that the Lord said to Moses: " Come up to Me into the mountain, and I will give thee the two tables of the covenant."

* " Spreadeth abroad her wings, taketh them, beareth them on her wings: so the Lord alone did lead him " [Israel].—The Song of Moses.

Just as the law was given to Moses and was written on tables of stone, so, on the day of Pentecost, a new law was written in the hearts of the faithful collected together when the fire appeared above them.

David (Ps. civ. 30).—" Thou sendest forth Thy Spirit; they are created."

Ezek. xxxvi. 27.—" I will put My Spirit within you."

1 Kings xviii. 38.—We read in the eighteenth chapter of the first book of Kings that when Elijah the prophet had placed the holocaust, that is, one bull, upon the wood, and in the presence of the people called upon the Lord; the fire coming down from heaven devoured everything: and so the people believed in the Lord. This fire from heaven signifies that Divine fire which, on the day of Pentecost, came upon the disciples, and cleansed them and devoured all their sin and wickedness.

Wisd. i. 7.—" For the Spirit of the Lord filleth the world."

Joel ii. 29.—" Upon the handmaids and upon the servants will I pour out My Spirit."

Coronation of the Virgin.

Vs. 1.—His mother cometh in: Solomon placeth her next himself.

Vs. 2.—Like as Esther cometh in and doeth honour to Ahasuerus.

Vs. 3.—By taking to thyself the holy Mary, do honour unto her.

1 Kings ii. 19.—We read in the first book of Kings (chap. ii.) that when Bathsheba, the mother of Solomon, had entered in unto him, into his palace, king Solomon commanded a throne to be placed for his mother next to his own throne. Bathsheba signifies the glorious Virgin, whose throne is placed next the throne of the true Solomon, that is—Jesus Christ.

David.—" All the rich among the people will pray not to see Thy face."

Isa. xxxv. 2.—" The glory of Lebanon is given to her, the excellency of Carmel and Sharon."

Esther ii. 17.—We read in the book of Esther (chap. ii.) that when queen Esther had come to king Ahasuerus into his palace, king Ahasuerus himself, to do her honour, placed her next himself; queen Esther signifies the Virgin Mary whom Ahasuerus—that is

Christ—in the day of the assumption, placed in heavenly glory next Himself.

Solomon's Song viii. 5.—"Who is this that cometh up from the wilderness?"

Wisd.—"O how fair is a chaste generation with love!"

The Last Judgment.

Vs. 1.—Solomon decrees that the child is justly to be given to its mother.

Vs. 2.—David thus judgeth him because of the Lord Christ.

Vs. 3.—I judge worthy of condemnation the wicked and the impious together.

1 Kings iii. 16-28.—We read in the third chapter of the first book of Kings that there came to Solomon the two mothers who were harlots, and pleaded before him as judge about the overlaid child and the living one, and when he could not judge otherwise, he said: "Bring me a sword and divide the living child;" and the bowels of the living child's mother went out unto him, and she said: "Give her the living child;" and she ceased from the trial. In the wise Solomon we see Christ, who judged the just and the unjust by the true judgment.

Eccles. iii. 17.—"God shall judge the righteous and the wicked."

Isa. ii. 4.—"He shall judge among the nations, and shall rebuke many people."

2 Sam. i. 15, 16.—We read in the second book of Samuel that King David, after the death of Saul, remained in Ziklag; and one coming from the land of the Amalekites boasted that he had slain the Lord's Anointed, to wit, king Saul; and sentence of death was passed upon him by king David because his mouth had spoken against him; and he said to his armour-bearer, "Fall upon him and slay him." David is a type of Christ, who will reward all nations with equity to each according to his sins, just as David is about to judge the Amalekite.

1 Sam. ii. 10.—"The Lord shall judge the ends of the earth."

Ezek. vii. 3.—"I will judge thee according to thy ways."

Hell.

Vs. 1.—These are given unto the earth because they serve not Christ.

Vs. 2.—For the sins of their lives thus are the men of Sodom given to destruction.

Vs. 3.—Thus are they afflicted and punished who follow wickedness.

Deut. xi. 6.—We read in the eleventh chapter of Deuteronomy that Dathan and Abiram, who lived in the middle of Israel, were swallowed up by the earth, with their houses and tents, because they kept not the commandments of God. By Dathan and Abiram are meant those sinners who, caring not for the Catholic Law nor the Law of the Decalogue, go down into hell, which is the place of sinners, full of guile and of fire, which will devour them; and with the devil they shall be punished.

Wisd. xviii. 11.—"And like as the king so suffered the common person."

Jer. xxv. 10.—" Moreover, I will take from them the voice of gladness."

Gen. xix. 24.—We read in the nineteenth chapter of Genesis that for the sins of the men of Sodom and Gomorrah the Lord sent fire from heaven upon those cities; and they were both overturned. By Sodom and Gomorrah are meant those sinners living upon earth according to the lusts of the flesh, which blind their eyes; and when the morning shall rise there will appear all the sinners on earth; and alive they will be doomed to hell and damned.

David (Ps. lxxv. 8).—" His dregs are not drained; all the sinners of the world shall drain them."

Job.—" Satiati sunt poenis meis." (" They are fulfilled with my pains.")

Christ with the souls of the blessed in His mantle.

Vs. 1.—The sons of Job rejoice because they are thus happily daring.

Vs. 2.—The angel appears; Jacob thereat rejoiceth greatly.

Vs. 3.—O Father in heaven, Thou wouldst lead me in green pastures!

Job. i. 4.—We read in the first chapter of the book of Job that his sons held feasts in their houses, each in his own house, and they sent for their sisters to eat and drink with them. The sons of Job are those righteous men who keep daily feasts, sending for those who shall be saved to come to the eternal happiness, and for ever to enjoy God. Amen.

David xxxiii. 1.—" Rejoice in the Lord, all ye just, and be proud, all ye that are true of heart."

Josh. i. 3.—" Every place that the sole of your foot shall tread upon [I have given you, as I said unto Moses]."

Gen. xxviii. 10-13.—We read in the twenty-eighth chapter of Genesis that when Jacob saw the sun setting, he found a stone, which he placed under his head; and in his dream he saw a ladder stretching from the earth to the heaven, and angels descending, and the Lord standing above it, saying to him, " The earth on which thou sleepest will I give unto thee and to thy seed for ever." By Jacob understand the faithful soul, which, when it sleeps upon a stone—that is, Christ—will gain the land flowing with milk and honey—that is, the kingdom of heaven.

Tobias xi. 9.—" Et flere ceperunt præ gaudio." ("And they begin to weep for joy.")

Isa. lxvi. 10.—" Rejoice ye with Jerusalem, and be glad with her, all ye that love her."

The reward of the righteous.

Vs. 1.—The praise of a true soul I have thought to rejoice in for my spouse.

Vs. 2.—The bridegroom loves his spouse; so doth Christ greatly love His fair bride.

Vs. 3.—Then souls rejoice in spirit when all good is given to them.

Solomon's Song iv. 7.—We read in the fourth chapter of Solomon's Song that the bridegroom addresses his spouse, taking her and saying, " Thou art all fair, my love; there is no spot in thee; come, my love, and thou shalt be crowned." That true Bridegroom is Christ, who, taking that bride, which is the soul, without spot of any sin, brings her to eternal rest, and crowns her with a crown of immortality.

David (Ps. xix. 5).—" Like a bridegroom coming from his chamber."

Ezek. xxiv. 17.—" Bind thy crown upon thine head, and put thy shoes upon thy feet."

Revelation.—We read in the Apocalypse (chap. xxi.) that the angel of God caught John the Evangelist when he was in the spirit, and, wishing to show him the secret things of God, said to him, "Come, I will show unto thee the bride, the Lamb's wife." The angel speaks to all in general to come in the spirit, and witness Christ, the innocent Lamb, crowning the innocent soul.

Isa. lxi. 10.—"He hath clothed me with the garments of salvation: as bridegroom, He hath crowned me with a crown."

Hosea ii. 19.—"I will betroth thee to Me for ever."

THE END.

DESCRIPTIVE LIST OF ILLUSTRATIONS.
VOL. I.

TITLE.	NATURE AND ORIGIN.	DATE.	PAGE
Charlemagne	Glass painting, Strasbourg	circ. 1100	23
Christ	Spec. Bibl. Nat., Lat. 9584, Paris	circ. 1300	24
St. John Evan.	Glass, St. Rèmi, Rheims	circ. 1100	29
God the Father	Fresco, Mt. Athos, Greece	circ. 1600	30
St. Gregory IV.	Mosaic. Roman	A.D. 828	31
Three Persons	Bibl. Sacra, 6829, Bibl. Roy., Paris	circ. 1250	32
Christ, head of	Bibl. Nat. 920, Paris	circ. 1500	33
Christ	Bibl. Nat., Paris	circ. 850	34
Apollo with rays	Antiq. Ex. Montfaucon.* Roman	. . .	35
Abraxas: Pantheic divinity.	Antiq. Ex. Montfaucon.† Gnostic gem	. . .	36
Trinity: three crucif. nimbi.	Heures du Duc d'Anjou, Bibl. Nat. Paris.	1250	39
Hindoo Maya	Religions de l'Antiquité.‡ Hindostan.	. . .	41
Lamb : cruc. nimbus	Bosio, Rom. Sott.§ Roman Catacombs	. . .	43
Christ in oval nimbus	Fresco, Montorio ch., near Vendôme.‖	. . .	44
Christ, Alpha and Omega.	Fresco, Meteora, Thessaly	circ. 1300	46
Christ's Ascension	Wood-carving, Italy (M. Durand's coll.).	circ. 1300	48
Christ, beardless	Fresco. Roman Catacombs	1st Xtian period.	51
Christ and the Earth	Sculpture sarcophagus, Vatican, Rome	1st Xtian period.	53
Abraham and Angels	Bible, MS., No. 6, Bibl. Nat., Paris	circ. 900	54
Divine Hand	Liber Precum, Bibl. Nat., Paris	circ. 800	55
Trinity	Fresco, Mt. Athos, Greece	. . .	60
God the Father	Spec. Hum. Sal., Bibl. Nat., Paris, Lat. 9584.	circ. 1300	64
Lamb, A and Ω	Sculpture, sarcophagus, Vatican, Rome	1st Xtian period.	67
John Baptist winged	Fresco, Kaiçariani, Mount Hymettus	. . .	70
Emp. Henry II.	Painted glass, Strasbourg cathedral	12th or 14th cent.	75
Pope Paschal	Mosaic, church of St. Cecilia, Rome	circ. 800	77

* Tom. I. p. 118, pl. 54.   † Tom. iv. p. 363.   ‡ Atlas, pl. 19, No. 103.
§ Ed. Rome, 1636. p. 627.
‖ See *Musée Egyptien, Louvre* ; *The Zodiac of Denderah* ; *Atlas des Religions de l'Antiquité* ; *Peintures et Ornements des Manuscrits*, being one among a collection of treatises (MS. de la Bibliothèque Royale fonds de St. Germain).

TITLE.	NATURE AND ORIGIN.	DATE.	PA
Bishop nimbed, with chalice.	Pont. MS. Latin, Bibl. de la Minerva, Rome.	c. 800	
St. Peter and Pope Leo III.	Mosaic. Triclinium, S. Giov. Laterano; now in Vatican Triclinium.	. . .	
Liberty	Sculptured figure, Chartres cathedral*	1250	
Diana with nimbus.	Sculpture, Rom. Montfaucon, Antiq. Ex., tom. ii. 414.	. . .	
Sun	Sculpture, Etruscan	. . .	
God with Adam and Eve.	Sculpture sarcophagus. Catacombs, Rome; Bosio, Rom. Sott. p. 295.	1st Xtian period.	
Christ with flat nimbus.	Wood-carving, Stalls, Amiens . . .	circ. 1500	1
Christ with nimbus	MS. 920, Bibl. Nat., Paris	circ. 1500	1(
Nimbus, a thread of light.	Raphael, Disputà, Rome	. . .	1(
God in aureole . .	Fresco, Auxerre cathedral, crypt . .	1150 to 1200	1(
The Lord in aureole of cloud.	MS. de St. Sever., Bibl. Nat., Paris	. . .	1
God in aureole . .	Fresco, Salamis convent	circ. 1700	1
Transfiguration . .	Painted glass, Chartres cathedral .	12th cent.	1
Christ in aureole .	Psalter St. Louis, Bibl. de l'Arsénal, 1186.	1200 to 1250	1:
Mary in oval . .	Liber Precum, Bibl. Nat., Paris . .	circ. 900	1:
Soul of St. Martin .	Painted glass, Cathedral, Chartres	13th cent.	1:
Mary and Infant .	MS., Bibl. de Ste. Geneviève, Paris	16th cent.	1:
Mercury nimbed .	Roman sculpture, Antiq. Exq. Montfaucon, tom. ii. pl. 223, p. 414.	. . .	1:
Persian king, nimbed	Persian MS., Bibl. Nat., Paris † . .	. . .	1:
Satan torments Job	MS. Bible, No. 6, Bibl. Nat, Paris .	circ. 950	1:
Beast with seven heads.	Psalterium cum figuris, No. 8846, Bibl. Nat., Paris.	12th cent.	1(
Christ as Creator .	Fresco and ivory, Gori, Thesaurus Vet. dipt. ii. p. 160	12th cent.	1'
Christ the Almighty	Fresco, Salamis	18th cent.	1'
Christ as St. Sophia	Miniature, Lyons	12th cent.	1'
Jehovah of battles .	MS. Psalter, Bibl. Nat. Suppl. fr. 1132, bis.	12th cent.	1:
Isaiah, Night & Day	Psalterium cum figuris, Bibl. Nat., Paris. Greek, No. 139.	10th cent. (classic.)	2(
Baptism of Christ .	Liber Precum, Bibl. Nat., Paris. Suppl. lat. 641.	9th cent.	2(
Divine hand . . .	Sculptured, Ferrara cathedral porch .	12th cent.	2(

* Nicolo Alemanni, De Lateranensibus Parietinis, Rome, 1625, p. 12 M. de Basta Peintures et Ornements des MSS. Engravings from Karez, Mt. Athos. Greek Iconograp note: Didron, vol. 1. p. 59.
† See Persian MS. Bibl. St. Geneviève ent. Medgialis; and Livre des Augures, a Turk MS., Bibl. Nat., Paris.

TITLE.	NATURE AND ORIGIN.	DATE.	PAGE
Divine hand and crown.	Mosaic, Santa Maria Nova, Rome, Vet. Monimenta, 2nd pt., fig. 53.	A.D. 848	206
Hand holding Souls	Fresco, Salamis	1100 or 1735	210
Face of Christ as God	Heures du Duc de Berri, fol. 65., Bibl. Nat. Paris	14th cent.	211
God, beardless	MS. treatise St. Augustine, Beauvais	11th cent.	212
Trinity	Psalter M.S, Bibl. de Chartres	circ. 1200	214
Trinity	Heures du Duc d'Anjou, Bib. Nat., Paris	circ. 1250	215
Trinity	Roman des trois Pèlerinages, Bibl. St. Geneviève, 226 fol.	1350	217
Creator as Pope	Painted glass, St. Madeleine de Troyes.	16th cent.	218
God as Pope, five crowns.	Painted glass, St. Martin ès Vignes, Troyes.	16th cent.	226
Jehovah	Wood-carving, Hautvilliers, Rheims	17th cent.	231
Creation of Angels	Psalterium cum figuris, Bibl. Nat. Suppl. fr. 1132.	1250	240
Christ as Apollo throned above world (personified)	Sculpture, tomb of Junius Bassus. Roman.	4th cent.	250
Christ the Judge	Orcagna, Campo Santo, Pisa*	14th cent.	263
Christ crucified	Ivory, Latin, but semi-Byzantine, Bib. Nat., Paris.	12th cent.	269
Christ triumphant	Ivory, lower side, ibid.	Ibid.	272
Temptation of Christ	Psalterium cum figuris, MS. Bibl. Nat., Paris.	12th cent.	277
The Mother & Jesus	Painted glass, Jouy, near Rheims	16th cent.	281
Jesus and archangels	Greek painting.	15th cent.	282
Mother and Jesus	Seal of Mt. Athos, Convent of St. Laura	. . .	284
Mary glorified	Fresco, Campo Santo, Pisa	14th cent.	286
Word of God (Mission of).	Miniature in Romant des trois Pèlerinages, Bibl. St. Geneviève, Paris.	A.D. 1358	296
Christ subdues serpent, basilisk and lion and dragon.	Ivory, Vatican Museum	10th cent.	298
Christ chains devil	Missal of Worms, Bibl. de l'Arsénal, Theol. Lat., No. 192, in fol.	9th or 10th cent.	300
Christ a pilgrim	Rom. trois Pèlerinages, Bibl. St. Geneviève.	A.D. 1358	301
Jesus shows the Father His wounds.	Spec. Hum. Salvationis, Bibl. Nat. Suppl. Lat. 9584.	circ. 1350	304
Christ as Archbishop in heaven.	Fresco, cupola of Greek church †	. . .	306
Triumph of Christ	Fresco on vault, cathedral, Auxerre, east crypt.	. . .	309

* Buffalmacco paints Christ as Creator at Pisa, p. 240.
† Similar subject at Rheims (*Divine Liturgy*), also in MS. du Duc d'Anjou, Lavall, 127 in Bibl. Nat. Origin of Raphael's Disputa. See p. 231, supra.

TITLE.	NATURE AND ORIGIN.	DATE.	PAG
Lamb of God ..	Copper-plate book-binding, Musée de Cluny, Paris.	1000	32
John Baptist carries Lamb.	Sculpture, cathedral, Chartres ..	13th cent.	32
John Baptist carries Lamb.	Painting, fol. 187, Rom. des trois Pèlerinages, St. eneviève, Paris.	A.D. 1358	32
Ram with Cross. .	Sculpture, Troyes cathedral . . .	13th cent.	32
Apostles as lambs .	Sculpture, sarcophagus, Vatican, Roma Sott., p. 63.	1st Xtian period.	32
The Lamb, use of .	Sculpture, Latin, Tomb of Junius Bassus, Musée Chrétienne, Rome.	4th cent.	33
Seven-eyed & seven-horned Lamb.	Miniature, Theol. Lat. Apocalypse, Bibl. de l'Arsénal.	13th cent.	35
The Good Shepherd	Fresco, Catacombs, Rome, Bosio, 351 .	1st Xtian period.	35
Tomb of oil-vendor	Sculpture, Latin, Roma Sott., Bosio, p. 302.	5th cent.	35
Tomb of architect .	Sculpture, Latin, Roma Sott., p. 505 .	1st Xtian period.	35
Tomb of sailor . .	Sculpture, Salviati Coll., Rome . .	1st Xtian period.	35
Tombs, various attributes on.	Sculpture and painting, Catacombs .	1st Xtian period.	35
Vine-dresser's grave	Sculpture, Catacombs, Bosio, Rom. Sott.., p. 505.	1st Xtian period.	36
Plan of Greek cross church.	Drawing by Bishop Arculfe, France, on waxen tablet.	7th cent.	37
Greek cross, two-armed.	Sculpture, Athenian	11th cent.	38
Descent into Hades .	Miniature, MS. Bibl. Nat., Paris . .	13th cent.	38
Cross of Lorraine .	Sculpture, Mount Athos, St. Laura Convent.	1st Xtian period.	38
Greek cross, two arms.	Sculpture, Athens	11th cent.	38
Cross quartered. .	Fresco, Catacombs	1st Xtian period.	3!
Greek crosses . .	Sculpture, Sarcophagi	1st Xtian period.	3!
Cross, six-branched.	Sculpture on capital, Ch. of Demetrius, Salonica.	4th cent.	3!
Cross, six-branched.	Sculpture. Salonica.	4th cent.	3!
Crosses, Greek and Latin.	Catacombs	1st Xtian period.	3'
Monogram and cross	Sculpture, Catacombs	1st Xtian period.	3'
Mystic cross . .	Engraved stone	. . .	3'
Starry cross. . .	Mosaic, Revenna, Ciampini, Vet. Mon. pt. i., pl. 24.	6th cent.	3!

TITLE.	NATURE AND ORIGIN.	DATE.	PAGE
Crosses, Greek and Latin.	Sculpture, Rheims; Laon, Berne . .	. . .	399
Dante's cross . .	Florentine engraving, Paradiso, canto xiv. 1. 94.	A.D. 1491	400
David and Intelligence.	Miniature, Psalterium cum figuris, Greek MS., No. 139.	10th cent.	432
Holy Ghost, Intelligence.	Miniature, Bibl. Nat., fonds Lavall .	14th cent.	435
Holy Ghost, Dove .	Miniature, Book of Hours, Bibl. de l'Arsénal, Theol. Fr. viii., fol. 3, verso.	15th cent.	442
Coronation of Virgin, Holy Ghost as Man.	Wood-carving, stalls, Amiens . . .	16th cent.	445
St. Gregory and Holy Ghost.	Sculpture, Chartres, Notre Dame de .	13th cent.	448
Standard, Holy Ghost	Miniature, Bibl. Nat., Paris; Heures du Duc de Berri.	15th cent.	450
Six-winged Angel .	Painting by Perugino, church of St. Gervais, Paris.	15th cent.	452
Tetramorph on wheels.	Mosaic, Vatopédi, Mount Athos . .	. . .	453
Youth (Spirit of) .	Miniature, Rom. des trois Pèlerinages. Bibl. de St. Geneviève, Paris.	14th cent.	454
Church (the), as a dove.	Miniature, Hortus Deliciarum of Herrade, Strasbourg.*	11th cent.	456
Demon as bird . .	Miniature, Herrade, Hortus Deliciarum, Strasbourg.	11th cent.	465
Demon as black insect.	Miniature, Cité de Dieu, Bibl. St. Geneviève, fol. 21.	16th cent.	466
Spirit as child on waters.	Miniature, service book, Suppl. i., 638. Bibl. Nat., Paris.	15th cent.	470
Spirit as child of eight years.	Miniature, Heures, Lat., Bibl. St. Geneviève, 464.	16th cent.	471
Virgin, Child, and doves.	Miniature, Bibl. Nat., Biblia Sacra, 6829.	14th cent.	476
Virgin, Child, six doves.	Painted window, Chartres, west porch, right side.	13th cent.	486
Coronation of Virgin	Sculpture, church of Verrières, dept. l'Aube.	16th cent.	494
Dove with cruciform nimbus.	Miniature, Bibl. Nat., MS. Latin, fonds Lavalle.	14th cent.	497
Dove radiating . .	Miniature, Heures, Bibl. Nat., Paris. .	15th cent.	498
Dove at creation .	Painted window, Auxerre cathedral, sanctuary.	13th cent.	500
Trinity	Painting, church of St. Riquier . .	15th cent.	505

* Dante and Herrade, note p. 458. Guizot's translation of *Hist. Eccl. Franc.*, vol. ii. p. 138. Taylor (Abaron) *Voyage Pittoresque dans l'Ancienne France.* Missal of Poitiers, Bibl. id. 833.

VOL. II.

TITLE.	NATURE AND ORIGIN.	DATE.	PAG
God and angel creating man.	Miniature, Psalterium cum figuris, Bibl. Nat.	13th cent.	1
Trinity, Behemoth.	Miniature, Psalterium cum figuris, Bibl. Nat.	13th cent.	1
Baptism, Trinity	Wood-carving, Italian, Durant Col.	14th cent.	1
Trinity of Evil.	Min., Bibl. Nat., French, Emblema. Biblica.	13th cent.	2
Trinity of Evil.	Min., France, Hist. St. Graal, Bibl. Nat., 6770.	15th cent.	2
Time, three-faced personification.	Miniature, Bibl. de l'Arsénal, MS. Theol. Lat. 133c., Officium Ecclesiastic.	14th cent.	2
Trinity at Creation.	Miniature, Hortus Deliciarum, Strasburg.	12th cent.	4
Three faces in one head.	Min., Spanish, Chron. d'Isidore de Seville, MS. Bibl. Nat. 7135.	13th cent.	4
Trinity as three circles.	Min. MS., Bibl. Chartres	13th cent.	4
Triplicity in Unity.	Engraving, German, Gruter, Cab. des Estampes, Bibl. Nat.	16th cent.	5
Three faces, one head	Printed on vellum, Hours, Simon Vostre, Paris.	1524	5
Three faces, one head	Min., French, MS. Henry II., Bibl. Nat.	16th cent.	5
Three divine Persons	Min., French, Cité de Dieu, MS. Bibl. St. Geneviève.	16th cent.	6
Trinity, Holy Ghost proceeding.	Min., French, MS. Duc d'Anjou, Bibl. Nat.	13th cent.	6
Trinity, Holy Ghost proceeding.	Min., French, MS. Bibl. Troyes, from Abb. Notre Dame aux Nonnains.	12th cent.	7
Trinity	Wood engraving	12th cent.	7
Three faces, one head	Wood engraving, Italian, Dante, printed, Par., fol. cclxxviii.	A.D. 1491	7
God and Universe.	Buffalmacco, fresco, Campo Santo, Pisa.	14th cent.	7
God holding scales and compasses.	Miniature, Psalterium cum figuris, Bibl. Nat.	13th cent.	7
Trinity, human forms.	. . . .	15th cent.	8
Seraph of St. Francis.	Min., Bibl. Nat., Hours of Anne of France.	. . .	9
Thrones	Fresco, Athens	13th cent.	9
Angel	Sculpture, Chartres	13th cent.	9
Wingless angels. .	Painting, Nat. Gall., London, Piero della Francesca.	14th cent.	9
Angel without legs	Fresco, Campo Santo, Pisa. . . .	14th cent.	9

LIST OF ILLUSTRATIONS.—VOL. II.

TITLE.	NATURE AND ORIGIN.	DATE.	PAGE
Angel of Ascension	Manuscript, Bibl. Nat., Paris	. . .	95
Six-winged Angel	Manuscript, Bibl. Nat., Biblia Sacra. Lat. 6. i.	12th cent.	97
Angel holds flames	Sculpture, Chartres	13th cent.	100
Angel holds globes	Sculpture, Chartres	13th cent.	100
Angel with sword	Sculpture, Chartres	13th cent.	101
Angel with sceptre	Sculpture, Chartres	13th cent.	101
Angel with trumpet	Sculpture, Chartres	13th cent.	102
Angel with book	Sculpture, Chartres	13th cent.	102
John Baptist, winged	Sculpture, Chartres	13th cent.	108
Lucifer before Fall	MS., Hortus Deliciarum, Strasburg	12th cent.	109
Fall of Lucifer	Miniature, Breviary of St. Louis and Blanche of Castille, Bibl. de l'Arsénal, Paris.	A.D. 1220	111
Fall of Lucifer	Miniature, Spec. Hum. Sal., Bibl. de l'Arsénal, Paris, No. 593.	A.D. 1340	112
Four-faced demon	Unknown	. . .	113
Liver personified	Unknown	. . .	115
Fire demon	Unknown	. . .	117
Satan and Hell	Miniature, Missal of Poitiers	. . .	119
Satan	Fresco, Campo Santo, Pisa	. . .	120
Persian devil	Miniature, Bibl. Nat., Paris, Turkish MS.	. . .	122
Egyptian devil	Engraving, Montfaucon, Antiq. Ex.	. . .	123
Turkish devil	Engraving, Montfaucon, Antiq. Ex.	. . .	124
Satan, serpent-horned.	MS. Bibl. Nat., Paris, Coll. Duc d'Anjou.	circ. 1200	125
The Abyss	MS. Bibl. Nat., Paris. Lat. 6	. . .	127
Devil as Professor	Miniature, Spec. Hum. Sal., Bibl. de l'Arsénal, Paris, No. 593.	1340	128
Temptation of St. Paphnutius	Fresco, Campo Santo, Pisa	. . .	129
Juliana and Devil	Miniature, unknown	1340	130
Demons on tomb of Dagobert.	Sculpture, church of St. Denis, Paris.	A.D. 1220	131
Devils as men	Painted glass, Chartres	. . .	133
Devil as Satyr	Ivory carving, Tournus	. . .	134
Apocalyptic dragon	Painted glass, St. Nizier, Troyes.	. . .	137
Temptation, serpent	Sculpture, sarcophagus, Vatican	. . .	139
Two-headed serpent	Miniature, Bibl. Nat., Bible Historiée, Paris, No. 9561, fol. 8ª.	. . .	139
Temptation of Eve and Adam.	Miniature, Bibl. Nat., Bible Historiée, Paris, No. 9561, fol. 8.	1340	140
Devil, vampire	Fresco, Campo Santo, Pisa	1340	141
Devil on helmet of Goliath.	Miniature, Initial P.	. . .	142
Devil	Sculpture, Amiens	. . .	143
Drinking devil	Sculpture, Amiens	1340	144

TITLE.	NATURE AND ORIGIN.	DATE.	PA(
Exorcism of devil	Miniature, MS., Bibl. de Chartres, 1380.	1340	1·
Lucifer on seal	Miniature, MS., Bib. de Chartres, 1380	1340	1·
Lucifer's handwriting.	Miniature, MS., Bibl. de Chartres, 1380.	1340	1·
Impiety	Sculpture, Amiens cathedral	1340	1·
Covetousness	Miniature, Rom. des trois Pèlerinages, Bibl. St. Geneviève, Paris.	circ. 1330	1:
Death, Thanatos	Sculpture, temple of Diana of Ephesus	B.C.	1:
Death-bed scene	Miniature, Miss Twining	B.C.	1:
Death as woman	Fresco, Campo Santo, Pisa	circ. 1330	1:
Death as woman			1:
Death as rider			1(
Death as rider			1(
Death demon	Fresco, Campo Santo, Pisa.	circ. 1330	1(
Death and soul	Fresco, Campo Santo, Pisa.	circ. 1330	1(
Satan of Job	Fresco, Francis da Volterra, Campo Santo, Pisa.	circ. 1330	1(
Ladder of soul			1(
Death as king			1(
Death as Ecce Homo			1(
Death and fool			1:
Death and shepherd	Gem, Coll., M. Badeigts de la Borde.		1:
Death as a skeleton	Onyx gem, King's Horace		1:
The soul, Psyche	Gem		1:
Soul as butterfly	Sculpt. (ancient), collection, P. Rascasius di Bigarris.		1:
The soul, Psyche	Mosaic, St. Mark's, Venice.	6th cent.	1:
Soul of St. Stephen	Sculpture, ch. of St. Trophimus, Arles.		1:
Soul borne by angels	Miniature, Greek Menologium of Basil.		1:
Souls weighed by Michael.	Miniature, MS., M. Dupasquier, col., Lyons.	A.D. 1300	1:
Souls weighed by Hermes.	Vase painting, Duc de Luynes.		1:
Hermes lifts soul from grave.	Onyx gem, coll., Duke of Orleans		1:
Hermes leads soul to Charon.	Gem, Uzielli collection		1:
Michael slays dragon	Miniature, Amiens	A.D. 1197	1:
Michael slays dragon	Miniature, Abbey of Prume	circ. 993, 1001	1:
Michael and seven-headed dragon.	Miniature, Psalterium cum figuris, Bibl. Nat., Paris.		1:
Adoration of Cross	Ancient gem, lapis lazuli, Alexandria.	1st. Xtian age.	1!
Descent into Hell	Miniature, Bibl. Pauperum	Mediæval	1:
Christ overcomes human-headed serpent	Ancient gem, C. W. King, Report Cambridge Antiq. Soc. v. 82		2·

TITLE.	NATURE AND ORIGIN.	DATE.	PAGE
Hercules overcomes the human-headed hydra.	Ancient coin, C. W. King, Report Cambridge Ant. Soc. v. 82.	. . .	202
Daniel among lions	Miniature, Spec. Hum. Sal., Library of Lord Coleridge.	A.D. 1350	210
Ostrich delivers its young.	Miniature, Spec. Hum. Sal., Library of Lord Coleridge.	A.D. 1350	215
Mass of Regulus, Bishop of Arles.	Miniature, Bibl. Nat., Paris, Lat. 5086.	14th cent.	239
Burial of Virgin Mary.	Sculpture, Notre Dame, Paris . . .	13th cent.	241

INDEX.

ABATEMENTS of honour, i. 78 n.
Abelard, i. 427; his denial of the spirit of fear in Christ, i. 487; on the relations of the Divine Persons of the Trinity, ii. 10
Abgarus, king of Edessa, and the traditional portrait of Christ, i. 245
Achilles, the shield of, and the snow-white rose of the 'Divina Commedia,' ii. 249
Ahriman, contest between Ormuzd and, i. 464; the Persian spirit of darkness, ii. 122
Allegorical beings, nimbus of, i. 83, 154; figures, Impiety, ii. 149; Covetousness, 150
Allegories and myths, difference between, i. 343
Amiens, cathedral of, early Christian art in the, i. 90, 101, 104, 130 n., 144, 149, 445, ii. 143, 283 n., 328 n., 383 n., 445; library of, i. 501
Angels, nimbus of, i. 66, ii. 96; assisting God the Father at the creation, ii. 14; *iconography of*, ii. 85; creation of, ii. 85; method of treatment in art, ii. 85; St. John Damascene's opinion of the period of their creation, ii. 87; St. Jerome's, ii. 87; Dante's, ii. 87; incorporeal nature of, ii. 88; angels in Ezekiel, ii. 89, 91, 96; Dante's description of, ii. 89; angels of Giotto and other painters, ii. 90; representation of, by Italians, ii. 92; by artists in the West, ii. 94; costume of, ii. 96; small horn or cross on the brow of, ii. 97; St.

Dionysius' classification of the angelic hierarchy and their symbols, ii. 98, 265; hierarchy of angels at Chartres, ii. 99; in the convent of Ivirôn, ii. 101; wingless, ii. 93, 154, 256; of Botticelli, ii. 256
Apocalypse, the seven gifts of the Spirit in the, i. 481; the dragon of the, ii. 123; order amongst the devils of the, ii. 137; how to represent the, ii. 336
Apostles, nimbus of the, i. 72; figured under the form of lambs, i. 327
Arezzo, fresco at, ii. 186
Arles, ch. of St. Trophimus at, i. 502, ii. 177
Art, influence of social life and ideas on works of, i. 228
Athos, Mt, i. 76 n.; government of, i. 285 n.; the Satan of, ii. 121; early Christian art in convents, &c., of, i. 30, 36 n., 58 n., 60 n., 284, 388, 453, ii. 106, 121, 245, 281 n., 305 n., 322 n., 330, 342 n., 345 n., 376 n., 383 n., 391 n., 392 n.
Aureole: restriction of the term, i. 25; derivation of the word, i. 107; nature, i. 107; other names, i. 108; *form of the aureole*, i. 110, 115, 137; its field, i. 111, 115; the, characteristic of the Deity, i. 111, 121; use of the stool supporting the feet of God i. 113; variations in form, i. 118; *application of*, i. 121; of the Virgin Mary, i. 121; degradation of the, i. 123; *history of*, i. 126; *colour of*, i. 163; not always symbolic, i. 165

Auvergne, churches of, decorated in fifth century, ii. 191
Auxerre, cathedral of, fresco-painting of the triumph of Christ in the, i. 308; early Christian art in the, i. 109, 335 n., 462, 500 n., ii. 336 n.

BEAUCE, cathedral of, i. 18
Beauvais, i. 71 n., 212, ii. 383
Behemoth, the, of Job, ii. 123, 128
Benediction, forms of, i. 406; the Greek, i. 407; the Latin, i. 408
'Bible Historiale,' i. 7, 9
'Biblia Pauperum,' the, ii. 202; St. Ansgar its supposed author, ii. 202; its plan, ii. 203; rarity of MS. copies of, ii. 203; *translation of the*, ii. 403; the annunciation, ii. 403 the nativity, ii. 404; adoration of the Magi, ii. 404; the purification, ii. 405; the flight into Egypt, ii. 405; the Holy Family in Egypt, ii. 406; murder of the Innocents, ii. 407; return from Egypt, ii. 408; John baptizing Christ, ii. 408; temptation of Christ, ii. 409; the raising of Lazarus, ii. 410; the transfiguration, ii. 410; Mary Magdalene at the feet of Christ, ii. 411; Christ's entry into Jerusalem, ii. 412; Christ driving the money-changers out of the temple, ii. 412; Judas Iscariot betrays Christ, ii. 413; Judas receiving the thirty pieces of silver, ii. 414; the Last Supper, ii. 414; Christ leaving his disciples in Gethsemane, ii. 415; Christ in the garden of Olives, ii. 416; Judas betraying Christ with a kiss, ii. 416; Pilate washing his hands, ii. 417; Christ crowned with thorns, ii. 418; bearing his cross, ii. 418; on the cross, ii. 419; the crucifixion and the soldier with a spear, ii. 420; entombment of Christ, ii. 420; the descent into hell, ii. 421; the resurrection, ii. 412; the three Maries and the angel at the tomb, ii. 422; Christ appearing to Mary Magdalene in the garden, ii. 423; to his disciples, ii. 423; the incredulity of Thomas, ii. 424; the ascension, ii. 425; descent of the Holy Ghost, ii. 425; coronation of the Virgin, ii. 426; the last judgment, ii. 427; hell, ii. 426; Christ with the souls of the blessed in his mantle, ii. 428; the reward of the righteous, ii. 429

Blessing, how to represent the hand in, ii. 395
Bossuet, ii. 8
Botticelli, Sandro, his painting of angels, ii. 256
Bourges, cathedral of, early Christian art in the, i. 69, 319 n., 370, ii. 209 n.
Brou, Notre Dame de, stained window, representing the triumph of Christ in the, i. 310. 417; early Christian art in, i. 95 n., 102, 318 n., 323, 417
Browning, Mrs. Barrett, on Gregory Nazianzen, ii. 236 n.
Buffamalco, ii. 86
Burton, Sir F., description of the winged Thanatos in the British Museum, ii. 153, 255
Byzantine 'Guide to Painting,' ii. 189; its date, ii. 189; compiled by Dionysius, ii. 190; copies of the, and its growth, ii. 190; the scheme of the, ii. 193; the scenes in chronological order, ii. 194; *translation of second part of the*, ii. 263; the nine choirs of angels, ii. 265; fall of Lucifer, ii. 266; how to represent scenes in the lives of Adam and Eve, ii. 266; of Cain and Abel, ii. 267; of Noah, ii 268; of Abraham, ii. 269; of Jacob, ii. 271; of Joseph, ii 271; of Moses and Aaron, ii. 273; of Joshua, ii. 276; of Gideon, ii. 277; of Samson, ii. 277; of Samuel, ii. 278; of David, ii. 279; of Solomon, ii.

280; of Elijah, ii. 280; of Elisha, ii. 282; of Isaiah, ii. 283; of Jeremiah, ii. 284; of Daniel, ii. 284; of Jonah, ii. 286; of Job, ii. 287; the Patriarchs, ii. 288; the sons of Jacob, ii. 289; other ancestors outside the genealogy, ii. 291; holy women of the Old Testament, ii. 291; the holy Prophets, ii. 292; other prophecies, ii. 294; the philosophers of Greece who have spoken of the incarnation of Christ, ii. 297; the tree of Jesse, ii. 298; the festivals of the Lord and other works and miracles of Christ according to the Holy Gospel, ii. 299; the Holy Passion, ii. 314; the parables. ii. 322; the Apocalypse, ii. 336; the second coming of our Lord, ii. 345; the feasts of the Divine Mother, ii. 347; the twenty-four stations of the Divine Mother, ii. 352; the faces of the twelve holy Apostles, ii. 356; the four evangelists, ii. 356; the exaltation of the cross, ii. 357; the seven holy synods, ii. 358; the miracles of the principal saints, ii. 361; of the archangel Michael, ii. 361; of the Harbinger, ii. 362; of St. Peter, ii. 366; of St. Paul, ii. 367; of St. Nicholas, ii. 368; of St. George, ii. 369; of St. Catherine, ii. 371; of St. Anthony, ii. 372; how to represent the seven martyrs of the year, ii. 374; allegories and moralities, ii. 378; how to paint the walls of a church, ii. 383; the narthex, ii. 389; the fountain, ii. 390; the refectory, ii. 391; a cruciform church with four vaults, ii. 393; a church roofed with a barrel vault, ii. 393; the method by which we have to paint the holy images, ii. 394; the face and body of our Lord, ii. 394; of the mother of God, ii. 395; how to represent the hand in blessing, ii. 395; inscriptions for Holy Trinity, ii. 395

CHARON, the Etruscan, ii. 155
Chartres, cathedral of, arrangement of statues on the outside of, i. 14; hierarchy of angels in, ii. 99; figures of, arranged in the order of the 'Speculum Universale,' ii. 221; the 'Mirror of Nature,' ii. 222; the 'Mirror of Doctrine,' ii. 223; the 'Historical Mirror,' ii. 225; early Christian art in, i. 16, 17, 18, 55 n., 56 n., 69, 71, 84, 88 n., 91, 100, 109, 112, 117, 123, 125, 154 n., 175, 177, 181, 195, 227, 319 n., 322, 371 n., 380 n., 406, 448, 485, 487, 488, 502, ii. 15, 74, 85, 86, 92, 99, 132, 221, 230, 337 n., 377 n.
Chosroes, king of the Persians, visit to Jerusalem, ii. 37; his mimicry of the Trinity, ii. 38; death, ii. 38
Christ: as the conqueror of death, ii. 168; legend of footprints of, on the Mount of Olives, ii. 217. *See also*: God the Son.
Christian Scheme, iconography of the, ii. 188; the Byzantine 'Guide to Painting,' ii. 189, 226; its scheme, ii. 193; early systems of iconography, ii. 194, 226; the 'Mirror of Human Salvation,' ii. 196, 226; its scheme, ii. 197; the 'Biblia Pauperum,' ii. 202, 206; St. Ansgar its supposed author, ii. 202; its plan, ii. 203
Christianity and imitative art, i. 1
Church, the, likened to a dove, i. 455
Churches, form of eastern, i. 377 of western, i. 378; plan of, revealed in visions, &c., i. 381; how to paint the walls, &c., of, ii. 385
Circle, emblematic of God, ii. 45 use of by Dante and Homer, *ib* 249, 250
Circles, three intersecting, used as a type of the Trinity, ii. 45
Classification, passion for, of knowledge in the middle ages, i. 8, 9
Codrus, king of Athens, voluntary sacrifice of, ii. 214
Coleridge, Lord, manuscript in library of, 206, 210, 215

Costa, Jean, ii. 206 n.
Covetousness, female figure symbolising, ii. 148, 150
Creation, angels assisting God the Father at the, ii. 14
Crescent, adoption of the, by the Turks, i. 159 n.
Crescenzio's triumph of death, ii. 161
Cross: use of the, in the nimbus of Christ, i. 40; form of the arms of, i. 45; inscription of the letters ὤν, i. 45; the, confined to the nimbus of the Deity, i. 47; *the cross a symbol of Christ*, i. 367; history of the, i. 366; virtue of the, i. 370; enthusiasm for the, and its form, i. 372; dedication of churches to the, i. 373; *varieties of the cross*, i. 374; 1. the 'tau,' i. 374; 2. the cross with a top and one transverse bar, i. 374; its different forms, i. 375; the Greek cross, i. 375; the Roman, i. 376; both types common to both churches, i. 376; form of eastern churches, i. 377; of western churches, i. 378; 3. the cross with double branches, i. 380, 387; English churches in this form, i. 380; 4. the cross with three transverse bars, i. 382; free crosses, i. 384; the cross of the Passion, i. 384; the Resurrection cross, i. 385; varieties of heraldic crosses, i. 386; forms of intertwined crosses, i. 387; animals represented at the foot of crosses in Greek churches, i. 390; crosses formed by the monogram of Christ, i. 392; other forms, i. 393; allegorical ornaments on crosses, i. 395; inscriptions on, i. 396; inhabited cross described by Dante, i. 399; *the sign of the cross*, i. 405, 414; instructions from early Fathers, i. 405; form of benediction, i. 406; the Greek benediction, i. 407; the Latin, i. 408; forms of signing the cross, i. 409, ii. 11; *the colour of the cross*, i. 412; of the historical cross, i. 412; of the ideal cross, i. 413; *the triumph of the cross*, i. 414; adoration of the cross, ii. 196

Cupola, adoption of the, by the Turks, i. 159
Cyrus, vision of Astyages before the birth of, legend of, ii. 211

DAGOBERT, legend of the death of, ii. 132
Daniel, bishop of Lacedæmon, ii. 11
Dante, description of the triumph of Christ, i. 317; on the creation of angels, ii. 87; description of angels, ii. 89; of Lucifer, ii. 113; influence of, upon mediæval art, ii. 250, 258; quoted, i. 137, 138, 139, 144, 145, 166, 224, 233. 237 n., 401, 457, 467, ii. 5, 9 n., 47, 217, 248, 259
Death, iconography of, ii. 153; Christian images of, borrowed from the Græco-Latin polytheism, ii. 153; statue of Thanatos, ii. 153; figure of the Etruscan Charon, ii. 155; Death depicted by Christians as a skeleton, ii. 156; Orcagna's treatment of Death, ii. 157; Death as a woman, Petrarch's, ii. 159; Death as a rider, ii. 161; Crescenzio's triumph of Death, ii. 161; Orcagna's illustrations of the 'Three Deaths and the Three Lives,' ii. 164; the chariot of, ii. 166; death of man figured in the 'Ladder of the Soul's Salvation,' ii. 166; the Moral Ladder, ii. 167; Christ as the conqueror of, ii. 168; Death as a crowned skeleton, ii. 169; Death and the Fool, ii. 169; the Dance of Death, ii. 171
Devils, iconography of, ii. 109; Lucifer before his fall, ii. 109; the fall of Lucifer, ii. 110, 265; Dante's description of Lucifer, ii. 113; personification of physical evils by the ancients, ii. 114; of earthquakes by the Scandinavians, ii. 115; the monster of the

Tarasque, ii. 116; the fire-demon; ii. 116; legend of St. Remi and the fire at Rheims, ii. 116; the Devil in Missal of Poitiers ii. 118; painting of the Devil in the Campo Santo, Pisa, ii. 118; in the convent of St. Gregory, Mt. Athos, ii. 121; Ahriman, ii. 122; Egyptian devils, ii. 122, 123; the dragon of the Apocalypse, ii. 123; the Behemoth of Job, ii. 123, 128; the genius of evil in the west, ii. 124; represented as a beggar, ii. 126; as a monk or doctor, ii, 127, 259; as a splendidly dressed woman, ii. 129, 261; as a holy angel, ii. 129; in human form, ii. 132; the type of the demon indicative of the country and epoch, ii. 132; nomenclature of the devil, ii. 135; in the east, ii. 135; in the west, ii. 136; order amongst the devils of the Apocalypse, ii. 137; the serpent in the temptation of Adam and Eve, ii. 139; the demons of the New Testament, ii. 142; belief in the devil during the Middle Ages, ii. 144; humorous conceptions of, ii. 144; bull of Innocent VIII., ii. 144; exorcism, ii. 145; men begotten of the Devil, ii. 145; seal of Lucifer, ii. 146; figures symbolising impiety and covetousness, ii. 148; demons of floods, ii. 259
Didron, M., referred to, ii. 84, 100, 107, 188; 189, 225, 239, 249
Dove, the, representing, the Holy Spirit, i. 451, 459; the Church, i. 455
Drama, object of the religious, i. 6; influence of the, on iconography, ii. 233, 242; St. Francis' celebration of the nativity of Christ, ii. 233; influence of games and dramas on Greek art, ii. 234
Durandus, G., i. 274, 329, 336, 371, 375, 384, 408, 436, ii. 29

EASTLAKE, Lady, ii. 188, 176
Editor's note, ii. 84

Egyptian idols, legend of the fall of, before the child Christ, ii 214, 301
Encyclopædias, passion for making in the middle ages, i. 8, ii. 220; superiority of Vincent de Beauvais', i. 17
Epigonation, the, i. 60, 61
Evangelists, nimbi of the evangelical symbols, i. 87; symbols of the, i. 318, ii. 267
Eve, creation of, i. 218
Evil, trinity of, ii. 22
Exorcism, ii. 145

FERGUSON, Sir Samuel, sonnet on Paul Veronese, ii. 219
Ferrara, cathedral, i. 205
Festivals of the church, inscriptions for the, ii. 399
Figures and symbols, difference between, i. 342, 351
Fish, the, a figure of Jesus Christ, i. 344, 351
Fletcher, Giles, description of the Tempter, ii. 128; his opening scene of Christ's temptation, ii. 219
Footprints of bull indicating ground plan of churches, i. 382
Footprints of Christ, legend of, on the mount of Olive's, ii. 217
Freiburg in Breisgau, i. 75, 429, 491, 492; ii. 328

GLORY, restriction of the term, i. 25; origin of the word, i. 129; application of the term, i. 130; *nature of the glory*, i. 131; light embodied in painting or sculpture, i. 131; illustrations from the Hindoos, i. 132; from the Greeks, i. 132; from the modern Persians, i. 133; from Virgil, i. 134; from the Christian shrines i. 134; from the Apocalypse, i. 136; from Dante's 'Paradiso,' i. 137, 144; from the New Testament, i. 139; representations in rose-windows, i. 143; *its origin and native country*, i. 146; use amongst the Hindoos, i. 146;

amongst the Egyptians, i. 146; amongst the Greeks and Romans, i. 147; origin in the east, i. 149, 151; borrowed by the Christian religion, i. 150; at first not given to holy persons, i. 151; *character of the glory*, i. 153

Gnosticism, influence of, on Christian arts, i. 191, 197

Gnostics, hatred borne by the, to Jehovah, i. 187, 243; earliest portraits of Christ made by, i. 243; gem, i. 36

God, nimbus of; *see* Nimbus.

God the Father, i. 167; most frequently manifested in the Old Testament, i. 167; represented by a small part of his person, i. 170, 179; but generally by entire portraits of Christ, i. 170; the rank assigned to him frequently inferior to that of the Son, i. 180, 183; causes of this treatment, i. 187; the hatred borne by the Gnostics to Jehovah, i. 187; the dread then prevalent of making an idol, i. 192; the supposed identity between Father and Son, i. 194; the incarnation of the Son, i. 195; the difficulty in representing God the Father, i. 197; the absence of any visible manifestation of, i. 198; *portraits of*, i. 201; represented at first by a hand alone, i. 201; then by a face issuing from a cloud i. 211; with features slightly differing from the Son, i. 215; lastly, by a face and figure with distinctive features, i. 216; *characteristic attributes of*, i. 221; a hand extended from clouds, i. 221; a globe of the world, i. 222; triangular or lozenge-shaped nimbus, i. 222, 232; age, i. 223; as pope, emperor, or king, i. 223; ideal treatmeant by Italian artists, i. 229; his name inscribed in a triangle, i. 231; no special festival in honour of, ii. 29

God the Son; most frequently manifested in the New Testament, i. 167; represented instead of God the Father, as creator, i. 171; as all-wise, i. 178; frequently more honoured in early monuments than God the Father, i. 180, 183; causes of this treatment, i. 187; portraits of, i. 204, 212, 214, 215, 217, 219, 239; honoured above the other persons of the Trinity, i. 234; in the 'Gloria,' i. 235; with the title of 'Our Lord,' i. 238; *history of the portraits of*, i. 242; causes of their number, i. 242; earliest portraits made by Gnostics, i. 243; miraculous images, i. 245, description of his appearance by Lentulus, i. 246; by St. John Damascene, i. 247; by St. Anschaire, i. 248; evidence from monuments, i. 248; growing age of the figure of, with the progress of Christianity, i. 249; successive divestment of drapery from the figure of the crucified, i. 260; Michelangelo's Christ in the last judgment, i. 261; portraits from the period of the Renaissance to the present day, i. 263; reaction against the materiality of the fifteenth and sixteenth centuries, i. 263; the beauty or ugliness of Christ, i. 264; view of the African church, i. 264; of the Latin church, i. 265; of Christian artists, i. 266; portraits, neither beautiful nor ugly, i. 266; description of Christ by Tertullian, i. 268; by St. Cyril of Alexandria, i. 268; presence or absence of the beard in figures of Christ, i. 268; *archæological signs characteristic of our Saviour*, i. 278; bare feet, i. 279; triangular aureole, i. 283; cruciform nimbus and monograms, i. 287; inscription of his sayings, i. 289; presence of seven doves symbolical of the spirits of God, i. 291; of actions in the life of Christ, i. 291; *the triumph of Christ*, i. 292; as treated in Greece, i. 293;

in the west, i. 294; the pilgrimage of Christ in the 'Romant des trois Pèlerinages,' i. 294; Greek representations of Christ after his return to heaven, i. 305; fresco-painting in the cathedral of Auxerre, i. 308; stained window in the Notre-Dame de Brou, i. 310; Dante's description in the 'Purgatorio,' i. 317; *Jesus Christ as a lamb*, i. 318; St. John the Baptist carrying the Lamb of God, i. 321; the Lamb of God depicted as a ram in the cathedral at Troyes, i. 325; decree of Justinian II. prohibiting the use of the lamb as a symbol of Christ, i. 332; effect of the decree, i. 333; the Lamb of God in the Apocalypse, i. 333; representation of Christ and the symbolic lamb on the same cross, i. 336; *Jesus as the good shepherd*, i. 337 treatment of the subject, i. 338; its popularity, i. 341; *Jesus Christ as lion*, i. 341; *Jesus figured by the fish*, i. 344, 351; evidence from monuments, i. 345; testimony of authors, i. 347; anagram from the word ΙΧΘΥΣ, i. 347; the fish not always a figure of Christ, i. 352; often a sign of trade when carved on monuments, i. 353; the natural explanation in such cases to be the first adopted, i. 361; epithets for God the Son, ii. 396

Gospel of Christ, inscriptions on the, ii. 397

Graal, history of the, i. 270

Gregory Nazianzen, ii. 236

Gregory of Tours, i. 425, 459, ii. 191

Gregory the Great, pope. inspired by the Holy Spirit, i. 447

Greek art, influence of games and dramas on, ii. 234

HEBRADE, i. 50, 207, 430, 455, 457, 465, 469, ii. 8, 34, 63, 167

Hercules and human-headed serpent ii. 201

Holy Ghost; portraits of the, i.

216, 219, 220; *history of the*, 417; *definition of the*, i. 418 Jehovah the God of strength, 418; Jesus the God of love, 419; the Holy Ghost the God of intelligence, i. 420; Charlemagne's hymn to the, i. 421 the, also possessing the attributes of the other persons of the Trinity, i. 422; the office of the i. 424; evidence from Scripture i. 424; testimony from legends i. 426; from history, i. 427; from art, 428; represented as the creator of sciences, i. 429; *worship of the*, i. 437; churches and monasteries dedicated to the, i 437; *manifestations of the*, i 440; scriptural, i. 440; legendary i. 443; at the coronation of th Virgin Mary, i. 444; legend o St. Joseph, i. 446; the, inspiring Gregory the Great, i. 447; St Jerome, i. 448; St. Theresa, i 449; directing the actions o kings, i. 449; as a dove embroidered on a standard, i. 450 *the Holy Spirit as a dove*, i. 60 120, 204, 451; a bird used t express rapidity, i. 451; there fore mind or spirit, i. 451; th dove selected as the image o the, i, 459; in Scripture, 459; in legends, i. 459; *th colour of the Holy Ghost represented as a dove*, i. 461; as see in the vision of Theutram, i. 463 *the Holy Ghost as man*, i. 467 late introduction and short dura tion of the type, i. 467; paps bull prohibiting its use, i. 468 varying age of the human form of the figure, i. 469; neglect c the use of the figure, i. 473 *qualities peculiar to the Hol Ghost*, i. 474; the seven spirits i Isaiah, i. 474; their order, i. 476 testimony of their order on mon uments to the social condition c the period and country, i. 477 wisdom the highest gift, i. 479 Rhaban Maur's arrangement c the seven gifts, i. 480; the seven gifts in the Apocalypse, i. 481; arrangement in manuscripts, i. 482; omission of one or more, i. 485; Abélard's omission of the spirit of fear in Christ, i. 487; colour and size of the seven doves, i. 490; *chronological iconography of the Holy Ghost*, i. 493; *the attributes of the Holy Ghost*, i. 496; character of the nimbus, i. 496; its frequent absence, i. 497; *heresies against the Holy Ghost*, i. 499; honour paid to the, i. 499; omission of the, in pictures of Pentecost, i. 501; in representations of the Trinity, i. 502; denial of the divinity of the, i. 506

Holy Ghost, order of the, i. 427
'Hortus Deliciarum,' the, i. 50 n., 72 n., 207, 430, 456 n., ii. 9, 34 n., 42, 109
Hugo de St. Victor, ii. 220
Hymettus, church on, i. 70, ii. 107

IMAGES, the number of, in French churches, i. 1; images and figures in churches nearly all religious, i. 2; defence of, by the curé of St. Nizier, i. 2; by Pope Sixtus, i. 3; by St. Benedict Biscop, i. 3; by St. John Damascene, i. 3, ii. 397; by the Synod of Arras, i. 4; by Bishop Geoffrey, i. 4; by St. Paulinus, i. 4; Byzantine Guide on the worship of, ii. 394
Impiety, female figure symbolising, ii. 148
Innocents, murder of the, ii. 407
Ivirôn, angelic hierarchy at, ii. 101–106; the portico, ii. 232

JAMESON, Mrs., quoted, ii. 107, 177, 184, 188
Janus, representations of, ii. 23
Joan of Arc, i. 461
Judas Iscariot, nimbus of, i. 156, 164; betrayal of Christ, ii. 413, 416
Judgment, Last, representations of the, i. 253, 254, 256, 257, ii. 70, 126, 228
Justinian II., decree of, prohibiting the use of the lamb as a symbol of Christ, i. 332; representative of Justice, ii. 251; Dante on, ii. 251; on capital in ducal palace, Venice, ii. 251

KING, C. W. on gems and coins, ii. 155, 171, 172, 174, 181, 196, 201, 202
Kings, the Holy Ghost directing the actions of, i. 449

LAMB, the, the symbol of Christ, sometimes encircled with a cruciform nimbus, i. 56; symbolic of Christ, i. 318; of prophets and apostles, i. 326; of the faithful, i. 328; of the actors in various biblical scenes, i. 330
Laon, cathedral of, i. 18, 155 n., ii. 328 n.
Lazarus, raising of, ii. 410
'Legenda Aurea,' the, referred to, i. 2, 8, 9. 68, 367, 370, 382, 397, 444, ii. 6, 183, 308, 365, 368 n.
Lentulus, description of the appearance of Christ, i. 246
Liberius, pope, nimbus of, i. 77
Limoges, ii. 336
Lion, the, the symbol of Christ, sometimes encircled with a cruciform nimbus, i. 56; the symbol of St. Mark, i. 341; of Christ, i. 341
Liturgy, Greek, i. 307, ii. 230
Living persons, nimbus of, i. 76
Loki, the Scandinavian god of evil, ii. 115
London, National Gallery, ii. 93, 108, 256, 258

MARCELLINA, i. 244
Martyrs of the year, how to represent the, ii. 374
Mary Magdalene, at the feet of Christ, ii. 411; with Christ in the garden, ii. 423
Mary, Virgin, nimbus of the, i. 71; aureole of the i. 121; coronation

of the, i. 444, ii. 426; endowed with the seven gifts of the Holy Spirit, i. 491; the Trinity represented in the womb of the, ii. 59; how to represent the feasts of the, ii. 347; the twenty-four stations of the, ii. 352; physiognomy of the, ii. 395; epithets for the, ii. 396, 398; the annunciation, ii. 403; the purification, ii. 405; Mirror of, 208

Maya, nimbus of, i. 40

Mediæval art and the antique, ii. 244; continued use of heathen images in Christian art, ii. 244; in illuminated manuscripts, ii. 245; in the monasteries of Mount Athos, &c., ii. 245; in the church of St. Michael, Ticino, ii. 245; in the pavement of Siena cathedral, ii. 246

Melchizedeck, nimbus of, i. 69, ii. 270, 414

Mercury and St. Michael, correspondence between, in Pagan and Christian religions, ii. 179, 180, 181, 262

Michael, dedication of rocks to, ii. 181; miracles of, 361

Michelangelo, portrait of Christ in the 'Last Judgment,' i. 261; use of the emblem of three intersecting circles as a seal, ii. 49; inspired by Dante, ii. 251; his 'Mirror of Human Salvation' in the Sistine Chapel, ii. 226

Miniature painting, early practice of, ii. 206; the origin of some Italian schools of artists, ii. 207; Byzantine miniatures on wood, ii. 209

Miracles, how to represent the, of Christ, ii. 303; of the principal saints, ii. 361

'Mirror of Human Salvation,' the, ii. 196; its scheme, ii. 197; correspondence with Milton's 'Paradise Regained,' ii. 200; correspondence of Christian with heathen types, ii. 201; MS. copies, ii. 204; mythological legends in the, ii. 211; legends from Pagan mythology used a types of Christ and the Virgin ii. 211; vision of Astyages before the birth of Cyrus, ii. 211 offering of the golden table in the temple of the sun-god, ii 211; Semiramis, ii. 212; the choice of Moses, ii. 212; fall o the Egyptian idols before th child Christ, ii. 214; voluntar sacrifice of Codrus, king c Athens, ii. 214; myth of th ostrich delivering her young on from a vase, ii. 215; simila legends, ii. 216; the vengeanc of queen Tomyris on the dea body of Cyrus, ii. 217; foot-print of Christ on the mount of Olive ii. 217; 'Universal Mirror,' i. 8 ii. 221

Monk, how to represent the life the true, ii. 378

Monuments, figures on early Chris tian, denoting trades, i. 352

Moon, nimbus of the, i. 86

Moses, choice of the child, legend of the, ii. 212

Mystery plays, ii. 233; St. Francis celebration of the nativity c Christ, ii. 233; at Ammergar ii. 235; 'Mary's Lament,' i 236; St. Avitus' play on the fa of Adam, ii. 237; other plays, i 237; the 'Acts of the Apostle and St. Dionysius the Areo pagite,' ii. 239; representation i a miniature from this play, i 239; mediæval stage direction. ii. 240

Myths and allegories, differenc between, i. 343

NAMATIUS, bishop, tomb of, ii. 19 Nimbus, the, used to denote a hol person, i. 22; its importance i Christian art, i. 22; restriction the term to that encircling th head, i. 24; *definition of the*, 25; etymology and meaning the word, i. 25; *form of the*, 28; difference in form in Christia and Pagan iconography, i. 3

application of the, i. 37; ordinarily the attribute of divinity, i. 37; exceptions, i. 37; *nimbus of God*, i. 38; distinguished by intersecting bars, i. 38; that of Christ sometimes by a cross, i. 40; at first simple and undecorated, i. 50; the hand of God the Father sometimes encircled by a cruciform nimbus, i. 55; generally round, i. 57; sometimes triangular or square, i. 58; the triangular form retained as an emblem of the Trinity, i. 58; sometimes bi-triangular, i. 59; the triangular form confined to the Deity, chiefly to God the Father, i. 59; variations of form in different countries, i. 62; the square form generally given to living persons, i. 63; but sometimes worn by God the Father, i. 63; explanation, i. 63; ornamentation of the field, i. 65; *nimbus of angels and saints*, i. 66, ii. 96; ornamentation, i. 66; nimbus of the patriarchs, i. 68; of Melchizedeck, i. 69; of prophets, i. 69, 154; of kings, i. 69; of St. John the Baptist, i. 70; of St. Joseph, i. 71; of the Virgin Mary, i. 71; of the Apostles, i. 72; decoration and material of the nimbus, i. 73; custom of writing the name or monogram of a saint on the edge, i. 74; *nimbus of persons living*, i. 76; inferiority of the square form, i. 77; the square form peculiar to Italy, i. 79; varieties in form, i. 79; hexagonal form, i. 81; *nimbus of allegorical beings*, i. 83, 154; of the virtues, i. 83; of the moon, i. 86; of the sun, i. 87; of the attributes of the four evangelists, i. 87; of Satan black, i. 88, 157, 164; *signification of the nimbus*, i. 89; in the east, power, i. 89, 153; in the west, holiness, i. 90, 161; inference from presence or absence of, i. 90; *history of the nimbus*, i. 92; preference of the head over the body, i. 92; the heads of chiefs and nobles adorned with crowns of different degrees, i. 94; the heads of saints and martyrs with nimbi of various forms, i. 96; sometimes employed by pagans, i. 96; phases in the history, i. 97; nimbus of Judas Iscariot black, i. 156, 164; of the dragon of the Apocalypse, i. 159; *colour of the*, i. 163; not always symbolic, i. 165

ORANTE, origin of the type, ii. 195
Orcagna, portrait of Christ in the 'Last Judgment,' i. 261; his treatment of death, ii. 157; his illustrations of the 'Three Deaths and Three Lives,' ii. 164
Ormuzd and Ahriman, contest between, i. 464

PALMIERI, Matteo, ii. 256
Parables, how to represent the, ii. 322
Paris, Notre Dame de, early Christian art in the, i. 71, 122, 183, 207, ii. 230, 241, 320, 328, 331; St. Denis, ii. 131, 337; St. Geneviève, i. 128, 217, 296, 301, 323, 454; St. Gervais, Perugino, 452
Patriarchs, nimbus of the, i. 68
Pesello, Francesco di, his painting of the Trinity, ii. 255
Petrarch's Triumph of Death, ii. 157, 259
Philosophers of Greece, how to represent the, who have spoken of the incarnation of Christ, ii. 297
Pisa, Campo Santo at, i. 262, 287, ii. 76, 94, 118, 120, 129, 141, 158, 159, 160, 161, 162, 164, 165, 209
Plato, his doctrine of the Trinity, ii. 1
Poitiers, missal of, the devil as ruler of hell in the, ii. 118.
Pope, the, represented by Dante in the form of a bird, i. 457
Procession of the Holy Ghost, doctrine of the, denied by the Greek church, ii. 72
Psyche, fable of, ii. 174

2 G

RAPHAEL, his 'Disputà,' referred to, i. 64, 74, 104, 230; frescoes of, in the Vatican, ii. 229; subject of Byzantine origin, the 'Mystagogia,' ii. 230; the 'Communion in Heaven,' ii. 230
Ravenna, i. 340 n., ii. 195
Ravenna, mosaic, i. 396
Renaissance, the, ii. 50, 244
Rhaban Maur, arrangement of the seven gifts of the Spirit, i. 480
Rheims cathedral, scenes from the life of Christ and the Apocalypse in, ii. 225; early Christian art in, i. 17, 29, 72, 156, 174, 177, 231, 279, 307, 323, 354, 371, 475, ii. 225, 280, 328, 336, 337, 340, 383; Jouy, near, 281
Richard de St. Victor, definition of Persons of Trinity, ii. 9
'Romant des trois Pèlerinages,' the, i. 294
Rome, ancient basilica of St. Peter at, i. 77; church of St. Cæcilia at, i. 76; San Giovanni in Laterano, i. 64, 65, 82; Sta. Maria Nova, mosaic, i. 206
Rose-window, i. 109, 143, ii. 249, 383

ST. AMBROSE, definition of the Persons of the Trinity, ii. 7
St. Angilbert, design of monastery of St. Riquier, ii. 32
St. Ansgar, description of the appearance of Christ, i. 248; the supposed author of the 'Biblia Pauperum,' ii. 202
St. Anthony, how to represent the miracles of, ii. 372
St. Augustine, definition of the Persons of the Trinity, ii. 7
St. Avitus, mystery play on the fall of Adam, ii. 237
St. Benedict Biscop, defence of images, i. 3, 17
St. Catherine of Alexandria, i. 428
St. Catherine, how to represent the miracles of, ii. 371
St. Christopher, represented as carrying the Trinity, ii. 59
St. Cyril of Alexandria, description of Christ, i. 268

St. Dionysius the Areopagite, definition of fire, i. 140; classification of the angelic hierarchy and symbols, ii. 98; quoted, i. 140
St. Dunstan, i. 426, 468, ii. 40
St. Francis, celebration of the nativity of Christ, ii. 233
St. George, how to represent the miracles of, ii. 369
St. Jerome, inspired by the Holy Spirit, i. 448; on the period of the creation of angels, ii. 87
St. John Damascene, defence of images. i. 3, ii. 397; on representations of the Deity, i. 198, 242, 256; description of the appearance of Christ, i. 247; on the period of the creation of angels, ii. 87
St. John the Baptist, nimbus of, i. 70; depicted as carrying the Lamb of God, i. 321; his place in the hierarchy of angels, ii. 104, 107; how to represent the miracles of, ii. 362; inscriptions for, ii. 398; baptizing Christ, ii. 408
St. Joseph, nimbus of, i. 71; the Holy Ghost as a white dove escaping from the flowering staff of, i. 446
St. Juliana, temptation of, by the devil disguised as an angel, ii. 130
St. Michael, order of, i. 427; his office at the judgment day, ii. 178; dedication of rocks and high places to, ii. 181; his part in the Hebrew religion and Christian drama, ii. 183; struggle of, and the dragon, ii. 185
St. Nicholas, how to represent the miracles of, ii. 368
St. Paphnutius, the temptation of, ii. 129, 261
St. Paul, how to represent the miracles of, ii. 367
St. Paulinus, defence of images, i. 4; description of a group of the Trinity, ii. 35, 39
St. Peter, how to represent the miracles of, ii. 366
St. Remi, i. 135, 150, 459; legend of, and the fire at Rheims, ii. 116

St. Riquier, monastery of, ii. 32
St. Sophia, legend of, and Faith, Hope, and Charity, ii. 33
St. Theresa, inspired by the Holy Spirit, i. 449
St. Thomas, legend of, ii. 5; illustrations of the doctrine of the Trinity, ii. 5
St. Thomas Aquinas, ii. 8
St. Veronica, description of angels, ii. 97
Salamis, church at, i. 114, 210
Salonica, i. 190, 393
Satan, nimbus of, i. 88, 157
Sayce, Mr., quoted, ii. 212, 219
Sedgeford church, ii. 59 n.
Semiramis, a type of the Virgin, ii. 211
Shakespeare, allusions to death and the fool in, ii. 170
Siena cathedral, pavement of, ii. 246
Sign of the cross: *see* Cross.
Sistine chapel, the scheme of the Old and New Law in the, ii. 226; Michelangelo's 'Mirror of Human Salvation' in the, ii. 226
Soul, iconography of the, ii. 173; Egyptian emblems of the, ii. 173; the, according to the ancients, delivered with the last breath through the mouth, ii. 173; the fable of Psyche, ii. 174; the, figured as little child, ii. 176; the weighing of souls in the balance at the Judgment Day the office at St. Michael, ii. 178; of Mercury in Pagan art, ii. 179
'Speculum Humanæ Salvationis': *see* 'Mirror of Human Salvation.'
'Speculum Universale,' i. 9, 10; excellence of its arrangement, i. 10; outline of, i. 11; the order of, followed by the sculptors of Chartres cathedral, ii. 221; the 'Mirror of Nature,' ii. 222; the 'Mirror of Doctrine,' ii. 223; the 'Historical Mirror,' ii. 225; date of the, ii. 225
Spinello, painting of Struggle of St. Michael and the dragon, ii. 186

Spirits, colours of good and evil, i. 465
Square form of nimbus, inferiority of, i. 77
Strasburg, cathedral of, i. 23, 74, 463, ii. 328 n.
Study of statues and effigies, i. 18
'Summa Theologiæ,' St. Thomas's, i. 9
Sun, nimbus of the, i. 87
Symbols and figures, difference between, i. 342, 351
Synods, the seven holy, how to represent the, ii. 358

TARASQUE, the monster of the, ii. 115, 259
Tau, the, a sign, i. 370
Temptation of Christ, representation of the, i. 276
Tertullian, description of Christ, i. 268
Thanatos, statue of, ii. 153
Thessaly, i. 46
Theutram, the vision of, i. 463
Three, the number, mystical properties of, ii. 3; sacredness of, ii. 26
Time, figures of, with three faces, ii. 24
Tomyris, queen, legend of the vengeance of, on the dead body of Cyrus, ii. 217
Toulouse, i. 370n
Trades, figures denoting, on early Christian monuments, i. 352
Triads of Britain, ii. 26
Triangle, symbolic properties of the, i. 59, 61; the, used as an image of the Trinity, ii. 41
Trinitarians, order of the, ii. 30
Trinity; *history of the doctrine of the*, ii. 1; vaguely known to the Pagans, ii. 1; Plato's doctrine, ii. 1; Seneca's, ii. 2; ideas of the Greeks, ii. 3; mystical properties of the number three, ii. 3; legend of St. Thomas, ii. 5; his illustrations of the doctrine of the Trinity, ii. 5; *definition of the Divine Persons of the*, ii. 6; St. Augustine's opinions, ii. 7; doc-

trine of St. Ambrose, ii. 7; of St. Thomas Aquinas, ii. 8; of Richard de St. Victor, ii. 9; of Abélard, ii. 10; the sign of the cross and the doctrine of the, ii. 11; mutual relations of the Divine Persons, ii. 12; *manifestations of the*, ii. 13; unsatisfactory evidence from the Old Testament, ii. 13; at the creation, ii. 13; at the visit of the three angels to Abraham, ii. 16; in the Psalms, ii. 16; Ananias, Misaël and Azarias typical of the Trinity, ii. 18; doctrine of the, in the New Testament, ii. 20; trinity of the human soul, ii. 21; trinity of evil, ii. 22; Janus, ii. 23; figures of time with three faces, ii. 24; sacredness of the number three, ii. 26; *the worship of the*, ii. 28; festival of the, ii. 28; order of the Trinitarians. ii. 28; churches and monasteries erected in honour of the Trinity, ii. 30; monastery of St. Riquier, ii. 32; *chronological iconography of the*, ii. 34; four periods, ii. 35; first period, of preparation, ii. 35; description by St. Paulinus of a group of the Trinity, ii. 36; the, dramatised by Chosroes, ii. 37; disposition of the symbols, ii. 39 : second period, ii. 39; human figures of the three Persons, ii. 40; the triangle used as an image of the, ii. 41; third period, ii. 43; the, represented by three heads on one body, ii. 44; three intersecting circles a type of the, ii. 45; Dante's adoption of it, ii. 47; its use as a seal by Michelangelo, ii. 49; fourth period, ii. 49; extended use of previous figures, ii. 50; St. Christopher represented as carrying the, ii. 59; the, represented in the womb of the Virgin, ii. 59; papal decree on representations of the, ii. 61; *attributes of the*, ii. 63, 255; differences in the figures, ii. 63; the three Persons at first isolated, ii. 65, 255; in contact, ii. 66 fusion into one body with three heads, ii. 67; fusion of the three heads into one with three faces, ii. 67; the Father sometimes placed on the right of the Son, ii. 68; the Holy Spirit in the centre, ii. 71; triangular nimbus round a grouped Trinity, ii. 73; head-dress of the, ii. 74; use of the globe in representations of the, ii. 77; inscriptions for the, ii. 80, 395; the three Persons represented with bare feet, ii. 81; exceptions, ii. 81, 255

Triumph of Christ: *see* God the Son.

Troyes, cathedral of St. Nizier de, early Christian art in, i. 154, 163, 226, 325, 326, 502, ii. 70, 137, 328 *n.*, 336 *n.*

Twining, Miss L., quoted, ii. 156, 168

Typhon, ii. 122, 123

VATICAN, frescoes of Raphael in the, ii. 229; the 'Mystagogia,' ii. 230; the 'Communion in Heaven,' ii. 230; early Christian art in the, i. 41, 53, 67, 86, 98, 172, 349, ii. 139

Vendôme, Montorio church, i. 44

Venice, St. Mark's at, ii.; Ducal Palace at, 251; St. Mark's, 176, 240

Verrières sur l'Aube, church of, 494

Vincent de Beauvais, i. 9, 10, ii. 221, 225

Virtues, nimbus of the, i. 83

Voragine, Jacques de, i. 8, 9, 68 ii. 5, 37, 38.

WALDSTEIN, Dr., quoted, ii. 218, 234

AN
ALPHABETICAL LIST

OF BOOKS CONTAINED IN

BOHN'S LIBRARIES.

Detailed Catalogue, arranged according to the various Libraries, will be sent on application.

ADDISON'S Works. With the Notes of Bishop Hurd, Portrait, and 8 Plates of Medals and Coins. Edited by H. G. Bohn. 6 vols. 3s. 6d. each.

ÆSCHYLUS, The Dramas of. Translated into English Verse by Anna Swanwick. 4th Edition, revised. 5s.

—— **The Tragedies of.** Translated into Prose by T. A. Buckley, B.A. 3s. 6d.

AGASSIZ and GOULD'S Outline of Comparative Physiology. Enlarged by Dr. Wright. With 390 Woodcuts. 5s.

ALFIERI'S Tragedies. Translated into English Verse by Edgar A. Bowring, C.B. 2 vols. 3s. 6d. each.

ALLEN'S (Joseph, R. N.) Battles of the British Navy. Revised Edition, with 57 Steel Engravings. 2 vols. 5s. each.

AMMIANUS MARCELLINUS. History of Rome during the Reigns of Constantius, Julian, Jovianus, Valentinian, and Valens.

Translated by Prof. C. D. Yonge, M.A. 7s. 6d.

ANDERSEN'S Danish Legends and Fairy Tales. Translated by Caroline Peachey. With 120 Wood Engravings. 5s.

ANTONINUS (M. Aurelius), The Thoughts of. Trans. literally, with Notes and Introduction by George Long, M.A. 3s. 6d.

APOLLONIUS RHODIUS. 'The Argonautica.' Translated by E. P. Coleridge, B.A.

APPIAN'S Roman History. Translated by Horace White, M.A., LL.D. With Maps and Illustrations. 2 vols. 6s. each.

APULEIUS, The Works of. Comprising the Golden Ass, God of Socrates, Florida, and Discourse of Magic. 5s.

ARIOSTO'S Orlando Furioso. Translated into English Verse by W. S. Rose. With Portrait, and 24 Steel Engravings. 2 vols. 5s. each.

ARISTOPHANES' Comedies. Translated by W. J. Hickie. 2 vols. 5s. each.

ARISTOTLE'S Nicomachean Ethics. Translated, with Introduction and Notes, by the Venerable Archdeacon Browne. 5s.

—— **Politics and Economics.** Translated by E. Walford, M.A., with Introduction by Dr. Gillies. 5s.

—— **Metaphysics.** Translated by the Rev. John H. M'Mahon, M.A. 5s.

—— **History of Animals.** Trans. by Richard Cresswell, M.A. 5s.

—— **Organon**; or, Logical Treatises, and the Introduction of Porphyry. Translated by the Rev. O. F. Owen, M.A. 2 vols. 3s. 6d. each.

—— **Rhetoric and Poetics.** Trans. by T. Buckley, B.A. 5s.

ARRIAN'S Anabasis of Alexander, together with the **Indica.** Translated by E. J. Chinnock, M.A., LL.D. With Maps and Plans. 5s.

ATHENÆUS. The Deipnosophists; or, the Banquet of the Learned. Trans. by Prof. C. D. Yonge, M.A. 3 vols. 5s. each.

BACON'S Moral and Historical Works, including the Essays, Apophthegms, Wisdom of the Ancients, New Atlantis, Henry VII., Henry VIII., Elizabeth, Henry Prince of Wales, History of Great Britain, Julius Cæsar, and Augustus Cæsar. Edited by J. Devey, M.A. 3s. 6d.

—— **Novum Organum** and **Advancement of Learning.** Edited by J. Devey, M.A. 5s.

BASS'S Lexicon to the Greek Testament. 2s.

BAX'S Manual of the History of Philosophy, for the use of Students. By E. Belfort Bax. 5s.

BEAUMONT and FLETCHER, their finest Scenes, Lyrics, and other Beauties, selected from the whole of their works, and edited by Leigh Hunt. 3s. 6d.

BECHSTEIN'S Cage and Chamber Birds, their Natural History, Habits, Food, Diseases, and Modes of Capture. Translated, with considerable additions on Structure, Migration, and Economy, by H. G. Adams. Together with SWEET BRITISH WARBLERS. With 43 coloured Plates and Woodcut Illustrations. 5s.

BEDE'S (Venerable) Ecclesiastical History of England. Together with the ANGLO-SAXON CHRONICLE. Edited by J. A. Giles, D.C.L. With Map. 5s.

BELL (Sir Charles). The Anatomy and Philosophy of Expression, as connected with the Fine Arts. By Sir Charles Bell, K.H. 7th edition, revised. 5s.

BERKELEY (George), Bishop of Cloyne, The Works of. Edited by George Sampson. With Biographical Introduction by the Right Hon. A. J. Balfour, M.P. 3 vols. 5s. each.

BION. See THEOCRITUS.

BJÖRNSON'S Arne and the Fisher Lassie. Translated by W. H. Low, M.A. 3s. 6d.

BLAIR'S Chronological Tables Revised and Enlarged. Comprehending the Chronology and History of the World, from the Earliest Times to the Russian Treaty of Peace, April 1856. By J. Willoughby Rosse. Double vol. 10s.

BLAIR'S Index of Dates. Comprehending the principal Facts in the Chronology and History of the World, alphabetically arranged; being a complete Index to Blair's Chronological Tables. By J. W. Rosse. 2 vols. 5s. each.

BLEEK, Introduction to the Old Testament. By Friedrich Bleek. Edited by Johann Bleek and Adolf Kamphausen. Translated by G. H. Venables, under the supervision of the Rev. Canon Venables. 2 vols. 5s. each.

BOETHIUS'S Consolation of Philosophy. King Alfred's Anglo-Saxon Version of. With a literal English Translation on opposite pages, Notes, Introduction, and Glossary, by Rev. S. Fox, M.A. 5s.

BOHN'S Dictionary of Poetical Quotations. 4th edition. 6s.

—— **Handbooks of Athletic Sports.** In 8 vols., each containing numerous Illustrations. 3s. 6d. each.
I.—Cricket, Lawn Tennis, Tennis, Rackets, Fives, Golf.
II.—Rowing and Sculling, Sailing, Swimming.
III.—Boxing, Broadsword, Single Stick, &c., Wrestling, Fencing.
IV.—Rugby Football, Association Football, Baseball, Rounders, Fieldball, Quoits, Skittles, Bowls,

BOHN'S Handbooks of Games. New edition. In 2 vols., with numerous Illustrations 3s. 6d. each.
Vol. I.—TABLE GAMES:—Billiards, Chess, Draughts, Backgammon, Dominoes, Solitaire, Reversi, Go-Bang, Rouge et Noir, Roulette, E.O., Hazard, Faro.
Vol. II. — CARD GAMES: — Whist, Solo Whist, Poker, Piquet, Ecarté, Euchre, Bézique, Cribbage, Loo, Vingt-et-un, Napoleon, Newmarket, Pope Joan, Speculation, &c., &c.

BOND'S A Handy Book of Rules and Tables for verifying Dates with the Christian Era, &c. Giving an account of the Chief Eras and Systems used by various Nations; with the easy Methods for determining the Corresponding Dates. By J. J. Bond. 5s.

BONOMI'S Nineveh and its Palaces. 7 Plates and 294 Woodcut Illustrations. 5s.

BOSWELL'S Life of Johnson, with the TOUR IN THE HEBRIDES and JOHNSONIANA. Edited by the Rev. A. Napier, M.A. With Frontispiece to each vol. 6 vols. 3s. 6d. each.

BRAND'S Popular Antiquities of England, Scotland, and Ireland. Arranged, revised, and greatly enlarged, by Sir Henry Ellis, K.H., F.R.S., &c., &c. 3 vols. 5s. each.

BREMER'S (Frederika) Works. Translated by Mary Howitt. 4 vols. 3s. 6d. each.

BRIDGWATER TREATISES *continued.*

Kidd on the Adaptation of External Nature to the Physical Condition of Man. 3s. 6d.

Chalmers on the Adaptation of External Nature to the Moral and Intellectual Constitution of Man. 5s.

BRINK (B. ten) Early English Literature. By Bernhard ten Brink. Vol. I. To Wyclif. Translated by Horace M. Kennedy. 3s. 6d.

Vol. II. Wyclif, Chaucer, Earliest Drama Renaissance. Translated by W. Clarke Robinson, Ph.D. 3s. 6d.

Vol. III. From the Fourteenth Century to the Death of Surrey. Edited by Dr. Alois Brandl. Trans. by L. Dora Schmitz. 3s. 6d.

—— Five Lectures on Shakespeare. Trans. by Julia Franklin. 3s. 6d.

BROWNE'S (Sir Thomas) Works Edited by Simon Wilkin. 3 vols. 3s. 6d. each.

BURKE'S Works. 8 vols. 3s. 6d. each.

I.—Vindication of Natural Society—Essay on the Sublime and Beautiful, and various Political Miscellanies.

II.—Reflections on the French Revolution— Letters relating to the Bristol Election— Speech on Fox's East India Bill, &c.

III.—Appeal from the New to the Old Whigs—On the Nabob of Arcot's Debts— The Catholic Claims, &c.

BURKE'S WORKS *continued.*

IV.—Report on the Affairs of India, and Articles of Charge against Warren Hastings.

V.—Conclusion of the Articles of Charge against Warren Hastings—Political Letters on the American War, on a Regicide Peace, to the Empress of Russia.

VI.—Miscellaneous Speeches— Letters and Fragments— Abridgments of English History, &c. With a General Index.

VII. & VIII.—Speeches on the Impeachment of Warren Hastings; and Letters. With Index. 2 vols. 3s. 6d. each.

—— Life. By Sir J. Prior. 3s. 6d.

BURNEY'S Evelina. By Frances Burney (Mme. D'Arblay). With an Introduction and Notes by A. R. Ellis. 3s. 6d.

—— Cecilia. With an Introduction and Notes by A. R. Ellis. 2 vols. 3s. 6d. each.

BURN (R.) Ancient Rome and its Neighbourhood. An Illustrated Handbook to the Ruins in the City and the Campagna, for the use of Travellers. By Robert Burn, M.A. With numerous Illustrations, Maps, and Plans. 7s. 6d.

BURNS (Robert), Life of. By J. G. Lockhart, D.C.L. A new and enlarged Edition. Revised by William Scott Douglas. 3s. 6d.

BURTON'S (Robert) Anatomy of Melancholy. Edited by the Rev. A. R. Shilleto, M.A. With Introduction by A. H. Bullen, and full Index. 3 vols. 3s. 6d. each.

BURTON (Sir R. F.) Personal Narrative of a Pilgrimage to Al-Madinah and Meccah. By Captain Sir Richard F. Burton, K.C.M.G. With an Introduction by Stanley Lane-Poole, and all the original Illustrations. 2 vols. 3s. 6d. each.

∗ This is the copyright edition, containing the author's latest notes.

BUTLER'S (Bishop) Analogy of Religion, Natural and Revealed, to the Constitution and Course of Nature; together with two Dissertations on Personal Identity and on the Nature of Virtue, and Fifteen Sermons. 3s. 6d.

BUTLER'S (Samuel) Hudibras. With Variorum Notes, a Biography, Portrait, and 28 Illustrations. 5s.

—— or, further Illustrated with 60 Outline Portraits. 2 vols. 5s. each.

CÆSAR. Commentaries on the Gallic and Civil Wars, Translated by W. A. McDevitte, B.A. 5s.

CAMOENS' Lusiad; or, the Discovery of India. An Epic Poem. Translated by W. J. Mickle. 5th Edition, revised by E. R. Hodges, M.C.P. 3s. 6d.

CARAFAS (The) of Maddaloni. Naples under Spanish Dominion. Translated from the German of Alfred de Reumont. 3s. 6d.

CARLYLE'S French Revolution. Edited by J. Holland Rose, Litt.D. Illus. 3 vols. 5s. each.

—— **Sartor Resartus.** With 75 Illustrations by Edmund J. Sullivan. 5s.

CARPENTER'S (Dr. W. B.) Zoology. Revised Edition, by W. S. Dallas, F.L.S. With very numerous Woodcuts. Vol. I. 6s. [Vol. II. out of print.

CARPENTER'S Mechanical Philosophy, Astronomy, and Horology. 181 Woodcuts. 5s.

—— **Vegetable Physiology and Systematic Botany.** Revised Edition, by E. Lankester, M.D., &c. With very numerous Woodcuts. 6s.

—— **Animal Physiology.** Revised Edition. With upwards of 300 Woodcuts. 6s.

CASTLE (E.) Schools and Masters of Fence, from the Middle Ages to the End of the Eighteenth Century. By Egerton Castle, M.A., F.S.A. With a Complete Bibliography. Illustrated with 140 Reproductions of Old Engravings and 6 Plates of Swords, showing 114 Examples. 6s.

CATTERMOLE'S Evenings at Haddon Hall. With 24 Engravings on Steel from designs by Cattermole, the Letterpress by the Baroness de Carabella. 5s.

CATULLUS, Tibullus, and the Vigil of Venus. A Literal Prose Translation. 5s.

CELLINI (Benvenuto). Memoirs of, written by Himself. Translated by Thomas Roscoe. 3s. 6d.

CERVANTES' Don Quixote de la Mancha. Motteaux's Translation revised. 2 vols. 3s. 6d. each.

—— **Galatea.** A Pastoral Romance. Translated by G. W. J. Gyll. 3s. 6d.

—— **Exemplary Novels.** Translated by Walter K. Kelly. 3s. 6d.

CHAUCER'S Poetical Works. Edited by Robert Bell. Revised Edition, with a Preliminary Essay by Prof. W. W. Skeat, M.A. 4 vols. 3s. 6d. each.

An Alphabetical List of Books

CHESS CONGRESS of 1862. A Collection of the Games played. Edited by J. Löwenthal. 5s.

CHEVREUL on Colour. Translated from the French by Charles Martel. Third Edition, with Plates, 5s.; or with an additional series of 16 Plates in Colours, 7s. 6d.

CHILLINGWORTH'S Religion of Protestants. A Safe Way to Salvation. 3s. 6d.

CHINA, Pictorial, Descriptive, and Historical. With Map and nearly 100 Illustrations. 5s.

CHRONICLES OF THE CRUSADES. Contemporary Narratives of the Crusade of Richard Cœur de Lion, by Richard of Devizes and Geoffrey de Vinsauf; and of the Crusade at St. Louis, by Lord John de Joinville. 5s.

CICERO'S Orations. Translated by Prof. C. D. Yonge, M.A. 4 vols. 5s. each.

—— **Letters.** Translated by Evelyn S. Shuckburgh. 4 vols. 5s. each.

—— **On Oratory and Orators.** With Letters to Quintus and Brutus. Translated by the Rev. J. S. Watson, M.A. 5s.

—— **On the Nature of the Gods,** Divination, Fate, Laws, a Republic, Consulship. Translated by Prof. C. D. Yonge, M.A., and Francis Barham. 5s.

—— **Academics,** De Finibus, and Tusculan Questions. By Prof. C. D. Yonge, M.A. 5s.

CICERO'S Offices; or, Moral Duties. Cato Major, an Essay on Old Age; Lælius, an Essay on Friendship; Scipio's Dream; Paradoxes; Letter to Quintus on Magistrates. Translated by C. R. Edmonds. 3s. 6d.

CORNELIUS NEPOS.—See JUSTIN.

CLARK'S (Hugh) Introduction to Heraldry. 18th Edition, Revised and Enlarged by J. R. Planché, Rouge Croix. With nearly 1000 Illustrations. 5s. Or with the Illustrations Coloured, 15s.

CLASSIC TALES, containing Rasselas, Vicar of Wakefield, Gulliver's Travels, and The Sentimental Journey. 3s. 6d.

COLERIDGE'S (S. T.) Friend. A Series of Essays on Morals, Politics, and Religion. 3s. 6d.

—— **Aids to Reflection,** and the CONFESSIONS OF AN INQUIRING SPIRIT, to which are added the ESSAYS ON FAITH and the BOOK OF COMMON PRAYER. 3s. 6d.

—— **Lectures and Notes on Shakespeare and other English Poets.** Edited by T. Ashe. 3s. 6d.

—— **Biographia Literaria;** together with Two Lay Sermons. 3s. 6d.

—— **Table-Talk and Omniana.** Edited by T. Ashe, B.A. 3s. 6d.

—— **Miscellanies, Æsthetic and Literary;** to which is added, THE THEORY OF LIFE. Collected and arranged by T. Ashe, B.A. 3s. 6d.

COMTE'S Positive Philosophy. Translated and condensed by Harriet Martineau. With Introduction by Frederic Harrison. 3 vols. 5s. each.

COMTE'S Philosophy of the Sciences, being an Exposition of the Principles of the *Cours de Philosophie Positive*. By G. H. Lewes. 5s.

CONDÉ'S History of the Dominion of the Arabs in Spain. Translated by Mrs. Foster. 3 vols. 3s. 6d. each.

COOPER'S Biographical Dictionary. Containing Concise Notices (upwards of 15,000) of Eminent Persons of all Ages and Countries. By Thompson Cooper, F.S.A. With a Supplement, bringing the work down to 1883. 2 vols. 5s. each.

COXE'S Memoirs of the Duke of Marlborough. With his original Correspondence. By W. Coxe, M.A., F.R.S. Revised edition by John Wade. 3 vols. 3s. 6d. each.

*** An Atlas of the plans of Marlborough's campaigns, 4to. 10s. 6d.

—— **History of the House of Austria** (1218-1792). With a Continuation from the Accession of Francis I. to the Revolution of 1848. 4 vols. 3s. 6d. each.

CRAIK'S (G. L.) Pursuit of Knowledge under Difficulties. Illustrated by Anecdotes and Memoirs. Revised edition, with numerous Woodcut Portraits and Plates. 5s.

CRUIKSHANK'S Punch and Judy. The Dialogue of the Puppet Show; an Account of its Origin, &c. With 24 Illustrations, and Coloured Plates, designed and engraved by G. Cruikshank. 5s.

CUNNINGHAM'S Lives of the Most Eminent British Painters. A New Edition, with Notes and Sixteen fresh Lives. By Mrs. Heaton. 3 vols. 3s. 6d. each.

DANTE. Divine Comedy. Translated by the Rev. H. F. Cary, M.A. 3s. 6d.

—— Translated into English Verse by I. C. Wright, M.A. 3rd Edition, revised. With Portrait, and 34 Illustrations on Steel, after Flaxman.

DANTE. The Inferno. A Literal Prose Translation, with the Text of the Original printed on the same page. By John A. Carlyle, M.D. 5s.

—— **The Purgatorio.** A Literal Prose Translation, with the Text printed on the same page. By W. S. Dugdale. 5s.

DE COMMINES (Philip), Memoirs of. Containing the Histories of Louis XI. and Charles VIII., Kings of France, and Charles the Bold, Duke of Burgundy. Together with the Scandalous Chronicle, or Secret History of Louis XI., by Jean de Troyes. Translated by Andrew R. Scoble. With Portraits. 2 vols. 3s. 6d. each.

DEFOE'S Novels and Miscellaneous Works. With Prefaces and Notes, including those attributed to Sir W. Scott. 7 vols. 3s. 6d. each.

I.—Captain Singleton, and Colonel Jack.

II.—Memoirs of a Cavalier, Captain Carleton, Dickory Cronke, &c.

III.—Moll Flanders, and the History of the Devil.

IV.—Roxana, and Life of Mrs. Christian Davies.

V.—History of the Great Plague of London, 1665; The Storm (1703); and the True-born Englishman.

VI.—Duncan Campbell, New Voyage round the World, and Political Tracts.

VII.—Robinson Crusoe.

DE LOLME on the Constitution of England. Edited by John Macgregor. 3s. 6d.

DEMMIN'S History of Arms and Armour. from the Earliest Period. By Auguste Demmin. Translated by C. C. Black, M.A. With nearly 2000 Illustrations. 7s. 6d.

DEMOSTHENES' Orations. Translated by C. Rann Kennedy. 5 vols. Vol. I., 3s. 6d.; Vols. II.–V., 5s. each.

DE STAËL'S Corinne or Italy. By Madame de Staël. Translated by Emily Baldwin and Paulina Driver. 3s. 6d.

DEVEY'S Logic, or the Science of Inference. A Popular Manual. By J. Devey. 5s.

DICTIONARY of Latin and Greek Quotations; including Proverbs, Maxims, Mottoes, Law Terms and Phrases. With all the Quantities marked, and English Translations. With Index Verborum (622 pages). 5s.

DICTIONARY of Obsolete and Provincial English. Compiled by Thomas Wright, M.A., F.S A., &c. 2 vols. 5s. each.

DIDRON·'S Christian Iconography: a History of Christian Art in the Middle Ages. Translated by E. J. Millington and completed by Margaret Stokes. With 240 Illustrations. 2 vols. 5s. each.

DIOGENES LAERTIUS. Lives and Opinions of the Ancient Philosophers. Translated by Prof. C. D. Yonge, M.A. 5s.

DOBREE'S Adversaria. Edited by the late Prof. Wagner. 2 vols. 5s. each.

DODD'S Epigrammatists. A Selection from the Epigrammatic Literature of Ancient, Mediæval, and Modern Times. By the Rev. Henry Philip Dodd, M.A. Oxford. 2nd Edition, revised and enlarged. 6s.

DONALDSON'S The Theatre of the Greeks. A Treatise on the History and Exhibition of the Greek Drama. With numerous Illustrations and 3 Plans. By John William Donaldson, D.D. 5s.

DRAPER'S History of the Intellectual Development of Europe. By John William Draper, M.D., LL.D. 2 vols. 5s. each.

DUNLOP'S History of Fiction. A new Edition. Revised by Henry Wilson. 2 vols. 5s. each.

DYER (Dr T. H.). Pompeii: its Buildings and Antiquities. By T. H. Dyer, LL.D. With nearly 300 Wood Engravings, a large Map, and a Plan of the Forum. 7s. 6d.

—— **The City of Rome**: its History and Monuments. With Illustrations. 5s.

DYER (T. F. T.) British Popular Customs, Present and Past. An Account of the various Games and Customs associated with Different Days of the Year in the British Isles, arranged according to the Calendar. By the Rev. T. F. Thiselton Dyer, M.A. 5s.

EBERS' Egyptian Princess. An Historical Novel. By George Ebers. Translated by E. S. Buchheim. 3s. 6d.

EDGEWORTH'S Stories for Children. With 8 Illustrations by L. Speed. 3s. 6d.

ELZE'S William Shakespeare. —*See* SHAKESPEARE.

EMERSON'S Works. 3 vols 3s. 6d. each.

I.—Essays, Lectures and Poems.

II.—English Traits, Nature, and Conduct of Life.

EMERSON'S WORKS *continued.*
III.—Society and Solitude—Letters and Social aims — Miscellaneous Papers (hitherto uncollected) — May Day, and other Poems.

ELLIS (G.) Specimens of Early English Metrical Romances. With an Historical Introduction on the Rise and Progress of Romantic Composition in France and England. Revised Edition. By J. O. Halliwell, F.R.S. 5s.

ENNEMOSER'S History of Magic. Translated by William Howitt. 2 vols. 5s. each.

EPICTETUS, The Discourses of. With the ENCHEIRIDION and Fragments. Translated by George Long, M.A. 5s.

EURIPIDES. A New Literal Translation in Prose. By E P. Coleridge, M.A. 2 vols. 5s. each.

EUTROPIUS.—*See* JUSTIN.

EUSEBIUS PAMPHILUS, Ecclesiastical History of. Translated by Rev. C. F. Cruse, M.A. 5s.

EVELYN'S Diary and Correspondendence. Edited from the Original MSS. by W. Bray, F.A.S. With 45 engravings. 4 vols. 5s. each.

FAIRHOLT'S Costume in England. A History of Dress to the end of the Eighteenth Century. 3rd Edition, revised, by Viscount Dillon, V.P.S.A. Illustrated with above 700 Engravings. 2 vols. 5s. each.

FIELDING'S Adventures of Joseph Andrews and his Friend Mr. Abraham Adams. With Cruikshank's Illustrations. 3s. 6d.

—— History of Tom Jones, a Foundling. With Cruikshank's Illustrations. 2 vols. 3s. 6d. each.

—— Amelia. With Cruikshank's Illustrations. 5s.

FLAXMAN'S Lectures on Sculpture. By John Flaxman, R.A. With Portrait and 53 Plates. 6s.

FLORENCE of WORCESTER'S Chronicle, with the Two Continuations: comprising Annals of English History, from the Departure of the Romans to the Reign of Edward I. Translated by Thomas Forester, M.A. 5s.

FOSTER'S (John) Life and Correspondence. Edited by J. E. Ryland. 2 vols. 3s. 6d. each.

—— Critical Essays. Edited by J. E. Ryland. 2 vols. 3s. 6d. each.

—— Essays: on Decision of Character; on a Man's writing Memoirs of Himself; on the epithet Romantic; on the aversion of Men of Taste to Evangelical Religion. 3s. 6d.

—— Essays on the Evils of Popular Ignorance; to which is added, a Discourse on the Propagation of Christianity in India. 3s. 6d.

—— Essays on the Improvement of Time. With NOTES OF SERMONS and other Pieces. 3s. 6d.

GASPARY'S History of Italian Literature. Translated by Herman Oelsner, M.A., Ph.D. Vol. I. 3s. 6d.

GEOFFREY OF MONMOUTH, Chronicle of.—*See Old English Chronicles.*

GESTA ROMANORUM, or Entertaining Moral Stories invented by the Monks. Translated by the Rev. Charles Swan. Revised Edition, by Wynnard Hooper, B.A. 5s.

GILDAS, Chronicles of.—*See Old English Chronicles.*

GIBBON'S Decline and Fall of the Roman Empire. Complete and Unabridged, with Variorum Notes. Edited by an English Churchman. With 2 Maps and Portrait. 7 vols. 3s. 6d. each.

GILBART'S History, Principles, and Practice of Banking. By the late J. W. Gilbart, F.R.S. New Edition, revised by A. S. Michie. 2 vols. 10s.

GIL BLAS, The Adventures of. Translated from the French of Lesage by Smollett. With 24 Engravings on Steel, after Smirke, and 10 Etchings by George Cruikshank. 6s.

GIRALDUS CAMBRENSIS' Historical Works. Translated by Th. Forester, M.A., and Sir R. Colt Hoare. Revised Edition, Edited by Thomas Wright, M.A., F.S.A. 5s.

GOETHE'S Faust. Part I. German Text with Hayward's Prose Translation and Notes. Revised by C. A. Buchheim, Ph.D. 5s.

GOETHE'S Works. Translated into English by various hands. 14 vols. 3s. 6d. each.
 I. and II.—Autobiography and Annals.
 III.—Faust. Two Parts, complete. (Swanwick.)
 IV.—Novels and Tales.
 V.—Wilhelm Meister's Apprenticeship.
 VI.—Conversations with Eckermann and Soret.
 VIII.—Dramatic Works.
 IX.—Wilhelm Meister's Travels.
 X.—Tour in Italy, and Second Residence in Rome.
 XI.—Miscellaneous Travels.
 XII.—Early and Miscellaneous Letters.
 XIII.—Correspondence with Zelter.
 XIV.—Reineke Fox, West-Eastern Divan and Achilleid.

GOLDSMITH'S Works. A new Edition, by J. W. M. Gibbs. 5 vols. 3s. 6d. each.

GRAMMONT'S Memoirs of the Court of Charles II. Edited by Sir Walter Scott. Together with the BOSCOBEL TRACTS, including two not before published, &c. New Edition. 5s.

GRAY'S Letters. Including the Correspondence of Gray and Mason. Edited by the Rev. D. C. Tovey, M.A. Vols. I. and II. 3s. 6d. each.

GREEK ANTHOLOGY. Translated by George Burges, M.A. 5s.

GREEK ROMANCES of Heliodorus, Longus, and Achilles Tatius—viz., The Adventures of Theagenes & Chariclea; Amours of Daphnis and Chloe; and Loves of Clitopho and Leucippe. Translated by Rev. R. Smith, M.A. 5s.

GREGORY'S Letters on the Evidences, Doctrines, & Duties of the Christian Religion. By Dr. Olinthus Gregory. 3s. 6d.

GREENE, MARLOWE, and BEN JONSON. Poems of. Edited by Robert Bell. 3s. 6d.

GRIMM'S TALES. With the Notes of the Original. Translated by Mrs. A. Hunt. With Introduction by Andrew Lang, M.A. 2 vols. 3s. 6d. each.

—— **Gammer Grethel**; or, German Fairy Tales and Popular Stories. Containing 42 Fairy Tales. Trans. by Edgar Taylor. With numerous Woodcuts after George Cruikshank and Ludwig Grimm. 3s. 6d.

GROSSI'S Marco Visconti. Translated by A. F. D. The Ballads rendered into English Verse by C. M. P. 3s. 6d.

GUIZOT'S History of the English Revolution of 1640. From the Accession of Charles I. to his Death. Translated by William Hazlitt. 3s. 6d.

—— **History of Civilisation**, from the Fall of the Roman Empire to the French Revolution. Translated by William Hazlitt. 3 vols. 3s. 6d. each.

HALL'S (Rev. Robert) Miscellaneous Works and Remains. 3s. 6d.

HAMPTON COURT: A Short History of the Manor and Palace. By Ernest Law, B.A. With numerous Illustrations. 5s.

HARDWICK'S History of the Articles of Religion. By the late C. Hardwick. Revised by the Rev. Francis Procter, M.A. 5s.

HAUFF'S Tales. The Caravan— The Sheik of Alexandria—The Inn in the Spessart. Trans. from the German by S. Mendel. 3s. 6d.

HAWTHORNE'S Tales. 4 vols. 3s. 6d. each.
I.—Twice-told Tales, and the Snow Image.
II.—Scarlet Letter, and the House with the Seven Gables.
III.—Transformation [The Marble Faun], and Blithedale Romance.
IV.—Mosses from an Old Manse.

HAZLITT'S Table-talk. Essays on Men and Manners. By W. Hazlitt. 3s. 6d.

—— **Lectures on the Literature of the Age of Elizabeth** and on Characters of Shakespeare's Plays. 3s. 6d.

—— **Lectures on the English Poets**, and on the English Comic Writers. 3s. 6d.

—— **The Plain Speaker.** Opinions on Books, Men, and Things. 3s. 6d.

—— **Round Table.** 3s. 6d.

HAZLITT'S Sketches and Essays. 3s. 6d.

—— **The Spirit of the Age**; or, Contemporary Portraits. Edited by W. Carew Hazlitt. 3s. 6d.

—— **View of the English Stage.** Edited by W. Spencer Jackson. 3s. 6d.

HEATON'S Concise History of Painting. New Edition, revised by Cosmo Monkhouse. 5s.

HEGEL'S Lectures on the Philosophy of History. Translated by J. Sibree, M.A.

HEINE'S Poems, Complete Translated by Edgar A. Bowring, C.B. 3s. 6d.

—— **Travel-Pictures**, including the Tour in the Harz, Norderney, and Book of Ideas, together with the Romantic School. Translated by Francis Storr. A New Edition, revised throughout. With Appendices and Maps. 3s. 6d.

HELP'S Life of Christopher Columbus, the Discoverer of America. By Sir Arthur Helps, K.C.B. 3s. 6d.

—— **Life of Hernando Cortes**, and the Conquest of Mexico. 2 vols. 3s. 6d. each.

—— **Life of Pizarro.** 3s. 6d.

—— **Life of Las Casas** the Apostle of the Indies. 3s. 6d.

HENDERSON (E.) Select Historical Documents of the Middle Ages, including the most famous Charters relating to England, the Empire, the Church, &c., from the 6th to the 14th Centuries. Translated from the Latin and edited by Ernest F. Henderson, A.B., A.M., Ph.D. 5s.

HENFREY'S Guide to English Coins, from the Conquest to the present time. New and revised Edition by C. F. Keary, M.A., F.S.A. 6s.

HENRY OF HUNTINGDON'S History of the English. Translated by T. Forester, M.A. 5s.

HENRY'S (Matthew) Exposition of the Book of the Psalms. 5*s*.

HELIODORUS. Theagenes and Chariclea. — *See* GREEK ROMANCES.

HERODOTUS. Translated by the Rev. Henry Cary, M.A. 3*s*. 6*d*.

—— **Notes** on, Original and Selected from the best Commentators. By D. W. Turner, M.A. With Coloured Map. 5*s*.

—— **Analysis and Summary** of By J. T. Wheeler. 5*s*.

HESIOD, CALLIMACHUS, and THEOGNIS. Translated by the Rev. J. Banks, M.A. 5*s*.

HOFFMANN'S (E. T. W.) The Serapion Brethren. Translated from the German by Lt.-Col. Alex. Ewing. 2 vols. 3*s*. 6*d*. each.

HOLBEIN'S Dance of Death and Bible Cuts. Upwards of 150 Subjects, engraved in facsimile, with Introduction and Descriptions by Francis Douce and Dr. Thomas Frognall Dibden. 5*s*.

HOMER'S Iliad. Translated into English Prose by T. A. Buckley, B.A. 5*s*.

—— **Odyssey.** Hymns, Epigrams, and Battle of the Frogs and Mice. Translated into English Prose by T. A. Buckley, B.A. 5*s*.

—— *See also* POPE.

HOOPER'S (G.) Waterloo: The Downfall of the First Napoleon: a History of the Campaign of 1815. By George Hooper. With Maps and Plans. 3*s*. 6*d*.

—— **The Campaign of Sedan:** The Downfall of the Second Empire, August – September, 1870. With General Map and Six Plans of Battle. 3*s*. 6*d*.

HORACE. A new literal Prose translation, by A. Hamilton Bryce, LL.D. 3*s*. 6*d*.

HUGO'S (Victor) Dramatic Works. Hernani—Ruy Blas—The King's Diversion. Translated by Mrs. Newton Crosland and F. L. Slous. 3*s*. 6*d*.

—— **Poems,** chiefly Lyrical. Translated by various Writers, now first collected by J. H. L. Williams. 3*s*. 6*d*.

HUMBOLDT'S Cosmos. Translated by E. C. Otté, B. H. Paul, and W. S. Dallas, F.L.S. 5 vols. 3*s*. 6*d*. each, excepting Vol. V. 5*s*.

—— **Personal Narrative** of his Travels to the Equinoctial Regions of America during the years 1799–1804. Translated by T. Ross. 3 vols. 5*s*. each.

—— **Views of Nature.** Translated by E. C. Otté and H. G. Bohn. 5*s*.

HUMPHREYS' Coin Collector's Manual. By H. N. Humphreys. with upwards of 140 Illustrations on Wood and Steel. 2 vols. 5*s*. each.

HUNGARY: its History and Revolution, together with a copious Memoir of Kossuth. 3*s*. 6*d*.

HUTCHINSON (Colonel). Memoirs of the Life of. By his Widow, Lucy: together with her Autobiography, and an Account of the Siege of Lathom House. 3*s*. 6*d*.

HUNT'S Poetry of Science. By Richard Hunt. 3rd Edition, revised and enlarged. 5*s*.

INDIA BEFORE THE SEPOY MUTINY. A Pictorial, Descriptive, and Historical Account, from the Earliest Times to the Annexation of the Punjab. with upwards of 100 Engravings on Wood, and a Map. 5*s*.

INGULPH'H Chronicles of the Abbey of Croyland, with the CONTINUATION by Peter of Blois and other Writers. Translated by H. T. Riley, M.A. 5*s*.

IRVING'S (Washington) Complete Works. 15 vols. With Portraits, &c. 3s. 6d. each.
I.—Salmagundi, Knickerbocker's History of New York.
II.—The Sketch-Book, and the Life of Oliver Goldsmith.
III.—Bracebridge Hall, Abbotsford and Newstead Abbey.
IV.—The Alhambra, Tales of a Traveller.
V.—Chronicle of the Conquest of Granada, Legends of the Conquest of Spain.
VI. & VII.—Life and Voyages of Columbus, together with the Voyages of his Companions.
VIII.—Astoria, A Tour on the Prairies.
XI.—Life of Mahomet, Lives of the Successors of Mahomet.
X.—Adventures of Captain Bonneville, U.S.A., Wolfert's Roost.
XI.—Biographies and Miscellaneous Papers.
XII.-XV.—Life of George Washington. 4 vols.

—— Life and Letters. By his Nephew, Pierre E. Irving. 2 vols. 3s. 6d. each.

ISOCRATES, The Orations of. Translated by J. H. Freese, M.A. Vol. I. 5s.

JAMES'S (G. P. R.) Life of Richard Cœur de Lion. 2 vols. 3s. 6d. each.

—— **The Life and Times of Louis XIV.** 2 vols. 3s. 6d. each.

JAMESON'S (Mrs.) Shakespeare's Heroines. Characteristics of Women: Moral, Poetical, and Historical. By Mrs. Jameson. 3s. 6d.

JESSE'S (E.) Anecdotes of Dogs. With 40 Woodcuts and 34 Steel Engravings. 5s.

JESSE'S (J. H.) Memoirs of the Court of England during the Reign of the Stuarts, including the Protectorate. 3 vols. With 42 Portraits. 5s. each.

—— **Memoirs of the Pretenders and their Adherents.** With 6 Portraits. 5s.

JOHNSON'S Lives of the Poets. Edited by Mrs. Alexander Napier, with Introduction by Professor Hales. 3 vols. 3s. 6d. each.

JOSEPHUS (Flavius), The Works of. Whiston's Translation, revised by Rev. A. R. Shilleto, M.A. With Topographical and Geographical Notes by Colonel Sir C. W. Wilson, K.C.B. 5 vols. 3s. 6d. each.

JOYCE'S Scientific Dialogues. With numerous Woodcuts. 5s.

JUKES-BROWNE (A. J.), The Building of the British Isles: a Study in Geographical Evolution. Illustrated by numerous Maps and Woodcuts. 2nd Edition, revised, 7s. 6d.

—— **Student's Handbook of Physical Geology.** With numerous Diagrams and Illustrations. 2nd Edition, much enlarged, 7s. 6d.

JULIAN, the Emperor. Containing Gregory Nazianzen's Two Invectives and Libanus' Monody, with Julian's extant Theosophical Works. Translated by C. W. King, M.A. 5s.

JUSTIN CORNELIUS NEPOS, and EUTROPIUS. Translated by the Rev. J. S. Watson, M.A. 5s.

JUVENAL, PERSIUS, SULPICIA and LUCILIUS. Translated by L. Evans, M.A. 5s.

JUNIUS'S Letters. With all the Notes of Woodfall's Edition, and important Additions. 2 vols. 3s. 6d. each.

KANT'S Critique of Pure Reason. Translated by J. M. D. Meiklejohn. 5s.
—— **Prolegomena and Metaphysical Foundations of Natural Science.** Translated by E. Belfort Bax. 5s.

KEIGHTLEY'S (Thomas) Mythology of Ancient Greece and Italy. 4th Edition, revised by Leonard Schmitz, Ph.D., LL.D. With 12 Plates from the Antique. 5s.
—— **Fairy Mythology,** illustrative of the Romance and Superstition of Various Countries. Revised Edition, with Frontispiece by Cruikshank. 5s.

LA FONTAINE'S Fables. Translated into English Verse by Elizur Wright. New Edition, with Notes by J. W. M. Gibbs. 3s. 6d.

LAMARTINE'S History of the Girondists. Translated by H. T. Ryde. 3 vols. 3s. 6d. each.
—— **History of the Restoration of Monarchy in France** (a Sequel to the History of the Girondists). 4 vols. 3s. 6d. each.
—— **History of the French Revolution of 1848.** 3s. 6d.

LAMB'S (Charles) Essays of Elia and Eliana. Complete Edition. 3s. 6d.
—— **Specimens of English Dramatic Poets of the Time of Elizabeth.** 3s. 6d.
—— **Memorials and Letters of Charles Lamb.** By Serjeant Talfourd. New Edition, revised, by W. Carew Hazlitt. 2 vols. 3s. 6d. each.
—— **Tales from Shakespeare** With Illustrations by Byam Shaw. 3s. 6d.

LANZI'S History of Painting in Italy, from the Period of the Revival of the Fine Arts to the End of the Eighteenth Century. Translated by Thomas Roscoe. 3 vols. 3s. 6d. each.

LAPPENBERG'S History of England under the Anglo-Saxon Kings. Translated by B. Thorpe, F.S.A. New edition, revised by E. C. Otté. 2 vols. 3s. 6d. each.

LECTURES ON PAINTING, by Barry, Opie, Fuseli. Edited by R. Wornum. 5s.

LEONARDO DA VINCI'S Treatise on Painting. Translated by J. F. Rigaud, R.A.; With a Life of Leonardo by John William Brown. With numerous Plates. 5s.

LEPSIUS'S Letters from Egypt, Ethiopia, and the Peninsula of Sinai. Translated by L. and J. B. Horner. With Maps. 5s.

LESSING'S Dramatic Works, Complete. Edited by Ernest Bell, M.A. With Memoir of Lessing by Helen Zimmern. 2 vols. 3s. 6d. each.
—— **Laokoon, Dramatic Notes, and the Representation of Death by the Ancients.** Translated by E. C. Beasley and Helen Zimmern. Edited by Edward Bell, M.A. With a Frontispiece of the Laokoon group. 3s. 6d.

LILLY'S Introduction to Astrology. With a GRAMMAR OF ASTROLOGY and Tables for Calculating Nativities, by Zadkiel. 5s.

LIVY'S History of Rome. Translated by Dr. Spillan, C. Edmonds, and others. 4 vols. 5s. each.

LOCKE'S Philosophical Works. Edited by J. A. St. John. 2 vols. 3s. 6d. each.
—— **Life and Letters:** By Lord King. 3s. 6d.

LOCKHART (J. G.)—See BURNS.

LODGE'S Portraits of Illustrious Personages of Great Britain, with Biographical and Historical Memoirs. 240 Portraits engraved on Steel, with the respective Biographies unabridged. 8 vols. 5s. each.

LONGFELLOW'S Prose Works. With 16 full-page Wood Engravings. 5s.

LOUDON'S (Mrs.) Natural History. Revised edition, by W. S. Dallas, F.L.S. With numerous Woodcut Illus. 5s.

LOWNDES' Bibliographer's Manual of English Literature. Enlarged Edition. By H. G. Bohn. 6 vols. cloth, 5s. each. Or 4 vols. half morocco, 2l. 2s.

LONGUS. Daphnis and Chloe. —*See* GREEK ROMANCES.

LUCAN'S Pharsalia. Translated by H. T. Riley, M.A. 5s.

LUCIAN'S Dialogues of the Gods, of the Sea Gods, and of the Dead. Translated by Howard Williams, M.A. 5s.

LUCRETIUS. Translated by the Rev. J. S. Watson, M.A. 5s.

LUTHER'S Table-Talk. Translated and Edited by William Hazlitt. 3s. 6d.

—— Autobiography. — *See* MICHELET.

MACHIAVELLI'S History of Florence, together with the Prince, Savonarola, various Historical Tracts, and a Memoir of Machiavelli. 3s. 6d.

MALLET'S Northern Antiquities, or an Historical Account of the Manners, Customs, Religions and Laws, Maritime Expeditions and Discoveries, Language and Literature, of the Ancient Scandinavians. Translated by Bishop Percy. Revised and Enlarged Edition, with a Translation of the PROSE EDDA, by J. A. Blackwell. 5s.

MANTELL'S (Dr.) Petrifactions and their Teachings. With numerous illustrative Woodcuts. 6s.

—— Wonders of Geology. 8th Edition, revised by T. Rupert Jones, F.G.S. With a coloured Geological Map of England, Plates, and upwards of 200 Woodcuts. 2 vols. 7s. 6d. each.

MANZONI. The Betrothed: being a Translation of 'I Promessi Sposi.' By Alessandro Manzoni. With numerous Woodcuts. 5s.

MARCO POLO'S Travels; the Translation of Marsden revised by T. Wright, M.A., F.S.A. 5s.

MARRYAT'S (Capt. R.N.) Masterman Ready. With 93 Woodcuts. 3s. 6d.

—— Mission; or, Scenes in Africa. Illustrated by Gilbert and Dalziel. 3s. 6d.

—— Pirate and Three Cutters. With 8 Steel Engravings, from Drawings by Clarkson Stanfield, R.A. 3s. 6d.

—— Privateersman. 8 Engravings on Steel. 3s. 6d.

—— Settlers in Canada. 10 Engravings by Gilbert and Dalziel. 3s. 6d.

—— Poor Jack. With 16 Illustrations after Clarkson Stansfield, R.A. 3s. 6d.

—— Peter Simple. With 8 full-page Illustrations. 3s. 6d.

—— Midshipman Easy. With 8 full-page Illustrations. 3s. 6d.

MARTIAL'S Epigrams, complete. Translated into Prose, each accompanied by one or more Verse Translations selected from the Works of English Poets, and other sources. 7s. 6d.

An Alphabetical List of Books

MARTINEAU'S (Harriet) History of England, from 1800–1815. 3s. 6d.

—— History of the Thirty Years' Peace, A.D. 1815-46. 4 vols. 3s. 6d. each.

—— *See Comte's Positive Philosophy.*

MATTHEW PARIS'S English History, from the Year 1235 to 1273. Translated by Rev. J. A. Giles, D.C.L. 3 vols. 5s. each.

MATTHEW OF WESTMINSTER'S Flowers of History, from the beginning of the World to A.D. 1307. Translated by C. D. Yonge, M.A. 2 vols. 5s. each.

MAXWELL'S Victories of Welington and the British Armies. Frontispiece and 5 Portraits. 5s.

MENZEL'S History of Germany, from the Earliest Period to 1842. 3 vols. 3s. 6d. each.

MICHAEL ANGELO AND RAPHAEL, their Lives and Works. By Duppa aud Quatremere de Quincy. With Portraits, and Engravings on Steel. 5s.

MICHELET'S Luther's Autobiography. Trans. by William Hazlitt. With an Appendix (110 pages) of Notes. 3s. 6d.

—— History of the French Revolution from its earliest indications to the flight of the King in 1791. 3s. 6d.

MIGNET'S History of the French Revolution, from 1789 to 1814. 3s. 6d.

MILL (J. S.). Early Essays by John Stuart Mill. Collected from various sources by J. W. M. Gibbs. 3s. 6d.

MILLER (Professor). History Philosophically Illustrated, from the Fall of the Roman Empire to the French Revolution. 4 vols. 3s. 6d. each.

MILTON'S Prose Works. Edited by J. A. St. John. 5 vols. 3s. 6d. each.

—— Poetical Works, with a Memoir and Critical Remarks by James Montgomery, an Index to Paradise Lost, Todd's Verbal Index to all the Poems, and a Selection of Explanatory Notes by Henry G. Bohn. Illustrated with 120 Wood Engravings from Drawings by W. Harvey. 2 vols. 3s. 6d. each.

MITFORD'S (Miss) Our Village Sketches of Rural Character and Scenery. With 2 Engravings on Steel. 2 vols. 3s. 6d. each.

MOLIERE'S Dramatic Works. A new Translation in English Prose, by C. H. Wall. 3 vols. 3s. 6d. each.

MONTAGU. The Letters and Works of Lady Mary Wortley Montagu. Edited by her great-grandson, Lord Wharncliffe's Edition, and revised by W. Moy Thomas. New Edition, revised, with 5 Portraits. 2 vols. 5s. each.

MONTAIGNE'S Essays. Cotton's Translation, revised by W. C. Hazlitt. New Edition. 3 vols. 3s. 6d. each.

MONTESQUIEU'S Spirit of Laws. New Edition, revised and corrected. By J. V. Pritchard, A.M. 2 vols. 3s. 6d. each.

MOTLEY (J. L.). The Rise of the Dutch Republic. A History. By John Lothrop Motley. New Edition, with Biographical Introduction by Moncure D. Conway. 3 vols. 3s. 6d. each.

MORPHY'S Games of Chess. Being the Matches and best Games played by the American Champion, with Explanatory and Analytical Notes by J. Löwenthal. 5s.

MUDIE'S British Birds; or, History of the Feathered Tribes of the British Islands. Revised by W. C. L. Martin. With 52 Figures of Birds and 7 Coloured Plates of Eggs. 2 vols.

NEANDER (Dr. A.). History of the Christian Religion and Church. Trans. from the German by J. Torrey. 10 vols. 3s. 6d. each.

—— **Life of Jesus Christ.** Translated by J. McClintock and C. Blumenthal. 3s. 6d.

—— **History of the Planting and Training of the Christian Church by the Apostles.** Translated by J. E. Ryland. 2 vols. 3s. 6d. each.

—— **Memorials of Christian Life in the Early and Middle Ages;** including Light in Dark Places. Trans. by J. E. Ryland. 3s. 6d.

NIBELUNGEN LIED. The Lay of the Nibelungs, metrically translated from the old German text by Alice Horton, and edited by Edward Bell, M.A. To which is prefixed the Essay on the Nibelungen Lied by Thomas Carlyle. 5s.

NEW TESTAMENT (The) in Greek. Griesbach's Text, with various Readings at the foot of the page, and Parallel References in the margin; also a Critical Introduction and Chronological Tables. By an eminent Scholar, with a Greek and English Lexicon. 3rd Edition, revised and corrected. Two Facsimiles of Greek Manuscripts. 900 pages. 5s.

The Lexicon may be had separately, price 2s.

NICOLINI'S History of the Jesuits: their Origin, Progress, Doctrines, and Designs. With 8 Portraits. 5s.

NORTH (R.) Lives of the Right Hon. Francis North, Baron Guildford, the Hon. Sir Dudley North, and the Hon. and Rev. Dr. John North. By the Hon. Roger North. Together with the Autobiography of the Author. Edited by Augustus Jessopp, D.D. 3 vols. 3s. 6d. each.

NUGENT'S (Lord) Memorials of Hampden, his Party and Times. With a Memoir of the Author, an Autograph Letter, and Portrait. 5s.

OCKLEY (S.) History of the Saracens and their Conquests in Syria, Persia, and Egypt. By Simon Ockley, B.D., Professor of Arabic in the University of Cambridge. 3s. 6d.

OLD ENGLISH CHRONICLES, including Ethelwerd's Chronicle, Asser's Life of Alfred, Geoffrey of Monmouth's British History, Gildas, Nennius, and the spurious chronicle of Richard of Cirencester. Edited by J. A. Giles, D.C.L. 5s.

OMAN (J. C.) The Great Indian Epics: the Stories of the RAMAYANA and the MAHABHARATA. By John Campbell Oman, Principal of Khalsa College, Amritsar. With Notes, Appendices, and Illustrations. 3s. 6d.

ORDERICUS VITALIS' Ecclesiastical History of England and Normandy. Translated by T. Forester, M.A. To which is added the CHRONICLE OF ST. EVROULT. 4 vols. 5s. each.

OVID'S Works, complete. Literally translated into Prose. 3 vols. 5s. each.

PASCAL'S Thoughts. Translated from the Text of M. Auguste Molinier by C. Kegan Paul. 3rd Edition. 3s. 6d.

PAULI'S (Dr. R.) Life of Alfred the Great. Translated from the German. To which is appended Alfred's ANGLO-SAXON VERSION OF OROSIUS. With a literal Translation interpaged, Notes, and an ANGLO-SAXON GRAMMAR and GLOSSARY, by B. Thorpe. 5s.

PAUSANIAS' Description of Greece. Newly translated by A. R. Shilleto, M.A. 2 vols. 5s. each.

PEARSON'S Exposition of the Creed. Edited by E. Walford, M.A. 5s.

PEPYS' Diary and Correspondence. Deciphered by the Rev. J. Smith, M.A., from the original Shorthand MS. in the Pepysian Library. Edited by Lord Braybrooke. 4 vols. With 31 Engravings. 5s. each.

PERCY'S Reliques of Ancient English Poetry. With an Essay on Ancient Minstrels and a Glossary. Edited by J. V. Pritchard, A.M. 2 vols. 3s. 6d. each.

PERSIUS.—See JUVENAL.

PETRARCH'S Sonnets, Triumphs, and other Poems. Translated into English Verse by various Hands. With a Life of the Poet by Thomas Campbell. With Portrait and 15 Steel Engravings. 5s.

PHILO - JUDÆUS, Works of. Translated by Prof. C. D. Yonge, M.A. 4 vols. 5s. each.

PICKERING'S History of the Races of Man, and their Geographical Distribution. With AN ANALYTICAL SYNOPSIS OF THE NATURAL HISTORY OF MAN by Dr. Hall. With a Map of the World and 12 coloured Plates. 5s.

PINDAR. Translated into Prose by Dawson W. Turner. To which is added the Metrical Version by Abraham Moore. 5s.

PLANCHE. History of British Costume, from the Earliest Time to the Close of the Eighteenth Century. By J. R. Planché, Somerset Herald. With upwards of 400 Illustrations. 5s.

PLATO'S Works. Literally translated, with Introduction and Notes. 6 vols. 5s. each.
  I.—The Apology of Socrates, Crito, Phædo, Gorgias, Protagoras, Phædrus, Theætetus, Euthyphron, Lysis. Translated by the Rev. H. Carey.
  II.—The Republic, Timæus, and Critias. Translated by Henry Davis.
  III.—Meno, Euthydemus, The Sophist, Statesman, Cratylus, Parmenides, and the Banquet. Translated by G. Burges.
  IV.—Philebus, Charmides, Laches, Menexenus, Hippias, Ion, The Two Alcibiades, Theages, Rivals, Hipparchus, Minos, Clitopho, Epistles. Translated by G. Burges.
  V.—The Laws. Translated by G. Burges.
  VI.—The Doubtful Works. Translated by G. Burges.
  —— Summary and Analysis of the Dialogues. With Analytical Index. By A. Day, LL.D. 5s.

PLAUTUS'S Comedies. Translated by H. T. Riley, M.A. 2 vols. 5s. each.

PLINY'S Natural History. Translated by the late John Bostock, M.D., F.R.S., and H. T. Riley, M.A. 6 vols. 5s. each.

PLINY. The Letters of Pliny the Younger. Melmoth's translation, revised by the Rev. F. C. T. Bosanquet, M.A. 5s.

PLOTINUS, Select Works of. Translated by Thomas Taylor. With an Introduction containing the substance of Porphyry's Plotinus. Edited by G. R. S. Mead, B.A., M.R.A.S. 5s.

Contained in Bohn's Libraries. 19

PLUTARCH'S Lives. Translated by A. Stewart, M.A., and George Long, M.A. 4 vols. 3s. 6d. each.

—— **Morals.** Theosophical Essays. Translated by C. W. King, M.A. 5s.

—— **Morals.** Ethical Essays. Translated by the Rev. A. R. Shilleto, M.A. 5s.

POETRY OF AMERICA. Selections from One Hundred American Poets, from 1776 to 1876. By W. J. Linton. 3s. 6d.

POLITICAL CYCLOPÆDIA. A Dictionary of Political, Constitutional, Statistical, and Forensic Knowledge; forming a Work of Reference on subjects of Civil Administration, Political Economy, Finance, Commerce, Laws, and Social Relations. 4 vols. 3s. 6d. each.

POPE'S Poetical Works. Edited, with copious Notes, by Robert Carruthers. With numerous Illustrations. 2 vols. 5s. each.

—— **Homer's Iliad.** Edited by the Rev. J. S. Watson, M.A. Illustrated by the entire Series of Flaxman's Designs. 5s.

—— **Homer's Odyssey**, with the Battle of Frogs and Mice, Hymns, &c., by other translators. Edited by the Rev. J. S. Watson, M.A. With the entire Series of Flaxman's Designs. 5s.

—— **Life**, including many of his Letters. By Robert Carruthers. With numerous Illustrations. 5s.

POUSHKIN'S Prose Tales: The Captain's Daughter—Doubrovsky — The Queen of Spades — An Amateur Peasant Girl—The Shot —The Snow Storm—The Postmaster — The Coffin Maker — Kirdjali—The Egyptian Nights— Peter the Great's Negro. Translated by T. Keane. 3s. 6d.

PRESCOTT'S Conquest of Mexico. Copyright edition, with the notes by John Foster Kirk, and an introduction by G. P. Winship. 3 vols. 3s. 6d. each.

—— **Conquest of Peru.** Copyright edition, with the notes of John Foster Kirk. 2 vols. 3s. 6d. each.

—— **Reign of Ferdinand and Isabella.** Copyright edition, with the notes of John Foster Kirk. 3 vols. 3s. 6d. each.

PROPERTIUS. Translated by Rev. P. J. F. Gantillon, M.A., and accompanied by Poetical Versions, from various sources. 3s. 6d.

PROVERBS, Handbook of. Containing an entire Republication of Ray's Collection of English Proverbs, with his additions from Foreign Languages and a complete Alphabetical Index; in which are introduced large additions as well of Proverbs as of Sayings, Sentences, Maxims, and Phrases, collected by H. G. Bohn. 5s.

PROVERBS, A Polyglot of Foreign. Comprising French, Italian, German, Dutch, Spanish, Portuguese, and Danish. With English Translations & a General Index by H. G. Bohn. 5s.

POTTERY AND PORCELAIN, and other Objects of Vertu. Comprising an Illustrated Catalogue of the Bernal Collection of Works of Art, with the prices at which they were sold by auction, and names of the possessors. To which are added, an Introductory Lecture on Pottery and Porcelain, and an Engraved List of all the known Marks and Monograms. By Henry G. Bohn. With numerous Wood Engravings, 5s.; or with Coloured Illustrations, 10s. 6d.

PROUT'S (Father) Reliques. Collected and arranged by Rev. F. Mahony. New issue, with 21 Etchings by D. Maclise, R.A. Nearly 600 pages. 5s.

QUINTILIAN'S Institutes of Oratory, or Education of an Orator. Translated by the Rev. J. S. Watson, M.A. 2 vols. 5*s* each.

RACINE'S (Jean) Dramatic Works. A metrical English version. By R. Bruce Boswell, M.A. Oxon. 2 vols. 3*s.* 6*d.* each.

RANKE'S History of the Popes, their Church and State, and especially of their Conflicts with Protestantism in the 16th and 17th centuries. Translated by E. Foster. 3 vols. 3*s.* 6*d.* each.

—— History of Servia and the Servian Revolution. With an Account of the Insurrection in Bosnia. Translated by Mrs. Kerr. 3*s.* 6*d.*

RECREATIONS in SHOOTING. By 'Craven.' With 62 Engravings on Wood after Harvey, and 9 Engravings on Steel, chiefly after A. Cooper, R.A. 5*s.*

RENNIE'S Insect Architecture. Revised and enlarged by Rev. J. G. Wood, M.A. With 186 Woodcut Illustrations. 5*s.*

REYNOLD'S (Sir J.) Literary Works. Edited by H. W. Beechy. 2 vols. 3*s.* 6*d.* each.

RICARDO on the Principles of Political Economy and Taxation. Edited by E. C. K. Gonner, M.A. 5*s.*

RICHTER (Jean Paul Friedrich). Levana, a Treatise on Education: together with the Autobiography (a Fragment), and a short Prefatory Memoir. 3*s.* 6*d.*

—— Flower, Fruit, and Thorn Pieces, or the Wedded Life, Death, and Marriage of Firmian Stanislaus Siebenkaes, Parish Advocate in the Parish of Kuhschnapptel. Newly translated by Lt.-Col. Alex. Ewing. 3*s.* 6*d.*

ROGER DE HOVEDEN'S Annals of English History, comprising the History of England and of other Countries of Europe from A.D. 732 to A.D. 1201. Translated by H. T. Riley, M.A. 2 vols. 5*s.* each.

ROGER OF WENDOVER'S Flowers of History, comprising the History of England from the Descent of the Saxons to A.D. 1235, formerly ascribed to Matthew Paris. Translated by J. A. Giles, D.C.L. 2 vols. 5*s.* each.

ROME in the NINETEENTH CENTURY. Containing a complete Account of the Ruins of the Ancient City, the Remains of the Middle Ages, and the Monuments of Modern Times. By C. A. Eaton. With 34 Steel Engravings. 2 vols. 5*s.* each.

—— See BURN and DYER.

ROSCOE'S (W.) Life and Pontificate of Leo X. Final edition, revised by Thomas Roscoe. 2 vols. 3*s.* 6*d.* each.

—— Life of Lorenzo de' Medici, called 'the Magnificent.' With his poems, letters, &c. 10th Edition, revised, with Memoir of Roscoe by his Son. 3*s.* 6*d.*

RUSSIA. History of, from the earliest Period, compiled from the most authentic sources by Walter K. Kelly. With Portraits. 2 vols. 3*s.* 6*d.* each.

SALLUST, FLORUS, and VELLEIUS PATERCULUS. Translated by J. S. Watson, M.A. 5*s.*

SCHILLER'S Works. Translated by various hands. 7 vols. 3*s.* 6*d.* each:—

I.—History of the Thirty Years' War.

SCHILLER'S WORKS *continued*.

II.—History of the Revolt in the Netherlands, the Trials of Counts Egmont and Horn, the Siege of Antwerp, and the Disturbances in France preceding the Reign of Henry IV.

III.—Don Carlos, Mary Stuart, Maid of Orleans, Bride of Messina, together with the Use of the Chorus in Tragedy (a short Essay).

These Dramas are all translated in metre.

IV.—Robbers (with Schiller's original Preface), Fiesco, Love and Intrigue, Demetrius, Ghost Seer, Sport of Divinity.

The Dramas in this volume are translated into Prose.

V.—Poems.

VI.—Essays, Æsthetical and Philosophical

VII.—Wallenstein's Camp, Piccolomini and Death of Wallenstein, William Tell.

SCHILLER and GOETHE. Correspondence between, from A.D. 1794-1805. Translated by L. Dora Schmitz. 2 vols. 3s. 6d. each.

SCHLEGEL'S (F.) Lectures on the Philosophy of Life and the Philosophy of Language. Translated by the Rev. A. J. W. Morrison, M.A. 3s. 6d.

—— Lectures on the History of Literature, Ancient and Modern. Translated from the German. 3s. 6d.

—— Lectures on the Philosophy of History. Translated by J. B. Robertson. 3s. 6d.

SCHLEGEL'S Lectures on Modern History, together with the Lectures entitled Cæsar and Alexander, and The Beginning of our History. Translated by L. Purcell and R. H. Whitetock. 3s. 6d.

—— Æsthetic and Miscellaneous Works. Translated by E. J. Millington. 3s. 6d.

SCHLEGEL (A. W.) Lectures on Dramatic Art and Literature. Translated by J. Black. Revised Edition, by the Rev. A. J. W. Morrison, M.A. 3s. 6d.

SCHOPENHAUER on the Fourfold Root of the Principle of Sufficient Reason, and On the Will in Nature. Translated by Madame Hillebrand. 5s.

—— Essays. Selected and Translated. With a Biographical Introduction and Sketch of his Philosophy, by E. Belfort Bax. 5s.

SCHOUW'S Earth, Plants, and Man. Translated by A. Henfrey. With coloured Map of the Geography of Plants. 5s.

SCHUMANN (Robert). His Life and Works, by August Reissmann. Translated by A. L. Alger. 3s. 6d.

—— Early Letters. Originally published by his Wife. Translated by May Herbert. With a Preface by Sir George Grove, D.C.L. 3s. 6d.

SENECA on Benefits. Newly translated by A. Stewart, M.A. 3s. 6d.

—— Minor Essays and On Clemency. Translated by A. Stewart, M.A. 5s.

SHAKESPEARE DOCUMENTS. Arranged by D. H. Lambert, B.A. 3s. 6d.

SHAKESPEARE'S Dramatic Art. The History and Character of Shakespeare's Plays. By Dr. Hermann Ulrici. Translated by L. Dora Schmitz. 2 vols. 3s. 6d. each.

SHAKESPEARE (William). A Literary Biography by Karl Elze, Ph.D., LL.D. Translated by L. Dora Schmitz. 5s.

SHARPE (S.) The History of Egypt, from the Earliest Times till the Conquest by the Arabs, A.D. 640. By Samuel Sharpe. 2 Maps and upwards of 400 Illustrative Woodcuts. 2 vols. 5s. each.

SHERIDAN'S Dramatic Works, Complete. With Life by G. G. S. 3s. 6d.

SISMONDI'S History of the Literature of the South of Europe. Translated by Thomas Roscoe. 2 vols. 3s. 6d. each.

SMITH'S Synonyms and Antonyms, or Kindred Words and their **Opposites.** Revised Edition. 5s.

—— **Synonyms Discriminated.** A Dictionary of Synonymous Words in the English Language, showing the Accurate signification of words of similar meaning. Edited by the Rev. H. Percy Smith, M.A. 6s.

SMITH'S (Adam) The Wealth of Nations. Edited by E. Belfort Bax. 2 vols. 3s. 6d. each.

—— **Theory of Moral Sentiments.** With a Memoir of the Author by Dugald Stewart. 3s. 6d.

SMYTH'S (Professor) Lectures on Modern History. 2 vols. 3s. 6d. each.

SMYTH'S (Professor) Lectures on the French Revolution. 2 vols. 3s. 6d. each.

SMITH'S (Pye) Geology and Scripture. 2nd Edition. 5s.

SMOLLETT'S Adventures of Roderick Random. With short Memoir and Bibliography, and Cruikshank's Illustrations. 3s. 6d.

SMOLLETT'S Adventures of Peregrine Pickle. With Bibliography and Cruikshank's Illustrations. 2 vols. 3s. 6d. each.

—— **The Expedition of Humphry Clinker.** With Bibliography and Cruikshank's Illustrations. 3s. 6d.

SOCRATES (surnamed 'Scholasticus'). The Ecclesiastical History of (A.D. 305-445). Translated from the Greek. 5s.

SOPHOCLES, The Tragedies of. A New Prose Translation, with Memoir, Notes, &c., by E. P. Coleridge, M.A. 5s.

SOUTHEY'S Life of Nelson. With Portraits, Plans, and upwards of 50 Engravings on Steel and Wood. 5s.

—— **Life of Wesley,** and the Rise and Progress of Methodism. 5s.

—— **Robert Southey.** The Story of his Life written in his Letters. Edited by John Dennis. 3s. 6d.

SOZOMEN'S Ecclesiastical History. Translated from the Greek. Together with the ECCLESIASTICAL HISTORY OF PHILOSTORGIUS, as epitomised by Photius. Translated by Rev. E. Walford, M.A. 5s.

SPINOZA'S Chief Works. Translated, with Introduction, by R.H.M. Elwes. 2 vols. 5s. each.

STANLEY'S Classified Synopsis of the Principal Painters of the Dutch and Flemish Schools. By George Stanley. 5s.

STARLING'S (Miss) Noble Deeds of Women. With 14 Steel Engravings. 5s.

STAUNTON'S Chess - Player's Handbook. 5s.

—— **Chess Praxis.** A Supplement to the Chess-player's Handbook. 5s.

Contained in Bohn's Libraries. 23

STAUNTON'S Chess - player's Companion. Comprising a Treatise on Odds, Collection of Match Games, and a Selection of Original Problems. 5s.

—— **Chess Tournament of 1851.** With Introduction and Notes. 5s.

STOCKHARDT'S Experimental Chemistry. Edited by C. W. Heaton, F.C.S. 5s.

STRABO'S Geography. Translated by W. Falconer, M.A., and H. C. Hamilton. 3 vols. 5s. each.

STRICKLAND'S (Agnes) Lives of the Queens of England, from the Norman Conquest. Revised Edition. With 6 Portraits. 6 vols. 5s. each.

—— **Life of Mary Queen of Scots.** 2 vols. 5s. each.

—— **Lives of the Tudor and Stuart Princesses.** With Portraits. 5s.

STUART and REVETT'S Antiquities of Athens, and other Monuments of Greece. With 71 Plates engraved on Steel, and numerous Woodcut Capitals. 5s.

SUETONIUS' Lives of the Twelve Cæsars and Lives of the Grammarians. Thomson's translation, revised by T. Forester. 5s.

SWIFT'S Prose Works. Edited by Temple Scott. With a Biographical Introduction by the Right Hon. W. E. H. Lecky, M.P. With Portraits and Facsimiles. 12 vols. 3s. 6d. each.
[*Vols. I.-X. ready.*

I.—A Tale of a Tub, The Battle of the Books, and other early works. Edited by Temple Scott. With a Biographical Introduction by W. E. H. Lecky.

II.— The Journal to Stella. Edited by Frederick Ryland, M.A. With 2 Portraits and Facsimile.

SWIFT'S PROSE WORKS *continued.*

III. & IV.—Writings on Religion and the Church.

V.—Historical and Political Tracts (English).

VI.—The Drapier's Letters. With facsimiles of Wood's Coinage, &c.

VII.—Historical and Political Tracts (Irish).

VIII.—Gulliver's Travels. Edited by G. R. Dennis. With Portrait and Maps.

IX.—Contributions to Periodicals.

X.—Historical Writings.

XI.—Literary Essays.
[*In preparation.*

XII.—Index and Bibliography.
[*In preparation.*

STOWE (Mrs. H. B.) Uncle Tom's Cabin. Illustrated. 3s. 6d.

TACITUS. The Works of. Literally translated. 2 vols. 5s. each.

TALES OF THE GENII. Translated from the Persian by Sir Charles Morell. Numerous Woodcuts and 12 Steel Engravings. 5s.

TASSO'S Jerusalem Delivered. Translated into English Spenserian Verse by J. H. Wiffen. With 8 Engravings on Steel and 24 Woodcuts by Thurston. 5s.

TAYLOR'S (Bishop Jeremy) Holy Living and Dying. 3s. 6d.

TEN BRINK.—*See* BRINK.

TERENCE and PHÆDRUS. Literally translated by H. T. Riley, M.A. To which is added, Smart's Metrical Version of Phædrus. 5s.

THEOCRITUS, BION, MOSCHUS, and TYRTÆUS. Literally translated by the Rev. J. Banks, M.A. To which are appended the Metrical Versions of Chapman. 5s.

THEODORET and EVAGRIUS. Histories of the Church from A.D. 332 to A.D. 427; and from A.D. 431 to A.D. 544. Translated. 5s.

THIERRY'S History of the Conquest of England by the Normans. Translated by William Hazlitt. 2 vols. 3s. 6d. each.

THUCYDIDES. The Peloponnesian War. Literally translated by the Rev. H. Dale. 2 vols. 3s. 6d. each.

—— **An Analysis and Summary of.** By J. T. Wheeler. 5s.

THUDICHUM (J. L. W.) A Treatise on Wines. Illustrated. 5s.

URE'S (Dr. A.) Cotton Manufacture of Great Britain. Edited by P. L. Simmonds. 2 vols. 5s. each.

—— **Philosophy of Manufactures.** Edited by P. L. Simmonds. 7s. 6d.

VASARI'S Lives of the most Eminent Painters, Sculptors, and Architects. Translated by Mrs. J. Foster, with a Commentary by J. P. Richter, Ph.D. 6 vols. 3s. 6d. each.

VIRGIL. A Literal Prose Translation by A. Hamilton Bryce, LL.D. With Portrait. 3s. 6d.

VOLTAIRE'S Tales. Translated by R. B. Boswell. Containing Bebouc, Memnon, Candide, L'Ingénu, and other Tales. 3s. 6d.

WALTON'S Complete Angler. Edited by Edward Jesse. With Portrait and 203 Engravings on Wood and 26 Engravings on Steel. 5s.

—— **Lives of Donne, Hooker, &c.** New Edition revised by A. H. Bullen, with a Memoir of Izaak Walton by Wm. Dowling. With numerous Illustrations. 5s.

WELLINGTON, Life of. By 'An Old Soldier.' From the materials of Maxwell. With Index and 18 Steel Engravings. 5s.

WELLINGTON, Victories of. See MAXWELL.

WERNER'S Templars in Cyprus. Translated by E. A. M. Lewis. 3s. 6d.

WESTROPP (H. M.) A Handbook of Archæology, Egyptian, Greek, Etruscan, Roman. Illustrated. 5s.

WHITE'S Natural History of Selborne. With Notes by Sir William Jardine. Edited by Edward Jesse. With 40 Portraits and coloured Plates. 5s.

WHEATLEY'S A Rational Illustration of the Book of Common Prayer. 3s. 6d.

WHEELER'S Noted Names of Fiction, Dictionary of. 5s.

WIESELER'S Chronological Synopsis of the Four Gospels. Translated by the Rev. Canon Venables. 3s. 6d.

WILLIAM of MALMESBURY'S Chronicle of the Kings of England. Translated by the Rev. J. Sharpe. Edited by J. A. Giles, D.C.L. 5s.

XENOPHON'S Works. Translated by the Rev. J. S. Watson, M.A., and the Rev. H. Dale. In 3 vols. 5s. each.

YOUNG (Arthur). Travels in France during the years 1787, 1788, and 1789. Edited by M. Betham Edwards. 3s. 6d.

—— **Tour in Ireland**, with General Observations on the state of the country during the years 1776-79. Edited by A. W. Hutton. With Complete Bibliography by J. P. Anderson, and Map. 2 vols. 3s. 6d. each.

YULE-TIDE STORIES. A Collection of Scandinavian and North-German Popular Tales and Traditions. Edited by B. Thorpe. 5s.

THE YORK LIBRARY
A NEW SERIES OF REPRINTS ON THIN PAPER.

The volumes are printed in a handy size ($6\frac{1}{2} \times 4\frac{1}{4}$ in.), on thin but opaque paper, and are simply and attractively bound.

Price, in cloth, 2s. net ; in leather, 3s. net.

'The York Library is noticeable by reason of the wisdom and intelligence displayed in the choice of unhackneyed classics. . . . A most attractive series of reprints. . . . The size and style of the volumes are exactly what they should be.'—*Bookman.*

' Charmingly tasteful.'—*Westminster Gazette.*

' Among favourite "thin paper" books none are better done than the admirable York Library. For a simple and attractive binding these volumes stand quite among the first of their kind. The price is two shillings net, and they are exceedingly good value for the money.'
St. James's Gazette.

' These books should find their way to every home that owns any cultivation.'—*Notes and Queries.*

' A series of books which for attractiveness and handiness would take a lot of beating.'—*Pall Mall Gazette.*

' One of the most beautiful series of books ever issued to the public, and marvellously cheap.'—*Manchester Courier.*

The following volumes are now ready :

BURNEY'S EVELINA. Edited, with an Introduction and Notes, by ANNIE RAINE ELLIS.

BURNEY'S CECILIA. Edited by ANNIE RAINE ELLIS. 2 vols.

BURTON'S ANATOMY OF MELANCHOLY. Edited by the Rev. A. R. SHILLETO, M.A., with Introduction by A. H. BULLEN. 3 vols.
' Admirers of " Burton's Anatomy " can hardly hope for a better edition.'
Morning Post.

CERVANTES' DON QUIXOTE. MOTTEUX'S Translation, revised. With LOCKHART'S Life and Notes. 2 vols.

COLERIDGE'S AIDS TO REFLECTION, and the Confessions of an Inquiring Spirit.

COLERIDGE'S FRIEND. A series of Essays on Morals, Politics, and Religion.

COLERIDGE'S TABLE TALK AND OMNIANA. Arranged and Edited by T. ASHE, B.A.

DRAPER'S HISTORY OF THE INTELLECTUAL DEVELOPMENT OF EUROPE. 2 vols.

THE YORK LIBRARY—*continued*.

EMERSON'S WORKS. A new edition in 5 volumes, with the Text edited and collated by GEORGE SAMPSON.
*** *The contents of the volumes are as follows*: *Vol. I.—Essays: Representative Men. Vol. II.—English Traits: Conduct of Life: Nature. Vol. III.—Society and Solitude: Letters and Social Aims: Addresses. Vol. IV.—Miscellaneous Pieces. Vol. V.—Poetical Works.*

FIELDING'S TOM JONES. 2 vols.

GESTA ROMANORUM, or Entertaining Moral Stories invented by the Monks. Translated from the Latin by the Rev. CHARLES SWAN. Revised edition, by WYNNARD HOOPER, M.A.
'To those whom things ancient delight, the book is a mine of enjoyment. Its appearance in so commodious a shape is a subject for congratulation . . . The "York Library" reprint is ideal.'—*Notes and Queries*.

GOETHE'S FAUST. Translated by ANNA SWANWICK, LL.D. Revised edition, with an Introduction and Bibliography by KARL BREUL, Litt.D., Ph.D.
'Will, we hope, be widely patronised, for the book has the great advantage of an admirable introduction and bibliography by Dr. Karl Breul. No one speaks with more authority on the subject.'—*Athenæum*.

HAWTHORNE'S TRANSFORMATION (THE MARBLE FAUN).

IRVING'S SKETCH BOOK.

JAMESON'S SHAKESPEARE'S HEROINES. Characteristics of Women : Moral, Poetical, and Historical.

LAMB'S ESSAYS. Including the Essays of Elia, Last Essays of Elia, and Eliana.

MARCUS AURELIUS ANTONINUS, THE THOUGHTS OF. Translated by GEORGE LONG, M.A. With an Essay on Marcus Aurelius by MATTHEW ARNOLD.

MONTAIGNE'S ESSAYS. Cotton's translation. Revised by W. C. HAZLITT. 3 vols.

MORE'S UTOPIA. With the Life of Sir Thomas More, by William Roper, and his Letters to Margaret Roper and others. Edited, with Introduction and Notes, by GEORGE SAMPSON. [*In the Press.*

MOTLEY'S RISE OF THE DUTCH REPUBLIC. With a Biographical Introduction by MONCURE D. CONWAY. 3 vols.

PASCAL'S THOUGHTS. Translated from the Text of M. AUGUSTE MOLINIER by C. KEGAN PAUL. Third edition.

PLUTARCH'S LIVES. Translated, with Notes and a Life by AUBREY STEWART, M.A., and GEORGE LONG, M.A. 4 vols.

SWIFT'S GULLIVER'S TRAVELS. Edited, with Introduction and Notes, by G. R. DENNIS, with facsimiles of the original illustrations.

SWIFT'S JOURNAL TO STELLA. Edited, with Introduction and Notes, by F. RYLAND, M.A.

ARTHUR YOUNG'S TRAVELS IN FRANCE, during the years 1787, 1788, and 1789. Edited with Introduction and Notes, by M. BETHAM EDWARDS.

Other Volumes are in Preparation.

BELL'S HANDBOOKS
OF
THE GREAT MASTERS
IN PAINTING AND SCULPTURE.
EDITED BY G. C. WILLIAMSON, LITT.D.

Post 8vo. With 40 Illustrations and Photogravure Frontispiece. 5s. net each.

The following Volumes have been issued:

BOTTICELLI. By A. STREETER. 2nd Edition.
BRUNELLESCHI. By LEADER SCOTT.
CORREGGIO. By SELWYN BRINTON, M.A. 2nd Edition.
CARLO CRIVELLI. By G. MCNEIL RUSHFORTH, M.A.
DELLA ROBBIA. By the MARCHESA BURLAMACCHI. 2nd Edition.
ANDREA DEL SARTO. By H. GUINNESS. 2nd Edition.
DONATELLO. By HOPE REA. 2nd Edition.
GERARD DOU. By Dr. W. MARTIN. Translated by Clara Bell.
GAUDENZIO FERRARI. By ETHEL HALSEY.
FRANCIA. By GEORGE C. WILLIAMSON, Litt.D.
GIORGIONE. By HERBERT COOK, M.A.
GIOTTO. By F. MASON PERKINS.
FRANS HALS. By GERALD S. DAVIES, M.A.
BERNARDINO LUINI. By GEORGE C. WILLIAMSON, Litt.D. 3rd Edition.
LEONARDO DA VINCI. By EDWARD MCCURDY, M.A.
MANTEGNA. By MAUD CRUTTWELL.
MEMLINC. By W. H. JAMES WEALE.
MICHEL ANGELO. By Lord RONALD SUTHERLAND GOWER, M.A., F.S.A.
PERUGINO. By G. C. WILLIAMSON, Litt.D. 2nd Edition.
PIERO DELLA FRANCESCA. By W. G. WATERS, M.A.
PINTORICCHIO. By EVELYN MARCH PHILLIPPS.
RAPHAEL. By H. STRACHEY. 2nd Edition.
REMBRANDT. By MALCOLM BELL. 2nd Edition.
RUBENS. By HOPE REA.
LUCA SIGNORELLI. By MAUD CRUTTWELL. 2nd Edition.
SODOMA. By the CONTESSA LORENZO PRIULI-BON.
TINTORETTO. By J. B. STOUGHTON HOLBORN, M.A.
VELASQUEZ. By R. A. M. STEVENSON. 3rd Edition.
WATTEAU. By EDGCUMBE STALEY, B.A.
WILKIE. By Lord RONALD SUTHERLAND GOWER, M.A., F.S.A.

Others to follow.

THE
CHISWICK SHAKESPEARE.

Illustrated by BYAM SHAW

WITH INTRODUCTIONS AND GLOSSARIES BY JOHN DENNIS.

Printed at the Chiswick Press, pott 8vo., price 1s. 6d. net per volume; also a cheaper edition, 1s. net per volume; or 2s. net in limp leather; also a few copies, on Japanese vellum, to be sold only in sets, price 5s. net per volume.

Now Complete in 39 Volumes.

ALL'S WELL THAT ENDS WELL.
ANTONY AND CLEOPATRA.
AS YOU LIKE IT.
COMEDY OF ERRORS.
CORIOLANUS.
CYMBELINE.
HAMLET.
JULIUS CÆSAR.
KING HENRY IV. Part I.
KING HENRY IV. Part II.
KING HENRY V.
KING HENRY VI. Part I.
KING HENRY VI. Part II.
KING HENRY VI. Part III.
KING HENRY VIII.
KING JOHN.
KING LEAR.
KING RICHARD II.
KING RICHARD III.
LOVE'S LABOUR'S LOST.
MACBETH.
MEASURE FOR MEASURE.
MERCHANT OF VENICE.
MERRY WIVES OF WINDSOR.
MIDSUMMER-NIGHT'S DREAM.
MUCH ADO ABOUT NOTHING.
OTHELLO.
PERICLES.
ROMEO AND JULIET.
THE TAMING OF THE SHREW.
THE TEMPEST.
TIMON OF ATHENS.
TITUS ANDRONICUS.
TROILUS AND CRESSIDA.
TWELFTH NIGHT.
TWO GENTLEMEN OF VERONA.
WINTER'S TALE.
POEMS.
SONNETS.

'A fascinating little edition.'—*Notes and Queries.*

'A cheap, very comely, and altogether desirable edition.'—*Westminster Gazette.*

But a few years ago such volumes would have been deemed worthy to be considered *éditions de luxe*. To-day, the low price at which they are offered to the public alone prevents them being so regarded.'—*Studio.*

'Handy in shape and size, wonderfully cheap, beautifully printed from the Cambridge text, and illustrated quaintly yet admirably by Mr. Byam Shaw, we have nothing but praise for it. No one who wants a good and convenient Shakespeare—without excursuses, discursuses, or even too many notes—can do better, in our opinion, than subscribe to this issue: which is saying a good deal in these days of cheap reprints.'—*Vanity Fair.*

'What we like about these elegant booklets is the attention that has been paid to the paper, as well as to the print and decoration; such stout laid paper will last for ages. On this account alone, the 'Chiswick' *should easily be first* among pocket Shakespeares.'—*Pall Mall Gazette.*

*** *The Chiswick Shakespeare may also be had bound in* 12 *volumes, full gilt back, price* 36s. *net.*

New Editions, fcap. 8vo. 2s. 6d. each net.

THE ALDINE EDITION

OF THE

BRITISH POETS.

'This excellent edition of the English classics, with their complete texts and scholarly introductions, are something very different from the cheap volumes of extracts which are just now so much too common.'—*St. James's Gazette.*

'An excellent series. Small, handy, and complete.'—*Saturday Review.*

Akenside. Edited by Rev. A. Dyce.

Beattie. Edited by Rev. A. Dyce.

*Blake. Edited by W. M. Rossetti.

*Burns. Edited by G. A. Aitken. 3 vols.

Butler. Edited by R. B. Johnson. 2 vols.

Campbell. Edited by His Son-in-law, the Rev. A. W. Hill. With Memoir by W. Allingham.

Chatterton. Edited by the Rev. W. W. Skeat, M.A. 2 vols.

Chaucer. Edited by Dr. R. Morris, with Memoir by Sir H. Nicolas. 6 vols.

Churchill. Edited by Jas. Hannay. 2 vols.

*Coleridge. Edited by T. Ashe, B.A. 2 vols.

Collins. Edited by W. Moy Thomas.

Cowper. Edited by John Bruce, F.S.A. 3 vols.

Dryden. Edited by the Rev. R. Hooper, M.A. 5 vols.

Goldsmith. Revised Edition by Austin Dobson. With Portrait.

*Gray. Edited by J. Bradshaw, LL.D.

Herbert. Edited by the Rev. A. B. Grosart.

*Herrick. Edited by George Saintsbury. 2 vols.

*Keats. Edited by the late Lord Houghton.

Kirke White. Edited, with a Memoir, by Sir H. Nicolas.

Milton. Edited by Dr. Bradshaw. 2 vols.

Parnell. Edited by G. A. Aitken.

Pope. Edited by G. R. Dennis. With Memoir by John Dennis. 3 vols.

Prior. Edited by R. B. Johnson. 2 vols.

Raleigh and Wotton. With Selections from the Writings of other COURTLY POETS from 1540 to 1650. Edited by Ven. Archdeacon Hannah, D.C.L.

Rogers. Edited by Edward Bell, M.A.

Scott. Edited by John Dennis. 5 vols.

Shakespeare's Poems. Edited by Rev. A. Dyce.

Shelley. Edited by H. Buxton Forman. 5 vols.

Spenser. Edited by J. Payne Collier. 5 vols.

Surrey. Edited by J. Yeowell.

Swift. Edited by the Rev. J. Mitford. 3 vols.

Thomson. Edited by the Rev. D. C. Tovey. 2 vols.

Vaughan. Sacred Poems and Pious Ejaculations. Edited by the Rev. H. Lyte.

Wordsworth. Edited by Prof. Dowden. 7 vols.

Wyatt. Edited by J. Yeowell.

Young. 2 vols. Edited by the Rev. J. Mitford.

These volumes may also be had bound in Irish linen, with design in gold on side and back by Gleeson White, and gilt top, 3s. 6d. each net.

THE ALL-ENGLAND SERIES.
HANDBOOKS OF ATHLETIC GAMES.
The only Series issued at a moderate price, by Writers who are in the first rank in their respective departments.

'The best instruction on games and sports by the best authorities, at the lowest prices.'—*Oxford Magazine*.

Small 8vo. cloth, Illustrated. Price 1s. each.

Cricket. By FRED C. HOLLAND.

Cricket. By the Hon. and Rev. E. LYTTELTON.

Croquet. By Lieut.-Col. the Hon. H. C. NEEDHAM.

Lawn Tennis. By H. W. W. WILBERFORCE. With a Chapter for Ladies, by Mrs. HILLYARD.

Squash Tennis. By EUSTACE H. MILES. Double vol. 2s.

Tennis and Rackets and Fives. By JULIAN MARSHALL, Major J. SPENS, and Rev. J. A. ARNAN TAIT.

Golf. By H. S. C. EVERARD. Double vol. 2s.

Rowing and Sculling. By GUY RIXON.

Rowing and Sculling. By W. B. WOODGATE.

Sailing. By E. F. KNIGHT, dbl. vol. 2s.

Swimming. By MARTIN and J. RACSTER COBBETT.

Camping out. By A. A. MACDONELL. Double vol. 2s.

Canoeing. By Dr. J. D. HAYWARD. Double vol. 2s.

Mountaineering. By Dr. CLAUDE WILSON. Double vol. 2s.

Athletics. By H. H. GRIFFIN.

Riding. By W. A. KERR, V.C. Double vol. 2s.

Ladies' Riding. By W.A. KERR, V.C.

Boxing. By R. G. ALLANSON-WINN. With Prefatory Note by Bat Mullins.

Fencing. By H. A. COLMORE DUNN.

Cycling. By H. H. GRIFFIN, L.A.C., N.C.U., C.T.C. With a Chapter for Ladies, by Miss AGNES WOOD. Double vol. 2s.

Wrestling. By WALTER ARMSTRONG. New Edition.

Broadsword and Singlestick. By R. G. ALLANSON-WINN and C. PHILLIPPS-WOLLEY.

Gymnastics. By A. F. JENKIN. Double vol. 2s.

Gymnastic Competition and Display Exercises. Compiled by F. GRAF.

Indian Clubs. By G. T. B. COBBETT and A. F. JENKIN.

Dumb-bells. By F. GRAF.

Football — Rugby Game. By HARRY VASSALL.

Football—Association Game. By C. W. ALCOCK. Revised Edition.

Hockey. By F. S. CRESWELL. New Edition.

Skating. By DOUGLAS ADAMS. With a Chapter for Ladies, by Miss L. CHEETHAM, and a Chapter on Speed Skating, by a Fen Skater. Dbl. vol. 2s.

Baseball. By NEWTON CRANE.

Rounders, Fieldball, Bowls, Quoits, Curling, Skittles, &c. By J. M. WALKER and C. C. MOTT.

Dancing. By EDWARD SCOTT. Double vol. 2s.

THE CLUB SERIES OF CARD AND TABLE GAMES.
'No well-regulated club or country house should be without this useful series of books.'

Small 8vo. cloth, Illustrated. Price 1s. each. *Globe.*

Bridge. By 'TEMPLAR.'

Whist. By Dr. WM. POLE, F.R.S.

Solo Whist. By ROBERT F. GREEN.

Billiards. By Major-Gen. A. W.

Dominoes and Solitaire. By 'BERKELEY.'

Bézique and Cribbage. By 'BERKELEY.'

BELL'S CATHEDRAL SERIES.
Profusely Illustrated, cloth, crown 8vo. 1s. 6d. net each.

ENGLISH CATHEDRALS. An Itinerary and Description. Compiled by JAMES G. GILCHRIST, A.M., M.D. Revised and edited with an Introduction on Cathedral Architecture by the Rev. T. PERKINS, M.A., F.R.A.S.
BRISTOL. By H. J. L. J. MASSÉ, M.A.
CANTERBURY. By HARTLEY WITHERS. 5th Edition.
CARLISLE. By C. KING ELEY.
CHESTER. By CHARLES HIATT. 3rd Edition.
CHICHESTER. By H. C. CORLETTE, A.R.I.B.A. 2nd Edition.
DURHAM. By J. E. BYGATE, A.R.C.A. 3rd Edition.
ELY. By Rev. W. D. SWEETING, M.A. 2nd Edition.
EXETER. By PERCY ADDLESHAW, B.A. 2nd Edition, revised.
GLOUCESTER. By H. J. L J. MASSÉ, M.A. 3rd Edition.
HEREFORD. By A. HUGH FISHER, A.R.E. 2nd Edition, revised.
LICHFIELD. By A. B. CLIFTON. 2nd Edition.
LINCOLN. By A. F. KENDRICK, B.A. 3rd Edition.
MANCHESTER. By Rev. T. PERKINS, M.A.
NORWICH. By C. H. B. QUENNELL. 2nd Edition.
OXFORD. By Rev. PERCY DEARMER, M.A. 2nd Edition, revised.
PETERBOROUGH. By Rev. W. D. SWEETING. 2nd Edition, revised.
RIPON. By CECIL HALLETT, B.A.
ROCHESTER. By G. H. PALMER, B.A. 2nd Edition, revised.
ST. ALBANS. By Rev. T. PERKINS, M.A.
ST. ASAPH. By P. B. IRONSIDE BAX.
ST. DAVID'S. By PHILIP ROBSON, A.R.I.B.A.
ST. PATRICK'S, DUBLIN. By Rev. J. H. BERNARD, M.A., D.D. 2nd Edition
ST. PAUL'S. By Rev. ARTHUR DIMOCK, M.A. 3rd Edition, revised.
ST. SAVIOUR'S, SOUTHWARK. By GEORGE WORLEY.
SALISBURY. By GLEESON WHITE. 3rd Edition, revised.
SOUTHWELL. By Rev. ARTHUR DIMOCK, M.A. 2nd Edition, revised.
WELLS. By PERCY DEARMER, M.A. 3rd Edition.
WINCHESTER. By P. W. SERGEANT. 3rd Edition.
WORCESTER. By E. F. STRANGE. 2nd Edition.
YORK. By A. CLUTTON-BROCK, M.A. 3rd Edition.

Uniform with above Series. Now ready. 1s. 6d. net each.
ST. MARTIN'S CHURCH, CANTERBURY. By the Rev. CANON ROUTLEDGE, M.A., F.S.A.
BEVERLEY MINSTER. By CHARLES HIATT.
WIMBORNE MINSTER and CHRISTCHURCH PRIORY. By the Rev. T. PERKINS, M.A.
TEWKESBURY ABBEY AND DEERHURST PRIORY. By H. J. L. J. MASSÉ, M.A.
BATH ABBEY, MALMESBURY ABBEY, and BRADFORD-ON-AVON CHURCH. By Rev. T. PERKINS, M.A.
WESTMINSTER ABBEY. By CHARLES HIATT.
STRATFORD-ON-AVON CHURCH. By HAROLD BAKER.

BELL'S HANDBOOKS TO CONTINENTAL CHURCHES.
Profusely Illustrated. Crown 8vo, cloth, 2s. 6d. net each.
AMIENS By the Rev. T. PERKINS, M.A.
BAYEUX. By the Rev. R. S. MYLNE.
CHARTRES : The Cathedral and Other Churches. By H. J. L. J. MASSÉ, M.A.
MONT ST. MICHEL. By H. J. L. J. MASSÉ, M.A.
PARIS (NOTRE-DAME). By CHARLES HIATT.
ROUEN : The Cathedral and Other Churches. By the Rev. T. PERKINS, M.A.

The Best Practical Working Dictionary of the
English Language.

WEBSTER'S
INTERNATIONAL
DICTIONARY.

2348 PAGES.   5000 ILLUSTRATIONS.

NEW EDITION, REVISED THROUGHOUT WITH A NEW SUPPLEMENT OF 25,000 ADDITIONAL WORDS AND PHRASES.

The Appendices comprise a Pronouncing Gazetteer of the World, Vocabularies of Scripture, Greek, Latin, and English Proper Names, a Dictionary of the Noted Names of Fiction, a Brief History of the English Language, a Dictionary of Foreign Quotations, Words, Phrases, Proverbs, &c., a Biographical Dictionary with 10,000 names, &c., &c.

Dr. MURRAY, Editor of the '*Oxford English Dictionary*,' says:—'In this its latest form, and with its large Supplement and numerous appendices, it is a wonderful volume, which well maintains its ground against all rivals on its own lines. The 'definitions,' or more properly, 'explanations of meaning' in 'Webster' have always struck me as particularly terse and well-put; and it is hard to see how anything better could be done within the limits.'

Professor JOSEPH WRIGHT, M.A., Ph.D., D.C.L., LL.D., Editor of the '*English Dialect Dictionary*,' says:—'The new edition of "Webster's International Dictionary" is undoubtedly the most useful and reliable work of its kind in any country. No one who has not examined the work carefully would believe that such a vast amount of lexicographical information could possibly be found within so small a compass.'

Professor A. H. SAYCE, LL.D., D.D., says:—'It is indeed a marvellous work; it is difficult to conceive of a Dictionary more exhaustive and complete. Everything is in it—not only what we might expect to find in such a work, but also what few of us would ever have thought of looking for.'

Rev. JOSEPH WOOD, D.D., *Head Master of Harrow*, says:—'I have always thought very highly of its merits. Indeed, I consider it to be far the most accurate English Dictionary in existence, and much more reliable than the "Century." For daily and hourly reference, "Webster" seems to me unrivalled.'

Prospectuses, with Prices and Specimen Pages, on Application.

LONDON: GEORGE BELL & SONS, YORK HOUSE,
PORTUGAL STREET, W.C.

www.ingramcontent.com/pod-product-compliance
Lightning Source LLC
Chambersburg PA
CBHW020833020526
44114CB00040B/603